SOURCES OF THE WEST

■ ■ ■

READINGS IN WESTERN CIVILIZATION

EIGHTH EDITION

VOLUME I
From the Beginning to 1715

Mark A. Kishlansky, Editor
Harvard University

with the assistance of
Victor L. Stater
Louisiana State University

PEARSON

Boston   Columbus   Indianapolis   New York   San Francisco   Upper Saddle River
Amsterdam   Cape Town   Dubai   London   Madrid   Milan   Munich   Paris   Montreal   Toronto
Delhi   Mexico City   Sao Paulo   Sydney   Hong Kong   Seoul   Singapore   Taipei   Tokyo

Executive Editor: Jeff Lasser
Editorial Project Manager: Rob DeGeorge
Editorial Assistant: Julia Feltus
Director of Marketing: Brandy Dawson
Senior Marketing Manager: Maureen
   E. Prado Roberts
Marketing Assistant: Samantha Bennett
Senior Managing Editor: Ann Marie
   McCarthy
Production Manager: Meghan DeMaio

Creative Director: Jayne Conte
Cover Designer: Suzanne Behnke
Manager, Visual Research: Beth Brenzel
**Full Service Project Management/
   Composition:** Abinaya Ragendran/
   Integra Software Services
   Pvt. Ltd.
Printer/Binder/Cover Printer:
   R. R. Donnelley & Sons
Text Font: 10/12 New Baskerville

Credits and acknowledgments borrowed from other sources and reproduced, with permission, in this textbook appear on pages 363 and 366.

Library of Congress Cataloging-in-Publication Data

Sources of the West: readings in Western civilization/Mark A. Kishlansky, editor; with the assistance of Victor L. Stater.—8th ed.
   v. cm.
Contents: v. 1. From the beginning to 1715.
ISBN-13: 978-0-205-05376-6 (alk. paper)
ISBN-10: 0-205-05376-9 (alk. paper)
1. Civilization, Western—History—Sources. I. Kishlansky, Mark A.
II. Stater, Victor Louis, 1959- III. Title.
CB245.S578 2012
909'.09821—dc22

                                          2011010621

11

ISBN 10: 0-205-05376-9
ISBN 13: 978-0-205-05376-6

CONTENTS

Preface   vii

How to Read a Document   x

PART I   THE ORIGINS OF WESTERN CIVILIZATION AND THE CLASSICAL WORLD   1

CREATION EPICS   **3**

1. *The Epic of Gilgamesh* (ca. 2000 B.C.E.)   3
2. *The Creation Epic* (ca. 2000 B.C.E.)   5
3. *The Book of Genesis* (ca. 10th–6th century B.C.E.)   10
4. Hesiod, *Works and Days* (ca. 700 B.C.E.)   16

THE ANCIENT NEAR EAST   **20**

5. *Code of Hammurabi* (early 18th century B.C.E.)   20
6. *The Book of the Dead* (ca. 16th century B.C.E.)   23
7. *The Book of Exodus* (ca. 10th–6th century B.C.E.)   26
8. *The Book of Isaiah* (ca. 8th–6th century B.C.E.)   31
9. *The Legacy of Cyrus the Great:* (6th century B.C.E.)   34

ANCIENT AND CLASSICAL GREECE   **38**

10. Homer, *Iliad* (9th–8th century B.C.E.)   38
11. Sappho of Lesbos, *Poems* (ca. 600 B.C.E.)   41
12. Thucydides, *History of the Peloponnesian War* (ca. 400 B.C.E.)   44
13. Xenophon, *The Spartan Constitution* (ca. 360 B.C.E.)   49
14. Plato, *Apology* (399 B.C.E.)   53
15. Plato, *The Republic* (ca. 327 B.C.E.)   57
16. Aristotle, *Politics* (4th century B.C.E.)   66
17. Plutarch, *The Life of Alexander* (ca. C.E. 116)   69

THE ROMAN WORLD   **77**

18. Polybius, *The Roman Constitution* (ca. 150 B.C.E.)   77
19. Cicero, *The Trial of Aulus Cluentius Habitus* (66 B.C.E.)   81
20. Virgil, *Aeneid* (30–19 B.C.E.)   86
21. Juvenal, *Satires* (ca. C.E. 116)   89
22. Plutarch, *The Life of Cato the Elder* (ca. C.E. 116)   93
23. Suetonius, *The Life of Augustus* (ca. C.E. 122)   97
24. *The Sermon on the Mount* (ca. C.E. 28–35)   101
25. St. Paul, *Epistle to the Romans* (ca. C.E. 57)   104

PART II   MEDIEVAL EUROPE   **109**

THE EARLY MIDDLE AGES   **111**

26. Tacitus, *Germania* (98)   111
27. Eusebius, *In Praise of Constantine* (336)   115
28. Augustine of Hippo, *The City of God* (413–426)   119
29. Benedict of Nursia, *Rule of Saint Benedict* (ca. 535–540)   124
30. *The Burgundian Code* (ca. 474)   128
31. Gregory of Tours, *History of the Franks* (ca. 581–591)   133
32. Bede, *The Ecclesiastical History of England* (731)   137
33. Einhard, *The Life of Charlemagne* (ca. 829–836)   141

ISLAM AND THE EASTERN EMPIRE   **144**

34. Justinian, *Code* (529–565)   144
35. Procopius, *Secret History* (ca. 560)   148
36. *The Koran* (7th century)   152
37. Michael Psellus, *Chronographia* (ca. 1075–1077)   156
38. Ibn Al-Qalanisi, *The Damascus Chronicle* (ca. 1150)   159
39. Ibn Ishaq, *The Life of Muhammad* (after 733)   162

THE HIGH MIDDLE AGES   **167**

40. *Feudal Documents* (11th–13th centuries)   167
41. Bernard of Angers, *Miracles of St. Foy* (ca. 1010)   171
42. Fulcher of Chartres, *The First Crusade and the Siege of Jerusalem* (1101–1127)   176
43. *The Song of Roland* (ca. 1100)   183
44. *Magna Carta* (1215)   186
45. Francis of Assisi, *Admonitions* (ca. 1220)   190
46. Thomas Aquinas, *Summa Theologica* (1266–1273)   195

47. Dante, *The Divine Comedy* (ca. 1320)   200
48. Catherine of Siena, *Letters* (1376)   204
49. Christine de Pisan, *The Book of the City of Ladies* (ca. 1405)   209
50. Margaret Paston, *Letters* (1441–1448)   215

PART III   RENAISSANCE AND REFORMATION   219

THE RENAISSANCE   **221**
51. Francesco Petrarca, *Letters* (ca. 1372)   221
52. Leon Battista Alberti, *On the Family* (1435–1444)   226
53. Giorgio Vasari, *The Life of Leonardo da Vinci* (1550)   232
54. Niccolò Machiavelli, *The Prince* (1513)   236
55. Desiderius Erasmus, *In Praise of Folly* (1509)   240
56. Sir Thomas More, *Utopia* (1516)   244

THE NEW WORLDS AND THE AGE OF EXPLORATION   **248**
57. Ibn Battuta, *Travels in Africa* (1354)   248
58. Christopher Columbus, *Letter from the First Voyage* (1493)   252
59. Gomes de Zurara, *Chronicle of Guinea* (1453)   256
60. Bartolomé de Las Casas, *Apologetic
    History of the Indies* (1566)   260
61. Bernal Díaz, *The True History of the Conquest
    of New Spain* (1552–1568)   264
62. Juan Gonzalez de Mendoza, *The History of the Great
    and Mightie Kingdom of China* (1585)   267

RELIGIOUS REFORM   **271**
63. Bernard Gui, *A Manual for Inquisitors* (1331)   271
64. Martin Luther, *The Freedom of a Christian* (1520)
    and *Of Marriage and Celibacy* (1566)   275
65. John Calvin, *Institutes of the Christian Religion* (1534)
    and *Catechism* (ca. 1540)   281
66. Ignatius Loyola, *Spiritual Exercises* (1548)   289
67. Teresa of Ávila, *The Life of St. Teresa* (1611)   294

THE EARLY MODERN WORLD   **298**
68. Anonymous, *Lazarillo De Tormes* (1554)   298
69. *The Twelve Articles of the Peasants of Swabia* (1524);
    Martin Luther, *Admonition to Peace* (1525)   301

70. Francis Xavier, *Letter from India* (1543) 307
71. Marguerite de Navarre, *Heptameron* (1558) 311
72. Philippe Duplessis-Mornay, *A Defense of Liberty Against Tyrants* (1579) 315
73. Magdalena and Balthasar Paumgartner, *Letters* (1592–1596) 320

PART IV   THE ANCIEN RÉGIME   325

THE WARS OF RELIGION

74. Henry IV, *The Edict of Nantes* (1598) 327
75. Cardinal Richelieu, *The Political Testament* (1638) 329
76. Hans von Grimmelshausen, *Simplicissimus* (1669) 332

SUBJECTS AND SOVEREIGNS

77. James I, *True Law of a Free Monarchy* (1598) 337
78. Thomas Hobbes, *Leviathan* (1651) 342
79. John Locke, *Second Treatise of Government* (1689) 345
80. *The English Bill of Rights* (1689) 349
81. Duc de Saint-Simon, *Memoirs* (1694–1723) 355
82. Napoleon Bonaparte, *The Napoleonic Code (The French Civil Code)* (1804) 358

Acknowledgments 363
Photo Credits 366

PREFACE

Sources of the West is a collection of documents designed to supplement textbooks and lectures in the teaching of Western Civilization. The use of primary materials is an essential component of the study of history. By hearing the voices of the past, students come to realize both the similarities and differences between their society and previous ones. In witnessing others ponder the same questions that rouse their own curiosity, students feel a connection between the past and the present. Moreover, by observing the ways in which such questions and experiences are worked out and described, they come to an understanding and respect for the integrity of other cultures. By confronting the materials of the past, students exercise an imagination that is at the heart of the teaching and learning of history.

Historical sources are the building blocks from which instructors and textbook writers have ultimately constructed their accounts and their explanations of Western historical development. It is essential that even beginning students learn that the past does not come to us prepackaged but is formed by historians who exercise their own imaginations on primary materials. Historical thinking involves examining the ideas of others, understanding past experiences on others' terms, and recognizing other points of view. This process makes everyone, student and instructor alike, a historian.

I have observed a number of principles in selecting the materials for this collection, which is designed for beginning-level college students. I believe strongly in the value of primary sources and feel that they should be made as accessible to contemporary students as possible. Thus, I have preferred to use up-to-date translations of many texts despite the costliness of acquiring their rights. Many of the late-nineteenth-century translations that are commonly used in source books present texts that are syntactically too complex for modern students to comprehend easily. I have also chosen to present longer selections than is usual in books of this type. Unlike works that contain snippets of hundreds of documents, *Sources of the West* presents a sizable amount of a small number of sources. It therefore allows students to gain a deeper feeling for authors and texts and to concentrate their energies and resources. No selection is so long that it cannot be easily read at a sitting and none so short as to defy recall. Each selection raises a significant issue around which classroom discussion can take place or to which lectures can refer. Some may even stimulate students to seek out the complete original works.

Two other principles lie behind the selections I have made. The first is that a steady diet of even the greatest thinkers of the Western tradition is unpalatable without other varieties of social and cultural materials. For this reason, I have tried to leaven the mass of intellectual history with materials that draw on social conditions or common experiences in past eras. These should not only aid students in making connections between past and present but also introduce them to the varieties of materials from which history is recreated. Second, I have been especially concerned to recover the voices or highlight the experiences of those who are not always adequately represented in surveys of Western Civilization. The explosion of work in social history, in the history of the family, and in the history of women has made possible the inclusion of materials here that were barely discovered a decade ago. While this effort can be clearly seen in the materials chosen for the modern sections, it is also apparent in the more traditional selections made from older documents.

By providing longer selections and by expanding the scope of the materials to be incorporated, I have necessarily been compelled to make some hard choices. There exists a superabundance of materials that demand inclusion in a collection such as this. I have chosen the principal texts that best illustrate the dominant themes of Western Civilization. Because Western Civilization is a basic course in the curriculum of most colleges and universities, it must carry the primary responsibility for introducing students to dominant historical events and personalities. But it is my conviction that it is the experience of using primary materials—more than the identity of the materials—that is vital. Thus, I have tried to provide a balance among constitutional documents, political theory, philosophy, imaginative literature, and social description. In all cases, I have made the pedagogical value of the specific texts the prime consideration, selecting for significance, readability, and variety.

The feature *How to Read a Document* is designed to introduce students to a disciplined approach of working with primary sources and to encourage them to use their imaginations in their historical studies. No brief introduction can pretend to be authoritative, and there are many other strategies and questions that can be adopted in training students to become critical readers. It is hoped that this introduction will remove some of the barriers that usually exist between student and source by walking students through a single exercise with a document in front of them. Any disciplined approach to source materials will sensitize students to the construction of historical documents, their content and meaning, and the ways in which they relate to modern experience. Individual instructors will easily be able to improve upon the example offered here.

NEW TO THIS EDITION

The eighth edition of *Sources of the West* reflects the continued effort to respond to requests for the inclusion of new documents from users and students. I have also wanted to continue to expand the range of materials that are represented in terms of both genre and scope. With this in mind, the following documents are new to the first volume of the eighth edition:

- The Legacy of Cyrus the Great: *The Cyrus Cylinder* (6th century B.C.E.) and *The Book of Ezra* (5th century B.C.E.)
- Ibn Battuta, *Travels in Africa* (1354)
- Bernard Gui, *A Manual for Inquisitors* (1331)
- Napoleon Bonaparte, *The Napoleonic Code (The French Civil Code)* (1804)

Each new document is accompanied by an introduction that provides crucial background information on the document and author as well as focus questions that bring to light important themes reflected in the document. These questions will also drive class discussion.

ACKNOWLEDGMENTS

In preparing this new edition of *Sources of the West,* I have been aided by innumerable suggestions from both adopters and users of the book. Letters from course heads and even some students have helped me in choosing new documents for this edition. The result, I hope, will be a stronger, more balanced, and more up-to-date collection. I have had the opportunity to include a number of works in the modern period that now seem to have greater relevance than they did when the first edition was compiled. I would like to thank the following reviewers for their thoughtful critiques: Arthur H. Auten, *University of Hartford;* Lawrence Backlund, *Montgomery County Community College* (PA); Andrew Barnes, *Carnegie Mellon University;* Melvin E. Bender, *Central Baptist College* (AR); George C. Browder, *SUNY, Fredonia;* Ronald G. Brown, *Charles County Community College;* Karen Bruhn, *Arizona State University;* Clea Bunch, *University of Arkansas;* Daniel F. Callahan, *University of Delaware;* Robert Caputi, *Rochester Institute of Technology;* Barbara Evans Clements, *University of Akron;* Thomas H. L. Cornman, *Moody Bible Institute;* Paul G. Cooper, *Sierra Community College;* Mary Cygan, *University of Connecticut;* Alexander DeGrand, *North Carolina State University;* Carol A. Devlin, *Marquette University;* Gregory P. Elder, *Riverside Community College;* Duane K. Everhart, *College of DuPage;* Constantina S. Gaddis, *Onondaga Community College;* Eliga Gould, *University of New Hampshire;* Kevin D. Hill, *Iowa State University;* Lloyd Johnson, *Campbell University*; John W. Langdon, *Le Moyne College;* Janine Lanza, *Appalachian State University;* Marshall Lee, *Pacific University;* Elizabeth A. Lehfeldt, *Cleveland State University;* Cameron A. MacKenzie, *Concordia Theological Seminary;* Fiona Mani, *West Virginia University*; Daniel Meissner, *Marquette University;* Jesus Mendez, *Barry University;* Elise Moentmann, *University of Portland;* Sean Farrell Moran, *Oakland University;* David T. Murphy, *Anderson University;* Richard A. Oehling, *Assumption College;* Steven R. Pointer, *Trinity College;* Martha Rampton, *Pacific University;* Kevin C. Robbins, *Indiana University–Purdue University at Indianapolis;* Pete Rottier, *Cleveland State University;* Nancy Rupprecht, *Middle Tennessee State University;* Hugo Schwyzer, *Pasadena City College;* Barbara H. Shepard, *Longwood University;* George H. Shriver, *Georgia Southern University;* David Silbey, *Alvernia University*; Timothy Sistrunk, *Chicago State University;* Fran Sternberg, *University of Missouri;* William Stockton, *Johnson County Community College;* Norman Wilson, *Xavier University;* Sally Vaughn, *University of Houston;* Michael Wilson, *University of Texas at Dallas.* Victor Stater was an indispensable assistant in reworking texts, consulting on new choices, and helping to edit the new documents over the course of editions.

MARK A. KISHLANSKY

HOW TO READ A DOCUMENT

Do you remember the first time you used a road map? After struggling to unfold it and find the right side up and the right way around, you were confronted by an astonishing amount of information. You could calculate the distance between places, from towns to cities, or cities to cities, even the distance between exits on the toll roads. You could observe relative population density and identify large and small places. You could even judge the quality of roads. Most likely, though, you opened that map to help you figure out how to get from one particular place to another, to find the best route for the trip you were making.

For the map to tell you that, you had to know how to ask the right questions. It all seems so obvious now: You put one finger on the place where you were and another on the place you wanted to get to, and then you found the best and most direct roads between them. But in order to do something this simple, you made a lot of assumptions about the map. First, you assumed that the map was directionally oriented—north at the top, east to the right, south and west opposite. Next, you assumed that the map was to scale—that the distance between places on the map was proportional to their distances in reality. Third, you assumed that intersections on the map represented intersections on the ground, that roads that appeared to cross on paper actually would cross when you reached them. These assumptions allowed you to draw conclusions about your route. Of course, if any of them were not true, you found out soon enough.

Learning to read a historical document is much like learning to read a map. It is important to ask the right questions and make the right assumptions. But unlike the real journey that the map makes possible, the journey that is made with an historical document is one of the imagination. It is not so easy to put your finger on the past. You will have to learn to test your assumptions and to sharpen your ability to ask questions before you can have any confidence that you are on the right road. As with anything else, mastery of these skills takes concentration and practice. You will have to discipline yourself to ask and answer questions about the document on three different levels. At first, you will need to identify the basic components of the document itself: who wrote it, when, and for what purpose. Then you will want to understand its form and content. Finally, you will want to know the ways in which it can be interpreted. At the beginning, you will be asking questions that you can answer directly; by the end, you will be asking questions that will give full play to your imagination and your skills as a historian. Let's take an example.

Read this document slowly and carefully.

To the King's Most Excellent Majesty

1 *Humbly show unto our sovereign Lord the King, the Lords*
2 *Spiritual and Temporal, and Commons in Parliament assembled,*
3 *that whereas it is declared and enacted by a statute made in the*
4 *time of the reign of King Edward the First, commonly called "The*
5 *Statute of No Taxation Without Consent," that no tallage or aid*
6 *shall be laid or levied by the King or his heirs in this realm, without*
7 *the goodwill and assent of the Archbishops, Bishops, Earls,*
8 *Barons, Knights, Burgesses, and other the freeman of the*
9 *commonalty of this realm: and by authority of Parliament holden in*
10 *the five and twentieth year of the reign of King Edward the Third*
11 *[1352], it is declared and enacted, that from thenceforth no*
12 *person shall be compelled to make any loans to the King against his*
13 *will, because such loans were against reason and the franchise*
14 *of the land; and by other laws of this realm it is provided, that*
15 *none should be charged by any charge or imposition, called a*
16 *Benevolence. . . . Your subjects have inherited this freedom, that*
17 *they should not be compelled to contribute to any tax, tallage,*
18 *aid, or other charge not met by common consent in Parliament.*
19 *   Yet nevertheless, of late divers commissions directed to*
20 *sundry Commissioners in several counties with instructions have*
21 *issued, by means whereof your people have been in divers places*
22 *assembled, and required to lend certain sums of money unto your*
23 *Majesty, and many of them upon their refusal so to do have had*
24 *an oath administered unto them, not warrantable by the laws or*
25 *statutes of this realm, and have been constrained to become bound*
26 *to make appearance and give attendance before your Privy*
27 *Council, and in other places, and others of them have been therefore*
28 *imprisoned, confined, and sundry other ways molested and*
29 *disquieted; and divers other charges have been laid and leveled upon*
30 *your people in several counties, by Lords Lieutenants, Deputy*
31 *Lieutenants, Commissioners for Muster, Justices of Peace and*
32 *others, by command or direction from your Majesty or your Privy*
33 *Council, against the laws and free customs of this realm.*
34 *   And where also by the statute called "The Great Charter of*
35 *the Liberties of England," it is declared and enacted, that no free*
36 *man may be taken or imprisoned or be disseised [dispossessed]*
37 *of freeholds or liberties, or his free customs, or be outlawed or*
38 *exiled; or in any manner destroyed, but by the lawful judgment*
39 *of his peers, or by the law of the land:*
40 *   And in the eight and twentieth year of the reign of King*
41 *Edward the Third [1355] it was declared and enacted by authority*
42 *of Parliament, that no man of what estate or condition that he*

43 be, should be put out of his lands or tenements, nor taken, nor
44 imprisoned, nor disinherited, nor put to death, without being
45 brought to answer by due process of law.
46   Nevertheless, against the tenor of the said statutes and other
47 good laws and statutes of your realm to that end provided, divers
48 of your subjects have of late been imprisoned without any cause
49 showed, and when for their deliverance they were brought before
50 your justices, by your Majesty's writs of Habeas Corpus, there to
51 undergo and receive as the Court should order, and their keepers
52 commanded to certify the causes of their detainer, no cause was
53 certified, but that they were detained by your Majesty's special
54 command, signified by the Lords of your Privy Council, and yet
55 were returned back to several prisons, without being charged with
56 anything to which they might make answer according to the law.
57   And whereas of late great companies of soldiers and mariners
58 have been dispersed into divers counties of the realm, and the
59 inhabitants against their wills have been compelled to receive
60 them into their houses, and there to suffer them to sojourn, against
61 the laws and customs of this realm, and to the great grievances
62 and vexation of the people:
63   And whereas also by authority of Parliament, in the 25th year
64 of the reign of King Edward the Third [1352] it was declared and
65 enacted, that no man shall be forejudged of life or limb against
66 the form of the Great Charter, and the law of the land and by the
67 said Great Charter . . . no man ought to be adjudged to death, but
68 by the laws established in this your realm . . . : and whereas no
69 offender of what kind soever is exempted from the proceedings
70 to be used, and punishments to be inflicted by the laws and
71 statutes of this your realm: nevertheless of late divers commissions
72 under your Majesty's Great Seal have issued forth, by which
73 certain persons have been assigned and appointed Commissioners
74 with power and authority to proceed within the land, according
75 to the justice of martial law against such soldiers and mariners,
76 or other dissolute persons joining with them, as should commit
77 any murder, robbery, felony, mutiny, or other outrage or
78 misdemeanor whatsoever, and by such summary course and order
79 as is agreeable to martial law, and is used in armies in time of
80 war, to proceed to the trial and condemnation of such offenders,
81 and them to cause to be executed and put to death according to
82 the law martial:
83   By pretext whereof, some of your Majesty's subjects have been
84 by some of the said Commissioners put to death, when and where,
85 if by the laws and statutes of the land they had deserved death,
86 by the same laws and statutes also they might, and by no other
87 ought to, have been adjudged and executed:
88   And also sundry grievous offenders by color thereof, claim-

89   *ing an exemption, have escaped the punishments due to them . . .*
90   *by reason that divers of your officers and ministers of justice have*
91   *unjustly refused, or forborne to proceed against such offenders*
92   *according to the same laws and statutes, upon pretense that the*
93   *said offenders were punishable only by martial law. . . .*
94   *They do therefore humbly pray for your Most Excellent*
95   *Majesty that no man hereafter be compelled to make or yield any*
96   *gift, loan, benevolence, tax, or such like charge, without common*
97   *consent by Act of Parliament; and that none be called to make*
98   *answer, or take such oath or to give attendance, or be confined,*
99   *or otherwise molested or disquieted concerning the same, or for*
100 *refusal thereof; and that no freeman, in any such manner as is*
101 *before-mentioned, be imprisoned or detained; and that your*
102 *Majesty will be pleased to remove the said soldiers and mariners,*
103 *and that your people may not be so burdened in time to come;*
104 *and that the foresaid commissions for proceeding by martial law,*
105 *may be revoked and annulled; and that hereafter no commissions*
106 *of like nature may issue forth to any person or persons whatsoever,*
107 *to be executed as aforesaid, lest by color of them any of your*
108 *Majesty's subjects be destroyed or put to death, contrary to the*
109 *laws and franchise of the land.*
110 *All which they most humbly pray of your Most Excellent*
111 *Majesty, as their rights and liberties according to the laws and*
112 *statutes of this realm: and that your Majesty would also vouchsafe*
113 *to declare that the awards, doings, and proceedings to the*
114 *prejudice of your people, in any of the premises shall not be drawn*
115 *hereafter into consequence or example: and that your Majesty*
116 *would be also graciously pleased, for the further comfort and*
117 *safety of your people, to declare your royal will and pleasure, that*
118 *in the things aforesaid all your officers and ministers shall serve*
119 *you according to the laws and statutes of this realm as they tender*
120 *the honor of your Majesty, and the prosperity of this kingdom.*

Now, what sense can we make out of all of that? You have just read a historical document known as the "Petition of Right." It was presented to King Charles I of England by his Parliament in 1628. In order to understand this document, you are going to need to find answers to a series of questions about it. Start at the beginning with a number of questions that might be designated "level-one" questions.

LEVEL ONE

The first set of questions that need to be addressed are those for which you should be able to find concrete answers. The answers to these questions will give you the basic information you need to begin the process of interpretation. Although "level-one" questions are seemingly straightforward, they contain important implications for deeper interpretation.

If you do not consciously ask these questions, you will deprive yourself of some of the most important evidence there is for understanding documents. Train yourself to underline or highlight the information that will allow you to answer the following questions.

1. Who Wrote This Document?

In the first place, you need to know how this document came to be created. Written historical records were created by individuals in a specific historical setting for a particular purpose. Until you know who created the document you have read, you cannot know why it was created or what meanings its author intended to impart by creating it. Nor is it enough simply to learn the name of the author; it is equally important to learn about authors as people, what social background they came from, what position they held, to what group they belonged. Although you will learn the identity of the author from the headnotes, you will learn much about that person or group from the document. In the case of the Petition of Right, you know that the document was written by the Lords Spiritual and Temporal and the Commons assembled in Parliament **(line 2).** This document is the work of a political body rather than of an individual, and you probably know from your own experience that such a document must have been written by a committee and revised and amended by the rest of the body before it was completed. Such authorship, unlike the work of an identifiable individual, suggests a wide degree of support and probably more than one compromise between those who wanted a stronger statement and those who wanted a weaker one. You will need to learn as much as you can about the authors of a document to help you answer more complicated questions.

2. Who Is the Intended Audience?

Identifying the intended audience of a document will tell you much about its language, about the amount of knowledge that the writer is assuming, even sometimes about the best form for the document to take. The relationship between author and audience is one of the most basic elements of communication and one that will tell you much about the purpose of the document. Think of the difference between the audience for a novel and that for a diary, or for a law and for a secret treaty. In each case, knowing the intended audience determines your view of what to expect from the document. Knowing the audience allows you to begin to ask important questions, such as, "Should I believe what I am being told?" In the Petition of Right, you know that the intended audience was the king of England **(line 1).** This knowledge helps you to establish the relationship between authors and audience, from which you can learn many things. In the Petition of Right, this relationship helps you understand the kind of language that is being used. You would expect Parliament to "most humbly pray" **(line 110)** when addressing the king. If you were reading a shopkeeper's bill to a customer or a mother's letter of advice to her daughter, you would be surprised by such language and alerted that something unusual was going on. The relationship between author and audience provides you with reasonable expectations, and it is well for you to ask if these are fulfilled. Is there language in the Petition of Right that is not appropriate to the relationship between a king and his parliament? Finally, you must remember that the writer may have intended to address more than one audience. Here, you might wonder if the Petition of Right was not also intended to be read by government officials, lawyers, and even the educated public. How would such multiple audiences affect the nature of the document?

3. What Is the Story Line?

The final "level-one" question has to do with the content of the document. You now know enough about it in a general way to pay attention to what it actually says. To learn the story line, you must take some notes while you are reading and underline or highlight important places in your text. The more often you ask yourself, "What is going on here?" the easier it will be to find out. No matter how obscure a document appears at first, deliberate attention to the story line will allow you to focus your reading. In this document, the story seems to be simple. Parliament has identified a number of violations of the laws of the realm. In their opinion, the king has attempted to raise taxes without parliamentary consent **(line 18)**; has imprisoned people without telling them the grounds for their imprisonment **(line 49)**; has quartered soldiers in the homes of citizens against their will **(line 60)**; and has allowed his agents to use the forms of martial law to try, convict, and punish unruly persons **(line 76)**. Parliament petitions the king to recognize that these are violations of the rights of citizens **(line 111),** that they be halted at once, that they not be used as precedent for future actions **(line 95),** and that those responsible be instructed to follow the laws of the realm more fully in the future **(line 119)**. While this is undoubtedly the "story" this document tells, you will soon see that while the story may be simple, its meaning may be very complicated. Notice how in trying to find the story line you were not concerned with the thick details of the document—those complicated facts and arguments that seemed so imposing when you first read it. It doesn't yet matter in which year in the reign of Edward III laws were passed **(line 41),** what a writ of Habeas Corpus is **(line 50),** or who the Lords of the Privy Council might have been **(line 54).** At this point, you want to know what this document is about, and unless understanding these thick details is absolutely essential to making any sense out of it at all, you are not going to be put off by them.

LEVEL TWO

If "level-one" questions allow you to identify the nature of the document and its author, "level-two" questions allow you to probe behind the essential facts. Now that you know who wrote the document, to whom it is addressed, and what it is about, you can begin to try to understand it. Since your goal is to learn what this document means, first in its historical context and then in your current context, you now want to study it from a more detached point of view, to be less accepting of "facts" and more critical in the questions you pose. At the first level, the document controlled you; at the second level, you will begin to control the document.

1. Why Was This Document Written?

Everything is written for a reason. You make notes to yourself to remember; you send cards to celebrate and sympathize; you correspond to convey or request information. The documents that historians traditionally study are more likely to have been written for public rather than for private purposes, but not always. Understanding the purpose of a historical document is critical to analyzing the strategies that the author employs within it. A document intended to convince will employ logic; a document intended to entertain will employ fancy; a document attempting to motivate will employ emotional appeals. In order to find these strategies, you must know what purpose this document was intended to serve. The Petition of Right was intended to persuade. The case for the abuses of which Parliament was complaining is set out logically with clear examples. By the end of the petition, the case seems irrefutable, though, of course, there was undoubtedly another side to the story.

2. What Type of Document Is This?

The form of a document is vital to its purpose. You would expect a telephone book to be alphabetized, a poem to be in meter, and a work of philosophy to be in prose. The form or genre in which a document appears is always carefully chosen. Genre contains its own conventions, which fulfill the expectations of author and audience. A prose map of how one travels from Chicago to Boston might be as effective as a conventional map, but it would not allow for much of the incidental information that a conventional map contains and would be much harder to consult. A map in poetry would be mind-boggling! Here you have a petition, and even if you don't know much about the form of a seventeenth-century petition, you can learn more than enough about it from the presentation itself. This document is obviously very formal and written in legal language. It specifies certain laws **(lines 5, 34)** and then asserts that they have been violated **(line 46).** It takes the form of a request, "humbly praying," that the king "your most Excellent Majesty" **(line 110)** will grant the desires expressed in the petition. You can learn a variety of things from the petition form: the relationship between Parliament and king, the powers of the king, the role of a parliament, the way in which the legal or legislative process works.

3. What Are the Basic Assumptions Made in This Document?

All documents make assumptions that are bound up with their intended audience, with the form in which they are written, and with their purpose. Some of these assumptions are so integral to the document that they are left unsaid, others are so important to establish that they form a part of the central argumentation. The Petition of Right assumes that king and Parliament share a legal system and that both recognize certain precedents in it as valid. This is why statutes from past realms are quoted as authorities. If the Petition of Right had been written by the English Parliament to the French king, such assumptions would be invalid and the document would be incomprehensible. Similarly, the assumption that law is binding on both king and subjects—an assumption that might have been contested in the seventeenth century—runs through the entire petition. Of course, the authors continually frame this assumption in the language of "Your Majesty's law" so as to persuade the king that the violations are as much against the king as against his subjects. Finally, the form of the petition assumes that both king and Parliament desire to eliminate the grievances of the nation. The petition would make no sense if the king could reply, "They are taking your property, imprisoning you without cause, and hanging you arbitrarily? Good! Let's have more of this efficiency in government."

LEVEL THREE

So far, you have been asking questions of your document that you can learn directly from it. Sometimes it is more difficult to know who composed a document or who the intended audience was than it has been with the Petition of Right. Sometimes you have to guess at the purpose of the document. But essentially questions on level one and level two are questions with direct answers. Once you have learned to ask them, you will have a great deal of information about the historical document at your disposal. You will then be able to think historically—that is, to pose your own questions about the past and to use the material the document presents to seek for answers. In level three, you will exercise your critical imagination, probing the material and developing your own assessment of its value. "Level-three" questions will not always have definite answers; in fact, they are the kind of questions that arouse disagreement and debate and that make for lively classroom discussion.

1. Can I Believe This Document?

To be successful, a document designed to persuade, to recount events, or to motivate people to action must be believable to its audience. For the critical historical reader, it is that very believability that must be examined. Every author has a point of view, and exposing the assumptions of the document is an essential task for the reader. You must treat all claims skeptically (even while admiring audacity, rhetorical tricks, and clever comparisons). One question you certainly want to ask is, "Is this a likely story?" Are you really persuaded that the king of England does not know the laws that the Petition of Right claims to be reasserting? Doesn't it seem that the authors want to have it both ways when they complain that martial law is too severe **(line 75)** but not severe enough **(line 93)**? Testing the credibility of a document means looking at it from the other side. How would the king of England respond to the Petition of Right, and what would his point of view be?

2. What Can I Learn About the Society That Produced This Document?

All documents unintentionally reveal things about their authors and about their era. It is the things that are embedded in the very language, structure, and assumptions of the document that can tell you the most about the historical period or event that you are studying. However angry the members of Parliament are about their grievances, they believe profoundly in monarchy. Look at the way they address their king **(lines 1, 94).** Notice how careful they are to blame everything on agents rather than on the monarch himself. You might think that this is just sweet-talking, that they know it is the king who is to blame, and that they have him dead to rights with all the violations of law that they have documented. But, of course, if they really believed that the king was in the wrong, why petition him to reassert their rights? What expectation could they have that he would grant these rights or respect them? Notice also the hierarchical structure of English government—the "Lords Spiritual and Temporal," the earls and the barons, and so forth **(line 7).** You can learn many things about seventeenth-century English society by reading *into* this document rather than by simply reading it.

3. What Does This Document Mean to Me?

So what? What does the Petition of Right, written over 350 years ago, have to do with you? Other than for the practical purpose of passing your exams and getting your degree, why should you be concerned with historical documents? What can you learn from them? Only you can answer those questions. But you won't be able to answer them until you have asked them. You should demand the meaning of each document you read: what it meant to the historical actors—authors, audience, and society—and what it means to your own society. In the case of the Petition of Right, the principles of freedom from arbitrary arrest, from the seizure of property, and the assurance of due process of law in criminal matters obviously have something to do with all of us. But not all documents will yield their meanings so easily.

Now that you have seen how to unfold the map of a historical document, you must get used to asking these questions by yourself. The temptation will be great to jump from level one to level three, to start in the middle, or to pose the questions in no sequence at all. After all, you probably have a ready-made answer to "What does this document mean to me?" But if you develop the discipline of asking all your questions in the proper order, you will soon find that you are able to gain command of a document on a single reading and that the complicated names and facts that ordinarily would confuse you will easily settle into a pattern around one or another of your questions. After a few weeks, reread these pages and ask yourself how careful you have been to maintain the discipline of posing historical questions. Think also about how much more comfortable you now feel about reading and discussing historical documents.

PART I

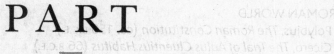

THE ORIGINS OF WESTERN CIVILIZATION
AND THE CLASSICAL WORLD

CREATION EPICS
1. *The Epic of Gilgamesh* (ca. 2000 B.C.E.)
2. *The Creation Epic* (ca. 2000 B.C.E.)
3. *The Book of Genesis* (ca. 10th–6th century B.C.E.)
4. *Hesiod, Works and Days* (ca. 700 B.C.E.)

THE ANCIENT NEAR EAST
5. *Code of Hammurabi* (early 18th century B.C.E.)
6. *The Book of the Dead* (ca. 16th century B.C.E.)
7. *The Book of Exodus* (ca. 10th–6th century B.C.E.)
8. *The Book of Isaiah* (ca. 8th–6th century B.C.E.)
9. The Legacy of Cyrus the Great: *The Cyrus Cylinder* (6th century B.C.E.)
    and *The Book of Ezra* (5th century B.C.E.)

ANCIENT AND CLASSICAL GREECE
10. Homer, *Iliad* (9th–8th century B.C.E.)
11. Sappho of Lesbos, *Poems* (ca. 600 B.C.E.)
12. Thucydides, *History of the Peloponnesian War* (ca. 400 B.C.E.)
13. Xenophon, *The Spartan Constitution* (ca. 360 B.C.E.)
14. Plato, *Apology* (399 B.C.E.)
15. Plato, *The Republic* (ca. 327 B.C.E.)
16. Aristotle, *Politics* (4th century B.C.E.)
17. Plutarch, *The Life of Alexander* (ca. C.E. 116)

THE ROMAN WORLD

18. Polybius, *The Roman Constitution* (ca. 150 B.C.E.)
19. Cicero, *The Trial of Aulus Cluentius Habitus* (66 B.C.E.)
20. Virgil, *Aeneid* (30–19 B.C.E.)
21. Juvenal, *Satires* (ca. C.E. 116)
22. Plutarch, *The Life of Cato the Elder* (ca. C.E. 116)
23. Suetonius, *The Life of Augustus* (ca. C.E. 122)
24. *The Sermon on the Mount* (ca. C.E. 28–35)
25. St. Paul, *Epistle to the Romans* (ca. C.E. 57)

CREATION EPICS

1

THE EPIC OF GILGAMESH

(CA. 2000 B.C.E.)

The Epic of Gilgamesh, the best-known of the Mesopotamian myths, is one of the world's oldest surviving pieces of literature. Only incomplete versions of the story have come down to us, the longest of which is a copy written on twelve tablets found in the Royal Library of Nineveh. The epic was probably composed about 2000 B.C.E. and tells the story of the wanderings of Gilgamesh, the part-human, part-divine king of Uruk. Uruk, one of the most important of the Mesopotamian city-states, was ruled by a King Gilgamesh around 2000 B.C.E., but it is impossible to be certain that the events recounted in the epic derive from his reign.

The peoples of the Ancient Near East lived precariously, always at the mercy of nature. Flood and drought were the most common natural disasters, and *The Epic of Gilgamesh* contains echoes of the great flood narrated in the Bible. Gilgamesh's search for the survivors of this great flood, who supposedly know the secret of everlasting life, motivates the hero's travels. The twin themes of the unpredictability of the gods and the inevitability of death dominate the epic.

THE STORY OF THE FLOOD

You know the city Shurrupak, it stands on the banks of Euphrates? That city grew old and the gods that were in it were old. There was Anu, lord of the firmament, their father, and warrior Enlil their counsellor, Ninurta the helper, and Ennugi watcher over canals; and with them also was Ea. In those days the world teemed, the people multiplied, the world bellowed like a wild bull, and the great god was aroused by the clamour. Enlil heard the clamour and he said to the gods in council, "The uproar of mankind is intolerable and sleep is no longer possible by reason of the babel." So the gods agreed to exterminate mankind. Enlil did this, but Ea because of his oath warned me in a dream.

He whispered their words to my house of reeds, "Reed-house, reed-house! Wall, O wall, hearken reed-house, wall reflect; O man of Shurrupak, son of Ubara-Tutu; tear down your house and build a boat, abandon possessions and look for life, despise worldly goods and save your soul alive. Tear down your house, I say, and build a boat. These are the measurements of the barque as you shall build her: let her beam equal her length, let her deck be roofed like the vault that covers the abyss; then take up into the boat the seed of all living creatures."

When I had understood I said to my lord, "Behold, what you have commanded I will honour and perform, but how shall I answer the people, the city, the elders?" Then Ea opened his mouth and said to me, his servant, "Tell them this: I have learnt that Enlil is wrathful against me, I dare no longer walk in his land nor live in his city; I will go down to the Gulf to dwell with Ea my lord. But on you he will rain down abundance, rare fish and shy wild-fowl, a rich harvest-tide. In the evening the rider of the storm will bring you wheat in torrents."

In the first light of dawn all my household gathered round me, the children brought pitch and the men whatever was necessary. On the fifth day I laid the keel and the ribs, then I made fast the planking. The ground-space was one acre, each side of the deck measured one hundred and twenty cubits, making a square. I built six decks below, seven in all, I divided them into nine sections with bulkheads between. I drove in wedges where needed, I saw to the punt-poles, and laid in supplies. The carriers brought oil in baskets, I poured pitch into the furnace and asphalt and oil; more oil was consumed in caulking, and more again the master of the boat took into his stores. I slaughtered bullocks for the people and every day I killed sheep. I gave the shipwrights wine to drink as though it were river water, raw wine and red wine and oil and white wine. There was feasting then as there is at the time of the New Year's festival; I myself anointed my head. On the seventh day the boat was complete.

Then was the launching full of difficulty; there was shifting of ballast above and below till two thirds was submerged. I loaded into her all that I had of gold and of living things, my family, my kin, the beast of the field both wild and tame, and all the craftsmen. I sent them on board, for the time that Shamash had ordained was already fulfilled when he said, "In the evening, when the rider of the storm sends down the destroying rain, enter the boat and batten her down." The time was fulfilled, the evening came, the rider of the storm sent down the rain. I looked out at the weather and it was terrible, so I too boarded the boat and battened her down. All was now complete, the battening and the caulking; so I handed the tiller to Puzur-Amurri the steersman, with the navigation and the care of the whole boat.

With the first light of dawn a black cloud came from the horizon; it thundered within where Adad, lord of the storm was riding. In front over hill and plain Shullat and Hanish, heralds of the storm, led on. Then the gods of the abyss rose up; Nergal pulled out the dams of the nether waters, Ninurta the war-lord threw down the dykes, and the seven judges of hell, the Annunaki, raised their torches, lighting the land with their livid flame. A stupor of despair went up to heaven when the god of the storm turned daylight to darkness, when he smashed the land like a cup. One whole day the tempest raged, gathering fury as it went, it poured over the people like the tides of battle; a man could not see his brother nor the people be seen from heaven. Even the gods were terrified at the flood, they fled to the highest heaven, the firmament of Anu; they crouched against the walls, cowering like curs. Then Ishtar the sweet-voiced Queen of Heaven cried out like a woman in travail: "Alas the days of old are turned to dust because I commanded evil; why did I command this evil in the council of all the gods? I commanded wars to destroy the people, but are they not my people, for I brought them forth? Now like the spawn of fish they float in the ocean." The great gods of heaven and of hell wept, they covered their mouths.

For six days and six nights the winds blew, torrent and tempest and flood overwhelmed the world, tempest and flood raged together like warring hosts. When the seventh day dawned the storm from the south subsided, the sea grew calm, the flood was stilled; I looked at the face of the world and there was silence, all mankind was turned to clay. The surface of the sea stretched as flat as a roof-top; I opened a hatch and the light fell on my face. Then I bowed low, I sat down and I wept, the tears streamed down my face, for on every side was the waste of water. I looked for land in vain, but fourteen leagues distant there appeared a mountain, and there the boat grounded; on the mountain of Nisir the boat held fast, she held fast and did not budge. One day she held, and a second day on the mountain of Nisir she held fast and did not budge. A third day, and a fourth day she held fast on the mountain and did not budge; a fifth day and a sixth day she held fast on the mountain. When the seventh day dawned I loosed a dove and let her go. She flew away, but finding no resting-place she returned. Then I loosed a swallow, and she flew away but finding no resting-place she returned. I loosed a raven, she saw that the water had retreated, she ate, she flew around, she cawed, and she did not come back. Then I threw everything open to the four winds, I made a sacrifice and poured out a libation on the mountain top. Seven and again seven cauldrons I set up on their stands, I heaped up wood and cane and cedar and myrtle. When the gods smelled the sweet savour, they gathered like flies over the sacrifice. Then, at last, Ishtar also came, she lifted her necklace with the jewels of heaven that once Anu had made to please her. "O you gods here present, by the lapis lazuli round my neck I shall remember these days as I remember the jewels of my throat; these last days I shall not forget. Let all the gods gather round the sacrifice, except Enlil. He shall not approach this offering, for without reflection he brought the flood; he consigned my people to destruction."

QUESTIONS

1. Why was there a great flood, according to the epic? Who or what caused it?

2. Compare the account of the flood in the *Epic of Gilgamesh* with that described in Genesis. How are they similar? How different?

3. What does the story of the flood reveal about Mesopotamian gods and people's attitudes toward them?

4. What do you think the epic tells us about the Mesopotamian view of life?

2

THE CREATION EPIC
(CA. 2000 B.C.E.)

Mesopotamian civilization emerged in a land that knew little continuity or order. Both climate and geography made life hazardous and unpredictable. In contrast to life in ancient Egypt, where the seasonal flooding of the Nile and the relative isolation of the country fostered a sense of regularity, Mesopotamians lived with uncertainty. The religion of the people reflects these environmental conditions. Faced by a world in which change was often rapid and violent, Mesopotamians sought an explanation for their social reality through a belief in the capriciousness of the gods.

The Creation Epic describes a bitter conflict between the gods Marduk and Tiamat that led to the creation of the world that the Mesopotamians knew.

Tiamat was the oldest of the gods, but she was also the patron of the primeval chaos. Marduk was the warrior god whose purpose was to institute order. The world that emerged from this battle maintained precarious stability—subject always to the whims of inexplicable divinity.

Tablet I

When on high, heaven was not named,
Below, dry land was not named.
Apsu, their first begetter,
Mummu [and] Tiamat, the mother of all of them,
Their waters combined together.
Field was not marked off, sprout had not
    come forth.
When none of the gods had yet come forth,
Had not borne a name,
No destinies had been fixed;
Then gods were created in the midst of heaven.
Lakhmu and Lakhamu came forth
Ages increased . . .
Anshar and Kishar were created.
After many days had passed by there came
    forth . . .
Anu, their son . . .
Anshar and Anu . . .
Anu . . .
Nudimmud whom his father, his mother, . . .
Of large intelligence, knowing [wise],
Exceeding strong . . .
Without a rival . . .
Then were established. . . .
Then Apsu, the begetter of the great gods,
Cried out, to Mummu, to his messenger,
    he spoke:
"Oh Mummu, joy of my liver,
Come, unto Tiamat let us go."
They went, and before Tiamat they crouched,
Hatching a plan with regard to the gods . . .
Apsu opened his mouth and spoke,
Unto Tiamat, the splendid one addressed a word:
" . . . their course against me
By day I have no rest, at night I cannot lie down,
    I wish to destroy their course,
So that clamor cease and we may again lie down
    to sleep."

When Tiamat [heard] this,
She raged and shrieked for [revenge?],
She herself became furiously enraged.
Evil she conceived in her heart.
"All that we have made let us destroy,
That their course may be full of misery so that
    we may have release."
Mummu answered and counselled Apsu,
Hostile was the counsel of Mummu.
"Come, their course is strong, destroy it!
Then by day thou wilt have rest,
At night thou wilt lie down."
Apsu [hearkened], and his face shone;
Evil he planned against the gods, his sons. . . .
They uttered curses and at the side of Tiamat
    advanced.
In fury and rage they devised plans ceaselessly
    night and day.
They rushed to the conflict, raging and furious.
They grouped themselves and ranged the
    battle array.
Ummu-Khubur, creator of all things,
Gathering invincible weapons, she brought
    forth huge monsters,
Sharp of tooth and merciless of fang.
With poison instead of blood she filled their
    bodies.
She clothed with terror the terrible dragons,
Decking them with brilliancy, giving them
    a lofty stature,
So that whoever beheld them would be
    overcome with terror.
With their bodies reared up, none could
    withstand their attack.
She brought forth great serpents, dragons and
    the Lakhami,
Hurricanes, raging dogs and scorpion men,
Mighty tempests, fish men, and rams,
Bearing cruel weapons, fearless in combat,

Mighty in command, irresistible.
In all eleven monsters of this kind she made.
Among the gods, the first born who formed
     the assembly,
She exalted Kingu, giving him high rank in
     their midst;
To march in advance and to direct the host;
To be foremost in arming for the attack,
To direct the fight in supreme control,
To his hand she confided. She decked him out
     in costly garments:
"I have uttered thy magic formula, in the
     assembly of the gods I have exalted thee."
The dominion over all the gods was entrusted
     unto his hands:
"Be thou exalted, my one and only husband;
May the Anunnaki exalt thy name above all
     the gods!"
She gave him the tablets of fate, to his breast
     she attached them.
"Oh, thou, thy command will be irresistible!
Firmly established be the utterance of thy mouth!
Now Kingu is exalted, endowed with the power
     of Anu;
Among the gods, his children, he fixes destinies.
By the word of thy mouth fire will be quenched;
The strong in battle will be increased in
     strength."

Tablet II

Tiamat finished her work.
[The evil that] she contrived against the gods
     her offspring,
To avenge Apsu, Tiamat planned evil.
When she had equipped her army, it was
     revealed to Ea;
Ea heard the words,
And was grievously afflicted, and overwhelmed
     with grief.
Days passed by and his anger was appeased.
To Anshar, his father, he took the way.
To Father Anshar who begot him he went.
All that Tiamat had planned he repeated to him.
"Tiamat our mother has taken a dislike for us,
She has assembled a host, she rages furiously.

All the gods are gathered to her,
Aye, even those whom thou hast created, march
     at her side."
[Anshar asks his son Marduk to fight Tiamat]
"Thou are my son of strong courage, . . . draw
     nigh to the battle!
 . . . at sight of thee there shall be peace."
The Lord rejoiced at the word of his father.
He drew nigh and stood in front of Anshar;
Anshar saw him and his heart was full of joy.
He kissed him on the mouth, and fear departed
     from him.
"[Oh my father], may the words of thy lips not
     be taken back,
May I go and accomplish the desire of thy
     heart!"
"Oh, my son, full of all knowledge,
Quiet Tiamat with thy supreme incantation;
Quickly proceed [on thy way]!
Thy blood will not be poured out, thou shalt
     surely return."
The Lord rejoiced at the word of his father.
His heart exulted and he spoke to his father.
"Oh Lord of the gods, [who fixes] the fate of
     the great gods,
If I become thy avenger,
Conquering Tiamat, and giving life to thee,
Call an assembly and proclaim the preeminence
     of my lot!
That when in Upshukkinaku thou joyfully
     seatest thyself,
My command in place of thine should fix fates.
What I do should be unaltered,
The word of my lips be never changed or
     annulled."

Tablet III

Then they gathered and went,
The great gods, all of them, who fix fates,
Came into the presence of Anshar, they filled
     [the assembly hall],
Embracing one another in the assembly [hall],
They prepared themselves to feast at the banquet.
They ate bread, they mixed the wine,
The sweet mead confused [their senses].

Babylonian cylinder seal imprint showing the slaughter of the monster Tiamat by the god Marduk, who is armed with a thunderbolt and other weapons. This scene is described on the fourth tablet of the Creation series.

Drunk, their bodies filled with drink,
They shouted aloud, with their spirits exalted,
For Marduk, their avenger, they fixed the destiny.

Tablet IV

They prepared for him a royal chamber,
In the presence of his fathers as ruler he stood.
"Thou art the weightiest among the great gods.
Thy [power of decreeing] fate is unrivalled, thy
    command is [like that of] Anu.
Oh Marduk, thou art mightiest among the
    great gods!
Thy power of decreeing fate unrivalled, thy
    word is like that of Anu!
From now on thy decree will not be altered,
Thine it shall be to raise up and to bring low,
Thy utterance be established, against thy
    command no rebellion!
None among the gods will transgress the limit
    [set by thee].
Abundance is pleasing to the shrines of the gods,
The place of their worship will be established as
    thy place.

Oh Marduk, thou art our avenger!
We give thee kingship over the entire universe,
Take thy seat in the assembly, thy word be
    exalted;
Thy weapon be not overcome, may it crush thy
    enemies.
Oh lord, the life of him who trusts in thee
    will be spared,
But pour out the life of the god who has
    planned evil." . . .
He sent forth the winds which he had created,
    the seven of them;
To trouble the spirit of Tiamat, they followed
    behind him.
Then the lord raised on high the Deluge, his
    mighty weapon.
He mounted the storm chariot, unequalled
    in power,
He harnessed and attached to it four horses,
Merciless, overwhelming, swiftly flying.
[Sharp of] teeth, bearing poison. . . .
Then the lord drew nigh, piercing Tiamat with
    his glance;
He saw the purpose of Kingu, her spouse,

As he [i.e., Marduk] gazed, he [i.e., Kingu]
    tottered in his gait. His mind was destroyed,
    his action upset,
And the gods, his helpers, marching at his side,
Saw [the terror of] the hero and leader.
But Tiamat [uttered a cry] and did not turn
    her back,
From her lips there gushed forth rebellious words
    . . . "coming to thee as lord of the gods,
As in their own sanctuaries they are gathered
    in thy sanctuary."
Then the lord raised on high the Deluge,
    the great weapon,
And against Tiamat, who was foaming with
    wrath, thus sent forth [his answer].
"Great art thou! Thou has exalted thyself greatly.
Thy heart hath prompted thee to arrange
    for battle. . . .
Thou has [exalted] Kingu to be thy husband,
[Thou hast given him power to issue] the
    decrees of Anu.
[Against the gods, my fathers], thou hast
    planned evil,
Against the gods, my fathers, thou hast
    planned evil.
Let thy army be equipped, thy weapons be
    girded on;
Stand; I and thou, let us join in battle."
When Tiamat heard this,
She was beside herself, she lost her reason.
Tiamat shouted in a paroxysm of fury,
Trembling to the root, shaking in her
    foundations.
She uttered an incantation, she pronounced
    a magic formula.
The gods of battle, appeal to their weapons.
Then stepped forth Tiamat and the leader of
    the gods, Marduk.
To the fight they advanced, to the battle they
    drew nigh.
The lord spread his net and encompassed her,
The evil wind stationed behind him he drove
    into her face.
Tiamat opened her mouth to its full extent.
He drove in the evil wind before she could close
    her lips.

The terrible winds filled her belly,
Her heart was seized, and she held her mouth
    wide open.
He drove in the spear and burst open her belly,
Cutting into her entrails, he slit her heart.
He overcame her and destroyed her life;
He cast down her carcass and stood upon it.
When he had thus subjected Tiamat, the leader,
Her host was scattered, her assembly was
    dissolved;
And the gods, her helpers, who marched
    beside her,
In fear and trembling turned about,
Taking to flight to save their lives.
But they were surrounded and could not escape.
He captured them and smashed their weapons,
They were cast into the net, and brought into
    the snare; . . .
After he [i.e., Marduk] had bound and cast
    down his enemies,
Had battered down the arrogant foe,
Had completely gained the victory of
    Anshar over the enemy,
The hero Marduk had attained the aim of
    Nudimmud,
He strengthened his hold over the captive gods.
To Tiamat, whom he had bound, he came back,
And the lord trampled under foot the
    foundation of Tiamat.
With his merciless weapon he smashed her skull,
He cut the channels of her blood,
And made the north wind carry them to secret
    places.
His fathers beheld and rejoiced exceeding glad,
Presents and gifts they brought to him.
Then the lord rested and looked at the carcass.
He divided the flesh of the monster, and
    created marvellous things.
He split her like a fish flattened into two halves;
One half he took and made it a covering for
    heaven.
He drew a bolt, he stationed a watchman,
Enjoining that the waters be not permitted to
    flow out.
He passed over the heavens, inspecting the
    regions [thereof],

And over against the Apsu, he set the dwelling
of Nudimmud.
The lord measured the structure of the Deep.
He established E-sharra as a palace
corresponding to it.
The palace E-sharra which he created as heaven,
He caused Anu, Enlil and Ea to inhabit their
districts.

Tablet V

He made stations for the great gods,
The stars, their counterparts, the twin stars he
fixed.
He fixed the year and divided it into divisions.
For the twelve months he fixed three stars.
Also for the days of the year [he had fashioned]
pictures. . . .

Tablet VI

Upon [Marduk's] hearing the word of the gods,
His heart led him to create [marvellous
things]
He opened his mouth and [spoke] to Ea
[What] he had conceived in his heart he
imparted to him;
"My blood I will take and bone I will [form].
I will set up man that man . . .
I will create man to inhabit [the earth],
That the worship of the gods be fixed, that
they may have shrines.
But I will alter the ways of the gods, I will
change . . .
They shall be joined in concert, unto evil shall
they" . . .
Ea answered him and spoke.

QUESTIONS

1. Conflict seems to be a major theme of the *Creation Epic*. What, in practical
   terms, does war among gods mean for mere mortals?

2. Mortals play little part in the struggles of the gods. Why? What assumptions
   about humanity and its relations to the gods are revealed in the epic?

3. Who won the battle between Marduk and Tiamat? What followed the end
   of that war?

4. Extreme violence marks much of the *Creation Epic*. What lessons might
   you draw from this about the nature of Mesopotamian society?

3

THE BOOK OF GENESIS

(CA. 10TH–6TH CENTURY B.C.E.)

Genesis is the first book of the Old Testament, as well as the first book of the
Hebrew Torah. Its subject is the creation of the world, the origins of humanity,
and the early history of the Hebrew people. Most scholars believe that the

book is the result of combining three different versions with roots in the distant past. They seem to have been written down between about 950 and 400 B.C.E., but the book contains much older traditions. Genesis contains echoes of other ancient texts and myths, such as *The Epic of Gilgamesh* and the Babylonian *Creation Epic*. This selection relates the story of the creation, the expulsion from the Garden of Eden, and the Flood.

1 In the beginning God created the heavens and the earth. [2]The earth was without form and void, and darkness was upon the face of the deep; and the Spirit of God was moving over the face of the waters.

[3]And God said, "Let there be light"; and there was light. [4]And God saw that the light was good; and God separated the light from the darkness. [5]God called the light Day, and the darkness he called Night. And there was evening and there was morning, one day.

[6]And God said, "Let there be a firmament in the midst of the waters, and let it separate the waters from the waters." [7]And God made the firmament and separated the waters which were under the firmament from the waters which were above the firmament. And it was so. [8]And God called the firmament Heaven. And there was evening and there was morning, a second day.

[9]And God said, "Let the waters under the heavens be gathered together into one place, and let the dry land appear." And it was so. [10]God called the dry land Earth, and the waters that were gathered together he called Seas. And God saw that it was good. [11]And God said, "Let the earth put forth vegetation, plants yielding seed, and fruit trees bearing fruit in which is their seed, each according to its kind, upon the earth." And it was so. [12]The earth brought forth vegetation, plants yielding seed according to their own kinds, and trees bearing fruit in which is their seed, each according to its kind. And God saw that it was good. [13]And there was evening and there was morning, a third day.

[14]And God said, "Let there be lights in the firmament of the heavens to separate the day from the night; and let them be for signs and for seasons and for days and years, [15]and let them be lights in the firmament of the heavens to give light upon the earth." And it was so. [16]And God made the two great lights, the greater light to rule the day, and the lesser light to rule the night; he made the stars also. [17]And God set them in the firmament of the heavens to give light upon the earth, [18]to rule over the day and over the night, and to separate the light from the darkness. And God saw that it was good. [19]And there was evening and there was morning, a fourth day.

[20]And God said, "Let the waters bring forth swarms of living creatures, and let birds fly above the earth across the firmament of the heavens." [21]So God created the great sea monsters and every living creature that moves, with which the waters swarm, according to their kinds, and every winged bird according to its kind. And God saw that it was good. [22]And God blessed them, saying, "Be fruitful and multiply and fill the waters in the seas, and let birds multiply on the earth." [23]And there was evening and there was morning, a fifth day.

[24]And God said, "Let the earth bring forth living creatures according to their kinds: cattle and creeping things and beasts of the earth according to their kinds." And it was so. [25]And God made the beasts of the earth according to their kinds and the cattle according to their kinds, and everything that creeps upon the ground according to its kind. And God saw that it was good.

[26]Then God said, "Let us make man in our image, after our likeness; and let them have dominion over the fish of the sea, and over the birds of the air, and over the cattle, and over all

the earth, and over every creeping thing that creeps upon the earth." [27]So God created man in his own image, in the image of God he created him; male and female he created them. [28]And God blessed them, and God said to them, "Be fruitful and multiply, and fill the earth and subdue it; and have dominion over the fish of the sea and over the birds of the air and over every living thing that moves upon the earth." [29]And God said, "Behold, I have given you every plant yielding seed which is upon the face of all the earth, and every tree with seed in its fruit; you shall have them for food. [30]And to every beast of the earth, and to every bird of the air, and to everything that creeps on the earth, everything that has the breath of life, I have given every green plant for food." And it was so. [31]And God saw everything that he had made, and behold, it was very good. And there was evening and there was morning, a sixth day.

2 Thus the heavens and the earth were finished, and all the host of them. [2]And on the seventh day God finished his work which he had done, and he rested on the seventh day from all his work which he had done. [3]So God blessed the seventh day and hallowed it, because on it God rested from all his work which he had done in creation.

[4]These are the generations of the heavens and the earth when they were created.

In the day that the LORD God made the earth and the heavens, [5]when no plant of the field was yet in the earth and no herb of the field had yet sprung up—for the LORD God had not caused it to rain upon the earth, and there was no man to till the ground; [6]but a mist went up from the earth and watered the whole face of the ground—[7]then the LORD God formed man of dust from the ground, and breathed into his nostrils the breath of life; and man became a living being. [8]And the LORD God planted a garden in Eden, in the east; and there he put the man whom he had formed. [9]And out of the ground the LORD God made to grow every tree that is pleasant to the sight and good for food, the tree of life also in the midst of the garden, and the tree of the knowledge of good and evil.

[10]A river flowed out of Eden to water the garden, and there it divided and became four rivers. [11]The name of the first is Pishon; it is the one which flows around the whole land of Hav'ilah, where there is gold; [12]and the gold of that land is good; bdellium and onyx stone are there. [13]The name of the second river is Gihon; it is the one which flows around the whole land of Cush. [14]And the name of the third river is Tigris, which flows east of Assyria. And the fourth river is the Euphra'tes.

[15]The LORD God took the man and put him in the garden of Eden to till it and keep it. [16]And the LORD God commanded the man, saying, "You may freely eat of every tree of the garden; [17]but of the tree of the knowledge of good and evil you shall not eat, for in the day that you eat of it you shall die."

[18]Then the LORD God said, "It is not good that the man should be alone; I will make him a helper fit for him." [19]So out of the ground the LORD God formed every beast of the field and every bird of the air, and brought them to the man to see what he would call them; and whatever the man called every living creature, that was its name. [20]The man gave names to all cattle, and to the birds of the air, and to every beast of the field; but for the man there was not found a helper fit for him. [21]So the LORD God caused a deep sleep to fall upon the man, and while he slept took one of his ribs and closed up its place with flesh; [22]and the rib which the LORD God had taken from the man he made into a woman and brought her to the man. [23]Then the man said,

"This at last is bone of my bones
    and flesh of my flesh;
she shall be called Woman,
    because she was taken out of Man."

[24]Therefore a man leaves his father and his mother and cleaves to his wife, and they become

one flesh. [25]And the man and his wife were both naked, and were not ashamed.

3 Now the serpent was more subtle than any other wild creature that the LORD God had made. He said to the woman, "Did God say, 'You shall not eat of any tree of the garden'?" [2]And the woman said to the serpent, "We may eat of the fruit of the trees of the garden; [3]but God said, 'You shall not eat of the fruit of the tree which is in the midst of the garden, neither shall you touch it, lest you die.' " [4]But the serpent said to the woman, "You will not die. [5]For God knows that when you eat of it your eyes will be opened, and you will be like God, knowing good and evil." [6]So when the woman saw that the tree was good for food, and that it was a delight to the eyes, and that the tree was to be desired to make one wise, she took of its fruit and ate; and she also gave some to her husband, and he ate. [7]Then the eyes of both were opened, and they knew that they were naked; and they sewed fig leaves together and made themselves aprons.

[8]And they heard the sound of the LORD God walking in the garden in the cool of the day, and the man and his wife hid themselves from the presence of the LORD God among the trees of the garden. [9]But the LORD God called to the man, and said to him, "Where are you?" [10]And he said, "I heard the sound of thee in the garden, and I was afraid, because I was naked; and I hid myself." [11]He said, "Who told you that you were naked? Have you eaten of the tree of which I commanded you not to eat?" [12]The man said, "The woman whom thou gavest to be with me, she gave me fruit of the tree, and I ate." [13]Then the LORD God said to the woman, "What is this that you have done?" The woman said, "The serpent beguiled me, and I ate." [14]The LORD God said to the serpent,

"Because you have done this,
        cursed are you above all cattle,
        and above all wild animals;
upon your belly you shall go,
        and dust you shall eat
        all the days of your life.
[15]I will put enmity between you and the woman,

and between your seed and her seed;
he shall bruise your head,
and you shall bruise his heel."

[16]To the woman he said,

"I will greatly multiply your pain in childbearing;
        in pain you shall bring forth children,
yet your desire shall be for your husband,
        and he shall rule over you."

[17]And to Adam he said,

"Because you have listened to the voice of
        your wife,
        and have eaten of the tree
of which I commanded you,
        'You shall not eat of it,'
cursed is the ground because of you;
        in toil you shall eat of it all the days of your
        life;
[18]thorns and thistles it shall bring forth to you;
and you shall eat the plants of the field.
[19]In the sweat of your face
you shall eat bread
till you return to the ground,
        for out of it you were taken;
you are dust,
and to dust you shall return."

[20]The man called his wife's name Eve, because she was the mother of all living. [21]And the LORD God made for Adam and for his wife garments of skins, and clothed them.

[22]Then the LORD God said, "Behold, the man has become like one of us, knowing good and evil; and now, lest he put forth his hand and take also of the tree of life, and eat, and live for ever"—[23]therefore the LORD God sent him forth from the garden of Eden, to till the ground from which he was taken. [24]He drove out the man; and at the east of the garden of Eden he placed the cherubim, and a flaming sword which turned every way, to guard the way to the tree of life.

• • •

6 When men began to multiply on the face of the ground, and daughters were born to them, [2]the sons of God saw that the daughters of men were fair; and they took to wife such of them as they chose. [3]Then the LORD said, "My spirit shall not abide in man for ever, for he is flesh, but his days shall be a hundred and twenty years." [4]The Nephilim were on the earth in those days, and also afterward, when the sons of God came in to the daughters of men, and they bore children to them. These were the mighty men that were of old, the men of renown.

[5]The LORD saw that the wickedness of man was great in the earth, and that every imagination of the thoughts of his heart was only evil continually. [6]And the LORD was sorry that he had made man on the earth, and it grieved him to his heart. [7]So the LORD said, "I will blot out man whom I have created from the face of the ground, man and beast and creeping things and birds of the air, for I am sorry that I have made them." [8]But Noah found favor in the eyes of the LORD. . . .

[11]Now the earth was corrupt in God's sight, and the earth was filled with violence. [12]And God saw the earth, and behold, it was corrupt; for all flesh had corrupted their way upon the earth. [13]And God said to Noah, "I have determined to make an end of all flesh; for the earth is filled with violence through them; behold, I will destroy them with the earth. [14]Make yourself an ark of gopher wood; make rooms in the ark, and cover it inside and out with pitch. For behold, I will bring a flood of waters upon the earth, to destroy all flesh in which is the breath of life from under heaven; everything that is on the earth shall die. [18]But I will establish my covenant with you; and you shall come into the ark, you, your sons, your wife, and your sons' wives with you. [19]And of every living thing of all flesh, you shall bring two of every sort into the ark, to keep them alive with you; they shall be male and female. [20]Of the birds according to their kinds, and of the animals according to their kinds, of every creeping thing of the ground according to its kind, two of every sort shall come in to you, to keep them alive. [21]Also take with you every sort of food that is eaten, and

store it up; and it shall serve as food for you and for them." [22]Noah did this; he did all that God commanded him.

7 Then the LORD said to Noah, "Go into the ark, you and all your household, for I have seen that you are righteous before me in this generation. [2]Take with you seven pairs of all clean animals, the male and his mate; and a pair of the animals that are not clean, the male and his mate; [3]and seven pairs of the birds of the air also, male and female, to keep their kind alive upon the face of all the earth. [4]For in seven days I will send rain upon the earth forty days and forty nights; and every living thing that I have made I will blot out from the face of the ground." [5]And Noah did all that the LORD had commanded him.

[6]Noah was six hundred years old when the flood of waters came upon the earth. [7]And Noah and his sons and his wife and his sons' wives with him went into the ark, to escape the waters of the flood. [8]Of clean animals, and of animals that are not clean, and of birds, and of everything that creeps, on the ground, [9]two and two, male and female, went into the ark with Noah, as God had commanded Noah. [10]And after seven days the waters of the flood came upon the earth.

. . . [12]And rain fell upon the earth forty days and forty nights. [13]On the very same day Noah and his sons, Shem and Ham and Japheth, and Noah's wife and the three wives of his sons with them entered the ark, [14]they and every beast according to its kind, and all the cattle according to their kinds, and every creeping thing that creeps on the earth according to its kind, and every bird according to its kind, every bird of every sort. [15]They went into the ark with Noah, two and two of all flesh in which there was the breath of life. [16]And they that entered, male and female of all flesh, went in as God had commanded him; and the LORD shut him in.

[17]The flood continued forty days upon the earth; and the waters increased, and bore up the ark, and it rose high above the earth. [18]The waters prevailed and increased greatly upon

the earth; and the ark floated on the face of the waters. [19]And the waters prevailed so mightily upon the earth that all the high mountains under the whole heaven were covered; [20]the waters prevailed above the mountains, covering them fifteen cubits deep. [21]And all flesh died that moved upon the earth, birds, cattle, beasts, all swarming creatures that swarm upon the earth, and every man; [22]everything on the dry land in whose nostrils was the breath of life died. [23]He blotted out every living thing that was upon the face of the ground, man and animals and creeping things and birds of the air; they were blotted out from the earth. Only Noah was left, and those that were with him in the ark. [24]And the waters prevailed upon the earth a hundred and fifty days. . . .

8 . . . [6]At the end of forty days Noah opened the window of the ark which he had made, [7]and sent forth a raven; and it went to and fro until the waters were dried up from the earth. [8]Then he sent forth a dove from him, to see if the waters had subsided from the face of the ground; [9]but the dove found no place to set her foot, and she returned to him to the ark, for the waters were still on the face of the whole earth. So he put forth his hand and took her and brought her into the ark with him. [10]He waited another seven days, and again he sent forth the dove out of the ark; [11]and the dove came back to him in the evening, and lo, in her mouth a freshly plucked olive leaf; so Noah knew that the waters had subsided from the earth. [12]Then he waited another seven days, and sent forth the dove; and she did not return to him any more. . . .

9 And God blessed Noah and his sons, and said to them, "Be fruitful and multiply, and fill the earth. [2]The fear of you and the dread of you shall be upon every beast of the earth, and upon every bird of the air, upon everything that creeps on the ground and all the fish of the sea; into your hand they are delivered. [3]Every moving thing that lives shall be food for you; and as I gave you the green plants, I give you everything.

QUESTIONS

1. How is Eve created? What do you think the story of the Garden of Eden reveals about gender relations in ancient times?

2. What does Genesis have in common with other creation myths? How does it differ?

3. According to Genesis, what is man's place in the natural world? What does humanity's relationship with nature reveal about ancient attitudes toward the environment?

4. God seems to expect a great deal of his human creations—do they live up to his high standards? What does he want from them?

5. Why do you think this book was written? What purpose might it have served?

4

■ *Hesiod* ■

WORKS AND DAYS

(CA. 700 B.C.E.)

Hesiod (lived ca. 700 B.C.E.) is one of the earliest known Greek poets. Although he was famous in his own time—his works were publicly performed throughout the Greek world—the actual facts of his life remain shadowy. It is believed that his father came from Asia Minor, though Hesiod himself was born in central Greece. He may have earned his living as a public reciter of songs and poetry, first the works of others and later his own. He performed at festivals and athletic events all over Greece.

Hesiod's fame as a poet was such that his contemporaries often gave his name to their own works, so it is difficult to determine what he actually wrote. He was most famous, however, for two epics: the *Theogony*, which told the story of the gods, and *Works and Days*, whose subjects were mere mortals. Addressed to his brother Perses, *Works and Days* offers advice for daily living.

"[Prometheus,] clever above all others, you are pleased at having stolen fire and outwitted me— a great calamity both for yourself and for men to come. To set against the fire I shall give them an affliction in which they will all delight as they embrace their own misfortune."

So saying, the father of gods and men laughed aloud; and he told renowned Hephaestus at once to mix earth with water, to add in a human voice and strength, and to model upon the immortal goddesses' aspect the fair lovely form of a maiden. Athene he told to teach her crafts, to weave the embroidered web, and golden Aphrodite to shower charm about her head, and painful yearning and consuming obsession; to put in a bitch's mind and a knavish nature, that was his instruction to Hermes the go-between, the dog-killer.

So he ordered, and they all obeyed the lord Zeus son of Kronos. At once the renowned Ambidexter moulded from earth the likeness of a modest maiden by Kronos' son's design, and the pale-eyed goddess Athene dressed and adorned her. The Graces and the lady Temptation put necklaces of gold about her body, and the lovely-haired spirits of ripeness garlanded her about with spring flowers. Pallas Athene arranged all the adornment on her body. In her breast the Go-between, the dog-killer, fashioned lies and wily pretences and a knavish nature by deep-thundering Zeus' design; and he put in a voice, did the herald of the gods, and he named this woman Pandora, Allgift, because all the dwellers on Olympus made her their gift—a calamity for men who live by bread.

When he had completed the precipitous, unmanageable trap, the father sent the renowned dog-killer to Epimetheus taking the gift, swift messenger of the gods. Epimetheus gave no thought to what Prometheus had told him, never to accept a gift from Olympian Zeus but to send it back lest some affliction befall mortals: he accepted, and had the bane before he realized it.

For formerly the tribes of men on earth lived remote from ills, without harsh toil and the grievous sicknesses that are deadly to men. But the woman unstopped the jar and let it all out, and brought grim cares upon mankind. Only Hope remained there inside in her secure dwelling, under the lip of the jar, and did not fly out, because the woman put the lid back in time by the providence of Zeus the cloud-gatherer who bears the aegis. But for the rest, countless troubles roam among men: full of ills is the earth, and full the sea. Sicknesses visit men by day, and others by night, uninvited, bringing ill to mortals, silently, because Zeus the resourceful deprived them of voice. Thus there is no way to evade the purpose of Zeus.

If you like, I will summarize another tale for you, well and skilfully—mind you take it in— telling how gods and mortal men have come from the same starting-point.

The race of men that the immortals who dwell on Olympus made first of all was of gold. They were in the time of Kronos, when he was king in heaven; and they lived like gods, with carefree heart, remote from toil and misery. Wretched old age did not affect them either, but with hands and feet ever unchanged they enjoyed themselves in feasting, beyond all ills, and they died as if overcome by sleep. All good things were theirs, and the grain-giving soil bore its fruits of its own accord in unstinted plenty, while they at their leisure harvested their fields in contentment amid abundance. Since the earth covered up that race, they have been divine spirits by great Zeus' design, good spirits on the face of the earth, watchers over mortal men, bestowers of wealth: such is the kingly honour that they received.

A second race after that, much inferior, the dwellers on Olympus made of silver. It resembled the golden one neither in body nor in disposition. For a hundred years a boy would stay in the care of his mother, playing childishly at home; but after reaching adolescence and the appointed span of youthful manhood, they lived but a little time, and in suffering, because of their witlessness. For they could not restrain themselves from crimes against each other, and they would not serve the immortals or sacrifice on the sacred altars of the blessed ones, as is laid down for men in their various homelands. They were put away by Zeus son of Kronos, angry because they did not offer honour to the blessed gods who occupy Olympus. Since the earth covered up this race in its turn, they have been called the mortal blessed below, second in rank, but still they too have honour.

Then Zeus the father made yet a third race of men, of bronze, not like the silver in anything. Out of ash-trees he made them, a terrible and fierce race, occupied with the woeful works of Ares and with acts of violence, no eaters of corn, their stern hearts being of adamant; unshapen hulks, with great strength and indescribable arms growing from their shoulders above their stalwart bodies. They had bronze armour, bronze houses, and with bronze they laboured, as dark iron was not available. They were laid low by their own hands, and they went to chill Hades' house of decay leaving no names: mighty though they were, dark death got them, and they left the bright sunlight.

After the earth covered up this race too, Zeus son of Kronos made yet a fourth one upon the rich-pastured earth, a more righteous and noble one, the godly race of the heroes who are called demigods, our predecessors on the boundless earth. And as for them, ugly war and fearful fighting destroyed them, some below seven-gated Thebes, the Cadmean country, as they battled for Oedipus' flocks, and others it led in ships over the great abyss of the sea to Troy on account of lovely-haired Helen. There some of them were engulfed by the consummation of death, but to some Zeus the father, son of Kronos, granted a life and home apart from men, and settled them at the ends of the earth. These dwell with carefree heart in the Isles of the Blessed Ones, beside deep-swirling Oceanus:

fortunate Heroes, for whom the grain-giving soil bears its honey-sweet fruits thrice a year.

Would that I were not then among the fifth men, but either dead earlier or born later! For now it is a race of iron; and they will never cease from toil and misery by day or night, in constant distress, and the gods will give them harsh troubles. Nevertheless, even they shall have good mixed with ill. Yet Zeus will destroy this race of men also, when at birth they turn out grey at the temples. Nor will father be like children nor children to father, nor guest to host or comrade to comrade, nor will a brother be friendly as in former times. Soon they will cease to respect their ageing parents, and will rail at them with harsh words, the ruffians, in ignorance of the gods' punishment; nor are they likely to repay their ageing parents for their nurture. Fist-law men; one will sack another's town, and there will be no thanks for the man who abides by his oath or for the righteous or worthy man, but instead they will honour the miscreant and the criminal. Law and decency will be in fists. The villain will do his better down by telling crooked tales, and will swear his oath upon it. Men in their misery will everywhere be dogged by the evil commotions of that Envy who exults in misfortune with a face full of hate. Then verily off to Olympus from the wide-pathed earth, veiling their fair faces with white robes, Decency and Moral Disapproval will go to join the family of the immortals, abandoning mankind; those grim woes will remain for mortal men, and there will be no help against evil.

Now I will tell a fable to the lords, although they can think for themselves. Here is how the hawk addressed the dapple-throat nightingale as he carried her high in the clouds, grasping her in his claws; impaled on the curved talons, she was weeping piteously, but he addressed her sternly:

"Goodness, why are you screaming? You are in the power of one much superior, and you will go whichever way I take you, singer though you are. I will make you my dinner if I like, or let you go. He is a fool who seeks to compete against the stronger: he both loses the struggle and suffers injury on top of insult."

So spoke the swift-flying hawk, the great winged bird. But you, Perses, must hearken to Right and not promote violence. For violence is bad for a lowly man; not even a man of worth can carry it easily, but he sinks under it when he runs into Blights. The road on the other side gives better passage, to righteousness: Right gets the upper hand over violence in the end. The fool learns only by experience. For Oath at once runs level with crooked judgments; there is angry murmuring when Right is dragged off wherever bribe-swallowers choose to take her as they give judgment with crooked verdicts; and she follows weeping to those people's town and territories clad in darkness, bringing ill to men who drive her out and do not dispense her straight.

As for those who give straight judgments to visitors and to their own people and do not deviate from what is just, their community flourishes, and the people blooms in it. Peace is about the land, fostering the young, and wide-seeing Zeus never marks out grievous war as their portion. Neither does Famine attend straight-judging men, nor Blight, and they feast on the crops they tend. For them Earth bears plentiful food, and on the mountains the oak carries acorns at its surface and bees at its centre. The fleecy sheep are laden down with wool; the womenfolk bear children that resemble their parents; they enjoy a continual sufficiency of good things. Nor do they ply on ships, but the grain-giving ploughland bears them fruit.

But for those who occupy themselves with violence and wickedness and brutal deeds, Kronos' son, wide-seeing Zeus, marks out retribution. Often a whole community together suffers in consequence of a bad man who does wrong and contrives evil. From heaven Kronos' son brings disaster upon them, famine and with it plague, and the people waste away. The womenfolk do not give birth, and households decline, by Olympian Zeus' design. At other times again he either destroys those men's broad army or city wall, or punishes their ships at sea.

You too, my lords, attend to this justice-doing of yours. For close at hand among men there are immortals taking note of all those who afflict each other with crooked judgments, heedless of the gods' punishment. Thrice countless are they on the rich-pastured earth, Zeus' immortal watchers of mortal men, who watch over judgments and wickedness, clothed in darkness, travelling about the land on every road. And there is that maiden Right, daughter of Zeus, esteemed and respected by the gods in Olympus; and whenever someone does her down with crooked abuse, at once she sits by Zeus her father, Kronos' son, and reports the men's unrighteous mind, so that the people may pay for the crimes of their lords who balefully divert justice from its course by pronouncing it crooked. Beware of this, lords, and keep your pronouncements straight, you bribe-swallowers, and forget your crooked judgments altogether.

A man fashions ill for himself who fashions ill for another, and the ill design is most ill for the designer.

The eye of Zeus, that sees everything and notices everything, observes even this situation if it chooses, and does not fail to perceive what kind of justice even this is that the community has within it. As things are, I cannot wish to be righteous in my dealings with men, either myself or a son of mine, since it is bad to be a righteous man if the less righteous is to have the greater right. Only I do not expect resourceful Zeus is bringing *this* to pass yet!

But you, Perses, must take in what I say and hearken to Right, forgetting force altogether. For this was the rule for men that Kronos' son laid down: whereas fish and beasts and flying birds would eat one another, because Right is not among them, to men he gave Right, which is much the best in practice. For if a man is willing to say what he knows to be just, to him wide-seeing Zeus gives prosperity; but whoever deliberately lies in his sworn testimony, therein, by injuring Right, he is blighted past healing; his family remains more obscure thereafter, while the true-sworn man's line gains in worth.

QUESTIONS

1. Hesiod describes men's relations with the gods in *Works and Days*—what are they like? How do they differ from those of other ancient peoples? How are they similar?

2. The story of Pandora has sometimes been compared to Adam and Eve's fall from grace in Eden. Do you see any similarities? Any differences?

3. *Works and Days* can be taken as an advice book for humanity—what is the author telling his audience about how to behave?

4. What kind of picture does Hesiod paint of the lives of mortals in *Works and Days?*

5. As in many ancient myths, part of Hesiod's subject is the nature of humanity—why are men not like beasts?

THE ANCIENT NEAR EAST

5

Written/recorded by King Hammurabi

CODE OF HAMMURABI

(EARLY 18TH CENTURY B.C.E.)

Hammurabi (d. 1750 B.C.E.) was a ruler of the Old Babylonian or Amorite dynasty from 1792 to 1750 B.C.E. His principal achievement was unifying his Mesopotamian kingdom by controlling the Euphrates River. Although little is known about either his family life or the events of his reign, Hammurabi's military achievements are undoubted.

Discovered in the early twentieth century, the Code of Hammurabi was hailed as the first law code in Western history. Its severe punishments for criminal offenses and its explicit statement of the doctrine of "an eye for an eye" also led to its connection with the Mosaic code. It is now clear that Hammurabi's code is a compendium of earlier laws rather than an innovation of this Babylonian ruler. Its influence on Hebrew law is also less direct than was once thought. What remains significant about Hammurabi's code, however, is what it tells us about the importance of writing and literacy among the elite of Babylonian society and about their well-developed notions of law and justice. In this translation, "seignior" is roughly equivalent to what we might call "lord" or "master."

THE LAWS *(Legal code)*

If a seignior accused a[nother] seignior and brought a charge of murder against him, but has not proved it, his accuser shall be put to death.

If a seignior brought a charge of sorcery against a[nother] seignior, but has not proved it, the one against whom the charge of sorcery was brought, upon going to the river, shall throw himself into the river, and if the river has then overpowered him, his accuser shall take over his estate; if the river has shown that seignior to be innocent and he has accordingly come forth safe, the one who brought the charge of sorcery against him shall be put to death, while the one who threw himself into the river shall take over the estate of his accuser.

If a seignior came forward with false testimony in a case, and has not proved the word which he spoke, if that case was a case involving life, that seignior shall be put to death.

If he came forward with [false] testimony concerning grain or money, he shall bear the penalty of that case.

If a seignior stole the property of church or state, that seignior shall be put to death; also the one who received the stolen goods from his hand shall be put to death.

If a seignior has purchased or has received for safekeeping either silver or gold or a male slave or a female slave or an ox or a sheep or an ass or any sort of thing from the hand of a seignior's son or a seignior's slave without witnesses and contracts, since that seignior is a thief, he shall be put to death.

If a seignior stole either an ox or a sheep or an ass or a pig or a boat, if it belonged to the church [or] if it belonged to the state, he shall make thirtyfold restitution; if it belonged to a private citizen, he shall make good tenfold. If the thief does not have sufficient to make restitution, he shall be put to death.

If a seignior has stolen the young son of a[nother] seignior, he shall be put to death.

If a seignior has helped either a male slave of the state or a female slave of the state or a male slave of a private citizen or a female slave of a private citizen to escape through the city-gate, he shall be put to death.

If a seignior has harbored in his house either a fugitive male or female slave belonging to the state or to a private citizen and has not brought him forth at the summons of the police, that householder shall be put to death.

If a seignior committed robbery and has been caught, that seignior shall be put to death.

If the robber has not been caught, the robbed seignior shall set forth the particulars regarding his lost property in the presence of god, and the city and governor, in whose territory and district the robbery was committed, shall make good to him his lost property.

If either a sergeant or a captain has obtained a soldier by conscription or he accepted and has sent a hired substitute for a campaign of the king, that sergeant or captain shall be put to death.

If either a sergeant or a captain has appropriated the household goods of a soldier, has wronged a soldier, has let a soldier for hire, has abandoned a soldier to a superior in a lawsuit, has appropriated the grant which the king gave to a soldier, that sergeant or captain shall be put to death.

If a seignior has bought from the hand of a soldier the cattle or sheep which the king gave to the soldier, he shall forfeit his money.

When a seignior borrowed money from a merchant and pledged to the merchant a field prepared for grain or sesame, if he said to him, "Cultivate the field, then harvest [and] take the grain or sesame that is produced," if the tenant has produced grain or sesame in the field, the owner of the field at harvest-time shall himself take the grain or sesame that was produced in the field and he shall give to the merchant grain for his money, which he borrowed from the merchant, together with its interest, and also for the cost of cultivation.

If he pledged a field planted with [grain] or a field planted with sesame, the owner of the field shall himself take the grain or sesame that was produced in the field and he shall pay back the money with its interest to the merchant.

If he does not have the money to pay back, [grain or] sesame at their market value in accordance with the ratio fixed by the king he shall give to the merchant for his money, which he borrowed from the merchant, together with its interest.

If the tenant has not produced grain or sesame in the field, he may not change his contract.

If a seignior was too lazy to make [the dike of] his field strong and did not make his dike strong and a break has opened up in his dike and he has accordingly let the water ravage the farmland, the seignior in whose dike the break was opened shall make good the grain that he let get destroyed.

If he is not able to make good the grain, they shall sell him and his goods, and the farmers whose grain the water carried off shall divide [the proceeds].

If a seignior, upon opening his canal for irrigation, became so lazy that he has let the water ravage a field adjoining his, he shall measure out grain on the basis of those adjoining his.

If a seignior pointed the finger at a nun or the wife of a[nother] seignior, but has proved nothing, they shall drag that seignior into the presence of the judges and also cut off half his [hair].

If a seignior acquired a wife, but did not draw up the contracts for her, that woman is no wife.

If the wife of a seignior has been caught while lying with another man, they shall bind them and throw them into the water. If the husband of the woman wishes to spare his wife, then the king in turn may spare his subject.

If a seignior bound the [betrothed] wife of a[nother] seignior, who had had no intercourse with a male and was still living in her father's house, and he has lain in her bosom and they have caught him, that seignior shall be put to death, while that woman shall go free.

If a seignior's wife was accused by her husband, but she was not caught while lying with another man, she shall make affirmation by god and return to her house.

If the finger was pointed at the wife of a seignior because of another man, but she has not been caught while lying with the other man, she shall throw herself into the river for the sake of her husband.

If a seignior was taken captive, but there was sufficient to live on in his house, his wife [shall not leave her house, but she shall take care of her person by not] entering [the house of another].

If that woman did not take care of her person, but has entered the house of another, they shall prove it against that woman and throw her into the water.

If the seignior was taken captive and there was not sufficient to live on in his house, his wife may enter the house of another, with that woman incurring no blame at all.

If, when a seignior was taken captive and there was not sufficient to live on in his house, his wife has then entered the house of another before his [return] and has borne children, [and] later her husband has returned and has reached his city, that woman shall return to her first husband, while the children shall go with their father.

If, when a seignior deserted his city and then ran away, his wife has entered the house of another after his [departure], if that seignior has returned and wishes to take back his wife, the wife of the fugitive shall not return to her husband because he scorned his city and ran away.

If a seignior wishes to divorce his wife who did not bear him children, he shall give her money to the full amount of her marriage-price and he shall also make good to her the dowry which she brought from her father's house and then he may divorce her.

If there was no marriage-price, he shall give her one mina of silver as the divorce-settlement.

If he is a peasant, he shall give her one-third mina of silver.

If a seignior's wife, who was living in the house of the seignior, has made up her mind to leave in order that she may engage in business, thus neglecting her house [and] humiliating her husband, they shall prove it against her; and if her husband has then decided on her divorce, he may divorce her, with nothing to be given her as her divorce-settlement upon her departure. If her husband has not decided on her divorce, her husband may marry another woman, with the former woman living in the house of her husband like a maidservant.

If a woman so hated her husband that she has declared, "You may not have me," her record shall be investigated at her city council, and if she was careful and was not at fault, even though her husband has been going out and disparaging her greatly, that woman, without incurring any blame at all, may take her dowry and go off to her father's house.

If she was not careful, but was a gadabout, thus neglecting her house [and] humiliating her husband, they shall throw that woman into the water.

If a seignior's wife has brought about the death of her husband because of another man, they shall impale that woman on stakes.

If a seignior has had intercourse with his daughter, they shall make that seignior leave the city.

If a seignior chose a bride for his son and his son had intercourse with her, but later he himself has lain in her bosom and they have caught him, they shall bind that seignior and throw him into the water.

If a seignior chose a bride for his son and his son did not have intercourse with her, but he himself has lain in her bosom, he shall pay to her one-half mina of silver and he shall also make good to her whatever she brought from her father's house in order that the man of her choice may marry her.

If a seignior has lain in the bosom of his mother after [the death of] his father, they shall burn both of them.

If a son has struck his father, they shall cut off his hand.

If a seignior has destroyed the eye of a member of the aristocracy, they shall destroy his eye.

If he has broken a[nother] seignior's bone, they shall break his bone.

If he has destroyed the eye of a commoner or broken the bone of a commoner, he shall pay one mina of silver.

If he has destroyed the eye of a seignior's slave or broken the bone of a seignior's slave, he shall pay one-half his value.

QUESTIONS

1. Many ancient law codes were transmitted orally, through memorization. What are some advantages of a written legal code? Can you think of some disadvantages?

2. The areas of society that are regulated often indicate something about what is important to those who make the laws. What seem to be the main concerns of this law code?

3. Does the code make distinctions among people? Are some more important than others? How are people of different status dealt with under the law?

4. The penalties for breaking the law in Babylon were often very harsh. Why do you think the code was so severe?

6

THE BOOK OF THE DEAD

(CA. 16TH CENTURY B.C.E.)

The *Book of the Dead* is a collection of spells and prayers that the Egyptians believed were crucial to well-being in the afterlife. Composed of some two hundred chapters, it contains charms from as early as 2400 B.C.E., as well as more recent incantations. Some time in the sixteenth century B.C.E. anonymous priests and scribes collected the chapters into a single volume. Many copies of the book have been found in tombs and burial chambers, where they were presumably placed for the use of the dead. They were copied on papyrus rolls and some surviving ones were elaborately illustrated.

The following selection is an incantation meant to prepare the deceased for the judgment of the gods. The chant provides much direct evidence of the manners and values of everyday life in ancient Egypt.

The Protestation of Guiltlessness

What is said on reaching the Broad-Hall of the Two Justices, absolving X of every sin which he has committed, and seeing the faces of the gods:

Hail to thee, O great god, lord of the Two Justices! I have come to thee, my lord, I have been brought that I might see thy beauty. I know thee; I know thy name and the names of the forty-two gods who are with thee in the Broad-Hall of the Two Justices, who live on them who preserve evil and who drink their blood on that day of reckoning up character in the presence of Wenofer. Behold, "Sati-mertifi, Lord of Justice," is thy name. I have come to thee; I have brought thee justice; I have expelled deceit for thee.

I have not committed evil against men.

I have not mistreated cattle.

I have not blasphemed a god.

I have not done violence to a poor man.

I have not done that which the gods abominate.

I have not defamed a slave to his superior.

I have not made [anyone] sick.

I have not made [anyone] weep.

I have not killed.

I have given no order to a killer.

I have not caused anyone suffering.

I have not cut down on the food [income] in the temples.

I have not damaged the bread of the gods.

I have not taken the loaves of the blessed [dead].

I have not had sexual relations with a boy.

I have not defiled myself.

I have neither increased or diminished the grain-measure.

I have not taken milk from the mouths of children.

I have not driven cattle away from their pasturage.

I have not snared the birds of the gods.

I have not caught fish in their marshes.

I have not held up the water in its season.

I have not built a dam against running water.

I have not driven away the cattle of the god's property.

I have not stopped a god on his procession.

I am pure! My purity is the purity of the great benu-bird which is in Herakleopolis, because I am really that nose of the Lord of Breath, who makes all men to live, on that day of filling out the Eye [of Horus] in Heliopolis, in the second month of the second season, the last day, in the presence of the lord of this land. I am the one who has seen the filling out of the Eye in Heliopolis. Evil will never happen to me in this land or in this Broad-Hall of the Two Justices, because I know the names of these gods who are in it, the followers of the great god.

O Wide-of-Stride, who comes forth from Heliopolis, I have not committed evil.

O Embracer-of-Fire, who comes forth from Babylon, I have not stolen.

O Nosey, who comes forth from Hermopolis, I have not been covetous.

O Swallower-of-Shadows, who comes forth from the pit, I have not robbed.

O Dangerous-of-Face, who came forth from *Rostau,* I have not killed men.

O *Ruti,* who comes forth from heaven, I have not damaged the grain-measure.

O Flamer, who comes forth backward, I have not stolen the property of a god.

O Breaker-of-Bones, who comes forth from Herakleopolis, I have not told lies.

O Commander-of-Fire, who comes forth from Memphis, I have not taken away food.

O Dweller-in-the-Pit, who comes forth from the west, I have not been contentious.

O White-of-Teeth, who comes forth from the Faiyum, I have not trespassed.

O Eater-of-Blood, who comes forth from the execution-block, I have not slain the cattle of the god.

O Eater-of-Entrails, who comes forth from the Thirty, I have not practised usury.

O Lord-of-Justice, who comes forth from Ma'ati, I have not stolen the bread-ration.

O Wanderer, who comes forth from Bubastis, I have not gossiped.

O Djudju-serpent, who comes forth from Busiris, I have not argued with some one summoned because of his property.

O Wamemti-serpent, who comes forth from the place of judgment, I have not committed adultery.

O Superior-of-the-Nobles, who comes forth from Imau, I have not caused terror.

O Wrecker, who comes forth from the Saite Nome, I have not trespassed.

O Mischief-Maker, who comes forth from the sanctuary, I have not been [over]heated.

O Child, who comes forth from the Heliopolitan Nome, I have not been unresponsive to a matter of justice.

O Ser-kheru, who comes forth from Wensi, I have not been quarrelsome.

O Dark-One, who comes forth from the darkness, I have not been abusive.

O Bringer-of-His-Peace, who comes forth from Sais, I have not been [over]-energetic.

O Lord-of-Faces, who comes forth from the Heroonpolite Nome, my heart has not been hasty.

O Tem-sep, who comes forth from Busiris, I have not been abusive against a king.

O Acting-with-His-Heart, who comes forth from Tjebu, I have not waded in water.

O Flowing-One, who comes forth from Nun, my voice has not been loud.

O Commander-of-the-People, who comes forth from his shrine, I have not been abusive against a god.

O In-af serpent, who comes forth from the cemetery, I have not blasphemed against my local god.

Words to be spoken by X:

Hail to you, ye gods who are in this Broad-Hall of the Two Justices! I know you; I know your names. I shall not fall for dread of you. Ye have not reported guilt of mine up to this god in whose retinue ye are; no deed of mine has come from you. Ye have spoken truth about me in the presence of the All-Lord, because I acted justly in Egypt.

Hail to you who are in the Broad-Hall of the Two Justices, who have no deceit in your bodies, who live on truth and who eat of truth in the presence of Horus, who is in his sun disc. May ye rescue me from Babi, who lives on the entrails of elders on that day of the great reckoning. Behold me—I have come to you without sin, without guilt, without evil, without a witness [against me], without one against whom I have taken action. I live on truth, and I eat of truth. I have done that which men said and that with which gods are content. I have satisfied a god with that which he desires. I have given bread to the hungry, water to the thirsty, clothing to the naked, and a ferry-boat to him who was marooned. I have provided divine offerings for the gods and mortuary offerings for the dead. [So] rescue me, you; protect me, you. Ye will not make report against me in the presence [of the great god.] I am one pure of mouth and pure of hands, one to whom "Welcome, welcome, in peace!" is said by those who see him. I am one who has a concern for the gods, who knows the nature of their bodies. I have come here to testify to justice and to bring the scales to their [proper] position in the cemetery.

O thou who art high upon his standard, Lord of the Atef-Crown, whose name has been made "Lord of Breath," mayest thou rescue me from thy messengers who give forth uncleanliness and create destruction, who have no covering up of their faces, because I have effected justice for the Lord of Justice, being pure—my front is pure, my rear is clean, my middle is in the flowing water of justice; there is no part of me free of justice.

Instructions for the Use of the Spell

To be done in conformance with what takes place in this Broad-Hall of the Two Justices. This spell is to be recited when one is clean and pure, clothed in [fresh] garments, shod with white sandals, painted with stibium, and anointed with myrrh, to whom cattle, fowl, incense, bread, beer, and vegetables have been offered. Then make thou this text in writing on a clean pavement with ochre smeared with earth upon which pigs and [other] small cattle have not trodden. As for him on whose behalf this book is made, he shall be prosperous and his children shall be prosperous, without greed, because he shall be a trusted man of the king and his courtiers. Loaves, jars, bread, and joints of meat shall be given to him from the altar of the great god. He cannot be held back at any door of the west, [but] he shall be ushered in with the Kings of Upper and Lower Egypt, and he shall be in the retinue of Osiris.

Right and true a million times.

QUESTIONS

1. Passing into the afterlife was not easy. What hurdles did the dead face before reaching safety?

2. Egyptian society obviously had a very well-developed sense of right and wrong. What kinds of things should a righteous person do? What are some of the sins a person might commit?

3. In what ways do Egyptian ideas of right and wrong resemble our own? How are they different?

4. The *Book of the Dead* was clearly thought to be a very important means to everlasting life by contemporary Egyptians, who often brought it with them to the tomb. How could it also have been useful for the living?

7

THE BOOK OF EXODUS

(CA. 10TH–6TH CENTURY B.C.E.)

The Book of Exodus is the second book of the Old Testament as well as the second book of the Hebrew Torah. It was probably composed between the tenth and sixth centuries B.C.E. Exodus tells the story of the enslavement of the Hebrew people at the hands of the Egyptians, of their liberation under the leadership of Moses, and of their journey into the promised land. The central actions are the confrontation between Moses and the pharaoh and God's deliverance of the Hebrews across the Red Sea. Much of the story takes place during the forty years when the Hebrews wandered in the desert and when a nation was forged through tribulation. At Mount Sinai, Moses received the Ten Commandments, the foundation of Judeo-Christian ethics.

19 On the third new moon after the people of Israel had gone forth out of the land of Egypt, on that day they came into the wilderness of Sinai.

[2]And when they set out from Rephi'dim and came into the wilderness of Sinai, they encamped in the wilderness; and there Israel encamped before the mountain. [3]And Moses went up to God, and the Lord called to him out of the mountain, saying, "Thus you shall say to the house of Jacob, and tell the people of Israel; [4]You have seen what I did to the Egyptians, and how I bore you on eagles' wings and brought you to myself. [5]Now therefore, if you will obey my voice and keep my covenant, you shall be my own possession among all peoples; for all the earth is mine, [6]and you shall be to me a kingdom of priests and a holy nation. These are the words which you shall speak to the children of Israel."

[7]So Moses came and called the elders of the people, and set before them all these words which the Lord had commanded him. [8]And all the people answered together and said, "All that the Lord has spoken we will do." And Moses reported the words of the people to the Lord. [9]And the Lord said to Moses, "Lo, I am coming to you in a thick cloud, that the people may hear when I speak with you, and may also believe you for ever." ....

[16]On the morning of the third day there were thunders and lightnings, and a thick cloud upon the mountain, and a very loud trumpet blast, so that all the people who were in the camp trembled. [17]Then Moses brought the people out of the camp to meet God; and they took their stand at the foot of the mountain. [18]And Mount Sinai was wrapped in smoke, because the Lord descended upon it in fire; and the smoke of it went up like the smoke of a kiln, and the whole mountain quaked greatly. [19]And as the sound of the trumpet grew louder and louder, Moses spoke, and God answered him in thunder. [20]And the Lord came down upon Mount Sinai, to the top of the mountain; and the Lord called Moses to the top of the mountain, and Moses went up. [21]And the Lord said to Moses, "Go down and warn the people, lest they break through to the Lord to gaze and many of them perish. [22]And also let the priests who come near to the Lord consecrate themselves, lest the Lord break out upon them."

[23]And Moses said to the Lord, "The people cannot come up to Mount Sinai; for thou thyself didst charge us, saying, 'Set bounds about the mountain, and consecrate it.' " [24]And the Lord said to him, "Go down, and come up bringing Aaron with you; but do not let the priests and the people break through to come up to the Lord, lest he break out against them." [25]So Moses went down to the people and told them.

20 And God spoke all these words, saying,

[2]"I am the Lord your God, who brought you out of the land of Egypt, out of the house of bondage.

[3]"You shall have no other gods before me.

[4]"You shall not make for yourself a graven image, or any likeness of anything that is in heaven above, or that is in the earth beneath, or that is in the water under the earth; [5]you shall not bow down to them or serve them; for I the Lord your God am a jealous God, visiting the iniquity

Miniature from an illuminated Haggadah showing Moses crossing the Red Sea (left) and Pharaoh with his warriors (right).

of the fathers upon the children to the third and the fourth generation of those who hate me, [6]but showing steadfast love to thousands of those who love me and keep my commandments.

[7]"You shall not take the name of the Lord your God in vain; for the Lord will not hold him guiltless who takes his name in vain.

[8]"Remember the sabbath day, to keep it holy. [9]Six days you shall labor, and do all your work; [10]but the seventh day is a sabbath to the Lord your God; in it you shall not do any work, you, or your son, or your daughter, your manservant, or your maidservant, or your cattle, or the sojourner who is within your gates; [11]for in six days the Lord made heaven and earth, the sea, and all that is in them, and rested the seventh day; therefore the Lord blessed the sabbath day and hallowed it.

[12]"Honor your father and your mother, that your days may be long in the land which the Lord your God gives you.

[13]"You shall not kill.

[14]"You shall not commit adultery.

[15]"You shall not steal.

[16]"You shall not bear false witness against your neighbor.

[17]"You shall not covet your neighbor's house; you shall not covet your neighbor's wife, or his manservant, or his maidservant, or his ox, or his ass, or anything that is your neighbor's."

[18]Now when all the people perceived the thunderings and the lightnings and the sound of the trumpet and the mountain smoking, the people were afraid and trembled; and they stood afar off, [19]and said to Moses, "You speak to us, and we will hear; but let not God speak to us, lest we die." [20]And Moses said to the people, "Do not fear; for God has come to prove you, and that the fear of him may be before your eyes, that you may not sin."

[21]And the people stood afar off, while Moses drew near to the thick darkness where God was. [22]And the Lord said to Moses, "Thus you shall say to the people of Israel: 'You have seen for yourselves that I have talked with you from heaven. [23]You shall not make gods of silver to be

with me, nor shall you make for yourselves gods of gold.' " . . .

32

When the people saw that Moses delayed to come down from the mountain, the people gathered themselves together to Aaron, and said to him, "Up, make us gods, who shall go before us; as for this Moses, the man who brought us up out of the land of Egypt, we do not know what has become of him." ²And Aaron said to them, "Take off the rings of gold which are in the ears of your wives, your sons, and your daughters, and bring them to me." ³So all the people took off the rings of gold which were in their ears, and brought them to Aaron. ⁴And he received the gold at their hand, and fashioned it with a graving tool, and made a molten calf; and they said, "These are your gods, O Israel, who brought you up out of the land of Egypt!" ⁵When Aaron saw this, he built an altar before it; and Aaron made proclamation and said, "Tomorrow shall be a feast to the Lord."

⁶And they rose up early on the morrow, and offered burnt offerings and brought peace offerings; and the people sat down to eat and drink and rose up to play.

⁷And the Lord said to Moses, "Go down; for your people, whom you brought up out of the land of Egypt, have corrupted themselves; ⁸they have turned aside quickly out of the way which I commanded them; they have made for themselves a molten calf, and have worshipped it and sacrificed to it, and said, 'These are your gods, O Israel, who brought you up out of the land of Egypt!' " ⁹And the Lord said to Moses, "I have seen this people, and behold, it is a stiff-necked people; now therefore let me alone, that my wrath may burn hot against them and I may consume them; but of you I will make a great nation."

¹⁰But Moses besought the Lord his God, and said, "O Lord, why does thy wrath burn hot against thy people, whom thou has brought forth out of the land of Egypt with great power and with a mighty hand? ¹¹Why should the Egyptians say, 'With evil intent did he bring

them forth, to slay them in the mountains, and to consume them from the face of the earth'? Turn from thy fierce wrath, and repent of this evil against thy people. ¹²Remember Abraham, Isaac, and Israel, thy servants, to whom thou didst swear by thine own self, and didst say to them, 'I will multiply your descendants as the stars of heaven, and all this land that I have promised I will give to your descendants, and they shall inherit it for ever'." ¹³And the Lord repented of the evil which he thought to do to his people.

¹⁴And Moses turned, and went down from the mountain with the two tables of the testimony in his hands, tables that were written on both sides; on the one side and on the other were they written. ¹⁵And the tables were the work of God, and the writing was the writing of God, graven upon the tables.

¹⁶When Joshua heard the noise of the people as they shouted, he said to Moses, "There is a noise of war in the camp." ¹⁷But he said, "It is not the sound of shouting for victory, or the sound of the cry of defeat, but the sound of singing that I hear." ¹⁸And as soon as he came near the camp and saw the calf and the dancing, Moses' anger burned hot, and he threw the tables out of his hands and broke them at the foot of the mountain. ¹⁹And he took the calf which they had made and burnt it with fire, and ground it to powder, and scattered it upon the water, and made the people of Israel drink it. . . .

³⁰On the morrow Moses said to the people, "You have sinned a great sin. And now I will go up to the Lord; perhaps I can make atonement for your sin." ³¹So Moses returned to the Lord and said, "Alas, this people have sinned a great sin; they have made for themselves gods of gold. ³²But now, if thou wilt forgive their sin—and if not, blot me, I pray thee, out of thy book which thou hast written." ³³But the Lord said to Moses, "Whoever has sinned against me, him will I blot out of my book. ³⁴But now go, lead the people to the place of which I have spoken to you; behold,

my angel shall go before you. Nevertheless, in the day when I visit, I will visit their sin upon them."

[35]And the Lord sent a plague upon the people, because they made the calf which Aaron made.

33 The Lord said to Moses, "Depart, go up hence, you and the people whom you have brought up out of the land of Egypt, to the land of which I swore to Abraham, Isaac, and Jacob, saying, 'To your descendants I will give it.' [2]And I will send an angel before you, and I will drive out the Canaanites, the Amorites, the Hittites, the Per'izzites, the Hivites, and the Jeb'usites. [3]Go up to a land flowing with milk and honey; but I will not go up among you, lest I consume you in the way, for you are a stiff-necked people."

[4]When the people heard these evil tidings, they mourned; and no man put on his ornaments. [5]For the Lord had said to Moses, "Say to the people of Israel, 'You are a stiff-necked people; if for a single moment I should go up among you, I would consume you. So now put off your ornaments from you, that I may know what to do with you.' " [6]Therefore the people of Israel stripped themselves of their ornaments, from Mount Horeb onward.

[7]Now Moses used to take the tent and pitch it outside the camp, far off from the camp; and he called it the tent of meeting. And every one who sought the Lord would go out to the tent of meeting, which was outside the camp. [8]Whenever Moses went out to the tent, all the people rose up, and every man stood at his tent door, and looked after Moses, until he had gone into the tent. [9]When Moses entered the tent, the pillar of cloud would descend and stand at the door of the tent, and the Lord would speak with Moses. [10]And when all the people saw the pillar of cloud standing at the door of the tent, all the people would rise up and worship, every man at his tent door. Thus the Lord used to speak to Moses face to face, as a man speaks to his friend.

QUESTIONS

1. Moses is the main intermediary between God and the Hebrew people. How does he manage his task? What problems does he face?

2. What is the relationship between God and the Hebrews like? Is it a smooth one?

3. The Ten Commandments were the basis of Hebrew law and later were incorporated into Christian thought. They also had contemporary utility. In what ways could they be useful to a tribe of nomads?

4. How does the story told in Exodus create a sense of identity and purpose for the Hebrews?

5. How different is the Hebrews' view of their God from those of other Near Eastern cultures, such as the Mesopotamians or Egyptians? Do you see any similarities?

8

THE BOOK OF ISAIAH

(CA. 8TH–6TH CENTURY B.C.E.)

Isaiah was a Hebrew prophet who lived and wrote prophecies in the kingdom of Judah in the eighth century B.C.E. His prophecies continued to be written down by his followers after his death. Together these writings form the Book of Isaiah, one of the most important works of the Old Testament. Written with a quiet poetic beauty, the Book of Isaiah has value as literature as well as theology.

Isaiah lived during a period when the Hebrew nation was under attack from enemies without and from an erosion of moral and spiritual values within. He took it as his mission to return the nation of Moses to the path of righteousness. In doing so, he carefully stated the core of Hebrew beliefs, stressing the monotheistic outlook and pointing the way for the coming of a savior. The prophecies of Isaiah thus became central to Christianity, and the Book of Isaiah is one of the most widely read of the Judeo-Christian scriptures.

42Behold my servant, whom I uphold, my chosen, in whom my soul delights; I have put my Spirit upon him, he will bring forth justice to the nations. [2]He will not cry or lift up his voice, or make it heard in the street; [3]a bruised reed he will not break, and a dimly burning wick he will not quench; he will faithfully bring forth justice. [4]He will not fail or be discouraged till he has established justice in the earth; and the coastlands wait for his law.

[5]Thus says God, the Lord, who created the heavens and stretched them out, who spread forth the earth and what comes from it who gives breath to the people upon it and spirit to those who walk in it: [6]"I am the Lord, I have called you in righteousness, I have taken you by the hand and kept you; I have given you as a covenant to the people, a light to the nations, [7]to open the eyes that are blind, to bring out the prisoners from the dungeon, from the prison those who sit in darkness. [8]I am the Lord, that is my name; my glory I give to no other, nor my praise to graven images." . . .

43But now thus says the Lord, he who created you, O Jacob, he who formed you, O Israel: "Fear not, for I have redeemed you; I have called you by name, you are mine. [2]When you pass through the waters I will be with you; and through the rivers, they shall not overwhelm you; when you walk through fire you shall not be burned, and the flame shall not consume you. [3]For I am the Lord your God, the Holy One of Israel, your Savior. I give Egypt as your ransom, Ethiopia and Seba in exchange for you. [4]Because you are precious in my eyes, and honored, and I love you, I give men in return for you, peoples in exchange for your life. [5]Fear not, for I am with you; I will bring your offspring from the east, and from the west I will gather you; [6]I will say to the north, Give up, and to the south, Do not withhold; bring my sons from afar and my daughters from the end of the earth, [7]every one who is called by my name, whom I created for my glory, who I formed and made."

[8]Bring forth the people who are blind, yet have eyes, who are deaf, yet have ears! [9]Let all the nations gather together, and let the peoples assemble. Who among them can declare this, and show us the former things? Let them bring their witnesses to justify them, and let them hear and say, It is true. [10]"You are my witnesses," says the Lord, "and my servant whom I have chosen, that you may know and believe me and understand that I am He. Before me no god was formed, nor shall there be any after me. [11]I, I am the Lord, and besides me there is no savior. [12]I declared and saved and proclaimed, when there was no strange god among you; and you are my witnesses" says the Lord. [13]"I am God, and also henceforth I am He; there is none who can deliver from my hand; I work and who can hinder it?

[14]Thus says the Lord, your Redeemer, the Holy One of Israel . . . [25]"I, I am He who blots out your transgressions for my own sake, and I will not remember your sins. [26]Put me in remembrance, let us argue together; set forth your case, that you may be proved right. [27]Your first father sinned, and your mediators transgressed against me. [28]Therefore I profaned the princes of the sanctuary, I delivered Jacob to utter destruction and Israel to reviling.

44"But now hear, O Jacob my servant, Israel whom I have chosen! [2]Thus says the Lord who made you, who formed you from the womb and will help you: Fear not, O Jacob my servant, Jeshu'run whom I have chosen. [3]For I will pour water on the thirsty land, and streams on the dry ground; I will pour my Spirit upon your descendants, and my blessing on your offspring. [4]They shall spring up like grass amid waters, like willows by flowing streams. [5]This one will say, 'I am the Lord's,' another will call himself by the name of Jacob, and another will write on his hand, 'The Lord's,' and surname himself by the name of Israel."

[6]Thus says the Lord, the King of Israel and his Redeemer, the Lord of hosts: "I am the first and I am the last; besides me there is no god.

[7]Who is like me? Let him proclaim it, let him declare and set it forth before me. Who has announced from of old the things to come? Let them tell us what is yet to be. [8]Fear not, nor be afraid; have I not told you from of old and declared it? And you are my witnesses! Is there a God besides me? There is no Rock; I know not any." . . . [21]Remember these things, O Jacob, and Israel, for you are my servant; I formed you, you are my servant; O Israel, you will not be forgotten by me. [22]I have swept away your transgressions like a cloud, and your sins like mist; return to me, for I have redeemed you. . . .

45Thus says the Lord to his anointed, to Cyrus, whose right hand I have grasped, to subdue nations before him and ungird the loins of kings, to open doors before him that gates may not be closed: [2]"I will go before you and level the mountains, I will break in pieces the doors of bronze, and cut asunder the bars of iron, [3]I will give you the treasures of darkness and the hoards in secret places, that you may know that it is I, the Lord, the God of Israel, who call you by your name, [4]For the sake of my servant Jacob, and Israel my chosen. I call you by your name, I surname you, though you do not know me. [5]I am the Lord, and there is no other, besides me there is no God; I gird you, though you do not know me, [6]that men may know, from the rising of the sun and from the west, that there is none besides me; I am the Lord, and there is no other." . . . [14]Thus says the Lord: "The wealth of Egypt and the merchandise of Ethiopia, and the Sabe'ans, men of stature, shall come over to you and be yours, they shall follow you; they shall come over in chains and bow down to you. They will make supplication to you, saying: 'God is with you only, and there is no other, no god besides him.'" [15]Truly, thou art a God who hidest thyself, O God of Israel, the Savior. [16]All of them are put to shame and confounded, the makers of idols go in confusion together. [17]But Israel is saved by the Lord with everlasting salvation; you shall not be put to shame or confounded to all eternity. . . .

49Listen to me, O coastlands, and hearken, you peoples from afar. The Lord called me from the womb, from the body of my mother he named my name. [2]He made my mouth like a sharp sword, in the shadow of his hand he hid me; he made me a polished arrow, in his quiver he hid me away. [3]And he said to me, "You are my servant. . . . "

[8]Thus says the Lord: "In a time of favor I have answered you, in a day of salvation I have helped you; I have kept you and given you as a covenant to the people, to establish the land, to apportion the desolate heritages; [9]saying to the prisoners, 'Come forth,' to those who are in darkness, 'Appear.' They shall feed along the ways, on all bare heights shall be their pasture; [10]they shall not hunger or thirst, neither scorching wind nor sun shall smite them, for he who has pity on them will lead them, and by springs of water will guide them. [11]And I will make all my mountains a way, and my highways shall be raised up. [12]Lo, these shall come from afar, and lo, these from the north and from the west, and these from the land of Syene." [13]Sing for joy, O heavens, and exult, O earth; break forth, O mountains, into singing! For the Lord has comforted his people, and will have compassion on his afflicted.

QUESTIONS

1.   What will Isaiah's prophesied savior do?

2.   Isaiah dwells on many of the things God has given the Hebrews. What are some of the things God has done for them?

3.   Other peoples are mentioned in Isaiah. What kind of relationship do these peoples seem to have with the Hebrews?

4.   Isaiah contains many images of the land. What sort of picture do these images paint of the ancient Near East?

5.   Is the God described in Isaiah very much like the one in Exodus? How are they alike? How do they differ?

6.   Why do you think the Judaeans were so interested in the possible coming of a savior? What causes a people to turn to the future, as Isaiah seems to be doing?

9

THE LEGACY OF CYRUS THE GREAT

(6TH CENTURY B.C.E.)

Under Cyrus II, commonly known as Cyrus the Great (D.C. 530 B.C.E.), the Persian Empire conquered nearly all of the Near East. Cyrus destroyed the Babylonian Empire that up until that time had been the ruler of the known world. He was a powerful military leader, but also paid attention to building the infrastructure of his own empire. He bequeathed a dynasty so strong as to survive two centuries as the largest and most powerful empire known in Europe. It did not fall until overwhelmed by Alexander the Great. Cyrus held his empire together by winning the hearts and minds of his conquered subjects by offering them unexpected freedoms, such as freedom of religion. He was a surprisingly tolerant emperor, issuing the Edict of Restoration that allowed the Jews, exiled in Babylonia, to return to Israel and rebuild their temple. Whether Cyrus himself was dedicated to the Zoroastrian religion, as were later Persian kings, is disputable. But he certainly promoted it as a sort of nonmandatory state religion in Persia.

The clay Cyrus Cylinder, written in Akkadian Cuneiform script, shows both the militaristic and the magnanimous sides of Cyrus's imperial program. Nineteenth-century archeologists excavating temples of the city of Babylon discovered it. The cylinder hails Cyrus's defeat of the Babylonians in 539 B.C.E., and recounts in first person (as if written by Cyrus himself) his glorious deeds and the genealogy of his house. But it also recounts Cyrus's generosity in restoring local temples and peoples to their original homelands. The Book of Ezra confirms this second aspect of Cyrus's program.

THE CYRUS CYLINDER
(6TH CENTURY B.C.E.)

(one line destroyed)

. . . [r]ims (of the world) . . . a weakling has been installed as the *enû*[2] of his country; [the correct images of the gods he removed from their thrones, imi]tations, he ordered to place upon them. A replica of the temple Esagila he has . . . for Ur and the other sacred cities inappropriate rituals . . . daily he did blabber [incorrect prayers]. He (furthermore) interrupted in a

fiendish way the regular offerings, he did . . . he established within the sacred cities. The worship of Marduk, the king of the gods, he [chang]ed into abomination, daily he used to do evil against his (i.e. Marduk's) city. . . . He [tormented] its [inhabitant]s with corvée-work (lit.: a yoke) without relief, he ruined them all.

Upon their complaints the lord of the gods became terribly angry and [he departed from] their region, (also) the (other) gods living among them left their mansions, wroth that he had brought (them) into Babylon (Š u . a n. n a[ki]).

(But) Marduk [who does care for] . . . on account of (the fact that) the sanctuaries of all their settlements were in ruins and the inhabitants of Sumer and Akkad had become like (living) dead, turned back (his countenance) [his] an[ger] [abated] and he had mercy (upon them). He scanned and looked (through) all the countries, searching for a righteous ruler willing to lead him (i.e. Marduk)-(in the annual procession). (Then) he pronounced the name of Cyrus (*Ku-ra-a Š*), king of Anshan, declared him (lit.: pronounced [his] name) to be(come) the ruler of all the world. He made the Guti country and all the Manda-hordes bow in submission to his (i.e. Cyrus') feet. And he (Cyrus) did always endeavour to treat according to justice the black-headed whom he (Marduk) has made him conquer. Marduk, the great lord, a protector of his people/worshipers, beheld with pleasure his (i.e. Cyrus') good deeds and his upright mind (lit.: heart) (and therefore) ordered him to march against his city Babylon (Ká.dingir.ra). He made him set out on the road to Babylon (DIN.TIR^ki) going at his side like a real friend. His widespread troops—their number, like that of the water of a river, could not be established—strolled along, their weapons packed away. Without any battle, he made him enter his town Babylon (Šu.an.na), sparing Babylon (Ká.dingir.ra^ki)[1] any calamity. He delivered into his (i.e. Cyrus') hands Nabonidus, the king who did not worship him (i.e. Marduk). All the inhabitants of Babylon (DIN.TIR^ki) as well as of the entire country of Sumer and Akkad, princes and governors (included), bowed to him (Cyrus) and kissed his feet, jubilant that he (had received) the kingship, and with shining faces. Happily they greeted him as a master through whose help they had come (again) to life from

death (and) had all been spared damage and disaster, and they worshiped his (very) name.

I am Cyrus, king of the world, great king, legitimate king, king of Babylon, king of Sumer and Akkad, king of the four rims (of the earth), son of Cambyses (*Ka-am-bu-zi-ia*), great king, king of Anshan, grandson of Cyrus, great king, king of Anshan, descendant of Teispes (*Ši-iš-pi-iš*), great king, king of Anshan, of a family (which) always (exercised) kingship; whose mile Bel and Nebo love, whom they want as king to please their hearts.

When I entered Babylon (DIN.TIR^ki) as a friend and (when) I established the seat of the government in the palace of the ruler under jubilation and rejoicing, Marduk, the great lord, [induced] the magnanimous inhabitants of Babylon (DIN.TIR^ki) [to love me], and I was daily endeavouring to worship him. My numerous troops walked around in Babylon (DIN.TIR^ki) in peace, I did not allow anybody to terrorize (any place) of the [country of Sumer] and Akkad. I strove for peace in Babylon (Ká.dingir.ra^ki) and in all his (other) sacred cities. As to the inhabitants of Babylon (DIN.TIR^ki), [who] against the will of the gods [had/were . . . , I abolished] the corvée (lit.: yoke) which was against their (social) standing. I brought relief to their dilapidated, housing, putting (thus) an end to their (main) complaints. Marduk, the great lord, was well pleased with my deeds and sent friendly blessings to myself, Cyrus, the king who worships him, to Cambyses, my son the offspring of [my] loins, as well as to all my troops, and we all [praised] his great [godhead] joyously, standing before him in peace.

All the kings of the entire world from the Upper to the Lower Sea, those who are seated in throne rooms, (those who) live in other [types of buildings as well as] all the kings of the West land living in tents,[2] brought their heavy tributes and kissed my feet in Babylon (Šu.an.na). (As to the region) from . . . as far as Ashur and Susa, Agade,

---

[1]The old Sumerian title appears here in a context which seems to indicate that the primitive concept concerning the intimate connection between the physical vitality of the ruler and the prosperity of the country, was still valid in the political speculations of the Babylonian clergy.

[2]This phrase refers either to the way of life of a nomadic or a primitive society in contradistinction to that of an urban.

Eshnunna, the towns Zamban, Me-Turnu, Der as well as the region of the Gutians, I returned to (these) sacred cities on the other side of the Tigris, the sanctuaries of which have been ruins for a long time, the images which (used) to live therein and established for them permanent sanctuaries. I (also) gathered all their (former) inhabitants and returned (to them) their habitations. Furthermore, I resettled upon the command of Marduk, the great lord, all the gods of Sumer and Akkad whom Nabonidus has brought into Babylon (Š u. a n. n a^{ki}) to the anger of the lord of the gods, unharmed, in their (former) chapels, the places which make them happy.

May all the gods whom I have resettled in their sacred cities ask daily Bel and Nebo for a long life for me and may they recommend me (to him); to Marduk, my lord, they may say this: "Cyrus, the king who worships you, and Cambyses, his son, . . . " . . . all of them I settled in a peaceful place . . . ducks and doves, . . . I endeavoured to fortify/repair their dwelling places. . . .

(six lines destroyed)

THE BOOK OF EZRA (5TH CENTURY B.C.E.)

End of the Babylonian Captivity

1 In the first year of King Cyrus of Persia, in order that the word of the LORD by the mouth of Jeremiah might be accomplished, the LORD stirred up the spirit of King Cyrus of Persia so that he sent a herald throughout all his kingdom, and also in a written edict declared:

2 "Thus says King Cyrus of Persia: The LORD, the God of heaven, has given me all the kingdoms of the earth, and he has charged me to build him a house at Jerusalem in Judah. ^{3}Any of those among you who are of his people—may their God be with them!—are now permitted to go up to Jerusalem in Judah, and rebuild the house of the LORD, the God of Israel—he is the God who is in Jerusalem; ^{4}and let all survivors, in whatever place they reside, be assisted by the people of their place with silver and gold, with goods and with animals, besides freewill offerings for the house of God in Jerusalem."

5 The heads of the families of Judah and Benjamin, and the priests and the Levites—everyone whose spirit God had stirred—got ready to go up and rebuild the house of the LORD in Jerusalem. ^{6}All their neighbors aided them with silver vessels, with gold, with goods with animals, and with valuable gifts, besides all that was freely offered. ^{7}King Cyrus himself brought out the vessels of the house of the LORD that Nebuchadnezzar had carried away from Jerusalem and placed in the house of his gods. ^{8}King Cyrus of Persia had them released into the charge of Mithredath the treasure who counted them out to Sheshbazzar the prince of Judah. ^{9}And this was the inventory gold basins, thirty; silver basins, one thousand; knives,[a] twenty-nine; ^{10}gold bowls thirty; other silver bowls, four hundred ten other vessels, one thousand; ^{11}the total of the gold and silver vessels was five thousand four hundred. All these Sheshbazzar brought up, when the exiles were brought up from Babylonia to Jerusalem.

QUESTIONS

1. Why do you think that Cyrus emphasized that he is the son of Cambyses, son of Cyrus, son of Teispes, all great kings, "of a family [which] always [exercised] kingship"? How does this compare to the Babylonian king?

---

[a]Vg: Meaning of Heb uncertain

2. How does Cyrus legitimate his rule as emperor? How does he rationalize his conquest of the Babylonians?

3. What role does religion play in Cyrus's rule? Can we separate the religious from the political realms here? Why or why not?

4. In what ways does the passage from the *Book of Ezra* confirm Cyrus's own declaration of his actions? In what ways does it differ?

5. If Cyrus calls on the Babylonian god Marduk in the cylinder, and on the Israelite god in the *Book of Ezra*, what are we to make of Cyrus's view of deities? How does ancient Persian religious understanding differ from our own conceptions of God/gods and religion?

ANCIENT AND CLASSICAL GREECE

10

■ *Homer* ■

ILIAD

(9TH–8TH CENTURY B.C.E.)

The two greatest epic poems in the Western tradition, the *Iliad* and the *Odyssey,* are traditionally attributed to Homer. Reputed to have been a blind poet, Homer is credited with the composition of the *Iliad* and with being the inspiration behind the *Odyssey,* the story of the travels of the Greek warrior Odysseus. It appears that Homer lived in either the ninth or eighth century B.C.E., if evidence from the epics can be used to date his life. The Homeric poems formed part of an oral tradition, changing in the process of retelling. The characteristic meter of the verses undoubtedly aided memory. Both works were written and codified during the Hellenistic period of Greek history.

The *Iliad* tells the story of the siege of Troy (*Illium* in Greek) by the forces of Greece after the abduction of Helen, the wife of Menelaus, the king of Sparta. The central actors in the story are Achilles and Hector, respectively the greatest Greek and Trojan warriors. The war serves as a backdrop for their personal confrontation and the story ends with the resolution of their conflict. The values of Greek and Trojan societies are readily identifiable in the final meeting between these two warriors, from which the following excerpt is taken.

So all through Troy the men who had fled like
    panicked fawns
were wiping off their sweat, drinking away their
    thirst,
leaning along the city's massive ramparts now
while Achaean troops, sloping shields to
    shoulders,
closed against the walls. But there stood
    Hector,
shackled fast by his deadly fate, holding his
    ground,
exposed in front of Troy and the Scaean Gates.

And now Apollo turned to taunt Achilles:
"Why are you chasing *me?* Why waste your
    speed?—
son of Peleus, you a mortal and I a deathless god.
You still don't know that I am immortal, do
    you?—
straining to catch me in your fury! Have you
    forgotten?
There's a war to fight with the Trojans you
    stampeded,
look, they're packed inside their city walls,
    but you,

you've slipped away out here. You can't kill *me*—
I can never die—it's not my fate!"
Enraged at that,
Achilles shouted in mid-stride, "You've
    blocked my way,
you distant, deadly Archer, deadliest god of all—
you made me swerve away from the rampart
    there.
Else what a mighty Trojan army had gnawed
    the dust
before they could ever straggle through their
    gates!
Now you've robbed me of great glory, saved
    their lives
with all your deathless ease. Nothing for you
    to fear,
no punishment to come. Oh I'd pay you back
if I only had the power at my command!"
No more words—he dashed toward the city,
heart racing for some great exploit, rushing on
like a champion stallion drawing a chariot full tilt,
sweeping across the plain in easy, tearing
    strides—
so Achilles hurtled on, driving legs and knees.
And old King Priam was first to see him coming,
surging over the plain, blazing like the star
that rears at harvest, flaming up in its brilliance,—
far outshining the countless stars in the night sky,
that star they call Orion's Dog—brightest of all
but a fatal sign emblazoned on the heavens,
it brings such killing fever down on wretched
    men.
So the bronze flared on his chest as on
    he raced—
and the old man moaned, flinging both hands
    high,
beating his head and groaning deep he called,
begging his dear son who stood before the gates,
unshakable, furious to fight Achilles to the death.
The old man cried, pitifully, hands reaching out
    to him,
"Oh Hector! Don't just stand there, don't,
    dear child,
waiting that man's attack—alone, cut off from
    friends!

You'll meet your doom at once, beaten down
    by Achilles,
so much stronger than you—that hard,
    headlong man.

• • •

Back, come back! Inside the walls, my boy!
Rescue the men of Troy and the Trojan women—
don't hand the great glory to Peleus' son,
of your own sweet life yourself.

• • •

So the old man groaned
and seizing his gray hair tore it out by the roots
but he could not shake the fixed resolve of
    Hector.
And his mother wailed now, standing beside
    Priam,
weeping freely, loosing her robes with one hand
and holding out her bare breast with the other,
her words pouring forth in a flight of grief
    and tears:
"Hector, my child! Look—have some respect
    for *this!*
Pity your mother too, if I ever gave you the
    breast
to soothe your troubles, remember it now,
    dear boy—
beat back that savage man from safe inside the
    walls!
Don't go forth, a champion pitted against him—
merciless, brutal man. If he kills you now,
how can I ever mourn you on your deathbed?—
dear branch in bloom, dear child I brought to
    birth!—
Neither I nor your wife, that warm, generous
    woman . . .
Now far beyond our reach, now by the Argive
    ships
the rushing dogs will tear you, bolt your flesh!"
So they wept, the two of them crying out
to their dear son, both pleading time and
    again

but they could not shake the fixed resolve
   of Hector.
No, he waited Achilles, coming on, gigantic
   in power.

•••

Hector looked up, saw him, started to tremble,
nerve gone, he could hold his ground no
   longer,
he left the gates behind and away he fled in
   fear—
and Achilles went for him, fast, sure of his speed
as the wild mountain hawk, the quickest thing
   on wings,
launching smoothly, swooping down on a
   cringing dove
and the dove flits out from under, the hawk
   screaming
over the quarry, plunging over and over, his fury
driving him down to beak and tear his kill—
so Achilles flew at him, breakneck on in fury
with Hector fleeing along the walls of Troy,
fast as his legs would go.

•••

And swift Achilles kept on coursing Hector,
   nonstop
as a hound in the mountains starts a fawn from
   its lair,
hunting him down the gorges, down the
   narrow glens
and the fawn goes to ground, hiding deep in
   brush
but the hound comes racing fast, nosing him out
until he lands his kill. So Hector could never
   throw
Achilles off his trail, the swift racer Achilles—
time and again he'd make a dash for the
   Dardan Gates,
trying to rush beneath the rock-built
   ramparts, hoping
men on the heights might save him, somehow,
   raining spears

but time and again Achilles would intercept
   him quickly,
heading him off, forcing him out across the plain
and always sprinting along the city side himself—
endless as in a dream . . .

•••

Athena luring him on with all her immortal
   cunning—
and now, at last, as the two came closing for
   the kill
it was tall Hector, helmet flashing, who led off:
"No more running from you in fear, Achilles!
Not as before. Three times I fled around
the great city of Priam—I lacked courage then
to stand your onslaught. Now my spirit stirs me
to meet you face-to-face. Now kill or be killed!"

•••

Shaft poised, he hurled and his spear's long
   shadow flew
and it struck Achilles' shield—a dead-center hit—
but off and away it glanced and Hector seethed,
his hurtling spear, his whole arm's power poured
in a wasted shot. He stood there, cast down . . .
he had no spear in reserve.

•••

[H]e drew the whetted sword that hung at his side,
tempered, massive, and gathering all his force
he swooped like a soaring eagle
launching down from the dark clouds to earth
to snatch some helpless lamb or trembling hare.
So Hector swooped now, swinging his whetted
   sword and
Achilles charged too, bursting with rage, barbaric,
guarding his chest with the well-wrought
   blazoned shield,
head tossing his gleaming helmet, four horns
   strong
and the golden plumes shook that the god of fire

drove in bristling thick along its ridge.
Bright as that star amid the stars in the night sky,
star of the evening, brightest star that rides the
    heavens,
so fire flared from the sharp point of the spear
    Achilles
brandished high in his right hand, bent on
    Hector's death,
scanning his splendid body—where to pierce
    it best?

• • •

[O]ne spot lay exposed,
where collarbones lift the neckbone off the
    shoulders,

the open throat, where the end of life comes
    quickest—*there*
as Hector charged in fury brilliant Achilles
    drove his spear
and the point went stabbing clean through
    the tender neck
but the heavy bronze weapon failed to slash the
    windpipe—
Hector could still gasp out some words, some
    last reply . . .
he crashed in the dust—
godlike Achilles gloried over him:
"Hector— . . . you fool! . . .
[T]he dogs and birds will maul you, shame your
    corpse[!]

QUESTIONS

1. What does the *Iliad* tell us about the Greek style of warfare?

2. What does the *Iliad* suggest is the nature of relations between city-states in Homer's time?

3. What role do the gods play in the lives of mortals? How closely involved are they in the outcome of the struggle between Hector and Achilles?

4. Judging from the story Homer tells, what might you say about the ideals of the Greek warrior? How do warriors behave?

11

■ *Sappho of Lesbos* ■

POEMS

(CA. 600 B.C.E.)

Sappho (ca. 610–580 B.C.E.) is one of the most admired of the Greek poets. She was born on the Aegean island of Lesbos, and she may have endured political exile in Sicily. It may be inferred from the fact that she refers to a daughter that she had been married, but we know virtually nothing about her life, her social position, or the poetic environment of the time. Sappho was probably free and wealthy, and therefore subject to fewer restraints than the majority of women in her time. It is also clear from the context of her poetry that she was bisexual, but more specific information about her sexuality is not available.

Sappho's poetry was famous throughout the ancient world and was extensively quoted by later classical authors, but very little survives today. Only one complete poem has been discovered; the rest of the work has come down to us only in fragments. Most of these relate, in one way or another, to Sappho's own social world and to matters of love and personal relationships. The personal nature and familiar themes of her work still move readers today.

V

Some say that an army of cavalry
Others that infantry
And others that a fleet of ships
Is what is most desirable
On this dark earth
But for me it is whatever
Inspires one's passionate love
One can make this readily
Comprehensible to anybody
For Helen who far excelled
Other humans in beauty
Deserted her excellent husband
And sailed away to Troy
Completely heedless of her child
And her own family
Instead Aphrodite exerted
Her influence right away
Which now makes me remember
Anactoria from whom I am apart
I would rather hear
Her beloved footfall
And see the shining
Radiance of her face
Than any Lydian chariots
Or soldiers fighting fully-armed

Anonymous female poet of the fourth century B.C.E.

IX

Just like a god he seems to me
That man who sits

Across from you so closely
Attentive to your sweet words
And your charming laugh that honestly
Makes my heart reel inside my breast
For when I briefly glance at you
Then speech becomes impossible
My tongue is shivered and at once
Soft flame infiltrates my skin
In my eyes no sight remains
And roaring fills my ears
Sweat cascades off me and

Tremor completely savages me
I am paler than dry grass
And in my craziness I seem
To have reached the threshold of death
But I must submit to everything

And sweetly on soft beds
You rapidly slaked
Your passion for young women
There was never music
We did not share
Never a shrine
We did not visit

XIX

I sincerely wish I were dead
She cried copiously when she left me
And she told me this:
"Ah Sappho how terribly we have suffered
Sure I am leaving you against my will"
And this was my answer to her:
"Go and good luck remember me
For you know how we cherished you
Otherwise I want to remind you
Of all our tender experiences
You wove many garlands
Of violets roses and tendrils of vine
Beside me to circle your brow
And you plaited many chaplets
Wreathed from flowers
To throw around your delicate neck
And you used to anoint yourself
All over with fresh perfumes
Whose scents were royal and rich

XXVIII

Fortunate bridegroom your marriage
Has been consummated as you prayed
And you have the young woman
For whom you prayed
Your appearance is beautiful
But your bride has honeyed eyes
And when she smiles
Love suffuses her radiant face
Aphrodite has graced you incomparably

XXXVII

Wealth in the absence of virtue
Is not an innocent neighbor
But the blending of both
Is the peak of good fortune

QUESTIONS

1. A poem can reveal much about its author, as well as something about that author's society. What do you think these poems reveal about Sappho and women like her?

2. Many of Sappho's poems are about love. What do they tell us about Greek attitudes toward love?

3. There are relatively few surviving literary works by women in the ancient world. Do you think that Sappho's gender had an important impact on her poetry?

4. Sappho's work has been praised for its ability to "create a close personal relationship" with her readers. Do you think this is true? Is this important?

12

■ *Thucydides* ■

HISTORY OF THE PELOPONNESIAN WAR

(CA. 400 B.C.E.)

Thucydides (ca. 455–400 B.C.E.) was born in Athens, of a prominent aristocratic family with roots in Thrace. Intelligent and very well educated in the sophist school, he was raised in the city. He inherited property and gold mines in Thrace, giving him sufficient independence to devote much of his time to the service of the state. When war broke out between Athens and Sparta in 431 B.C.E., he joined the Athenian navy. After surviving a bout of the plague, he continued his military career. In 424–423, he was elected General of Athen's forces, but in 422, he failed to prevent a Spartan victory at Amphipolis. This setback ended his command and led to his exile from Athens. He spent the rest of the war in Thrace, gathering materials for his history. He returned to Athens briefly around 403, after the Spartan conquest of the city, but is thought to have died in Thrace.

The *History of the Peloponnesian War* tells the story of the monumental struggle between Athens and Sparta, based upon Thucydides' personal experiences and research. Thucydides avoided reporting myth as fact, and has been called the first "objective" and "scientific" historian. The famous passage included here is the Melian dialogue. The Athenians demanded the surrender of the island of Melos, which had been settled by Spartan (or Lacedaemonian) colonists. The Melians had remained neutral in the war and hoped to avoid conflict with Athens.

The Athenians next made an expedition against the island of Melos with thirty ships of their own, six Chian, and two Lesbian, twelve hundred hoplites and three hundred archers besides twenty mounted archers of their own, and about fifteen hundred hoplites furnished by their allies in the islands. The Melians are colonists of the Lacedaemonians who would not submit to Athens like other islanders. At first they were neutral and took no part. But when the Athenians tried to coerce them by ravaging their lands, they were driven into open hostilities.

The generals, Cleomedes the son of Lycomedes and Tisias the son of Tisimachus, encamped with Athenian forces on the island. But before they did the country any harm they sent envoys to negotiate with the Melians. Instead of bringing these envoys before the people, the Melians desired them to explain their errand to the magistrates and to the chief men. They spoke as follows:—

'Since we are not allowed to speak to the people, lest, forsooth they should be deceived by seductive and unanswerable arguments which they would hear set forth in a single uninterrupted oration (for we are perfectly aware that this is what you mean in bringing us before a select few), you who are sitting here may as well make assurance yet surer. Let us have no set speeches at all, but do you reply to each several statement of which you disapprove, and criticise it at once. Say first of all how you like this mode of proceeding.'

The Melian representatives answered:— 'The quiet interchange of explanations is a reasonable thing, and we do not object to that. But your warlike movements, which are present not only to our fears but to our eyes, seem to belie your words. We see that, although you may reason with us, you mean to our judges; and that at the end of the discussion, if the justice of our cause prevail and we therefore refuse to yield, we may expect war; if we are convinced by you, slavery.'

Ath. 'Nay, but if you are only going to argue from fancies about the future, or if you meet us with any other purpose than that of looking your circumstances in the face and saving your city, we have done; if this is your intention we will proceed.'

Mel. 'It is an excusable and natural thing that men in our position should have much to say and should indulge in many fancies. But we admit that this conference has met to consider the question of our preservation; and therefore let the argument proceed in the manner which you propose.'

Ath. 'Well, then we Athenians will use no fine words; we will not go out of our way to prove at length that we have a right to rule, because we overthrew the Persians; or that we attack you now because we are suffering any injury at your hands. We should not convince you if we did; nor must you expect to convince us by arguing that, although a colony of the Lacedaemonians, you have taken no part in their expeditions, or that you have never done us any wrong. But you and we should say what we really think, and aim only at what is possible, for we both alike know

that into the discussion of human affairs the question of justice only enters where the pressure of necessity is equal, and that the powerful exact what they can, and the weak grant what they must.'

Mel. 'Well, then, since you set aside justice and invite us to speak of expediency, in our judgment it is certainly expedient that you should respect a principle which is for the common good; and that to every man when in peril a reasonable claim should be accounted a claim of right, and any plea which he is disposed to urge, even if failing of the point a little, should help his cause. Your interest in this principle is quite as great as ours, inasmuch as you, if you fall, will incur the heaviest vengeance, and will be the most terrible example to mankind.'

Ath. 'The fall of our empire, if it should fall, is not an event to which we look forward with dismay; for ruling states such as Lacedaemon are not cruel to their vanquished enemies. And we are fighting not so much against the Lacedaemonians, as against our own subjects who may some day rise up and overcome their former masters. But this is a danger which you may leave to us. And we will now endeavour to show that we have come in the interests of our empire, and that in what we are about to say we are only seeking the preservation of your city. For we want to make you ours with the least trouble to ourselves, and it is for the interests of us both that you should not be destroyed.'

Mel. 'It may be your interest to be our masters, but how can it be ours to be your slaves?'

Ath. 'To you the gain will be that by submission you will avert the worst; and we shall be all the richer for your preservation.'

Mel. 'But must we be your enemies? Will you not receive us as friends if we are neutral and remain at peace with you?'

Ath. 'No, your enmity is not half so mischievous to us as your friendship; for the one is in the eyes of our subjects an argument of our power, the other of our weakness.'

Mel. 'But are your subjects really unable to distinguish between states in which you have no concern, and those which are chiefly your own colonies, and in some cases have revolted and been subdued by you?'

Ath. 'Why, then do not doubt that both of them have a good deal to say for themselves on the score of justice, but they think that states like yours are left free because they are able to defend themselves, and that we do not attack them because we dare not. So that your subjection will give us an increase of security, as well as an extension of empire. For we are masters of the sea, and you who are islanders, and insignificant islanders too, must not be allowed to escape us.'

Mel. 'But do you not recognise another danger? For, once more, since you drive us from the plea of justice and press upon us your doctrine of expediency, we must show you what is for our interest, and, if it be for yours also, may hope to convince you:—Will you not be making enemies of all who are now neutrals? When they see how you are treating us they will expect you someday to turn against them; and if so, are you not strengthening the enemies whom you already have, and bringing upon you others who, if they could help, would never dream of being your enemies at all?'

Ath. 'We do not consider our really dangerous enemies to be any of the peoples inhabiting the mainland who, secure in their freedom, may defer indefinitely any measures of precaution which they take against us, but islanders who, like you, happen to be under no control, and all who may be already irritated by the necessity of submission to our empire—these are our real enemies, for they are the most reckless and most likely to bring themselves as well as us into a danger which they cannot but foresee.'

Mel. 'Surely then, if you and your subjects will brave all this risk, you to preserve your empire and they to be quit of it, how base and cowardly would it be in us, who retain our freedom, not to do and suffer anything rather than be your slaves.'

Ath. 'Not so, if you calmly reflect: for you are not fighting against equals to whom you cannot yield without disgrace, but you are taking counsel whether or no you shall resist an overwhelming force. The question is not one of honour but of prudence.'

Mel. 'But we know that the fortune of war is sometimes impartial, and not always on the side of numbers. If we yield now, all is over; but if we fight, there is yet a hope that we may stand upright.'

Ath. 'Hope is a good comforter in the hour of danger, and when men have something else to depend upon, although hurtful, she is not ruinous. But when her spendthrift nature has induced them to stake their all, they see her as she is in the moment of their fall, and not till then. While the knowledge of her might enable them to beware of her, she never fails. You are weak and a single turn of the scale might be your ruin. Do not you be thus deluded; avoid the error of which so many are guilty, who, although they might still be saved if they would take the natural means, when visible grounds of confidence forsake them, have recourse to the invisible, to prophecies and oracles and the like, which ruin men by the hopes which they inspire in them.'

Mel. 'We know only too well how hard the struggle must be against your power, and against fortune, if she does not mean to be impartial. Nevertheless we do not despair of fortune; for we hope to stand as high as you in the favour of heaven, because we are righteous, and you against whom we contend are unrighteous; and we are satisfied that our deficiency in power will be compensated by the aid of our allies the Lacedaemonians; they cannot refuse to help us, if only because we are their kinsmen, and for the sake of their own honour. And therefore our confidence is not so utterly blind as you suppose.'

Ath. 'As for the Gods, we expect to have quite as much of their favour as you: for we are not doing or claiming anything which goes beyond common opinion about divine or men's desires about human things. For of the Gods we believe, and of men we know, that by a law of their nature wherever they can rule they will. This law was not made by us, and we are not the first who have acted upon it; we did but inherit it, and shall bequeath it to all time, and we know that you and all mankind, if you were as strong as we are, would do as we do. So much for the Gods; we have told you why we expect to stand as high in their good opinion as you. And then as to the Lacedaemonians—when you imagine that out of very shame they will assist you, we admire the simplicity of your idea, but we do not envy you the folly of it. The Lacedaemonians are exceedingly virtuous among themselves, and according to their national standard of morality. But, in respect of their dealings with others, although many things might be said, a word is enough to describe them,—of all men whom we know they are the most notorious for identifying what is pleasant with what is honourable, and what is expedient with what is just. But how inconsistent is such a character with your present blind hope of deliverance!'

Mel. 'That is the very reason why we trust them; they will look to their interest, and therefore will not be willing to betray the Melians, who are their own colonists, lest they should be distrusted by their friends in Hellas and play into the hands of their enemies.'

Ath. 'But do you not see that the path of expediency is safe, whereas justice and honour involve danger in practice, and such dangers the Lacedaemonians seldom care to face?'

Mel. 'On the other hand, we think that whatever perils there may be, they will be ready to face them for our sakes, and will consider danger less dangerous where we are concerned. For if they need our aid we are close at hand, and they can better trust our loyal feeling because we are their kinsmen.'

Ath. 'Yes, but what encourages men who are invited to join in a conflict is clearly not the goodwill of those who summon them to their side, but a decided superiority in real power. To this no men look more keenly than the Lacedaemonians;

so little confidence have they in their own resources, that they only attack their neighbours when they have numerous allies, and therefore they are not likely to find their way by themselves to an island, when we are masters of the sea.'

Mel. 'But they may send their allies: the Cretan sea is a large place; and the masters of the sea will have more difficulty in overtaking vessels which want to escape than the pursued in escaping. If the attempt should fail they may invade Attica itself, and find their way to allies of yours whom Brasidas did not reach: and then you will have to fight, not for the conquest of a land in which you have no concern, but nearer home, for the preservation of your confederacy and of your own territory.'

Ath. 'Help may come from Lacedaemon to you as it has come to others, and should you ever have actual experience of it, then you will know that never once have the Athenians retired from a siege through fear of a foe elsewhere. You told us that the safety of your city would be your first care, but we remark that, in this long discussion, not a word has been uttered by you which would give a reasonable man expectation of deliverance. Your strongest grounds are hopes deferred, and what power you have is not to be compared with that which is already arrayed against you. Unless after we have withdrawn you mean to come, as even now you may, to a wiser conclusion, you are showing a great want of sense. For surely you cannot dream of flying to that false sense of honour which has been the ruin of so many when danger and dishonour were staring them in the face. Many men with their eyes still open to the consequences have found the word "honour" too much for them, and have suffered a mere name to lure them on, until it has drawn down upon them real and irretrievable calamities; through their own folly they have incurred a worse dishonour than fortune would have inflicted upon them. If you are wise you will not run this risk; you ought to see that there can be no disgrace in yielding to a great city which invites you to become her ally on reasonable terms, keeping your own land, and merely paying tribute; and that you will certainly gain honour if, having to choose between two alternatives, safety and war, you obstinately prefer the worse. To maintain our rights against equals, to be politic with superiors, and to be moderate towards inferiors is the path of safety. Reflect once more when we have withdrawn, and say to yourselves over and over again that you are deliberating about your one and only country, which may be saved or may be destroyed by a single decision.'

The Athenians left the conference: the Melians, after consulting among themselves, resolved to persevere in their refusal, and made answer as follows:—'Men of Athens, our resolution is unchanged; and we will not in a moment surrender that liberty which our city, founded seven hundred years ago, still enjoys; we will trust to the good-fortune which, by the favour of the Gods, has hitherto preserved us, and for human help to the Lacedaemonians, and endeavour to save ourselves.'

Such was the answer of the Melians; the Athenians, as they quitted the conference, spoke as follows:—'Well, we must say, judging from the decision at which you have arrived, that you are the only men who deem the future to be more certain than the present, and regard things unseen as already realised in your fond anticipation, and that the more you cast yourselves upon the Lacedaemonians and fortune, and hope, and trust them, the more complete will be your ruin.'

The Athenian envoys returned to the army; and the generals, when they found that the Melians would not yield, immediately commenced hostilities. They surrounded the town of Melos with a wall, dividing the work among several contingents. They then left troops of their own and of their allies to keep guard both by land and by sea, and retired with the greater part of their army; the remainder carried on the blockade.

The Melians took another part of the Athenian wall; for the fortifications were insufficiently guarded. Whereupon the Athenians sent fresh troops, under the command of Philocrates the son of Demeas. The place was now closely invested, and there was treachery among the citizens themselves. So the Melians were induced to surrender at discretion. The Athenians thereupon put to death all who were of military age, and made slaves of the women and children. They then colonised the island, sending thither five hundred settlers of their own.

QUESTIONS

1. Why do the Athenians believe that Melos must be conquered?

2. Why, according to the Melians, should Athens allow Melos its independence?

3. Why, according to the Athenians, should the Melians give in and surrender?

4. What are the opposing views of justice and right as presented by the Athenians and Melians here?

5. Judging from the outcome of the struggle between Melos and Athens, do you believe the Athenians' arguments were correct?

13

■ *Xenophon* ■

THE SPARTAN CONSTITUTION

(CA. 360 B.C.E.)

[handwritten annotation: Xenophon - was an Athenian aristocrat. Disliked the policies of Athenian Democracy, favoring the oligarchy of Sparta. He became a military leader after Cyrus was killed. Earned an estate near Olympia after serving with the Spartans for 5 years.]

Xenophon (ca. 430–354 B.C.E.) was an Athenian aristocrat who came of age during the disastrous Peloponnesian War between Athens and Sparta. He disliked the policies of the Athenian democracy, favoring the oligarchic faction and became sympathetic to Sparta. After the war, he joined those Greeks who were fighting for the Persian prince Cyrus and traveled far into the Persian Empire. He became a military leader after Cyrus and his commanders were killed and successfully led them back to Greek territory. After serving with the Spartans for five years, he was awarded an estate near Olympia, where he retired. He wrote his major works, *The Persian Expedition* and *A History of My Own Times*, there and in Corinth, where he died after witnessing the final collapse of Sparta. His works are the major source for the history of his times.

This selection from the Constitution of Sparta attempts to answer the question, why did the Spartans succeed? Xenophon's admiration for Lycurgus led him to accumulate examples of his special social and military practices. He gave these great weight in explaining Sparta's success.

CONSTITUTION OF THE LACEDAEMONIANS

[handwritten annotation: Sparta - small populated but very powerful.]

I.

It occurred to me one day that Sparta, though among the most thinly populated of states, was evidently the most powerful and most celebrated city in Greece; and I fell to wondering how this could have happened. But when I considered the institutions of the Spartans, I wondered no longer.

Lycurgus, who gave them the laws that they obey, and to which they owe their prosperity, I do regard with wonder; and I think that he reached the utmost limit of wisdom. For it was not by imitating other states, but by devising a system utterly different from that of most others, that he made his country pre-eminently prosperous.

[handwritten annotation: Lycurgus → Sparta did not imitate other Greek states but devised a different system.]

First, to begin at the beginning, I will take the begetting of children. In other states the girls who are destined to become mothers and are brought up in the approved fashion, live on the very plainest fare, with a most meagre allowance of delicacies. Wine is either withheld altogether, or, if allowed them, is diluted with water. The rest of the Greeks expect their girls to imitate the sedentary life that is typical of handicraftsmen—to keep quiet and do wool-work. How, then, is it to be expected that women so brought up will bear fine children?

But Lycurgus thought the labour of slave women sufficient to supply clothing. He believed motherhood to be the most important function of freeborn woman. Therefore, in the first place, he insisted on physical training for the female no less than for the male sex: moreover, he

[handwritten annotation: Unlike other Greek states Lycurgus and Sparta put a larger emphasis on the roles of females in society.]

instituted races and trials of strength for women competitors as for men, believing that if both parents are strong they produce more vigorous offspring.

He noticed, too, that, during the time immediately succeeding marriage, it was usual elsewhere for the husband to have unlimited intercourse with his wife. The rule that he adopted was the opposite of this: for he laid it down that the husband should be ashamed to be seen entering his wife's room or leaving it. With this restriction on intercourse the desire of the one for the other must necessarily be increased, and their offspring was bound to be more vigorous than if they were surfeited with one another. In addition to this, he withdrew from men the right to take a wife whenever they chose, and insisted on their marrying in the prime of their manhood, believing that this too promoted the production of fine children. It might happen, however, that an old man had a young wife; and he observed that old men keep a very jealous watch over their young wives. To meet these cases he instituted an entirely different system by requiring the elderly husband to introduce into his house some man whose physical and moral qualities he admired, in order to beget children. On the other hand, in case a man did not want to cohabit with his wife and nevertheless desired children of whom he could be proud, he made it lawful for him to choose a woman who was the mother of a fine family and of high birth, and if he obtained her husband's consent, to make her the mother of his children.

He gave his sanction to many similar arrangements. For the wives want to take charge of two households, and the husbands want to get brothers for their sons, brothers who are members of the family and share in its influence, but claim no part of the money.

Thus his regulations with regard to the begetting of children were in sharp contrast with those of other states. Whether he succeeded in populating Sparta with a race of men remarkable for their size and strength anyone who chooses may judge for himself.

Lycurgus had different ideas on the subject of marriage, birth and education.

II.

Having dealt with the subject of birth, I wish next to explain the educational system of Lycurgus, and how it differs from other systems.

In the other Greek states parents who profess to give their sons the best education place their boys under the care and control of a moral tutor as soon as they can understand what is said to them, and send them to a school to learn letters, music and the exercises of the wrestling-ground. Moreover, they soften the children's feet by giving them sandals, and pamper their bodies with changes of clothing; and it is customary to allow them as much food as they can eat.

Lycurgus, on the contrary, instead of leaving each father to appoint a slave to act as tutor, gave the duty of controlling the boys to a member of the class from which the highest offices are filled, in fact to the "Warden" as he is called. He gave this person authority to gather the boys together, to take charge of them and to punish them severely in case of misconduct. He also assigned to him a staff of youths provided with whips to chastise them when necessary; and the result is that modesty and obedience are inseparable companions at Sparta. Instead of softening the boys' feet with sandals he required them to harden their feet by going without shoes. He believed that if this habit were cultivated it would enable them to climb hills more easily and descend steep inclines with less danger, and that a youth who had accustomed himself to go barefoot would leap and jump and run more nimbly than a boy in sandals. And instead of letting them be pampered in the matter of clothing, he introduced the custom of wearing one garment throughout the year, believing that they would thus be better prepared to face changes of heat and cold. As to the food, he required the prefect to bring with him such a moderate amount of it that the boys would never suffer from repletion, and would know what it was to go with their hunger unsatisfied; for he believed that those who underwent this training would be better able to continue working on an empty stomach; if necessary, and would be capable of carrying on longer without extra food, if the word of command were given to do so: they would want fewer delicacies and would accommodate themselves more readily to anything put before them, and at the same time would enjoy better health. He also thought that a diet which made their bodies slim would do more to increase their height than one that consisted of flesh-forming food.

On the other hand, lest they should feel too much the pinch of hunger, while not giving them the opportunity of taking what they wanted without trouble he allowed them to alleviate their hunger by stealing something. It was not on account of a difficulty in providing for them that he encouraged them to get their food by their own cunning. No one, I suppose, can fail to see that. Obviously a man who intends to take to thieving must spend sleepless nights and play the deceiver and lie in ambush by day, and moreover, if he means to make a capture, he must have spies ready. There can be no doubt then, that all this education was planned by him in order to make the boys more resourceful in getting supplies, and better fighting men.

Someone may ask: But why, if he believed stealing to be a fine thing, did he have the boy who was caught beaten with many stripes? I reply: Because in all cases men punish a learner for not carrying out properly whatever he is taught to do. So the Spartans chastise those who get caught for stealing badly. He made it a point of honour to steal as many cheeses as possible, but appointed others to scourge the thieves, meaning to show thereby that by enduring pain for a short time one may win lasting fame and felicity. It is shown herein that where there is need of swiftness, the slothful, as usual, gets little profit and many troubles.

In order that the boys might never lack a ruler even when the Warden was away, he gave authority to any citizen who chanced to be present to require them to do anything that he

thought right, and to punish them for any misconduct. This had the effect of making the boys more respectful; in fact boys and men alike respect their rulers above everything. And that a ruler might not be lacking to the boys even when no grown man happened to be present, he selected the keenest of the prefects, and gave to each the command of a division. And so at Sparta the boys are never without a ruler.

I think I ought to say something also about intimacy with boys, since this matter also has a bearing on education. In other Greek states, for instance among the Boeotians, man and boy live together, like married people; elsewhere, among the Eleians, for example, consent is won by means of favours. Some, on the other hand, entirely forbid suitors to talk with boys.

The customs instituted by Lycurgus were opposed to all of these. If someone, being himself an honest man, admired a boy's soul and tried to make of him an ideal friend without reproach and to associate with him, he approved, and believed in the excellence of this kind of training. But if it was clear that the attraction lay in the boy's outward beauty, he banned the connection as an abomination; and thus he purged the relationship of all impurity, so that in Lacedaemon it resembled parental and brotherly love.

I am not surprised, however, that people refuse to believe this. For in many states the laws are not opposed to the indulgence of these appetites.

I have now dealt with the Spartan system of education, and that of the other Greek states. Which system turns out men more obedient, more respectful, and more strictly temperate, anyone who chooses may once more judge for himself.

III.

When a boy ceases to be a child, and begins to be a lad, others release him from his moral tutor and his schoolmaster: he is then no longer under a ruler and is allowed to go his own way.

When a boy is no longer a boy, lycurgus believes a keen appetite for pleasures possession him, so it is important they are tasked allday.

Here again Lycurgus introduced a wholly different system. For he observed that at this time of life self-will makes strong root in a boy's mind, a tendency to insolence manifests itself, and a keen appetite for pleasure in different forms takes possession of him. At this stage, therefore, he imposed on him a ceaseless round of work, and contrived a constant round of occupation. The penalty for shirking the duties was exclusion from all future honours. He thus caused not only the public authorities, but their relations also to take pains that the lads did not incur the contempt of their fellow citizens by flinching from their tasks.

Moreover, wishing modesty to be firmly rooted in them, he required them to keep their hands under their cloaks, to walk in silence, not to look about them, but to fix their eyes on the ground. The effect of this rule has been to prove that even in the matter of decorum the male is stronger than the female sex. At any rate you would expect a stone image to utter a sound sooner than those lads; you would sooner attract the attention of a bronze figure; you might think them more modest even than a young bride in the bridal chamber. When they have taken their place at a public meal, you must be content if you can get an answer to a question.

Such was the care that he bestowed on the growing lads.

IV.

For those who had reached the prime of life he showed by far the deepest solicitude. For he believed that if these were of the right stamp they must exercise a powerful influence for good on the state. He saw that where the spirit of rivalry is strongest among the people, there the choruses are most worth hearing and the athletic contests afford the finest spectacle. He believed, therefore, that if he could match the young men together in a strife of valour, they too would reach a high level of manly excellence. I will proceed to explain, therefore, how he instituted matches between the young men.

The Ephors, then, pick out three of the very best among them. These three are called Commanders of the Guard. Each of them enrolls a hundred others, stating his reasons for preferring one and rejecting another. The result is that those who fail to win the honour are at war both with those who sent them away and with their successful rivals; and they are on the watch for any lapse from the code of honour.

Here then you find that kind of strife that is dearest to the gods, and in the highest sense political—the strife that sets the standard of a brave man's conduct; and in which either party exerts itself to the end that it may never fall below its best, and that, when the time comes, every member of it may support the state with all his might. And they are bound, too, to keep themselves fit, for one effect of the strife is that they spar whenever they meet; but anyone present has a right to part the combatants. If anyone refuses to obey the mediator the Warden takes him to the Ephors; and they fine him heavily, in order to make him realize that he must never yield to a sudden impulse to disobey the laws.

QUESTIONS

1. Why does Xenophon begin with procreation?

2. What was the purpose of Lycurgus's code of sexual conduct?

3. What was the purpose of Spartan education?

4. How did Lycurgus instill competition among the Spartans?

14

■ *Plato* ■

APOLOGY

(399 B.C.E.)

The *Apology* recounts Socrates's trial for heresy and corrupting the morals of
the youth of Athens. Socrates (469–399 B.C.E.) lived his entire life as an
Athenian. He served as an armored soldier in the Peloponnesian Wars but did
not enter state service as might have been expected of one of his intellectual
skills. Rather he took to walking throughout Athens, questioning those who
followed him about the things they saw and delving for the underlying principles of human life. He took particular delight in showing that individuals
reputed to be wise or honorable were nothing of the sort. Although Socrates
was not officially a teacher—that is, he received no fees and worked in no
fixed school—he instructed hundreds of Athenians in the technique of critical questioning that we now call the Socratic method. Among his pupils was
Plato, a devoted follower who was present at the trial and who went into self-
imposed exile after Socrates's death.

   The *Apology,* which means defense rather than retraction, relates the
speech that Socrates made to the jury at his trial, both before and after a verdict was reached by the 501 Athenian citizens who heard the evidence against
him. Socrates was seventy at the time, and the imposition of the death penalty
came as a shock to many of his admirers. The death of Socrates is narrated in
another work of Plato's, *Phaedo.*

How you have felt, O men of Athens, at hearing
the speeches of my accusers, I cannot tell; but I
know that their persuasive words almost made
me forget who I was—such was the effect of
them; and yet they have hardly spoken a word of
truth. But many as their falsehoods were, there
was one of them which quite amazed me—I
mean when they told you to be upon your
guard, and not to let yourselves be deceived by
the force of my eloquence. They ought to have
been ashamed of saying this, because they were
sure to be detected as soon as I opened my lips

and displayed my deficiency: they certainly did
appear to be most shameless in saying this,
unless by the force of eloquence they mean the
force of truth; for then I do indeed admit that
I am eloquent. But in how different a way from
theirs! I must beg of you to grant me one favor,
which is this—If you hear me using the same
words in my defence which I have been in
the habit of using, and which most of you may
have heard in the agora, and at the tables of
the money-changers, or anywhere else, I would
ask you not to be surprised at this, and not to

interrupt me. For I am more than seventy years of age, and this is the first time that I have ever appeared in a court of law, and I am quite a stranger to the ways of the place; and therefore I would have you regard me as if I were really a stranger, whom you would excuse if he spoke in his native tongue, and after the fashion of his country; that I think is not an unfair request. Never mind the manner, which may or may not be good; but think only of the justice of my cause, and give heed to that: let the judge decide justly and the speaker speak truly.

And first, I have to reply to the older charges and to my first accusers, and then I will go on to the later ones. For I have had many accusers, who accused me of old, and their false charges have continued during many years; and I am more afraid of them than of Anytus and his associates, who are dangerous, too, in their own way. But far more dangerous are these, who began when you were children, and took possession of your minds with their falsehoods, telling of one Socrates, a wise man, who speculated about the heaven above, and searched into the earth beneath, and made the worse appear the better cause. These are the accusers whom I dread; for they are the circulators of this rumor, and their hearers are too apt to fancy that speculators of this sort do not believe in the gods.

There is another thing: young men of the richer classes, who have not much to do, come about me of their own accord; they like to hear the pretenders examined, and they often imitate me, and examine others themselves; there are plenty of persons, as they soon enough discover, who think that they know something, but really know little or nothing; and then those who are examined by them instead of being angry with themselves are angry with me: This confounded Socrates, they say; this villainous misleader of youth!—and then if somebody asks them, Why, what evil does he practise or teach? they do not know, and can not tell; but in order that they may not appear to be at a loss, they repeat the ready-made charges which are used against all philosophers about teaching things up in the clouds and under the earth, and having no gods, and making the worse appear the better cause; for they do not like to confess that their pretence of knowledge has been detected—which is the truth; and as they are numerous and ambitious and energetic, and are all in battle array and have persuasive tongues, they have filled your ears with their loud and inveterate calumnies.

Some one will say: And are you not ashamed, Socrates, of a course of life which is likely to bring you to an untimely end? To him I may fairly answer: There you are mistaken: a man who is good for anything ought not to calculate the chance of living or dying; he ought only to consider whether in doing anything he is doing right or wrong—acting the part of a good man or of a bad. For this fear of death is indeed the pretence of wisdom, and not real wisdom, being the appearance of knowing the unknown; since no one knows whether death, which they in their fear apprehend to be the greatest evil, may not be the greatest good. Is there not here conceit of knowledge, which is a disgraceful sort of ignorance? And this is the point in which, as I think, I am superior to men in general, and in which I might perhaps fancy myself wiser than other men,—that whereas I know but little of the world below, I do not suppose that I know; but I do know that injustice and disobedience to a better, whether God or man, is evil and dishonorable, and I will never fear or avoid a possible good rather than a certain evil. If you say to me, Socrates, this time we will let you off, but upon one condition, that you are not to inquire and speculate in this way any more, and that if you are caught doing this again you shall die—if this was the condition on which you let me go, I should reply: Men of Athens, I honor and love you; but I shall obey God rather than you, and while I have life and strength I shall never cease from the practice and teaching of philosophy, exhorting any one whom I meet after my manner, and convincing him, saying: O my friend, why do you, who are a citizen of the great and mighty and wise city of Athens, care so much about laying up the greatest amount of money and honor and reputation, and so little about wisdom and truth and the greatest improvement of the soul, which you never regard or heed at all? Are you not ashamed of this? And if the person with whom I am arguing, says: Yes, but I do care; I do not depart or let him go at once; I interrogate and examine and cross-examine him, and if I think that he has no virtue, but only says that he has, I reproach him with undervaluing the greater, and overvaluing the less. And this I should say to every one whom I meet, young and old, citizen and alien, but especially to the citizens, inasmuch as they are my brethren. For this is the command to God, as I would have you know; and I believe that to this day no greater good has ever happened in the state than my service to the God. For I do nothing but go about persuading you all, old and young alike, not to take thought for your persons or your properties, but first and chiefly to care about the greatest improvement of the soul. I tell you that virtue is not given by money, but that from virtue come money and every other good of man, public as well as private. This is my teaching, and if this is the doctrine which corrupts the youth, my influence is ruinous indeed. But if any one says that this is not my teaching, he is speaking an untruth. Wherefore, O men of Athens, I say to you, do as Anytus bids or not as Anytus bids, and either acquit me or not; but whatever you do, know that I shall never alter my ways, not even if I have to die many times.

And now, Athenians, I am not going to argue for my own sake, as you may think, but for yours, that you may not sin against the God, or lightly reject his boon by condemning me. For if you kill me you will not easily find another like me, who, if I may use such a ludicrous figure of speech, am a sort of gadfly, given to the state by the God; and the state is like a great and noble steed who is tardy in his motions owing to his every size, and requires to be stirred into life. I am that gadfly which God has given the state, and all day long and in all places am always fastening upon you, arousing and persuading and reproaching you. And as you will not easily find another like me, I would advise you to spare me. I dare say that you

may feel irritated at being suddenly awakened when you are caught napping; and you may think that if you were to strike me dead, which you easily might, then you would sleep on for the remainder of your lives, unless God in his care of you gives you another gadfly. And that I am given to you by God is proved by this: that if I had been like other men, I should not have neglected all my own concerns or patiently seen the neglect of them during all these years, and have been doing yours, coming to you individually like a father or elder brother, exhorting you to regard virtue; this, I say, would not be like human nature. And had I gained anything, or if my exhortations had been paid, there would have been some sense in that; but now, as you will perceive, not even the impudence of my accusers dares to say that I have ever exacted or sought pay of any one; they have no witness of that. And I have a witness of the truth of what I say; my poverty is a sufficient witness.

There are many reasons why I am not grieved, O men of Athens, at the vote of condemnation. I expected this, and am only surprised that the votes are so nearly equal; for I had thought that the majority against me would have been far larger; but now, had thirty votes gone over to the other side, I should have been acquitted.

And so [the death penalty is proposed.] And what shall I propose on my part, O men of Athens? Clearly that which is my due. And what is that which I ought to pay or to receive? What shall be done to the man who has never had the wit to be idle during his whole life; but has been careless of what the many care about—wealth, and family interests, and military offices, and speaking in the assembly, and magistracies, and plots, and parties. Reflecting that I was really too honest a man to follow in this way and live, I did not go where I could do the greatest good privately to every one of you, thither I went, and sought to persuade every man among you, that he must look to himself, and seek virtue and wisdom before he looks to his private interests, and look to the state before he looks to the interests of the state; and that this should be the order which he observes in all his actions. What shall be done to such a one? Doubtless some good thing, O men of Athens, if he has his reward; and the good should be of a kind suitable to him. What would be a reward suitable to a poor man who is your benefactor, who desires leisure that he may instruct you? There can be no more fitting reward than maintenance in the Prytaneum, O men of Athens, a reward which he deserves far more than the citizen who has won the prize at Olympia in the horse or chariot race, whether the chariots were drawn by two horses or by many. For I am in want, and he has enough; and he only gives you the appearance of happiness, and I give you the reality. And if I am to estimate the penalty justly, I say that maintenance in the Prytaneum is the just return.

Not much time will be gained, O Athenians, in return for the evil name which you will get from the detractors of the city, who will say that you killed Socrates, a wise man; for they will call me wise even although I am not wise when they want to reproach you. If you had waited a little while, your desire would have been fulfilled in the course of nature. For I am far advanced in years, as you may perceive, and not far from death. I am speaking now only to those of you who have condemned me to death. And I have another thing to say to them: You think that I was convicted through deficiency of words—I mean, that if I had thought fit to leave nothing undone, nothing unsaid, I might have gained an acquittal. Not so; the deficiency which led to my conviction was not of words—certainly not. But I had not the boldness or impudence or inclination to address you as you would have liked me to address you, weeping and wailing and lamenting, and saying and doing many things which you have been accustomed to hear from others, and which, as I say, are unworthy of me. But I thought that I ought not to do anything common or mean in the hour of danger: nor do I now repent of the manner of my defence, and I would rather die having spoken after my manner, than speak in your manner and live. For neither in war nor yet at law ought any man to use every way of escaping death. For often

in battle there is no doubt that if a man will throw away his arms, and fall on his knees before his pursuers, he may escape death; and in other dangers there are other ways of escaping death, if a man is willing to say and do anything. The difficulty, my friends, is not in avoiding death, but in avoiding unrighteousness; for that runs faster than death. I am old and move slowly, and the slower runner has overtaken me, and my accusers are keen and quick, and the faster runner, who is unrighteousness, has overtaken them. And now I depart hence condemned by you to suffer the penalty of death, and they too go their ways condemned by the truth to suffer the penalty of villainy and wrong; and I must abide by my award—let them abide by theirs. I suppose that these things may be regarded as fated,—and I think that they are well.

And now, O men who have condemned me, I would fain prophesy to you; for I am about to die, and that is the hour in which men are gifted with prophetic power. And I prophesy to you who are my murderers, that immediately after my death punishment far heavier than you have inflicted on me will surely await you. Me you have killed because you wanted to escape the accuser, and not to give an account of your lives. But that will not be as you suppose: far otherwise. For I say that there will be more accusers of you than there are now; accusers whom hitherto I have restrained: and as they are younger they will be more severe with you, and you will be more offended at them. For if you think that by killing men you can avoid the accuser censuring your lives, you are mistaken; that is not a way of escape which is either possible or honorable; the easiest and the noblest way is not to be crushing others but to be improving yourselves. This is the prophecy which I utter before my departure to the judges who have condemned me.

Wherefore, O judges, be of good cheer about death, and know this of a truth—that no evil can happen to a good man, either in life or after death. He and his are not neglected by the gods; nor has my own approaching end happened by mere chance. But I see clearly that to die and be released was better for me; and therefore the oracle gave no sign. For which reason, also, I am not angry with my accusers or my condemners; they have done me no harm, although neither of them meant to do me any good; and for this I may gently blame them.

Still I have a favor to ask of them. When my sons are grown up, I would ask you, O my friends, to punish them; and I would have you trouble them, as I have troubled you, if they seem to care about riches, or anything, more than about virtue; or if they pretend to be something when they are really nothing, then reprove them, as I have reproved you, for not caring about that for which they ought to care, and thinking that they are something when they are really nothing. And if you do this, I and my sons will have received justice at your hands.

The hour of departure has arrived, and we go our ways—I to die, and you to live. Which is better God only knows.

QUESTIONS

1. What impressions do you get of Socrates from his *Apology*?

2. Socrates considers himself to be a philosopher. What does that mean? What does a philosopher do?

3. What, according to Socrates, was Athens losing by condemning him to death? What will be the consequences for the city?

4. Why did many Athenians think Socrates was such a dangerous man?

5. What fate did Socrates predict for those who condemned him?

6. The *Apology* presents a very sympathetic view of Socrates. If you were one of his accusers, how might you have put your case?

15

▪ *Plato* ▪

THE REPUBLIC

(CA. 327 B.C.E.)

Plato (428–347 B.C.E.), a member of an aristocratic Athenian family, studied under Socrates, whose ideas and methods of teaching he was later to immortalize. Plato trained for a career in politics, but the turbulent events of the late fifth century B.C.E. turned him against the ruling regime. After the death of

Socrates in 399 B.C.E., Plato began to travel and remained away from Athens for over a decade. He returned as a teacher and philosopher, spreading the views that had been taught to him by his master. In keeping with his idea that the state should be ruled by philosopher-kings, Plato founded an Academy for philosophical and political study. During this time he wrote extensively, producing his famous *Dialogues*. His philosophy centered on the belief that a fixed reality existed beyond the experience of the senses. Although a polytheist, Plato believed in a single, universal Good.

The Republic, one of the most important philosophical tracts in Western history, takes the form of a dialogue about the composition of a perfect society ruled by a philosopher-king who always strives to achieve the Good. The dialogue between Socrates and Glaucon presents Plato's ideas about the proper education of women in the republic. Part of Book VII, which uses analogy to illustrate Plato's belief that good government comes through the wisdom of philosophers, is reprinted here.

I suppose that I must retrace my steps and say what I perhaps ought to have said before in the proper place. The part of the men has been played out, and now properly enough comes the turn of the women. Of them I will proceed to speak, and the more readily since I am invited by you.

For men born and educated like our citizens, the only way, in my opinion, of arriving at a right conclusion about the possession and use of women and children is to follow the path on which we originally started, when we said that the men were to be the guardians and watchdogs of the herd.

True.

Let us further suppose the birth and education of our women to be subject to similar or nearly similar regulations; then we shall see whether the result accords with our design.

What do you mean?

What I mean may be put into the form of a question, I said: Are dogs divided into hes and shes, or do they both share equally in hunting and in keeping watch and in the other duties of dogs? or do we entrust to the males the entire and exclusive care of the flocks, while we leave the females at home, under the idea that the bearing and suckling their puppies is labour enough for them?

No, he said, they share alike; the only difference between them is that the males are stronger and the females weaker.

But can you use different animals for the same purpose, unless they are bred and fed in the same way?

You cannot.

Then, if women are to have the same duties as men, they must have the same nurture and education?

Yes.

The education which was assigned to the men was music and gymnastic.

Yes.

Then women must be taught music and gymnastic and also the art of war, which they must practise like the men?

That is the inference, I suppose.

I should rather expect, I said, that several of our proposals, if they are carried out, being unusual, may appear ridiculous.

No doubt of it.

Yes, and the most ridiculous thing of all will be the sight of women naked in the palaestra, exercising with the men, especially when they are no longer young; they certainly will not be a vision of beauty, any more than the enthusiastic old men who in spite of wrinkles and ugliness continue to frequent the gymnasia.

Yes, indeed, he said: according to present notions the proposal would be thought ridiculous.

But then, I said, as we have determined to speak our minds, we must not fear the jests of the wits which will be directed against this sort of innovation; how they will talk of women's attainments both in music and gymnastic, and above all about their wearing armour and riding upon horseback!

Very true, he replied.

First, then, whether the question is to be put in jest or in earnest, let us come to an understanding about the nature of woman: Is she capable of sharing either wholly or partially in the actions of men, or not at all? And is the art of war one of those arts in which she can or can not share? That will be the best way of commencing the enquiry, and will probably lead to the fairest conclusion.

That will be much the best way.

Shall we take the other side first and begin by arguing against ourselves; in this manner the adversary's position will not be undefended.

Why not? he said.

Then let us put a speech into the mouths of our opponents. They will say: "Socrates and Glaucon, no adversary need convict you, for you yourselves, at the first foundation of the State, admitted the principle that everybody was to do the one work suited to his own nature." And certainly, if I am not mistaken, such an admission was made by us. "And do not the natures of men and women differ very much indeed?" And we shall reply: Of course they do. Then we shall be asked, "Whether the tasks assigned to men and to women should not be different, and such as are agreeable to their different natures?" Certainly they should. "But if so, have you not fallen into a serious inconsistency in saying that men and women, whose natures are so entirely different, ought to perform the same actions?"—What

defence will you make for us, my good Sir, against any one who offers these objections?

That is not an easy question to answer when asked suddenly; and I shall and I do beg of you to draw out the case on our side.

These are the objections, Glaucon, and there are many others of a like kind, which I foresaw long ago; they made me afraid and reluctant to take in hand any law about the possession and nurture of women and children.

By Zeus, he said, the problem to be solved is anything but easy.

Why yes, I said, but the fact is that when a man is out of his depth, whether he has fallen into a little swimming bath or into mid ocean, he has to swim all the same.

Very true.

And must not we swim and try to reach the shore: we will hope that Arion's dolphin or some other miraculous help may save us?

I suppose so, he said.

Well then, let us see if any way of escape can be found. We acknowledged—did we not? that different natures ought to have different pursuits, and that men's and women's natures are different. And now what are we saying?—that different natures ought to have the same pursuits, this is the inconsistency which is charged upon us.

Precisely.

Verily, Glaucon, I said, glorious is the power of the art of contradiction!

Why do you say so?

Because I think that many a man falls into the practice against his will. When he thinks that he is reasoning he is really disputing, just because he cannot define and divide, and so know that of which he is speaking; and he will pursue a merely verbal opposition in the spirit of contention and not of fair discussion.

Yes, he replied, such is very often the case; but what has that to do with us and our argument?

A great deal; for there is certainly a danger of our getting unintentionally into a verbal opposition.

In what way?

Why we valiantly and pugnaciously insist upon the verbal truth, that different natures ought to have different pursuits, but we never considered at all what was the meaning of sameness or difference of nature, or why we distinguished them when we assigned different pursuits to different natures and the same to the same natures.

Why, no, he said, that was never considered by us.

I said: Suppose that by way of illustration we were to ask the question whether there is not an opposition in nature between bald men and hairy men; and if this is admitted by us, then, if bald men are cobblers, we should forbid the hairy men to be cobblers, and conversely?

That would be a jest, he said.

Yes, I said, a jest; and why? because were never meant when we constructed the State, that the opposition of natures should extend to every difference, but only to those differences which affected the pursuit in which the individual is engaged; we should have argued, for example, that a physician and one who is in mind a physician may be said to have the same nature.

True.

Whereas the physician and the carpenter have different natures?

Certainly.

And if, I said, the male and female sex appear to differ in their fitness for any art or pursuit, we should say that such pursuit or art ought to be assigned to one or the other of them; but if the difference consists only in women bearing and men begetting children, this does not amount to a proof that a woman differs from a man in respect of the sort of education she should receive; and we shall therefore continue to maintain that our guardians and their wives ought to have the same pursuits.

Very true, he said.

Next, we shall ask our opponent how, in reference to any of the pursuits or arts of civic life, the nature of a woman differs from that of a man?

That will be quite fair.

And perhaps he, like yourself, will reply that to give a sufficient answer on the instant is not easy; but after a little reflection there is no difficulty.

Yes, perhaps.

Suppose then that we invite him to accompany us in the argument, and then we may hope to show him that there is nothing peculiar in the constitution of women which would affect them in the administration of the State.

By all means.

Let us say to him: Come now, and we will ask you a question—when you spoke of a nature gifted or not gifted in any respect, did you mean to say that one man will acquire a thing easily, another with difficulty; a little learning will lead the one to discover a great deal; whereas the other, after much study and application, no sooner learns than he forgets; or again, did you mean, that the one has a body which is a good servant to his mind, while the body of the other is a hindrance to him? Would not these be the sort of differences which distinguish the man gifted by nature from the one who is ungifted?

No one will deny that.

And can you mention any pursuit of mankind in which the male sex has not all these gifts and qualities in a higher degree than the female? Need I waste time in speaking of the art of weaving, and the management of pancakes and preserves, in which womankind does really appear to be great, and in which for her to be beaten by a man is of all things the most absurd?

You are quite right, he replied, in maintaining the general inferiority of the female sex: although many women are in many things superior to men, yet on the whole what you say is true.

And if so, my friend, I said, there is no special faculty of administration in a state which a woman has because she is a woman, or which a man has by virtue of his sex, but the gifts of nature are alike diffused in both; all the pursuits of men are the pursuits of women also, but in all of them a woman is inferior to a man.

Very true.

Then are we to impose all our enactments on men and none of them on women?

That will never do.

One woman has a gift of healing, another not; one is a musician, and another has no music in her nature?

Very true.

And one woman has a turn for gymnastic and military exercises, and another is unwarlike and hates gymnastics?

Certainly.

And one woman is a philosopher, and another is an enemy of philosophy; one has spirit, and another is without spirit?

That is also true.

Then one woman will have the temper of a guardian, and another not. Was not the selection of the male guardians determined by differences of this sort?

Yes.

Men and women alike possess the qualities which make a guardian; they differ only in their comparative strength or weakness.

Obviously.

And those women who have such qualities are to be selected as the companions and colleagues of men who have similar qualities and whom they resemble in capacity and in character?

Very true.

And ought not the same natures to have the same pursuits?

They ought.

Then, as we were saying before, there is nothing unnatural in assigning music and gymnastic to the wives of the guardians—to that point we come round again.

Certainly not.

The law which we then enacted was agreeable to nature, and therefore not an impossibility or mere aspiration; and the contrary practice, which prevails at present, is in reality a violation of nature.

That appears to be true.

We had to consider, first, whether our proposals were possible, and secondly whether they were the most beneficial?

Yes.

And the possibility has been acknowledged?

Yes.

The very great benefit has next to be established?

Quite so.

You will admit that the same education which makes a man a good guardian will make a woman a good guardian; for their original nature is the same?

Yes.

I should like to ask you a question.

What is it?

Would you say that all men are equal in excellence, or is one man better than another?

The latter.

And in the commonwealth which we were founding do you conceive the guardians who have been brought up on our model system to be more perfect men, or the cobblers whose education has been cobbling?

What a ridiculous question!

You have answered me, I replied: Well, and may we not further say that our guardians are the best of our citizens?

By far the best.

And will not their wives be the best women?

Yes, by far the best.

And can there be anything better for the interests of the State than that of the men and women of a State should be as good as possible?

There can be nothing better.

And this is what the art of music and gymnastic, when present in such manner as we have described, will accomplish?

Certainly.

Then we have made an enactment not only possible but in the highest degree beneficial to the State?

True.

Then let the wives of our guardians strip, for their virtue will be their robe, and let them share in the toils of war and the defence of their country; only in the distribution of labours the lighter are to be assigned to the women, who are the weaker natures, but in other respects their duties are to be the same. And as for the man who laughs at naked women exercising their bodies from the best of motives, in his laughter he is plucking "A fruit of unripe wisdom," and he himself is ignorant of what he is laughing at, or what he is about; for that is, and ever will be, the best of sayings, *That the useful is the noble and the hurtful is the base.*

BOOK VII

And now, I said, let me show in a figure how far our nature is enlightened or unenlightened:— Behold! human beings living in an underground den, which has a mouth open towards the light and reaching all along the den; here they have been from their childhood, and have their legs and necks chained so that they cannot move, and can only see before them, being prevented by the chains from turning round their heads. Above and behind them a fire is blazing at a distance, and between the fire and the prisoners there is a raised way; and you will see, if you look, a low wall built along the way, like the screen which marionette players have in front of them, over which they show the puppets.

I see.

And do you see, I said, men passing along the wall carrying all sorts of vessels, and statues and figures of animals made of wood and stone and various materials, which appear over the wall? Some of them are talking, others silent.

You have shown me a strange image, and they are strange prisoners.

Like ourselves, I replied; and they see only their own shadows, or the shadows of one another, which the fire throws on the opposite wall of the cave?

True, he said; how could they see anything but the shadows if they were never allowed to move their heads?

And of the objects which are being carried in like manner they would only see the shadows?

Yes, he said.

And if they were able to converse with one another, would they not suppose that they were naming what was actually before them?

Very true.

And suppose further that the prison had an echo which came from the other side, would they not be sure to fancy when one of the passers-by spoke that the voice which they heard came from the passing shadow?

No question, he replied.

To them, I said, the truth would be literally nothing but the shadows of the images.

That is certain.

And now look again, and see what will naturally follow if the prisoners are released and disabused of their error. At first, when any of them is liberated and compelled suddenly to stand up and turn his neck round and walk and look towards the light, he will suffer sharp pains; the glare will distress him, and he will be unable to see the realities of which in his former state he had seen the shadows; and then conceive some one saying to him, that what he saw before was an illusion, but that now, when he is approaching nearer to being and his eye is turned towards more real existence, he has a clearer vision,— what will be his reply? And you may further imagine that his instructor is pointing to the objects as they pass and requiring him to name them,— will he not be perplexed? Will he not fancy that the shadows which he formerly saw are truer than the objects which are now shown to him?

Far truer.

And if he is compelled to look straight at the light, will he not have a pain in his eyes which will make him turn away to take refuge in the objects of vision which he can see, and which he will conceive to be in reality clearer than the things which are now being shown to him?

True, he said. . . .

He will require to grow accustomed to the sight of the upper world. And first he will see the shadows best, next the reflections of men and other objects in the water, and then the objects themselves; then he will gaze upon the light of the moon and the stars and the spangled heaven; and he will see the sky and the stars by night better than the sun or the light of the sun by day?

Certainly.

Last of all he will be able to see the sun, and not mere reflections of him in the water, but he will see him in his own proper place, and not in another; and he will contemplate him as he is. . . .

And when he remembered his old habitation, and the wisdom of the den and his fellow-prisoners, do you not suppose that he would felicitate himself on the change, and pity them?

Certainly, he would.

And if they were in the habit of conferring honours among themselves on those who were quickest to observe the passing shadows and to remark which of them went before, and which followed after, and which were together; and who were therefore best able to draw conclusions as to the future, do you think that he would care for such honours and glories, or envy the possessors of them? Would he not say with Homer,

'Better to be the poor servant of a poor master,' and to endure anything, rather than think as they do and live after their manner?

Yes, he said, I think that he would rather suffer anything than entertain these false notions and live in this miserable manner.

Imagine once more, I said, such an one coming suddenly out of the sun to be replaced in his old situation; would he not be certain to have his eyes full of darkness?

To be sure, he said.

And if there were a contest, and he had to compete in measuring the shadows with the prisoners who had never moved out of the den, while his sight was still weak, and before his eyes had become steady (and the time which would be needed to acquire this new habit of sight might be very considerable), would he not be ridiculous? Men would say of him that up he went and down he came without his eyes; and that it was better not even to think of ascending; and if any one tried to loose another and lead him up to the light, let them only catch the offender, and they would put him to death.

No question, he said.

This entire allegory, I said, you may now append, dear Glaucon, to the previous argument; the prison-house is the world of sight, the light of the fire is the sun, and you will not misapprehend me if you interpret the journey upwards to be the ascent of the soul into the intellectual world according to my poor belief, which, at your desire, I have expressed—whether rightly or wrongly God knows. But, whether true or false, my opinion is that in the world of knowledge the idea of good appears last of all, and is seen only with an effort; and, when seen, is also inferred to be the universal author of all things beautiful and right, parent of light and of the lord of light in this visible world, and the immediate source of reason and truth in the intellectual; and that this is the power upon which he who would act rationally either in public or private life must have his eye fixed.

I agree, he said, as far as I am able to understand you.

Moreover, I said, you must not wonder that those who attain to this beatific vision are unwilling to descend to human affairs; for their souls are ever hastening into the upper world where they desire to dwell; which desire of theirs is very natural, if our allegory may be trusted.

Yes, very natural.

And is there anything surprising in one who passes from divine contemplations to the evil state of man, misbehaving himself in a ridiculous manner; if, while his eyes are blinking and before he has become accustomed to the surrounding darkness, he is compelled to fight in courts of law, or in other places, about the images or the shadows of images of justice, and is endeavouring to meet the conceptions of those who have never yet seen absolute justice?

Anything but surprising, he replied.

Any one who has common sense will remember that the bewilderments of the eyes are of two kinds, and arise from two causes, either from coming out of the light or from going into the light, which is true of the mind's eye, quite as much as of the bodily eye; and he who remembers this when he sees any one whose vision is perplexed and weak, will not be too ready to laugh; he will first ask whether that soul of man has come out of the brighter life, and is unable to see because unaccustomed to the dark, or having turned from darkness to the day is dazzled by excess of light. And he will count the one happy in his condition and state of being, and he will pity the other; or, if he have a mind to laugh at the soul which comes from below into the light, there will be more reason in this than in the laugh which greets him who returns from above out of the light into the den.

That, he said, is a very just distinction.

But then, if I am right, certain professors of education must be wrong when they say that they can put a knowledge into the soul which was not there before, like sight into blind eyes.

They undoubtedly say this, he replied.

Whereas, our argument shows that the power and capacity of learning exists in the soul already; and that just as the eye was unable to turn from darkness to light without the whole body, so too the instrument of knowledge can only by the movement of the whole soul be turned from the world of becoming into that of being, and learn by degrees to endure the sight of being, and of the brightest and best of being, or in other words, of the good.

Very true.

And must there not be some art which will effect conversion in the easiest and quickest manner; not implanting the faculty of sight, for that exists already, but has been turned in the wrong direction, and is looking away from the truth?

Yes, he said, such an art may be presumed.

And whereas the other so-called virtues of the soul seem to be akin to bodily qualities, for even when they are not originally innate they can be implanted later by habit and exercise, the virtue of wisdom more than anything else contains a divine element which always remains, and by this conversion is rendered useful and profitable; or, on the other hand, hurtful and useless. Did you never observe the narrow intelligence flashing from the keen eye of a clever rogue—how eager he is, how clearly his paltry soul sees the way to his end; he is the reverse of blind, but his keen eye-sight is forced into the service of evil, and he is mischievous in proportion to his cleverness?

Very true, he said.

But what if there had been a circumcision of such natures in the days of their youth; and they had been severed from those sensual pleasures, such as eating and drinking, which, like leaden weights, were attached to them at their birth, and which drag them down and turn the vision of their souls upon the things that are below—if, I say, they had been released from these impediments and turned in the opposite direction, the very same faculty in them would have seen the truth as keenly as they see what their eyes are turned to now.

Very likely.

Yes, I said; and there is another thing which is likely, or rather a necessary inference from what has preceded, that neither the uneducated and uninformed of the truth, nor yet those who never make an end of their education, will be able ministers of State; not the former, because they have no single aim of duty which is the rule of all their actions, private as well as public; nor the latter, because they will not act at all except upon compulsion, fancying that they are already dwelling apart in the islands of the blest.

Very true, he replied.

Then, I said, the business of us who are the founders of the State will be to compel the best minds to attain that knowledge which we have already shown to be the greatest of all—they must continue to ascend until they arrive at the good; but when they have ascended and seen enough we must not allow them to do as they do now.

What do you mean?

I mean that they remain in the upper world: but this must not be allowed; they must be made to descend again among the prisoners in the den, and partake of their labours and honours, whether they are worth having or not.

But is not this unjust? he said; ought we to give them a worse life, when they might have a better?

You have again forgotten, my friend, I said, the intention of the legislator, who did not aim at making any one class in the State happy above the rest; the happiness was to be in the whole State, and he held the citizens together by persuasion and necessity, making them benefactors of the State, and therefore benefactors of one another; to this end he created them, not to please themselves, but to be his instruments in binding up the State.

True, he said, I had forgotten.

Observe, Glaucon, that there will be no injustice in compelling our philosophers to have a care and providence of others; we shall explain to them that in other States, men of their class are not obliged to share in the toils of politics: and this is reasonable, for they grow up at their own sweet will, and the government would rather not have them. Being self taught, they cannot be expected to show any gratitude for a culture which they have never received. But we have brought you into the world to be rulers of the hive, kings of yourselves and of the other citizens, and have educated you far better and more perfectly than they have been educated, and you are better able to share in the double duty. Wherefore each of you, when his turn comes, must go down to the general underground abode, and get the habit of seeing in the dark. When you have acquired the habit, you will see ten thousand times better than the inhabitants of the den, and you will know what the several images are, and what they represent, because you have seen the beautiful and just and good in their truth. And thus our State, which is also yours, will be a reality, and not a dream only, and will be administered in a spirit unlike that of other States, in which men fight with one another about shadows only and are distracted in the struggle for power, which in their eyes is a great good. Whereas the truth is that the State in which the rulers are most reluctant to govern is always the best and most quietly governed, and the State in which they are most eager, the worst.

QUESTIONS

1. Does Plato believe that the perfect society should be bound by tradition or convention?

2. Why, according to the conventional argument, should women be kept to their own "separate sphere"? Are men and women equal in Plato's Republic? What are the differences between them?

3. How should the state educate women? How does Plato's plan differ from the Greek reality?

4. In Book VII, what does Plato mean when he talks about people living in the cave? What does living in darkness do to their understanding? Plato implies that the light can be dangerous—what does he mean?

5. "Seeing the light" has become a cliché: What does it mean in this context? What are the responsibilities of those who have seen the light toward those still in the cave?

6. Why do you think Plato chose to teach through analogy and dialogue? Do they work? Why or why not?

16

■ *Aristotle* ■

POLITICS

(4TH CENTURY B.C.E.)

Aristotle (384–322 B.C.E.) was the third of the great Greek philosophers and was arguably the most influential of all. The son of a physician, Aristotle was taught medicine and biology from an early age. He was sent to Athens specifically to be educated at Plato's Academy and there he imbibed the wisdom of Socrates as well. Aristotle's original philosophical achievements are nearly beyond comprehension. His scientific works include major treatises on astronomy, botany, physics, and zoology. His philosophical works include discourses on cosmology, ethics, logic, poetry, and politics. Like Plato, Aristotle founded a school in Athens, the Lyceum, but he taught by lecture rather than by Socratic cross-questioning. Aristotle's works were neither written nor published during his lifetime. They consisted mostly of lecture notes taken by his students and brought together into treatises. Thirty such works survive today, although it is believed that there were nearly two hundred in existence in ancient times.

The *Politics* was an attempt to establish principles of government along scientific lines. Aristotle was the first philosopher to explore the basic forms of government and to discuss their inherent strengths and weaknesses.

As what has already been said finishes the preface of this subject, and as we have considered at large the nature of all other states, it now remains that I should first say what ought to be the form laid down as that of the state which is in accordance with our idea; for no good state can exist without a proportionate supply of what is necessary. Many things therefore ought to be previously laid down as objects desirable, but none of them such as are impossible; I mean, relative to the number of citizens, and the extent of the territory. For as other artificers, such as the weaver and the shipwright, ought to have such materials as are fit for their work, so also ought the legislator and politician to endeavour to procure proper materials for the business they have in hand. Now the first and principal instrument of the politician is the number of people; he should therefore know how many and what they naturally ought to be; in like manner as to the country, how large and of what kind it ought to be. Most persons think that it is necessary for a city to be large in order to be happy; but even should this be true, still they cannot tell what is a large one and what a small one. For they estimate its greatness according to the multitude of its inhabitants, but they ought rather to look to its strengths than to its numbers. But even if it were proper to determine the strength of the city from the number of its inhabitants, it should never be inferred from the multitude in general who may happen to be in it—(for in a city there must necessarily be many slaves, sojourners, and foreigners)—but from those who are really part of the state, and properly constitute the members of it. A multitude of these is indeed a proof that the city is large, but where a large number of mechanics dwell, and but few soldiers, such a state cannot be great; for a great city and a populous one are not the same thing. This too is evident from the fact that it is very difficult, if not impossible, properly to govern a very numerous body of men; for of all the states which appear well governed, we find not one where the rights of a citizen are laid open to the entire multitude. And this is also made evident by proof from the nature of the thing; for as law is a certain order, so good law is of course a certain good order; but too large a multitude is incapable of this. For this is in very truth the prerogative of that Divine Power which comprehends the universe. Not but that, as quantity and greatness are usually essential to beauty, the perfection of a city consists in its being large, if only consistent with that order already mentioned. But still there is a determinate size to all cities, as well as every thing else, whether animals, plants, or machines; for each of these have their proper powers, if they are

neither too little nor too large; but when they have not their due growth, or are badly constructed, so it is with a city. One that is too small has not in itself the power of self-defence, but this power is essential to a city: one that is too large is capable of self-defence in what is necessary, in the same way as a nation, but then it is not a city; for it will be difficult to find a form of government for it. The first thing therefore necessary is, that a city should consist of the lowest numbers which will be sufficient to enable the inhabitants to live happily in their political community. And it follows, that the more the inhabitants exceed that necessary number, the greater will the city be. But, as we have already said, this must not be without bounds; but what is the proper limit of the excess, experience will easily show, and this experience is to be collected from the actions both of the governors and the governed. Now, as it belongs to the first to direct the inferior magistrates and to act as judges, it follows that they can neither determine causes with justice, nor issue their orders with propriety, without they know the characters of their fellow-citizens: so that whenever this happens to be impossible in these two particulars, the state must of necessity be badly managed; for in both of them it is unjust to determine too hastily, and without proper knowledge, which must evidently be the case where the number of the citizens is too many. Besides, it is more easy for strangers and sojourners to assume the rights of citizens, as they will easily escape detection owing to the greatness of the multitude. It is evident then, that the best boundary for a city is that wherein the numbers are the greatest possible, that they may be the better able to be sufficient in themselves, while they are not too large to be under the eye of the magistrates. And thus let us determine the extent of a city.

As to the extent of a country, it should be such as may enable the inhabitants to live at their ease with freedom and temperance. What the situation of the country should be, is not difficult to determine; but in some particulars respecting this point, we ought to be advised by those who are skilful in military affairs. It should be difficult of access to an enemy, but easy of egress to the inhabitants; and, as we said that the number of inhabitants ought to be such as can come under the eye of the magistrate, so should it be with the country; for by that means the country is easily defended. As to the position of the city, if one could place it to one's wish, it ought to lie well both for sea and land. One situation which it ought to have has been already mentioned; for it should be so placed as easily to give assistance to all parts, and also to receive the necessaries of life from every quarter; as also it should be accessible for the carriage of wood, or any other materials of the like kind which may happen to be in the country.

We now proceed to point out of what natural disposition the citizens ought to be: but this surely any one would easily perceive who casts his eye over those states of Greece which bear a high repute, and indeed over all the habitable world, as it is divided among the nations. Those who live in cold countries, as the north of Europe, are full of courage, but wanting in understanding and in art; therefore they remain free for a long time; but, not being versed in the political science, they cannot reduce their neighbours under their power. But the Asiatics, whose understandings are quick, and who are conversant in the arts, are deficient in courage; and therefore they continue to be always conquered, and the slaves of others. But the Greeks, placed as it were between these two parts, partake of the nature of both, so as to be at the same time both courageous and intellectual; for which reason Greece continues free, and governed in the best manner possible, and capable of commanding the whole world, could it be combined into one system of policy. The races of the Greeks have the very same difference among themselves: for part of them possess but one of these qualities, whereas in the other they are both happily blended together. Hence it is evident, that those persons ought to be both intelligent and courageous who will be readily obedient to a legislator, whose object is virtue.

We are now to consider what those things are without which a city cannot possibly exist; for what we call parts of the city must of necessity be inherent in it. And this we shall more plainly understand, if we know the number of things necessary to a city. First, the inhabitants must have food: secondly, arts, for many instruments are necessary in life: thirdly, arms, for it is necessary that the community should have an armed force within themselves, both to support their government against the disaffected of themselves, and also to defend it from those who seek to attack it from without: fourthly, a certain revenue, as well for the internal necessities of the state, as for the business of war: fifthly, and indeed chief of all, the care of the service of gods: sixthly in order, but most necessary of all, a court to determine both civil and criminal causes. These things are matters which are absolutely required, so to speak, in every state: for a city is a number of people, not accidentally met together, but with a purpose of insuring to themselves sufficient independency and self-protection; and if any thing necessary for these purposes is wanting, it is impossible that in such a situation these ends can be obtained. It is necessary therefore that a city should be composed with reference to these various trades; for this purpose a proper number of husbandmen are necessary to procure food; as also artificers and soldiers, and rich men, and priests, and judges, to determine what is necessary and beneficial.

Since we are inquiring what is the best government possible, and as it is admitted to be that in which the citizens are happy, and that, as we have already said, it is impossible to obtain happiness without virtue; it follows, that in the best governed states, where the citizens are really men of intrinsic and not relative goodness, none of them should be permitted to exercise any low mechanical employment or traffic, as being ignoble and destructive to virtue: neither should they who are destined for office be husbandmen; for leisure is necessary in order to improve in virtue, and to perform the duty which they owe to the state.

It is necessary that the citizens should be rich, and these are the men proper for citizens; for no low mechanic ought to be admitted to the rights of a citizen, nor any other sort of people, whose employment is not productive of virtue.

QUESTIONS

1. Why is size an important consideration in the construction of a state? What are the advantages and disadvantages of large and small cities? What is the best size?

2. Using the *Politics* as a guide, what seems to be the ideal physical setting for a city-state? Could you make some broader generalization about Greek city-states with this knowledge?

3. Why does Aristotle feel that the Greeks are more successful than other peoples in the ancient world?

4. What does a city-state require to survive?

5. Who is excluded from citizenship in the state? Why?

6. Compare Aristotle's view of politics and the state with Plato's in *The Republic*. How do their approaches differ? Are there any similarities that you can identify?

17

■ *Plutarch* ■

THE LIFE OF ALEXANDER

(CA. C.E. 116)

Plutarch (ca. C.E. 46–119) was a Greek philosopher and biographer and is one of the best-known sources for information about ancient personalities. Educated in Athens, he traveled throughout the Roman Empire, perhaps making the acquaintance of Roman emperors, and held a priesthood while directing a school of ethics. Plutarch was prolific, writing 227 works, the best known of which is the *Parallel Lives*, in which he wrote biographies of great Greeks and great Romans and compared the two. These biographies were didactic and based on impressive research.

Alexander of Macedon (336–323 B.C.E.) was the subject of one of Plutarch's most important biographies. He inherited his father's rule over Macedonia and expanded his holdings considerably. In less than thirteen years as king, Alexander consolidated Macedonia's prominence in Greece, overthrew the Persian Empire, conquered as far eastward as the Punjab, and founded over seventy new cities. Unfortunately, he had failed to establish a succession, and not twenty years after Alexander's death, the empire he had built had fragmented into many small, independent provinces.

On one occasion some ambassadors from the King of Persia arrived in Macedon, and since Philip was absent, Alexander received them in his place. He talked freely with them and quite won them over, not only by the friendliness of his manner, but also because he did not trouble them with any childish or trivial inquiries, but questioned them about the distances they had travelled by road, the nature of the journey into the interior of Persia, the character of the king, his experience in war, and the military strength and prowess of the Persians. The ambassadors were filled with admiration. They came away convinced that Philip's celebrated astuteness was as nothing compared to the adventurous spirit and lofty ambitions of his son. At any rate, whenever he heard that Philip had captured some famous city or won an overwhelming victory, Alexander would show no pleasure at the news, but would declare to his friends, "Boys, my father will forestall me in everything. There will be nothing great or spectacular for you and me to show the world." He cared nothing for pleasure or wealth but only for deeds of valour and glory, and this was why he believed that the more he received from his father, the less would be left for him to conquer. And so every success that was gained by Macedonia inspired in Alexander the dread that another opportunity for action had been squandered on his father.

There came a day when Philoneicus the Thessalian brought Philip a horse named Bucephalas, which he offered to sell for thirteen talents. The king and his friends went down to the plain to watch the horse's trials, and came to the conclusion that he was wild and quite unmanageable, for he would allow no one to mount him, nor would he endure the shouts of Philip's grooms, but reared up against anyone who approached him. The king became angry at being offered such a vicious animal unbroken, and ordered it to be led away. But Alexander, who was standing close by, remarked, "What a horse they are losing, and all because they don't know how to handle him, or dare not try!" Philip kept quiet at first, but when he heard Alexander repeat these words several times and saw that he was upset, he asked him, "Are you finding fault with your elders because you think you know more than they do, or can manage a horse better?" "At least I could manage this one better," retorted Alexander. "And if you cannot," said his father, "What penalty will you pay for being so impertinent?" "I will pay the price of the horse," answered the boy. At this the whole company burst out laughing, and then as soon as the father and son had settled the terms of the bet, Alexander went quickly up to Bucephalas, took hold of his bridle, and turned him towards the sun, for he had noticed that the horse was shying at the sight of his own shadow, as it fell in front of him and constantly moved whenever he did. He ran alongside the animal for a little way, calming him down by stroking him, and then, when he saw he was full of spirit and courage, he quietly threw aside his cloak and with a light spring vaulted safely on to his back. For a little while he kept feeling the bit with the reins, without jarring or tearing his mouth, and got him collected. Finally, when he saw that the horse was free of his fears and impatient to show his speed, he gave him his head and urged him forward, using a commanding voice and a touch of the foot.

At first Philip and his friends held their breath and looked on in an agony of suspense, until they saw Alexander reach the end of his gallop, turn in full control, and ride back triumphant and exulting in his success. Thereupon the rest of the company broke into loud applause, while his father, we are told, actually wept for joy, and when Alexander had dismounted he kissed him and said, "My boy, you must find a kingdom big enough for your ambitions. Macedonia is too small for you."

Philip had noticed that his son was self-willed, and that while it was very difficult to influence him by force, he could easily be guided towards his duty by an appeal to reason, and he therefore made a point of trying to persuade the boy rather than giving him orders. Besides this he considered that the task of training and educating his son was too important to be entrusted to the ordinary run of teachers of poetry, music and general education: it required, as Sophocles puts it

The rudder's guidance and the curb's restraint,

and so he sent for Aristotle, the most famous and learned of the philosophers of his time, and rewarded him with the generosity that his reputation deserved. Aristotle was a native of the city of Stageira, which Philip had himself destroyed. He now repopulated it and brought back all the citizens who had been enslaved or driven into exile.

He gave Aristotle and his pupil the temple of the Nymphs near Mieza as a place where they could study and converse, and to this day they show you the stone seats and shady walks which Aristotle used. It seems clear too that Alexander was instructed by his teacher not only in the principles of ethics and politics, but also in those secret and more esoteric studies which philosophers do not impart to the general run of students, but only by word of mouth to a select circle of the initiated.

• • •

He was also devoted by nature to all kinds of learning and was a lover of books. He regarded the *Iliad* as a handbook of the art of war and took with him on his campaigns a text annotated by Aristotle, . . . which he always kept under his pillow together with his dagger.

. . . Alexander never lost the devotion to philosophy which had been innate in him from the first, and which matured as he grew older. . . .

• • •

Alexander was only twenty years old when he inherited his kingdom, which at that moment was beset by formidable jealousies and feuds, and external dangers on every side. The neighbouring barbarian tribes were eager to throw off the Macedonian yoke and longed for the rule of their native kings: as for the Greek states, although Philip had defeated them in battle, he had not had time to subdue them or accustom them to his authority. He had swept away the existing governments, and then, having prepared their peoples for drastic changes, had left them in turmoil and confusion, because he had created a situation which was completely unfamiliar to them. Alexander's Macedonian advisers feared that a crisis was at hand and urged the young king to leave the Greek states to their own devices and refrain from using any force against them. As for the barbarian tribes, they considered that he should try to win them back to their allegiance by using milder methods, and forestall the first signs of revolt by offering them concessions. Alexander, however, chose precisely the opposite course, and decided that the only way to make his kingdom safe was to act with audacity and a lofty spirit, for he was certain that if he were seen to yield even a fraction of his authority, all his enemies would attack him at once. He swiftly crushed the uprisings among the barbarians. . . . Then when the news reached him that the Thebans had revolted and were being supported by the Athenians, he immediately marched south through the pass of Thermopylae. "Demosthenes," he said, "called me a boy while I was in Illyria and among the Triballi, and a youth when I was marching through Thessaly; I will show him I am a man by the time I reach the walls of Athens."

When he arrived before Thebes, he wished to give the citizens the opportunity to repent of their actions, and so he merely demanded the surrender of their leaders . . . and offered an amnesty to all the rest if they would come over to his side. The Thebans countered by demanding the surrender of Philotas and Antipater and appealing to all who wished to liberate Greece to range themselves on their side, and at this Alexander ordered his troops to prepare for battle. The Thebans, although greatly outnumbered, fought with a superhuman courage and spirit, but when the Macedonian garrison which had been posted in the citadel of the Cadmeia made a sortie and fell upon them from the rear, the greater part of their army was encircled, they were slaughtered where they stood, and the city was stormed, plundered and razed to the ground. Alexander's principal object in permitting the sack of Thebes was to frighten the rest of the Greeks into submission by making a terrible example. But he also put forward the excuse that he was redressing the wrongs done to his allies, for the Plataeans and Phocians had both complained of the actions of the Thebans against them. As for the population of Thebes, he singled out the priests, a few citizens who had friendly connections with Macedonia, the

descendants of the poet Pindar, and those who had opposed the revolt to be spared: all the rest were publicly sold into slavery to the number of twenty thousand. Those who were killed in the battle numbered more than six thousand.

•••

In later years Alexander often felt distressed, we are told, at the harsh fate of the Thebans, and the recollection of it made him milder in his treatment of many other peoples. Certainly he believed that the murder of Cleitus, which he committed when he was drunk, and the cowardly refusal of the Macedonians to cross the Ganges and attack the Indians, which cut short his campaign and robbed him of its crowning achievement, were both caused by the anger of the god Dionysus, who wished to avenge the destruction of his favorite city. And of those Thebans who survived, it was remarked that all who came to him with a request were granted whatever they asked. So much for Alexander's dealings with Thebes.

In the previous year a congress of the Greek states had been held at the Isthmus of Corinth: here a vote had been passed that the states should join forces with Alexander in invading Persia and that he should be commander-in-chief of the expedition. Many of the Greek statesmen and philosophers visited him to offer their congratulations, and he hoped that Diogenes of Sinope, who was at that time living in Corinth, would do the same. However since he paid no attention whatever to Alexander, but continued to live at leisure . . . Alexander went in person to see him and found him basking at full length in the sun. When he saw so many people approaching him, Diogenes raised himself a little on his elbow and fixed his gaze upon Alexander. The king greeted him and inquired whether he could do anything for him. "Yes," replied the philosopher, "you can stand a little to one side out of my sun." Alexander is said to have been greatly impressed by this answer and full of admiration for the hauteur and independence of mind of a man who could look down on him with such condescension. So much so that he remarked to his followers, who were laughing and mocking the philosopher as they went away, "You may say what you like, but if I were not Alexander, I would be Diogenes."

• • •

As for the size of his army, the lowest estimate puts its strength at 30,000 infantry and 4,000 cavalry and the highest 43,000 infantry and 4,000 cavalry. According to Aristobulus the money available for the army's supplies amounted to no more than seventy talents, Douris says that there were supplies for only thirty days, and Onesicritus that Alexander was already two hundred talents in debt. Yet although he set out with such slender resources, he would not go aboard his ship until he had discovered the circumstances of all his companions and had assigned an estate to one, a village to another, or the revenues of some port or community to a third. When he had shared out or signed away almost all the property of the crown, Perdiccas asked him, "But your majesty, what are you leaving for yourself?" "My hopes!" replied Alexander, "Very well, then," answered Perdiccas, "those who serve with you will share those too." With this, he declined to accept the prize which had been allotted to him, and several of Alexander's other friends did the same. However those who accepted or requested rewards were lavishly provided for, so that in the end Alexander distributed among them most of what he possessed in Macedonia. These were his preparations and this was the adventurous spirit in which he crossed the Hellespont.

• • •

The Persians are said to have lost twenty thousand infantry and two thousand five hundred cavalry, whereas on Alexander's side, according to Aristobulus, only thirty-four soldiers in all were killed, nine of them belonging to the infantry. Alexander gave orders that each of these men should have his statue set up in bronze and the

work was carried out by Lysippus. At the same time he was anxious to give the other Greek states a share in the victory. He therefore sent the Athenians in particular three hundred of the shields captured from the enemy, and over the rest of the spoils he had this proud inscription engraved:

Alexander, the son of Philip, and all the Greeks, with the exception of the Spartans, won these spoils of war from the barbarians who dwell in Asia.

As for the drinking vessels, purple hangings and other such plunder, he sent it all with the exception of a few items to his mother.

• • •

Next he marched into Pisidia where he subdued any resistance which he encountered, and then made himself master of Phrygia. When he captured Gordium, which is reputed to have been the home of the ancient king Midas, he saw the celebrated chariot which was fastened to its yoke by the bark of the cornel-tree, and heard the legend which was believed by all the barbarians, that the fates had decreed that the man who untied the knot was destined to become the ruler of the whole world. According to most writers the fastenings were so elaborately intertwined and coiled upon one another that their ends were hidden: in consequence Alexander did not know what to do, and in the end loosened the knot by cutting through it with his sword, whereupon the many ends sprang into view. But according to Aristobulus he unfastened it quite easily by removing the pin which secured the yoke to the pole of the chariot, and then pulling out the yoke itself.

After this Alexander marched northward and won over the peoples of Cappadocia and Paphlagonia. He also learned of the death of Memnon, the general to whom Darius had entrusted the defence of mountain passes and [regaining his mountain passes.] He already saw the mistake he had made by advancing into country which was hemmed in by the sea on one side and the mountains on the other, and divided by the river Pinarus which ran between them. Here the ground prevented him from using his cavalry, forced him to split up his army into small groups, and favoured his opponent's inferior numbers. Fortune certainly presented Alexander with the ideal terrain for the battle, but it was his own generalship which did most to win the victory. For although he was so heavily outnumbered, he not only gave the enemy no opportunity to encircle him, but leading his own right wing in person, he managed to extend it round the enemy's left, outflanked it, and fighting in the foremost ranks, put the barbarians to flight. In this action he received a sword wound in the thigh: according to Chares this was given him by Darius, with whom he engaged in hand to hand combat. Alexander sent a letter to Antipater describing the battle, but made no mention in it of who had given him the wound: he said no more than that he had been stabbed in the thigh with a dagger and that the wound was not a dangerous one.

The result of this battle was a brilliant victory for Alexander. His men killed one hundred and ten thousand of the enemy, but he could not catch Darius, who had got a start of half a mile or more, although he captured the king's chariot and his bow before he returned from the pursuit. He found the Macedonians busy carrying off the spoils from the enemy's camp, for this contained an immense wealth of possessions, despite the fact that the Persians had marched into battle lightly equipped and had left most of their baggage in Damascus. Darius' tent which was full of many treasures, luxurious furniture, and lavishly dressed servants had been set aside for Alexander himself. As soon as he arrived, he unbuckled his armour and went to the bath, saying "Let us wash off the sweat of battle in Darius's bath." "No, in Alexander's bath, now," remarked one of his companions. "The Conqueror takes over the possessions of the conquered and they should be called his."

When Alexander entered the bath-room he saw that the basins, the pitchers, the baths themselves and the caskets containing unguents were all made of gold and elaborately carved, and noticed that the whole room was marvellously fragrant with spices and perfumes, and then passing from this into a spacious and lofty tent, he observed the magnificence of the dining-couches, the tables and the banquet which had been set out for him. He turned to his companions and remarked, "So this, it seems, is what it is to be a king."

As he was about to sit down to supper, word was brought to him that the mother, the wife and the two unmarried daughters of Darius were among the prisoners, and that at the sight of the Persian king's bow and chariot they had beaten their breasts and cried out, since they supposed that he must be dead. When he heard this Alexander was silent for some time, for he was evidently more affected by the women's grief than by his own triumph. Then he sent Leonnatus to tell them that Darius was not dead and that they need have no fear of Alexander: he was fighting Darius for the empire of Asia, but they should be provided with everything they had been accustomed to regard as their due when Darius was king. This kindly and reassuring message for Darius' womenfolk was followed by still more generous actions. Alexander gave them leave to bury as many of the Persians as they wished, and to take from the plunder any clothes and ornaments they thought fit and use them for this purpose. He also allowed them to keep the same attendants and privileges that they had previously enjoyed and even increased their revenues. But the most honourable and truly regal service which he rendered to these chaste and noble women was to ensure that they should never hear, suspect nor have cause to fear anything which could disgrace them: they lived out of sight and earshot of the soldiers, as though they were guarded in some inviolable retreat set aside for virgin priestesses rather than in an enemy's camp. This was the more remarkable because the wife of Darius was said to have been the most beautiful princess of her time, just as Darius himself was the tallest and handsomest man in Asia, and their daughters resembled their parents.

At any rate Alexander, so it seems, thought it more worthy of a king to subdue his own passions than to conquer his enemies, and so he never came near these women, nor did he associate with any other before his marriage, with the exception only of Barsine. This woman, the widow of Memnon, the Greek mercenary commander, was captured at Damascus. She had received a Greek education, was of a gentle disposition, and could claim royal descent, since her father was Artabazus who had married one of the Persian King's daughters. These qualities made Alexander the more willing—he was encouraged by Parmenio, so Aristobulus tells us—to form an attachment to a woman of such beauty and noble lineage. As for the other prisoners, when Alexander saw their handsome and stately appearance, he took no more notice of them than to say jokingly, "These Persian women are a torment for our eyes." He was determined to make such a show of his chastity and self-control as to eclipse the beauty of their appearance, and so he passed them by as if they had been so many lifeless images cut out of stone.

When Philoxenus, the commander of his forces on the sea coast, wrote to say that he had with him a slave merchant from Tarentum named Theodorus who was offering exceptionally handsome boys for sale and asked whether Alexander wished to buy them, the king was furious and angrily demanded of his friends what signs of degeneracy Philoxenus had ever noticed in him that he should waste his time procuring such debased creatures. He wrote a letter to Philoxenus telling him what he thought of him and ordering him to send Theodorus and his merchandise to the devil. He also sharply rebuked Hagnon, who had written that he wanted to buy as a present for him a young man named Crobylus, whose good looks were famous in Corinth. And when he discovered that Damon and Timotheus, two Macedonian soldiers who were serving under Parmenio, had seduced the wives of some of the Greek mercenaries, he sent orders to Parmenio that if the two men were found guilty, they should be put to death as wild beasts which are born to prey upon mankind. In the same letter he wrote of himself: "In my own case it will be found not only that I have never seen nor wished to see Darius' wife, but that I have not even allowed her beauty to be mentioned in my presence." He also used to say that it was sleep and sexual intercourse which more than anything else, reminded him that he was mortal; by this he meant that both exhaustion and pleasure proceed from the same weakness of human nature.

He was exceptionally temperate in what he ate, as he showed in many different ways, but above all in the answer he gave to Queen Ada, whom he honoured with the official title of Mother and made Queen of Caria. To show her affection for him she had formed the habit of sending him delicacies and sweetmeats every day, and finally offered him bakers and cooks who were supposed to be the most skilful in the country. Alexander's reply was that he did not need them, because his tutor Leonidas had provided him with better cooks than these, that is a night march to prepare him for breakfast, and a light breakfast to give him an appetite for supper. "This same Leonidas," he went on, "would often come and open my chests of bedding and clothes, to see whether my mother had not hidden some luxury inside."

Alexander was also more moderate in his drinking than was generally supposed. The impression that he was a heavy drinker arose because when he had nothing else to do, he liked to linger over each cup, but in fact he was usually talking rather than drinking: he enjoyed holding long conversations, but only when he had plenty of leisure. Whenever there was urgent business to attend to, neither wine, nor sleep, nor sport, nor sex, nor spectacle, could

ever distract his attention, as they did for other generals. The proof of this is his life-span, which although so short, was filled to overflowing with the most prodigious achievements.

QUESTIONS

1. Was Alexander an educated man?

2. How would you characterize Alexander's relationship with his father, Philip?

3. Was Alexander's leadership effective? Does he deserve the title "Alexander the Great"?

4. Why does Plutarch emphasize Alexander's self-discipline?

THE ROMAN WORLD

18

■ *Polybius* ■

THE ROMAN CONSTITUTION

(CA. 150 B.C.E.)

Polybius (200–118 B.C.E.) was an Achaean, well educated in the employ of his government when he was taken captive after the Romans defeated the Macedonians in 168 B.C.E. He was taken to Rome as a prisoner and resided there for the following nineteen years. His experience in government made his services valuable, and he gained the confidence of a number of influential Roman citizens including politicians and military leaders. His natural curiosity led him to explore the nature of Roman rule and attempt to understand how Rome had become the greatest empire on earth. He returned to Greece sometime about 150 B.C.E., and there he began to compose a history of Rome that was designed to explain to his countrymen the dramatic nature of Rome's rise through an analysis of its institutions, particularly its government and military. His *History* was thus composed in Greek. Polybius was himself involved in a number of Roman military incursions, and he believed that the historian should have the experience of those about whom he wrote.

The *History* that he wrote after returning to Greece began with an account of the Punic Wars but also contained descriptions of key Roman institutions. Polybius wrote about both the distant and the recent past, including a history of events in which he had personally taken part. In the following passage, Polybius explains the strengths of the Roman Constitution with its checks and balances of power.

ON THE ROMAN CONSTITUTION AT ITS PRIME

From the crossing of Xerxes to Greece . . . and for thirty years after this period, it was always one of those polities which was an object of special study, and it was at its best and nearest to perfection at the time of the Hannibalic war, the period at which I interrupted my narrative to deal with it. Therefore now that I have described its growth, I will explain what were the conditions at the time when by their defeat at Cannae the Romans were brought face to face with disaster.

I am quite aware that to those who have been born and bred under the Roman Republic my account of it will seem somewhat imperfect owing to the omission of certain details. For as they have complete knowledge of it and practical acquaintance with all its parts, having been familiar with these customs and institutions from childhood, they will not be struck by the extent of the information I give but will demand in addition all I have omitted: they will not think that the author has purposely omitted small peculiarities, but that owing to ignorance he has been silent regarding the origins of many things and some points of capital importance. Had I mentioned them, they would not have been impressed by my doing so, regarding them as small and trivial points, but as they are omitted they will demand their inclusion as if they were vital matters, through a desire themselves to appear better informed than the author. Now a good critic should not judge authors by what they omit, but by what they relate, and if he finds any falsehood in this, he may conclude that the omissions are due to ignorance; but if all the writer says is true, he should admit that he has been silent about these matters deliberately and not from ignorance.

These remarks are meant for those who find fault with authors in a cavilling rather than just spirit . . . .

In so far as any view of a matter we form applies to the right occasion, so far expressions of approval or blame are sound. [When circumstances change, and when applied to these changed conditions, the most excellent and true reflections of authors seem often not only not acceptable, but utterly offensive . . .].

The three kinds of government that I spoke of above all shared in the control of the Roman state. And such fairness and propriety in all respects was shown in the use of these three elements for drawing up the constitution and in its subsequent administration that it was impossible even for a native to pronounce with certainty whether the whole system was aristocratic, democratic, or monarchical. This was indeed only natural. For if one fixed one's eyes on the power of the consuls,

the constitution seemed completely monarchical and royal; if on that of the senate it seemed again to be aristocratic; and when one looked at the power of the masses, it seemed clearly to be a democracy. The parts of the state falling under the control of each element were and with a few modifications still are as follows.

The consuls, previous to leading out their legions, exercise authority in Rome over all public affairs, since all the other magistrates except the tribunes are under them and bound to obey them, and it is they who introduce embassies to the senate. Besides this it is they who consult the senate on matters of urgency, they who carry out in detail the provisions of its decrees. Again as concerns all affairs of state administered by the people it is their duty to take these under their charge, to summon assemblies, to introduce measures, and to preside over the execution of the popular decrees. As for preparation for war and the general conduct of operations in the field, here their power is almost uncontrolled; for they are empowered to make what demands they choose on the allies, to appoint military tribunes, to levy soldiers and select those who are fittest for service. They also have the right of inflicting, when on active service, punishment on anyone under their command; and they are authorized to spend any sum they decide upon from the public funds, being accompanied by a quaestor who faithfully executes their instructions. So that if one looks at this part of the administration alone, one may reasonably pronounce the constitution to be a pure monarchy or kingship. I may remark that any changes in these matters or in others of which I am about to speak that may be made in present or future times do not in any way affect the truth of the views I here state.

To pass to the senate. In the first place it has the control of the treasury, all revenue and expenditure being regulated by it. For with the exception of payments made to the consuls, the quaestors are not allowed to disburse for any particular object without a decree of the senate. And even the item of expenditure which is far heavier and more important than any other—the outlay every five years by the sensors on public works, whether constructions or repairs—is under the control of the senate, which makes a grant to the censors for the purpose. Similarly crimes committed in Italy which require a public investigation, such as treason, conspiracy, poisoning, and assassination, are under the jurisdiction of the senate. Also if any private person or community in Italy is in need of arbitration or indeed claims damages or requires succour or protection, the senate attends to all such matters. It also occupies itself with the dispatch of all embassies sent to countries outside of Italy for the purpose either of settling differences, or of offering friendly advice, or indeed of imposing demands, or of receiving submission, or of declaring war; and in like manner with respect to embassies arriving in Rome it decides what reception and what answer should be given to them. All these matters are in the hands of the senate, nor have the people anything whatever to do with them. So that again to one residing in Rome during the absence of the consuls the constitution appears to be entirely aristocratic; and this is the conviction of many Greek states and many of the kings, as the senate manages all business connected with them.

After this we are naturally inclined to ask what part in the constitution is left for the people, considering that the senate controls all the particular matters I mentioned, and, what is most important, manages all matters of revenue and expenditure, and considering that the consuls again have uncontrolled authority as regards armaments and operations in the field. But nevertheless there is a part and a very important part left for the people. For it is the people which alone has the right to confer honours and inflict punishment, the only bonds by which kingdoms and states, and in a word human society in general are held together. For where the distinction between these is overlooked or is observed but ill applied, no affairs can be properly administered. How indeed is this possible when good and evil men are held in equal estimation? It is by the people, then, in many cases that offences punishable by a fine are tried when the accused have held the highest office; and they are the only court which may try on capital charges. As regards the latter they have a practice which is praiseworthy and should be mentioned. Their usage allows those on trial for their lives when found guilty liberty to depart openly, thus inflicting voluntary exile on themselves, if even only one of the tribes that pronounce the verdict has not yet voted. Such exiles enjoy safety in the territories of Naples, Praeneste, Tibur, and other *civitates foederatae*. Again it is the people who bestow office on the deserving, the noblest reward of virtue in a state; the people have the power of approving or rejecting laws, and what is most important of all, they deliberate on the question of war and peace. Further in the case of alliances, terms of peace, and treaties, it is the people who ratify all these or the reverse. Thus here again one might plausibly say that the people's share in the government is the greatest, and that the constitution is a democratic one.

Having stated how political power is distributed among the different parts of the state, I will now explain how each of the three parts is enabled, if they wish, to counteract or co-operate with the others. The consul, when he leaves with his army invested with the powers I mentioned, appears indeed to have absolute authority in all matters necessary for carrying out his purpose; but in fact he requires the support of the people and the senate, and is not able to bring his operations to a conclusion without them. For it is obvious that the legions require constant supplies, and without the consent of the senate, neither corn, clothing, nor pay can be provided; so that the commander's plans come to nothing, if the senate chooses to be deliberately negligent and obstructive. It also depends on the senate whether or not a general can carry out completely his conceptions and designs, since it has the right of either superseding him when his year's term of office has expired or of retaining him in command. Again it is in its power to celebrate with pomp and to magnify the successes of a general or on the other hand to obscure and belittle them. For the processions they call triumphs, in which the generals bring the actual spectacle of their achievements before the eyes of their fellow-citizens, cannot be properly organized and sometimes even cannot be held at all, unless the senate consents and provides the requisite funds. As for the people it is most indispensable for the consuls to conciliate them, however far away from home they may be; for, as I said, it is the people which ratifies or annuls terms of peace and treaties, and what is most important, on laying down office the consuls are obliged to account for their actions to the people. So that in no respect is it safe for the consuls to neglect keeping in favour with both the senate and the people.

The senate again, which possesses such great power, is obliged in the first place to pay attention to the commons in public affairs and respect the wishes of the people, and it cannot carry out inquiries into the most grave and important offences against the state, punishable with death, and their correction, unless the *senatus consultum* is confirmed by the people. The same is the case in matters which directly affect the senate itself. For if anyone introduces a law meant to deprive the senate of some of its traditional authority, or to abolish the precedence and other distinctions of the senators or even to curtail them of their private fortunes, it is the people alone which has the power of passing or rejecting any such measure. And what is most important is that if a single one of the tribunes interposes, the senate is unable to decide finally about any matter, and cannot even meet and hold sittings; and here it is to be observed that the tribunes are always obliged to act as the people decree and to pay every attention to their wishes. Therefore for all these reasons the senate is afraid of the masses and must pay due attention to the popular will.

Similarly, again, the people must be submissive to the senate and respect its members both in public and in private. Through the whole of Italy a vast number of contracts, which it would not be easy to enumerate, are given out by the censors for the construction and repair of public buildings, and besides this there are many things which are farmed, such as navigable rivers, harbours, gardens, mines, lands, in fact everything that forms part of the Roman dominion. Now all these matters are undertaken by the people, and one may almost say that everyone is interested in these contracts and the work they involve. For certain people are the actual purchasers from the censors of the contracts, others are the partners of these first, others stand surety for them, others pledge their own fortunes to the state for this purpose. Now in all these matters the senate is supreme. It can grant extension of time; it can relieve the contractor if any accident occurs; and if the work proves to be absolutely impossible to carry out it can liberate him from his contract. There are in fact many ways in which the senate can either benefit or injure those who manage public property, as all these matters are referred to it. What is even more important is that the judges in most civil trials, whether public or private, are appointed from its members, where the action involves large interests. So that all citizens being at the mercy of the senate, and looking forward with alarm to the uncertainty of litigation, are very shy of obstructing or resisting its decisions. Similarly everyone is reluctant to oppose the projects of the consuls as all are generally and individually under their authority when in the field.

Such being the power that each part has of hampering the others or co-operating with them, their union is adequate to all emergencies, so that it is impossible to find a better political system than this. For whenever the menace of some common danger from abroad compels them to act in concord and support each other, so great does the strength of the state become, that nothing which is requisite can be neglected, as all are zealously competing in devising means of meeting the need of the hour, nor can any decision arrived at fail to be executed promptly, as all are co-operating both in public and in private to the accomplishment of the task they have set themselves; and consequently this peculiar form of constitution possesses an irresistible power of attaining every object upon which it is resolved. When again they are freed from external menace, and reap the harvest of good fortune and affluence which is the result of their success, and in the enjoyment of this prosperity are corrupted by flattery and idleness and wax insolent and overbearing, as indeed happens often enough, it is then especially that we see the state providing itself a remedy for the evil from which it suffers. For when one part having grown out of proportion to the others aims at supremacy and tends to become too predominant, it is evident that, as for the reasons above given none of the three is absolute, but the purpose of the one can be counterworked and thwarted by the others, none of them will excessively outgrow the others or treat them with contempt. All in fact remains *in statu quo,* on the one hand, because any aggressive impulse is sure to be checked and from the outset each estate stands in dread of being interfered with by the others. . . .

QUESTIONS

1. Which of the three forms of government (monarchy, aristocracy, and democracy) dominates the Roman Constitution?

2. What is the power of the consuls?

3. Who controls revenue in the Roman system?

4. What does Polybius think about the checks and balances in the Roman Constitution?

19

■ *Cicero* ■

THE TRIAL OF AULUS CLUENTIUS HABITUS

(66 B.C.E.)

Marcus Tullius Cicero (106–43 B.C.E.) is remembered as the greatest orator and rhetorician of the ancient world. He was born in the Italian countryside to a well-off family, although not one of the highest social ranking. Cicero's family moved to Rome, where he received an exceptional education, especially in law. In 80 B.C.E., he spoke on his first legal case and was an immediate sensation. He embarked upon a political career that was helped at every step by his remarkable rhetorical skills. Most unusually, given his class background, Cicero was elected consul in 63 B.C.E. He served with honor and achieved much before he fell victim to the factious politics surrounding Julius Caesar's rise to power. Although he took no part in Caesar's assassination, Cicero was condemned by Mark Antony and murdered.

Cicero's summation at Habitus's trial is his most famous speech. Habitus was accused of murdering his stepfather, Oppianicus, and Cicero's defense managed to ignore evidence against his client (of which there was a considerable amount) and fixed blame on Habitus's mother. Cluentius was acquitted, thanks to Cicero's brilliant confusion of the issues. Cicero later bragged that he had successfully "thrown dirt in the eyes of the jury."

Gentlemen: Aulus Cluentius Habitus Senior, the father of my client, was a man whose personal qualities, reputation and birth alike combined to make him the most distinguished person not only in the town of Larinum, to which he belonged, but in the entire district and neighbourhood. He died during the consulship of Sulla and Pompeius Rufus, leaving a son aged fifteen, who is my present client. Cluentius Senior also left a grown-up marriageable daughter, who shortly after her father's death wedded her mother's nephew, Aulus Aurius Melinus, a young man who stood high among his contemporaries in character and position.

The marriage was proceeding on a perfectly respectable and happy course when suddenly there burst onto the scene the evil passion of a woman devoid of natural human characteristics—and the results were terrible dishonour and crime. The woman was Sassia, the mother of my client Cluentius here. Yes, I shall go on describing her as his mother throughout this speech: his mother she will have to be called, for even the recital of her appalling misdeeds cannot deprive her of the name which nature has given her. But the associations of love and tenderness which the word normally conveys will not fail to intensify the violent abhorrence you must feel for so unspeakable a mother who, at this very moment as for many years past, is set upon nothing less than the murder of her own son.

For what happened was that this woman Sassia, Cluentius' mother, conceived a perverted love for the young Aulus Aurius Melinus, the husband of her daughter Cluentia. At first, as best she could, Sassia somehow managed to suppress her craving, but not for long. For soon she became madly infatuated—consumed and carried away by lecherous transports against which considerations of modesty and decency counted as nothing. Family feeling, duty, public opinion, all failed to exercise the slightest restraint over her; the grief of her son, the misery of her daughter were wholly without effect. The young man was too immature to feel the strengthening influence of wisdom and understanding, and she, therefore, employing all the arts which have the power to ensnare and captivate a youth of that age, went on to complete his seduction. As for her daughter Cluentia, she was not only tormented by the anguish which any woman would feel when her husband had wronged her, but found the spectacle of her own mother as his mistress so completely beyond endurance that even to utter a protest about such a horror seemed to her an unthinkable sin. She decided, therefore, that the disaster which had befallen her must remain her own secret, and so, clasped in the arms of her deeply devoted brother, who is my client, she consumed the best years of her life in tears and lamentations.

But finally, suddenly, she arranged a divorce. Now, at long last, there seemed a good chance that her troubles would come to an end; for she went away and parted from Melinus—neither sorry to do so after everything she had suffered, nor glad, since he had been her husband. But now this marvellous, exemplary mother of hers began to exult openly in her delight and to revel in the victory she had won, a victory in which it was not her lusts that had been vanquished but her daughter. Unwilling, evidently, that the suspicions which were damaging her reputation should remain in any way unconfirmed, she actually gave orders that the identical marriage-bed which she herself had prepared, two years previously, for the wedding of her own daughter should now be got ready and adorned for herself, in the very home from which her daughter had been expelled and hounded out. And so mother-in-law married son-in-law, with no one to . . . give the bride away, amid the gloomiest forebodings from everyone.

What unbelievably atrocious behaviour that woman displayed! Indeed, her conduct must surely be quite unparalleled and unique. Her sexual desires must truly have been insatiable. Even if the might of the gods, the judgement of mankind, did not frighten her, it is strange indeed that she did not feel overawed by the torches, by the threshold of the bridal chamber which contained her own daughter's bridal bed, by the very walls themselves which had gazed upon that other union. In her sensual frenzy there was no obstacle which she forebore to break through and trample down out of her way. Modesty was overcome by passionate lust, caution by unbridled recklessness, reason by mania uncontrollable.

Her son Cluentius took it badly. The disgrace had fearful repercussions upon his family, his kinsmen, and his own good name. And to add to his troubles there were his sister's daily lamentations and unceasing tears. Nevertheless, in spite of his mother's outrageous and inexcusable conduct, he decided that all he would do was to stop treating her as a mother. For if he maintained the filial relationship with his mother—whom he could not even so much as look at any longer without feelings of profound anguish—it would have seemed as if he were not just turning his gaze upon her, but condoning what she had done.

This, then, was how the enmity between my client and his mother originated . . . .

Throughout his entire life all the calamities that Aulus Cluentius has ever had to undergo, all the mortal menaces that have ever threatened him, all the miseries which have ever engulfed him, have been due without exception to the contrivance and instigation of his own mother. And yet, even so, he would not, today, say so much as a single word about any of these misfortunes, he would allow the veil, not perhaps of oblivion, but at least of silence, to cover every single one of them, were it not for the total impossibility, in the position in which he is placed, of maintaining such a silence. For this trial, this peril which it imposes upon him, this accusation, this host of witnesses who are shortly to appear—this whole situation, in every one of

Cicero, statesman of the Roman republic.

its aspects, was created by this mother of his, and is still being organized by his mother today, and promoted by all the resources and riches that she can command. And indeed she herself has just come hastening from Larinum to Rome, in person, with the express purpose of destroying her own son. Here she is!—violent, wealthy and cruel. It is she who is directing the prosecution; it is herself who marshals the witnesses. Her son's neglected appearance and shabby clothes inspire her to feel not pity, but exultation. She longs for his ruin. She is willing to squander every single drop of her own blood if only she can see his blood shed first. . . .

My first question is this. What motive could Cluentius have had for murdering Oppianicus? I admit that they did not get on well with one another. But if a man hopes for the death of his enemy, it is because he either fears him or hates him. Now, as to the former, it is quite impossible to point to any fear which could conceivably have induced Cluentius to undertake the responsibility of so appalling a crime. Indeed, there was no longer any reason for anyone to be afraid of Oppianicus at all, now that he had paid the penalty for his misdeeds—expulsion from the community. For what was there, in fact, to be frightened about? An attack from a ruined man, an accusation from a convicted criminal, the evidence of an outlaw? these presented no perils whatsoever. Or alternatively, seeing that the two men were enemies, let us imagine for a moment that Cluentius was so blinded by hatred that he could not bear Oppianicus to stay alive. But surely he cannot have been stupid enough not to realize that the life which Oppianicus was living at that time could scarcely be described as a life at all. For his existence was that of a condemned man, an outcast, an individual whom everyone had abandoned; a scoundrel so repulsive that no one would accept him under his roof, or go near him, or even speak to him; no one would so much as give him a single glance.

Cluentius was not going to grudge a man like that his life. On the contrary, if he really hated Oppianicus as ferociously and intensely as all that, he ought to have been eager that the man should go on living for as long as possible. . . .

In any case, this alleged use of bread for purposes of poisoning is exceedingly unusual, and strange, and unlikely. Surely the application of poison in this fashion, hidden away in some corner of a piece of bread, would mean that the fatal dose was unlikely to permeate the victim's veins and frame nearly as quickly as if it were mixed with some liquid that could be drunk instead of eaten. Furthermore, once suspicion was aroused, it would have been considerably easier to detect the presence of poison in the bread than if it were dissolved in a liquid, in which case its detection might well be impossible.

You make the point that Oppianicus died very suddenly. Well, suppose he did. And so do many other people too: but that does not necessarily mean that they have been poisoned! Besides, even if he did die suddenly, even if the suddenness aroused some suspicion, it would be directed against others before it ever fell upon Cluentius. But actually this story of his sudden death is a barefaced fabrication. To prove that this is so, let me tell you the true facts about Oppianicus' death—and let me tell you also how, after he was dead, Cluentius' mother made every effort to pin the responsibility falsely upon her own son . . . .

When Sassia held her inquiry, many of his father's and mother's friends, and people they had exchanged hospitality with, were requested to attend—all respectable, reputable figures. The proceedings included a rigorous examination of the slaves, in which various forms of torture was applied. Although every pressure, in the form of promises and threats alike, was brought to bear on them in the hope that they would give something away, they were so greatly overawed—by the authority of the gathering, I suppose—that they persisted in telling the truth and refused to admit that they knew anything whatever about any plot to murder Oppianicus. Finally, at the suggestion of the assembled friends of the family, the inquiry was called off for that day. But after a considerable interval they were invited to attend once again, and the examination was repeated.

Tortures of the most unpleasant nature were employed. Finally, when the witnesses felt unable to endure the spectacle any longer, they protested. In the heart of the savage, unnatural Sassia the only feeling was rage, because her scheme had totally miscarried. However, at long last, when the torturer and even his instruments of torture were worn out, and still she showed not the slightest intention of calling a halt, one of the men who had been summoned as witnesses, a person of high position and unimpeachable character, declared he had come to the conclusion that the purpose of her inquiry was not to find the truth at all: it was to force the slaves to say something untrue. There was a general agreement with this, and it was unanimously resolved that the investigation must go no further. . . .

. . . In heaven's name, was there ever such an awful phenomenon as that woman? One would think that in all the world there could be no region capable of producing or harbouring a monstrosity so appalling, a criminality so detestable and unnatural. Surely it must be clear to you by now, gentlemen, that when I referred to my client's mother in the first words of this speech I was absolutely right. For from the very beginning, without cessation, there has been no conceivable kind of evil and wickedness that she has not longed for, and hankered after, and plotted, and perpetrated against her own son. . . .

And so Sassia herself came to Rome; and I can tell you what her journey was like. Since the people of Aquinum and Fabrateria are my neighbours, many bystanders have told me all the details, and I know exactly how it all happened. You must imagine great crowds of men and women assembling, and a mighty groan issuing from every throat, as they all gazed upon this female, furnished with a vast retinue and loaded with huge sums of money, hastening along the road from Larinum, hastening all the way from the Adriatic coast to Rome itself, for the specific purpose of striking down her own son on a capital charge and causing his utter destruction. Among all those spectators, I truly believe that there was not a single one who felt that any place where she had set her foot would ever be clean again until it was subjected to solemn rites of purification: they were convinced, one and all, that the very earth itself, the common mother of every one of us, had become utterly polluted wherever that most abominable of mothers had trod. And so there was not a town which allowed her to tarry, not an inn where the innkeeper did not shrink from the contagion of her baleful eye. No hostelry, no city, could bring itself to receive her; night and solitude were her lot. . . .

Gentlemen, you . . . by the force of circumstances, have been placed in the position of gods, since the entire future of my client lies wholly within your power today. Protect his life, I implore you, from his unspeakable mother. In times gone by, many a judge has thought fit to dismiss the wrongdoings of children because he felt sympathy for their parents. What I am begging you to do is something strangely different: I am begging you not to sacrifice my client's wholly blameless life to a mother who is utterly inhuman.

QUESTIONS

1. Judging from what you have read of Cicero's speech, what verdict would you render as one of Habitus's judges?

2. Sassia, the defendant's mother, is the focus of Cicero's defense. Why do you think he set his sights on her?

3.   Sassia and her son obviously were not likely to be held up as a model family—what sort of lessons about family life might Romans have drawn from this affair?

4.   What do the facts presented reveal about Roman society?

5.   Why do you think this speech was so famous?

20

■ *Virgil* ■

AENEID
(30–19 B.C.E.)

Publius Virgilius Maro, known as Virgil (70–19 B.C.E.), was born near Mantua to a peasant family. Remarkably, given his family background, he was able to receive an education, first at local schools and then in Rome. He was especially skilled in rhetoric and philosophy, the two central subjects of the time. Unlike most other distinguished Romans, Virgil never aspired to public life but devoted himself entirely to writing poetry. His early works were merely preparation for the creation of an epic, regarded as the highest form of poetic expression.

This work was the *Aeneid,* Virgil's story of the founding of Rome and the fulfillment of its great destiny. Initially, the poem was meant to honor the Emperor; in it, Augustus was compared favorably to the mythical founder of Rome, Aeneas, after whom the poem was named. Virgil worked on the *Aeneid* for over a decade and it remained unfinished at his death. The following selection comes from the opening stanzas of the poem.

Arms and the man I sing, who first made way,
Predestined exile, from the Trojan shore
To Italy, the blest Lavinian strand.
Smitten of storms he was on land and sea
By violence of Heaven, to satisfy
Stern Juno's sleepless wrath; and much in war
He suffered, seeking at the last to found

The city, and bring o'er his fathers' gods
To safe abode in Latium; whence arose
The Latin race, old Alba's reverend lords,
And from her hills wide-walled, imperial Rome.
O Muse, the causes tell! What sacrilege,
Or vengeful sorrow, moved the heavenly Queen
To thrust on dangers dark and endless toil

A man whose largest honor in men's eyes
Was serving Heaven? Can gods such anger feel?
In ages gone an ancient city stood—
Carthage, a Tyrian seat, which from afar
Made front on Italy and on the mouths
Of Tiber's stream; its wealth and revenues
Were vast, and ruthless was its quest of war.
'T' is said that Juno, of all lands she loved,
Most cherished this—not Samos' self so dear.
Here were her arms, her chariot; even then
A throne of power o'er nations near and far,
If Fate opposed not, 't was her darling hope
To 'stablish here; but anxiously she heard
That of the Trojan blood there was a breed
Then rising, which upon the destined day
Should utterly o'erwhelm her Tyrian towers;
A people of wide sway and conquest proud
Should compass Libya's doom; such was the web
The Fatal Sisters spun.
Aeneas' wave-worn crew now landward made,
And took the nearest passage, whither lay
The coast of Libya. A haven there
Walled in by bold sides of a rocky isle,
Offers a spacious and secure retreat,
Where every billow from the distant main
Breaks, and in many a rippling curve retires.
Huge crags and two confronted promontories
Frown heaven-high, beneath whose brows out-
    spread
The silent, sheltered waters; on the heights
The bright and glimmering foliage seems to show
A woodland amphitheatre; and yet higher
Rises a straight-stemmed grove of dense,
    dark shade.
Fronting on these a grotto may be seen,
O'erhung by steep cliffs; from its inmost wall
Clear springs gush out; and shelving seats it has
Of unhewn stone, a place the wood-nymphs love.
In such a port, a weary ship rides free
Of weight of firm-fluked anchor or strong chain.
Hither Aeneas, of his scattered fleet
Saving but seven, into harbor sailed;
With passionate longing for the touch of land,
Forth leap the Trojans to the welcome shore,
And fling their dripping limbs along the ground.

Then good Achates smote a flinty stone,
Secured a flashing spark, heaped on light leaves,
And with dry branches nursed the mounting
    flame.
Then Ceres' gift from the corrupting sea
They bring away; and wearied utterly
Ply Ceres' cunning on the rescued corn,
And parch in flames, and mill 'twixt two smooth
    stones.
"Companions mine, we have not failed to feel
Calamity till now. O, ye have borne
Far heavier sorrow: Jove will make an end
Also of this. Ye sailed a course hard by
Infuriate Scylla's howling cliffs and caves.
Ye knew the Cyclops' crags. Lift up your hearts!
No more complaint and fear! It well may be
Some happier hour will find this memory fair.
Through chance and change and hazard
    without end,
Our goal is Latium; where our destinies
Beckon to blest abodes, and have ordained
That Troy shall rise new-born! Have patience all!
And bide expectantly that golden day."
Such was his word, but vexed with grief and care,
Feigned hopes upon his forehead firm he wore,
And locked within his heart a hero's pain.
After these things were past, exalted Jove,
From his ethereal sky surveying clear
The seas all winged with sails, lands widely spread,
And nations populous from shore to shore,
Paused on the peak of heaven, and fixed his gaze
On Libya. But while he anxious mused,
Near him, her radiant eyes all dim with tears,
Nor smiling any more, Venus approached,
And thus complained: "O thou who dost control
Things human and divine by changeless laws,
Enthroned in awful thunder! What huge wrong
Could my Aeneas and his Trojans few
Achieve against thy power? For they have borne
Unnumbered deaths, and, failing Italy,
The gates of all the world again them close.
Hast thou not give us thy covenant
That hence the Romans when the rolling years
Have come full cycle, shall arise to power
From Troy's regenerate seed, and rule supreme

The unresisted lords of land and sea?
O sire, what swerves thy will? How oft have I
In Troy's most lamentable wreck and woe.
Consoled my heart with this, and balanced oft
Our destined good against our destined ill!
But the same stormful fortune still pursues
My band of heroes on their perilous way.
When shall these labors cease, O glorious King?
Antenor, though th' Achoeans pressed him sore,
Found his way forth, and entered unassailed
Illyria's haven, and the guarded land
Of the Liburni. Straight up stream he sailed
Where like a swollen sea Timavus pours
A nine-fold flood from roaring mountain gorge,
And whelms with voiceful wave the fields below.
He built Patavium there, and fixed abodes
For Troy's far-exiled sons; he gave a name
To a new land and race; the Trojan arms
Were hung on temple walls; and, to this day,
Lying in perfect peace, the hero sleeps.
But we of thine own seed, to whom thou dost
A station in the arch of heaven assign,
Behold our navy vilely wrecked, because
A single god is angry; we endure
This treachery and violence, whereby
Wide seas divide us from th' Hesperian shore.
Is this what piety receives? Or thus
Doth Heaven's decree restore our fallen thrones?"
Smiling reply, the Sire of gods and men,
With such a look as clears the skies of storm,
Chastely his daughter kissed, and thus spake on:
"Let Cythera cast her fears away!
Irrevocably blest the fortunes be
Of thee and thine. Nor shalt thou fail to see
That City, and the proud predestined wall
Encompassing Lavinium. Thyself
Shall starward to the heights of heaven bear
Aeneas the great-hearted. Nothing swerves
My will once uttered. Since such carking cares
Consume thee, I this hour speak freely forth,
And leaf by leaf the book of fate unfold.
Thy son in Italy shall wage vast war
And quell its nations wild; his city-wall
And sacred laws shall be a mighty bond
About his gathered people. Summers three

Shall Latium call him king; and three times pass
The winter o'er Rutulia's vanquished hills.
His heir, Ascanius, now Iulus called
(Ilus it was while Ilium's kingdom stood),
Full thirty months shall reign, then move the
    throne
From the Lavinian citadel, and build
For Alba Longa its well-bastioned wall.
Here three full centuries shall Hector's race
Have kingly power; till a priestess queen,
By Mars conceiving, her twin offspring bear;
Then Romulus, wolf-nursed and proudly clad
In tawny wolf-skin mantle, shall receive
The sceptre of his race. He shall uprear
The war-god's citadel and lofty wall,
And on his Romans his own name bestow.
To these I give no bounded times or power,
But empire without end. Yea, even my Queen,
Juno, who now chastiseth land and sea
With her dread frown, will find a wiser way,
And at my sovereign side protect and bless
The Romans, masters of the whole round world,
Who, clad in peaceful toga, judge mankind.
Such my decree! In lapse of seasons due,
The heirs of Ilium's kings shall bind in chains
Mycenae's glory and Achilles' towers,
And over prostrate Argos sit supreme.
Of Trojan stock illustriously sprung,
Lo, Caesar comes! whose power the ocean
    bounds,
Whose fame, the skies. He shall receive the name
Iulus nobly bore, great Julius, he.
Him to the skies, in Orient trophies dight,
Thou shalt with smiles receive; and he, like us,
Shall hear at his own shrines the suppliant vow.
Then will the world grow mild; the battle-sound
Will be forgot; for olden Honor then,
With spotless Vesta, and the brothers twain,
Remus and Romulus, at strife no more,
Will publish sacred laws. The dreadful gates
Whence issueth war, shall with close-jointed steel
Be barred impregnably; and prisoned there
The heaven-offending Fury, throned on swords,
And fettered by a hundred brazen chains,
Shall belch vain curses from his lips of gore."

QUESTIONS

1. The *Aeneid* offered Romans an explanation of their origins. Why would such a myth have been useful? What purpose might it have served?

2. What is Rome's destiny as foretold in the *Aeneid?* What stands in the way of success?

3. Virgil gives us a glimpse of what the Romans thought they were like. What sort of people do the founders of Rome appear to be?

4. Why do you think Virgil chose to tell his story in the form of an epic poem?

5. The links between the *Aeneid* and the works of Homer seem very clear. Why did the Romans want to connect themselves so closely with Homeric legends?

21

■ *Juvenal* ■

SATIRES
(CA. C.E. 116)

The *Satires* of Decimus Junius Juvenal (ca. C.E. 60–128) give us an unforgettable picture of the decline of the Roman Empire. Little can be established about Juvenal's life. He was probably born in central Italy, where he received an excellent education in rhetoric and philosophy. He may have made his living as a lawyer, though there is a tradition suggesting that he was a soldier. He was certainly in Rome during the reign of the cruel Emperor Domitian, and the *Satires* began to appear shortly afterward. It is thought that Juvenal died in Egypt.

The *Satires* examine all manner of human failings and display the author's zest for the absurd and the erotic. They are not without their serious side, despite the mocking tone employed throughout. The sixth satire, the satire on women, is typical in tone and style, although the subject matter gives full play to ancient myths about women.

In Address to Postumus Ursidius

And are you, at our time of life and in
    our day,
you contemplating betrothal and a lawyer
    to pay
and a formal ceremony, just to get into bed?
Really, you need someone to look at your
    head.
Are you off to the master-barber? On her
    finger
perhaps you've already fitted that fatal ring?
What, *you* to fall
to be at a female's beck and call!
Haven't you any longer got what it takes?
Have you heard of Tisiphone and her coiffure
    of snakes?
There are plenty of halters in Rome
and dizzy windows to chuck yourself from—
not to mention the Aemilian bridge
and the red light district.
Or you want a nice little heir? Are you sane?
The plump turtle-doves, the bearded mullets
and such little tit-bits the legacy-hunters
bring from the market you won't see again.
If you can marry, there are no laws of Nature.
Why, you who of late well deserved the renown
of the most considerable lecher in town—
so often concealed with a price on his head
in a wardrobe or under the bed
as in those triangular farces—
now make matrimonial passes
and stick your poor neck out right into the net!
And you must have a wife
who is leading a life
of something they used to call virtue?
My dear little man, what a charming idea—
but I fear
they must puncture your veins till they
    hurt you.
Prostrate yourself at the threshold of Tarpeian
    Jove,
sacrifice to Juno a heifer with gilded horns—
to find a lady if you can—

really innocent of man.
She may be quite a priestess—in one place—
her father fears to kiss her on the face.
Wreathe for the portal garlands
and thick clusters of ivy—
that's if you really imagine
one man enough for the lady
but you might more easily win her consent
to have only one eye.
Oh, she has such a good reputation—
she lives at her own country seat?
Could you be sure of a single woman in all the
    arcades?

Marriage à la Mode

'My lady wife's the best of wives' says a certain
    gentleman.
You may lift an eyebrow, knowing perhaps . . .
But the answer's easy
She brought him a hundred thousand—
not a bad price
for a mere reputation. It's not through the
    quiver of Venus
he looks so thin, that's not the torch that he
    carries.
It's from the dowry the fires are lit, thence come
    the arrows.
She has purchased her right to do what she will,
to flirt and make her assignments right under
    his eyes.
A wife with a fortune is free as the birds of
    the air.
Take the other side of the medal and ask
    (if a woman)
'Why is Sertorius so madly in love with the
    Bibula?
They're so disparate.'
Well you *do* know though you wouldn't
    admit—
she's so pretty
which is what the man sees, he doesn't see into
    her heart.
Let but three wrinkles creep up on her face,

let her chin sag
let her teeth go black, or the lustre go out of
    her eyes,
'Pack up your bags' he'll send his freedman to
    tell her 'and *go!*
I can't bear the way your nose runs—and be
    quick about it.
Thank goodness another who's more appetising
    is coming.'
But until that day comes, the gold-digger's a
    shrew.
She flies off in fits, she bullies her husband,
must have her pound of flesh . . . . .
But in the mid-winter month,
the time of present giving
then she really goes to town—vases of crystal
vases of agate, a fabulous diamond
costing the more for having been worn by
    a queen
marked 'Herod Agrippa to his loving
    sister,'—
it was his 'Thanks for the incest' to
    Berenice
in that curious land where bare-footed
    kings
keep Sabbath as a *fiesta,* and pigs
unlike kings, to conform with tradition
are allowed to live out their days.
See Ogulnia off to the games—what a
    beautiful dress!
So many attendants escorting her chair—a fine
    cushion
to sit on, a neat little blonde as *soubrette,* and
    even a 'nurse'—
old family retainer of course—all hired for
    the day!
What's left of the family plate she presents to
    the athletes—
she can't resist the gleam of their well-oiled
    limbs.
There is many and many a woman of limited
    fortune, none
who is modest enough to admit it and cut her
    coat to her cloth.

Sometimes at least men do look to the
    future
and learn from the ant a proper respect for
    hunger and cold.
These women take no account of a daily
    diminishing fortune,
as if it would sprout afresh
like a plant from the exhausted safe
and she was helping herself from a pile that
    never grew less,
nor ever stop to consider
how much their pleasure cost.
Even she's not so bad as the tough type
who likes to barge in on men's talk,
who runs round the town, embarrassing
    her man,
telling uniformed generals where they get off.
She knows all that goes on in the world
what the Chinese and Russians are up to
the secrets of mother and son
who's in love with whom, who's the escort
    in fashion
who made that widow pregnant
and how many months gone,
what so-and-so says in bed.
She is always the first to have seen
the comet that portends God knows what
for some Oriental king.
She is always the first to snatch up the news
that's latest arrived—or invent it—
the first to have heard
of flooded Niphates, the acres it covers
the thousands made homeless, the cities
    destroyed
by the earthquake—embroidering the tale
once again for every new comer.
Yet I'd rather have even that old battle-axe
than one who presumes to be literate—
who fairly astounds the company
by discovering, if you please
that Virgil is *good!* As if anyone called for
    her views
on the *to-be-or-not-to-be* of Carthage's queen.
Poets she'll match and compare, Homer v. Maro

like a pair of horses. Politicians and dons
have to take a back seat, reduced to unnatural
    silence.
Not even our Learned Counsel can get a
    word in—
not even another female.
Such a torrent of words, like the clamour
of so many basins and bells!
Don't send for trumpet and drum
to fend off an eclipse of the moon—
send for *her*.
(Even best things are better better controlled.)
This would-be Portia should wear a man's tunic;
give a pig to men's god, Sylvanus; bathe at
    men's prices.
The marriage-bed's no place for oratorical flights

or bowling rounded syllogisms with a spin.
Oh for some chink in her proud armour of
    knowledge
some history, some play she has *not* read!
How I dislike a woman who never seems to tire
of studying some exhaustive—and exhausting—
    treatise—
who keeps the rules and precepts of 'you can be
    a speaker'
and quotes from ancient poets lines I never
    heard.
She'll jump down a friend's throat for getting
    one word wrong.
What right has she to criticise, if *you* don't mind?
Let her poor husband make a slip in syntax if
    he likes!

QUESTIONS

1. How does Juvenal depict upper-class Roman life? How do wealthy Romans amuse themselves?

2. Juvenal's women are cunning and faithless. Why—do they have to be, given the nature of Roman society? What strategies do they employ in their everyday relations with men?

3. Who are the main targets of Juvenal's satire? What are the flaws he exposes in both men and women?

4. Although often meant to amuse, satire can also have a serious purpose. How might the *Satires* have taught a useful lesson to the Roman audience?

5. What are some of the stereotypes Juvenal employs in his *Satires*? Are they still common today?

22

■ *Plutarch* ■

THE LIFE OF CATO THE ELDER

(CA. C.E. 116)

Plutarch (C.E. 46–124) was a Greek philosopher and biographer and is one of the best-known sources for information about ancient personalities. Although educated in Athens, Plutarch traveled extensively in the Roman Empire and may even have achieved high office within it. Little is known of his life until he returned to Greece, where he was a teacher and a priest at the oracle of Apollo at Delphi. Plutarch wrote extensively on ethical and philosophical issues, but his most popular work was *Lives,* which he began in middle age.

Plutarch considered himself a biographer rather than a historian. He paired the life of a Greek with that of a Roman and then wrote an explicit comparison of the two. Twenty-two such pairs survive, each using narrative, description, and anecdote to provide a portrait. Plutarch's *Lives* were enormously popular in the Roman world and became a vital source of knowledge about the ancients after they were rediscovered in the sixteenth century. Shakespeare relied upon the *Lives* heavily for his Roman plays.

Marcus Cato, we are told, was born at Tusculum, though (till he betook himself to civil and military affairs) he lived and was bred up in the country of the Sabines, where his father's estate lay. His ancestors seeming almost entirely unknown, he himself praises his father Marcus, as a worthy man and a brave soldier, and Cato, his great grandfather too, as one who had often obtained military prizes, and who, having lost five horses under him, received, on the account of his valor, the worth of them out of the public exchequer.

He gained, in early life, a good habit of body by working with his own hands, and living temperately, and serving in war; and seemed to have an equal proportion both of health and strength. And he exerted and practiced his eloquence through all the neighborhood and little villages; thinking it as requisite as a second body, and an all but necessary organ to one who looks forward to something above a mere humble and inactive life. He would never refuse to be counsel for those who needed him, and was, indeed, early reckoned a good lawyer, and, ere long, a capable orator.

Hence his solidity and depth of character showed itself gradually, more and more to those with whom he was concerned, and claimed, as it were, employment in great affairs, and places of public command. Nor did he merely abstain from taking fees for his counsel and pleading but did not even seem to put any high price on the honor which proceeded from such kind of combats, seeming much more desirous to signalize himself in the camp and in real fights; and while yet but a youth, had his breast covered with scars he had received from the enemy; being (as he himself says) but seventeen years old, when he made his first campaign; in the time when Hannibal, in the height of his success, was burning and pillaging all Italy. In engagements he would strike boldly, without flinching, stand firm to his ground, fix a bold countenance upon his enemies, and with a harsh threatening voice accost them, justly thinking himself and telling others, that such a rugged kind of behavior sometimes terrifies the enemy more than the sword itself. In his marches, he bore his own arms on foot, whilst one servant only followed, to carry the provisions for his table, with whom he is said never to have been angry or hasty, whilst he made ready his dinner or supper, but would, for the most part, when he was free from military duty, assist and help him himself to dress it. When he was with the army, he used to drink only water; unless, perhaps, when extremely thirsty, he might mingle it with a little vinegar; or if he found his strength fail him, take a little wine.

There was a man of the highest rank, and very influential among the Romans, called Valerius Flaccus, who was singularly skillful in discerning excellence yet in the bud, and, also, much disposed to nourish and advance it. He, it seems, had lands bordering upon Cato's; nor could he but admire, when he understood from his servants the manner of his living, how he labored with his own hands, went on foot betimes in the morning to the courts to assist those who wanted his counsel; how, returning home again, when it was winter, he would throw a loose frock, over his shoulders, and in the summer time would work without any thing on among his domestics, sit down with them, eat of the same bread, and drink of the same wine. When they spoke, also, of other good qualities, his fair dealing and moderation, mentioning also some of his wise sayings, he ordered, that he should be invited to supper; and thus becoming personally assured of his fine temper and his superior character which, like a plant, seemed

only to require culture and a better situation, he urged and persuaded him to apply himself to state affairs at Rome. Thither, therefore, he went, and by his pleading soon gained many friends and admirers; but, Valerius chiefly assisting his promotion, he first of all got appointed tribune in the army, and afterwards was made quaestor, or treasurer. And now becoming eminent and noted, he passed, with Valerius himself, through the greatest commands, being first his colleague as consul, and then censor. But among all the ancient senators, he most attached himself to Fabius Maximus; not so much for the honor of his person, and greatness of his power, as that he might have before him his habit and manner of life, as the best examples to follow: and so he did not hesitate to oppose Scipio the Great, who, being then but a young man, seemed to set himself against the power of Fabius, and to be envied by him. For being sent together with him as treasurer, when he saw him, according to his natural custom, make great expenses, and distribute among the soldiers without sparing, he freely told him that the expense in itself was not the greatest thing to be considered, but that he was corrupting the ancient frugality of the soldiers, by giving them the means to abandon themselves to unnecessary pleasures and luxuries. Scipio answered, that he had no need for so accurate a treasurer (bearing on as he was, so to say, full sail to the war), and that he owed the people an account of his actions, and not of the money he spent.

Cato grew more and more powerful by his eloquence, so that he was commonly called the Roman Demosthenes, but his manner of life was yet more famous and talked of. For oratorical skill was, as an accomplishment, commonly studied and sought after by all young men; but he was very rare who would cultivate the old habits of bodily labor, or prefer a light supper, and a breakfast which never saw the fire; or be in love with poor clothes and a homely lodging, or could set his ambition rather on doing without luxuries than on possessing them. For now the state, unable to keep its purity by reason of its greatness, and having so many affairs, and people from all parts under its government, was fain to admit many mixed customs, and new examples of living. With reason, therefore, everybody admired Cato, when they saw others sink under labors, and grow effeminate by pleasures; and yet beheld him unconquered by either, and that not only when he was young and desirous of honor, but also when old and greyheaded, after a consulship and triumph; like some famous victor in the games, persevering in his exercise and maintaining his character to the very last.

He gave most general annoyance, by retrenching people's luxury; for though (most of the youth being thereby already corrupted) it seemed almost impossible to take it away with an open hand and directly, yet going, as it were, obliquely around, he caused all dress, carriages, women's ornaments, household furniture, whose price exceeded one thousand five hundred drachmas, to be rated at ten times as much as they were worth; intending by thus making the assessments greater, to increase the taxes paid upon them. And thus, on the one side, not only those were disgusted at Cato, who bore the taxes for the sake of their luxury, but those, too, who on the other side laid by their luxury for fear of the taxes. For people in general reckon, that an order not to display their riches, is equivalent to the taking away their riches; because riches are seen much more in superfluous, than in necessary, things.

Cato, notwithstanding, being little solicitous as to those who exclaimed against him, increased his austerity. He caused the pipes, through which some persons brought the public water into their own houses and gardens, to be cut, and threw down all buildings which jutted out into the common streets. He beat down also the price in contracts for public works to the lowest, and raised it in contracts for farming the taxes to the highest sum; by

which proceedings he drew a great deal of hatred on himself. Those who were of Titus Flamininus's party cancelled in the senate all the bargains and contracts made by him for the repairing and carrying on of the sacred and public buildings, as unadvantageous to the commonwealth. They incited also the boldest of the tribunes of the people to accuse him, and to fine him two talents. They likewise much opposed him in building the court or basilica, which he caused to be erected at the common charge, just by the senate-house, in the market-place, and called by his own name, the Porcian. However, the people, it seems, liked his censorship wondrously well; for, setting up a statue for him in the temple of the goddess of Health, they put an inscription under it, not recording his commands in war or his triumph, but to the effect, that this was Cato the Censor, who, by his good discipline and wise and temperate ordinances, reclaimed the Roman commonwealth when it was declining and sinking down into vice.

He was also a good father, an excellent husband to his wife, and an extraordinary economist; and as he did not manage his affairs of this kind carelessly, and as things of little moment, I think I ought to record a little further whatever was commendable in him in these points. He married a wife more noble than rich; being of opinion, that the rich and the high-born are equally haughty and proud; but that those of noble blood, would be more ashamed of base things, and consequently more obedient to their husbands in all that was fit and right. A man who beat his wife or child, laid violent hands, he said, on what was most sacred; and a good husband he reckoned worthy of more praise than a great senator; and he admired the ancient Socrates for nothing so much, as for having lived a temperate and contented life with a wife who was a scold, and children who were half-witted.

Some will have the overthrow of Carthage to have been one of his last acts of state; when, indeed, Scipio the younger, did by his valor give it the last blow, but the war, chiefly by the counsel and advice of Cato, was undertaken on the following occasion. Cato was sent to the Carthaginians and Masinissa, king of Numidia, who were at war with one another, to know the cause of their difference. He, it seems, had been a friend of the Romans from the beginning; and they, too, since they were conquered by Scipio, were of the Roman confederacy, having been shorn of their power by loss of territory, and a heavy tax. Finding Carthage, not (as the Romans thought) low and in an ill condition, but well manned, full of riches and all sorts of arms and ammunition, and perceiving the Carthaginians carry it high, he conceived that it was not a time for the Romans to adjust affairs between them and Masinissa; but rather that they themselves would fall into danger, unless they should find means to check this rapid new growth of Rome's ancient irreconcilable enemy. Therefore, returning quickly to Rome, he acquainted the senate, that the former defeats and blows given to the Carthaginians, had not so much diminished their strength, as it had abated their imprudence and folly; that they were not become weaker, but more experienced in war, and did only skirmish with the Numidians, to exercise themselves the better to cope with the Romans: that the peace and league they had made was but a kind of suspension of war which awaited a fairer opportunity to break out again.

Moreover, they say that, shaking his gown, he took occasion to let drop some African figs before the senate. And on their admiring the size and beauty of them, he presently added, that the place that bore them was but three days' sail from Rome. Nay, he never after this gave his opinion, but at the end he would be sure to come out with this sentence, "Also, Carthage, methinks, ought utterly to be destroyed."

Thus Cato, they say, stirred up the third and last war against the Carthaginians: but no sooner was the said war begun, than he died.

QUESTIONS

1. How might a Roman gentleman like Cato rise in politics?

2. What were the qualities that made Cato the model of the noble Roman?

3. Why did Cato create so many enemies while he held political office?

4. Plutarch clearly meant his biography of Cato to be an inspiration for his readers. Could you argue that Cato was not the best role model Plutarch might have chosen? Does Cato have any flaws?

23

■ *Suetonius* ■

THE LIFE OF AUGUSTUS
(CA. C.E. 122)

Gaius Suetonius Tranquillus (ca. C.E. 69–122) gained fame for his biographies of the first twelve Roman emperors. The son of a knightly family, Suetonius studied but never practiced law. He saw military and diplomatic service before entering the government of Emperor Hadrian. Suetonius's historical interests shaped his public career and he soon became the imperial archivist, the director of the Roman libraries, and a cultural advisor to the emperor. In 121, Suetonius rose to the key position of imperial secretary but was dismissed from office for failing to abide by court etiquette. He spent the rest of his life writing biographies.

The Life of Augustus is one of the best known of the Lives of the Twelve Caesars. It was Suetonius's purpose to provide both a vivid portrayal of his subject and an account of the social environment in which Augustus lived.

In military affairs he made many alterations, introducing some practices entirely new, and reviving others, which had become obsolete. He maintained the strictest discipline among the troops; and would not allow even his lieutenants the liberty to visit their wives, except reluctantly, and in the winter season only. A Roman knight having cut off the thumbs of his two young sons, to render them incapable of serving in the wars, he exposed both him and his estate to public sale. But upon observing the farmers of the revenue very greedy for the purchase, he assigned him to a freedman of his own, that he might send him into the country, and suffer him to retain his freedom. The tenth legion becoming mutinous, he disbanded it with ignominy; and did the same by some others which petulantly demanded their discharge; withholding from them the rewards usually bestowed on those who had served their stated time in the wars. The

[handwritten note: Didn't want his sons to go to war]

cohorts which yielded their ground in time of action, he decimated, and fed with barley. Centurions, as well as common sentinels, who deserted their posts when on guard, he punished with death. For other misdemeanors he inflicted upon them various kinds of disgrace; such as obliging them to stand all day before the praetorium, sometimes in their tunics only, and without their belts, sometimes to carry poles ten feet long, or sods of turf.

He was advanced to public offices before the age at which he was legally qualified for them: and to some, also, of a new kind, and for life. He seized the consulship in the twentieth year of his age, quartering his legions in a threatening manner near the city, and sending deputies to demand it for him in the name of the army. When the senate demurred, a centurion, named Cornelius, who was at the head of the chief deputation, throwing back his cloak, and shewing the

[handwritten note: became consul at 20]

hilt of his sword, had the presumption to say in the senate-house, "This will make him consul, if ye will not." His second consulship he filled nine years afterwards; his third, after the interval of only one year, and held the same office every year successively until the eleventh. From this period, although the consulship was frequently offered him, he always declined it, until, after a long interval, not less than seventeen years, he voluntarily stood for the twelfth, and two years after that, for a thirteenth; that he might successively introduce into the forum, on their entering public life, his two sons, Caius and Lucius, while he was invested with the highest office in the state.

He accepted of the tribunitian power for life, but more than once chose a colleague in that office for ten years successively. He also had the supervision of morality and observance of the laws, for life, but without the title of censor; yet he thrice took a census of the people, the first and third time with a colleague, but the second by himself.

He twice entertained thoughts of restoring the republic; first, immediately after he had crushed Antony, remembering that he had often charged him with being the obstacle to its restoration. The second time was in consequence of a long illness, when he sent for the magistrates and the senate to his own house, and delivered them a particular account of the state of the empire. But reflecting at the same time that it would be both hazardous to himself to return to the condition of a private person, and might be dangerous to the public to have the government placed again under the control of the people, he resolved to keep it in his own hands, whether with the better event or intention, is hard to say. His good intentions he often affirmed in private discourse, and also published an edict, in which it was declared in the following terms: "May it be permitted me to have the happiness of establishing the commonwealth on a safe and sound basis, and thus enjoy the reward of which I am ambitious, that of being celebrated for moulding it into the form best adapted to present circumstances; so that, on my leaving the world,

I may carry with me the hope that the foundations which I have laid for its future government, will stand firm and stable."

The city, which was not built in a manner suitable to the grandeur of the empire, and was liable to inundations of the Tiber, as well as to fires, was so much improved under his administration, that he boasted, not without reason, that he "found it of brick, but left it of marble." He also rendered it secure for the time to come against such disasters, as far as could be effected by human foresight. A great number of public buildings were erected by him, the most considerable of which were a forum, containing the temple of Mars the Avenger, the temple of Apollo on the Palatine hill, and the temple of Jupiter Tonans in the capitol. The reason of his building a new forum was the vast increase in the population, and the number of cases to be tried in the courts, for which, the two already existing not affording sufficient space, it was thought necessary to have a third. It was therefore opened for public use before the temple of Mars was completely finished; and a law was passed, that cases should be tried, and judges chosen by lot, in that place.

He corrected many ill practices, which, to the detriment of the public, had either survived the licentious habits of the late civil wars, or else originated in the long peace. Bands of robbers shewed themselves openly, completely armed, under colour of self-defence; and in different parts of the country, travellers, freemen and slaves without distinction, were forcibly carried off, and kept to work in the houses of correction. Several associations were formed under the specious name of a new college, which banded together for the perpetration of all kinds of villainy. The bandits he quelled by establishing posts of soldiers in suitable stations for the purpose; the houses of correction were subjected to a strict superintendence; all associations, those only excepted which were of ancient standing, and recognised by the laws, were dissolved. He burnt all the notes of those who had been a long time in arrear with the treasury, as being the principal source of vexatious suits and prosecutions. Places in the city claimed by the public, where the right was doubtful, he adjudged to the actual possessors. He struck out of the list of criminals the names of those over whom prosecutions had been long impending, where nothing further was intended by the informers than to gratify their own malice, by seeing their enemies humiliated; laying it down as a rule, that if any one chose to renew a prosecution, he should incur the risk of the punishment which he sought to inflict. And that crimes might not escape punishment, nor business be neglected by delay, he ordered the courts to sit during the thirty days which were spent in celebrating honorary games.

He was desirous that his friends should be great and powerful in the state, but have no exclusive privileges, or be exempt from the laws which governed others. When Asprenas Nonius, an intimate friend of his, was tried upon a charge of administering poison at the instance of Cassius Severus, he consulted the senate for their opinion what was his duty under the circumstances: "For," said he, "I am afraid, lest, if I should stand by him in the cause, I may be supposed to screen a guilty man; and if I do not, to desert and prejudge a friend." With the unanimous concurrence, therefore, of the senate, he took his seat amongst his advocates for several hours, but without giving him the benefit of speaking to character, as was usual. He likewise appeared for his clients; as on behalf of Scutarius, an old soldier of his, who brought an action for slander. He never relieved any one from prosecution but in a single instance, in the case of a man who had given information of the conspiracy of Muraena; and that he did only by prevailing upon the accuser, in open court, to drop his prosecution.

The whole body of the people, upon a sudden impulse, and with unanimous consent, offered him the title of Father of His Country. It was announced to him first at Antium, by a deputation from the people, and upon his declining the

honour, they repeated their offer on his return to Rome, in a full theatre, when they were crowned with laurel. The senate soon afterwards adopted the proposal, not in the way of acclamation or decree, but by commissioning M. Messala, in an unanimous vote, to compliment him with it in the following terms: "With hearty wishes for the happiness and prosperity of yourself and your family, Caesar Augustus, (for we think we thus most effectually pray for the lasting welfare of the state), the senate, in agreement with the Roman people, salute you by the title of Father of Your Country." To this compliment Augustus replied, with tears in his eyes, in these words (for I give them exactly as I have done those of Messala): "Having now arrived at the summit of my wishes, O Conscript Fathers, what else have I to beg of the Immortal Gods, but the continuance of this your affection for me to the last moments of my life?"

In person he was handsome and graceful, through every period of his life. But he was negligent in his dress; and so careless about dressing his hair, that he usually had it done in great haste, by several barbers at a time. His beard he sometimes clipped, and sometimes shaved; and either read or wrote during the operation. His countenance, either when discoursing or silent, was so calm and serene, that a Gaul of the first rank declared amongst his friends, that he was so softened by it, as to be restrained from throwing him down a precipice, in his passage over the Alps, when he had been admitted to approach him, under pretence of conferring with him. His eyes were bright and piercing; and he was willing it should be thought that there was something of a divine vigour in them. He was likewise not a little pleased to see people, upon his looking steadfastly at them, lower their countenances, as if the sun shone in their eyes. But in his old age, he saw very imperfectly with his left eye. His teeth were thin set, small and scaly, his hair a little curled, and inclining to a yellow colour. His eyebrows met; his ears were small, and he had an aquiline nose. His complexion was betwixt brown and fair;

his stature but low; though Julius Marathus, his freedman, says he was five feet and nine inches in height. This, however, was so much concealed by the just proportion of his limbs, that it was only perceivable upon comparison with some taller person standing by him.

He expired in the same room in which his father Octavius had died, when the two Sextus's, Pompey and Apuleius, were consuls, upon the fourteenth of the calends of September [the 19th August], at the ninth hour of the day, being seventy-six years of age, wanting only thirty-five days. His remains were carried by the magistrates of the municipal towns and colonies, from Nola to Bovillae, and in the night-time, because of the season of the year. During the intervals, the body lay in some basilica, or great temple, of each town. At Bovillae it was met by the Equestrian Order, who carried it to the city, and deposited it in the vestibule of his own house. The senate proceeded with so much zeal in the arrangement of his funeral, and paying honour to his memory, that, amongst several other proposals, some were for having the funeral procession made through the triumphal gate, preceded by the image of Victory which is in the senate-house, and the children of highest rank and of both sexes singing the funeral dirge.

Others proposed, that on the day of the funeral, they should lay aside their gold rings, and wear rings of iron; and others, that his bones should be collected by the priests of the principal colleges. One likewise proposed to transfer the name of August to September, because he was born in the latter, but died in the former. Another moved, that the whole period of time, from his birth to his death, should be called the Augustan age, and be inserted in the calendar under that title. But at last it was judged proper to be moderate in the honours paid to his memory. Two funeral orations were pronounced in his praise, one before the temple of Julius, by Tiberius; and the other before the rostra, under the old shops, by Drusus, Tiberius's son. The body was then carried upon the shoulders of senators into the Campus Martius, and there burnt. A man of praetorian rank affirmed upon oath, that he saw his spirit ascend from the funeral pile to heaven. The most distinguished persons of the equestrian order, bare-footed, and with their tunics loose, gathered up his relics, and deposited them in the mausoleum, which had been built in his sixth consulship between the Flaminian Way and the bank of the Tiber; at which time likewise he gave the groves and walks about it for the use of the people.

QUESTIONS

1. What did Augustus accomplish as emperor?

2. How did Augustus attempt to avoid appearing as a dictator? Can you cite an example from Suetonius's *Life*?

3. Would an author such as Suetonius be limited in his freedom to write a biography of a Roman emperor? What factors might he have considered in assessing Augustus's accomplishments?

4. What skills did Augustus need to manipulate the extremely complex Roman political system? How did he manage?

5. Was Augustus's regime appreciated? How did Rome show its gratitude toward the emperor?

24

THE SERMON ON THE MOUNT

(CA. C.E. 28–35)

The Sermon on the Mount was delivered by Jesus sometime after the beginning of his ministry in C.E. 27 and was recorded by the Apostle Matthew. It is a classic example of Jesus' method of teaching, but more importantly its message lies at the heart of the religion that he founded. Unlike most teachers and prophets of his day, Jesus did not teach in a synagogue; rather he brought his message directly to the people by traveling to various centers of population where he would preach in the open air. Thus the setting of the Sermon on the Mount, while unusual in the context of his contemporaries, was typical of Jesus' style.

The message in the Sermon is set firmly within the Jewish tradition. Jesus urges his listeners to a commitment to righteousness, which he defines with poignant simplicity.

Then Jesus was led up by the Spirit into the wilderness to be tempted by the devil. And he fasted forty days and forty nights, and afterward he was hungry. And the tempter came and said to him, "If you are the Son of God, command these stones to become loaves of bread." But he answered, "It is written,

'Man shall not live by bread alone,
    but by every word that proceeds from the mouth of God'."

Then the devil took him to the holy city, and set him on the pinnacle of the temple, and said to him, "If you are the Son of God, throw yourself down; for it is written,

'He will give his angels charge of you,'
and
'On their hands they will bear you up,
    lest you strike your foot against a stone'."

Jesus said to him, "Again it is written, 'You shall not tempt the Lord your God.' " Again, the devil took him to a very high mountain, and showed him all the kingdoms of the world and the glory of them; and he said to him, "All these I will give you, if you will fall down and worship me." Then Jesus said to him, "Begone, Satan! for it is written,

'You shall worship the Lord your God
    and him only shall you serve.' "

Then the devil left him, and behold, angels came and ministered to him.

From that time Jesus began to preach, saying, "Repent, for the kingdom of heaven is at hand."

As he walked by the Sea of Galilee, he saw two brothers, Simon who is called Peter and Andrew his brother, casting a net into the sea; for they were fishermen. And he said to them, "Follow me, and I will make you fishers of men." Immediately they left their nets and followed him. And going on from there he saw two other brothers, James the son of Zebedee and John his brother, in the boat with Zebedee their father, mending their nets, and he called them. Immediately they left the boat and their father, and followed him.

And he went about all Galilee, teaching in their synagogues and preaching the gospel of the kingdom and healing every disease and every infirmity among the people. So his fame spread throughout all Syria, and they brought him all the sick, those afflicted with various diseases and pains, demoniacs, epileptics, and paralytics, and he healed them. And great crowds followed him from Galilee and the Decapolis and Jerusalem and Judea and from beyond the Jordan.

Seeing the crowds, he went up on the mountain, and when he sat down his disciples came to him. And he opened his mouth and taught them, saying:

"Blessed are the poor in spirit, for theirs is the kingdom of heaven.

"Blessed are those who mourn, for they shall be comforted.

"Blessed are the meek, for they shall inherit the earth.

"Blessed are those who hunger and thirst for righteousness, for they shall be satisfied.

"Blessed are the merciful, for they shall obtain mercy.

"Blessed are the pure in heart, for they shall see God.

"Blessed are the peacemakers, for they shall be called sons of God.

"Blessed are those who are persecuted for righteousness' sake, for theirs is the kingdom of heaven.

"Blessed are you when men revile you and persecute you and utter all kinds of evil against you falsely on my account. Rejoice and be glad, for your reward is great in heaven, for so men persecuted the prophets who were before you.

"You are the salt of the earth; but if salt has lost its taste, how shall its saltness be restored? It is no longer good for anything except to be thrown out and trodden under foot by men.

"You are the light of the world. A city set on a hill cannot be hid. Nor do men light a lamp and put it under a bushel, but on a stand, and it gives light to all in the house. Let your light so shine before men, that they may see your good works and give glory to your Father who is in heaven.

"Think not that I have come to abolish the law and the prophets; I have come not to abolish them but to fulfill them. For truly, I say to you, till heaven and earth pass away, not an iota, not a dot, will pass from the law until all is accomplished. Whoever then relaxes one of the least of these commandments and teaches men so, shall be called least in the kingdom of heaven; but he who does them and teaches them shall be called great in the kingdom of heaven. For I tell you, unless your righteousness exceeds that of the scribes and Pharisees, you will never enter the kingdom of heaven.

"You have heard that it was said to the men of old, 'You shall not kill; and whoever kills shall be liable to judgment.' But I say to you that every one who is angry with his brother shall be liable to judgment; whoever insults his brother shall be liable to the council, and whoever says, 'You fool!' shall be liable to the hell of fire. So if you are offering your gift at the altar, and there remember that your brother has something against you, leave your gift there before the altar and go; first be reconciled to your brother, and them come and offer your gift. Make friends quickly with your accuser, while you are going with him to court, lest your accuser hand you over to the judge, and the judge to the guard, and you be put in prison; truly, I say to you, you will never get out till you have paid the last penny.

"You have heard that it was said, 'You shall not commit adultery.' But I say to you that every one who looks at a woman lustfully has already committed adultery with her in his heart.

"If your right eye causes you to sin, pluck it out and throw it away; it is better that you lose one of your members than that your whole body be thrown into hell. And if your right hand causes you to sin, cut it off and throw it away; it is better that you lose one of your members than that your whole body go into hell.

"It was also said, 'Whoever divorces his wife, let him give her a certificate of divorce.' But I say to you that every one who divorces his wife, except on the ground of unchastity, makes her an adulteress; and whoever marries a divorced woman commits adultery.

"Again you have heard that it was said to the men of old, 'You shall not swear falsely, but shall perform to the Lord what you have sworn.' But I say to you, Do not swear at all, either by heaven, for it is the throne of God, or by the earth, for it is his footstool, or by Jerusalem, for it is the city of the great King. And do not swear by your head, for you cannot make one hair white or black. Let what you say be simply 'Yes' or 'No'; anything more than this comes from evil.

"You have heard that it was said, 'An eye for an eye and a tooth for a tooth.' But I say to you,

Do not resist one who is evil. But if any one strikes you on the right cheek, turn to him the other also; and if any one would sue you and take your coat, let him have your cloak as well; and if any one forces you to go one mile, go with him two miles. Give to him who begs from you, and do not refuse him who would borrow from you.

"You have heard that it was said, 'You shall love your neighbor and hate your enemy.' But I say to you, Love your enemies and pray for those who persecute you, so that you may be sons of your Father who is in heaven; for he makes his sun rise on the evil and on the good, and sends rain on the just and on the unjust. For if you love those who love you, what reward have you? Do not even the tax collectors do the same? And if you salute only your brethren, what more are you doing than others? Do not even the Gentiles do the same? You, therefore, must be perfect, as your heavenly Father is perfect.

QUESTIONS

1. The Sermon on the Mount was written down and preserved for later generations but it had originally been delivered orally. How might the transformation of the spoken to the written word affect the impact of the original message?

2. How does the Sermon resemble earlier expressions of the Jewish moral tradition?

3. How does Jesus elaborate on the Hebrew law?

4. To whom is Jesus' message principally directed? Is it to the rich and powerful or the humble? What is his advice?

5. Jesus taught his message through sermons, but he also demonstrated special powers. How did he do this?

25

■ *St. Paul* ■

EPISTLE TO THE ROMANS

(CA. C.E. 57)

Paul was born in the city of Tarsus in Asia Minor sometime in the first century. His family were Romanized Jews, and Paul may have been trained as a rabbi as well as in the trade of tent-making, which he later practiced. Though there is little evidence to suggest that Paul ever met Jesus, he came into contact with Jesus' teachings while in Jerusalem. He was initially of the common opinion that Jesus was a heretic and a troublemaker, but after Jesus' crucifixion, Paul began to rethink his position. His conversion to Christianity came while he was on a trip to Damascus. After retreating to the desert to meditate, Paul embarked upon a series of missions to help spread the Gospel of Jesus throughout the Roman world. He was received no better than was Jesus by the Roman authorities, who beat and imprisoned him for his opinions. Paul is thought to have met his death at the hands of Emperor Nero in C.E. 64.

While traveling, Paul wrote letters to the small congregations of Christians that he had visited. These epistles were probably meant to be read aloud during services; through them Paul sought to settle points of doctrine and to exhort the listeners to lead a Christian life. The Epistle to the Romans was sent to one of the Christian congregations in Rome and set out many of Paul's central theological views.

To all God's beloved in Rome, who are called to be saints:

Grace to you and peace from God our Father and the Lord Jesus Christ.

First, I thank my God through Jesus Christ for all of you, because your faith is proclaimed in all the world. For God is my witness, whom I serve with my spirit in the gospel of his Son, that without ceasing I mention you always in my prayers, asking that somehow by God's will I may now at last succeed in coming to you. For I long to see you, that I may impart to you some spiritual gift to strengthen you, that is, that we may be mutually encouraged by each other's faith, both yours and mine. I want you to know, brethren, that I have often intended to come to you (but thus far have been prevented), in order that I may reap some harvest among you as well as among the rest of the Gentiles.

I am under obligation both to Greeks and to barbarians, both to the wise and to the foolish: so I am eager to preach the gospel to you also who are in Rome.

For I am not ashamed of the gospel: it is the power of God for salvation to every one who has faith, to the Jew first and also to the Greek.

For in it the righteousness of God is revealed through faith for faith; as it is written, "He who through faith is righteous shall live."

For the wrath of God is revealed from heaven against all ungodliness and wickedness of men who by their wickedness suppress the truth. For what can be known about God is plain to them, because God has shown it to them. Ever since the creation of the world his invisible nature, namely, his eternal power and deity, has been clearly perceived in the things that have been made. So they are without excuse; for although they knew God they did not honor him as God or give thanks to him, but they became futile in their thinking and their senseless minds were darkened. Claiming to be wise, they became fools, and exchanged the glory of the immortal God for images resembling mortal man or birds or animals or reptiles.

Therefore God gave them up in the lusts of their hearts to impurity, to the dishonoring of their bodies among themselves, because they exchanged the truth about God for a lie and worshiped and served the creature rather than the Creator, who is blessed for ever! Amen.

For this reason God gave them up to dishonorable passions. Their women exchanged natural relations for unnatural, and the men likewise gave up natural relations with women and were consumed with passion for one another, men committing shameless acts with men and receiving in their own persons the due penalty for their error.

And since they did not see fit to acknowledge God, God gave them up to a base mind and to improper conduct. They were filled with all manner of wickedness, evil, covetousness, malice. Full of envy, murder, strife, deceit, malignity, they are gossips, slanderers, haters of God, insolent, haughty, boastful, inventors of evil, disobedient to parents, foolish, faithless, heartless, ruthless. Though they know God's decree that those who do such things deserve to die, they not only do them but approve those who practice them.

There is therefore now no condemnation for those who are in Christ Jesus. For the law of the Spirit of life in Christ Jesus has set me free from the law of sin and death. For God has done what the law, weakened by the flesh, could not do: sending his own Son in the likeness of sinful flesh and for sin, he condemned sin in the flesh, in order that the just requirement of the law might be fulfilled in us, who walk not according to the flesh but according to the Spirit. For those who live according to the flesh set their minds on the things of the flesh, but those who live according to the Spirit set their minds on the things of the Spirit. To set the mind on the flesh is death, but to set the mind on the Spirit is life and peace. For the mind that is set on the flesh is hostile to God; it does not submit to God's law, indeed it cannot; and those who are in the flesh cannot please God.

But you are not in the flesh, you are in the Spirit, if the Spirit of God really dwells in you. Any one who does not have the Spirit of Christ does not belong to him. But if Christ is in you, although your bodies are dead because of sin, your spirits are alive because of righteousness. If the Spirit of him who raised Jesus from the dead dwells in you, he who raised Christ Jesus from the dead will give life to your mortal bodies also through his Spirit which dwells in you.

So then, brethren, we are debtors, not to the flesh, to live according to the flesh—for if you live according to the flesh you will die, but if by the Spirit you put to death the deeds of the body you will live. For all who are led by the Spirit of God are sons of God. For you did not receive the spirit of slavery to fall back into fear, but you have received the spirit of sonship. When we cry, "Abba! Father!" it is the Spirit himself bearing witness with our spirit that we are children of God, and if children, then heirs, heirs of God and fellow heirs with Christ, provided we suffer with him in order that we may also be glorified with him.

I consider that the sufferings of this present time are not worth comparing with the glory that is to be revealed to us. For the creation waits with eager longing for the revealing of the sons of God; for the creation was subjected to futility, not of its own will but by the will of him who subjected it in hope; because the creation itself will be set free from its bondage to decay and obtain the glorious liberty of the children of God.

We know that the whole creation has been groaning in travail together until now; and not only the creation, but we ourselves, who have the first fruits of the Spirit, groan inwardly as we wait for adoption as sons, the redemption of our bodies. For in this hope we were saved. Now hope that is seen is not hope. For who hopes for what he sees? But if we hope for what we do not see, we wait for it with patience.

Likewise the Spirit helps us in our weakness, for we do not know how to pray as we ought, but the Spirit himself intercedes for us with sighs too deep for words. And he who searches the hearts of men knows what is the mind of the Spirit, because the Spirit intercedes for the saints according to the will of God.

We know that in everything God works for good with those who love him, who are called according to his purpose. For those whom he foreknew he also predestined to be conformed to the image of his Son, in order that he might be the first-born among many brethren. And those whom he predestined he also called; and those whom he called he also justified; and those whom he justified he also glorified.

What then shall we say to this? If God is for us, who is against us? He who did not spare his own Son but gave him up for us all, will he not also give us all things with him? Who shall bring any charge against God's elect? It is God who justifies; who is to condemn? It is Christ Jesus, who died, yes, who was raised from the dead, who is at the right hand of God, who indeed intercedes for us? Who shall separate us from the love of Christ? Shall tribulation, or distress, or persecution, or famine, or nakedness, or peril, or sword? As it is written,

"For thy sake we are being killed all the day long; we are regarded as sheep to be slaughtered."

No, in all these things we are more than conquerors through him who loved us. For I am sure that neither death, nor life, nor angels, nor principalities, nor things present, nor things to come, nor powers, nor height, nor depth, nor anything else in all creation, will be able to separate us from the love of God in Christ Jesus our Lord.

I appeal to you therefore, brethren, by the mercies of God, to present your bodies as a living sacrifice, holy and acceptable to God, which is your spiritual worship. Do not be conformed to this world, but be transformed by the renewal of your mind, that you may prove what is the will of God, what is good and acceptable and perfect.

For by the grace given to me I bid every one among you not to think of himself more highly than he ought to think, but to think with sober judgment, each according to the measure of faith which God has assigned him. For as in one body we have many members, and all the members do not have the same function, so we, though many, are one body in Christ, and individually members one of another. Having gifts that differ according to the grace given to us, let us use them: if prophecy, in proportion to our faith; if service, in our serving; he who teaches, in his teaching; he who exhorts, in his exhortation; he who contributes, in liberality; he who gives aid, with zeal; he who does acts of mercy, with cheerfulness.

Let love be genuine; hate what is evil, hold fast to what is good; love one another with brotherly affection; outdo one another in showing honor. Never flag in zeal, be aglow with the Spirit, serve the Lord. Rejoice in your hope, be patient in tribulation, be constant in prayer. Contribute to the needs of the saints, practice hospitality.

Bless those who persecute you; bless and do not curse them. Rejoice with those who rejoice, weep with those who weep. Live in harmony with one another; do not be haughty, but associate with the lowly; never be conceited. Repay no one evil for evil but take thought for what is noble in the sight of all. If possible, so far as it depends upon you, live peaceably with all. Beloved, never avenge yourselves, but leave it to the wrath of God; for it is written, "Vengeance is mine, I will repay, says the Lord."

No, "if your enemy is hungry, feed him; if he is thirsty, give him drink; for by so doing you will heap burning coals upon his head." Do not be overcome by evil, but overcome evil with good.

Let every person be subject to the governing authorities. For there is no authority except from God, and those that exist have been instituted by God. Therefore he who resists the authorities resists what God has appointed, and those who resist will incur judgment. For rulers are not a terror to good conduct, but to bad. Would you have no fear of him who is in authority? Then do what is good, and you will receive his approval, for he is God's servant for your good. But if you do wrong, be afraid, for he does not bear the sword in vain; he is the servant of God to execute his wrath on the wrong-doer. Therefore one must be subject, not only to avoid God's wrath but also for the sake of conscience.

For the same reason you also pay taxes, for the authorities are ministers of God, attending to this very thing. Pay all of them their dues, taxes to whom taxes are due, revenue to whom revenue is due, respect to whom respect is due, honor to whom honor is due.

Owe no one anything, except to love one another; for he who loves his neighbor has fulfilled the law. The commandments, "You shall not commit adultery, You shall not kill, You shall not steal, You shall not covet," and any other commandment, are summed up in this sentence, "You shall love your neighbor as yourself."

Love does no wrong to a neighbor; therefore love is the fulfilling of the law.

Besides this you know what hour it is, how it is full time now for you to wake from sleep. For salvation is nearer to us now than when we first believed; the night is far gone, the day is at hand. Let us then cast off the works of darkness and put on the armor of light; let us conduct ourselves becomingly as in the day, not in reveling and drunkenness, not in debauchery and licentiousness, not in quarreling and jealousy. But put on the Lord Jesus Christ, and make no provision for the flesh, to gratify its desires.

QUESTIONS

1. How different is the tone and content of Paul's message from that of Jesus in the Sermon on the Mount?

2. What, according to Paul, is the fate of the nonbeliever?

3. How does the status of Christians as a persecuted minority in the Roman Empire affect Paul's thinking? How might this status be reflected in their beliefs? How should Christians cope with persecution?

4. What does Paul teach about secular authority? Is this a sensible attitude in view of the situation of Christians at the time?

5. Paul himself was raised in the Jewish tradition. Does this play a role in his religious thought?

Owe no one anything, except to love one another; for he who loves his neighbor has fulfilled the law. The commandments, "You shall not commit adultery, You shall not kill, You shall not steal, You shall not covet," and any other commandment, are summed up in this sentence, "You shall love your neighbor as yourself."...

2. What according to Paul, is the fate of the nonbeliever?

PART

II

■ ■ ■

MEDIEVAL EUROPE

THE EARLY MIDDLE AGES
26. Tacitus, *Germania* (98)
27. Eusebius, *In Praise of Constantine* (336)
28. Augustine of Hippo, *The City of God* (413–426)
29. Benedict of Nursia, *Rule of Saint Benedict* (ca. 535–540)
30. *The Burgundian Code* (ca. 474)
31. Gregory of Tours, *History of the Franks* (ca. 581–591)
32. Bede, *The Ecclesiastical History of England* (731)
33. Einhard, *The Life of Charlemagne* (ca. 829–836)

ISLAM AND THE EASTERN EMPIRE
34. Justinian, *Code* (529–565)
35. Procopius, *Secret History* (ca. 560)
36. *The Koran* (7th century)
37. Michael Psellus, *Chronographia* (ca. 1075–1077)
38. Ibn Al-Qalanisi, *The Damascus Chronicle* (ca. 1150)
39. Ibn Ishaq, *The Life of Muhammad* (after 733)

THE HIGH MIDDLE AGES
40. *Feudal Documents* (11th–13th centuries)
41. Bernard of Angers, *Miracles of St. Foy* (ca. 1010)
42. Fulcher of Chartres, *The First Crusade and the Siege of Jerusalem* (1101–1127)
43. *The Song of Roland* (ca. 1100)
44. *Magna Carta* (1215)
45. Francis of Assisi, *Admonitions* (ca. 1220)

46. Thomas Aquinas, *Summa Theologica* (1266–1273)
47. Dante, *The Divine Comedy* (ca. 1320)
48. Catherine of Siena, *Letters* (1376)
49. Christine de Pisan, *The Book of the City of Ladies* (ca. 1405)
50. Margaret Paston, *Letters* (1441–1448)

THE EARLY MIDDLE AGES

26

■ *Tacitus* ■

GERMANIA

(98)

Cornelius Tacitus (ca. 56–120) was the greatest of the Roman historians. Little is known of his early life, but he must have come from comfortable surroundings, since he was trained for a public career. He practiced law and moved up the ranks of public service, benefiting from his marriage to the daughter of Julius Agricola, governor of Britain. Elected consul in 97, Tacitus distinguished himself by his oratory. It appears that soon afterward he retired from public life to devote himself to writing, although he served as proconsul of Asia in 112. Both a biographer and a scholar of recent Roman history, Tacitus prepared a biography of his father-in-law as well as his *History,* which ended just before his consulship.

The *Germania* (C.E. 98) was one of Tacitus' earliest works, describing firsthand the customs and characteristics of the Germanic tribes living on the Roman frontier. It remains a principal source for understanding Roman attitudes toward other peoples and for re-creating early Germanic life. *Germania*'s description of German society is the most detailed we have before the tribes converted to Christianity, and therefore has often been cited by scholars interested in periods considerably later than when Tacitus wrote.

The people of Germany appear to me indigenous, and free from intermixture with foreigners, either as settlers or casual visitants. For the emigrants of former ages performed their expeditions not by land, but by water; and that immense, and, if I may so call it, hostile ocean, is rarely navigated by ships from our world. Then, besides the dangers of a boisterous and unknown sea, who would relinquish Asia, Africa, or Italy, for Germany, a land rude in its surface, rigorous in its climate, cheerless to every beholder and cultivator, except a native?

In the election of kings they have regard to birth; in that of generals, to valor. Their kings have not an absolute or unlimited power; and their generals command less through the force of authority than of example. If they are daring, adventurous, and conspicuous in action, they procure obedience from the admiration they inspire. None, however, but the priests are permitted to judge offenders, to inflict bonds or stripes; so that chastisement appears not as an act of military discipline, but as the instigation of the god whom they suppose present with warriors. They also carry with them to battle certain images and standards taken from the sacred groves.

Tradition relates that armies beginning to give way have been rallied by the females, through the earnestness of their supplications, the interposition of their bodies, and the pictures they have drawn of impending slavery, a calamity which these people bear with more impatience for their women than themselves; so that those states who have been obliged to give among their hostages the daughters of noble families, are the most effectually bound to fidelity. They even suppose somewhat of sanctity and prescience to be inherent in the female sex; and therefore neither despise their counsels, nor disregard their responses. We have beheld, in the reign of Vespasian, Veleda, long reverenced by many as a deity. Aurima, moreover, and several others, were formerly held in equal veneration, but not with a servile flattery, nor as though they made them goddesses.

No people are more addicted to divination by omens and lots. The latter is performed in the following simple manner. They cut a twig from a fruit-tree, and divide it into small pieces, which, distinguished by certain marks, are thrown promiscuously upon a white garment. Then, the priest of the canton, if the occasion be public; if private, the master of the family; after an invocation of the gods, with his eyes lifted up to heaven, thrice takes out each piece, and, as they come up, interprets their signification according to the marks fixed upon them. If the result prove unfavorable, there is no more consultation on the same affair that day; if propitious, a confirmation by omens is still required. In common with other nations, the Germans are acquainted with the practice of auguring from the notes and flight of birds; but it is peculiar to them to derive admonitions and presages from

horses also. Certain of these animals, milk-white, and untouched by earthly labor, are pastured at the public expense in the sacred woods and groves. These, yoked to a consecrated chariot, are accompanied by the priest, and king, or chief person of the community, who attentively observe their manner of neighing and snorting; and no kind of augury is more credited, not only among the populace, but among the nobles and priests. For the latter consider themselves as the ministers of the gods, and the horses, as privy to the divine will. Another kind of divination, by which they explore the event of momentous wars, is to oblige a prisoner, taken by any means whatsoever from the nation with whom they are at variance, to fight with a picked man of their own, each with his own country's arms; and, according as the victory falls, they presage success to the one or to the other party.

The Germans transact no business, public or private, without being armed: but it is not customary for any person to assume arms till the state has approved his ability to use them. Then, in the midst of the assembly, either one of the chiefs, or the father, or a relation, equips the youth with a shield and javelin. These are to them the manly gown; this is the first honor conferred on youth; before this they are considered as part of a household: afterward, of the state. The dignity of chieftain is bestowed even on mere lads, whose descent is eminently illustrious, or whose fathers have performed signal services to the public; they are associated, however, with those of mature strength, who have already been declared capable of service; nor do they blush to be seen in the rank of companions. For the state of companionship itself has its several degrees, determined by the judgment of him whom they follow; and there is a great emulation among the companions, which shall possess the highest place in the favor of their chief; and among the chiefs, which shall excel in the number and valor of his companions. It is their dignity, their strength, to be always surrounded with a large body of select youth, an ornament in peace, a bulwark in war. And not in his own country alone, but among the neighboring states, the fame and glory of each chief consists in being distinguished for the number and bravery of his companions. Such chiefs are courted by embassies; distinguished by presents; and often by their reputation alone decide a war.

In the field of battle, it is disgraceful for the chief to be surpassed in valor; it is disgraceful for the companions not to equal their chief; but it is reproach and infamy during a whole succeeding life to retreat from the field surviving him. To aid, to protect him; to place their own gallant actions to the account of his glory, is their first and most sacred engagement. The chiefs fight for victory; the companions for their chief. If their native country be long sunk in peace and inaction, many of the young nobles repair to some other state then engaged in war. For, besides that repose is unwelcome to their race, and toils and perils afford them a better opportunity of distinguishing themselves; they are unable, without war and violence, to maintain a large train of followers. The companion requires from the liberality of his chief, the warlike steed, the bloody and conquering spear; and in place of pay he expects to be supplied with a table, homely indeed, but plentiful. The funds for this munificence must be found in war and rapine; nor are they so easily persuaded to cultivate the earth, and await the produce of the seasons, as to challenge the foe, and expose themselves to wounds; nay, they even think it base and spiritless to earn by sweat what they might purchase with blood.

During the intervals of war, they pass their time less in hunting than in a sluggish repose, divided between sleep and the table. All the bravest of the warriors, committing the care of the house, the family affairs, and the lands, to the women, old men, and weaker part of the domestics, stupefy themselves in inaction: so wonderful is the contrast presented by nature, that

the same persons love indolence, and hate tranquility! It is customary for the several states to present, by voluntary and individual contributions, cattle or grain to their chiefs; which are accepted as honorary gifts, while they serve as necessary supplies. They are peculiarly pleased with presents from neighboring nations, offered not only by individuals, but by the community at large; such as fine horses, heavy armor, rich housing, and gold chains. We have now taught them also to accept of money.

It is well known that none of the German nations inhabit cities, or even admit of contiguous settlements. They dwell scattered and separate, as a spring, a meadow, or a grove may chance to invite them. Their villages are laid out, not like ours in rows of adjoining buildings; but every one surrounds his house with a vacant space, either by way of security against fire, or through ignorance of the art of building. For, indeed, they are unacquainted with the use of mortar and tiles; and for every purpose employ rude unshapen timber, fashioned with no regard to pleasing the eye. They bestow more than ordinary pains in coating certain parts of their buildings with a kind of earth, so pure and shining that it gives the appearance of painting.

The dress of the women does not differ from that of the men; except that they more frequently wear linen, which they stain with purple, and do not lengthen their upper garment into sleeves, but leave exposed the whole arm, and part of the breast.

The matrimonial bond is, nevertheless, strict and severe among them; nor is there any thing in their manners more commendable than this. Almost singly among the barbarians, they content themselves with one wife; a very few of them excepted, who, not through incontinence, but because their alliance is solicited on account of their rank, practice polygamy. The wife does not bring a dowry to her husband, but receives one from him. The parents and relations assemble, and pass their approbation on the presents—presents not adapted to please a female taste, or decorate the bride; but oxen, a caparisoned steed, a shield, a spear, and sword. By virtue of these, the wife is espoused; and she in her turn makes a present of some arms to her husband. This they consider as the firmest bond of union; these, the sacred mysteries, the conjugal deities. That the woman may not think herself excused from exertions of fortitude, or exempt from the casualties of war, she is admonished by the very ceremonial of her marriage, that she comes to her husband as a partner in toils and dangers; to suffer and to dare equally with him, in peace and in war; this is indicated by the yoked oxen, the harnessed steed, the offered arms. Thus she is to live; thus to die. She receives what she is to return inviolate and honored to her children; what her daughters-in-law are to receive, and again transmit to her grandchildren.

They live, therefore, fenced around with chastity, corrupted by no seductive spectacles, no convivial incitements. Men and women are alike unacquainted with clandestine correspondence. Adultery is extremely rare among so numerous a people. Its punishment is instant, and at the pleasure of the husband. He cuts off the hair of the offender, strips her, and in presence of her relations expels her from his house, and pursues her with stripes through the whole village. Nor is any indulgence shown to a prostitute. Neither beauty, youth, nor riches can procure her a husband; for none there looks on vice with a smile, or calls mutual seduction the way of the world. Still more exemplary is the practice of those states in which none but virgins marry, and the expectations and wishes of a wife are at once brought to a period. Thus, they take one husband as one body and one life; that no thought, no desire, may extend beyond him; and he may be loved not only as their husband, but as their marriage. To limit the increase of children, or put to death any of the later progeny, is accounted infamous: and good habits have there more influence than good laws elsewhere.

QUESTIONS

1. Tacitus's view of the Germans is that of an outsider looking in. How might his background affect his description?

2. How is German society organized? Who bears authority within it, and how do they achieve power?

3. Why is German society so warlike? What purpose does warfare serve among the Germanic tribes?

4. What is the family life of the Germans like?

5. Implicit in Tacitus's account of the morals of the Germans is a comment on the Romans of his own time. What do you think he is trying to say?

27

■ *Eusebius* ■

IN PRAISE OF CONSTANTINE
(336)

Eusebius of Caesarea (ca. 260–339), bishop and historian, was born in Palestine. Very little is known about his early life though there is some reason to believe that he was imprisoned as a Christian during the persecutions of Emperor Diocletian in 303. Eusebius lived and wrote in the twilight period often described as "the late antique": an age when the certainties of the old Roman order were beginning to give way as the advance of Christianity and barbarian invasions shattered the empire, creating a new kind of society. Active as a Christian teacher, Eusebius wrote one of the first histories of the Christian Church. He became bishop of Palestine in 313, and during his time there took part in the controversy over Arianism—which claimed that Jesus was not of the same substance as God. Eusebius was briefly excommunicated for his Arian views.

The Only-Begotten Logos of God endures with His Father as co-ruler from ages that have no beginning to ages that have no end. Similarly, His friend, supplied from above by royal streams and confirmed in the name of a divine calling, rules on earth for long periods of years. As the Universal Savior renders the entire heaven and earth and highest kingdom fit for His Father, so His friend, leading his subjects on earth to the Only-Begotten and Savior Logos, makes them suitable for His kingdom. Again, our common Universal Savior, by invisible and divine power, keeps the rebellious powers—all those who used to fly through the earth's air and infect men's souls—at a distance, just as a good shepherd keeps wild beasts from his flock. And His friend, armed against his enemies with standards from Him above, subdues and chastizes the visible opponents of truth by the law of combat.

This man now honored by the All-Ruling God with a triple period of decades, alone, of all who ever have ruled the Empire of the Romans, concludes this Jubilee not in the ancient way with offerings to the nether spirits, nor to the spectres of demons who deceive the people, nor to the foolish deceits of godless men, but rather to the One who has honored him. Aware of the benefits bestowed on him, he makes repayment, not by polluting the royal halls in the ancient way with blood and gore, nor by appeasing the underworld demons with smoke and fire and sacrifices of wholly burnt beasts, but by the sacrifice pleasing and fitting to this same Universal Sovereign, that is, by dedicating to Him his own royal soul and a mind thoroughly worthy of God. For that sacrifice alone is pleasing to Him which our own sovereign has, through reckoning purified to accord with the intent, learned to make acceptable without fire and bloodshed. Strengthening the dictates of piety with his soul's unerring doctrines, he honors the divine Reason with the best of human reasons, seeking to emulate in royal deeds the benevolence of the Higher Power. Entirely dedicated to Him, he has himself rendered a great offering, the firstfruit of the world with which he is entrusted, himself. This greatest sacrifice the sovereign performs on behalf of all together.

And He, delighting in such an offering and welcoming gladly the gift, values the minister of a sacrifice both holy and fit, and bestows on him additional long periods of rule, increasing the benefits in return for the rites paid Him. And He allows him to carry out every one of his celebrations with great relief from the burden of sole rule, having readied some one of his sons for partnership in the royal throne at each tenth anniversary, as if to prolong the bloom of a flourishing plant. He enlarges his Imperial power by the ungrudging association of his relatives. And so, by the appointment of the Caesars, He fulfills the predictions of the divine prophets, which ages and ages ago proclaimed that "the saints of the Most High, shall take up the kingdom." Thus surely has God Himself, the Ruler of All, who has given this bounty of years and offspring to the most God-beloved ruler, made his leadership of the peoples on earth to be young and blooming as if just now beginning to bear. He Himself makes possible this celebration, since He has designated him Victor over all rivals and foreign foes, and thus revealed a model of piety and truth to all on earth. Meanwhile, as the light of the sun shines upon settlers in the most remote lands by the rays sent off from itself into the distance, so too does he assign, like beacons and lamps of the brilliance emanating from himself, this son here to us who inhabit the East, an offspring worthy of himself; and another of his sons to the other division of mankind, and yet another elsewhere. Thus, having yoked the four valiant Caesars like colts beneath the single yoke of the Imperial chariot, he controls them with the reins of holy harmony and concord. Holding the reins high above them, he rides along, traversing all lands alike that the sun gazes upon, himself present everywhere and watching over everything.

Thus outfitted in the likeness of the kingdom of heaven, he pilots affairs below with an upward gaze, to steer by the archetypal form. He grows strong in his model of monarchic rule, which the Ruler of All has given to the race of man alone of those on earth. For this is the law of royal authority, the law which decrees one rule over everybody. Monarchy excels all other kinds of constitution and government. For rather do anarchy and civil war result from the alternative, a polyarchy based on equality. For which reason there is One God, not two or three or even more. For strictly speaking, belief in many gods is godless. There is one Sovereign, and His Logos and royal law is one, not expressed in words or syllables nor eroded by time in books or tables, but the living and actual God the Logos, who directs His Father's kingdom for all those under and beneath Him. Heavenly armies encircle Him, an infinite number of supernatural troops, including God's attendant angels and those invisible spirits within heaven who see to the order of the whole cosmos—over all of whom the royal Logos takes precedence as a kind of prefect of the Supreme Sovereign. Him the voices of men learned in God have acclaimed in prophecy as Supreme Commander and Chief High Priest, Prophet of the Father and Carrier of Great Counsel, Radiance of the Paternal Light and Sole-Begotten Son, and by countless other titles. He it is whom His Parent ordained living Logos, law and wisdom, and fruition of every good, and gave to all in His domain, a gift of the highest quality. And He, pervading the whole and travelling everywhere, unfolding His Father's favors ungrudgingly to all, has provided a model of the royal power even unto reasoning beings on earth by outfitting the soul of man, which is fashioned according to His own image, with divine powers, so that it is able to partake of all the other benefits that flow from the divine stream. For He who alone is God alone is wisdom. He alone is good in His very essence. He alone is strong in real strength, and the Parent of Justice itself, the Father of Reason and Wisdom, the Source of light and life, the Holder of Truth and Virtue, and so the Leader of the Empire itself, and of every form of rule and power.

But how came it to man to perceive these things? Who brought them to human hearing? How can matters that are not of flesh and the body be elucidated by a tongue of flesh? Who has seen the Invisible Sovereign and beheld these powers in Him? By physical senses we comprehend kindred elements and compounds made of these, but no one ever has prided himself on having seen the invisible, transcendent kingdom with mortal eyes, nor has human nature comprehended Wisdom in its own beauty. Who has looked on the face of Justice with his physical senses? So how did the concepts of legitimate authority and royal power ever penetrate men's minds? How does the principle of autocracy occur to solid flesh and blood? Who made known to those on earth Ideas, which are invisible and formless, or Essence, incorporeal and shapeless? So there had to be a medium for these things, the one, all-pervading Logos of God, the Father of the rational and intellectual faculty in men, alone endowed with the Father's divinity, who channels the paternal emanations into His own progeny. Hence the natural and instinctive reasoning powers in all men, alike Greek and barbarian; hence the concepts of Reason and Wisdom; hence the seeds of Prudence and Justice; hence apprehension of skills; hence knowledge of Virtue and the sweet name of Wisdom, and noble passion for the training of philosophy; hence knowledge of all goodness and beauty; hence the ability to conceive of God Himself, and a life worthy of God's service; hence man's regal force and irresistible sway over everything on earth. Wherefore let the friend of the All-Ruling God be proclaimed our sole sovereign with truth as witness, the only one who is truly free, or rather truly a lord. Above care for money, stronger than the passion for women, victor of physical pleasures and demands, the conqueror, not the captive, of ill-temper and wrath, this man truly is the Autokrator, bearing the title that conforms to his moral conduct. Really a Victor is he who has triumphed over the passions which have overcome mankind, who has modelled himself after the archetypal form of the Supreme Sovereign, whose thoughts mirror its virtuous rays, by which he has been made perfectly wise, good, just, courageous, pious, and God-loving. Truly, therefore, is only this man a philosopher-king, who knows himself and understands the showers of every blessing which descend on him from outside, or rather, from heaven. He makes manifest the august title of monarchical authority in the remarkable fabric of his robes, since he alone deserves to wear the royal purple which so becomes him. This is a sovereign who calls on the Heavenly Father night and day, who petitions Him in his prayers, who yearns for the highest kingdom. Far from thinking his present state comparable to that of the All-Ruling God, he is aware that the mortal and perishable state is like a river, ever-flowing and vanishing. And so he longs for the incorruptible and spiritual kingdom of God, and he prays to come into it. Through exalted contemplation he has raised his thoughts beyond the heavenly vault, and now he cherishes in his heart an indescribable longing for the lights there, by comparison with which he judges the honors of his present life to be no more than darkness. For he recognizes that rule over men is a small and fleeting authority over a mortal and temporary life, not much greater than the rule exercised by goatherds or shepherds or cowherds—in fact, he considers the job more troublesome and the creatures harder to satisfy. The cheers of the crowds and the voices of flatterers he holds more a nuisance than a pleasure, because of his stern character and the upright rearing of his soul.

Not even the sight of his entourage of attendants, the myriads of his armies, the subservient and obedient multitudes of heavy-armed men both on foot and horse alike, excites him, nor is he made swell-headed by his rule over all these. Turning his attention inward, he sees in himself the nature common to all. He laughs at his raiment, interwoven with gold, finished with intricate blossoms, his royal robe with the diadem itself, when he sees the people astounded and marvelling at the sight, like children at a hobgoblin. He himself has experienced no such sensation, but through acquaintance with the divine he clothes his soul in raiment embroidered with temperance and justice, piety and the remaining virtues, truly the fitting attire for a sovereign. As for those valuables longed for by the many, I mean gold and silver and that type of stone that makes men gape, these he takes for exactly what they are: simple stones, useless and worthless stuff, in no way able to provide defense against evil. For what power have these things to provide relief from illness or escape from death? All the same, even though he knows this, with dispassionate reasoning he skillfully arranges for their use out of regard for his subjects' sense of proper style, all the while amused at those who in their naïveté are distracted by such things. Yet from drinking bouts and drunkenness and delicate dishes such as are relished by gluttons he abstains, assuming that these things may be suitable for others, but not for himself. For he is convinced such things cause damage to higher faculties and impair the intellectual part of the soul. Because of all these things, the high-minded sovereign, learned in divine matters, pursues things higher than his present life, calling on the Father who is in heaven and longing for His kingdom, doing all things with piety and holding out to his subjects, just as if they were students of a good teacher, the holy knowledge of the Supreme Sovereign.

And now accounts, teachings, and exhortations to a moderate and God-fearing life are heralded for all nations to hear, and the sovereign himself is the herald. Yes, this is surely the greatest miracle—that so great a sovereign has cried out at the top of his voice to the whole world and, like some interpreter of the All-Ruling God, has summoned all under his care alike to knowledge of The Being. No longer as formerly do the babblings of godless men fill the royal chambers, but rather priests and celebrants of God now keep solemn festival with hymns to the royal piety. The One God Himself, the Universal Sovereign, is proclaimed to all, and the joyous word of His benefits binds the race of mankind to the Ruler of All, bringing the good news that the Heavenly Father is gracious and loving to His sons on earth. Choruses of all kinds honor Him with victory odes, and the entire moral race chimes in with the angelic revellers in heaven. As through musical instruments, rational souls send up to Him through the bodies which enclose them fitting hymns and due praise. Together with those who live in the East, those allotted the West are trained in His teaching at the same moment of time, and with those in the South those allotted the Northern sphere sing out a harmonious strain: to pursue the pious life under the same customs and laws; to praise one God who is over all; to acknowledge one Only-Begotten Savior, the cause of all good things; and to recognize also one sovereign, rector of the earth, and his sons beloved of God.

He, meanwhile, like some wise pilot riding on high over the rudder to pursue a direct route, steers by a favorable Sign and conveys all under him to a safe and calm anchorage. So God Himself, the Supreme Sovereign, stretches out His right hand to him from above and confirms him victor over every pretender and aggressor. Augmenting the sway of his kingdom by long periods of years, He intends to declare him a partner of greater goods, to confirm to him with deeds those personal promises which the present occasion does not permit me to discuss further, but which must await the journey thither, because surely it is not possible for the divine nature to be comprehended by mortal eyes and ears of flesh.

QUESTIONS

1. What is the status of the emperor? Where does his authority come from?

2. What is the emperor's primary duty to God? To his subjects?

3. Do you think that Eusebius's work pleased Constantine? How might the emperor use Eusebius's work to his own advantage?

4. In what way is Eusebius's message advantageous for the Christian Church?

5. What does Eusebius believe is the best form of government? Why does he think so?

6. What are the qualities of the perfect Christian monarch?

28

■ *Augustine of Hippo* ■

THE CITY OF GOD

(413–426)

North Africa

Augustine of Hippo (354–430) was the most important Christian philosopher and theologian of late antiquity. Born in Roman North Africa, the son of a pagan father and a devoutly Christian mother, Augustine himself remained pagan until adulthood. Although his family was not rich, he was sent for schooling at Carthage, where he developed a taste and aptitude for philosophy. At the age of thirty-two, he converted to Christianity and became a priest in 391. He recounted the story of his inner struggles in *The Confessions* (ca. 400), one of the most famous of all Christian autobiographies. In 396, Augustine was consecrated Bishop of Hippo, a position he held until his death. There he combined pastoral duties with the writing of major theological and philosophical works. His great achievement was a synthesis of classical and Christian traditions. He died when Hippo was besieged by the Vandals in 430.

The City of God (413–426) was Augustine's major work. It provides a summary of Christian thought at the moment when the Roman Empire was under siege and has become the heart of the Catholic Church's doctrines. His work was particularly important to Catholics in the Middle Ages. Augustine contrasts the world of corruption and sin inhabited by humans with God's world of blissful perfection. *heaven*

City of ~~heaven heaven~~ and City of men

Of that part of the work wherein the demonstration of the beginnings and ends of the two cities, the heavenly and the earthly, are declared

We give the name of the city of God unto that society whereof that scripture bears witness, which has gained the most exalted authority and pre-eminence over all other works whatsoever, by the disposing of the divine providence, not the chance decisions of men's judgments. For there it is said: 'Glorious things are spoken of thee, thou city of God': and in another place: 'Great is the Lord, and greatly to be praised in the city of our God, even upon His holy mountain, increasing the joy of all the earth.' And by and by in the same psalm: 'As we have heard, so have we seen in the city of the Lord of Hosts, in the city of our God: God has established it for ever.' And in another: 'The rivers' streams shall make glad the city of God, the most High sanctified His tabernacle, God is in the midst of it unmoved.' These testimonies, and thousands more, teach us that there is a city of God, whereof His inspired love makes us desire to be members. The earthly citizens prefer their gods before this heavenly city's holy Founder, knowing not that He is the God of gods, not of those false, wicked, and proud ones, (which lacking His light so universal and unchangeable, and being thereby reduced to a state of extreme need, each one follows his own state, as it were, and begs divine honours of his deluded servants), but of the godly and holy ones, who select their own submission to Him, rather than the world's to them, and love rather to worship Him their God, than to be worshipped for gods themselves. And now, knowing what is next expected of me, as my promise—viz. to dispute (as far as my poor talent allows) of the origin, progress, and consummation of the two cities that in this world lie confusedly together, by the assistance of the same God and King of ours, I set pen to paper, intending first to show the beginning of these two, arising from the difference between the angelical powers.

The state of the two cities, the heavenly and the earthly

Two loves therefore have given origin to these two cities, self-love in contempt of God unto the earthly, love of God in contempt of one's self to the heavenly. The first seeks the glory of men, and the latter desires God only as the testimony of the conscience, the greatest glory. That glories in itself, and this in God. That exalts itself in self-glory: this says to God: 'My glory and the lifter up of my head.' That boasts of the ambitious conquerors led by the lust of sovereignty: in this all serve each other in charity, both the rulers in counselling and the subjects in obeying. That loves worldly virtue in the potentates: this says unto God: 'I will love thee, O Lord, my strength.' And the wise men of that follow either the good things of the body, or mind, or both: living according to the flesh; and such as might know God; 'honoured Him not as God, nor were thankful, but became vain in their own imaginations, and their foolish heart was darkened; for professing themselves to be wise, that is, extolling themselves proudly in their wisdom, they became fools; changing the glory of the incorruptible God to the likeness of the image of a corruptible man, and of birds and four-footed beasts and serpents': for they were the people's guides or followers unto all those idolatries, and served the creature more than the Creator who is blessed for ever. But in this other, this heavenly city, there is no wisdom of man, but only the piety that serves the true God and expects a reward in the society of the holy angels, and men, that God may be all in all.

Of the two contrary courses taken by the human race from the beginning

Of the place and felicity of the local paradise, together with man's life and fall therein, there are many opinions, many assertions, and many books, as several men thought, spoke, and wrote. What we held hereof, or could gather out of holy scriptures, correspondent unto their truth and authority, we related in some of the foregoing books. If they be farther looked into, they will give birth to more questions and longer disputations than we have now room for. Our time is not so large as to permit us to argue scrupulously upon every question that may be asked by busy heads that are more curious of inquiry than capable of understanding. I think we have sufficiently discussed the doubts concerning the beginning of the world, the soul, and mankind; which last is divided into two sorts, such as live according to man, and such as live according to God. These we mystically call two cities or societies, the one predestined to being eternally with God, the other condemned in perpetual torment with the devil. This is their end, of which hereafter. Now seeing we have said sufficient concerning their origin, both in the angels whose number we know not, and in the two first parents of mankind, I think it fit to pass on to their progression from man's first offspring until he cease to beget anymore. All the time included between these two points, wherein the livers ever succeed the diers, is the progression of these two cities. Cain therefore was the first begotten of those two that were mankind's parents, and he belongs to the city man; Abel was the later, and he belongs to the city of God. For as we see that in an individual man (as the apostle says) that which is spiritual is not first, but that which is natural first, and then the spiritual (whereupon all that comes from Adam's corrupted nature must needs be evil and carnal at first, and then if a man be regenerate by Christ, becomes good and spiritual afterward): so in the first propagation of man, and progression of the two cities of which we dispute, the carnal citizen was born first, and the pilgrim on earth or heavenly citizen afterwards, being by grace predestined, and by grace elected, by grace a pilgrim upon earth, and by grace a citizen in heaven. For as for his birth; it was out of the same corrupted mass that was condemned from the beginning; but God like a potter (for this simile the apostle himself

uses) out of the same lump, made 'one vessel to honour and another to reproach.' The vessel of reproach was made first, and the vessel of honour afterwards. For in each individual, as I said, there is first reprobation, whence we must needs begin (and wherein we need not remain), and afterwards goodness, to which we come by profiting, and coming thither therein make our abode. Whereupon it follows that no one can be good that has not first been evil, though all that be evil become not good; but the sooner a man betters himself the quicker does this name follow him, abolishing the memory of the other. Therefore, it is recorded of Cain that he built a city, but Abel was a pilgrim, and built none. For the city of the saints is above, though it have citizens here upon earth, wherein it lives as a pilgrim until the time of the kingdom come; and then it gathers all the citizens together in the resurrection of the body, and gives them a kingdom to reign in with their King for ever and ever.

Of the sons of the flesh and the sons of promise

The shadow and prophetical image of this city (not making it present but signifying it) served here upon earth, at the time when such a foreshadowing was needed; and was called the holy city, because it was a symbol of the city that was to be, though not the reality. Of this city serving as an image, and the free city herein prefigured, the apostle speaks thus unto the Galatians: 'Tell me, ye that desire to be under the law, do ye not hear the law? For it is written that Abraham had two sons, one by a bondwoman, and the other by a free: but the son of the bondwoman was born of the flesh, and the son of the freewoman by promise. Which things are an allegory: for these are the two Testaments, the one given from Mount Sinai, begetting man in servitude, which is Hagar; for Sinai is a mountain in Arabia, joined to the Jerusalem on earth, for it serves with her children. But our mother the celestial Jerusalem is free, for it is written: "Rejoice, thou barren that

Augustine of Hippo as depicted by Pinturicchio.

bearest not: break forth into joy, and cry out, thou that travailest not with child, for the desolate hath many more children than the married wife." But we, brethren, are the sons of promise to Isaac. But as then he that was born of the flesh persecuted him that was born after the spirit, even so it is now. But what says the scripture? "Cast out the bondwoman and her son, for the bondwoman's son shall not be heir with the freewoman's." Then, brethren, we are not children of the bondwoman, but of the free. Thus the apostle authorizes us to conceive of the Old and New Testaments. For a part of the earthly city was made an image of the heavenly, not signifying itself but another, and therefore serving: for it was not ordained

to signify itself but another, and itself was signified by another precedent type; for Hagar, Sarah's servant, and her son, were an image hereof. And because, when the light comes, the shadows must flee away, Sarah the freewoman signifying the free city (which that shadow of the earthly Jerusalem signified in another manner) said: 'Cast out the bondwoman and her son: for the bondwoman's son shall not be heir with my son Isaac': whom the apostle calls the freewoman's son. Thus then we find this earthly city in two forms; the one presenting itself, and the other prefiguring the celestial city, and serving it. Our nature corrupted by sin produces citizens of earth; and grace freeing us from the sin of nature makes us citizens of heaven: the first are called the vessels of wrath, the last of mercy. And this was signified in the two sons of Abraham, the one of whom being born of the bondwoman was called Ishmael, being the son of the flesh; the other, the freewoman's, Isaac, the son of promise. Both were Abraham's sons; but natural custom begot the first, and gracious promise the latter. In the first was a demonstration of man's use, in the second was a revelation of God's goodness.

Of the eternal felicity of the city of God, and the perpetual sabbath

How great shall that felicity be, where there shall be no evil thing, where no good thing shall lie hidden, where we shall have leisure to utter forth the praises of God, which shall be all things in all! There shall be true glory, where no man shall be praised for error or flattery. True honour, which shall be denied unto none which is worthy, shall be given unto none unworthy. But neither shall any unworthy person covet after it, where none is permitted to be but he who is worthy. There is true peace, where no man suffers anything which may molest him, either from himself or from any other. He Himself shall be reward of virtue, who has given virtue, and has promised Himself unto him, than whom nothing can be better and greater. For what other thing is that which He has said by the prophet: 'I will be their God, and they shall be My people; but 'I will be whereby they shall be satisfied: I will be whatsoever is lawfully desired of men, life, health, food, abundance, glory, honour, peace, and all good things'? For so also is that rightly understood, which the apostle says: 'That God may be all in all.' He shall be the end of our desires, who shall be seen without end, who shall be loved without any disgust, and praised without any tediousness. This function, this affection, this action verily shall be unto all, as the eternal life shall be common to all. But who is sufficient to think, much less to utter, what degrees there shall also be of the rewards for merits, of the honours and glories? But we must not doubt but that there shall be degrees. And also that blessed city shall see this in itself—that no inferior shall envy his superior, even as now the other angels do not envy the archangels; as every one will not wish to be what he has not received, although he be bound in a most peaceable bond of concord with him who has received, even as the finger does not wish to be the eye in the body, since a peaceable conjunction and knitting together of the whole flesh contains both members. Therefore one shall so have a gift less than another has, that he also has this further gift that he does not wish to have any more. By Him being restored and perfected with a greater grace we shall rest for ever, seeing that He is God, with whom we shall be replenished, when He shall be all in all.

QUESTIONS

1. How do you think that Augustine's background as an urban Roman affected his thought?

2. What is the difference between the city of God and the earthly city?

3. How, according to Augustine, do people become "residents" of the city of God?

4. Augustine does not envisage a community of social equals in the city of God. Would this, in Augustine's view, lead to conflict? Why or why not?

5. There are several clues in *The City of God* about the nature of society in late classical cities: Augustine makes assumptions about social status, for example. Judging from his work, what might you say about the real cities that Augustine knew?

29

■ *Benedict of Nursia* ■

RULE OF SAINT BENEDICT

(CA. 535–540)

Benedict of Nursia (ca. 480–547), the patron saint of Europe, played a key role in the foundation of Christian monasteries throughout the continent. Benedict came from a prosperous Italian family and was sent to Rome for his education. He grew up during a period of social and political disorder as the Roman world was fast vanishing. Benedict was shocked by the immorality and corruption that he witnessed in Rome, and in reaction he retreated to a cave outside of the city, where he lived as a hermit for three years. During this time his reputation as a holy man spread, and he was persuaded to take charge of a local monastery. Monasticism, which made its first appearance in Egypt in the fourth century, was a movement in which men and women removed themselves from worldly affairs in an attempt to create a closer bond with God. Monastics hoped to perfect their spirituality through self-mortification and scrupulous piety. His attempts to reform the monastery were not altogether successful and Benedict narrowly escaped being poisoned there. He subsequently founded his own monastery at Monte Cassino, which became the model for the Benedictine order.

Benedict's Rule was a system of regulations for a monastic order. It is a guide to life in a religious community and enjoins the residents to prayer, hard work, obedience, and hospitality. The Rule became the constitution of countless monasteries and nunneries in succeeding centuries.

What are the Instruments of Good Works.

1. First Instrument: in the first place to love the Lord God with all one's heart, all one's soul, and all one's strength.
2. Then, one's neighbour as oneself.
3. Then not to kill.
4. Not to commit adultery.
5. Not to steal.
6. Not to covet.
7. Not to bear false witness.
8. To honour all men.
9. Not to do to another what one would not have done to oneself.
10. To deny oneself, in order to follow Christ.
11. To chastise the body.
12. Not to seek after delicate living.
13. To love fasting.
14. To relieve the poor.
15. To clothe the naked.
16. To visit the sick.
17. To bury the dead.
18. To help in affliction.

19. To console the sorrowing.
20. To keep aloof from worldly actions.
21. To prefer nothing to the love of Christ.
22. Not to gratify anger.
23. Not to harbour a desire of revenge.
24. Not to foster guile in one's heart.
25. Not to make a feigned peace.
26. Not to forsake charity.
27. Not to swear, lest perchance, one forswear oneself.
28. To utter truth from heart and mouth.
29. Not to render evil for evil.
30. To do no wrong to anyone, yea, to bear, patiently wrong done to oneself.
31. To love one's enemies.
32. Not to render cursing for cursing, but rather blessing.
33. To bear persecution for justice's sake.
34. Not to be proud.
35. Not given to wine.
36. Not a glutton.
37. Not drowsy.
38. Not slothful.
39. Not a murmurer.
40. Not a detractor.
41. To put one's hope in God.
42. To attribute any good that one sees in oneself to God and not to oneself.
43. But to recognize and always impute to oneself the evil that one does.
44. To fear the Day of Judgement.
45. To be in dread of hell.
46. To desire with all spiritual longing everlasting life.
47. To keep death daily before one's eyes.
48. To keep guard at all times over the actions of one's life.
49. To know for certain that God sees one everywhere.
50. To dash down at the feet of Christ one's evil thoughts, the instant that they come into the heart.
51. And to lay them open to one's spiritual father.
52. To keep one's mouth from evil and wicked words.
53. Not to love much speaking.
54. Not to speak vain words or such as move to laughter.
55. Not to love much or excessive laughter.
56. To listen willingly to holy reading.
57. To apply oneself frequently to prayer.
58. Daily to confess in prayer one's past sins with tears and sighs to God, and to amend them for the time to come.
59. Not to fulfill the desires of the flesh: to hate one's own will.
60. To obey in all things the commands of the Abbot, even though he himself (which God forbid) should act otherwise; being mindful of that precept of the Lord: "What they say, do ye; but what they do, do ye not."
61. Not to wish to be called holy before one is so; but first to be holy, that one may be truly so called.
62. Daily to fulfill by one's deeds the Commandments of God.
63. To love chastity.
64. To hate no man.
65. Not to be jealous, nor to give way to envy.
66. Not to love strife.
67. To fly from vainglory.
68. To reverence seniors.
69. To love juniors.
70. To pray for one's enemies in the love of Christ.
71. To make peace with an adversary before the setting of the sun.
72. And never to despair of God's mercy.

Behold, these are the tools of the spiritual craft, which, if they be constantly employed day and night, and duly given back on the Day of Judgement, will gain for us from the Lord that reward which He Himself has promised— "which eye hath not seen, nor ear heard; nor hath it entered into the heart of man to conceive what God hath prepared for them that love him." And the workshop where we are to labour diligently at all these things is the cloister of the monastery, and stability in the community.

Of Obedience

The first degree of humility is obedience without delay. This becomes those who hold nothing dearer to them than Christ, and who on account of the holy servitude which they have taken upon them, and for fear of hell, and for the glory of life everlasting, as soon as anything is ordered by the superior, just as if it had been commanded by God Himself, are unable to bear delay in doing it. It is of these that the Lord says: "At the hearing of the ear he hath obeyed me." And again, to teachers he saith: "He that heareth you heareth me."

The Spirit of Silence

Let us do as says the prophet: "I said, I will take heed to my ways, that I sin not with my tongue: I have placed a watch over my mouth; I became dumb, and was silent, and held my peace even from good things." Here the prophet shows that if we ought to refrain even from good words for the sake of silence, how much more ought we to abstain from evil words, on account of the punishment due to sin!

Therefore, on account of the importance of silence, let leave to speak be seldom granted even to perfect disciples, although their conversation be good and holy and tending to edification; because it is written: "In much speaking thou shalt not avoid sin;" and elsewhere: "Death and life are in the power of the tongue." For it becomes the master to speak and to teach, but it beseems the disciple to be silent and to listen.

And, therefore, if anything has to be asked of a superior, let it be done with all humility and subjection of reverence, lest he seem to say more than is expedient.

But as for buffoonery or silly words, such as move to laughter, we utterly condemn them in

every place, nor do we allow the disciple to open his mouth in such discourse.

Of Humility

The Holy Scripture cries out to us, brethren, saying: "Everyone that exalteth himself shall be humbled, and he that humbleth himself shall be exalted." In saying this, it teaches us that all exaltation is a kind of pride, against which the prophet shows himself to be on his guard when he says: "Lord, my heart is not exalted nor mine eyes lifted up; nor have I walked in great things, nor in wonders above me." And why? "If I did not think humbly, but exalted my soul: like a child that is weaned from his mother, so wilt thou requite my soul."

Whence, brethen, if we wish to arrive at the highest point of humility and speedily to reach that heavenly exaltation to which we can only ascend by the humility of this present life, we must by our ever-ascending actions erect such a ladder as that which Jacob beheld his dream, by which the angels appeared to him descending and ascending. This descent and ascent signify nothing else than that we descend by exaltation and ascend by humility. And the ladder thus erected is our life in the world, which, if the heart be humbled, is lifted up by the Lord to heaven. The sides of the same ladder we understand to be our body and soul, in which the call of God has placed various degrees of humility or discipline, which we must ascend.

How the Monks Are to Sleep

Let them sleep each one in a separate bed, receiving bedding suitable to their manner of life, as the Abbot shall appoint.

If it be possible, let all sleep in one place; but if the number do not permit of this, let them repose by tens or twenties with the seniors who have charge of them. Let a candle burn constantly in the cell until morning.

Let them sleep clothed, and girded with belts or cords—but not with knives at their sides, lest perchance they wound themselves in their sleep—and thus be always ready, so that when the signal is given they rise without delay, and hasten each to forestall the other in going to the Work of God, yet with all gravity and modesty.

Let not the younger brethren have their beds by themselves, but among those of the seniors. And when they rise for the Work of God, let them gently encourage one another, because of the excuses of the drowsy.

Of the Daily Manual Labour

Idleness is the enemy of the soul. Therefore should the brethren be occupied at stated times in manual labour, and at other fixed hours in sacred reading.

We think, therefore, that the times for each may be disposed as follow: from Easter to the Calends of October, on coming out in the morning let them labour at whatever is necessary from the first until about the fourth hour. From the fourth hour until close upon the sixth let them apply themselves to reading. After the sixth hour, when they rise from table, let them rest on their beds in all silence; or if anyone chance to wish to read to himself, let him so read as not to disturb anyone else. Let None be said rather

soon, at the middle of the eighth hour; and then let them again work at whatever has to be done until Vespers.

If, however, the needs of the place or poverty require them to labour themselves in gathering in the harvest, let them not grieve at that; for then are they truly monks when they live by the labour of their hands, as our Fathers and the Apostles did. But let all things be done in moderation for the sake of the faint-hearted.

From the Calends of October until the beginning of Lent let the brethren devote themselves to reading till the end of the second hour. At the second hour let Terce be said, after which they shall all labour at their appointed work until None. At the first signal for the hour of None all shall cease from their work, and be ready as soon as the second signal is sounded. After their meal let them occupy themselves in their reading or with the psalms.

Of the Reception of Guests

Let all guests that come be received like Christ Himself, for He will say: "I was a stranger and ye took me in." And let fitting honour be shown to all, especially, however, to such as are of the household of the faith and to pilgrims.

QUESTIONS

1. The creation of the Rule is a comment on Benedict's view of the nature of humanity. What are people like, and what good is the Rule?

2. Benedict has taken great care to order the lives of his monks in great detail. What is their daily life like?

3. Why does Benedict have such a high regard for silence? Why is talk dangerous?

4. Monasteries that kept to Benedict's Rule could be very useful institutions. How?

5. Every monastery reflected something about the society of which it was a part. What does the Rule tell us about the social and economic structure of the time?

30

THE BURGUNDIAN CODE

(CA. 474)

The Burgundians were a Germanic tribe that moved westward across the Rhine River until they were stopped by the Roman army. In the fourth century, they were incorporated into the Roman Empire and settled north of Lake Geneva. During the reign of Gundobad (474–516), one of the greatest Burgundian kings, the tribe occupied the largest amount of territory in its history and became a major power in northwestern Europe, even defeating the Franks. After his death, the kingdom contracted and was soon absorbed into the Frankish empire.

Gundobad's codification, known as the Burgundian Code, was undoubtedly a combination of older laws and those current in the late fifth century. Because Romans and Burgundians had been neighbors for over a century, procedures such as those outlined here must have developed slowly.

1. In the name of God in the second year of the reign of our lord the most glorious king Gundobad, this book concerning laws past and present, and to be preserved throughout all future time, has been issued on the fourth day before the Kalends of April [March 29] at Lyons.

2. For the love of justice, through which God is pleased and the power of earthly kingdoms acquired, we have obtained the consent of our counts and leaders, and have desired to establish such laws that the integrity and equity of those judging may exclude all rewards and corruptions from themselves.

3. Therefore all administrators and judges must judge from the present time on between Burgundians and Romans according to our laws which have been set forth and corrected by a common method, to the end that no one may hope or presume to receive anything by way of reward or emolument from any party as the result of the suits or decisions; but let him whose case is

deserving obtain justice and let the integrity of the judge alone suffice to accomplish this.

4. We believe the condition of this law should be imposed on us that no one may presume to tempt our integrity in any kind of case with favors or rewards; first, since our zeal for equity repudiates from ourselves those things which we forbid to all judges under our rule, let our treasury accept nothing more than has been established in the laws concerning the payment of fines.

5. Therefore let all nobles, counsellors, bailiffs, mayors of our palace, chancellors, counts of the cities or villages, Burgundian as well as Roman, and all appointed judges and military judges know that nothing can be accepted in connection with those suits which have been acted upon or decided, and that nothing can be sought in the name of promise or reward from those litigating; nor can the parties [to the suit] be compelled by the judge to make a payment in order that they may receive anything [from their suit].

Of Murders

1. If anyone presumes with boldness or rashness bent on injury to kill a native freeman of our people of any nation or a servant of the king, in any case a man of barbarian tribe, let him make restitution for the committed crime not otherwise than by the shedding of his own blood.

2. We decree that this rule be added to the law by a reasonable provision, that if violence shall have been done by anyone to any person, so that he is injured by blows of lashes or by wounds, and if he pursues his persecutor and overcome by grief and indignation kills him, proof of the deed shall be afforded by the act itself or by suitable witnesses who can be believed. Then the guilty party shall be compelled to pay to the relatives of the person killed half his wergeld [value] according to the status of the person: that is, if he shall have killed a noble of the highest class, we decree that the payment be set at one hundred fifty solidi, i.e., half his wergeld; if a person of middle class, one hundred solidi; if a person of the lowest class, seventy-five solidi.

3. If a slave unknown to his master presumes to kill a native freeman, let the slave be handed over to death, and let the master not be made liable for damages.

4. If the master knows of the deed, let both be handed over to death.

5. If the slave himself flees after the deed, let his master be compelled to pay thirty solidi to the relatives of the man killed for the wergeld of the slave.

Of the Commission of Crimes Which Are Charged Against Native Freemen

1. If a native freeman, either barbarian or Roman, is accused of a crime through suspicion, let him render oath, and let him swear with his wife and sons and twelve relatives: if indeed he does not have wife and sons and he has mother or father, let him complete the designated number with father and mother. But if he has neither father nor mother, let him complete the oath with twelve relatives.

2. But if he who must take oath wishes to take it with raised hand, and if those who are ordered to hear the oath—those three whom we always command to be delegated by the judges for hearing an oath—before they enter the church declare they do not wish to receive the oath, then he who was about to take oath is not permitted to do so after this statement, but they [the judges] are hereby directed by us to commit the matter to the judgment of God [i.e., to ordeal].

3. If however, having received permission, he has taken the oath, and if he has been convicted after the oath, let him know that he must make restitution by a ninefold payment to those in whose presence the judge ordered him to give his oath.

4. But if they [those appointed to hear the oath] fail to come to the place on the appointed day, and if they shall not have been detained by any illness or public duty, let them pay a fine of six solidi. But if they were detained by any illness or duty, let them make this known to the judge or send other persons in their place whom they can trust to receive the oath for them.

5. If moreover he who is about to take the oath does not come to the place, let the other party wait until the sixth hour of the day; but if he has not come by the sixth hour, let the case be dismissed without delay.

6. But if the other [the accusing party] does not come, let him who was about to take the oath depart without loss.

Let Burgundians and Romans Be Held Under the Same Condition in the Matter of Killing Slaves

1. If anyone kills a slave, barbarian by birth, a trained [select] house servant or messenger, let him compound sixty solidi; moreover, let the amount of the fine be twelve solidi. If anyone kills another's slave, Roman or

barbarian, either ploughman or swine-herd, let him pay thirty solidi.

2. Whoever kills a skilled goldsmith, let him pay two hundred solidi.

3. Whoever kills a silversmith, let him pay one hundred solidi.

4. Whoever kills a blacksmith, let him pay fifty solidi.

5. Whoever kills a carpenter, let him pay forty solidi.

Of the Stealing of Girls

1. If anyone shall steal a girl, let him be compelled to pay the price set for such a girl ninefold, and let him pay a fine to the amount of twelve solidi.

2. If a girl who has been seized returns uncorrupted to her parents, let the abductor compound six times the wergeld of the girl; moreover, let the fine be set at twelve solidi.

3. But if the abductor does not have the means to make the above-mentioned payment, let him be given over to the parents of the girl that they may have the power of doing to him whatever they choose.

4. If indeed, the girl seeks the man of her own will and comes to his house, and he has intercourse with her, let him pay her marriage price threefold; if moreover, she returns uncorrupted to her home, let her return with all blame removed from him.

5. If indeed a Roman girl, without the consent or knowledge of her parents, unites in marriage with a Burgundian, let her know she will have none of the property of her parents.

Of Succession

1. Among Burgundians we wish it to be observed that if anyone does not leave a son, let a daughter succeed to the inheritance of the father and mother in place of the son.

2. If by chance the dead leave neither a son or daughter, let the inheritance go to the sisters or nearest relatives.

3. It is pleasing that it be contained in the present law that if a woman having a husband dies without children, the husband of the dead wife may not demand back the marriage price which had been given for her.

4. Likewise, let neither the woman nor the relatives of the woman seek back that which a woman pays when she comes to her husband if the husband dies without children.

5. Concerning those women who are vowed to God and remain in chastity, we order that if they have two brothers they receive a third portion of the inheritance of the father, that is, of that land which the father, possessing by the right of sors [allotment], left at the time of his death. Likewise, if she has four or five brothers, let her receive the portion due to her.

6. If moreover she has but one brother, let not a half, but a third part go to her on the condition that, after the death of her who is a woman and a nun, whatever she possesses in usufruct from her father's property shall go to the nearest relatives, and she will have no power of transferring anything therefrom, unless perhaps from her mother's goods, that is, from her clothing or things of the cell, or what she has acquired by her own labor.

7. We decree that this should be observed only by those whose fathers have not given them portions; but if they shall have received from their father a place where they can live, let them have full freedom of disposing of it at their will.

Of Those Things Which Happen by Chance

1. If any animal by chance, or if any dog by bite, cause death to a man, we order that among Burgundians the ancient rule of blame be removed henceforth: because what happens by

chance ought not to conduce to the loss or discomfiture of man. So that if among animals, a horse kills a horse unexpectedly, or an ox gores an ox, or a dog gnaws a dog, so that it is crippled, let the owner hand over the animal or dog through which the loss is seen to have been committed to him who suffers the loss.

2. In truth, if a lance or any kind of weapon shall have been thrown upon the ground or set there without intent to do harm, and if by accident a man or animal impales himself thereupon, we order that he to whom the weapon belongs shall pay nothing unless by chance he held the weapon in his own hands in such a manner that it could cause harm to a man.

Of Burgundian Women Entering a Second or Third Marriage

1. If any Burgundian woman, as is the custom, enters a second or third marriage after the death of her husband, and she has children by each husband, let her possess the marriage gift in usufruct while she lives; after her death, let what his father gave her be given to each son, with the further provision that the mother has the power neither of giving, selling, or transferring any of the things which she received in the marriage gift.

2. If by chance the woman has no children, after her death let her relatives receive half of whatever has come to her by way of marriage gift, and let the relatives of the dead husband who was the donor receive half.

3. But if perchance children shall have been born and they shall have died after the death of their father, we command that the inheritance of the husband or children belong wholly to the mother. Moreover, after the death of the mother, we decree that what she holds in usufruct by inheritance from her children shall belong to the legal heirs of her children. Also we command that she protect the property of her children dying intestate.

4. If any son has given his mother something by will or by gift, let the mother have the power of doing whatever she wishes therewith; if she dies intestate, let the relatives of the woman claim the inheritance as their possession.

5. If any Burgundian has sons [children?] to whom he has given their portions, let him have the power of giving or selling that which he has reserved for himself to whomever he wishes.

Of Injuries Which Are Suffered by Women

1. If any native freewoman has her hair cut off and is humiliated without cause [when innocent] by any native freeman in her home or on the road, and this can be proved with witnesses, let the doer of the deed pay her twelve solidi, and let the amount of the fine be twelve solidi.

2. If this was done to a freedwoman, let him pay her six solidi.

3. If this was done to a maidservant, let him pay her three solidi, and let the amount of the fine be three solidi.

4. If this injury [shame, disgrace] is inflicted by a slave on a native freewoman, let him receive two hundred blows; if a freedwoman, let him receive a hundred blows; if a maidservant, let him receive seventy-five blows.

5. If indeed the woman whose injury we have ordered to be punished in this manner commits fornication voluntarily [i.e., if she yields], let nothing be sought for the injury suffered.

Of Divorces

1. If any woman leaves (puts aside) her husband to whom she is legally married, let her be smothered in mire.

2. If anyone wishes to put away his wife without cause, let him give her another payment such as he gave for her marriage price, and let the amount of the fine be twelve solidi.

3. If by chance a man wishes to put away his wife, and is able to prove one of these three crimes against her, that is, adultery, witchcraft, or violation of graves, let him have full right to put her away; and let the judge pronounce the sentence of the law against her, just as should be done against criminals.

4. But if she admits none of these three crimes, let no man be permitted to put away his wife for any other crime. But if he chooses, he may go away from the home, leaving all household property behind, and his wife with their children may possess the property of her husband.

Of the Punishment of Slaves Who Commit a Criminal Assault on Freeborn Women

1. If any slave does violence to a native freewoman, and if she complains and is clearly able to prove this, let the slave be killed for the crime committed.

2. If indeed a native free girl unites voluntarily with a slave, we order both to be killed.

3. But if the relatives of the girl do not wish to punish their own relative, let the girl be deprived of her free status and delivered into servitude to the king.

Of Incestuous Adultery

If anyone has been taken in adultery with his relative or with his wife's sister, let him be compelled to pay her wergeld, according to her status, to him who is the nearest relative of the woman with whom he committed adultery; and let the amount of the fine be twelve solidi. Further, we order the adulteress to be placed in servitude to the king.

Of the Inheritance of Those Who Die Without Children

1. Although we have ordered many things in former laws concerning the inheritance of those who die without children, nevertheless after considering the matter thoroughly, we perceive it to be just that some of those things which were ordered before should be corrected. Therefore we decree in the present constitution that if a woman whose husband has died without children has not taken her vows a second time, let her possess securely a third of all the property of her husband to the day of her death; with the further provision that after her death, all will revert to the legitimate heirs of her husband.

2. Let that remain in effect which has been stated previously concerning the morning gift. For if she wishes to marry within a year from the time of the death of her first husband, let her have full right to do so, but let her give up that third part of the property which she had been permitted to possess. However, if she wishes to take a husband after a year or two have passed, let her give up all as has been stated above which she received from her first husband, and let the heirs in whose portion the inheritance of her former husband belongs receive the price which must be paid for her [second] marriage.

QUESTIONS

1. How free is Gundobad to make laws? What limits are there upon his authority as king?

2. How does the Code distinguish between classes of people? Does social status matter?

3. What principles underlie the Burgundian view of crime and punishment? How do the Burgundians punish criminals, and how do they determine guilt?

4. The Code says a great deal about women and family matters. What is the status of women in Burgundian society?

5. You have read several excerpts from legal codes in earlier parts of this book. What are the sorts of things that seem common to these codes in general? Can you think of ways in which the Burgundian Code is quite different?

31

■ *Gregory of Tours* ■

HISTORY OF THE FRANKS

(CA. 581–591)

Gregory of Tours (ca. 538–595) was born into an aristocratic family in what is now central France. There were several bishops in his family line and Gregory was selected early on to enter the clergy. He was educated by one of his successful relatives and ultimately succeeded his cousin as Bishop of Tours in 573. He entered this office during a turbulent period in Frankish history—the kingdom of Clovis had just been split three ways, and a period of fratricidal warfare had begun. As a bishop, Gregory had to remain studiously neutral in the controversies among the three brothers. His overriding aim was to maintain the autonomy of the Church, a task in which he achieved considerable success. He died in 595 and was later canonized by the Roman Catholic Church.

Gregory produced a host of writings, lives of saints and biblical commentaries especially, but his most famous work was his *History of the Franks*. Writing over a period of ten years, Gregory recalled the events through which he had lived and narrated the struggles of Clovis and his successors. Although frequently disjointed, the narrative is a vivid account of life within the Germanic tribes that ultimately settled in France.

After these events Childeric died and Clovis his son reigned in his stead. In the fifth year of his reign Siagrius, king of the Romans, son of Egidius, had his seat in the city of Soissons which Egidius, who has been mentioned before, once held. And Clovis came against him with Ragnachar, his kinsman, because he used to possess the kingdom, and demanded that they make ready a battle-field. And Siagrius did not delay nor was he afraid to resist. And so they fought against each other and Siagrius, seeing his army crushed, turned his back and fled swiftly to king Alaric at Toulouse. And Clovis sent to Alaric to send him back, otherwise he was to know that Clovis would make war on him for his refusal. And Alaric was afraid that he would incur the anger of the Franks on account of Siagrius, seeing it is the fashion of the Goths to be terrified, and he surrendered him in chains to Clovis' envoys. And Clovis took him and gave orders to put him under guard, and when he had got his kingdom he directed that he be executed secretly. At that time many churches were despoiled by Clovis' army, since he was as yet involved in heathen error. Now the army had taken from a certain church a vase of wonderful size and beauty, along with the remainder of the utensils for the service of the church. And the bishop of the church sent messengers to the king asking that the vase at least be returned, if he could not get back any more of the sacred dishes. On hearing this the king said to the messenger: "Follow us as far as Soissons, because all that has been taken is to be divided there and when the lot assigns me that dish I will do what the father asks." Then when he came to Soissons and all the booty was set in their midst, the king said: "I ask of you, brave warriors, not to refuse to grant me in addition to my share, yonder dish," that is, he was speaking of the vase just mentioned. In answer to the speech of the king those of more sense replied: "Glorious king, all that we see is yours, and we ourselves are subject to your rule. Now do what seems well-pleasing to you; for no one is able to resist your power." When they said this a foolish, envious and excitable fellow lifted his battle-ax and struck the vase, and cried in a loud voice: "You shall get nothing here except what the lot fairly bestows on you." At this all were stupefied, but the king endured the insult with the gentleness of patience, and taking the vase he handed it over to the messenger of the church, nursing the wound deep in his heart. And at the end of the year he ordered the whole army to come with their equipment of armor, to show the brightness of their arms on the field of March. And when he was reviewing them all carefully, he came to the man who struck the vase, and said to him: "No one has brought armor so carelessly kept as you; for neither your spear nor sword nor ax is in serviceable condition." And seizing his ax he cast it to the earth, and when the other had bent over somewhat to pick it up, the king raised his hands and drove his own ax into the man's head. "This," said he, "is what you did at Soissons to the vase." Upon the death of this man, he ordered the rest to depart, raising great dread of himself by this action. He made many wars and gained many victories. In the tenth year of his reign he made war on the Thuringi and brought them under his dominion.

Clovis had a first-born son by queen Clotilda, and as his wife wished to consecrate him in baptism, she tried unceasingly to persuade her husband, saying: "The gods you worship are nothing, and they will be unable to help themselves or any one else. For they are graven out of stone or wood or some metal. And the names you have given them are names of men and not of gods, as Saturn, who is declared to have fled in fear of being banished from his kingdom by his son; as Jove himself, the foul perpetrator of all shameful crimes, committing incest with men, mocking at his kinswomen, not able to refrain from intercourse with his own sister. What could Mars or Mercury do? They are endowed rather with the magic arts than with the power of the divine name. But he ought rather to be worshipped who created by his word heaven and earth, the sea and all that in them is out of a state of nothingness, who made the sun shine, and adorned the heavens with stars, who filled the waters with creeping things, the earth with living things and the air with creatures that fly, at whose nod the earth is decked with growing crops, the trees with fruit, the vines with grapes, by whose hand mankind was created, by whose generosity all that creation serves and helps man whom he created as his own." But though the queen said this the spirit of the king was by no means moved to belief, and he said: "It was at the command of our gods that all things were created and came forth, and it is plain that your God has no power and, what is more, he is proven not to belong to the family of the gods." Meantime the faithful queen made her son ready for baptism; she gave command to adorn the church with hangings and curtains, in order that he who could not be moved by persuasion might be urged to belief by this mystery. The boy, whom they named Ingomer, died after being baptized, still wearing the white garments in which he became regenerate. At this the king was violently angry, and reproached the queen harshly, saying: "If the boy had been dedicated in the name of my gods he would certainly have lived; but as it is, since he was baptized in the name of your God, he could not live at all." To this the queen said: "I give thanks to the omnipotent God, creator of all, who has judged me not wholly unworthy, that he should deign to take to his kingdom one born from my womb. My soul is not stricken with grief for his sake, because I know that, summoned from this world as he was in his baptismal garments, he will be fed by the vision of God."

After this she bore another son, whom she named Cholodomer at baptism; and when he fell sick, the king said: "It is impossible that anything else should happen to him than happened to his brother, namely, that being baptized in the name of your Christ, he should die at once." But through the prayers of his mother, and the Lord's command, he became well.

The queen did not cease to urge him to recognize the true God and cease worshiping idols. But he could not be influenced in any way to this belief, until at last a war arose with the Alamanni, in which he was driven by necessity to confess what before he had of his free will denied. It came about that as the two armies were fighting fiercely, there was much slaughter, and Clovis's army began to be in danger of destruction. He saw it and raised his eyes to heaven, and with remorse in his heart he burst into tears and cried: "Jesus Christ, whom Clotilda asserts to be the son of the living God, who art said to give aid to those in distress, and to bestow victory on those who hope in thee, I beseech the glory of thy aid, with the vow that if thou wilt grant me victory over these enemies, and I shall know that power which she says that people dedicated in thy name have had from thee, I will believe in thee and be baptized in thy name. For I have invoked my own gods, but, as I find, they have withdrawn from aiding me; and therefore I believe that they possess no power, since they do not help those who obey them. I now call upon thee, I desire to believe thee, only let me be rescued from my adversaries." And when he said this, the Alamanni turned their backs, and began to disperse in flight. And when they saw that their king was killed, they submitted to the dominion of Clovis, saying: "Let not the people perish further, we pray; we are yours now." And he stopped the fighting, and after encouraging his men, retired in peace and told the queen how he had had merit to win the victory by calling on the name of Christ. This happened in the fifteenth year of his reign.

Then the queen asked saint Remi, bishop of Rheims, to summon Clovis secretly, urging him to introduce the king to the word of salvation. And the bishop sent for him secretly and began to urge him to believe in the true God, maker of heaven and earth, and to cease worshiping idols, which could help neither themselves nor any one else. But the king said: "I gladly hear you, most holy father; but there remains one thing: the people who follow me cannot endure to abandon their gods; but I shall go and speak to them according to your words." He met with his followers, but before he could speak the power of God anticipated him, and all the people cried out together: "O pious king, we reject our mortal gods, and we are ready to follow the immortal God whom Remi preaches." This was reported to the bishop, who was greatly rejoiced, and bade them get ready the baptismal font. The squares were shaded with tapestried canopies, the churches adorned with white curtains, the baptistery set in order, the aroma of incense spread, candles of fragrant odor burned brightly, and the whole shrine of the baptistery was filled with a divine fragrance: and the Lord gave such grace to those who stood by

that they thought they were placed amid the odors of paradise. And the king was the first to ask to be baptized by the bishop. Another Constantine advanced to the baptismal font, to terminate the disease of ancient leprosy and wash away with fresh water the foul spots that had long been borne. And when he entered to be baptized, the saint of God began with ready speech: "Gently bend your neck, Sigamber; worship what you burned; burn what you worshipped." The holy bishop Remi was a man of excellent wisdom and especially trained in rhetorical studies, and of such surpassing holiness that he equalled the miracles of Silvester. For there is extant a book of his life which tells that he raised a dead man. And so the king confessed all-powerful God in the Trinity, and was baptized in the name of the Father, Son and holy Spirit, and was anointed with the holy ointment with the sign of the cross of Christ. And of his army more than 3000 were baptized.

QUESTIONS

1. Gregory's story illustrates competing ideas about the nature of kingship among the Franks. Define these ideas. Which view seems to triumph?

2. Christians such as Queen Clotilda went to great lengths to convert the pagans around them. What arguments did they use to convince nonbelievers? How might nonbelievers have responded?

3. How would Gregory's position as a Christian and a bishop of the Church affect his presentation of the history of the Franks?

4. Converting the Franks to Christianity was more than a matter of persuasion. How was it accomplished?

5. Many of Clovis's subjects converted to Christianity. What conclusions could you draw about the process of conversion from Gregory's account?

32

■ *Bede* ■

THE ECCLESIASTICAL HISTORY OF ENGLAND

(731)

The Venerable Bede (673–735) was born in northern England, and, it seems, orphaned at an early age. When he was seven, he was taken in hand by Benedict Biscop, abbot of Wearmouth, beginning a lifelong career in the church. Bede spent most of his life as a monk in the famous Benedictine monastery at Jarrow, where he won a reputation as a scholar and teacher. He devoted much of his time to writing and meditations on the Scriptures, working, legend, has it, in a solitary stone hut. In addition to his Latin, Bede was familiar with Greek, and, unusual for his time, had some Hebrew. He knew the ancient classics, and was intimately familiar with the works of the fathers of the Church. Bede was also a talented teacher, and many of his students came to occupy important places in the Church. He continued his lectures until the day of his much lamented death on May 26, 735.

Although Bede wrote other texts, he is best known for his *Ecclesiastical History*, which tells the story of Christianity in Britain from the time of the Romans until his own day. This selection is from his account of St. Augustine of Canterbury's sixth century mission to Kent. Pope Gregory commanded Augustine to bring the faith back to Britain, where Christianity had collapsed with the Roman Empire centuries before.

On the east of Kent is the large Isle of Thanet. In this island landed the servant of our Lord, Augustine, and his companions, being, as is reported, nearly forty men. The king having heard this, ordered them to stay in that island where they had landed, and that they should be furnished with all necessaries, till he should consider what to do with them. For he had before heard of the Christian religion, having a Christian wife of the royal family of the Franks, called Bertha; whom he had received from her parents, upon condition that she should be permitted to practise her religion. Some days after, the king came into the island, and sitting in the open air, ordered Augustine and his companions to be brought into his presence. For he had taken precaution that they should not come to him in any house, lest, according to an ancient superstition, if they practised any magical arts, they might impose upon him, and so get the better of him. But they came furnished with Divine, not with magic virtue, bearing a silver cross for their banner, and the image of our Lord and Saviour painted on a board; and singing the litany, they offered up their prayers to the Lord for the eternal salvation both of themselves and of those to whom they were come. When he had sat down, pursuant to the king's commands, and preached to him and his attendants there present, the word of life, the king answered thus:—"Your words and promises are very fair, but as they are new to us, and of uncertain import, I cannot approve of them so far as to forsake that which I have so long followed with the whole English nation. But because you are come from far into my kingdom, and, as I conceive, are desirous to impart to us those things which you believe to be true, and most beneficial, we will not molest you, but give you favourable entertainment, and take care to supply you with necessary sustenance; nor do we forbid you to preach and gain as many as you can to your religion."

As soon as they entered the dwelling-place assigned them, they began to imitate the course of life practised in the primitive church; applying themselves to frequent prayer, watching and fasting; preaching the word of life to as many as they could; despising all worldly things, as not belonging to them; receiving only their necessary food from those they taught; living themselves in all respects conformably to what they prescribed to others, and being always disposed to suffer any adversity, and even to die for that truth which they preached. In short, several believed and were baptized, admiring the simplicity of their innocent life, and the sweetness of their heavenly doctrine. There was on the east side of the city, a church dedicated to the honour of St. Martin, built whilst the Romans were still in the island, wherein the queen, who, as has been said before, was a Christian, used to pray. In this they first began to meet, to sing, to pray, to say mass, to preach, and to baptize, till the king, being converted to the faith, allowed them to preach openly, and build or repair churches in all places.

When he, among the rest, induced by the unspotted life of these holy men, and their delightful promises, which by many miracles, they proved to be most certain, believed and was baptized, greater numbers began daily to flock together to hear the word, and, forsaking their heathen rites, to associate themselves, by believing, to the unity of the church of Christ. Their conversion the king so far encouraged, as that he compelled none to embrace Christianity, but only showed more affection to the believers, as to his fellow citizens in the heavenly kingdom. For he had learned from his instructors and leaders to salvation, that the service of Christ ought to be voluntary, not by compulsion. Nor was it long before he gave his teachers a settled residence in his metropolis of Canterbury, with such possessions of different kinds as were necessary for their subsistence.

At the same time, Augustine desired his solution of some doubts that occurred to him. He soon received proper answers to his questions, which we have also thought fit to insert in this our history:—

Augustine's Second Question.—Whereas the faith is one and the same, why are there different customs in different churches? and why is one custom of masses observed in the holy Roman church, and another in the Gallican church?

Pope Gregory Answers.—You know, my brother, the custom of the Roman church in which you remember you were bred up. But it pleases me, that if you have found anything, either in the Roman, or the Gallican, or any other church, which may be more acceptable to Almighty God, you carefully make choice of the same, and sedulously teach the church for the English, which as yet is new in the faith, whatsoever you can gather from the several churches. For things are not to be loved for the sake of places, but places for the sake of good things. Choose, therefore, from every church those things that are pious, religious, and upright, and when you have, as it were, made them up into one body, let the minds of the English be accustomed thereto.

Augustine's Fifth Question.—To what degree may the faithful marry with their kindred? and whether it is lawful for men to marry their stepmothers and relations?

Gregory Answers.—To marry with one's stepmother is a heinous crime, because it is written in the Law, "Thou shalt not uncover the nakedness of thy father:" now the son, indeed, cannot uncover his father's nakedness; but in regard that is written, "They shall be two in one flesh," he that presumes to uncover the nakedness of his stepmother, who was one flesh with his father, certainly uncovers the nakedness of his father. It is also prohibited to marry with a sister-in-law because by the former union she is become the brother's flesh.

But forasmuch as there are many of the English, who, whilst they were still in infidelity, are said to have been joined in this execrable matrimony, when they come to the faith they are to be admonished to abstain, and be made to know that this is a grievous sin. Let them fear the dreadful judgment of God, lest, for the gratification for their carnal appetites, they incur the torments of eternal punishment. Yet they are not on this account to be deprived of the communion of the body and blood of Christ, lest they seem to be punished for those things which they did through ignorance before they had received baptism. For at this time the Holy Church chastises some things through zeal, and tolerates some through meekness, and connives at some things through discretion, that so she may often, by this forbearance and connivance, suppress the evil which she disapproves. But all that come to the faith are to be admonished not to do such things. And if any shall be guilty of them, they are to be excluded from the communion of the body and blood of Christ. For as the offence is, in some measure, to be tolerated in those who did it through ignorance, so it is to be strenuously prosecuted in those who do not fear to sin knowingly.

Augustine's Eighth Question.—Whether a woman with child ought to be baptized? Or how long after she has brought forth, may she come into the church? As also, after how many days the infant born may be baptized, lest he be prevented by death? Or how long after her husband may have carnal knowledge of her? Or whether it is lawful for her to come into the church when she has her courses? Or to receive the holy sacrament of communion? All which things are requisite to be known by the rude nation of the English.

Gregory Answers.—I do not doubt but that these questions have been put to you, my brother, and I think I have already answered you therein. But I believe you would wish the opinion which you yourself might give to be confirmed by mine also. Why should not a woman with child be baptized, since the fruitfulness of the flesh is no offence in the eyes of Almighty God? For when our first parents sinned in Paradise, they forfeited the immortality which they had received, by the just judgment of God. Because, therefore, Almighty God would not for their fault wholly destroy the human race, he both deprived man of immortality for his sin, and, at the same time, of his great goodness, reserved to him the power of propagating his race after him. On what account then can that which is preserved to the human race, by the free gift of Almighty God, be excluded from the privilege of baptism? For it is very foolish to imagine that the gift of grace opposes that mystery in which all sin is blotted out. When a woman is delivered, after how many days she may come into the church, you have been informed by reading the Old Testament, viz. that she is to abstain for a male child thirty-three days, and sixty-six for a female. Now you must know that this is to be taken in a mystery; for if she enters the church the very hour she is delivered, to return thanks, she is not guilty of any sin; because the pleasure of the flesh is in fault, and not the pain; but the pleasure is in the copulation of the flesh, whereas there is pain in bringing forth the child. Wherefore it is said to the first mother of all, "In sorrow shalt thou bring forth children." If, therefore, we forbid a woman that has brought forth, to enter the church, we make a crime of her very punishment. To baptize either a woman who has brought forth, if there be danger of death, even the very hour that she brings forth or that which she has brought forth the very hour it is born, is no way prohibited, because, as the grace of the holy mystery is to be with much discretion provided for the living and understanding, so is it to be without any delay offered to the dying; lest, while a further time is sought to confer the mystery of redemption, a small delay intervening, the person that is to be redeemed is dead and gone.

Her husband is not to approach her, till the infant born be weaned. A bad custom is sprung up in the behaviour of married people, that is, that women disdain to suckle the children which they bring forth, and give them to other women to suckle; which seems to have been invented on no other account but incontinency; because, as they will not be continent, they will not suckle the children which they bear. Those women, therefore, who, from bad custom, give their children to others to bring up, must not approach their husbands till the time of purification is past. For even when there has been no child-birth, women are forbidden to do so, whilst they have their monthly courses, insomuch that the Law condemns to death any man that shall approach unto a woman during her uncleanness. Yet the woman, nevertheless, must not be forbidden to come into the church whilst she has her monthly courses; because the superfluity of nature cannot be imputed to her as a crime; and it is not just that she should be refused admittance into the church, for that which she suffers against her will. For we know, that the woman who has the issue of blood, humbly approaching behind our Lord's back, touched the hem of his garment, and her distemper immediately departed from her. If, therefore, she that had issue of blood might commendably touch the garment of our Lord, why may not she, who has the monthly courses, lawfully enter into the church of God? But you may say, Her distemper compelled her, whereas these we speak of are bound by custom. Consider, then, most dear brother, that all we suffer in this mortal flesh, through the infirmity of our nature is ordained by the just judgment of God after the fall; for to hunger, to thirst, to be hot, to be cold, to be weary, is from the infirmity of our nature; and what else is it to seek food against hunger, drink against thirst, air against heat, clothes against cold, rest against weariness, than to procure a remedy against distempers? Thus to a woman her monthly courses are distemper. If, therefore, it was a commendable boldness in her, who in her disease touched our Lord's garment, why may not that which is allowed to one infirm person, be granted to all women, who, through the fault of their nature, are distempered?

She must not, therefore, be forbidden to receive the mystery of the holy communion during those days. But if any one out of profound respect does not presume to do it, she is to be commended; yet if she receives it, she is not to be judged.

QUESTIONS

1. How does Augustine go about converting the English? What methods does he use?

2. How does the Church deal with local customs that conflict with Christian teachings?

3. How important is the King in the process of conversion? Would Augustine's mission have succeeded without royal assistance?

4. What is Pope Gregory's attitude toward women?

5. How might Bede's position as a Christian monk affect the way he tells the story of Augustine's mission to the English?

33

■ *Einhard* ■

THE LIFE OF CHARLEMAGNE
(CA. 829–836)

Einhard (ca. 770–840) was a prominent scholar and historian of the reign of Charlemagne. Little has been preserved concerning Einhard's youth, although it is supposed that he was born in Germany near the monastery of Fulda where he was educated. While at Fulda, he developed a reputation as a brilliant scholar, and he soon entered Charlemagne's court in the city of Aachen, which was renowned for its intellectual sophistication—despite the fact that the emperor himself could not write—and where many promising young scholars came to serve. Einhard took a position as a teacher in the school that trained the children of the nobility. Einhard grew to become one of the emperor's most trusted advisors.

The Life of Charlemagne was written during Einhard's retirement, between 829 and 836. It was produced as a token of gratitude to the emperor as well as to teach Charlemagne's sons about the achievements of their father. Although it is based on classical models, *The Life* was the first medieval biography of a layman. It became one of the most frequently copied works of the Middle Ages.

Private Life and Character of Charlemagne

I have shown, then, how Charles protected and expanded his kingdom and also what splendour he gave to it. I shall now go on to speak of his mental endowments, of his steadiness of purpose under whatever circumstances of prosperity or adversity, and of all that concerns his private and domestic life.

In educating his children he determined to train them, both sons and daughters, in those liberal studies to which he himself paid great attention. Further, he made his sons, as soon as their age permitted it, learn to ride like true Franks, and practise the use of arms and hunting. He ordered his daughters to learn wool work and devote attention to the spindle and distaff, for the avoidance of idleness and lethargy, and to be trained to the adoption of high principles.

He bore the deaths of his two sons and of his daughters with less patience than might have been expected from his usual stoutness of heart, for his domestic affection, a quality for which he was as remarkable as for courage, forced him to shed tears. Moreover, when the death of Hadrian, the Roman Pontiff, whom he reckoned as the chief of his friends, was announced to him, he wept for him as though he had lost a brother or a very dear son. For he showed a very fine disposition in his friendships: he embraced them readily and maintained them faithfully, and he treated with the utmost respect all whom he had admitted into the circle of his friends.

He had such care of the upbringing of his sons and daughters that he never dined without them when he was at home, and never travelled without them. His sons rode along with him, and his daughters followed in the rear. Some of his guards, chosen for this very purpose, watched the end of the line of march where his daughters travelled. They were very beautiful, and much beloved by their father, and, therefore, it is strange that he would give them in marriage to no one, either among his own people or of a foreign state. But up to his death he kept them all at home, saying that he could not forgo their society. And hence the good fortune that followed him in all other respects was here broken by the touch of scandal and failure. He shut his eyes, however, to everything, and acted as though no suspicion of anything amiss had reached him, or as if the rumour of it had been discredited.

He had a great love for foreigners, and took such pains to entertain them that their numbers were justly reckoned to be a burden not only to the palace but to the kingdom at large. But, with his usual loftiness of spirit, he took little note of such charges, for he found in the reputation of generosity and in the good fame that

followed such actions a compensation even for grave inconveniences.

He paid the greatest attention to the liberal arts, and showed the greatest respect and bestowed high honours upon those who taught them. For his lessons in grammar he listened to the instruction of Deacon Peter of Pisa, an old man; but for all other subjects Albinus, called Alcuin, also a deacon, was his teacher—a man from Britain, of the Saxon race, and the most learned man of his time. Charles spent much time and labour in learning rhetoric and dialectic, and especially astronomy, from Alcuin. He learnt, too, the art of reckoning, and with close application scrutinised most carefully the course of the stars. He tried also to learn to write, and for this purpose used to carry with him and keep under the pillow of his couch tablets and writing-sheets that he might in his spare moments accustom himself to the formation of letters. But he made little advance in this strange task, which was begun too late in life.

He paid the most devout and pious regard to the Christian religion, in which he had been brought up from infancy. And, therefore, he built the great and most beautiful church at Aix, and decorated it with gold and silver and candelabras and with wicket-gates and doors of solid brass. And, since he could not procure marble columns elsewhere for the building of it, he had them brought from Rome and Ravenna. As long as his health permitted it he used diligently to attend the church both in the morning and evening, and during the night, and at the time of the Sacrifice. He took the greatest care to have all the services of the church performed with the utmost dignity, and constantly warned the keepers of the building not to allow anything improper or dirty either to be brought into or to remain in the building. He provided so great a quantity of gold and silver vessels, and so large a supply of priestly vestments, that at the religious services not even the doorkeepers, who form the lowest ecclesiastical order, had to officiate in their ordinary dress. He carefully reformed the manner of reading and singing; for he was thoroughly instructed in both, though he never read publicly himself, nor sang except in a low voice, and with the rest of the congregation.

He was most devout in relieving the poor and in those free gifts which the Greeks call alms. For he gave it his attention not only in his own country and in his own kingdom, but he also used to send money across the sea to Syria, to Egypt, to Africa—to Jerusalem, Alexandria, and Carthage—in compassion for the poverty of any Christians whose miserable condition in those countries came to his ears. It was for this reason chiefly that he cultivated the friendship of kings beyond the sea, hoping thereby to win for the Christians living beneath their sway some succour and relief.

Beyond all other sacred and venerable places he loved the church of the holy Apostle Peter at Rome, and he poured into its treasury great wealth in silver and gold and precious stones. He sent innumerable gifts to the Pope; and during the whole course of his reign he strove with all his might (and, indeed, no object was nearer to his heart than this) to restore to the city of Rome her ancient authority, and not merely to defend the church of Saint Peter but to decorate and enrich it out of his resources above all other churches. But although he valued Rome so much, still, during all the forty-seven years that he reigned, he only went there four times to pay his vows and offer up his prayers.

When he had taken the imperial title he noticed many defects in the legal systems of his people; for the Franks have two legal systems, differing in many points very widely from one another, and he, therefore, determined to add what was lacking, to reconcile the differences, and to amend anything that was wrong or wrongly expressed. He completed nothing of all his designs beyond adding a few capitularies, and those unfinished. But he gave orders that the laws and rules of all nations comprised within his dominions which were not already written out should be collected and committed to writing.

He also wrote out the barbarous and ancient songs, in which the acts of the kings and their wars were sung, and committed them to memory. He also began a grammar of his native language.

QUESTIONS

1. What does Einhard's biography tell us about the education and upbringing of royal children? How does Charlemagne treat his children, and is he, by the standards of the time, a successful father?

2. Although Charlemagne was never literate, Einhard still counted him a learned man. How did the emperor qualify for this distinction?

3. In what ways was Charlemagne a model king?

4. Einhard based his work on the biographies of ancient rulers, such as Suetonius's *Life of Augustus*. Can you detect any similarities with such classical biographies?

5. What would you say is the message that Einhard is trying to put across with his work? How does he do it?

ISLAM AND THE EASTERN EMPIRE

34

■ *Justinian* ■

CODE
(529–565)

Eustinian I (483–565) began life as a peasant although his uncle Justin, born a swineherd, had already become a Byzantine general. Justin ultimately rose to become emperor in 518, and, since he had no children of his own, he brought his nephew Justinian to Constantinople to be groomed as his successor. Justinian was named emperor in 527 only a few months before his uncle died. Justinian's rule was characterized by his desire to expand the borders of his empire and to reform its civil administration, but he was more successful as a reformer than a conqueror. He undertook a series of governmental reforms, began a public works program, and finally codified Byzantine law.

The Justinian Code was compiled at the emperor's command between 529 and 565. The state of Roman and Byzantine law had grown increasingly chaotic over the centuries, with a vast accumulation of contradictory laws and statutes. The Code was designed to remove these anomalies by examining every known law to reduce duplication and contradiction. Teams of lawyers worked for decades on the project, and the result surpassed even the most optimistic hopes of the emperor. The Code formed the basis of European law for centuries. The section reproduced here relates to family law and covers marriage, divorce, and the responsibilities of parents and children.

Formation of Marriage

Marriage is the union of a man and a woman, a partnership for life involving divine as well as human law.

Marriage cannot take place unless everyone involved consents, that is, those who are being united and those in whose power they are.

According to Pomponius, if I have a grandson by one son and a granddaughter by another who are both in my power, my authority alone will be enough to allow them to marry, and this is correct.

A girl who was less than twelve years old when she married will not be a lawful wife until she reaches that age while living with her husband.

Where a grandson marries, his father must also consent; but if a granddaughter gets married, the consent and authority of the grandfather will suffice. Insanity prevents marriage being contracted, because consent is required; but once validly contracted, it does not invalidate the marriage.

When the relationship of brother and sister arises because of adoption, it is an impediment to marriage while the adoption lasts. So I will be able to marry a girl whom my father adopted and then emancipated. Similarly, if she is kept in his power and I am emancipated, we can be married. It is advisable, then, for someone who wishes to adopt his son-in-law to emancipate his daughter-in-law and for someone who wished to adopt his daughter-in-law to emancipate his son. We are not allowed to marry our paternal or maternal aunts or paternal or maternal great-aunts although paternal and maternal great-aunts are related in the fourth degree. Again, we are not allowed to marry a paternal aunt or great-aunt, even though they are related to us by adoption.

People who wrongfully prevent children in their power from marrying, or who refuse to provide a dowry for them can be forced by proconsuls and provincial governors to arrange marriages and provide dowries for them. Those who do not try to arrange marriages are held to prevent them.

Where he marries someone because his father forces him to do so and he would not have married her if the choice had been his, the marriage will nevertheless be valid, because marriage cannot take place without the consent of the parties; he is held to have chosen this course of action.

The *lex Papia* provides that all freeborn men, apart from senators and their children, can marry freedwomen.

Living with a freewoman implies marriage, not concubinage, as long as she does not make money out of prostitution.

An emancipated son can marry without his father's consent, and any son he has will be his heir.

Women accused of adultery cannot marry during the lifetime of their husbands, even before conviction.

Women who live in a shameful way and make money out of prostitution, even where it is not done openly, are held in disgrace. If a woman lives as a concubine with anyone other than her patron, I would say that she lacks the character of the mother of a household.

As far as marriages are concerned, it is always necessary to consider not just what is lawful but also what is decent. If the daughter, granddaughter, or great-granddaughter of a senator marries a freedman or someone who was an actor, or whose father or mother were actors, the marriage will be void.

Divorces and Repudiations

Marriage is dissolved by the divorce, death, captivity, or other kind of slavery of either of the parties.

The word "divorce" derives from either the diversity of views it involves or because people who dissolve their marriage go in different directions. Where repudiation, that is, renunciation, is involved, these words are used: "Keep your things to yourself"; or "Look after your own things." It is agreed that in order to end betrothals a renunciation must be made. Here the established words are: "I do not accept your conditions." It makes no difference whether the repudiation is made in the presence of the other party.

A true divorce does not take place unless an intention to remain apart permanently is present. So things said or done in anger are not effective until the parties show by their persistence that they are an indication of their considered opinion. So where repudiation takes place in anger and the wife returns shortly afterward, she is not held to have divorced her husband.

Julian asks in the eighteenth book of his *Digest* whether an insane woman can repudiate her husband or be repudiated by him. He writes that an insane woman can be repudiated, because she is in the same position as a person who does not know of the repudiation. But she could not repudiate her husband because of her madness, and her curator cannot do this either but her father can repudiate for her. He would not have dealt with repudiation here unless it was established that the marriage was to continue. This opinion seems to me to be correct.

The wives of people who fall into enemy hands can still be considered married women only in that other men cannot marry them hastily. Generally, as long as it is certain that a husband who is in captivity is still alive, his wife does not have the right to contract another marriage, unless she herself has given some ground for repudiation. But if it is not certain whether the husband in captivity is alive or has died, then if five years have passed since his capture, his wife has the right to marry again so that the first marriage will be held to have been dissolved with the consent of the parties and each of the parties will have their rights withdrawn. The same rule applies where a husband stays at home and his wife is captured.

Where someone who has given the other party written notice of divorce regrets having done this and the notice is served in ignorance of the change of mind, the marriage is held to remain valid, unless the person who receives the notice is aware of the change of mind and wants to end the marriage himself. Then the marriage will be dissolved by the person who received the notice.

The Recognition of Children

It is not just a person who smothers a child who is held to kill it but also the person who abandons it, denies it food, or puts it on show in public places to excite pity which he himself does not have.

If anyone asks his children to support him or children seek support from their father, a judge should look into the question. Should a father be forced to support only children in his power or should he also support children who have been emancipated or have become independent in some other way? I think it is better to say that even where children are not in power, they must be supported by their parents and they, on the other hand, must support their parents. Must we support only our fathers, our paternal grandfathers, paternal great-grandfathers, and other relatives of the male sex, or are we compelled to support our mothers and other relatives in the maternal line? It is better to say that in each case the judge should intervene so as to give relief to the necessities of some of them and the infirmity of others. Since this obligation is based on justice and affection between blood relations, the judge should balance the claims of each person involved. The same is true in the maintenance of children by their parents. So we force a mother to support her illegitimate children and them to support her. The deified Pius also says that a maternal grandfather is compelled to support his grandchildren. He also stated in a rescript that a father must support his daughter, if it is proved in court that he was really her father. But where a son can support himself, judges should decide not to compel the provision of maintenance for him. So the Emperor Pius stated: "The appropriate judges before whom you will appear must order you to be supported by your father according to his means, provided that where you claim you are a tradesman, it is your ill health which makes you incapable of supporting yourself by your own labor." If a father denies that the person seeking support is his son and so maintains that he need not provide it, or where a son denies that the person seeking support is his father, the judges must decide this summarily. If it is established that the person is a son or a father, they must order him to be supported. But if this is not proved, they should not award maintenance. Remember if the judges declare that support must be provided, this does not affect the truth of the matter; for they did not declare that the person was the man's son, but only that he must be supported. If anyone refuses to provide support, the judges must determine the maintenance according to his means. If he fails to provide this, he can be forced to comply with the judgment by the seizing of his property in execution and selling it. The judge must also decide whether a relative or a father has any good reason for not supporting his children.

Concubines

Can a woman living in concubinage leave her patron against his will and either marry someone else or become his concubine? I think that a concubine should not be granted the right to marry if she leaves her patron without his consent, since it is more respectable for a freedwoman to be her patron's concubine rather than the mother of a family. I agree with the view of Atilicinus that it is only women who have not been debauched that can be kept as concubines without fear of committing a crime. Where a man keeps a woman who has been convicted of adultery as a concubine, I do not think the *lex Julia* on adultery will apply, although it will if he marries her. If a woman has been her patron's concubine and then becomes his son's or grandson's or vice versa, I do not think she is behaving properly, since a relationship of this kind is almost criminal. So this sort of bad behavior is prohibited. Clearly, a man can keep a concubine of any age unless she is less than twelve years old.

If a patron who has a freedwoman as his concubine becomes insane, it is more humane to say that she is still his concubine.

Another person's freedwoman can be kept as a concubine as well as a freeborn woman, especially where she is of low birth or has been a prostitute. But if a man would rather have a freeborn woman with respectable background as his concubine, he will not be allowed to do this unless he clearly states the position in front of witnesses. But it will be necessary for him to marry her, or if he refuses, to commit debauchery with her. A person does not commit adultery by having a concubine; for because concubinage exists because of statute law, it is not penalized by statute.

A man can have a concubine in the province where he holds office.

QUESTIONS

1. What does the Code reveal about the status of women in Justinian's time?

2. Upon what grounds could a divorce be procured under the Code?

3. The law has a great deal to say about the parent–child relationship. Could you make some generalization about parents and children in Byzantium from the Code?

4. The Code talks about concubines and wives alike. How were they different? What rights did each have?

5. Judging from the Code's discussion of marriage, could you offer any generalizations about the institution in Justinian's time?

35

■ *Procopius* ■

SECRET HISTORY

(CA. 560)

Procopius was a Byzantine civil servant and historian whose works provide important information about the reign of Emperor Justinian. Procopius was probably born in Palestine sometime between 490 and 510. After his early education, he sought a career in civil service and migrated to Constantinople, then the center of the Roman Empire. He served on a general's staff and was thus able to travel to Persia, Italy, and Africa, so his experience of Byzantine administration was extensive and firsthand. He had apparently returned to Constantinople by 540, but there is no trace of him thereafter.

Procopius wrote several official histories during his career, of which the most important is an account of the military campaigns of Justinian's reign entitled *On the Wars*. He also left a description of Justinian's public works projects called *The Buildings*. His most famous work, however, was published after his death. This was the *Secret History*, a highly personal account of Justinian and Empress Theodora. Whether Procopius's point of view was unique or common among Byzantine civil servants remains an open question. As biased as Procopius was against the emperor, the *Secret History* is nevertheless an important view of the Byzantine court from the inside. The use of the word "Byzantine" as a synonym for a "treacherous" or "complex" political system is more understandable after reading Procopius. The *Secret History* provides a very interesting contrast between the rational lawgiver Justinian of the Code (in the previous document) and the monster Procopius claims to have known.

I think this is as good a time as any to describe the personal appearance of the man. Now in physique he was neither tall nor short, but of average height; not thin, but moderately plump; his face was round, and not bad looking, for he had good color, even when he fasted for two days. To make a long description short, he much resembled Domitian, Vespasian's son.

Now such was Justinian in appearance; but his character was something I could not fully describe. For he was at once villainous and amenable; as people say colloquially, a moron. He was never truthful with anyone, but always guileful in what he said and did, yet easily hoodwinked by any who wanted to deceive him. His nature was an unnatural mixture of folly and wickedness. What in olden times a peripatetic philosopher said was also true of him, that opposite qualities combine in a man as in the mixing of colors. I will try to portray him, however, insofar as I can fathom his complexity.

This Emperor, then, was deceitful, devious, false, hypocritical, two-faced, cruel, skilled in dissembling his thought, never moved to tears by either joy or pain, though he could summon them artfully at will when the occasion demanded, a liar always, not only offhand, but in writing, and when he swore sacred oaths to his subjects in their very hearing. Then he would immediately break his agreements and pledges, like the vilest of slaves, whom indeed only the fear of torture drives to confess their perjury. A faithless friend, he was a treacherous enemy, insane for murder and plunder, quarrelsome and revolutionary, easily led to anything evil, but never willing to listen to good counsel, quick to plan mischief and carry it out, but finding even the hearing of anything good distasteful to his ears.

How could anyone put Justinian's ways into words? These and many even worse vices were disclosed in him as in no other mortal: nature seemed to have taken the wickedness of all other men combined and planted it in this man's soul. And besides this, he was too prone to listen to accusations; and too quick to punish. For he decided such cases without full examination, naming the punishment when he had heard only the accuser's side of the matter. Without hesitation he wrote decrees for the plundering of countries, sacking of cities, and slavery of whole nations, for no cause whatever. So that if one wished to take all the calamities which had befallen the Romans before this time and weigh them against his crimes, I think it would be found that more men had been murdered by this single man than in all previous history.

He had no scruples about appropriating other people's property, and did not even think any excuse necessary, legal or illegal, for confiscating what did not belong to him. And when it was his, he was more than ready to squander it in insane display, or give it as an unnecessary bribe to the barbarians. In short, he neither held on to any money himself nor let anyone else keep any: as if his reason were not avarice, but jealousy of those who had riches. Driving all wealth from the country of the Romans in this manner, he became the cause of universal poverty.

Now this was the character of Justinian, so far as I can portray it.

As soon as Justinian came into power he turned everything upside down. Whatever had before been forbidden by law he now introduced into the government, while he revoked all established customs: as if he had been given the robes of an Emperor on the condition he would turn everything topsy-turvy. Existing offices he abolished, and invented new ones for the management of public affairs. He did the same thing to the laws and to the regulations of the army; and his reason was not any improvement of justice or any advantage, but simply that everything might be new and named after himself. And whatever was beyond his power to abolish, he renamed after himself anyway.

Of the plundering of property or the murder of men, no weariness ever overtook him. As soon as he had looted all the houses of the wealthy, he looked around for others; meanwhile throwing away the spoils of his previous robberies in subsidies to barbarians or senseless building extravagances. And when he had ruined perhaps myriads in this mad looting, he immediately sat down to plan how he could do likewise to others in even greater number.

As the Romans were now at peace with all the world and he had no other means of satisfying his lust for slaughter, he set the barbarians all to fighting each other. And for no reason at all he sent for the Hun chieftains, and with idiotic magnanimity gave them large sums of money, alleging he did this to secure their friendship. These Huns, as soon as they had got this money, sent it together with their soldiers to others of their chieftains, with the word to make inroads into the land of the Emperor: so that they might collect further tribute from him, to buy them off in a second peace. Thus the Huns enslaved the

Roman Empire, and were paid by the Emperor to keep on doing it.

This encouraged still others of them to rob the poor Romans; and after their pillaging, they too were further rewarded by the gracious Emperor. In this way all the Huns, for when it was not one tribe of them it was another, continuously overran and laid waste the Empire. For the barbarians were led by many different chieftains, and the war, thanks to Justinian's senseless generosity, was thus endlessly protracted. Consequently no place, mountain or cave, or any other spot in Roman territory, during this time remained uninjured; and many regions were pillaged more than five times.

These misfortunes, and those that were caused by the Medes, Saracens, Slavs, Antes, and the rest of the barbarians, I described in my previous works. But, as I said in the preface to this narrative, the real cause of these calamities remained to be told here.

Moreover, while he was encouraging civil strife and frontier warfare to confound the Romans, with only one thought in his mind, that the earth should run red with human blood and he might acquire more and more booty, he invented a new means of murdering his subjects. Now among the Christians in the entire Roman Empire, there are many with dissenting doctrines, which are called heresies by the established church: such as those of the Montanists and Sabbatians, and whatever others cause the minds of men to wander from the true path. All of these beliefs he ordered to be abolished, and their place taken by the orthodox dogma: threatening, among the punishments for disobedience, loss of the heretic's right to will property to his children or other relatives.

Now the churches of these so-called heretics, especially those belonging to the Arian dissenters, were almost incredibly wealthy. Neither all the Senate put together nor the greatest other unit of the Roman Empire, had anything in property comparable to that of these churches. For their gold and silver treasures, and stores of precious stones, were beyond telling or numbering: they owned mansions and whole villages, land all over the world, and everything else that is counted as wealth among men.

As none of the previous Emperors had molested these churches, many men, even those of the orthodox faith, got their livelihood by working on their estates. But the Emperor Justinian, in confiscating these properties, at the same time took away what for many people had been their only means of earning a living.

Agents were sent everywhere to force whomever they chanced upon to renounce the faith of their fathers. This, which seemed impious to rustic people, caused them to rebel against those who gave them such an order. Thus many perished at the hands of the persecuting faction, and others did away with themselves, foolishly thinking this the holier course of two evils; but most of them by far quitted the land of their fathers, and fled the country. The Montanists, who dwelt in Phrygia, shut themselves up in their churches, set them on fire, and ascended to glory in the flames. And thenceforth the whole Roman Empire was a scene of massacre and flight.

A similar law was then passed against the Samaritans, which threw Palestine into an indescribable turmoil. Those, indeed, who lived in my own Caesarea and in the other cities, deciding it silly to suffer harsh treatment over a ridiculous trifle of dogma, took the name of Christians in exchange for the one they had borne before, by which precaution they were able to avoid the perils of the new law. The most reputable and better class of these citizens, once they had adopted this religion, decided to remain faithful to it; the majority, however, as if in spite for having not voluntarily, but by the compulsion of law, abandoned the belief of their fathers, soon slipped away into the Manichean sect and what is known as polytheism.

The country people, however, banded together and determined to take arms against the Emperor: choosing as their candidate for the throne a bandit named Julian, son of

Sabarus. And for a time they held their own against the imperial troops; but finally, defeated in battle, were cut down, together with their leader. Ten myriads of men are said to have perished in this engagement, and the most fertile country on earth thus became destitute of farmers. To the Christian owners of these lands, the affair brought great hardship: for while their profits from these properties were annihilated, they had to pay heavy annual taxes on them to the Emperor for the rest of their lives, and secured no remission of this burden.

Next he turned his attention to those called Gentiles, torturing their persons and plundering their lands. Of this group, those who decided to become nominal Christians saved themselves for the time being; but it was not long before these, too, were caught performing libations and sacrifices and other unholy rites. And how he treated the Christians shall be told hereafter.

After this he passed a law prohibiting pederasty: a law pointed not at offenses committed after this decree, but at those who could be convicted of having practised the vice in the past. The conduct of the prosecution was utterly illegal. Sentence was passed when there was no accuser:

the word of one man or boy, and that perhaps a slave, compelled against his will to bear witness against his owner, was defined as sufficient evidence. Those who were convicted were castrated and then exhibited in a public parade. At the start, this persecution was directed only at those who were of the Green party, were reputed to be especially wealthy, or had otherwise aroused jealousy.

The Emperor's malice was also directed against the astrologer. Accordingly, magistrates appointed to punish thieves also abused the astrologers, for no other reason than that they belonged to this profession: whipping them on the back and parading them on camels throughout the city, though they were old men, and in every way respectable, with no reproach against them except that they studied the science of the stars while living in such a city.

Consequently there was a constant stream of emigration not only to the land of the barbarians but to places farthest remote from the Romans; and in every country and city one could see crowds of foreigners. For in order to escape persecution, each would lightly exchange his native land for another, as if his own country had been taken by an enemy.

QUESTIONS

1. What are the emperor's principal failings, according to Procopius?

2. Do Justinian's character flaws affect his ability to rule?

3. Justinian is criticized for his reforms by Procopius, a professional civil servant. If the emperor were to speak in his own defense, how might he answer the charges?

4. Why does Justinian's foreign policy fail? What do you think he was trying to accomplish?

5. Procopius presents us with an extremely biased picture of Justinian. Can such an unfair portrayal teach us anything of value about Justinian?

6. What does Procopius's bias tell us about him? Could you say something about his own views, given the picture he gives us of Justinian?

36

THE KORAN

(7TH CENTURY)

The Koran is the Holy Book of Islam. Reported to have been revealed by God to Muhammad (ca. 570–632) over the course of two decades beginning in 610, it is the foundation upon which Islam was built. Believers consider the book to be literally true in all respects and to be the final authority on all moral and legal questions.

Roughly the same length as the New Testament, the Koran contains many references to both the Jewish and Christian traditions. It recognizes the contribution of biblical figures such as Noah and Moses and the importance of Jesus as a prophet. Nevertheless, it contains much that is unique. The Koran emphasizes the singularity of God as well as His divine plan. It also includes a system of ritual laws and ethics. Each man, for example, is allowed to marry no more than four wives. Followers are presented with a strict moral and dietary code and are required to make a pilgrimage to Mecca, the center of Islam. They are also required to treat all persons, believers and infidels, with compassion.

In the name of God, the most merciful and
    compassionate.
Praise be to God, the Lord of the worlds;
The most merciful, the compassionate;
The king of the day of Judgment.
Thee do we worship, and of Thee do we
    beg assistance.
Direct us on the right way,
The way of those to whom Thou has been
    gracious; not of those against whom Thou
    art angry, nor of those who go astray.

In the name of God, the most merciful and compassionate.

Praise the name of thy Lord, the Most High, Who hath created and completely formed His creatures: Who determineth them to various ends, and directeth them to attain the same, Who produceth the pastures for cattle, and afterwards rendereth the same dry stubble of a dusky hue.

God will enable thee to rehearse His revelations, and thou shalt not forget any part thereof, except what God shall please, for He knoweth that which is manifest, and that which is hidden. And God will facilitate unto thee the most easy way. Therefore admonish thy people, if thy admonition shall be profitable unto them.

Whosoever feareth God, he will be admonished: but the most wretched unbeliever will turn away from it; who shall be cast to be broiled in the greater fire of hell, wherein he shall not die, neither shall he live.

Now hath he attained felicity who is purified by faith, and who remembereth the name of his Lord, and prayeth. But ye prefer this present life: yet the life to come is better, and more durable.

Verily this is written in the ancient Books, the Books of Abraham and Moses.

God! There is no god but Him, the Living, the Self-subsisting: He hath sent down unto thee the Book of the Koran with truth, confirming that which was revealed before it; For He had formerly sent down the Law and the Gospel, a guidance unto men; and He had also sent down the Salvation.

Verily those who believe not the signs of God shall suffer a grievous punishment; for God is mighty, able to revenge.

Surely nothing is hidden from God, of that which is on earth, or in the heavens; it is He who formeth you in the wombs, as He pleaseth; there is no God but Him, the Mighty, the Wise.

It is He who hath sent down unto thee the Book, wherein are some verses clear to be understood; they are the foundation of the Book; and others are parabolical. But they whose hearts are perverse will follow that which is parabolical therein, out of love of schism, and a desire of the interpretation thereof; yet none knoweth the interpretation thereof, except God. But they who are well grounded in knowledge say, We believe therein, the whole is from our Lord; and none will consider except the prudent.

The Doctrine of One God

God! There is no God but Him; the Living, the Self-subsisting: neither slumber nor sleep seizeth Him; to Him belongeth whatsoever is in the heavens, and on earth. Who is he that can intercede with Him, but through His good pleasure? He knoweth that which is past, and that which is to come unto them, and they shall not comprehend anything of His knowledge, but so far as He pleaseth. His throne is extended over the heavens and the earth; and the preservation of both is no burden unto Him. He is the High, the Mighty.

Let there be no compulsion in religion. Now is right direction manifestly distinguished from deceit: whoever therefore shall deny Tagut [Satan] and believe in God, he shall surely take hold on a strong handle, which shall not be broken; God is He who heareth and seeth.

God is the patron of those who believe; He shall lead them out of darkness into light; but as to those who believe not, their patrons are Tagut; they shall lead them from the light into darkness; they shall be the companions of hell fire, they shall remain therein forever.

Alms to the Poor

Who is he that will lend unto God an acceptable loan? For God will double the same unto him, and he shall receive moreover an honorable reward.

Verily as to those who give alms, both men and women, and those who lend unto God an acceptable loan, He will double the same unto them; and they shall moreover receive an honorable reward.

And they who believe in God and His apostles, these are the men of veracity and the witnesses in the presence of their Lord: they shall have their reward and their light. But as to those who believe not, and lie about God's signs; they shall be the companions of hell.

Know ye that this present life is only a play and a vain amusement; and worldly pomp, and the affectation of glory among you, and the multiplying of riches and children, are as the plants nourished by the rain, the springing up whereof delighteth the husbandmen; then they wither, so that thou seest the same turn yellow, and at length they become dry stubble. But in the life to come will be a severe punishment for those who covet worldly grandeur; and pardon from God, and favor for those who renounce it: for this present life is no other than a deceitful provision.

Hasten with emulation to obtain pardon from your Lord, and Paradise, the extent whereof equaleth the extent of heaven and earth, prepared for those who believe in God and His apostles. Such is the bounty of God; He will give the same unto whom He pleaseth; and God is endured with great bounty.

It is not righteousness that ye turn your faces in prayer towards the East and the West, but righteousness is of him who believeth in God and the last day, and the angels and the Scriptures, and the prophets; who giveth money for God's sake unto his kindred, and unto orphans, and the needy, and the wayfarer, and those who ask, and for the redemption of captives; who is constant in prayer, and giveth alms; and of those who perform their promises which they have made, and who behave themselves patiently in adversity, and hardships, and in time of violence: these are they who are true, and these are they who fear God.

The Devil threateneth you with poverty, and commandeth you filthy covetousness; but God promiseth you pardon from Himself and abundance: God is Bounteous and Wise. He giveth wisdom unto whom He pleaseth; and he unto whom wisdom is given, hath received much good: but none will consider it, except the wise of heart.

And whatever alms ye shall give, or whatever vow ye shall vow, verily God knoweth it; but the ungodly shall have none to help them. If ye make your alms to appear, it is well; but if ye conceal them, and give them unto the poor, this will be better for you, and will remove some of your sins: and God is well informed of that which ye do.

The guidance of them belongeth not unto thee [O Apostle]; but God guideth whom He pleaseth. The good that ye shall give in alms shall redound unto yourselves; and ye shall not give unless out of desire of seeing the face of God. And what good things ye shall give in alms, it shall be repaid you, and ye shall not be treated unjustly.

Alms unto the poor who are wholly employed in fighting for the religion of God, and cannot freely travel in the land; the ignorant man thinketh them rich, because of their modesty: thou shalt know them by this mark, they ask not men with importunity; and what good ye shall give them in alms, verily God knoweth it.

They who distribute alms of their substance night and day, in private and in public, shall have their reward with the Lord; on them shall no fear come, neither shall they be grieved.

Wine and Gambling

O true believers! surely wine, and gambling and images, and divining arrows, are an abomination of the work of Satan; therefore avoid them, that ye may prosper.

Satan seeketh to sow dissension and hatred among you, by means of wine and gambling, and to divert you from remembering God, and from prayer; will ye not therefore abstain from them?

Obey God, and obey the Apostle, and take heed to yourselves; but if ye turn back, know that the duty of God's Apostle is only to preach publicly.

On those who believe and do good works, it is no sin that they have tasted wine or gambled before they were forbidden; if they fear God, and believe, and do good works, and shall for the future fear God, and believe, and shall persevere to fear him, and to do good, for God loveth those who do good.

Paradise

The description of Paradise, which is promised unto the pious: therein are rivers of incorruptible water; and rivers of milk, the taste whereof changeth not; and rivers of wine, pleasant unto those who drink; and rivers of clarified honey. And therein shall they have plenty of all kinds of fruits; and pardon from their Lord. Shall the man for whom these things are prepared, be as they who must dwell forever in hell fire, and will have the boiling water given them to drink, which shall burst their bowels?

They [the righteous] shall repose on couches, the linings thereof shall be of thick silk interwoven with gold: and the fruit of the two gardens shall be near at hand to gather.

Which, therefore, of your Lord's benefits will ye ungratefully deny?

Therein shall be damsels, refraining their eyes from beholding any besides their spouses: whom no man or Jinni shall have touched before them,

Which, therefore, of your Lord's benefits will ye ungratefully deny?

Having complexions like rubies and pearls.

Which, therefore, of your Lord's benefits will ye ungratefully deny?

Shall the reward of good works be any other than good?

Which, therefore, of your Lord's benefits will ye ungratefully deny?

And besides these there shall be two other gardens.

Which, therefore, of your Lord's benefits will ye ungratefully deny?

Of a dark green color.

Which, therefore, of your Lord's benefits will ye ungratefully deny?

In each of them shall be two fountains pouring forth plenty of water.

Which, therefore, of your Lord's benefits will ye ungratefully deny?

In each of them shall be fruits, and palm trees, and pomegranates.

Which, therefore, of your Lord's benefits will ye ungratefully deny?

Therein shall be agreeable and beauteous damsels.

Which, therefore, of your Lord's benefits will ye ungratefully deny?

Having fine black eyes; and kept in pavilions from public view.

Which, therefore, of your Lord's benefits will ye ungratefully deny?

Whom no man shall have touched before their destined spouses, nor any Jinni.

Which, therefore, of your Lord's benefits will ye ungratefully deny?

Therein shall they delight themselves, lying on green cushions and beautiful carpets.

Which, therefore, of your Lord's benefits will ye ungratefully deny?

Blessed be the name of thy Lord, possessed of Glory and Honor!

QUESTIONS

1. What are some of the characteristics shared by Islam, Christianity, and Judaism?

2. What is the responsibility of the believer toward the poor?

3. In what way is the Koran a code of conduct for everyday life?

4. What does the Koran teach should be done to the nonbeliever?

5. What does paradise look like? Why do you think the Koran portrays paradise as it does?

37

■ *Michael Psellus* ■

CHRONOGRAPHIA

(CA. 1075–1077)

Michael Psellus (ca.1018–1080) was a Byzantine statesman and counselor to emperors. Psellus came from an aristocratic family and was educated in both Athens and Constantinople. He was a particularly skilled public orator at a time when oration was equated with wisdom. He was widely reputed to be one of the great minds of his age and was made professor of rhetoric at the newly founded University of Constantinople. There he was responsible for a revival of learning in numerous subjects and was widely recognized as the intellectual giant of the age. Though he pursued his scholarly studies, Psellus also played a central role in court politics and helped engineer the succession of his boyhood friend Constantine X. Psellus became Constantine's closest advisor, tutor to his son, and ultimately the most powerful individual at his court. Unfortunately, Psellus was a better politician than statesman, and the advice he gave to Constantine and his son Michael VII was disastrous. It was during their reigns that Byzantium lost its position as a great power. After Michael VII was deposed in 1078, Psellus fled the court and died in obscurity.

The most famous among Psellus's published works was the *Chronographia* (ca. 1075–1077), which combined both a history of Byzantium during the previous century and an autobiography. In this passage, Psellus describes his own early education.

At the time I was in my twenty-fifth year and engaged in serious studies. My efforts were concentrated on two objects: to train my tongue by rhetoric, so as to become a fine speaker, and to refine my mind by a course of philosophy. I soon mastered the rhetoric enough to be able to distinguish the central theme of an argument and logically connect it with my main and secondary points. I also learnt not to stand in complete awe of the art, nor to follow its precepts in everything like a child, and I even made certain contributions of a minor character myself. Then I applied myself to the study of philosophy, and having

acquainted myself thoroughly with the art of reasoning, both *deductive*, from cause to immediate effect, and *inductive*, tracing causes from all manner of effects, I turned to natural science and aspired to a knowledge of the fundamental principles of philosophy through mathematics.

If the reader does not find me boring in this and will allow me to go on, I will add to what I have already said concerning my own activities. The fact to which I am about to refer will undoubtedly win for me high approval among men of learning, quite apart from all other considerations. And you, who read my history today, will bear witness to the truth of my words. Philosophy, when I first studied it, was moribund as far as its professors were concerned, and I alone revived it, untutored by any masters worthy of mention, and despite my thorough search finding no germ of philosophy either in Greece or in the barbarian world. I had heard that the Greeks had a great reputation for philosophy, expressed in simple words and simple propositions, and their work in this field set a standard and criterion for the future. There were some who belittled the simplicity of the Greeks, but I sought to learn more, and, as I met some of the experts in the art, I was instructed by them how to pursue my studies in a methodical way. One passed me to another for tuition, the lesser light to the greater, and he again recommended me to a third, and he to Aristotle and Plato. Doubtless my former teachers were well satisfied to take second place to these two.

Starting from these authors I completed a cycle, so to speak, by coming down to Plotinus, Porphyry, and Iamblichus. Then, continuing my voyage, I put in at the mighty harbour of the admirable Proclus, eagerly picking up there his doctrine of perception, both in its broad principles and in its exact interpretation. From Proclus I intended to proceed to more advanced studies—metaphysics, with an introduction to pure science—so I began with an examination of abstract conceptions in the so-called mathematics, which hold a position midway between the science of corporeal nature, with the external apprehension of these bodies, and the ideas themselves, the object of pure thought. I hoped from this study to apprehend something that was beyond the reach of mind, something that was not subject to the limitations of substance.

It was therefore consonant with this plan that I should pay especial attention to systems of number and examine geometrical proofs, which some call "logical necessities." Moreover, I devoted time to the study of music and astronomy, as well as to their various subsidiary arts. First I would concentrate on each study by itself, then synthesize my knowledge, in the belief that the several branches of learning would by their individual contributions lead me to one simple goal, according to the teaching of Plato's *Epinomis*. So, thanks to these sciences, I was able to launch out into the more advanced studies.

I had heard it said by the most learned philosophers that there is a wisdom which is beyond all demonstration, apprehensible only by the intellect of a wise man, in moments of inspiration. Even here my resolution did not falter. I read some of the mystic books and grasped their meaning (as far as human nature allowed, of course, for I myself could never claim that I had an accurate understanding of these things, nor would I believe anyone else who said he had). On the other hand, it is by no means beyond our natural capacity to dwell on one science, as a special subject, and for sake of research to make excursions, as it were, into other branches of learning in a general survey, returning later to one's original starting-point.

Literature has two branches. One comprises the works of the orators, and the philosophers have arrogated the other. The first, knowing nothing of the deeper things, issues forth merely in a mighty torrent of noisy words; it concerns itself with the composition of speeches, sets forth certain rules for the arrangement of arguments on political subjects and for the various divisions of political orations, lends distinction to the spoken word, and in general beautifies the language of politics. Philosophy is less concerned with the embellishments of words. Its aim is rather to explore the nature of the universe, to unravel its secrets. Its lofty dictums are not even confined to the visible world, for with great subtlety it praises the glory of that realm, whatever it be, that lies beyond the heaven. Now I had no mind to follow the example of most other men, and emulate their experiences—men who study the art of the orator while despising the science of the philosopher, or else engross themselves in philosophy and enjoy the riches to be found in the marvels of thought, but condemn the glories of rhetoric and the skill required to arrange and divide the various parts of a speech. Thus, from time to time, when I compose an oration, I introduce some scientific proof, not without some elegance. Many persons have reproached me for this and they dislike the way I brighten a philosophic discourse with the graceful arts of rhetoric. My purpose in this is to assist the reader when he finds it difficult to absorb some deep thought, and so to prevent his losing the thread of philosophic argument.

But there is a new philosophy, based on the mystery of our Christian religion, which transcends the ancient systems. This mystery, too, has a dual aspect, in nature (human and divine), and in time (finite and infinite), not to mention a further dualism when one considers how it is capable of proof and yet the object of faith and divinely inspired into men's consciousness. It was this philosophy rather than the profane which became the object of my special study. In some respects I agreed with the doctrine of the great Fathers of the Church, but I also made some contribution to the corpus of divine teaching on my own account. I say this in all sincerity and without boastfulness: if any man should feel constrained to praise my literary works, I would beg him not to commend my researches in the field of religion, not to extol my extensive reading (I am not deluded by a false impression of my own importance, nor am I ignorant of my own limitations; my capacity is very small when compared with the ability of the orators and philosophers who have surpassed me). No, if anyone praises my efforts, let it be rather because I drew my small measure of wisdom from no living fount: the sources I discovered were choked up, and I had to open and cleanse them myself. Their waters, too, were hidden in the depths and only brought to the surface after I had expended much energy.

Today, in fact, neither Athens, nor Nicomedia, nor Alexandria in Egypt, nor Phoenicia, nor even the two Romes (the ancient and lesser Rome, and the later, more powerful city), nor any other State glories any longer in literary achievement. The golden streams of the past, and baser silver, and streams of metal more worthless still, all are blocked and choked up: their damming is complete. So, since I was unable to reach the living sources themselves, I perforce studied their images. These second-hand imitations I greedily devoured in my mind, and, having collected the knowledge, I grudged no one else a share of what I myself had acquired at the cost of much labour. Everybody was welcome to learn from me, and far from demanding a fee for my lessons, I was even prepared to help keen students with money from my own purse. But that story must wait until later.

In my career, even before the fruit was ripe, the blossom gave promise of a brilliant future. Certainly the emperor did not know me yet, but I was well known to all his bodyguard and they spoke of me in his presence, some recounting one quality, and others stressing another. They told him, moreover, that I was an eloquent orator. I would like to say something on this subject here. At the time of our birth, we are endowed with certain natural virtues, or their opposites. When I use the word "virtue" in this connexion, I am not referring to moral virtue, nor to political virtue, nor to the virtue which excels these others and attains to the pattern or perfection of the Creator; but just as some bodies, from the moment of birth, are endowed with beauty, while on others nature from their very beginning bestows blemishes and wrinkles, so with souls too, some are distinguished at once with extreme grace and attractiveness, while others leave a trail of sombre and deep gloom. As time goes on, the innate graces of the first sort become more and more apparent, but in the second everything goes wrong and even the reason functions poorly.

However that may be, even in simple utterances I have been told that my language is peculiarly graceful, and though I do not strive after effect, there is in my words a certain natural beauty. Of course, I would not know this myself, had not many folk told me so in the course of conversation and had they not listened with rapt attention while I talked with them. Anyhow, it was this characteristic that first won me access to the emperor, and it was the eloquence of my tongue that, so to speak, proved to be my forerunner, giving him a foretaste of the spirit deep-hidden within me.

At that first interview, my words were distinguished neither by their fluency nor by their elegance, but I told him about my family and the sort of education I had received in literature. As for Constantine, he was affected by a strange feeling of pleasure, as inexplicable as the divinely-inspired utterance of men in a trance. So influenced was he at the first sound of my voice that he almost embraced me. Other men had the right of access to him at set times and for a limited period, but to me his heart's doors were now thrown wide open, and gradually, as I became more intimate with him, he shared with me all his secrets. Please do not blame me if I have wandered somewhat from the main theme of my history, and please do not imagine that this digression is mere self-advertisement. If I have indulged in a certain amount of personal reminiscence, at least it is all directly concerned with the central thread of the story. Without disclosing the reason for it, it would have been impossible for me to speak of that first interview; and, of course, if I wished to explain the reason, it was essential to introduce some remarks on my own career. My history must be written in a methodical way: first the reference to my source, then the sifting of evidence, and finally the account of subsequent events. That is why so long a preface was necessary. Now that I have introduced myself with such a wealth of detail into this part of the history, I can assure you that my evidence will avoid all falsehood; whatever is not said, will remain hidden, but none of the things I am going to say will be of doubtful veracity.

QUESTIONS

1. What were the two objects of Psellus's education?

2. What is Psellus's attitude toward literature?

3. How did Psellus become a great orator?

4. What is your impression of Psellus's personality?

38

■ *Ibn Al-Qalanisi* ■

THE DAMASCUS CHRONICLE

(CA. 1150)

Ibn Al-Qalanisi (d. 1160) was a member of one of Damascus's most prominent families. Probably a young adult when the Christian infidels invaded his homeland, Al-Qalanisi was a witness of the fury of the First Crusade. Although he evidently did not take the field as a soldier, he did serve his faith in other ways.

Highly educated and very cultured, Al-Qalanisi worked in his government's secretariat and served as mayor of Damascus twice. His post in the secretariat involved him in diplomacy and central administration as the struggle over the Holy Land raged. Although he wrote some poetry, it is his *Chronicle* that has captured the interest of historians. As an eyewitness, and thanks to his access to official papers, Al-Qalanisi was in a good position to write about the Crusade from the Muslim perspective.

Al-Qalanisi's *Chronicle* is a superb picture of the deadly fighting between the Christian Franks, as Europeans were described, and the Muslims. He provides many details about siege warfare, diplomacy, and the human cost of war absent in other accounts. This selection describes the Christian assault on the Muslim city of Tyre.

In First Jumādā of this year [15th November to 14th December, 1110] the Sultan Ghiyāth al-Dunyā wal-Dīn Muhammad, son of Malik-Shāh, arrived at Baghdād from Hamadhān. Here he received letters and envoys from Syria, acquainting him with the state of affairs and the activities of the Franks after their return from the Euphrates, and the disaster at Sidon and al-Athārib and in the districts of Aleppo. On the first Friday of Sha 'bān [17th February, 1111] a certain Hāshimite sharīf from Aleppo and a company of Sūfīs, merchants and theologians presented themselves at the Sultan's mosque, and appealed for assistance. They drove the preacher from the pulpit and broke it in pieces, clamouring and weeping for the misfortunes that had befallen Islām at the hands of the Franks, the slaughter of men, and enslavement of women and children. They prevented the people from carrying out the service, while the attendants and leaders, to quieten them, promised them on behalf of the Sultan to dispatch armies and to vindicate Islām against the Franks and the infidels. On the following Friday they assembled again, went to the Caliph's mosque, and repeated their performance with much weeping and clamour and appealing for help, and lamenting. Shortly afterwards the princess, the Sultan's daughter and wife of the Caliph, arrived at Baghdād from Isfahān, in such magnificence and with such quantities of

jewellery, moneys, utensils, carriages and riding beasts of all kinds, furniture, varieties of gorgeous raiment, attendants, guards, slave-girls, and followers, as exceeds all reckoning. Her arrival coincided with these appeals for assistance, and the tranquillity of the city and joy at her coming were marred and disturbed. The Caliph, al-Mustazhir B'illāh, Commander of the Faithful, was indignant at what had happened, and determined to seek out him who had been its instigator and cause, in order to mete out to him condign punishment. The Sultan prevented him from doing so, and excused the action of those people, and directed the amīrs and commanders to return to their governments and make preparations for setting out to the Holy War against the infidels, the enemies of God. . . .

In this year king Baldwin assembled all whom he could of the Franks and marched to the port of Tyre. The governor 'Izz al-Mulk and the citizens wrote in haste to Zahīr al-Dīn Atābek at Damascus, asking him for help and reinforcement and promising to surrender the city to him. They besought him to make haste to send a large number of Turks and urged that they should come to them speedily to assist and strengthen them, for should there be any delay in sending them assistance necessity would compel them to surrender the city to the Franks, as they despaired of help from al-Afdal, the ruler of Egypt. The atābek dispatched with all speed a large contingent of Turks, consisting of over two hundred horsemen, archers of proved worth, with full equipment. In addition to this contingent, the citizens were reinforced by numbers of footsoldiers from Tyre and Jabal 'Amilah who embraced their cause, together with footsoldiers from Damascus. The atābek also prepared to dispatch another detachment. When Baldwin learned of the arrangement between the atābek and the people of Tyre, he made haste to invest it with the forces which he had assembled, on 25th First Jumādā 505 [29th November]. He ordered the fruit trees and palms to be cut down and constructed permanent dwellings before the city, and delivered regular assaults upon it on several occasions, only to retire discomfited and frustrated in his object. It is said that in one attack the people of Tyre discharged twenty thousand arrows in a single day.

Zahīr al-Dīn on learning that the Franks had invested Tyre marched out and made his camp at Bānyās, whence he dispatched his squadrons together with bands of brigands into the territories of the Franks with a free hand to plunder, kill, rob, destroy and burn, with the object of causing them vexation and forcing them to abandon the siege. The second contingent which he sent to Tyre attempted to enter the town but was unable to gain entrance. Zahīr al-Dīn himself marched to al-Habīs, a strong and forbidding castle in the Sawād, and after a vigorous attack captured it by the sword and put the entire garrison to death. The Franks set about constructing two wooden towers with which to make the assault on the wall of Tyre, and Zahīr al-Dīn deployed his forces against them several times in order to distract them so that the troops in Tyre might make a sortie and burn the towers. The Franks became aware of his object in these manœuvres, and having dug a trench around them on all sides, posted armed men along it to defend both it and the towers, paying no heed either to what he might do or to the raids which were made upon their territories and the slaughter of their inhabitants. When the winter storms commenced, they did no harm to the Franks since they were encamped on hard, sandy soil, while the Turks on the contrary suffered great hardships and bitter distress in their position, yet they did not cease from raiding and making booty, and cutting off supplies and provisions from the Franks, and seizing all that was conveyed to them. . . .

The construction of the two towers and the battering-rams to be placed within them was completed in about seventy-five days, and on 10th Sha 'bān [11th February] they began to be moved forward and employed in the attack. They were brought up close to the city wall and fierce fighting went on round about them. . . . On 1st Ramadān [2nd March] the men of Tyre made a sortie from the bastions with greek fire, firewood, pitch, and incendiary equipment, and being unable to penetrate to either of the towers, threw the fire close to the smaller one where the Franks could not protect it from the flames. The wind blew the fire on to the smaller tower, which was completely burned after severe fighting around it and a hand-to-hand struggle in its defence. Many coats of mail, long shields, and other objects were recovered from it as booty. . . . The Franks then made a vigorous attack upon them [the Muslims], drove them clear of the tower, and put out the fire that had caught hold of it. . . .

Thereupon the Franks despaired of capturing the city and prepared to retire. They burned the houses which they had built in their camp to dwell in, as well as many of the vessels belonging to them on the shore, since they had removed their masts, rudders, and equipment for their towers. The number of these vessels was about two hundred, large and small, about thirty of them being war vessels, and they used some of them for the transport of their light baggage. They departed on 10th Shawwāl of this year [10th April], having prosecuted the siege of Tyre for the space of four and a half months, and proceeding to 'Akkā dispersed to their own provinces. The men of Tyre came out and seized as booty everything belonging to them that they could find, and the Turks who had been sent to assist them returned to Damascus. The Tyrians, however, did not carry out their promise to surrender the city to Zahīr al-Dīn Atābek, and he did not openly demand it of them, but said, "What I have done I have done only for the sake of God and the Muslims, not out of desire for wealth or kingdom."

Blessings and thanks were showered upon him for his noble action, and he promised them that when a similar danger should threaten them, he would hasten to the city and do his utmost to assist it. He then returned to Damascus, having suffered great hardship in warring against the Franks until God delivered the men of Tyre from their distress.

QUESTIONS

1. Ibn Al-Qalanisi gives us a clear view of fighting in the Crusades. What was it like?

2. Why do the Muslims fight? Are their reasons any different from those of the Christian forces?

3. The Muslim side in the Crusade is often depicted as monolithic. From your reading of the *Chronicle,* does this seem true?

4. Why do you suppose this document was written? What purposes might it have served?

39

■ *IBN Ishaq* ■

THE LIFE OF MUHAMMAD

(AFTER 733)

Ibn Ishaq (ca. 704–767) was born in Medina, now in Saudi Arabia, at the beginning of the eighth century. His father and uncles were all Islamic scholars who collected information about the life of the prophet Muhammad, especially during his time in Medina. Ibn Ishaq followed in the family tradition, becoming expert on Muhammad's military campaigns. Little is known about his life except that he studied in Alexandria and some-time after 733 moved to Iraq, finally settling in Baghdad. It was during his travels that he collected information on the life of Muhammad, particularly upon his military campaigns and his establishment of Islam in Medina.

As Ibn Ishaq lived nearly a century after his subject, nearly all of the stories he collected were second- and third-hand accounts handed down from generation to generation. He was particularly careful to identify the source of the stories he recounted though he has been criticized for his uncritical acceptance of them.

The Life of Muhammad, also called the Sirah, is an account of the Prophet's early life, his military campaigns, and his establishment of the religion of Islam. It was never finished as a complete literary work, and only two manuscript copies were left at Ibn Ishaq's death. It was ultimately edited by Ibn Hisham and presumably reordered into a biographical form. The following section is drawn from Ibn Ishaq's description of the revelation to Muhammad that he was the Prophet of Allah.

THE REVELATION

Like the Jews and Christians, the Arab soothsayers also spoke of the coming of an apostle, but their people paid no heed until Allah actually sent him, when, the prophecies made by the soothsayers having been fulfilled, the people became aware of their significance. Whereas the Jews and Christians culled their Prophecies from scripture, the Arab soothsayers received their foreknowledge of most events from the djinns, spirits of the air who stole information by listening close to heaven. But when the coming of the apostle was close at hand meteors from heaven were hurled at all the djinns and they were driven away from the places where they used to sit and listen; and they realized that this was by the command of Allah.

The first Arabs to be struck with fear at the sight of the shooting starts—for that was how the meteors thrown at the djinns appeared on earth—went to the wisest man of their tribe and said, "Have you seen what happened in the sky and the falling of some of the stars?" He replied, "If the stars thrown down were those which serve as signs and guides by land and sea, those by which the seasons of summer and winter are defined and by which the various affairs of mankind are regulated, then by Allah the world has come to an end with all the people thereof; but if those stars remain in their places and it is others which have been hurled down, then Allah has a different intention and does not mean to destroy creation."

Afterwards, the apostle of Allah asked some men of Medina what had been said there about the falling stars and was told: "We said, 'A king has died or has begun to reign; a child has been born, or has died.'" The apostle of Allah replied: "It was not so. When Allah reaches any decision concerning His people He is heard by the bearers of His throne, who praise Him; and this praise is taken up by the angels below them, and by others still further below; and the praise continues to descend until it reaches the sky of this world, where other angels also praise. Then these ask each other why they praise, and the question ascends gradually till it reaches the bearers of the throne. They then, tell of the decree of Allah concerning His people, and the news travels down by degrees until it reaches the heaven of this world, where the angels discuss it. But the evil djinns, who used to listen to such discussions by stealth, sometimes misheard, and what they retailed to soothsayers on earth was sometimes true and sometimes false. The soothsayers also conversed about these matters, some giving true and some false accounts. So, when the coming of the apostle was being discussed by the angels, Allah foiled the evil djinns by hurling meteors, and from that time onwards an end was made to soothsayers."

When Muhammad was forty years old Allah sent him as a prophet of mercy to the people of the visible and of the invisible worlds, and to all mankind. With every prophet whom Allah had sent before the time of Muhammad, He had made a covenant, binding each of them to the coming of Muhammad, to declare him a true apostle, to aid him against every opponent, and to testify to every man who believed in the truth of their own prophetic missions that the mission of Muhammad was still to come. They complied, according to His command, and spread the covenant of Allah to all who believed in them, so that many men who believed in the Old or the New Testament believed also in the truth of this covenant.

According to his wife, the first prophetic sign shown by the apostle of Allah—after Allah determined to honor him and, through him, to show mercy to His servants—took the form of true visions. That is to say, the apostle of Allah never had a vision in his sleep; instead, it came like the break of day. She also said that Allah made him love solitude, so that he loved nothing more than to be alone.

When Allah had determined on the coming of the apostle of Allah, Muhammad went out on some business at such a distance that he left human habitation behind and came to deep valleys. He did not pass by a stone or a tree but it said "Salutation to thee, o apostle of Allah!" The apostle turned to his right, to his left, and looked behind, but saw nothing except trees and stones. Thus he remained for some time looking and listening, till Gabriel came to him with that revelation which the grace of Allah was to bestow upon him when he was at Hira during the month of Ramadan.

Every year the apostle of Allah spent a month praying at Hira and fed the poor who came to him; and when he returned to Mecca he walked round the Kaba seven or more times, as it pleased Allah, before entering his own house. In the month of Ramadan, in the year when Allah designed to bestow grace upon him, the apostle of allah went to Hira as usual, and his family accompanied him. In the night the angel Gabriel came with the command of Allah. The apostle of Allah later said, "He came while I was asleep, with a cloth of brocade whereon there was writing, and he said, 'Read.' I replied, 'I cannot read it.' Then he pressed the cloth on me till I thought I was dying; he released his hold and said, 'Read.' I replied, 'I cannot read it.' And he pressed me again with it, till I thought I was dying. Then he loosed his hold of me and said, 'Read.' I replied, 'I cannot read it.' Once more he pressed me and said, 'Read.' Then I asked, 'What shall I read?' And I said this because I feared he would press me again. Then he said, 'Read in the name of the Lord thy creator; who created man from a drop of blood. Read, the Lord is the most bountiful, who taught by means of the pen, taught man what he knew not.' Accordingly I read these words, and he had finished his task and departed from me. I awoke from my sleep, and felt as if words had been graven on my heart."

Afterwards I went out, and when I was on the centre of the mountain, I heard a voice from heaven, saying, "O Muhammad! Thou art the prophet of Allah, and I am Gabriel." I raised my head to look at the sky, and lo! I beheld Gabriel in the shape of a man with extended wings, standing in the firmament, with his feet touching the ground. And he said again, "O Muhammad! Thou art the apostle of Allah, and I am Gabriel." I continued to gaze at him, neither advancing nor retreating. Then I turned my face away from him to other parts of the sky, but in whatever direction I looked I saw him in the same form. I remained thus neither advancing nor retreating, and Khadija sent messengers to search for me. They went as far as the highest part of Mecca and again returned to her, while I remained standing on the same spot, until the angel departed from me and I returned to my family.

When I came to Khadija I narrated to her what I had seen, and she said, "Be of good cheer and comfort thyself! I swear by him whose hand the life of Khadija is, that I hope thou wilt be the prophet of this nation!" Then she rose, collected her garments around her and departed to Waraqa. She described to him what the apostle of Allah had seen and heard, and Waraqa exclaimed, "Holy! Holy! I swear to Him in whose hands the life of Waraqa is that the Law of Moses has been bestowed on him and he is the prophet of this nation! Tell him to stand firm." Khadija then returned to the apostle of Allah and informed him of what Waraqa had said.

When the apostle of Allah ended his sojourn at Hira he departed to Mecca and went first round the Kaba, as was his habit. And he was met by Waraqa, who said, "Thou wilt be accused of falsehood, thou wilt be persecuted, exiled, and attacked." Then Waraqa bent his head towards the apostle and kissed him on the crown of the head, and the apostle of Allah departed to his house.

But the revelations were not continued and the apostle became much downcast, until Gabriel came to him with a message from Allah saying that He had not abandoned Muhammad; "By brightness, and by the night when it is dark, thy Lord has not forsaken nor hated thee, and the next life will be better for thee than the first. The Lord will give these victory in this world and reward in the next. Did He not find thee an orphan and procure thee shelter? He found thee erring and guided thee; He found thee needy and enriched thee." The message to Muhammad continued: "Declare the goodness of thy Lord; declare what has come to thee from Allah, and declare His bounty and grace in thy mission; mention it, record it, and pray for manifestations of it." Accordingly the apostle of Allah began, at first in secret to those of his family whom he trusted, to promulgate the gospel bestowed by Allah on him, and on mankind through his agency.

Prayer was made an ordinance to Muhammad, and accordingly he prayed. The apostle of Allah was first commanded to make two prayer-flexions [prostrations] for every prayer, but later Allah commanded four prayer-flexions for those who were at home, although He confirmed the first ordinance of two prayer-flexions for those who were on a journey.

When Prayer was made obligatory to the apostle of Allah, Gabriel came to him when he was in the highest part of Mecca, and spurred his heel into the ground towards the valley; a spring gushed forth and Gabriel performed religious ablutions. The apostle of Allah observed how purification for prayers was to be made, and washed himself likewise. Then Gabriel rose and prayed, and the apostle of Allah did so after him, and then Gabriel departed. When the apostle of Allah came to Khadija he performed the religious ablution in her presence to show her how purity was attained, just as Gabriel had done. And she, too, washed as she had been shown. Then the apostle prayed as Gabriel had prayed, and Khadija prayed after him.

Then Gabriel came to him and held noon-prayers when the sun passed the zenith; and prayed the afternoon prayers with him when his shadow was the same length as his own body. Then he prayed the sunset prayers when the sun disappeared, and the last evening prayer when the twilight disappeared. Next day he held morning prayers with the apostle at dawn; then the midday prayers when the shadow was one with him; and the afternoon prayers when it was twice as long as he; then the sunset orisons when the sun disappeared, as on the preceding day. Then he prayed with him the last evening prayers when the first third of the night had elapsed, and lastly the morning prayers, when the morning dawned but the sun had not yet risen. Then he said, 'O Muhammad! The time of prayer is between thy prayers of yesterday and today.' . . .

When the season of pilgrimage was at hand, the Quraysh assembled to agree on the attitude they should display about the apostle. They asked, "Shall we call him a soothsayer?" but al-Walid, the chief, replied, "He is not a soothsayer. We have seen soothsayers; he does not murmur and rhyme as they do." They continued, "Then we shall say that he is possessed by djinns." He replied, "He is not possessed. We have seen lunatics and know them. He does not gasp, nor roll his eyes, nor mutter." They said, "Then we shall say that he is a poet." Al-Walid replied, "He is not a poet. We know all the poets and their styles. He is not a poet." They asked, "Then what shall we say?" Al-Walid replied, "You cannot say any of these things, for it will be known that they are false. The best will be to say that he is a sorcerer, because he has come with words which are sorcery and which separate a man from his father or from his brother, or from his wife, or from his family."

When the season of the pilgrimage arrived, the Quraysh sat by the roadside and allowed no man to pass without warning about Muhammad. And the Arab pilgrims carried away from Mecca news of the apostle of Allah, so that his fame spread over the whole country.

When Islam began to spread in Mecca, the Quraysh imprisoned its believers or sought to turn them away from Islam. The nobles sent for Muhammad in order to justify themselves, and the apostle of Allah hastened to them in the hope that they had conceived a favorable opinion of

what he had told them. But they only accused him once more of seeking riches and power. This he denied, and reaffirmed his mission from Allah. Then they said, "You know that no people are in greater want of land, of and of food than we are. Ask the Lord who has sent you to take away these mountains which confine us and to level out the country, to cause rivers to gush forth like the rivers of Syria, resurrect our ancestors that we may ask them whether what you say is true or false. If they declare you to be truthful and if you do what we have asked, we shall believe you and shall know that Allah has sent you to be an apostle." He replied, "I have not been sent to you with this, but I have brought to you from Allah the revelation He has sent. if you reject it, I appeal in this affair to Allah, that He decide between me and you."

They continued, "Ask, then, your Lord to send an angel to bear witness to your veracity. Ask Him to give you gardens, and treasures of gold and silver to enrich you; we know you go now to the markets to procure food as we procure it. Then we shall know your rank and station with Allah." The apostle of Allah said, "I shall not do this, nor ask for this. I was not sent to you for this; but Allah has sent me as a bearer of glad tidings and a preacher."

QUESTIONS

1. What persuaded Muhammad that he was the prophet sent by Allah?

2. What was the significance of water for the apostle?

3. Where did Muhammad find his first convert?

4. What were Muhammad's tribulations?

THE HIGH MIDDLE AGES

40

FEUDAL DOCUMENTS

(11TH–13TH CENTURIES)

The feudal system, the name usually given to medieval social organization, developed as a result of the need for security in a violent and disorderly world. Based on deeply felt concepts of obligation and justice, the heart of the system lay in the relationship between lord and vassal, as well as in an implicit belief in the active presence of God in everyday life.

A letter from the Bishop of Chartres, written in 1020, offers a brief account of the mutual duties of lords and vassals to serve and protect one another. Both lord and vassal benefited from the system. As the charter of homage between the monastery of Saint Mary of Grasse and Bernard Atton (1110) illustrates, promises of service were rewarded with a *fief*—that is, lands the vassal could use to support himself and his family.

The contract between lord and vassal was a sacred one and was enforced by appeals to God. The importance of God to all human endeavors, especially in the creation of feudal bonds and in the execution of justice, was never questioned. This belief in divine intervention in everyday life justified the use of the ordeal in criminal trials. During the ordeal, called the Judgment of God, authorities relied on heavenly signs to determine guilt or innocence. Reprinted here is a tract written either in the twelfth or thirteenth century that describes the procedure to be followed in the ordeal of boiling water.

Duties of Vassals and Lords

To William most glorious duke of the Aquitanians, bishop Fulbert the favor of his prayers.

Asked to write something concerning the form of fealty, I have noted briefly for you on the authority of the books the things which follow. He who swears fealty to his lord ought always to have these six things in memory; what is harmless, safe, honorable, useful, easy, practicable. Harmless, that is to say that he should not be injurious to his lord in his body; safe, that he should not be injurious to him in his secrets or in the defences through which he is able to be secure; honorable, that he should not be injurious to him in his justice or in other matters that pertain to his honor; useful, that he should not be injurious to him in his possessions; easy or practicable, that that good which his lord is able to do easily, he make not difficult, nor that which is practicable he make impossible to him.

However, that the faithful vassal should avoid these injuries is proper, but not for this does he deserve his holding; for it is not sufficient to abstain from evil, unless what is good is done also. It remains, therefore, that in the same six things mentioned above he should faithfully counsel and aid his lord, if he wishes to be looked upon as worthy of his benefice and to be safe concerning the fealty which he has sworn.

The lord also ought to act toward his faithful vassal reciprocally in all these things. And if he does not do this he will be justly considered guilty of bad faith, just as the former, if he should be detected in the avoidance of or the doing of or the consenting to them, would be perfidious and perjured.

I would have written to you at greater length, if I had not been occupied with many other things, including the rebuilding of our city and church which was lately entirely consumed in a great fire; from which loss though we could not for a while be diverted, yet by the hope of the comfort of God and of you we breathe again.

Charter of Homage and Fealty, C.E. 1110

In the name of the Lord, I, Bernard Atton, Viscount of Carcassonne, in the presence of my sons, Roger and Trencavel, and of Peter Roger of Barbazan, and William Hugo, and Raymond Mantellini, and Peter de Vietry, nobles, and of many other honorable men, who have come to the monastery of St. Mary of Grasse, to the honor of the festival of the august St. Mary: since lord Leo, abbot of the said monastery, has asked me, in the presence of all those above mentioned, to acknowledge to him the fealty and homage for the castles, manors, and places which the patrons, my ancestors, held from him and his predecessors and from the said monastery as a fief, and which I ought to hold as they held, I have made to the lord abbot Leo acknowledgment and homage as I ought to do.

Therefore, let all present and to come know that I the said Bernard Atton, lord and viscount of Carcassonne, acknowledge verily to thee my lord Leo, by the grace of God, abbot of St. Mary of Grasse, and to thy successors that I hold and

ought to hold as a fief in Carcassonne the following: that is to say, the castles of Confoles, of Leocque, of Capendes (which is otherwise known as St. Martin of Sussagues); and the manors of Mairac, of Albars and of Musso; also, in the valley of Aquitaine, Rieux, Traverina, Hérault, Archas, Servians, Villatritoes, Tansiraus, Presler, Cornelles. Moreover, I acknowledge that I hold from thee and from the said monastery as a fief the castle of Termes in Narbonne; and in Minerve the castle of Ventaion, and the manors of Cassanolles, and of Ferral and Aiohars; and in Le Rogés, the little village of Longville; for each and all of which I make homage and fealty with hands and with mouth to thee my said lord abbot Leo and to thy successors, and I swear upon these four gospels of God that I will always be a faithful vassal to thee and to thy successors and to St. Mary of Grasse in all things in which a vassal is required to be faithful to his lord, and I will defend thee, my lord, and all thy successors, and the said monastery and the monks present and to come and the castles and manors and all your men and their possessions against all malefactors and invaders, at my request and that of my successors at my own cost; and I will give to thee power over all the castles and manors above described, in peace and in war, whenever they shall be claimed by thee or by thy successors.

Moreover I acknowledge that, as a recognition of the above fiefs, I and my successors ought to come to the said monastery, at our own expense, as often as a new abbot shall have been made, and there do homage and return to him the power over all the fiefs described above. And when the abbot shall mount his horse I and my heirs, viscounts of Carcassonne, and our successors ought to hold the stirrup for the honor of the dominion of St. Mary of Grasse; and to him and all who come with him, to as many as two hundred beasts, we should make the abbot's purveyance in the borough of St. Michael of Carcassonne, the first time he enters Carcassonne, with the best fish and meat and with eggs and cheese, honorably according to his will, and pay the expense of shoeing of the horses, and for straw and fodder as the season shall require.

And if I or my sons or their successors do not observe to thee or to thy successors each and all the things declared above, and should come against these things, we wish that all the aforesaid fiefs should by that very fact be handed over to thee and to the said monastery of St. Mary of Grasse and to thy successors.

I, therefore, the aforesaid lord Leo, by the grace of God abbot of St. Mary of Grasse, receive the homage and fealty for all the fiefs of castles and manors and places which are described above; in the way and with the agreements and understandings written above; and likewise I concede to thee and thy heirs and their successors, the viscounts of Carcassonne, all the castles and manors and places aforesaid, as a fief, along with this present charter, divided through the alphabet. And I promise to thee and thy heirs and successors, viscounts of Carcassonne, under the religion of my order, that I will be good and faithful lord concerning all those things described above.

Moreover, I, the aforesaid viscount, acknowledge that the little villages of Cannetis, Maironis, Villamagna, Aiglino, Villadasas, Villafrancos, Villadenz, Villaudriz, St. Genese, Conguste and Mata, with the farm-house of Mathus and the chateaux of Villalauro and Claromont, with the little villages of St. Stephen of Surlac, and of Upper and Lower Agrifolio, ought to belong to the said monastery, and whoever holds anything there holds from the same monastery, as we have seen and have heard read in the privileges and charters of the monastery, and as was there written.

Made in the year of the Incarnation of the Lord 1110, in the reign of Louis. Seal of Bernard Atton, viscount of Carcassonne, seal of Raymond Mantellini, seal of Peter Roger of Barbazon, seal of Roger, son of the said viscount of Carcassonne, seal of Peter de Vitry, seal of Trencavel, son of the said viscount of Carcassonne, seal of William

Hugo, seal of lord abbot Leo, who has accepted this acknowledgment of the homage of the said viscount.

And I, the monk John, have written this charter at the command of the said lord Bernard Atton, viscount of Carcassonne and of his sons, on the day and year given above, in the presence and witness of all those named above.

Formula for Conducting the Ordeal of Boiling Water

Let the priest go to the church with the prosecutors and with him who is about to be tried. And while the rest wait in the vestibule of the church let the priest enter and put on the sacred garments except the chasuble and, taking the Gospel and the chrismarium and the relics of the saints and the chalice, let him go to the altar and speak thus to all the people standing near: Behold, brethren, the offices of the Christian religion. Behold the law in which is hope and remission of sins, the holy oil of the chrisma, the consecration of the body and blood of our Lord. Look that ye be not deprived of the heritage of such great blessing and of participation in it by implicating yourselves in the crime of another, for it is written, not only are they worthy of death who do these things, but they that have pleasure in them that do them.

Then let him thus address the one who is to undertake the ordeal: I command thee, N., in the presence of all, by the Father, the Son, and the Holy Ghost, by the tremendous day of judgment, by the ministry of baptism, by thy veneration for the saints, that, if thou art guilty of this matter charged against thee, if thou hast done it, or consented to it, or hast knowingly seen the perpetrators of this crime, thou enter not into the church nor mingle in the company of Christians unless thou wilt confess and admit thy guilt before thou are examined in public judgment.

Then he shall designate a spot in the vestibule where the fire is to be made for the water, and shall first sprinkle the place with holy water, and shall also sprinkle the kettle when it is ready to be hung and the water in it, to guard against the illusions of the devil. Then, entering the church with the others, he shall celebrate the ordeal mass. After the celebration let the priest go with the people to the place of the ordeal, the Gospel in his left hand, the cross, censer and relics of the saints being carried ahead, and let him chant seven penitential psalms with a litany.

Prayer over the boiling water: O God, just judge, firm and patient, who art the Author of peace, and judgest truly, determine what is right, O Lord, and make known Thy righteous judgment. O Omnipotent God, Thou that lookest upon the earth and makest it to tremble, Thou that by the gift of Thy Son, our Lord Jesus Christ, didst save the world and by His most holy passion didst redeem the human race, sanctify, O Lord, this water being heated by fire. Thou that didst save the three youths, Sidrac, Misac, and Abednago, cast into the fiery furnace at the command of Nebuchadnezzar, and didst lead them forth unharmed by the hand of Thy angel, do Thou O clement and most holy Ruler, give aid if he shall plunge his hand into the boiling water, being innocent, and, as Thou didst liberate the three youths from the fiery furnace and didst free Susanna from the false charge, so, O Lord, bring forth his hand safe and unharmed from this water. But if he be guilty and presume to plunge in his hand, the devil hardening his heart, let Thy holy justice deign to declare it, that Thy virtue may be manifest in his body and his soul be saved by penitence and confession. And if the guilty man shall try to hide his sins by the use of herbs or any magic, let Thy right hand deign to bring it to no account. Through Thy only begotten Son, our Lord Jesus Christ, who dwelleth with Thee.

Benediction of the water: I bless thee, O creature of water, boiling above the fire, in the name of the Father, and of the Son, and of the Holy Ghost, from whom all things proceed; I adjure thee by Him who ordered thee to water the whole earth from the four rivers, and who summoned thee forth from the rock, and who changed thee into wine, that no wiles of the devil or magic of men be able to separate thee from thy virtues as a medium of judgment; but mayest thou punish the vile and the wicked, and purify the innocent. Through Him whom hidden things do not escape and who sent thee in the flood over the whole earth to destroy the wicked and who will yet come to judge the quick and the dead and the world by fire. Amen.

Prayer: Omnipotent, Eternal God, we humbly beseech Thee in behalf of this investigation which we are about to undertake here amongst us that iniquity may not overcome justice but that falsehood may be subjected to truth. And if any one seek to hinder or obscure this examination by any magic or by herbs of the earth, deign to ring it to naught by Thy right hand, O upright Judge.

Then let the man who is to be tried, as well as the kettle or pot in which is the boiling water, be fumed with the incense of myrrh, and let this prayer be spoken: O God, Thou who within this substance of water hast hidden Thy most solemn sacraments, be graciously present with us who invoke Thee, and upon this element made ready by much purification pour down the virtue of Thy benediction that this creature, obedient to Thy mysteries, may be endued with Thy grace to detect diabolical and human fallacies, to confute their inventions and arguments, and to overcome their multiform arts. May all the wiles of the hidden enemy be brought to naught that we may clearly perceive the truth regarding those things which we with finite senses and simple hearts are seeking from Thy judgment through invocation of Thy holy name. Let not the innocent, we beseech Thee, be unjustly condemned, or the guilty be able to delude with safety those who seek the truth from Thee, who art the true Light, who seest in the shadowy darkness, and who makest our darkness light. O Thou who perceivest hidden things and knowest what is secret, show and declare this by Thy grace and make the knowledge of the truth manifest to us who believe in Thee.

Then let the hand that is to be placed in the water be washed with soap and let it be carefully examined whether it be sound; and before it is thrust in let the priest say: I adjure thee, O vessel, by the Father, and the Son, and the Holy Ghost, and by the holy resurrection, and by the tremendous day of judgment, and by the four Evangelists, that if this man be guilty of this crime either by deed or by consent, let the water boil violently, and do thou, O vessel, turn and swing.

After this let the man who is to be tried plunge in his hand, and afterwards let it be immediately sealed up. After the ordeal let him take a drink of holy water. Up to the time of the decision regarding the ordeal it is a good thing to mix salt and holy water with all his food and drink.

QUESTIONS

1. Bishop Fulbert describes the ideal relationship between a lord and his vassal. What should each expect from the other?

2. What might you deduce from these documents about the position of the Church in feudal society?

3. Feudal relationships often involved some kind of symbolic gesture of submission on the part of a vassal. How does Bernard, viscount of Carcassonne, demonstrate his vassalage?

4. How do these documents demonstrate the medieval belief of the presence of God in everyday life?

5. Why do you think people relied upon the ordeal as a method of justice?

41

■ *Bernard of Angers* ■

MIRACLES OF ST. FOY
(CA. 1010)

Bernard of Angers (lived ca. 1020) was a French scholar and cleric, and the director of the bishop's school in Angers. Although he was at first skeptical about the claims made in St. Foy's behalf, he found himself convinced after three trips to her shrine. Bernard subsequently collected all the stories of miracles attributed to the saint, and his book was circulated throughout Europe, making St. Foy a very popular figure. His book was used by many others as a model for their own accounts of the lives of local saints. The veneration of saints, who medieval Christians believed could intercede for them with a stern God, was one of the most important aspects of medieval Christianity. People traveled long distances to view the relics of these holy men and women, and anxiously sought as much information about them as they could, encouraging monks to write their biographies—or hagiographies, as they were called.

Little is known about the actual St. Foy. She was supposedly martyred at the age of twelve in the fourth century C.E., and her relics had arrived in Conques, where Bernard saw them, in the ninth century. They had been captured by the monks during a raid on a rival monastery in search of relics.

Concerning Vuitbert Whose Eyes, Having Been Gouged Out, Were Restored by Saint Foy

In the region of Rodez where reposes the blessed virgin Foy, in the vicus of Conques, there lived a priest named Gerald, who is still alive. He had a godson who was attached to him both by kinship and by episcopal confirmation named Vuitbert, who was his domestic servant and a competent administrator of his property. Once this Vuitbert went to Conques to celebrate the feast. When the solemn vigil was completed the next morning, that is the very day of the feast, as he was returning home, by bad fortune he encountered his lord who had been moved against him by an inexplicable evil zeal. This priest, when he saw him in the garb of a pilgrim, began with words of peace, but then was roused to aggressive abuse: "Well, Vuitbert, I see you have become a Roman" (this was the way the people of the area called pilgrims). He answered, "Yes, master, I am returning from the feast of Saint Foy." Then after speaking amicably of various things, the priest gave him permission to depart. But after he had gone on a little way, looking over his back this priest of the Jewish treason, if one can call one contaminated by such a sacrilege a priest, ordered his servant to wait a bit for him. Vuitbert complied and

suddenly the priest ordered him to be encircled and held by his men.

When he saw this, shaking with fear, he asked of what crime he was accused, but the evil man gave only this response: "You did me wrong and are planning even worse things. This is why I want for reparations nothing less than your own eyes," and would not describe any more openly the nature of the offense as if from modesty. It is unjust for a priest to make judgment based on his own jealousy since the cause of this evil had arisen from the suspicion of debauchery with women. Vuitbert, since he was ignorant of the affair, confidently offered to vindicate himself of all culpability. "My lord," he said, "if you would openly indicate all the crimes of which you suspect me, I am prepared to refute them legally. I am unable to determine by what law I ought to incur your wrath and that of your followers." The priest replied, "Enough, enough, of your superficial excuses; the sentence has been pronounced: your eyes will be torn out."

But Vuitbert, seeing the priest stand firm in his gladiatorial resolve and seeing the hour of his irreparable destruction imminent, and discerning no other opportunity of defending himself but prayer, although despairing of his safety, made this plea: "Lord, pardon me! If not for my innocence, at least for the love of God and of Saint Foy for the love of whom I am now wearing the holy habit of a pilgrim."

At these words the wild monster, not taking seriously either God or his saint, contorted by rage, vomited forth the poison of blasphemy which he had in his heart: "Neither God nor Saint Foy will save you today! You will not be able to escape my hands by invoking them. And don't expect that out of reverence for the habit of a pilgrim I would consider you worthy and inviolable since you have so evilly harmed me." This said, he ordered the man be thrown down and that his eyes be torn out. But when he could force none of his three men whose names we omit because of the horror of this barbarity, to carry out such a deed, ordering them at least to hold him down and descending from his horse, he tore out the eyes of his godson with the same fingers which were consecrated to holding the body of Christ and tossed them away.

These things did not happen without the presence of the heavenly power, which does not abandon men who call upon divine assistance and is always near those calling on it in truth and which passes judgment for those enduring injury. Those who were present immediately saw a snow white dove, or as the doer of this evil deed claimed, a magpie. This magpie or dove took up the bloody eyes of the poor unfortunate and rising high above the earth carried them toward Conques . . . .

A year passed. The day before the vigil of Saint Foy, he [Vuitbert] had fallen to sleep when he saw before him a young girl of indescribable beauty. Her appearance was like that of an angel. Her face shone and appeared with droplets of rose and scarlet. Her expression surpassed all human beauty. Her size was as had been read that it was in the time of her passion, that of an adolescent, not yet of mature age. She wore majestic clothing entirely brocaded of gold and surrounded by a variety of subtle colors. Her wide sleeves, carefully pleated, fell to her feet. She wore on her head a diadem decorated with four gems from which radiated extraordinary light. The smallness of her body seems to me to have signified nothing more than that at the time of her passion, as we have said, one reads that she had been a youth . . . .

Thus the saint, leaning on the bedpost, softly touched the right cheek of the sleeper and whispered to him, "Vuitbert, are you asleep?" He answered, "Who is there?" "I am Saint Foy," she replied. "My lady, why have you come to me?" "Simply to see you." Vuitbert thanked her, and Saint Foy replied, "Do you know me?" He recognized her as if he had already seen her and answered, "Yes, I see you well, my lady, and I recognize you perfectly." "Tell me how you are and how your affairs are doing." "Very well, my Lady, and all is going very well. Everything succeeds for me by the grace of God." "What," she said, "how can all be going well when you cannot see the light of the heavens?" But he, as happens in dreams, thought that he could see although he could not. This last question reminded him of his torn out eyes. "How could I see," he asked, "when, last year, while returning from your feast, alas, I lost my eyes by the brutality of an unjust master?" The saint said, "He offended God too much and raised the anger of the Creator, he who harmed you so seriously in your body without your having merited it. But if tomorrow, on the vigil of my martyrdom, you go to Conques, and you buy two candles and place one before the altar of the Holy Savior, the other before the altar where my bodily clay is placed, you will merit to enjoy the complete restoration of your eyes. For with a great supplication concerning the injury done you I moved the piety of the divine Judge to mercy. I bothered God by my incessant prayers until I obtained for you this cure." After these words she still insisted and urged him to go to Conques and encouraged him because he hesitated before the expense. "A thousand people, whom you have never before seen," she said, "will give to you. Besides, so that you can easily complete the present business, go quickly at dawn to the church of this parish, (this was

Statue-reliquary of St. Foy from the Abbey Treasury,
Conques, France (ninth–tenth century).

the parish of he who had deprived him of his eyes
which since ancient times was called Espeyrac)
and hear Mass there, and you will receive six
pence." He thanked her as a benefactor deserved
and the celestial power left him.

He awoke immediately and went to the
church where he told his vision. People thought
that he was delirious. But not at all discouraged,
he went through the crowd asking each in
order to obtain twelve pence. Finally a certain
Hugo, moving apart from the others, opened
his purse and offered him six pence and one
obole, that is, a little more than the vision had

announced. This first success increased his confidence. What more can I say? He arrived at
Conques, told his vision to the monks, bought
the candles, presented them to the altar, and
started the vigil before the golden statue of the
holy martyr.

Around midnight it seemed to him that he
could see as though two small glowing berries,
no larger than the fruit of a laurel, came from
above and buried themselves deeply into his
gouged eye sockets. At the shock, his thoughts
became muddled and he fell asleep. But at the
hour of lauds the chanting of the psalms awoke
him and he seemed to see spots of light and the
silhouettes of people moving about, but he had
an unbelievable headache and only half
conscious he thought that he was dreaming . . . .
He raised his hands to his eyes and touched
those windows of his flesh returned to the light
and entirely reconstituted. He went to tell his
neighbors and broke forth in praises for the
immeasurable magnificence of Christ. This
causes an indescribable rejoicing. Each person
asked himself if he was dreaming or if he had
actually seen an extraordinary miracle . . . .

Concerning Those Who, Robbing St. Foy, Suddenly Perished in the Collapse of a Roof

There was another miracle of divine vengeance,
but in a time before my arrival, which
encourages the ecclesiastics and those devotedly
serving the divine cult in the house of God and
which terrified those who violently rob the
goods of the holy church of God or who claim
the inheritance of the saints as their own right.
For in this time there are many whom we can
justly term antichrists, who are so blinded by
ambition that they dare to invade church rights,
that they not only do not revere the offices of
sacred ministry but they even attack them not
only with invective and with beatings, but even
afflict them with death. We have seen canons,
monks and abbots despoiled of their honor and

deprived of their goods and destroyed by death. We have seen bishops, some condemned by proscription, others expelled from their bishopric without cause, others cut down with the sword, and even burned by Christians in terrible flames for the defense of ecclesiastical rights, if in truth one can call those people Christians, who attack the order of Christian religion, they who stand opposed to Christ and to truth in all things. Because these undergo no punishment in the present life, they are not terrified by celestial vengeance. Rather they hope that there will never be any vengeance and there are even those who do not believe in a future judgment because in doing evil they have always enjoyed success and in following their own wills they have always escaped punishment. They have never experienced any hint of vengeance and therefore what they hear about vengeance of Christ they consider to be fables. Therefore it is necessary that the divine avenger punish some of them even in this world, lest they becomes so elated by their impunity that it appear a trivial thing to irritate God. It is also needed so that prowling folly, which rejects the sweet yoke of Christ and disdains the warnings of holy correction might be so bridled by the suffering of present punishments that it will impose a limit on its own malice lest it be more severely punished or that it might repent altogether and return to health. Then those who prepared their soul similarly for a like deed might be terrified by such an example and might repent of their intended evil, and might hurry in penance to the society of the sons of light. But having spoken about these things first, let us come now to that end toward which we hurry.

There was in the region of Cahors a noble woman, Doda, lord of Castelnau on the Dordogne. She had unjustly occupied an estate of Saint Foy which is called Alans. At the moment of her death, concerned about the salvation of her soul, she returned this property to the monastery of Conques. Hildegar, the son of her daughter, succeeded her, rich in the abundance of wealth as well as in the honor of office. He ruled from this famous castle in the territory of Albi called Penne, and he again dared to invade once more the same property and to take it from the monastery of Conques. For this reason the monks, in order to recover their property through the justice of the divine judge from the hand of this most violent robber, as was their custom, decided to go to in procession with the populace carrying as was the custom, the venerable effigy of the holy virgin. I shall explain later my feelings about this image, which might appear to be an object of superstition. There it happened that a knight of Hildegar (the grandson of Doda), whose name we forget and right now we are not able to return to Conques in order to ask for it, was reveling on Christmas, was dining in the midst of splendid knights and a succession of servants. Having consumed more wine than he was accustomed, among other things bodily abused the servants of Saint Foy, called them vile manure, protesting that he was amused to see the monks carrying their statue, a mask or sham worthy of ridicule and spittle, onto the contested estate. He would not be scared away by this nor would he defend his lord's rights any less violently and strenuously. Rather it seemed simple if he were to show how altogether vile this statue was by trampling it under foot. It would be tedious to tell how many times, three and four or more, he repeated such insults and laughter, when suddenly, the terrible sound of a divine storm was heard. It suddenly destroyed the balcony, the structure of the upper story collapsed, and all of the roof fell in. However, of the whole multitude who were present, only the blasphemer, his wife, and his five servants were killed. And so that no one might think that the house collapsed and that these men were killed by chance; the seven bodies were found thrown far out of the windows. Their remains lie in the cemetery of Saint-Antoin in the region of Albi.

Listen, robbers and devastators of Christian estates: the punishments of God are ineluctable and just are his judgments. His vengeance cedes place to no power; if it hold back for a time, it will strike with more force in the future. If you escape it in the present, a harsher punishment awaits you: that of eternal fire.

QUESTIONS

1. How did St. Foy restore Vuitbert's sight? What role did the saint play in Vuitbert's relationship with God?

2. A skeptic might have doubted the truth of St. Foy's miracles, but most people took them for granted. Why do you think such accounts convinced so many people?

3. What does this document reveal about relations between the church and the laity?

4. Vuitbert's story leaves an impression of what eleventh-century life might have been like for a common person. What is your impression?

5. Why do you think that neither Vuitbert nor the monks at Conques turn to the law to vindicate themselves?

42

■ *Fulcher of Chartres* ■

THE FIRST CRUSADE AND THE SIEGE OF JERUSALE
(1101–1127)

Fulcher (1057–1127) was born in Chartres and was probably trained and accepted into the priesthood there. Little is known of his early life before he attended the Council of Clermont in 1095 where he heard Pope Urban II call for a crusade against the Turks who held Jerusalem. Fulcher was so stirred by the call to arms that he joined the forces of Count Stephen of Blois and the Duke of Normandy. He crossed Italy and the Balkans with them and was present at the bloody siege of Nicaea. Fulcher was among the forces led by Count Baldwin who became the first Frankish prince in the east. It was as a member of Baldwin's army that Fulcher gathered the information that formed his history of the siege. Though he was not personally present, his sources were eyewitnesses and the accounts he used were first hand. Fulcher became Baldwin's chaplain, remained in Jerusalem, and possibly became the Prior of the Mount of Olives.

The History of Jerusalem was probably begun in 1101 but was not finished until 1127. It is the key account of the First Crusade and the most reliable account of Pope Urban's speech at the Council of Clermont. In this selection, Fulcher states his principles in writing the History and narrates the events that led to the First Crusade and culminated in the bloody siege of Jerusalem.

The Prologue of the Following Work of Fulcher the Cleric

1. It is especially pleasing to the living, and it is even beneficial to the dead, when the deeds of brave men, (particularly of those serving as soldiers of God), are either read from writings or soberly recounted from memory among the faithful. For, after hearing of the deeds of faithful predecessors who rejected the beauties and pleasures of the world and clung to God, and in accordance with the precept of the Gospel, left their parents and wives and possessions, however great, to follow Him, those here on earth are inspired to serve Him more eagerly in that same spirit. It is beneficial to the dead, especially to those dead in the Lord, when the living, upon hearing of their good and devoted works, bless their faithful souls, and out of love bestow alms with prayers on their behalf whether they were known to them, or not.

2. Therefore, induced by the promptings of certain of my companions on several occasions, I carefully arrange the deeds, most distinguished in the Lord, of the armies of the Franks who, by God's ordination, made a pilgrimage to Jerusalem. I have recorded in my unpolished style, as truthfully as possible, what is worth remembering and what I saw with my own eyes on that journey.

3. Although I do not dare to compare this labor with that of the Israelites or Maccabees or any other chosen people whom God has blessed

with many and brilliant victories, yet I have taken care to record it, since it is not to be judged greatly inferior, because often, in this labor, too, God's miracles are evident. Indeed, these [Franks] are not unequal to those Israelites or Maccabees. In the very lands [of the Israelites and Maccabees], we ourselves actually saw, or heard, how the Franks were dismembered, crucified, excoriated, shot with arrows, cut to pieces, and consumed by diverse means of martyrdom. Neither could they be overcome by any threats or temptation; nay, rather, if the assassin's sword had been present, many of our people would not have refused to be destroyed out of love for Christ.

4. Oh, how many thousands met a martyr's blessed death on this expedition! Is there anyone with heart so stony who hears of these acts of God and is not moved by bowels of compassion to burst forth in praises to Him? Can there be anyone who does not marvel how we, a few people in the realms of so many of our enemies, could not only remain but could even thrive? Who has ever heard of such things? Here Egypt and Ethiopia, here Arabia and Chaldea and Syria, here Assyria and Medea, here Parthia and Mesopotamia, here Persia and Scythia, here, even, the great sea shut us off from Christianity; and just as God permitted it, enclosed us in the hands of the butchers. However, out of pity, He protected us in His strong arm. "For blessed is the nation whose God is the Lord!"

5. The history which follows will reveal how this work was begun, and how all the people of the West, aroused to perform such a great journey, very willingly extended hand and mind to it.

The Council of Clermont

1. In the year 1095 from the Lord's Incarnation, with Henry reigning in Germany as so-called emperor, and with Philip as king in France, manifold evils were growing in all parts of Europe because of wavering faith. In Rome rule Pope Urban II, a man distinguished in life and character, who always strove wisely and actively to raise the status of the Holy Church above all things.

2. He saw that the faith of Christianity was being destroyed to excess by everybody, by the clergy as well as by the laity. He saw that peace was altogether discarded by the princes of the world, who were engaged in incessant warlike contention and quarreling among themselves. He saw the wealth of the land being pillaged continuously. He saw many of the vanquished, wrongfully taken prisoner and very cruelly thrown into foulest dungeons, either ransomed for a high price or, tortured by the triple torments of hunger, thirst, and cold, blotted out by a death hidden from the world. He saw holy places violated; monasteries and villas burned. He saw that no one was spared of any human suffering, and that things divine and human alike were held in derision.

3. He heard, too, that the interior regions of Romania, where the Turks ruled over the Christians, had been perniciously subjected in a savage attack. Moved by long-suffering compassion and by love of God's will, he descended the mountains to Gaul, and in Auvergne he called for a council to congregate from all sides at a suitable time at a city called Clermont. Three hundred and ten bishops and abbots, who had been advised beforehand by messengers, were present.

4. Then, on the day set aside for it, he called them together to himself and, in an eloquent address, carefully made the cause of the meeting known to them. In the plaintive voice of an aggrieved Church, he expressed great lamentation, and held a long discourse with them about the raging tempests of the world, which have been mentioned, because faith was undermined.

5. One after another, he beseechingly exhorted them all, with renewed faith, to spur themselves in great earnestness to overcome the Devil's devices and to try to restore the Holy Church, most unmercifully weakened by the wicked, to its former honorable status.

The Decree of Pope Urban in the Council

1. "Most beloved brethren," he said, "by God's permission placed over the whole world with the papal crown, I, Urban, as the messenger of divine admonition, have been compelled by an unavoidable occasion to come here to you servants of God. I desired those whom I judged to be stewards of God's ministries to be true stewards and faithful, with all hypocrisy rejected.

2. "But with temperance in reason and justice being remote, I, with divine aid, shall strive carefully to root out any crookedness or distortion which might obstruct God's law. For the Lord appointed you temporarily as stewards over His family to serve it nourishment seasoned with a modest savor. Moreover, blessed will you be if at last the Overseer find you faithful.

3. "You are also called shepherds; see that you are not occupied after the manner of mercenaries. Be true shepherds, always holding your crooks in your hands; and sleeping not, guard on every side the flock entrusted to you.

4. "For if through your carelessness or negligence, some wolf seizes a sheep, you doubtless will lose the reward prepared for you by our Lord. Nay, first most cruelly beaten by the whips of the lictors, you afterwards will be angrily cast into the keeping of a deadly place.

5. "Likewise, according to the evangelical sermon, you are the 'salt of the earth'. But if you fail, it will be disputed wherewith it was salted. O how much saltiness, indeed, is necessary for you to salt the people in correcting them with the salt of wisdom, people who are ignorant and panting with desire after the wantonness of the world; so that, unsalted, they might not be rotten with sins and stink whenever the Lord might wish to exhort them.

6. "For if because of the sloth of your management, He should find in them worms, that is, sin, straightway, He will order that they, despised, be cast into the dungheap. And because you could not make restoration for such a great loss, He will banish you, utterly condemned in judgment, from the familiarity of His love.

7. "It behooves saltiness of this kind to be wise, provident, temperate, learned, peacemaking, truth-seeking, pious, just, equitable, pure. For how will the unlearned be able to make men learned, the intemperate make them temperate, the impure make them pure? If one despises peace, how will he appease? Or it one has dirty hands, how will he be able to wipe the filth off another one defiled? For it is read, 'If the blind lead the blind, both shall fall into a ditch.'

8. "Set yourselves right before you do others, so that you can blamelessly correct your subjects. If you wish to be friends of God, gladly practise those things which you feel will please Him.

9. "Especially establish ecclesiastical affairs firm in their own right, so that no simoniac heresy will take root among you. Take care lest the vendors and moneychangers, flayed by the scourges of the Lord, be miserably driven out into the narrow streets of destruction.

10. "Uphold the Church in its own ranks, altogether free from all secular power. See that the tithes of all those who cultivate the earth are given faithfully to God; let them not be sold or held back.

11. "Let him who has seized a bishop be considered an outlaw. Let him who has seized or robbed monks, clerics, nuns and their servants, pilgrims, or merchants, be excommunicated. Let the robbers and burners of homes and their accomplices, banished from the Church, be smitten with excommunication.

12. "It must be considered very carefully, as Gregory says, by what penalty he must be punished who seizes other men's property, if he who does not bestow his own liberally is condemned to Hell. For so it happened to the rich man in the well-known Gospel, who on that account was not punished because he had taken away the property of others, but because he had misused that which he had received.

13. "And so by these iniquities, most beloved, you have seen the world disturbed too long; so long, as it was told to us by those reporting, that perhaps because of the weakness of your justice in some parts of your provinces, no one dares to walk in the streets with safety, lest he be kidnapped by robbers by day or thieves by night, either by force or trickery, at home or outside.

14. "Wherefore the Truce, as it is commonly called, now for a long time established by the Holy Fathers, must be renewed. In admonition, I entreat you to adhere to it most firmly in your own bishopric. But if anyone affected by avarice or pride breaks it of his own free will, let him be excommunicated by God's authority and by the sanction of the decrees of this Holy Council."

The Pope's Exhortation Concerning the Expedition to Jerusalem

1. "These and many other things having been suitably disposed of, all those present, both clergy and people, at the words of Lord Urban, the Pope, voluntarily gave thanks to God and confirmed by a faithful promise that his decrees would be well kept. But straightway he added that another thing not less than the tribulation already spoken of, but even greater and more oppressive, was injuring Christianity in another part of the world, saying:

2. "Now that you, O sons of God, have consecrated yourselves to God to maintain peace

among yourselves more vigorously and to uphold the laws of the Church faithfully, there is work to do, for you must turn the strength of your sincerity, now that you are aroused by divine correction, to another affair that concerns you and God. Hastening to the way, you must help your brothers living in the Orient, who need your aid for which they have already cried out many times.

3. "For, as most of you have been told, the Turks, a race of Persians, who have penetrated within the boundaries of Romania even to the Mediterranean to that point which they call the Arm of Saint George, in occupying more and more of the lands of the Christians, have overcome them, already victims of seven battles, and have killed and captured them, have overthrown churches, and have laid waste God's kingdom. If you permit this supinely for very long, God's faithful ones will be still further subjected.

4. "Concerning this affair, I, with suppliant prayer—not I, but the Lord—exhort you, heralds of Christ, to persuade all of whatever class, both knights and footmen, both rich and poor, in numerous edicts, to strive to help expel that wicked race from our Christian lands before it is too late.

5. "I speak to those present, I send word to those not here; moreover, Christ commands it. Remission of sins will be granted for those going thither, if they end a shackled life either on land or in crossing the sea, or in struggling against the heathen. I, being vested with that gift from God, grant this to those who go.

6. "O what a shame, if a people, so despised, degenerate, and enslaved by demons would thus overcome a people endowed with the trust of almighty God, and shining in the name of Christ! O how many evils will be imputed to you by the Lord Himself, if you do not help those who, like you, profess Christianity!

7. "Let those," he said, "who are accustomed to wage private wars wastefully even against Believers, go forth against the Infidels in a battle worthy to be undertaken now and to be finished in victory. Now, let those, who until recently existed

as plunderers, be soldiers of Christ; now, let those, who formerly contended against brothers and relations, rightly fight barbarians; now, let those, who recently were hired for a few pieces of silver, win their eternal reward. Let those, who wearied themselves to the detriment of body and soul, labor for a twofold honor. Nay, more, the sorrowful here will be glad there, the poor here will be rich there, and the enemies of the Lord here will be His friends there.

8. "Let no delay postpone the journey of those about to go, but when they have collected the money owed to them and the expenses for the journey, and when winter has ended and spring has come, let them enter the crossroads courageously with the Lord going on before."

The Siege of the City of Jerusalem

1. When the Franks viewed the city, and saw that it would be difficult to take, our princes ordered wooden ladders to be made. By erecting them against the wall they hoped to scale it, and by a fierce attack enter the city, with God helping.

2. After they had done this, when the leaders gave the signal and the trumpets sounded, in morning's bright light of the seventh day following they rushed upon the city from all sides in an astonishing attack. But when they had rushed upon it until the sixth hour of the day, and were unable to enter by means of the scaling ladders because there were few of them, they sadly abandoned the assault.

3. After consultation, craftsmen were ordered to make machines, so that by moving them to the walls they might, with God's aid, obtain the desired end. So this was done.

4. Meanwhile they suffered lack of neither bread nor meat; but, because that place was dry, unirrigated, and without rivers, both the men and the beasts of burden were very much in need of water to drink. This necessity forced them to seek water at a distance, and daily they laboriously carried it in skins from four or five miles to the siege.

5. After the machines were prepared, namely, the battering-rams and the sows, they again prepared to assail the city. In addition to other kinds of siege craft, they constructed a tower from small pieces of wood, because large pieces could not be secured in those regions. When the order was given, they carried the tower piecemeal to a corner of the city. Early in the same morning, when they had gathered the machines and other auxiliary weapons, they very quickly erected the tower in compact shape not far from the wall. After it was set up and well covered by hides on the outside, by pushing it they slowly moved it nearer to the wall.

6. Then a few but brave soldiers, at a signal from the horn, climbed on the tower. Nevertheless the Saracens defended themselves from these soldiers and, with slings, hurled firebrands dipped in oil and grease at the tower and at the solders, who were in it. Thereafter death was present and sudden for many on both sides.

7. From their position on Mount Zion, Count Raymond and his men likewise made a great assault with their machines. From another position, where Duke Godfrey, Robert, Count of the Normans, and Robert of Flanders, were situated, an even greater assault was made on the wall. This was what was done on that day.

8. On the following day, at the blast of the trumpets, they undertook the same work more vigorously, so that by hammering in one place with the battering-rams, they breached the wall. The Saracens had suspended two beams before the battlement and secured them by ropes as a protection against the stones hurled at them by their assailants. But what they did for their advantage later turned to their detriment, with God's providence. For when the tower was moved to the wall, the ropes, by which the aforesaid beams were suspended, were cut by falchions, and the Franks constructed a bridge for themselves out of the same timber, which they cleverly extended from the tower to the wall.

9. Already one stone tower on the wall, at which those working our machines had thrown flaming firebrands, was afire. The fire, little by little replenished by the wooden material in the tower, produced so much smoke and flame that not one of the citizens on guard could remain near it.

10. Then the Franks entered the city magnificently at the noonday hour on Friday, the day of the week when Christ redeemed the whole world on the cross. With trumpets sounding and with everything in an uproar, exclaiming: "Help, God!" they vigorously pushed into the city, and straightway raised the banner on the top of the wall. All the heathen, completely terrified, changed their boldness to swift flight through the narrow streets of the quarters. The more quickly they fled, the more quickly they were put to flight.

11. Count Raymond and his men, who were bravely assailing the city in another section, did not perceive this until they saw the Saracens jumping from the top of the wall. Seeing this, they joyfully ran to the city as quickly as they could, and helped the others pursue and kill the wicked enemy.

12. Then some, both Arabs and Ethiopians, fled into the Tower of David; others shut themselves in the Temple of the Lord and of Solomon, where in the halls a very great attack was made on them. Nowhere was there a place where the Saracens could escape the swordsmen.

13. On the top of Solomon's Temple, to which they had climbed in fleeing, many were shot to death with arrows and cast down headlong from the roof. Within this Temple about ten thousand were beheaded. If you had been there, your feet would have stained up to the ankles with the blood of the slain. What more shall I tell? Not one of them was allowed to live. They did not spare the women and children.

The Spoils Which the Christians Took

1. After they had discovered the cleverness of the Saracens, it was an extraordinary thing to see our squires and poorer people split the

...ead Saracens, so that they might ...rom their intestines, which they ...wn their horrible gullets while ...ter several days, they made a great heap of their bodies and burned them to ashes, and in these ashes they found the gold more easily.

2. Tancred rushed into the Temple of the Lord, and seized much of the gold and silver and precious stones. But he restored it, and returned everything or something of equal value to its holy place. I say "holy," although nothing divine was practised there at the time when the Saracens exercised their form of idolatry in religious ritual and never allowed a single Christian to enter.

3. With drawn swords, our people ran through the city; Nor did they spare anyone, not even those pleading for mercy. The crowd was struck to the ground, just as rotten fruit Falls from shaken branches, and acorns from a windblown oak.

The Sojourn of the Christians in the City

1. After this great massacre, they entered the homes of the citizens, seizing whatever they found in them. It was done systematically, so that whoever had entered the home first, whether he was rich or poor, was not to be harmed by anyone else in any way. He was to have and to hold the house or palace and whatever he had found in it entirely as his own. Since they mutually agreed to maintain this rule, many poor men became rich.

2. Then, going to the Sepulchre of the Lord and His glorious Temple, the clerics and also the laity, singing a new song unto the Lord in a high-sounding voice of exultation, and making offerings and most humble supplications, joyously visited the Holy Place as they had so long desired to do.

3. Oh, time so longed for! Oh, time remembered among all others! Oh, deed to be preferred before all deeds! Truly longed for since it had always been desired by all worshippers of the Catholic faith with an inward yearning of the soul. This was the place, where the Creator of all creatures, God made man, in His manifold mercy for the human race, brought the gift of spiritual rebirth. Here He was born, died, and rose. Cleansed from the contagion of the heathen inhabiting it at one time or another, so long contaminated by their superstition, it was restored to its former rank by those believing and trusting in Him.

4. And truly memorable and rightly remembered, because those things which the Lord God our Jesus Christ, as a man abiding among men on earth, practised and taught have often been recalled and repeated in doctrines. And, likewise, what the Lord wished to be fulfilled, I believe, by this people so dear, both His disciple and servant and predestined for this task, will resound and continue in a memorial of all the languages of the universe to the end of the ages.

QUESTIONS

1. What are Fulcher's goals in writing his history?

2. What is Pope Urban II's message to the Council at Clermont?

3. How will the Crusaders be rewarded?

4. How did the Christians behave in Jerusalem?

43

THE SONG OF ROLAND

(CA. 1100)

The Song of Roland is one of the most important epic poems in the Western tradition. It was part of the extensive mythology that grew up around the figure of Charlemagne, though its form and poetry transcend the actual historical event which it describes—a battle in 778 between troops of the Frankish king and the treacherous Gascons who had been allied to them. As Charlemagne's army, laden with booty from victories over the Saracens, returned across the passes of the Pyrenees, a Gascon force lay in wait. It attacked the rear of the column (where the treasure was kept) and killed all of the defenders, including Roland, Charlemagne's nephew. The story appears to have been part of the oral tradition that celebrated the life of Charlemagne. It was probably sung in an abbreviated form for several centuries before it came to be written down in its present style and length.

The Song of Roland, like the *Iliad* and the *Aeneid,* blends historical and contemporary images and values. The three centuries that separated the reign of Charlemagne from the composition of the epic are bridged by this remarkable poem.

Roland is bold, Olivier is wise,
and both of them are marvelously brave.
When they are armed and mounted on their
    horses,
not even death can make them shy from battle;
these counts are worthy men, their speech is
    proud.
The vicious pagans ride on in great fury.
Olivier says: "Roland, look at them;
they're close to us, but Charles is now too far.
You wouldn't deign to sound your ivory horn:
but were the king here, we would be unharmed.
Just take a look up toward the Spanish pass;
you there can see the desolate rear guard;
the men in it will never form another."
"Don't talk such nonsense!" Roland answers him.
"The heart that quavers in the breast be damned!
We'll stand our ground right here upon the field;
here *we'll* provide the carnage and the slaughter."

When Roland sees that there will be a battle,
he is fiercer than a leopard or a lion.
He hails the Franks, then calls Olivier:
"My lord companion, friend, don't talk that way!
The emperor, who left these Franks with us—
some twenty thousand of them he detached—
made sure there was no coward in the lot.
A man should suffer hardships for his lord,
and persevere through dreadful heat and cold;
a man should lose, if need be, flesh and blood.
So ply your lance, as I shall Durendal,
my well-made sword the king once gave to me.
If I should die here, then whoever gets it
can say a noble vassal owned it once."
Olivier says: "I've no heart for words.
You neither deigned to sound your ivory horn,
nor wanted any help at all from Charles.
It's not that brave man's fault, for he knows
    nothing,

nor may those here be blamed in any way.
So go ahead and ride for all you're worth.
—My lords and barons, hold the battlefield!
I beg of you, for God's sake be resolved
to strike, and give as well as you receive!
Let's not forget the battle cry of Charles."
And with this word the Frenchmen raised the cry.
Whoever might have heard them shout
"Monjoy!"
would be reminded of their vassalage.
And then they ride!—my God, with such
    defiance!
They spur to make their horses run all out,
and go to strike—what else are they to do?
The Saracens are not all afraid.
Now look: the pagans and the Franks engage.
Count Roland gallops through the battlefield
with slicing, cleaving Durendal in hand:
he plays great havoc with the Saracens.
Could you but see him piling corpse on corpse,
while pools of bright blood spread out on the
    ground!
His hauberk's drenched with gore, and both
    his arms,
the withers and the neck of his good horse.
Olivier does not decline to fight,
nor will the twelve peers need to be reproached,
nor all the French who fight and slaughter there.
The pagans die, and many of them faint.
The archbishop says: "A blessing on our
    barons!"
and shouts "Monjoy!"—the battle cry of
    Charles.
The battle is incredible and grim.
Olivier and Roland fight quite well,
the archbishop strikes a thousand blows
    and more,
the dozen peers do not let up a bit;
the Frenchmen who are there all fight together.
By hundreds and by thousands, pagans die; no
one who doesn't flee is safe from death—
like it or not, their time has all run out.
The Frenchmen lose their finest ornaments:
they'll never see their fathers nor their kin,
nor Charlemagne, who awaits them at the pass.

In France there is a very awesome tempest,
a raging storm of thunder, of high winds,
of rainfall, and of hail beyond all measure.
The thunderbolts crash down repeatedly—
in fact, there is a trembling of the earth.
From Saint Michael of the Peril down to Seinz,
from Besançon to the harbor of Guitsand,
no house remains whose walls have not been
    cracked.
Around midday a widespread darkness falls,
and light comes only when the skies are torn.
No one can witness this without great fear,
and many say: "It is the final judgment—
the end of all Creation is at hand."
They do not know, nor do they speak the truth:
it is the requiem for Roland's death.
See Roland, who has fainted on his horse,
and, wounded unto death, Olivier,
his vision so impaired by loss of blood
that, whether near or far, he cannot see
enough to recognize a living man;
and so, when he encounters his companion,
he hits him on his jeweled golden casque
and splits it wide apart from crown to nasal,
but doesn't cut into his head at all.
On being struck so, Roland studied him,
then asked him in a soft and gentle voice:
"My lord companion, did you mean to do that?
It's Roland, who has been your friend so long:
you gave no sign that you had challenged me."
Olivier says: "Now I hear you speak.
Since I can't see you, God keep you in sight!
I hit you, and I beg you to forgive me."
And Roland says: "I've not been hurt at all,
and here before the Lord I pardon you."
And with these words, they bowed to one
    another:
in friendship such as this you see them apart.
Olivier feels death-pangs coming on;
his eyes have both rolled back into his head,
and his sight and hearing are completely gone.
Dismounting, he lies down upon the ground,
and then confesses all his sins aloud,
with both hands clasped and lifted up toward
    heaven.

He prays that God may grant him Paradise
and give His blessing to sweet France and
    Charles
and, most of all, to his companion Roland.
His heart fails; his helmet tumbles down;
his body lies outstretched upon the ground.
The count is dead—he could endure no more.
The baron Roland weeps for him and mourns:
on earth you'll never hear a sadder man.
Now Roland, when he sees his friend is dead
and lying there face down upon the ground,
quite softly starts to say farewell to him:
"Your valor was for naught, my lord companion!
We've been together through the days and years,
and never have you wronged me, nor I you;
since you are dead, it saddens me to live."
And having said these words, the marquis faints
upon his horse, whose name is Veillantif;
but his stirrups of fine gold still hold him on:
whichever way he leans, he cannot fall.
Count Roland realizes death is near:
his brains begin to ooze out through his ears.
He prays to God to summon all his peers,
and to the angel Gabriel, himself.
Eschewing blame, he takes the horn in hand
and in the other Durendal, his sword,
and farther than a crossbow fires a bolt,
heads out across a fallow field toward Spain
and climbs a rise. Beneath two lovely trees
stand four enormous marble monoliths.
Upon the green grass he has fallen backward
and fainted, for his death is near at hand.
Now Roland is aware his time is up:
he lies upon a steep hill, facing Spain,
and with one hand he beats upon his chest:
"Oh God, against Thy power I have sinned,
because of my transgressions, great and small,
committed since the hour I was born
until this day when I have been struck down!"
He lifted up his right-hand glove to God:
from Heaven angels came to him down there.
Count Roland lay down underneath a pine,
his face turned so that it would point toward
    Spain:
he was caught up in the memory of things—

of many lands he'd valiantly subdued,
of sweet France, of the members of his line,
of Charlemagne, his lord, who brought him up;
he cannot help but weep and sigh for these.
But he does not intend to slight himself;
confessing all his sins, he begs God's mercy:
"True Father, Who hath never told a lie,
Who resurrected Lazarus from the dead,
and Who protected Daniel from the lions,
protect the soul in me from every peril
brought on by wrongs I've done throughout
    my life!"
He offered up his right-hand glove to God:
Saint Gabriel removed it from his hand.
And with his head inclined upon his arm,
hands clasped together, he has met his end.
Then God sent down his angel Cherubin
and Saint Michael of the Sea and of the Peril;
together with Saint Gabriel they came
and took the count's soul into Paradise.
There's not a chevalier or baron there
who fails to shed embittered tears of grief;
they mourn their sons, their brothers, and their
    nephews,
together with their liege-lords and their friends;
and many fall unconscious to the ground.
Duke Naimes displayed his courage through
    all this,
for he was first to tell the emperor:
"Look up ahead of us, two leagues away—
along the main road you can see the dust,
so many of the pagan host are there.
So ride! Take vengeance for this massacre!"
"Oh God!" says Charles, "already they're so far!
Permit me what is mine by right and honor;
they've robbed me of the flower of sweet
    France."
The emperor has had his trumpets sounded;
then, with his mighty host, the brave lord rides.
The men from Spain have turned their backs
    to them;
they all ride out together in pursuit.
The king, on seeing dusk begin to fall,
dismounts upon the green grass in a field,
prostrates himself, and prays Almighty God

that He will make the sun stand still for him,
hold back the night, and let the day go on.
An angel he had spoken with before
came instantly and gave him this command:
"Ride on, Charles, for the light shall not
    desert you.
God knows that you have lost the flower of France;
you may take vengeance on the guilty race."
And at these words, the emperor remounts.

For Charlemagne God worked a miracle,
because the sun is standing motionless.
The pagans flee, the Franks pursue them hard,
and overtake them at Val-Tenebrus.
They fight them on the run toward Saragossa;
with mighty blows they kill them as they go.
The night is clear, the moon is radiant:
though Charles is lying down, he grieves for
    Roland.

QUESTIONS

1.   What are the qualities of a chivalrous knight?

2.   Considering the account given in *The Song of Roland,* could you describe a
     medieval battle?

3.   What sort of audience do you think would have found *The Song of Roland*
     most appealing? How do you think this might have affected the story itself?

4.   Roland quarrels with his friend Olivier. Why? What does the quarrel
     reveal about Roland's personality?

5.   Although Roland is slain, Charlemagne wins a great victory. How? What
     does the outcome reveal about medieval attitudes toward God and divine
     intervention?

44

MAGNA CARTA

(1215)

The Magna Carta "Great Charter" was a series of concessions made by King
John of England to his rebellious barons in 1215. English participation in the
Third Crusade had disastrous consequences for England's internal stability;
not only had the great barons of the realm been forced to pay for the army led
by King Richard I, they were also faced with the expense of ransoming him
back from Germany. Failures of English policy in France and dispute between
John and the Catholic Church added to the problems of this unpopular ruler.
Finally, under the leadership of the Archbishop of Canterbury, a segment

of the aristocracy rebelled and asserted the nobles' traditional rights against the monarchy. These were conceded in the Magna Carta.

The Great Charter was not a bill of rights, nor did it institute any major reforms in the relationship between kings and their subjects. Its original purpose was to bind the king to respect the privileges of the barons—especially in matters of taxation—and the Church. But its significance in constitutional history was that it formally defined these rights for posterity. Over the centuries, the Magna Carta has been seen as the bedrock for the protection of the rights of subjects against arbitrary rule by the crown.

John, by the Grace of God, King of England, Lord of Ireland, Duke of Normandy and Acquitaine, and Earl of Anjou, to his Archbishops, Bishops, Abbots, Earls, Barons, Justiciaries, Foresters, Sheriffs, Governors, Officers, and to all Bailiffs, and his faithful subjects—Greeting. Know ye, that We, in the presence of God, and for the salvation of our own soul, and of the souls of all our ancestors, and of our heirs, to the honour of God, and the exaltation of the Holy Church and amendment of our Kingdom, by this our present Charter, have confirmed, for us and our heirs forever:

1. That the English Church shall be free, and shall have her whole rights and her liberties inviolable; and we will this to be observed in such a manner, that it may appear from thence, that the freedom of elections, which was reputed most requisite to the English Church, which we granted, and by our Charter confirmed, and obtained the Confirmation of the same, from our Lord Pope Innocent the Third, before the rupture between us and our Barons, was of our own free will; which Charter we shall observe, and we will it to be observed with good faith, by our heirs forever.

We have also granted to all the freemen of our Kingdom, for us and our heirs forever, all the underwritten Liberties, to be enjoyed and held by them and by their heirs, from us and from our heirs.

2. If any of our Earls or Barons, or others who hold of us in chief by military service, shall die, and at his death his heir shall be of full age, and shall owe a relief, he shall have his inheritance by the ancient relief; that is to say, the heir or heirs of an Earl, a whole Earl's Baron, for one hundred pounds; the heir or heirs of a Baron, for a whole Barony, by one hundred pounds; the heir or heirs of a Knight, for a whole Knight's fee, by one hundred shillings at most and he who owes less, shall give less, according to the ancient custom of fees.

3. But if the heir of any such be under age, and in wardship, when he comes to age he shall have his inheritance without relief and without fine.

4. The warden of the land of such heir who shall be under age, shall not take from the lands of the heir any but reasonable issues, and reasonable customs, and reasonable services, and that without destruction and waste of the men or goods. . . .

5. Heirs shall be married without disparagement, so that before the marriage be contracted it shall be notified to the relations of the heir by consanguinity.

6. A widow after the death of her husband shall immediately, and without difficulty, have her marriage and her inheritance; nor shall she give anything for her dower, or for her marriage, or for her inheritance, which her husband and she held at the day of his death; and she may remain in her husband's house forty days after his death, within which time her dower shall be assigned.

8. No widow shall be distrained to marry herself, while she is willing to live without a husband; but yet she shall give security that she will not marry herself without our consent, if she hold of us, or without the consent of the lord of whom she does hold, if she hold of another. . . .

12. No scutage nor aid shall be imposed in our kingdom, unless by the common council of our kingdom; excepting to redeem our person, to make our eldest son a knight, and once to marry our eldest daughter, and not for these, unless a reasonable aid shall be demanded.

13. In like manner let it be concerning the aids of the City of London. And the City of London shall have all its ancient liberties, and its free customs, as well by land as by water. Furthermore, we will and grant that all other Cities, Burghs, and Towns, and Ports, should have all their liberties and free customs.

14. And also to have the common council of the kingdom, to assess and aid, otherwise than in the three cases aforesaid: and for the assessing of scutages, we will cause to be summoned the Archbishops, Bishops, Abbots, Earls, and great Barons, individually by our letters. And besides, we will cause to be summoned in general by our Sheriffs and Bailiffs, all those who hold of us in chief, at a certain day, that is to say at the distance of forty days (before their meeting), at the least, and to a certain place; and in all the letters of summons, we will express the cause of the summons; and the summons being thus made, the business shall proceed on the day appointed, according to the counsel of those who shall be present, although all who have been summoned have not come. . . .

27. If any free-man shall die intestate, his chattels shall be distributed by the hands of his nearest relations and friends, by the view of the Church, saving to every one the debts which the defunct owed.

28. No Constable nor other Bailiff of ours shall take the corn or other goods of any one without instantly paying money for them,

unless he can obtain respite from the free-will of the seller.

29. No Constable (Governor of a Castle) shall distrain any Knight to give money for castle-guard, if he be willing to perform it in his own person, or by another able man, if he cannot perform it himself, for a reasonable cause; and if we have carried or sent him into the army he shall be excused from castle-guard, according to the time that he shall be in the army by our command.

30. No Sheriff nor Bailiff of ours, nor any other person shall take the horses or carts of any free-man for the purpose of carriage, without the consent of the said free-man.

31. Neither we, nor our Bailiffs, will take another man's wood, for our castles or other uses, unless by the consent of him to whom the wood belongs. . . .

35. There shall be one measure of wine throughout all our kingdom, and one measure of ale, and one measure of corn, namely, the quarter of London; and one breadth of dyed cloth, and of russets, and of halberjects, namely, two ells within the lists. Also it shall be the same with weights as with measures. . . .

39. No free-man shall be seized, or imprisoned, or dispossessed, or outlawed, or in any way destroyed; nor will we condemn him, nor will we commit him to prison, excepting by the legal judgment of his peers, or by the laws of the land.

40. To none will we sell, to none will we deny, to none will we delay right or justice.

41. All Merchants shall have safety and security in coming into England, and going out of England, and in staying and in traveling through England, as well by land as by water, to buy and sell, without any unjust exactions, according to ancient and right customs, excepting in the time of war. . . .

54. No man shall be apprehended or imprisoned on the appeal of a woman for the death of any other man than her husband. . . .

61. But since we have granted all these things aforesaid, for God and for the amendment of our kingdom, and for the better extinguishing the discord which has arisen between us and our Barons, we being desirous that these things should possess entire and unshaken stability forever, give and grant to them the security underwritten, namely, that the Barons may elect twenty-five Barons of the kingdom, whom they please, who shall with their whole power, observe, keep, and cause to be observed, the peace and liberties which we have granted to them, and have confirmed by this, our present charter, in this manner; that is to say, if we, or our Justiciary, or our bailiffs or any of our officers, shall have injured any one in anything, or shall have violated any article of the peace or security, and the injury shall have been shown to four of the aforesaid twenty-five Barons, the said four Barons shall come to us, or to our Justiciary if we be out of the kingdom, and making known to us the excess committed, petition that we cause that excess to be redressed without delay. And if we shall not have redressed the excess, or, if we have been out of the kingdom, our Justiciary shall not have redressed it within the term of forty days, computing from the time when it shall have been made known to us, or to our Justiciary, if we have been out of the kingdom, the aforesaid four Barons shall lay that cause before the residue of the twenty-five Barons; and they, the twenty-five Barons, with the community of the whole land, shall distress and harass us by all the ways in which they are able; that is to say, by the taking of our castles, lands and possessions, and by any other means in their power, until the excess shall have been redressed, according to their verdict, saving harmless our person and the persons of our Queen and children, and when it hath been redressed they shall behave to us as they have done before. . . .

62. And we have fully remitted and pardoned to all men all the ill-will, rancour and resentments which have arisen between us and our subjects, both clergy and laity, from the commencement of the discord.

63. Wherefore our will is, and we firmly command that the Church of England be free, and that the men in our kingdom have and hold the aforesaid liberties, rights and concessions, well in peace, freely and quietly, fully and entirely, to them and their heirs, of us and our heirs, in all things and places for ever, as is aforesaid. It is also sworn, both on our part and on that of the Barons, that all the aforesaid shall be observed in good faith and without any evil intention. Witnessed by the above and many others. Given by our hand in the Meadow which is called Running-mead, between Windsor and Staines, this 15th day of June, in the 17th year of our reign.

QUESTIONS

1. Who do you think the chief beneficiaries of the charter were?

2. What are the general issues that seem to concern the barons most? How has the king infringed upon the rights of the barons?

3. Some historians have said that the real importance of the charter is that it made the king subject to the laws. How does the Charter do that, and why is this important?

4. There are several important clauses in the Magna Carta that deal with the king's powers over the family lives of his nobility. What was the king's interest in these matters?

5. Do you think that the barons thought the king was trustworthy? How were the provisions of the charter to be enforced?

6. In what areas can you see the Magna Carta as an ancestor of later views about individual freedom?

45

■ *Francis of Assisi* ■

ADMONITIONS
(CA. 1220)

Francis of Assisi (1181 or 1182–1226) was one of the best-loved and most influential saints of the medieval church. The son of an Italian cloth merchant, Francis was a typical youth of a rich family. He was taught to read and write Latin as a boy, and as he grew up, he became a popular figure in his hometown. Not especially religious in his youth, he was briefly a soldier and a prisoner of war in 1202. In 1205, a vision turned his thoughts to religion and he renounced all of his material possessions, donned a hair shirt, and set out to preach to the unconverted. Francis's charm and magnetic personality quickly drew a large following. After receiving the Pope's blessing, Francis became the leader of a new order of monks, the Franciscans. Unlike other monastic orders, the friars, as they were known, had no abbeys or property of any kind. They traveled the highways, first of Italy and later of all of Europe, preaching the gospel and living from the alms of the people. In his later years, Francis received the stigmata, or the imprint of the wounds of Christ, and suffered from a series of painful illnesses. His fame grew, as did his order. He was canonized only two years after his death, a measure of his popularity and holiness.

The *Admonitions* were probably written around the time of the foundation of the Franciscan order. They are a simple prescription for a Christian life, meant for his fellow Franciscans. In these instructions, Francis emphasizes the virtues of humility, obedience, and poverty.

The Blessed Sacrament

Our Lord Jesus told his disciples, I am the way, and the truth, and the life. No one comes to the Father but through me. If you had known me, you would also have known my Father.

Sacred Scripture tells us that the Father dwells in *light inaccessible* and that *God is spirit*, and St. John adds, *No one at any time has seen God*. Because God is a spirit, he can be seen only in spirit; *It is the spirit that gives life; the flesh profits nothing*. But God the Son is equal to the Father and so he too can be seen only in the same way as the Father and the Holy Spirit. That is why all those were condemned who saw our Lord Jesus Christ in his humanity but did not see or believe in spirit in his divinity, that he was the true Son of God. In the same way now, all those are damned who see the sacrament of the Body of Christ which is consecrated on the altar in the form of bread and wine by the words of our Lord in the hands of the priest, and do not see or believe in spirit and in God that this is really the most holy Body and Blood of our Lord Jesus Christ. It is the Most High himself who has told us, This is my Body and Blood *of the new covenant*, and, *He who eats my flesh and drinks my blood has life everlasting*.

And so it is really the Spirit of God who dwells in his faithful who receive the most holy Body and Blood of our Lord. Anyone who does not have this Spirit and presumes to receive him *eats and drinks judgement to himself*. And so we may ask in the words of Scripture, *Men of rank, how long will you be dull of heart?* Why do you refuse to recognize the truth *and believe in the Son of God?* Every day he humbles himself just as he did when he came from his *heavenly throne* into the Virgin's womb; every day he comes to us and lets us see him in abjection, when he descends from the bosom of the Father into the hands of the priest at the altar. He shows himself to us in this sacred bread just as he once appeared to his apostles in real flesh. With their own eyes they saw only his flesh, but they believed that he was God, because they contemplated him with the eyes of the spirit. We, too, with our own eyes, see only bread and wine, but we must see further and firmly believe that this is his most holy Body and Blood, living and true. In this way our Lord remains continually with his followers, as he promised, *Behold, I am with you all days, even unto the consummation of the world.*

Perfect and Imperfect Obedience

Our Lord tells us in the Gospel, *Everyone of you who does not renounce all that he possesses cannot be my disciple*, and, *He who would save his life will lose it*. A man takes leave of all that he possesses and loses both his body and his life when he gives himself up completely to obedience in the hands of his superior. Any good that he says or does which he knows is not against the will of his superior is true obedience. A subject may realize that there are many courses of action that would be better and more profitable to his soul than what his superior commands. In that case he should make an offering of his own will to God, and do his best to carry out what the superior has enjoined. This is true and loving obedience which is pleasing to God and one's neighbour.

If a superior commands his subject anything that is against his conscience, the subject should not spurn his authority, even though he cannot obey him. If anyone persecutes him because of this, he should love him all the more, for God's sake. A religious who prefers to suffer persecution rather than be separated from his confrères certainly perseveres in true obedience, because he lays down his life for his brethren. There are many religious who under the pretext of doing something more perfect than what their superior commands look behind and go back to their own will that they have given up. People like that are murderers, and by their bad example they cause the loss of many souls.

No One Should Claim the Office of Superior as His Own

I did *not come to be served but to serve,* our Lord tells us. Those who are put in charge of others should be no prouder of their office than if they had been appointed to wash the feet of their confrères. They should be no more upset at the loss of their authority than they would be if they were deprived of the task of washing feet. The more they are upset, the greater the risk they incur to their souls.

No One Should Give Way to Pride but Boast Only in the Cross of the Lord

Try to realize the dignity God has conferred on you. He created and formed your body in the image of his beloved Son, and your soul in his own likeness. And yet every creature under heaven serves and acknowledges and obeys its Creator in its own way better than you do. Even the devils were not solely responsible for crucifying him; it was you who crucified him with them and you continue to crucify him by taking pleasure in your vices and sins.

What have you to be proud of? If you were so clever and learned that you knew everything and could speak every language, so that the things of heaven were an open book to you, still you could not boast of that. Any of the devils knew more about the things of heaven, and knows more about the things of earth, than any human being, even one who might have received from God a special revelation of the highest wisdom. If you were the most handsome and the richest man in the world, and could work wonders and drive out devils, all that would be something extrinsic to you; it would not belong to you and you could not boast of it. But there is one thing of which we can all boast; we can boast of our humiliations and in taking up daily the holy cross of our Lord Jesus Christ.

The Imitation of Christ

Look at the Good Shepherd, my brothers. To save his sheep he endured the agony of the cross. They followed him in trials and persecutions, in ignominy, hunger, and thirst, in humiliations and temptations, and so on. And for this God rewarded them with eternal life. We ought to be ashamed of ourselves; the saints endured all that, but we who are servants of God try to win honour and glory by recounting and making known what they have done.

Good Works Must Follow Knowledge

St. Paul tells us, *The letter kills, but the spirit gives life.* A man has been killed by the letter when he wants to know quotation only so that people will think he is very learned and he can make money to give to his relatives and friends. A religious has been killed by the letter when he has no desire to follow the spirit of Sacred Scripture, but wants to know what it says only so that he can explain it to others. On the other hand, those have received life from the spirit of Sacred Scripture who, by their words and example, refer to the most high God, to whom belongs all good, all that they know or wish to know, and do not allow their knowledge to become a source of self-complacency.

Beware the Sin of Envy

St. Paul tells us, *No one can say Jesus is Lord, except in the Holy Spirit* and, *There is none who does good, no, not even one.* And so when a man envies his brother the good God says or does through him, it is like committing a sin of blasphemy, because he is really envying God, who is the only source of every good.

Charity

Our Lord says in the Gospel, *Love your enemies.* A man really loves his enemy when he is not offended by the injury done to himself, but for love of God feels burning sorrow for the sin his enemy has brought on his own soul, and proves his love in a practical way.

No One Should Be Scandalized at Another's Fall

Nothing should upset a religious except sin. And even then, no matter what kind of sin has been committed, if he is upset or angry for any other reason except charity, he is only drawing blame upon himself. A religious lives a good life and avoids sin when he is never angry or disturbed at anything. Blessed the man who keeps nothing for himself, but renders *to Caesar the things that are Caesar's, and to God the things that are God's.*

How to Know the Spirit of God

We can be sure that a man is a true religious and has the spirit of God if his lower nature does not give way to pride when God accomplishes some good through him, and if he seems all the more worthless and inferior to others in his own eyes. Our lower nature is opposed to every good.

Patience

We can never tell how patient or humble a person is when everything is going well with him. But when those who should co-operate with him do the exact opposite, then we can tell. A man has as much patience and humility as he has then, and no more.

Poverty of Spirit

Blessed are the poor in spirit, for theirs is the kingdom of heaven. There are many people who spend all their time at their prayers and other religious exercises and mortify themselves by long fasts and so on. But if anyone says as much as a word that implies a reflection on their self-esteem or takes something from them, they are immediately up in arms and annoyed. These people are not really poor in spirit. A person is really poor in spirit when he hates himself and loves those who strike him in the face.

The Humble Religious

Blessed the religious who takes no more pride in the good that God says and does through him, than in that which he says and does through someone else. It is wrong for anyone to be anxious to receive more from his neighbour than he himself is willing to give to God.

Compassion for One's Neighbour

Blessed the man who is patient with his neighbour's shortcomings as he would like him to be if he were in a similar position himself.

The Virtuous and Humble Religious

Blessed the religious who has no more regard for himself when people praise him and make much of him than when they despise and revile him and say that he is ignorant. What a man is before God, that he is and no more. Woe to that religious who, after he has been put in a position of authority by others, is not anxious to leave it of his own free will. On the other hand, blessed is that religious who is elected to office against his will but always wants to be subject to others.

The Happy and the Silly Religious

Blessed that religious who finds all his joy and happiness in the words and deeds of our Lord and uses them to make people love God gladly. Woe to the religious who amuses himself with silly gossip, trying to make people laugh.

The Talkative Religious

Blessed that religious who never says anything just for what he can get out of it. He should never be *hasty in his words* or open his heart to everyone, but he should think hard before he speaks. Woe to that religious who does not keep the favours God has given him to himself; people should see them only through his good works, but he wants to tell everybody about them, hoping he will get something out of it. In this way he has received his reward, and it does not do his listeners any good.

True Correction

Blessed that religious who takes blame, accusation, or punishment from another as patiently as if it were coming from himself. Blessed the religious who obeys quietly when he is corrected, confesses his fault humbly and makes atonement cheerfully. Blessed the religious who is in no hurry to make excuses, but accepts the embarrassment and blame for some fault he did not commit.

True Love

Blessed that friar who loves his brother as much when he is sick and can be of no use to him as when he is well and can be of use to him. Blessed that friar who loves and respects his brother as much when he is absent as when he is present and who would not say anything behind his back that he could not say charitably to his face.

Religious Should be Respectful
Towards the Clergy

Blessed is that servant of God who has confidence in priests who live according to the laws of the holy Roman Church. Woe to those who despise them. Even if they fall into sin, no one should pass judgement on them, for God has reserved judgement on them to himself. They are in a privileged position because they have charge of the Body and Blood of our Lord Jesus Christ, which they receive and which they alone administer to others, and so anyone who sins against them commits a greater crime than if he sinned against anyone else in the whole world.

Virtue and Vice

Where there is Love and Wisdom,
there is neither Fear nor Ignorance.
Where there is Patience and Humility,
there is neither Anger nor Annoyance.
Where there is Poverty and Joy,
there is neither Cupidity nor Avarice.
Where there is Peace and Contemplation,
there is neither Care nor Restlessness.
Where there is the Fear of God to guard
the dwelling,
there no enemy can enter.
Where there is Mercy and Prudence,
there is neither Excess nor Harshness.

QUESTIONS

1. Whom do you think St. Francis was addressing in his *Admonitions*? How might his message differ if it were meant for a different audience?

2. What qualities does Francis seem to admire most?

3. What seems to be Francis's opinion about material things?

4. Several of the sections of the *Admonitions* deal with relationships between superiors and subordinates. What should these relationships be like?

5. Does Francis give clergymen and monks a special place in society? Are his expectations different for them?

46

■ *Thomas Aquinas* ■

SUMMA THEOLOGICA

(1266–1273)

Thomas Aquinas (1225–1274) was born in Italy near the town of Aquino, from which he took his name. His family were minor nobility, but Thomas was destined for a career in the Church from an early age. He was sent to a monastery to be trained as a monk, but his outstanding intellectual abilities led to further education. He studied first at the University of Naples and then, after he joined the newly formed Dominican order, at the University of Paris. At Paris, Aquinas studied philosophy and theology. His special interest was in ancient Greek thought, especially that of Aristotle, which he did much to popularize at the university. His reputation, however, was derived from his theological knowledge, which was unsurpassed within his generation. He was summoned to Rome in 1259 to become a theological advisor to the pope. He died in 1274 on his way to a Church council called to heal the split between the Roman and Eastern churches. Canonized in 1323, he is widely regarded as the most important philosopher of Catholicism.

The *Summa Theologica* is a massive compilation of Aquinas's learning. It treats the entire range of subjects with which the Church dealt, from the existence of God to the definition of a just war. The *Summa* takes the form of questions and answers. The answer sections provide pros and cons of the views expressed by the Church and clarified by Aquinas. As its importance grew over the next four hundred years, it became the central work of Catholicism.

Whether It Can Be Demonstrated that God Exists?

Objection 1. It seems that the existence of God cannot be demonstrated. For it is an article of faith that God exists. But what is of faith cannot be demonstrated, because a demonstration produces scientific knowledge; whereas faith is of the unseen. Therefore it cannot be demonstrated that God exists. . . .

Obj. 3. Further, if the existence of God were demonstrated, this could only be from His effects. But His effects are not proportionate to Him, since He is infinite and His effects are finite; and between the finite and infinite there is no proportion. Therefore, since a cause cannot be demonstrated by an effect not proportionate to it, it seems that the existence of God cannot be demonstrated.

On the contrary, The Apostle says: *The invisible things of Him are clearly seen, being understood by the things that are made.* But this would not be unless the existence of God could be demonstrated through the things that are made; for the first thing we must know of anything is, whether it exists.

I answer that, Demonstration can be made in two ways: One is through the cause, and is called *a priori,* and this is to argue from what is prior absolutely. The other is through the effect, and is called a demonstration *a posteriori;* this is to argue from what is prior relatively only to us. When an effect is better known to us than its cause, from the effect we proceed to the knowledge of the cause. And from every effect the existence of its proper cause can be demonstrated, so long as its effects are better known to us; because since every effect depends upon its cause, if the effect exists, the cause must pre-exist. Hence the existence of God, in so far as it is not self-evident to us, can be demonstrated from those of His effects which are known to us.

Reply Obj. 1. The existence of God and other like truths about God, which can be known by natural reason, are not articles of faith, but are preambles to the articles; for faith presupposes natural knowledge, even as grace presupposes nature, and perfection supposes something that can be perfected. Nevertheless, there is nothing to prevent a man, who cannot grasp a proof, accepting, as a matter of faith, something which in itself is capable of being scientifically known and demonstrated . . . .

Reply Obj. 3. From effects not proportionate to the cause no perfect knowledge of that cause can be obtained. Yet from every effect the existence of the cause can be clearly demonstrated, and so we can demonstrate the existence of God from His effects; though from them we cannot perfectly know God as He is in His essence.

We must now consider war, under which head there are four points of inquiry: Whether some kind of war is lawful? Whether it is lawful for clerics to fight? Whether it is lawful to fight on holy days?

Whether It Is Always Sinful to Wage War?

Objection 1. It would seem that it is always sinful to wage war. Because punishment is not inflicted except for sin. Now those who wage war are threatened by Our Lord with punishment, according to Matth. xxvi. 52: *All that take the sword shall perish with the sword.* Therefore all wars are unlawful.

Obj. 2. Further, whatever is contrary to a Divine precept is a sin. But war is contrary to a Divine precept, for it is written: *But I say to you not to resist evil; and: Not revenging yourselves, my dearly beloved, but give place unto wrath.* Therefore war is always sinful.

Obj. 3. Further, nothing, except sin, is contrary to an act of virtue. But war is contrary to peace. Therefore war is always a sin.

Obj. 4. Further, the exercise of a lawful thing is itself lawful, as is evident in scientific exercises. But warlike exercises which take place in tournaments are forbidden by the Church, since those who are slain in these trials are deprived of ecclesiastical burial. Therefore it seems that war is a sin in itself.

On the contrary, Augustine says in a sermon on the son of the centurion: *If the Christian Religion forbade war altogether, those who sought salutary advice in the Gospel would rather have been counselled to cast aside their arms, and to give up soldiering altogether. On the contrary, they were told: "Do violence to no man; . . . and be content with your pay."* If he commanded them to be content with their pay, he did not forbid soldiering.

I answer that, In order for a war to be just, three things are necessary. First, the authority of the sovereign by whose command the war is to be waged. For it is not the business of a private individual to declare war, because he can seek for redress of his rights from the tribunal of his superior. Moreover it is not the business of a private individual to summon together the people, which has to be done in wartime. And as the care of the common weal is committed to those who are in authority, it is their business to watch over the common weal of the city, kingdom or province subject to them. And just as it is lawful for them to have recourse to the sword in defending that common weal against internal disturbances, when they punish evil-doers, according to the words of the Apostle: *He beareth not the sword in vain: for he is God's minister, an avenger to execute wrath upon him that doth evil;* so too, it is their business to have recourse to the sword of war in defending the common weal against external enemies. Hence it is said to those who are in authority: *Rescue the poor: and deliver the needy out of the hand of the sinner;* and for this reason Augustine says: *The natural order conducive to peace among mortals demands that the power to declare and counsel war should be in the hands of those who hold the supreme authority.*

Secondly, a just cause is required, namely that those who are attacked, should be attacked because they deserve in on account of some fault. Wherefore Augustine says: *A just war is wont to be described as one that avenges wrongs, when a nation or state has to be punished, for refusing to make amends for the wrongs inflicted by its subjects, or to restore what it has seized unjustly.*

Thirdly, it is necessary that the belligerents should have a rightful intention, so that they intend the advancement of good, or the avoidance of evil. Hence Augustine says: *True religion looks upon as peaceful those wars that are waged not for motives of aggrandizement, or cruelty, but with the object of securing peace, of punishing evil-doers, and of uplifting the good.* For it may happen that the war is declared by the legitimate authority, and for a just cause, and yet be rendered unlawful through a wicked intention. Hence Augustine says: *The passion for inflicting harm, the cruel thirst for vengeance, an unpacific and relentless spirit, the fever of revolt,* the lust of power, and such like things, all these are rightly condemned in war.

Reply Obj. 1. As Augustine says: *To take the sword is to arm oneself in order to take the life of anyone, without the command or permission of superior or lawful authority.* On the other hand, to have recourse to the sword (as a private person) by the authority of the sovereign or judge, or (as a public person) through zeal for justice, and by the authority, so to speak, of God, is not to *take the sword,* but to use it as commissioned by another, wherefore it does not deserve punishment. And yet even those who make sinful use of the sword are not always slain with the sword, yet they always perish with their own sword, because, unless they repent, they are punished eternally for their sinful use of the sword.

Reply Obj. 2. Such like precepts, as Augustine observes should always be borne in readiness of mind, so that we be ready to obey them, and, if necessary, to refrain from resistance or self-defence. Nevertheless it is necessary sometimes for a man to act otherwise for the common good, or for the good of those with whom he is fighting. Hence Augustine says: *Those whom we have to punish with a kindly severity, it is necessary to handle in many ways against their will. For when we are stripping a man of the lawlessness of sin, it is good for him to be vanquished, since nothing is more hopeless than the happiness of sinners, whence arises a guilty impunity, and an evil will, like an internal enemy.*

Reply Obj. 3. Those who wage war justly aim at peace, and so they are not opposed to peace, except to the evil peace, which Our Lord *came not to send upon earth.* Hence Augustine says: *We do not seek peace in order to be at war, but we go to war that we may have peace. Be peaceful, therefore, in warring, so that you may vanquish those whom you war against, and bring them to the prosperity of peace.*

Reply Obj. 4. Manly exercises in warlike feats of arms are not all forbidden, but those which are inordinate and perilous, and end in slaying or plundering. In olden times warlike exercises presented no such danger, and hence they were called *exercises of arms* or *bloodless wars,* as Jerome states in an epistle.

Whether It Is Lawful for Clerics and Bishops to Fight?

Objection 1. It would seem lawful for clerics and bishops to fight. For, as stated above, wars are lawful and just in so far as they protect the poor and the entire common weal from suffering at the hands of the foe. Now this seems to be above all the duty of prelates, for Gregory says: *The wolf comes upon the sheep, when any unjust and rapacious man oppresses those who are faithful and humble. But he who was thought to be the shepherd, and was not, leaveth the sheep, and flieth, for he fears lest the wolf hurt him, and dares not stand up against his injustice.* Therefore it is lawful for prelates and clerics to fight.

Obj. 2. Further, Pope Leo IV writes: *As untoward tidings had frequently come from the Saracen side, some said that the Saracens would come to the port of Rome secretly and covertly; for which reason we commanded our people to gather together, and ordered them to go down to the seashore.* Therefore it is lawful for bishops to fight.

Obj. 3. Further, apparently, it comes to the same whether a man does a thing himself, or consents to its being done by another, according to Rom. i. 32: *They who do such things, are worthy of death, and not only they that do them, but they also that consent to them that do them.* Now those, above all, seem to consent to a thing, who induce others to do it. But it is lawful for bishops and clerics to induce others to fight: for it is written that Charles went to war with the Lombards at the instance and entreaty of Adrian, bishop of Rome. Therefore they also are allowed to fight.

Obj. 4. Further, whatever is right and meritorious in itself, is lawful for prelates and clerics. Now it is sometimes right and meritorious to make war, for it is written that if *a man die for the true faith, or to save his country, or in defense of Christians, God will give him a heavenly reward.* Therefore it is lawful for bishops and clerics to fight.

On the contrary, It was said to Peter as representing bishops and clerics: *Put up again thy sword into the scabbard.* Therefore it is not lawful for them to fight.

I answer that, Several things are requisite for the good of a human society: and a number of things are done better and quicker by a number of persons than by one, as the Philosopher observes, while certain occupations are so inconsistent with one another, that they cannot be fittingly exercised at the same time; wherefore those who are deputed to important duties are forbidden to occupy themselves with things of small importance. Thus according to human laws, soldiers who are deputed to warlike pursuits are forbidden to engage in commerce.

Now warlike pursuits are altogether incompatible with the duties of a bishop and a cleric, for two reasons. The first reason is a general one, because, to wit, warlike pursuits are full of unrest, so that they hinder the mind very much from the contemplation of Divine things, the praise of God, and prayers for the people, which belong to the duties of a cleric. Wherefore just as commercial enterprises are forbidden to clerics, because they unsettle the mind too much, so too are warlike pursuits, according to 2 Tim. ii.4: *No man being a soldier to God, entangleth himself with secular business.* The second reason is a special one, because, to wit, all the clerical Orders are directed to the ministry of the altar, on which the Passion of Christ is represented sacramentally, according to 1 Cor. xi. 26: *As often as you shall eat this bread, and drink the chalice, you shall show the death of the Lord, until He come.* Wherefore it is unbecoming for them to slay or shed blood, and it is more fitting that they should be ready to shed their own blood for Christ, so as to imitate in deed what they portray in their ministry. For this reason it has been decreed that those who shed blood, even without sin, become irregular. Now no man who has a certain duty to perform, can lawfully do that which renders him unfit for that duty. Wherefore it is altogether unlawful for clerics to fight, because war is directed to the shedding of blood.

Reply Obj. 1. Prelates ought to withstand not only the wolf who brings spiritual death upon the flock, but also the pillager and the oppressor who work bodily harm; not, however, by having recourse themselves to material arms, but by means of spiritual weapons, according to the saying of the Apostle: *The weapons of our warfare are not carnal, but mighty through God.* Such are salutary warnings, devout prayers, and, for those who are obstinate, the sentence of excommunication.

Reply Obj. 2. Prelates and clerics may, by the authority of their superiors, take part in wars, not indeed by taking up arms themselves, but by affording spiritual help to those who fight justly, by exhorting and absolving them, and by other like spiritual helps. Thus in the Old Testament the priests were commanded to sound the sacred trumpets in the battle. It was for this purpose that bishops or clerics were first allowed to go to the front: and it is an abuse of this permission, if any of them take up arms themselves.

Reply Obj. 3. As stated above every power, art or virtue that regards the end, has to dispose that which is directed to the end. Now, among the faithful, carnal wars should be considered as having for their end the Divine spiritual good to which clerics are deputed. Wherefore it is the duty of clerics to dispose and counsel other men to engage in just wars. For they are forbidden to take up arms, not as though it were a sin, but because such an occupation is unbecoming their personality.

Reply Obj. 4. Although it is meritorious to wage a just war, nevertheless it is rendered unlawful for clerics, by reason of their being deputed to works more meritorious still. Thus the marriage act may be meritorious; and yet it becomes reprehensible in those who have vowed virginity, because they are bound to a yet greater good.

Whether It Is Lawful to Fight on Holy Days?

Objection 1. It would seem unlawful to fight on holy days. For holy days are instituted that we may have our time to the things of God. Hence they are included in the keeping of the Sabbath prescribed in Exod. xx. 8: for *sabbath* is interpreted *rest.* But wars are full of unrest. Therefore by no means is it lawful to fight on holy days.

Obj. 2. Further, certain persons are reproached because on fast-days they exacted what was owing to them, were guilty of strife, and of smiting with the fist. Much more, therefore, is it unlawful to fight on holy days.

Obj. 3. Further, no ill deed should be done to avoid temporal harm. But fighting on a holy day seems in itself to be an ill deed. Therefore no one should fight on a holy day even through the need of avoiding temporal harm.

On the contrary, It is written: The Jews rightly determined. . . saying: *Whosoever shall come up against us to fight on the Sabbath-day, we will fight against him.*

I answer that, The observance of holy days is no hindrance to those things which are ordained to man's safety, even that of his body. Hence Our Lord argued with the Jews, saying: *Are you angry at Me because I have healed the whole man on the Sabbath-day?* Hence physicians may lawfully attend to their patients on holy days. Now there is much more reason for safeguarding the common weal (whereby many are saved from being slain, and innumerable evils both temporal and spiritual prevented), than the bodily safety of an individual. Therefore, for the purpose of safeguarding the common weal of the faithful, it is lawful to carry on a war on holy days, provided there be need for doing so: because it would be to tempt God, if notwithstanding such a need, one were to choose to refrain from fighting.

However, as soon as the need ceases, it is no longer lawful to fight on a holy day, for the reasons given: wherefore this suffices for the *Replies* to the *Objections.*

QUESTIONS

1. How does Thomas prove the existence of God?

2. What are Aquinas's views about war? What is a just war?

3. War is, of course, a political act. What are the political assumptions Thomas makes in his discussion of war?

4. How does Christianity limit war?

5. Who do you think Thomas was trying to persuade with his book? What kind of audience would have been suited for this method of argument?

47

■ *Dante* ■

THE DIVINE COMEDY

(CA. 1320)

Dante Aligheri (1265–1321) is the father of Italian poetry. He was born into a Florentine family of lesser nobility, and both of his parents died while he was still a youth. He probably was educated at Church schools, but little is known about his life before he entered Florentine politics. His wife's family was among the most powerful in the city, and Dante served Florence in a number of capacities before he became involved in a bitter factional dispute that erupted into civil war. After the defeat of his party, he was exiled in 1302 and never returned to Florence. By that time he had already established his literary reputation and had begun work on *The Divine Comedy,* an endeavor that was to occupy the last twenty years of his life.

The Divine Comedy describes Dante's spiritual journey into heaven, purgatory, and hell. His guide into hell is Virgil, the greatest of the Roman poets. In Limbo, the first circle of hell, Dante meets the great ancient poets and thinkers. On his journey into heaven, he is accompanied by Beatrice, his ideal of female perfection. In heaven, Dante sees the orders of angels.

Inferno, Canto IV Argument

The Poet, being roused by a clap of thunder, and following his guide onwards, descends into Limbo, which is the first circle of Hell, where he finds the souls of those, who, although they have lived virtuously and have not to suffer for great sins, nevertheless, through lack of baptism, merit not the bliss of Paradise. Hence he is led on by Virgil to descend into the second circle.

Broke the deep slumber in my brain a crash
Of heavy thunder, that I shook myself,
As one by main force roused. Risen upright,
My rested eyes I moved around, and search'd,
With fixed ken, to know what place it was
Wherein I stood. For certain, on the brink
I found me of the lamentable vale,
The dread abyss, that joins a thundrous sound
Of plaints innumerable. Dark and deep,
And thick with clouds o'erspread, mine eye
    in vain
Explored its bottom, nor could aught discern.
"Now let us to the blind world there beneath
Descend;" the bard began, all pale of look:
"I go the first, and thou shalt follow next."
Then I, his alter'd hue perceiving, thus:
"How may I speed, if thou yieldest to dread,
Who still art wont to comfort me in doubt?"
He then: "The anguish of that race below
With pity stains my cheek, which thou for fear
Mistakest. Let us on. Our length of way
Urges to haste." Onward, this said, he moved;
And entering led me with him, on the bounds
Of the first circle that surrounds the abyss.
Here, as mine ear could not, no plaint was heard
Except of sighs, that made the eternal air
Tremble, not caused by tortures, but from grief
Felt by those multitudes, many and vast,
Of men, women, and infants. Then to me
The gentle guide: "Inquirest thou not what
    spirits
Are these which thou beholdest? Ere thou pass
Farther, I would thou know, that these of sin
Were blameless; and if aught they merited,
It profits not, since baptism was not theirs,
The portal to their faith. If they before
The Gospel lived, they served not God aright;
And among such am I. For these defects,
And for no other evil, we are lost;
Only so far afflicted, that we live
Desiring without hope." Sore grief assail'd

My heart at hearing this, for well I knew
Suspended in that Limbo many a soul
Of mighty worth. "O tell me, sire revered!
Tell me, my master!" I began, through wish
Of full assurance in that holy faith
Which vanquishes all error; "say, did e'er
Any, or through his own or other's merit,
Come forth from thence, who afterward
    was blest?"
Piercing the secret purport of my speech,
He answer'd: "I was new to that estate,
When I beheld a puissand one arrive
Amongst us, with victorious trophy crown'd.
He forth the shade of our first parent drew,
Abel his child, and Noah righteous man,
Of Moses lawgiver for faith approved,
Of patriarch Abraham, and David king,
Israel with his sire and with his sons,
Nor without Rachel whom so hard he won,
And others many more, whom He to bliss
Exalted. Before these, be thou assured,
No spirit of human kind was ever saved."
We, while he spake, ceased not our onward road,
Still passing through the wood; for so I name
Those spirits thick beset. We were not far
On this side from the summit, when I kenn'd
A flame, that o'er the darken'd hemisphere
Prevailing shined. Yet we a little space
Were distant, not so far but I in part
Discover'd that a tribe in honour high
That place possess'd. "O thou, who every art
And science valuest! who are these, that boast
Such honour, separate from all the rest?"
He answer'd: "The renown of their great names,
That echoes through your world above, acquires
Favour in Heaven, which holds them thus
    advanced."
Meantime a voice I heard: "Honour the bard
Sublime! his shade returns, that left us late!"
No sooner ceased the sound, that I beheld
Four mighty spirits toward us bend their steps,
Of semblance neither sorrowful nor glad.
When thus my master kind began: "Mark him,
Who in his right hand bears that falchion keen,
The other three preceding, as their lord.

This is that Homer, of all bards supreme:
Flaccus the next, in satire's vein excelling;
The third is Naso; Lucan is the last.
Because they all that appellation own,
With which the voice singly accosted me,
Honouring they greet me thus, and well
    they judge."
So I beheld united the bright school
Of him the monarch of sublimest song,
That o'er the others like a eagle soars.
When they together short discourse had held,
They turn'd to me, with salutation kind
Beckoning me; at the which my master
    smiled:
Nor was this all; but greater honour still
They gave me, for they made me of their tribe;
And I was sixth amid so learn'd a band.
Then when a little more I raised my brow,
I spied the master of the sapient throng,
Seated amid the philosophic train.
Him all admire, all pay him reverence due.
There Socrates and Plato both I mark'd
Nearest to him in rank, Democritus,
Who sets the world at chance, Diogenes,
With Heraclitus, and Empedocles,
And Anaxagoras, and Thales sage,
Zeno, and Dioscorides well read
In nature's secret lore. Orpheus I mark'd
And Linus, Tully and moral Seneca,
Euclid and Ptolemy, Hippocrates,
Galenus, Avicen, and him who made
That commentary vast, Averroes.
Of all to speak at full were vain attempt;
For my wide theme so urges, that oft-times
My words fall short of what bechanced. In two
The six associates part. Another way
My sage guide leads me, from that air serene,
Into a climate ever vex'd with storms:
And to a part I come, where no light shines.

Paradiso, Canto XXVIII Argument

Still in the ninth Heaven, our Poet is permitted
to behold the Divine Essence; and then sees, in
three hierarchies, the nine choirs of Angels.
Beatrice clears some difficulties which occur to
him on this occasion.

As I turn'd:
And that which none, who in that volume looks,
Can miss of, in itself apparent, struck
My view, a point I saw, that darted light
So sharp, no lid, unclosing, may bear up
Against its keeness. The least star we ken
From hence, had seem'd a moon; set by its side,
As star by side of star. And so far off,
Perchance, as is the halo from the light
Which paints it, when most dense the vapour
    spreads;
There wheel'd about the point a circle of fire,
More rapid than the motion which surrounds,
Speediest, the world. Another this enring'd;
And that a third; the third a fourth, and that
A fifth emcompass'd; which a sixth next bound;
And over this, a seventh, following, reach'd
Circumference so ample, that its bow,
Within the span of Juno's messenger,
Had scarce been held entire. Beyond the seventh,
Ensued yet other two. And every one,
As more in number distant from the first,
Was tardier in motion: and that glow'd
With flame most pure, that to the sparkle of truth,
Was nearest; as partaking most, methinks,
Of its reality. The guide beloved
Saw me in anxious thought suspense, and spake:
"Heaven, and all nature, hangs upon that point.
The circle thereto most conjoin'd observe;
And know, that by intenser love its course
Is, to this swiftness, wing'd." To whom I thus:
"It were enough; nor should I further seek,
Had I but witness'd order, in the world
Appointed, such as in these wheels is seen.
But in the sensible world such difference is,
That in each round shows more divinity,
As each is wider from the center. Hence,
If in this wondrous and angelic temple,
That hath, for confine, only light and love,
My wish may have completion, I must know

Wherefore such disagreement is between
The exemplar and its copy: for myself,
Contemplating, I fail to pierce the cause."
"It is no marvel, if thy fingers foil'd
Do leave the knot untied: so hard 'tis grown
For want of tenting." Thus she said: "But take,"
She added, "if thou wish thy cure, my words,
And entertain them subtly. Every orb,
Corporeal, doth proportion its extent
Unto the virtue through its parts diffused.
The greater blessedness preserves the more:
The greater is the body (if all parts
Share equally) the more is to preserve.
Therefore the circle, whose swift course
    enwheels
The universal frame, answers to that
Which is supreme in knowledge and in love.
Thus by the virtue, not the seeming breadth
Of substance, measuring, thou shalt see the
    Heavens,
Each to the intelligence that ruleth it,
Greater to more, and smaller unto less,
Suited in strict and wondrous harmony."
As when the north blows from his milder cheek
A blast, that scours the sky, forthwith our air,
Clear'd of the rack that hung on it before,
Glitters; and, with his beauties all unveil'd,
The firmament looks forth serene, and smiles:
Such was my cheer, when Beatrice drove
With clear reply the shadows back, and truth
Was manifested, as a star in Heaven.
And when the words were ended, not unlike
To iron in the furnace, every cirque,
Ebullient, shot forth scintillating fires:
And every sparkle shivering to new blaze,
In number did outmillion the account
Reduplicate upon the chequer'd board.
Then heard I echoing on, from choir to choir,
"Hosanna," to the fixed point, that holds,
And shall for ever hold them to their place,
From everlasting, irremovable.
Musing awhile I stood: and she, who saw
My inward meditations, thus began:
"In the first circles, they, whom thou beheld'st,

Are Seraphim and Cherubim. Thus swift
Follow their hoops, in likeness to the point,
Near as they can, approaching; and they can
The more, the loftier their vision. Those
That round them fleet, gazing the Godhead next,
Are Thrones; in whom the first trine ends.
    And all
Are blessed, even as their sight descends
Deeper into the Truth, wherein rest is
For every mind. Thus happiness hath root
In seeing, not in loving, which of sight
Is aftergrowth. And of the seeing such
The meed, as unto each, in due degree,
Grace and good-will their measure have
    assign'd.
The other trine, that with still opening buds
In this eternal springtide blossom fair,
Fearless of bruising from the nightly ram,
Breathe up in warbled melodies threefold
Hosannas, blending ever; from the three,
Transmitted, hierarchy of gods, for aye
Rejoicing; Dominations first; next them,
Virtues; and Powers the third; the next
    to whom
Are Princedoms and Archangels, with glad
    round
To tread their festal ring; and last, the band
Angelical, disporting in their sphere.
All, as they circle in their orders, look
Aloft; and, downward, with such sway prevail,
That all with mutual impulse tend to God.
These once a mortal view beheld. Desire,
In Dionysius, so intensely wrought,
That he, as I have done, ranged them; and named
Their orders, marshal'd in his thought.
    From him,
Dissentient, one refused his sacred read;
But soon as in this Heaven his doubting eyes
Were open'd, Gregory at his error smiled.
Nor marvel, that a denizen of earth
Should scan such secret truth; for he had
    learnt
Both this and much beside of these our orbs,
From an eye-witness to Heaven's mysteries."

QUESTIONS

1. What is the place of eminent pre-Christians in the afterlife? What sort of attitude does *The Divine Comedy* display toward the classical past?

2. What is the punishment of the inhabitants of the first circle of Hell?

3. Dante's society was one in which hierarchy and order were highly prized. How are these values apparent in *The Divine Comedy*?

4. What is paradise like? What rewards await the virtuous?

5. Many medieval accounts of heaven and hell were written by priests, but Dante is not a clergyman. How do you think this affects his view?

48

■ *Catherine of Siena* ■

LETTERS
(1376)

Catherine Benincasa (1347–1380), better known as Catherine of Siena, was the most famous of the fourteenth-century mystics. Born in Tuscany, she became a Dominican nun at the age of sixteen. Her devout lifestyle, especially her regimen of prayer and fasting, gained her a reputation for holiness that spread beyond her order. Catherine was deeply distressed by the divisions within the Catholic Church. In 1376, she traveled to Avignon to attempt to persuade the Pope to initiate a crusade against the Muslims that would help reunite the warring Christian factions. Her appeal failed, but she continued to take part in papal politics, traveling to the court in Rome in hope of ending the Great Schism. She died in Rome in 1380. Catherine was canonized in 1461 and was named patron saint of Italy in 1939.

Catherine's importance lay in her experiences as a mystical teacher of Catholicism rather than in her efforts at church reform. Her letters reveal the intensity of her devotion.

To Monna Bartolomea di Salvatico of Lucca

In the name of Jesus Christ crucified and of gentle Mary, mother of God's Son.

Dearest and very loved daughter in Christ Jesus,

I Caterina, servant and slave of the servants of Jesus Christ, am writing to you in his precious blood. I long to see you always feeding and nursing at the breast of the gentle mother, charity, for I am convinced no one can have life without the milk this glorious mother gives us. She is so sweet and mild to souls who taste her that in her everything bitter becomes sweet, and every heavy burden light. This doesn't surprise me, because when we live in this charity and love, we are living in God. So says Saint John: "God is charity, and when we live in charity we are living in God, and God in us." So if we have God we cannot have any bitterness, since God is supreme delight, supreme sweetness and joy.

This is why God's servants are always happy. If they are ill or hungry, thirsty, poor, afflicted, troubled, or persecuted by others, they are happy. It doesn't bother God's servants if their reputation is torn to shreds. They are happy, jubilant about everything because they have God, who is all the rest they need, and they have tasted the milk of divine charity. And just as a baby draws milk through its mother's breast, so souls in love with God draw him to themselves through Christ crucified. They always follow in his footsteps, choosing to follow him along the road of disgrace, suffering, and abuse. They want to find their delight only in Christ crucified, and they refuse to boast of anything but the cross. Such people say with Saint Paul, "I glory in difficulties for love of my Lord Jesus Christ, through whom the world is crucified to me, and I to the world." So they embrace the wood of the most holy cross and with the face of holy desire upturned, gaze on the consummate blazing love that has torn open his body, which in love is pouring out blood from every part.

I'm not surprised, then, that these souls are patient in difficulties, since in love and with a free will they have rejected worldly consolations, and have become close friends with toil and persecution. For they have seen that this was the garment of God's Son, the garment he chose as the most precious and glorious he could find. This is the pearl our gentle Savior tells us of, that a person, after discovering it, sells all he or she has to buy it. What is this thing that is ours, given us by God, that neither the devil nor anyone else can take from us? It is our will. To whom shall we sell this treasure, our will? To Christ crucified. I mean that voluntarily and with wholesome patience we will renounce our perverse will, which, when it is set on God, is a treasure. And with this treasure we will buy the pearl of suffering, and from it in patience draw the fruit we eat at the table of everlasting life. Now it is to this food, this table, this milk that I am inviting you, my dearest daughter, and I beg you to accept it eagerly. Rise from the sleep of indifference, for I don't want you to be caught sleeping when you are summoned by First Truth. Oh sweet gentle summons that relieves us of our body's heaviness, that perverse interloper that has always rebelled against its Creator by ill-ordered indulgence and pleasure, making of these a god for us!

We used to be so blind that we didn't see our nothingness. Proud as we were, we thought we could get through the narrow door loaded with the baggage of our pathetic perverse love of the world, which is the death of our soul. So I want us to get rid of the baggage of all worldly vanity and selfish love for ourselves. Do you know why he says that the door through which we must pass is narrow? Because we have to narrow down our love and desires for all worldly pleasure and consolation, and transform ourselves in our sweet mother charity, as I've said. I say we have to bow our head because the door is low, and if we carry our head high we will crack it. We have to be willing to bow down in true holy humility, seeing that God stooped down to us.

I want you to regard yourself, as you should, as the lowest of all. And mind you don't turn back for anything whatever—neither for the devil's deceits nor for anything your husband or anyone else might say. Persevere courageously in your holy resolution. For you know that Christ says, "Do not turn back to look at what you've plowed." It is perseverance that is crowned. Turn in affectionate love, with the dear loving Magdalen, and embrace the sweet venerable cross. There you will find all the sweet solid virtues, since it is there we find the God-Man. Reflect that the fire of divine charity has so crushed that venerable and tender body that it pours out blood from every part. He is so patient and loving that not a cry of complaint is heard from this Lamb, humble and despised, sated with disgrace. Let your heart and soul burst with the heat of love [as you drink] at this breast of charity through the flesh of Christ crucified. There is no other way you can taste or have virtue, because he *is* the way and the truth, and whoever holds to this way and truth cannot be deceived.

Realize that the whole world is against you. Don't turn back, but with heart courageous and true prepare yourself ahead of time, with shield in hand, to receive the blows. You know that a shield is three-sided; so you need to have three virtues. You need hatred and contempt for the sins you have committed against your Creator, particularly in the past when you were a devil because you were following in the devil's footsteps. Next I am saying that you need to have love, considering the goodness of God, who has loved you so much, and not because he had to but gratuitously. Moved by his ineffable love, he did not take your soul from your body while you were rebelling against him. No, the gentle Jesus snatched you from the devil's hands and brought you grace. And I tell you, as soon as you have this perfect love and hatred, the third virtue will be born to you. I mean patience, so that not only will you not be saddened by any hurtful words or actions, nor

moved to impatience by any suffering you may have to bear, but you will endure these things joyfully, holding them in reverence and considering yourself unworthy of such grace. There will be no blow, from the devil or anyone else, that can harm you if you have this shield of hatred, love, and true patience. For these are the three sturdy pillars that free the soul from weakness and keep it strong.

The dear Magdalen took up this shield in such a way that she thought no more of herself but with true heart clothed herself in Christ crucified. She no longer turned to prestige or grandeur or her own vanities. She took no more pleasure or delight in the world. She didn't think or worry about anything but how she could follow Christ. No sooner had she set her affection on him and come to know herself than she embraced him and took the path of lowliness. For God's sake she despised herself, for she saw that there is no other way to follow or to please him. She realized that she was the lowliest of all people. She was no more self-conscious than a drunken woman, whether alone or with others. Otherwise she would never have been among those soldiers of Pilate, nor would she have gone and stayed alone at the tomb. Love kept her from thinking, "What will it look like? Will people speak ill of me because I am rich and beautiful?" Her thoughts weren't here, but only on how she might find and follow her Master. She, then, is the companion I am giving you. I want you to follow her because she knew the way so well that she has been made our teacher.

Run, my daughter and my daughters! Don't fall asleep on me any more, for time is racing on and won't wait even a moment for you. I don't want to say any more. . . . .

To Louis, Duke of Anjou

In the name of Jesus Christ crucified and of gentle Mary.

Dearest lord and brother in Christ gentle Jesus,

I Caterina, servant and slave of the servants of Jesus Christ, am writing to you in his precious blood. I long to see your heart nailed fast to the cross, to see your desire so grow that soon you will be ready and eager to raise the standard of the most holy cross against the unbelievers. If you look at the Lamb slain and consumed with love on the cross to free you from death and give you the life of grace, I am certain this holy memory will fire you with longing to do it soon, and will curb any unruly pleasure and earthly vanity in your heart and soul. Such pleasure passes away like the wind and always leaves death in the souls of its possessors. Unless it is set in order it leads them at death into eternal death, for they have by their sin given up seeing God and have made themselves worthy of seeing and associating with the devils. And it is fitting that those who sin against God, the infinite Good, should suffer infinite punishment.

I am talking about those who spend their whole lives in pleasure and in sumptuous living, looking for luxuries and for great honor at huge banquets. They spend everything they have on nothing but such things. The poor are dying of hunger, but they are busy looking for plenty of big meals, elegant dishes, expensive tables, and fine fancy clothes. They don't care that their wretched souls are dying of starvation because they deprive them of their food: holy virtue, holy confession, and God's holy Word—I mean the Word incarnate, God's only-begotten Son. We should by our affection and love be following in that Word's footsteps, loving what he loves, seeking what he sought. We should be loving virtue and despising vice, seeking God's honor and our own and our neighbors' salvation. This is why Christ said we do not live on bread alone but on God's Word.

So I want you, dear lord and brother in Christ gentle Jesus, to follow this gracious Word, Christ crucified, in true virtue. Don't let yourself be deceived by the world or by the strength of your youth. For if we follow only the world, what Christ said of the Jews could be said of us: "They are like tombs, beautiful and whitened on the outside, but inside full of the bones and stench of the dead." Oh how well does gentle First Truth speak! It is indeed so, for on the outside they seem beautiful in all their finery, but their heart and affection are filled with these dead transitory things that give off the disgusting stench of bodily and spiritual corruption. But I trust that by God's goodness you will make such an effort to amend your life that those words will not apply to you. No, with tremendously blazing love you will take up the cross, where the death of deadly sin was spent and destroyed, where we won life. And here is what it will do for you: when you take up the cross, all your past sins against God will be taken away. And then God will say to you, "Come, my beloved son. You have worked hard for me. Now I will relieve you; I will lead you to the wedding feast of everlasting life, where there is satiety without boredom, hunger without pain, pleasure without discord." Earthly wedding feasts and banquets are not like this. They are costly, but we gain nothing from them, and the more we stuff ourselves at them, the more empty we become, and our enjoyment becomes a source of sadness.

You had a good example of that yesterday, when you gave a banquet that was so festive yet turned out to be such a great sorrow for you. God permitted this because of his very great love for your soul. He wanted to show you and the others who were there what sort of thing our empty revelry is. And God showed how little he liked what was going on—the words, the actions, the manners, the plottings.

Ah, but I'm very much afraid our obtuseness is such that it doesn't even let us think about divine judgment! I'm telling you in the name of Christ crucified never to forget yesterday, so that your affairs will always be conducted in good order, with virtue and fear of God, rather than with no fear of God. Take heart, take heart, for I trust that he in his goodness will do this for you. Let your grief over what happened not be crippling; rather let it be the healing pain of a holy self-knowledge. Let it be a holy restraint to hold in check any disordered vanity in you—just as you do to your running horse when you pull in the reins to keep him on course.

Up now, my dear son in Christ our gentle Jesus! Embrace the most holy cross. Answer God, who is using this cross to call you. This is how you will fulfill his will and my desire. And this is why I said I long to see your heart and your desire nailed fast to the cross. Before the holy father leaves, see that you reaffirm your holy desire by taking the holy cross in his holiness' presence, and the sooner the better, for the Christian people as well and for the unbelievers. Be sure to do it soon; don't put it off any longer. Be willing to do without material things rather than lose the spiritual, especially in this dear holy work that God has put into your hands. He is making you worthy of what he in his goodness usually does for his great servants.

I'll say no more. Remember, my lord, that you will surely die, and you don't know when. Keep living in God's holy and tender love. Forgive my presumption.

Jesus, gentle Jesus!

QUESTIONS

1. Catherine's first letter was to a pious Italian woman, and her second to a powerful noble. How do the two letters differ in tone and style? Do the identities of the recipient seem to matter to Catherine?

2. What is Catherine's view of human nature?

3. Who is most responsible for the state of the Church?

4. Catherine employs some interesting images in her work. How does her gender shape her writing?

5. Catherine was treated with great respect by her contemporaries. Why was she so popular?

49

■ *Christine de Pisan* ■

THE BOOK OF THE CITY OF LADIES

(CA. 1405)

Christine de Pisan (1365–ca. 1430) was born in Italy, daughter of the court astrologer to the king of France. With her father's encouragement (though not her mother's), Christine received the education designed for sons of the court nobility. She married a court official but his premature death left Christine a twenty-five-year-old widow with three small children. She turned to literary pursuits in an effort to support herself and her family. She wrote both poetry and prose, and a number of her works were commissioned and paid for by patrons. Christine is widely believed to be the first "feminist author"—that is, the first woman to write in her own name in defense of women.

The Book of the City of Ladies takes the form of a dialogue between Christine and Reason in one part and Christine and Rectitude in another. It is a history of the achievements of women from classical times to the Middle Ages, but it is also a refutation of the traditional myths about women's capacities and achievements.

Christine asks Reason why women do not hold judicial offices; and Reason's response

[*Christine*] "Most noble and honored lady, your fine words satisfy my thinking. But tell me, if you please, why women do not plead cases in courts of justice, do not judge legal disputes, and do not hand down sentences? For men say that it is on account of a certain woman (whose identity I do not know) who governed unwisely from the seat of justice."

[*Reason*] "My daughter, everything told about this woman is frivolous and contrived out of malice. But whoever would ask the causes of all things would have to deal with too much in this question. Even Aristotle would not be fully equipped for it, in spite of all the arguments that he gives in his *Problemata* and *Categoriae*. Now, as to your question,

dear friend, one could just as well ask why God did not ordain that men take up the offices of women and women the offices of men. I must answer this question by saying that just as a wise and well-organized master orders his domain into departments so that what one servant accomplishes the other does not bother with, so God has ordained man and woman to serve Him in different offices and also to help one another, each in their proper task. He has given to each sex a fitting nature for its duties. God gives men strong and hardy bodies for coming and going as well as for speaking boldly. That is why men learn the laws—and they must do so in order to maintain justice in the world. In case anyone does not wish to obey the laws established by justice, men are needed to enforce them with physical power and strength of arms, a task that women could not accomplish. Although God has given many women great intelligence and endowed them with honesty, it would not be appropriate for women, given their nature, to appear brazenly in court like men because there are already enough men who do so. What would be accomplished by sending three men to lift a weight that two could carry easily? But if anyone states that women do not possess enough intelligence to learn the laws, the opposite is evident from the proof given by experience, proof that is manifest and has been manifest in many women, some of whom have been great philosophers and have mastered disciplines far more complicated and lofty than the study of the laws and human institutions. Moreover, in case anyone says that women do not have good sense in politics, I will give you the examples of many great female rulers who have lived in past times. And for your intellectual benefit, I will remind you of some female rulers of your own time whose skill in governing their affairs after the deaths of their husbands provides obvious proof that an intelligent woman is capable of anything."

Christine asks Reason whether God has ever ennobled the mind of a woman with the loftiness of the Sciences; and Reason's answer

[*Christine*] After hearing these things, I replied to the lady who spoke infallibly, "My lady, God has truly given wonderful strength to the women whom you describe. But please inform me whether it has ever pleased this God, who has bestowed so many favors on women, to honor the feminine sex with the privilege of enlightenment and learning. Do women have minds well suited for this? I wish to know because men maintain that the mind of women has a limited capacity."

She answered, "My daughter, since I told you before, you ought to know that the opposite of their opinion is true. To show you this even more clearly, I will give you some examples. I tell you again, and you should not doubt it, if it were customary to send young girls to school and if they were then taught the sciences as the boys learn them, they would learn as perfectly and understand the subtleties of all the arts and sciences as well as the boys. And by chance such women do appear sometimes. As I mentioned before, just as women have more delicate bodies than men, bodies which are weaker and less able to perform some tasks, so do they have minds that are livelier and more penetrating whenever they apply themselves."

[*Christine*] "My lady, what are you saying? With all due respect, could you explain this point? Certainly men would never admit your statement as true, unless you explained it better, for they would say that it is obvious that men know much more than women do."

She answered, "Do you know why women know less?"

[*Christine*] "Only if you tell me, my lady."

"Without a doubt, it is because they are not involved in many things, but stay at home, where it is enough for them to run the household. There is nothing which so instructs a reasonable creature as the exercise and experience of many different things."

[*Christine*] "My lady, if women have minds that are skilled in conceptualizing and learning, just like men, why don't women learn more?"

Her answer: "Because, my daughter, the state does not require them to be active in the affairs which men are commissioned to execute, as I said before. It is enough for women to perform their usual duties. As for judging from experience, since women usually know less than men, they understand less. Consider men who live in remote rural areas or in the mountains. You will find that in many countries they seem like animals because they are so ignorant. All the same, there is no doubt that Nature has endowed them with the qualities of body and mind found in the wisest and most educated men living in the cities. All of this stems from a lack of education, though, as I told you before, among men and women, some possess better minds than others. I shall tell you about women who have possessed great learning and profound understanding and I shall discuss the question of the similarity of women's minds to men's."

She [Reason] begins to discuss several ladies who were enlightened with great knowledge, and first of all the noble maiden Cornificia

"The noble maiden Cornificia was sent at an early age to school by her parents along with her brother Cornificius, thanks to an act of deception. This girl, endowed with an excellent mind, devoted herself to study and began to enjoy the sweet taste of knowledge acquired through study. It was not easy to take her away from this joy. She applied herself more and more and neglected all other feminine activities. After some time she became an accomplished poet. She was not only brilliant and learned in the craft of poetry but also seemed to have been nourished with the very milk of philosophy. She wanted to hear and know about every branch of learning. She mastered them so thoroughly that she surpassed the erudition of her brother, who was also a consummate poet.

"But knowledge was not enough for her. She put her mind in action and her pen to paper and wrote several remarkable books. These works, as well as her poems, had a high reputation during the time of Saint Gregory and he himself mentions them. The Italian, Boccaccio, a great poet, praised this woman: 'O great honor to this woman who abandoned feminine activities and devoted her mind like the greatest scholars!' Boccaccio also talks about the attitude of women who despise themselves and their own capacities. These women are like ignorant and uncouth people born in the mountains; they become discouraged easily. They say that they are valuable only for embracing men and raising children. But God has given them fine minds to develop, if they wish, in any of the fields that outstanding men pursue. If they wish to study these things, which are as appropriate for them as for men, they can, through hard work, gain

the same fame that great men seek. My dear daughter, you can see how this author Boccaccio supports what I have told you and how he praises and defends learning in women."

Christine asks Reason whether any woman ever discovered previously unknown knowledge

I, Christine, after hearing these explanations of Lady Reason, inquired of her: "My lady, I can see that there are numerous cases of women learned in the sciences and the arts. But I would like to know whether any women, through the power of insight and intellectual subtlety, have themselves discovered any new arts and useful sciences which had not been discovered or known before. For it is not so great an achievement to learn a discipline that is already established. It is greater to discover something new and unfamiliar to others."

Her answer: "Have no doubt that many noteworthy and great sciences and arts have been discovered through the intellect and insight of women, both in the speculative disciplines which can be demonstrated in writing, and in the arts, which are demonstrated in manual works of labor. And here are several examples.

"First, I will tell you of the noble Nicostrata, known to the Italians as Carmentis. This lady was the daughter of the king of Arcadia, named Pallas. She had a marvellous intellect. God endowed her with special gifts of understanding. She was a great scholar in Greek. She had such beautiful prose and a venerable style that the poets of her time claimed that she was the lover of the god Mercury. They stated that her son, who became very learned, was the son of this god. This lady, because of certain events that occurred in her country, departed in a large boat for the land of Italy. Her son and many other people followed her. She arrived at the Tiber River and proceeded to climb a high hill which she named the Palentine Hill after her father. The city of Rome was later founded in this place. There, this lady and her son and all those who had followed her built a castle. She found that the men of this country were all savages, so she composed laws and enjoined them to live according to rules and maxims based on justice. And she was the first to establish laws in that country. These laws eventually became famous and served as the model for many other statutes.

"This lady knew through divine inspiration and the gift of prophecy, which she possessed along with the other graces, how in the future this land would become great and famous above all the countries of the world. It seemed to her that when the greatness of the Roman Empire, which was destined to master the entire world, had been established, it would not be proper for the Romans to employ the strange and inferior letters and characters of another country. In order to show her wisdom and the excellence of her mind to future centuries, she worked so hard that she invented her own letters, which were utterly different from those of other nations. She made the Latin alphabet, spelling, the difference between vowels, and consonants, and a complete introduction to the science of grammar. These letters she taught to the people and wished that they be widely known. This was hardly a small or unprofitable form of learning. She deserved much gratitude, for thanks to the subtlety of her work and the great utility and profit which have since accrued to the world, one can say that nothing more worthy in the world was ever invented than the Latin language.

"The Italians were grateful for this benefit, and for good reason. For them this discovery was so marvellous that they not only considered this woman greater than any man, they also considered her a goddess and honored her during her lifetime with divine honors. After her death they dedicated a temple to her at the foot of the hill where she had lived. To ensure a perpetual memory of her, they used many names taken from the science she had discovered and gave her own name to many things.

The inhabitants of this country even called themselves Latins in honor of the science of Latin developed by this lady. Moreover, because *ita*, which means *oui* in French, is the strongest affirmation in the Latin language, they were not satisfied calling their country the 'Latin land.' They wanted all the territory beyond the mountains, which is large and contains many diverse parts, to be called *Italy*. In honor of Carmentis, poems were named *carmen*. Even the Romans who lived long afterward, named one of the gates of the city of Rome the *Carmentalis*. And regardless of the prosperity which the Romans enjoyed and the greatness of some of their emperors, they did not change these names, which still survive.

"So what more do you want, fair daughter? Can one say anything more worthy about any man born of woman? And do not believe that she was the only woman in the world who discovered new branches of learning."

About Queen Ceres, who discovered the art of cultivating the earth and many other arts

[*Reason*] "Ceres was in very ancient times the queen of the kingdom of the Sicilians. She first discovered the art of agriculture and invented the necessary tools. She taught her subjects to tame and raise oxen as well as to train them to the yoke. She invented the plow and showed her subjects how to plow the earth and how to carry out all the accompanying tasks. She also taught them how to cast seeds on this ground and cover it over. Later, after the seed had grown and multiplied, she showed them how to reap the grains and how to sift them by beating them with flails. Then she ingeniously taught them how to grind the grain between hard stone and in mills and then how to make bread. Thus this woman instructed men who had been living like beasts, eating acorns, wild grains, and fruits, to make use of more convenient foods.

"This lady did even more. The people of that time were living in the forest, wandering here and there like beasts. She had them gather into communities. She taught them to build cities and permanent dwellings where they could reside together. Thanks to her, the world turned from savage living to a rational and human way of life. The poets claimed that Ceres' daughter was ravished by Pluto, the god of Hell. And because of the authority of her knowledge and the great good she brought to the world, the people of that time worshipped her and called her the goddess of grain."

Concerning the benefits brought to the world by these women

[*Christine*] "My lady, I have great admiration for what you have said about the good that has come into the world through the intelligence of women. Many men say that women's knowledge is worthless. For example, when someone says something ridiculous, the response is often that this is a wive's tale. In short, the typical opinion of men is that women are useful in the world only for bearing children and sewing."

Her answer: "Now you can recognize the ingratitude of men who talk that way. That are like people who live off the work of others without appreciating it and without thanking anyone. You can also clearly see how God, who does nothing without a purpose, wished to show men that He does not despise the feminine sex because it pleased Him to place such great intelligence in their heads that they are talented enough not only to learn and retain the sciences but also to discover new sciences themselves, indeed sciences of such great utility for the world that nothing has been more necessary. You have heard me speak of Carmentis, who invented the Latin alphabet, toward which God has been so favorable and which he has spread across the world so that it has effaced even some of the glory of the Hebrew and Greek languages. Hebrew and Greek used to enjoy great esteem, but now all of Europe, which contains a large part of the world, uses the Latin script. An endless number of books on all subjects have been written in Latin. The actions of man and the noble and excellent glories of God, as well as the sciences

and the arts, have been rendered immortal in Latin. And let no one say that I am telling you these things out of bias, for they are Boccaccio's own words, and his credibility is established.

"You can thus conclude that the benefits realized by this woman are endless. Thanks to her, men have been brought out of ignorance and led to knowledge. Thanks to her they possess the means to send their thoughts and intentions as far away as they wish, to announce and to report whatever they wish anywhere, and to know the past, present, and future. Moreover, because of this woman's learning, men can make treaties and maintain friendships with distant people. Through the exchange of texts, they can know one another without even meeting. In short, all the good which comes from the alphabet is endless; for written language describes the world and helps us to understand God, celestial things, the sea, the earth, all people, and all things. I ask you: Has any man accomplished anything more?"

On the same topic

[*Reason*] "Similarly, was there ever a man from whom more good came into the world than from the noble queen Ceres whom I have just discussed with you? Could anyone ever achieve anything more important than leading savage men, who were living in the woods like wild animals without the rule of justice, into cities and teaching them to make use of law and securing better food for them than acorns, wild apples, and wild grains and cereals? Thanks to this food, men have more beautiful bodies and stronger and more flexible limbs because this food is more healthy for humans. And who could do anything better than she did when she showed men how to clear the land, which had been overgrown with thistles, shrubs, and trees, and how to sow seeds so that wild land became domesticated through cultivation to the benefit of everyone. Because of this lady, humanity benefitted from the transformation of the barbarous world into a civilized place. The minds of vagabond and lazy men changed. They were drawn from the depths of ignorance to the heights of contemplation and proper behavior. She ordered certain men to perform field work and made it possible for so many cities to be populated and for their inhabitants, who perform the other works necessary for life, to be supported.

"The same is true for Isis and gardening. No one can overestimate the great good which she procured for the world by inventing the process of grafting and enabling people to raise so many fruits and herbs that nourish humankind. Minerva, too, from her wisdom provided humanity with so many necessary objects, like woolen clothing which replaced animal skins. She also alleviated the hardship of transporting provisions in one's arms from one place to another by inventing wagons and carts. And she taught men how to make armor and cover their bodies for greater protection in war. She developed better looking, stronger, and more practical armor than they had possessed before, which had only consisted of leather."

[*Christine*] Then I said to her, "At last, my lady, I understand why you spoke of the enormous ingratitude and ignorance of these men who malign women. The fact that the mother of every man is a woman is reason enough not to attack women, not to mention the other good deeds which one can clearly see that women do for men. Truly, there are many benefits afforded by women to men. Henceforth, let all writers be silent who speak poorly of women, including those who have attacked women in their books and poems, and all their accomplices. Let them lower their eyes out of shame for daring to speak so falsely. The noble lady, Carmentis, through the greatness of her intelligence taught men like a schoolmistress—and they cannot deny it—the lesson thanks to which they consider themselves so superior and honored. It was she who taught them the Latin alphabet!"

[*Reason*] "But what can all the nobles and knights say, who generally slander all women? Let them keep their mouths shut from now on and remember that the customs of bearing arms, of fighting in an organized unit—an activity for which they consider themselves so great—came to them from a woman. And all men who live on bread, or who live in a civilized manner in cities in accordance with laws, or who cultivate the earth—do they have any reason to criticize and rebuff women, given these extraordinary benefits? Certainly not, because thanks to women such as Minerva, Ceres, and Isis, many good things have added honor to life, and these things must always be kept in mind."

[*Christine*] "Doubtless, my lady. It seems to me that neither in the teaching of Aristotle, which has been so profitable to human intelligence and which is rightly esteemed, nor in the teachings of all the other philosophers who have ever lived, could an equal benefit for the world be found as that which has come, and still comes, through the works of the ladies you have mentioned."

QUESTIONS

1. According to Christine, where would men be without women?

2. What are some of the myths about women that Christine is battling against?

3. How does Christine refute some of these myths?

4. How important is the classical tradition for Christine? To what uses does she put examples of antiquity? Why do you suppose she ignores more contemporary examples?

5. Do you think Christine de Pisan would be considered a feminist today? Why or why not?

50

■ *Margaret Pastan* ■

LETTERS
(1441–1448)

John (1421–1466) and Margaret (d. ca. 1482) Paston belonged to a family of English landowners. Their fame has less to do with their deeds than the extraordinary collection of their letters that somehow survived the centuries. Extant personal letters written in English before the sixteenth century are extremely rare, and the Pastons have left more than any of their contemporaries. John's grandfather had been no more than a relatively successful farmer, but his father, William, became a prosperous lawyer and judge. William invested his money in land, and his son John, who was also trained as a lawyer, inherited a handsome estate. Margaret also came from a wealthy family, though much less is known about her background. She long outlived her husband, and lived out her widowhood as a respected local landowner.

All of the letters here were written by Margaret, who was an active woman, fully involved in the affairs of her family and her local community. Beginning with her first pregnancy (she eventually had seven children), her letters follow the course of landowning life in the turbulent fifteenth century. Many of these letters revolve around the Pastons' dispute with a neighboring noble, Lord Moleyns.

14 [?] December, 1441

Right reverend and worshipful husband, I commend myself to you, desiring heartily to hear of your welfare, thanking you for the token that you sent me by Edmund Perys. Please let me tell you that my mother sent to my father in London for some grey woollen gown cloth, to make me a gown, and he told my mother and me when he came home that he had instructed you to buy it after you left London. If it is not yet bought, please be so kind as to buy it and send it home as soon as you can, for I have no gown to wear this winter except my black and green one with tapes, and that is so cumbersome that I am tired of wearing it.

As to the girdle that my father promised me, I spoke to him about it a little while before he last went to London, and he said to me that it was your fault, because you would not think about having it made: but I expect that it is not so—he said it just as an excuse. I ask you, if you dare take it upon you, to be so good as to have it made in time for your return home, for I never needed it more than I do now, for I have grown so fat that no belt or girdle that I have will go round me.

Elisabeth Peverel has lain sick for fifteen or sixteen weeks with sciatica, but she sent my mother word by Kate that she would come here when God sent time, even if she had to be wheeled in a barrow.

John Damme was here, and my mother revealed my secret to him and he said by his troth that he was not so pleased by anything he had heard for the last twelve months as he was by that news. I can no longer live by cunning; my secret is revealed to everyone who sees me. I sent you word of all the other things that you desired me to send word of in a letter I wrote on Our Lady's day last [8 December].

The Holy Trinity have you in their keeping. Written at Oxnead in very great haste on the Thursday before St Thomas' day.

Please wear the ring with the image of St. Margaret that I sent you as a keepsake until you come home. You have left me such a keepsake as makes me think of you both day and night when I want to sleep.

Yours, M.P.

8 July, 1444

Right reverend and worshipful husband, I commend myself to you, desiring with all my heart to hear that you are well, and thanking you for your letter and for the things that you sent me with it. And as for John Estegate, he has neither come nor sent anything here yet, so I expect I shall have to borrow money soon if you do not come home soon, because I do not think I shall get any from him. God help me, I have only 4s, and I owe almost as much money as comes to that amount.

I have done your errands to your mother and my uncle. And I have also delivered the other thing that you sent me sealed in the box as you ordered me to, and the man I delivered it to says that he wants nothing of the deal except such things as were done before he came there, which you told him about. He says he would not want to be troubled with any such thing as that is, or to have it done in his time, for twenty

marks. I expect he will let you know shortly what he will do.

Please be kind enough to buy me some lace like that enclosed as samples in this letter, and one piece of black lace. As for the caps you sent me for the children, they are too small for them. Please buy finer and bigger caps than those. Please remember me to my father- and mother-in-law, and tell them that all their children are well, blessed be God.

Heydon's wife had her child on Saint Peter's day. I have heard since that her husband wants nothing to do with her, nor with the child she has just had either. I heard it said that he said that if she came into his presence to make her excuse, he would cut off her nose so that everyone would know what she was, and if the child came into his presence, he would kill it. He will not be persuaded to have her back on any account, so I hear.

The Holy Trinity have you in their keeping and send you health. Written at Geldeston on Wednesday after St Thomas's day.

By yours, M. Paston

19 May, 1448

Right worshipful husband, I commend myself to you. This is to let you know last Friday before noon, while the parson of Oxnead was at mass in our parish church [in Norwich], before the elevation of the Host, James Gloys, who had been in the town, came home by Wymondham's gate. Wymondham was standing in his gateway, with John Norwood, his man, by him, and Thomas Hawes, his other man, stood in the street by the side of the street drain. And James Gloys came with his hat on his head between both his men. And when Gloys was opposite Wymondham, Wymondham said: "Uncover thy head!" and Gloys replied "So I will, for thou!" [the use of "thou" instead of the formal "you" would have been an insult]. And when Gloys was three or four paces past him, Wymondham drew out his dagger and said "Wilt thou, knave?" And at that Gloys turned and drew his dagger and defended himself, fleeing into my mother's place; and Wymondham and his man Hawes threw stones and drove Gloys into my mother's place. And Hawes followed him into my mother's and threw a stone as big as a farthing loaf into the hall after Gloys, and then ran out of the place again. And Gloys followed him out and stood outside the gate; then Wymondham called Gloys a thief and said he would kill him, and Gloys said he lied and called him a churl, and told him to come on himself or send the best man he had, and Gloys would match him, one against one. And then Hawes ran into Wymondham's place and fetched a spear and a sword, and took his master his sword. With the noise of this affray and assault my mother and I came out of the church at the consecration, and I told Gloys to go back into my mother's place; and he did so.

And then Wymondham called my mother and myself strong whores, and said the Pastons and all their family were [gap in manuscript] said he lied, knave and churl that he was. And he used much strong language, as I will tell you later.

In the afternoon, my mother and I went to the prior of Norwich and told him the whole incident, and the prior sent for Wymondham. We went home again, and Pagrave came home with us. And while Wymondham was with the prior, Gloys was standing in the street at my mother's gate, and Hawes saw him there as he stood in Lady Hastings' [Wymondham's wife's] chamber. Soon he came down again with a two-handed sword and assaulted Gloys again, and Thomas my mother's man. He let fly a blow at Thomas, and grazed his hand with his sword. As for this later assault, the parson of Oxnead saw it and will vouch for it. And much else was done, as Gloys will tell you. And because of the dangers that might ensue from all this, on my mother's advice and that of the others I am sending you Gloys to be with you for a time, for my own peace of mind. In good faith, I would not have such trouble again for forty pounds . . . .

No more at this time, but Almighty God have you in his keeping. Written in haste on Trinity Sunday at evening.

Yours, Margaret Paston

1448

Right worshipful husband, I commend myself to you and ask you to get some crossbows, and windlasses to wind them with, and crossbow bolts, for your houses here are so low that no one can shoot out of them with a longbow, however much we needed to. I expect you can get such things from Sir John Fastolf if you were to send to him. And I would also like you to get two or three short pole-axes to keep indoors, and as many leather jackets, if you can.

Partridge [Moleyns' bailiff] and his companions are very much afraid that you will try to reclaim possession from them, and have made great defences within the house, so I am told. They have made bars to bar the doors crosswise, and loopholes at every corner of the house out of which to shoot, both with bows and hand-guns; and the holes that have been made for hand-guns are barely knee high from the floor, and five such holes have been made. No one could shoot out from them with hand bows.

Purry made friends with William Hasard at Querles' house and told him that he would come and drink with Partridge and him; and he said he would be welcome. That afternoon he went there to see what they did and what company they had with them. When he came there the doors were bolted fast and there was no one with them but Margaret and Capron and his wife and Querles' wife, and sanother man in black, who walked with a limp; I think from what he said that it was Norfolk of Gimingham. And Purry saw all this, and Marriott and his company boasted greatly; but I will tell you about that when you come home.

Please be so kind as to buy me a pound of almonds, a pound of sugar, and buy some frieze-cloth to make gowns for your children. You will get the cheapest and the best choice from Hay's wife, I am told.

Please buy a yard of black broadcloth for a hood for me, at 3s 8d or 4s a yard, for there is neither good cloth nor frieze in this town. As for the children's gowns, if I have cloth I will have them made. The Trinity have you in their keeping and send you good fortune in all your affairs.

QUESTIONS

1. Judging from her letters, what would you say Margaret's relationship with her husband is like?

2. Historians have identified fifteenth-century England as an exceptionally violent place. Would you agree? What do the Pastons' disputes seem to be about?

3. What do the letters reveal about the Pastons' place in the social order? What clues can you find to their social position in the letters?

4. Do you think that Margaret was the "ideal wife"? What was her role in the family?

5. What seem to be Margaret's primary concerns in her letters to her husband?

PART

III

■ ■ ■

RENAISSANCE AND REFORMATION

THE RENAISSANCE
51. Francesco Petrarca, *Letters* (ca. 1372)
52. Leon Battista Alberti, *On the Family* (1435–1444)
53. Giorgio Vasari, *The Life of Leonardo da Vinci* (1550)
54. Niccolò Machiavelli, *The Prince* (1513)
55. Desiderius Erasmus, *In Praise of Folly* (1509)
56. Sir Thomas More, *Utopia* (1516)

THE NEW WORLDS AND THE AGE OF EXPLORATION
57. Ibn Battuta, *Travels in Africa* (1354)
58. Christopher Columbus, *Letter from the First Voyage* (1493)
59. Gomes de Zurara, *Chronicle of Guinea* (1453)
60. Bartolomé de Las Casas, *Apologetic History of the Indies* (1566)
61. Bernal Díaz, *The True History of the Conquest of New Spain* (1552–1568)
62. Juan Gonzalez de Mendoza, *The History of the Great and Mightie Kingdom of China* (1585)

RELIGIOUS REFORM
63. Bernard Gui, *A Manual for Inquisitors* (1331)
64. Martin Luther, *The Freedom of a Christian* (1520) and *Of Marriage and Celibacy* (1566)
65. John Calvin, *Institutes of the Christian Religion* (1534) and *Catechism* (ca. 1540)
66. Ignatius Loyola, *Spiritual Exercises* (1548)
67. Teresa of Ávila, *The Life of St. Teresa* (1611)

THE EARLY MODERN WORLD

68. Anonymous, *Lazarillo de Tormes* (1554)
69. *The Twelve Articles of the Peasants of Swabia* (1524); Martin Luther, *Admonition to Peace* (1525)
70. Francis Xavier, *Letter from India* (1543)
71. Marguerite de Navarre, *Heptameron* (1558)
72. Philippe Duplessis-Mornay, *A Defense of Liberty Against Tyrants* (1579)
73. Magdalena and Balthasar Paumgartner, *Letters* (1592–1596)

THE RENAISSANCE

51

■ *Francesco Petrarca* ■

LETTERS
(CA. 1372)

Francesco Petrarca (1304–1374), or Petrarch, is considered the greatest inspiration behind Italian humanism. Famed as a poet, historian, and scholar, Petrarch was absorbed with the classics and introduced them to his contemporaries. He spent much time in monastic libraries ferreting out the works of the ancients; but Petrarca was not just an antiquarian, lost in visions of the past—he was most decidedly a man of affairs. He lived at the papal court in Avignon (where the papacy established residence in 1305) and was an accomplished diplomat and political advisor. His love poetry—written in Italian rather than Latin—made him renowned throughout Italy. In 1341, he was crowned with a laurel wreath to symbolize his poetic greatness.

Petrarca maintained a wide correspondence with writers and thinkers whom he admired. Rather curiously, he also pretended to be in communication with the great classical intellectuals, of whom he ranked Cicero highest. The following excerpts are from his *Letter to Posterity*, written in the last few years of his life; a letter to the great writer Boccaccio; and two letters to the shade of Cicero.

Francesco Petrarca to Posterity

Greeting. It is possible that some word of me may have come to you, though even this is doubtful, since an insignificant and obscure name will scarcely penetrate far in either time or space. If, however, you should have heard of me, you may desire to know what manner of man I was, or what was the outcome of my labours, especially those of which some description or, at any rate, the bare titles may have reached you. To begin with myself, then, the utterances of men concerning me will differ widely, since in

passing judgment almost every one is influenced not so much by truth as by preference, and good and evil report alike know no bounds. I was, in truth, a poor mortal like yourself, neither very exalted in my origin, nor, on the other hand, of the most humble birth, but belonging, as Augustus Caesar says of himself, to an ancient family. As to my disposition, I was not naturally perverse or wanting in modesty, however the contagion of evil associations may have corrupted me. My youth was gone before I realised it; I was carried away by the strength of manhood; but a riper age brought me to my senses and taught me by experience the truth I had long before read in books, that youth and pleasure are vanity—nay, that the Author of all ages and times permits us miserable mortals, puffed up with emptiness, thus to wander about, until finally, coming to a tardy consciousness of our sins, we shall learn to know ourselves. In my prime I was blessed with a quick and active body, although not exceptionally strong; and while I do not lay claim to remarkable personal beauty, I was comely enough in my best days. I was possessed of a clear complexion, between light and dark, lively eyes, and for long years a keen vision, which however deserted me, contrary to my hopes, after I reached my sixtieth birthday, and forced me, to my great annoyance, to resort to glasses. Although I had previously enjoyed perfect health, old age brought with it the usual array of discomforts.

My parents were honourable folk, Florentine in their origin, of medium fortune, or, I may as well admit it, in a condition verging upon poverty. They had been expelled from their native city, and consequently I was born in exile. I have always possessed an extreme contempt for wealth; not that riches are not desirable in themselves, but because I hate the anxiety and care which are invariably associated with them. I certainly do not long to be able to give gorgeous banquets. So-called *convivia,* which are but vulgar bouts, sinning against sobriety and good manners, have always been repugnant to me. I have ever felt that it was irksome and profitless to invite others to such affairs, and not less so to be bidden to them myself. On the other hand, the pleasure of dining with one's friends is so great that nothing has ever given me more delight than their unexpected arrival, nor have I ever willingly sat down to table without a companion. Nothing displeases me more than display, for not only is it bad in itself, and opposed to humility, but it is troublesome and distracting.

I have taken pride in others, never in myself, and however insignificant I may have been,

I have always been still less important in my own judgment. My anger has very often injured myself, but never others. I have always been most desirous of honourable friendships, and have faithfully cherished them. I make this boast without fear, since I am confident that I speak truly. While I am very prone to take offence, I am equally quick to forget injuries, and have a memory tenacious of benefits. In my familiar associations with kings and princes, and in my friendship with noble personages, my good fortune has been such as to excite envy. But it is the cruel fate of those who are growing old that they can commonly only weep for friends who have passed away. The greatest kings of this age have loved and courted me. They may know why; I certainly do not. With some of them I was on such terms that they seemed in a certain sense my guests rather than I theirs; their lofty position in no way embarrassing me, but, on the contrary, bringing with it many advantages. I fled, however, from many of those to whom I was greatly attached; and such was my innate longing for liberty, that I studiously avoided those whose very name seemed incompatible with the freedom that I loved.

I possessed a well-balanced rather than a keen intellect, one prone to all kinds of good and wholesome study, but especially inclined to moral philosophy and the art of poetry. The latter, indeed, I neglected as time went on, and took delight in sacred literature. Finding in that a hidden sweetness which I had once esteemed but lightly, I came to regard the works of the poets as only amenities. Among the many subjects which interested me, I dwelt especially upon antiquity, for our own age has always repelled me, so that, had it not been for the love of those dear to me, I should have preferred to have been born in any other period than our own. In order to forget my own times, I have constantly striven to place myself in spirit in other ages, and consequently I delighted in history; not that the conflicting statements did not offend me, but when in doubt I accepted what appeared to me most probable, or yielded to the authority of the writer.

My style, as many claimed, was clear and forcible; but to me it seemed weak and obscure. In ordinary conversation with friends, or with those about me, I never gave any thought to my language, and I have always wondered that Augustus Caesar should have taken such pains in this respect. When, however, the subject itself, or the place or listener, seemed to demand it, I gave some attention to style, with what success I cannot pretend to say; let them judge in whose presence I spoke. If only I have lived well, it matters little to me how I talked. Mere elegance of language can produce at best but an empty renown.

To Boccaccio (1366)

To be sure, the Latin, in both prose and poetry, is undoubtedly the nobler language, but for that very reason it has been so thoroughly developed by earlier writers that neither we nor anyone else may expect to add very much to it. The vernacular, on the other hand, has but recently been discovered, and, though it has been ravaged by many, it still remains uncultivated, in spite of a few earnest labourers, and still shows itself capable of much improvement and enrichment. Stimulated by this thought, and by the enterprise of youth, I began an extensive work in that language. I laid the foundations of the structure, and got together my lime and stones and wood. And then I began to consider a little more carefully the times in which we live, the fact that our age is the mother of pride and indolence, and that the ability of the vainglorious fellows who would be my judges, and their peculiar grace of delivery is such that they can hardly be said to recite the writings of others, but rather to mangle them. Hearing their performances again and again, and turning the matter over in my mind, I concluded at length that I was building upon unstable earth and shifting sand, and should simply waste my labours and see the work

of my hands levelled by the common herd. Like one who finds a great serpent across his track, I stopped and changed my route—for a higher and more direct one, I hope. Although the short things I once wrote in the vulgar tongue are, as I have said, so scattered that they now belong to the public rather than to me, I shall take precautions against having my more important works torn to pieces in the same way.

And yet why should I find fault with the unenlightenment of the common people, when those who call themselves learned afford so much more just and serious a ground for complaint? Besides many other ridiculous peculiarities, these people add to their gross ignorance an exaggerated and most disgusting pride. It is this that leads them to carp at the reputation of those whose most trivial sayings they were once proud to comprehend, in even the most fragmentary fashion. O inglorious age! that scorns antiquity, its mother, to whom it owes every noble art, that dares to declare itself not only equal but superior to the glorious past. I say nothing of the vulgar, the dregs of mankind, whose sayings and opinions may raise a laugh but hardly merit serious censure. I will say nothing of the military class and the leaders in war, who do not blush to assert that their time has beheld the culmination and perfection of military art, when there is no doubt that this art has degenerated and is utterly going to ruin in their hands. They have neither skill nor intelligence, but rely entirely upon indolence and chance. They go to war decked out as if for a wedding, bent on meat and drink and the gratification of their lust. They think much more of flight than they do of victory. Their skill lies not in striking the adversary, but in holding out the hand of submission; not in terrifying the enemy, but in pleasing the eyes of their mistresses. But even these false notions may be excused in view of the utter ignorance and want of instruction on the part of those who hold them.

Such are the times, my friend, upon which we have fallen; such is the period in which we live and are growing old. Such are the critics of today, as I so often have occasion to lament and complain—men who are innocent of knowledge or virtue, and yet harbour the most exalted opinion of themselves. Not content with losing the words of the ancients, they must attack their genius and their ashes. They rejoice in their ignorance, as if what they did not know were not worth knowing.

To Marcus Tullius Cicero (1345)

Your letters I sought for long and diligently; and finally, where I least expected it, I found them. At once I read them, over and over, with the utmost eagerness. And as I read I seemed to hear your bodily voice, O Marcus Tullius, saying many things, uttering many lamentations, ranging through many phases of thought and feeling. I long had known how excellent a guide you have proved for others; at last I was to learn what sort of guidance you gave yourself.

Now it is your turn to be the listener. Hearken, wherever you are, to the words of advice, or rather of sorrow and regret, that fall, not unaccompanied by tears, from the lips of one of your successors, who loves you faithfully and cherishes your name. O spirit ever restless and perturbed! in old age—I am but using your own words—self-involved in calamities and ruin! what good could you think would come from your incessant wrangling, from all this wasteful strife and enmity? Where were the peace and quiet that befitted your years, your profession, your station in life? What Will-o'-the-wisp tempted you away, with a delusive hope of glory; involved you, in your declining years, in the wars of younger men; and, after exposing you to every form of misfortune, hurled you down to a death that is was unseemly for a philosopher to die? Alas! the wise counsel that you gave your brother and the salutary advice of your great masters, you forgot. You were like a traveller in the night, whose torch lights up for others the path where he himself has miserably fallen.

Of Dionysius I forbear to speak; of your brother and nephew, too; of Dolabella even, if you like. At one moment you praise them all to the skies; at the next fall upon them with sudden maledictions. This, however, could perhaps be pardoned. I will pass by Julius Caesar, too, whose well-approved clemency was a harbour of refuge for the very men who were warring against him. Great Pompey, likewise, I refrain from mentioning. His affection for you was such that you could do with him what you would. But what insanity led you to hurl yourself upon Antony? Love of the republic, you would probably say. But the republic had fallen before this into irretrievable ruin, as you had yourself admitted. Still, it is possible that a lofty sense of duty, and love of liberty, constrained you to do as you did, hopeless though the effort was. That we can easily believe of so great a man. But why, then, were you so friendly with Augustus? What answer can you give to Brutus? If you accept Octavius, said he, we must conclude that you are not so anxious to be rid of all tyrants as to find a tyrant who will be well-disposed toward yourself. Now, unhappy man, you were to take the last false step, the last and most deplorable. You began to speak ill of the very friend whom you had so lauded, although he was not doing any ill to you, but merely refusing to prevent others who were. I grieve, dear friend, at such fickleness. These shortcomings fill me with pity and shame. Like Brutus, I feel no confidence in the arts in which you are so proficient. What, pray, does it profit a man to teach others, and to be prating always about virtue, in high-sounding words, if he fails to give heed to his own instructions? Ah! How much better it would have been, how much more fitting for a philosopher, to have grown old peacefully in the country, meditating, as you yourself have somewhere said, upon the life that endures for ever, and not upon this poor fragment of life; to have known no fasces, yearned for no triumphs, found no Catilines to fill the soul with ambitious longings! All this, however, is vain. Farewell, forever, my Cicero.

Written in the land of the living; on the right bank of the Adige, in Verona, a city of Transpadane Italy; on the 16th of June, and in the year of that God whom you never knew the 1345th.

To Marcus Tullius Cicero

If my earlier letter gave you offence—for, as you often have remarked, the saying of your contemporary in the *Andria* is a faithful one, that compliance begets friends, truth only hatred—you shall listen now to words that will soothe your wounded feelings and prove that the truth need not always be hateful. For, if censure that is true angers us, true praise, on the other hand, gives us delight.

You lived then, Cicero, if I may be permitted to say it, like a mere man, but spoke like an orator, wrote like a philosopher. It was your life that I criticised; not your mind, nor your tongue; for the one fills me with admiration, the other with amazement. And even in your life I feel the lack of nothing but stability, and the love of quiet that should go with your philosophic professions, and abstention from civil war, when liberty had been extinguished and the republic buried and its dirge sung.

See how different my treatment of you is from yours of Epicurus, in your works at large, and especially in the *De Finibus*. You are continually praising his life, but his talents you ridicule. I ridicule in you nothing at all. Your life does awaken my pity, as I have said; but your talents and your eloquence call for nothing but congratulation. O great father of Roman eloquence! not I alone but all who deck themselves with the flowers of Latin speech render thanks unto you. It is from your well-springs that we draw the streams that water our meads. You, we freely acknowledge, are the leader who marshals us; yours are the words of encouragement that sustain us; yours is the light that illumines the path before us. In a word, it is under your auspices that we have attained to such little skill in this art of writing as we may possess. . . .

You have heard what I think of your life and your genius. Are you hoping to hear of your books also; what fate has befallen them, how they are esteemed by the masses and among scholars? They still are in existence, glorious volumes, but we of today are too feeble a folk to read them, or even to be acquainted with their mere titles. Your fame extends far and wide; your name is mighty, and fills the ears of men; and yet those who really know you are very few, be it because the times are unfavourable, or because men's minds are slow and dull, or, as I am the more inclined to believe, because the love of money forces our thoughts in other directions. Consequently right in our own day, unless I am much mistaken, some of your books have disappeared, I fear beyond recovery. It is a great grief to me, a great disgrace to this generation, a great wrong done to posterity. The shame of failing to cultivate our own talents, thereby depriving the future of the fruits that they might have yielded, is not enough for us; we must waste and spoil, through our cruel and insufferable neglect, the fruits of your labours too, and of those of your fellows as well, for the fate that I lament in the case of your own books has befallen the works of many another illustrious man.

QUESTIONS

1. How do you think Petrarca's origins might have affected his outlook as a writer?

2. Why did Petrarca look back to the classical period with such fondness?

3. Petrarca was one of the first Renaissance writers to compose in his own language. Why did he choose to do so? How do you think this change might have affected how literature was read and received?

4. How has Cicero let Petrarca down?

5. Although Petrarca is very harsh in his judgment of Cicero, how does the Roman redeem himself, and how do Petrarca's contemporaries fail Cicero?

52

■ *Leon Battista Alberti* ■

ON THE FAMILY
(1435–1444)

Leon Battista Alberti (1404–1472) was one of the great virtuosi of the Renaissance. The illegitimate son of one of the wealthiest Florentine merchants, Alberti was an outstanding athlete and man of action as well as an influential writer. After having studied law and entering the service of the Church, he achieved his greatest fame as an architect, designing a number of exquisite private mansions. His writings include classic works on the principles of painting and architecture.

On the Family is an exploration of the duties, obligations, and benefits of family life. Alberti uses the popular dialogue form to elaborate on the themes of parental responsibility, love, marriage, and the management of the household. He views the family from a variety of perspectives: as a kinship group, an economic unit, and a political body.

In our discussion we may establish four general precepts as sound and firm foundation for all the other points to be developed or added. I shall name them. In the family the number of men must not diminish but augment; possessions must not grow less, but more; all forms of disgrace are to be shunned—a good name and fine reputation is precious and worth pursuing;

hatreds, enmities, rancor must be carefully avoided, while good will, numerous acquaintances, and friendships are something to look for, augment, and cultivate.

We shall take up these four points of wisdom in order to see how men become rich, good, and well-beloved. First we must begin by seeing how a family becomes, as we may say, populous.

We shall give some thought to the reasons for a decline in numbers. Then we shall turn to the second point. I am delighted to find that by some providential chance we happened to begin our talk with a kind of prelude to all this, in which I urged you to avoid all lust and lascivious greed. Did I not intend to be brief in this matter, as before so in what is to come? Perhaps I would show you more clearly how in all four things that remain to our consideration, sensual pleasure and lascivious love are the most destructive cause of total ruin. Another time and place for this discussion may arise, while you, I know, need no persuasion to make you keep to your education, your noble pursuits, and your studies, and avoid idleness and less than honorable desires. So let us return to our subject. There we shall speak as lucidly and simply as we can, without any elegant and very polished rhetoric. I think among ourselves good thoughts are far more important than a pretty style. Listen to me.

Families increase in population no differently than do countries, regions, and the whole world. As anyone who uses his imagination will quickly realize, the number of mortal men has grown from a small number to the present almost infinite multitude through the procreation and rearing of children. And, for the procreation of children, no one can deny that man requires woman. Since a child comes into the world as a tender and delicate creature, he needs someone to whose care and devotion he comes as a cherished trust. This person must nourish him with diligence and love and must defend him from harm. Too much cold or too much sun, rain, and the wild blowing of a storm are harmful to children. Woman, therefore, did first find a roof under which to nourish and protect herself and her offspring. There she remained, busy in the shadow, nourishing and caring for her children. And since woman was busy guarding and taking care of the heir, she was not in a position to go out and find what she and her children required for the maintenance of their life. Man, however, was by nature more energetic and industrious, and he went out to find things and bring what seemed to him necessary. Sometimes the man remained away from home and did not return as soon as his family expected. Because of this, when he came back laden, the woman learned to save things up in order to make sure that if in the future her husband stayed away for a time, neither she nor her children would suffer. In this way it seems clear to me that nature and human reason taught mankind the necessity of having a spouse, both to increase and continue generations and to nourish and preserve those already born. It also became clear that careful gathering and diligent preserving were essential to the maintenance of human life in the married state.

Nature showed, further, that this relationship could not be permitted with more than one wife at a time, since man was by no means able to provide and bring home more than was needed for himself and one wife and children. Had he wished to find food and to gather goods for more wives and families, one or another of them would certainly sometimes have lacked some of the necessities. And the woman who found herself lacking what are or ought to be the necessities of life, would she not have had sufficient reason even to abandon her offspring in order to preserve her own life? Perhaps under pressure of such need she would even have had the right to seek out another companion. Marriage, therefore, was instituted by nature, our most excellent and divine teacher of all things, with the provision that there should be one constant life's companion for a man, and one only. With her he should dwell under one roof, her he should not forget or leave all alone, but to her return, bearing things with him and ordering matters so that his family might have all that was necessary and sufficient. The wife was to preserve in the house the things he brought to her. To satisfy nature, then, a man need only choose a woman with whom he can dwell in tranquillity under one roof all his life.

Young people, however, very often do not cherish the good of the family enough to do this. Marriage, perhaps, seems to them to take away their present liberty and freedom. It may be, as the comic poets like to tell us, that they are held back and dissuaded by some mistress. Sometimes, too, young men find it hard enough to manage one life, and fear as an excessive and undesirable burden the task of supporting a wife and children besides. They may doubt their capacity to maintain in honorable estate a family which grows in needs from day to day. Viewing the conjugal bed as a troublesome responsibility, they then avoid the legitimate and honorable path to the increase of a family.

If a family is not to fall for these reasons into what we have described as the most unfortunate condition of decline, but is to grow, instead, in fame and in the prosperous multitude of its youth, we must persuade our young men to take wives. We must use every argument for this purpose, offer incentive, promise reward, employ all our wit, persistence, and cunning. A most appropriate reason for taking a wife may be found in what we were saying before, about the evil of sensual indulgence, for the condemnation of such things may lead young men to desire honorable satisfactions. As other incentives, we may also speak to them of the delights of this primary and natural companionship of marriage. Children act as pledges and securities of marital love and kindness. At the same time they offer a focus for all a man's hopes and desires. Sad, indeed, is the man who has labored to get wealth and power and lands, and then has no true heir and perpetuator of his memory. No one can be more suited than a man's true and legitimate sons to gain advantages by virtue of his character, position, and authority, and to enjoy the fruits and rewards of his labor. If a man leaves such heirs, furthermore, he need not consider himself wholly dead and gone. His children keep his own position and his true image in the family.

It will serve our purpose, also, to remind the young of the dignity conferred on the father in the ancient world. Fathers of families wore precious jewels and were given other tokens of dignity forbidden to any who had not added by his progeny to the population of the republic. It may also help to recall to young men how often profligates and hopeless prodigals have been restored to a better life by the presence of a wife in the house. Add to this what a great help sons can be as hands to get work done—how they give zealous and loyal aid and support when fortune is hard and men unkind—and how your sons more than anyone spring to your defense and are ready to avenge the injury and harm inflicted upon you by evil and outrageous men. Likewise, our children are our comfort and are apt at every age to make us happy and give us great joys and satisfactions. These things it is good to tell them. It also helps to point out how much children come to mean in old age, when we live under the pressure of various needs.

Let it be the responsibility of the whole house to see that once they have the desire they have also the ability honorably to establish a family. Let the entire family contribute, as if to purchase its own growth, and let them all join by gathering something from each member to put up a sufficient sum for a fund which will support those who shall be born. In this way an expense which would have been disastrously heavy for one alone shall be shared among many and become merely a light obligatory payment. It seems to me that in a family where good customs prevail, no one would be unwilling to pay any amount to ransom back from slavery a humble member, not even of his own family but of his country and language. No attempt should be made, therefore, to evade the light expense which might restore a greater number to one's own blood and to one's family. Year after year you give wages to strangers, to various outsiders. You feed and clothe both foreigners and slaves, not so much to enjoy the fruit of their labor as to have a large company in your household. To contribute to a single charity which would support your own kinsmen would cost you far less. The company of your own relatives will yield you more honor and more pleasure than that of strangers. Cherished and faithful kinsmen will do more useful work and suit your household better than the workers you have taken into your service, whose loyalty you have merely bought. One should show such kindness and charity toward one's family, then, so that a father may be sure his children need never want for the necessities of life.

Perhaps it will help to put our young people under some compulsion like this: fathers could say in their wills, "If you do not marry when you reach the appropriate age, you are no heir of mine." As to what is the appropriate time of life to take a wife, to relate all the ancient opinions on this matter would take a long time. Hesiod would have a man marry at thirty; Lycurgus wanted fatherhood to begin at thirty-seven; to our modern minds it seems to be practical for a man to marry at twenty-five. Everyone at least agrees that to give this kind of responsibility to the willful and ardent youth under twenty-five is dangerous. A man of that age spends his fire and force better in establishing and strengthening his own position than in procreating. The youthful seed, moreover, seems faulty and frail and less full of vigor than that which is ripened. Let men wait for solid maturity.

When, by the urging and counsel of their elders and of the whole family, young men have arrived at the point of marriage, their mothers and other female relatives and friends, who have known the virgins of the neighborhood from earliest childhood and know the way their upbringing has formed them, should select all the well-born and well-brought-up girls and present that list to the new groom-to-be. He can then choose the one who suits him best. The elders of the house and all of the family shall reject no daughter-in-law unless she is tainted with the breath of scandal or bad reputation. Aside from that, let the man who will have to satisfy her satisfy himself. He should act as do wise heads of families before they acquire some

property—they like to look it over several times before they actually sign a contract. It is good in the case of any purchase and contract to inform oneself fully and to take counsel. One should consult a good number of persons and be very careful in order to avoid belated regrets. The man who has decided to marry must be still more cautious. I recommend that he examine and anticipate in every way, and consider for many days, what sort of person it is he is to live with for all his years as husband and companion. Let him be minded to marry for two purposes: first to perpetuate himself in his children, and second to have a steady and constant companion all his life. A woman is needed, therefore, who is likely to bear children and who is desirable as a perpetual mate.

They say that in choosing a wife one looks for beauty, parentage, and riches. The beauty of a man accustomed to arms, it seems to me, lies in his having a presence betokening pride, limbs full of strength, and the gestures of one who is skilled and adept in all forms of exercise. The beauty of an old man, I think, lies in his prudence, his amiability, and the reasoned judgment which permeates all his words and his counsel. Whatever else may be thought beautiful in an old man, certainly it differs sharply from what constitutes beauty in a young cavalier. I think that beauty in a woman, likewise, must be judged not only by the charm and refinement of her face, but still more by the grace of her person and her aptitude for bearing and giving birth to many fine children.

Among the most essential criteria of beauty in a woman is an honorable manner. Even a wild, prodigal, greasy, drunken woman may be beautiful of feature, but no one would call her a beautiful wife. A woman worthy of praise must show first of all in her conduct, modesty, and purity. Marius, the illustrious Roman, said in that first speech of his to the Roman people: "Of women we require purity, of men labor." And I certainly agree. There is nothing more disgusting than a coarse and dirty woman. Who is stupid enough not to see clearly that a woman who does not care for neatness and cleanliness in her appearance, not only in her dress and body but in all her behavior and language, is by no means well mannered? How can it be anything but obvious that a bad mannered woman is also rarely virtuous? We shall consider elsewhere the harm that comes to a family from women who lack virtue, for I myself do not know which is the worse fate for a family, total celibacy or a single dishonored woman. In a bride, therefore, a man must first seek beauty of mind, that is, good conduct and virtue.

In her body he must seek not only loveliness, grace, and charm but must also choose a woman who is well made for bearing children, with the kind of constitution that promises to make them strong and big. There's an old proverb, "When you pick your wife, you choose your children." All her virtues will in fact shine brighter still in beautiful children. It is a well-known saying among poets: "Beautiful character dwells in a beautiful body." The natural philosophers require that a woman be neither thin nor very fat. Those laden with fat are subject to coldness and constipation and slow to conceive. They say that a woman should have a joyful nature, fresh and lively in her blood and her whole being. They have no objections to a dark girl. They do reject girls with a frowning black visage, however. They have no liking for either the undersized or the overlarge and lean. They find that a woman is most suited to bear children if she is fairly big and has limbs of ample length. They always have a preference for youth, based on a number of arguments which I need not expound here, but particularly on the point that a young girl has a more adaptable mind. Young girls are pure by virtue of their age and have not developed any spitefulness. They are by nature modest and free of vice. They quickly learn to accept affectionately and unresistingly the habits and wishes of their husbands.

Now we have spoken of beauty. Let us next consider parentage, and what are the qualities to look for there. I think the first problem in choosing a family is to investigate closely the customs and habits of one's new relatives. Many marriages have ruined the family, as one may hear and read every day, because they involved union with a litigious, quarrelsome, arrogant, and malevolent set of men. For brevity's sake I cite no examples here. I think that no one is so great a fool that he would not rather remain unmarried than burden himself with terrible relatives. Sometimes the links of family have proved a trouble and disaster to the man, who has had to support both his own family and that of the girl he married. Not infrequently it happens that the new family, because they really are so unfortunate, all settle down in the house of their new kinsman. As the new husband you cannot keep them without harm to yourself, nor can you send them away without incurring censure.

To sum up this whole subject in a few words, for I want above all to be brief on this point, let a man get himself new kinsmen of better than plebeian blood, of a fortune more than diminutive, of a decent occupation, and of modest and respectable habits. Let them not be too far above himself, lest their greatness overshadow his own honor and position. Too high a family may disturb his own and his family's peace and tranquillity, and also, if one of them falls, you cannot help to support him without collapsing or wearing yourself out as you stagger under a weight too great for your arms and your strength. I also do not want the new relatives to rank too low, for while the first error puts you in a position of servitude, the second causes expense. Let them be equals, then, and, to repeat, modest and respectable people.

The matter of dowry is next, which I would like to see middling in size, certain and prompt rather than large, vague, or promised for an indefinite future. I know not why everyone, as if corrupted by a common vice, takes advantage of delay to grow lazy in paying debts. Sometimes, in cases of marriage, people are further tempted because they hope to evade payment altogether. As your wife spends her first year in your house, it seems impossible not to reinforce the new bonds of kinship by frequent visiting and parties. But it will be thought rude if, in the middle of a gathering of kinsmen, you put yourself forward to insist and complain. If, as new husbands usually do, you don't want to lose their still precarious favor, you may ask your in-laws in restrained and casual words. Then you are forced to accept any little excuse they may offer. If you make a more forthright demand for what is your own, they will explain to you their many obligations, will complain of fortune, blame the conditions of the time, complain of other men, and say that they hope to be able to ask much of you in greater difficulties. As long as they can, in fact, they will promise you bounteous repayment at an ever-receding date. They will beg you, and overwhelm you, nor will it seem possible for you to spurn the prayers of people you have accepted as your own family. Finally, you will be put in a position where you must either suffer the loss in silence or enter upon expensive litigation and create enmity.

What is more, it will seem that you can never put an end to the pressure from your wife on this point. She will weep many tears, and the pleadings and insistent prayers of a new love that has just begun are apt to have a certain force. However hard and twisted your temperament you can hardly impose silence on someone who pleads with an outsider, thus softly and tearfully, for the sake of her own father and brothers. Then imagine how impossible for you to turn a deaf ear on your own wife doing so in your own house, in your own room. You are bound, in the end, to suffer either financial loss or loss of affection. This is why the dowry should be precisely set, promptly paid, and not too high. The larger the payments are to be and the longer they are to be carried, the more discussion you will be forced into, the more reluctantly you will be paid, and the more obliged you will feel to spend inordinate sums for all sorts of things. There will be indescribable bitterness and often totally ruinous results in setting dowries very high. We have said now how a wife is to be selected from outside and how she is to be received into the house. It remains to be seen how she is to be treated once she is within.

QUESTIONS

1. Many historians view the Renaissance as a period of increasing secularization. How does Alberti's work reflect this trend?

2. How did Alberti define the role of the father in a family? Where does he get his examples?

3. In what ways is the family like a state?

4. How, according to Alberti, does nature shape the role of women in the family?

5. What are the qualities of a good wife? Why do you think Alberti has nothing to say about the qualifications of a good husband?

53

■ *Giorgio Vasari* ■

THE LIFE OF LEONARDO DA VINCI

(1550)

Giorgio Vasari (1511–1574) celebrated the achievements of hundreds of artists in his *Lives of the Most Eminent Italian Architects, Painters, and Sculptors,* which he published first in 1550 and then in an enlarged edition eighteen years later. Vasari undertook his project not as a historian or biographer, but as an artist. He believed that only a creative artist could understand the momentous accomplishments of the Renaissance.

Vasari's father was a potter; his uncle, with whom he lived as a teenager, was a painter. Apprenticed at an early age, Giorgio studied for a time in Michelangelo's studio. He secured the backing of powerful patrons and was soon in demand throughout the Italian peninsula. As he traveled, he collected materials for his *Lives*. His biography of Leonardo is one of the best known and shows Vasari's concern for detail, anecdote, and instruction.

Life of Leonardo da Vinci

Painter and Sculptor of Florence

The greatest gifts are often seen, in the course of nature, rained by celestial influences on human creatures; and sometimes, in supernatural fashion, beauty, grace, and talent are united beyond measure in one single person, in a manner that to whatever such [a] one turns his attention, his every action is so divine, that, surpassing all other men, it makes itself clearly known as a thing bestowed by God (as it is), and not acquired by human art. This was seen by all mankind in Leonardo da Vinci, in whom, besides a beauty of body never sufficiently extolled, there was an infinite grace in all his actions; and so great was his genius, and such its growth, that to whatever difficulties he turned

his mind, he solved them with ease. In him was great bodily strength, joined to dexterity, with a spirit and courage ever royal and magnanimous; and the fame of his name so increased, that not only in his lifetime was he held in esteem, but his reputation became even greater among posterity after his death.

Truly marvellous and celestial was Leonardo, the son of Ser Piero da Vinci; and in learning and in the rudiments of letters he would have made great proficience, if he had not been so variable and unstable, for he set himself to learn many things, and then, after having begun them, abandoned them. Thus, in arithmetic, during the few months that he studied it, he made so much progress, that, by continually suggesting doubts and difficulties to the master who was teaching him, he would very often bewilder him. He gave some little attention to music, and quickly resolved to learn to play the lyre, as one who had by nature a spirit most lofty and full of refinement: wherefore he sang divinely to that instrument, improvising upon it. Nevertheless, although he occupied himself with such a variety of things, he never ceased drawing and working in relief, pursuits which suited his fancy more than any other. Ser Piero, having observed this, and having considered the loftiness of his intellect, one day took some of his drawings and carried them to Andrea del Verrocchio, who was much his friend, and besought him straitly to tell him whether Leonardo, by devoting himself to drawing, would make any proficience. Andrea was astonished to see the extraordinary beginnings of Leonardo, and urged Ser Piero that he should make him study it; wherefore he arranged with Leonardo that he should enter the workshop of Andrea, which Leonardo did with the greatest willingness in the world. And he practised not one branch of art only, but all those in which drawing played a part; and having an intellect so divine and marvellous that he was also an excellent geometrician, he not only worked in sculpture, making in his youth, in clay, some heads of women that are smiling, of which plaster casts are still taken, and likewise some heads of boys which appeared to have issued from the hand of a master; but in architecture, also, he made many drawings both of ground-plans and of other designs of buildings; and he was the first, although but a youth, who suggested the plan of reducing the river Arno to a navigable canal from Pisa to Florence. He made designs of flour-mills, fulling-mills, and engines, which might be driven by the force of water: and since he wished that his profession should be painting, he studied much in drawing after nature, and sometimes in making models of figures in clay, over which he would lay soft pieces of cloth dipped in clay, and then set himself patiently to draw them on a certain kind of very fine Rheims cloth, or prepared linen; and he executed them in black and white with the point of his brush, so that it was a marvel, as some

of them by his hand, which I have in our book of drawings, still bear witness; besides which, he drew on paper with such diligence and so well, that there is no one who has ever equalled him in perfection of finish; and I have one, a head drawn with the style in chiaroscuro, which is divine.

And there was infused in that brain such grace from God, and a power of expression in such sublime accord with the intellect and memory that served it, and he knew so well how to express his conceptions by draughtmanship, that he vanquished with his discourse, and confuted with his reasoning, every valiant wit. And he was continually making models and designs to show men how to remove mountains with ease, and how to bore them in order to pass from one level to another; and by means of levers, windlasses, and screws, he showed the way to raise and draw great weights, together with methods for emptying harbours, and pumps for removing water from low places, things which his brain never ceased from devising.

It is clear that Leonardo, through his comprehension of art, began many things and never finished one of them, since it seemed to him that the hand was not able to attain to the perfection of art in carrying out the things which he imagined; for the reason that he conceived in idea difficulties so subtle and so marvellous, that they could never be expressed by the hands, be they ever so excellent. And so many were his caprices, that, philosophizing of natural things, he set himself to seek out the properties of herbs, going on even to observe the motions of the heavens, the path of the moon, and the courses of the sun. . . .

He also painted in Milan, for the Friars of S. Dominic, at S. Maria dell Grazie, a Last Supper, a most beautiful and marvellous thing; and to the heads of the Apostles he gave such majesty and beauty, that he left the head of Christ unfinished, not believing that he was able to give it that divine air which is essential to the image of Christ. This work, remaining thus all but finished, has ever

been held by the Milanese in the greatest veneration, and also by strangers as well; for Leonardo
imagined and succeeded in expressing that
anxiety which had seized the Apostles in wishing
to know who should betray their Master. For
which reason in all their faces are seen love, fear,
and wrath, or rather, sorrow, at not being able to
understand the meaning of Christ; which thing
excites no less marvel than the sight, in contrast
to it, of obstinacy, hatred, and treachery in Judas;
not to mention that every least part of the work
displays an incredible diligence, seeing that even
in the tablecloth the texture of the stuff is counterfeited in such a manner that linen itself could
not seem more real.

It is said that the Prior of that place kept
pressing Leonardo, in a most importunate
manner, to finish the work; for it seemed
strange to him to see Leonardo sometimes
stand half a day at a time, lost in contemplation, and he would have liked him to go on like
the labourers hoeing in his garden, without
ever stopping his brush. And not content with
this, he complained of it to the Duke, and that
so warmly, that he was constrained to send for
Leonardo and delicately urged him to work,
contriving nevertheless to show him that he was
doing all this because of the importunity of the
Prior. Leonardo, knowing that the intellect of
that Prince was acute and discerning, was
pleased to discourse at large with the Duke on
the subject, a thing which he had never done
with the Prior: and he reasoned much with him
about art, and made him understand that men
of lofty genius sometimes accomplish the most
when they work the least, seeking out inventions with the mind, and forming those perfect
ideas which the hands afterwards express and
reproduce from the images already conceived
in the brain. And he added that two heads were
still wanting for him to paint; that of Christ,
which he did not wish to seek on earth; and he
could not think that it was possible to conceive

in the imagination that beauty and heavenly
grace which should be the mark of God incarnate. Next, there was wanting that of Judas,
which was also troubling him, not thinking
himself capable of imagining features that
should represent the countenance of him who,
after so many benefits received, had a mind so
cruel as to resolve to betray his Lord, the
Creator of the world. However, he would seek
out a model for the latter; but if in the end he
could not find a better, he should not want that
of the importunate and tactless Prior. This
thing moved the Duke wondrously to laughter,
and he said that Leonardo had a thousand
reasons on his side. And so the poor Prior, in
confusion, confined himself to urging on the
work in the garden, and left Leonardo in
peace, who finished only the head of Judas,
which seems the very embodiment of treachery
and inhumanity; but that of Christ, as has been
said, remained unfinished.

Leonardo undertook to execute, for
Francesco del Giocondo, the portrait of Mona
Lisa, his wife; and after toiling over it for four
years, he left it unfinished; and the work is now
in the collection of King Frances of France, at
Fontainebleau. In this head, whoever wished to
see how closely art could imitate nature, was
able to comprehend it with ease; for in it were
counterfeited all the minutenesses that with
subtlety are able to be painted, seeing that the
eyes had that lustre and watery sheen which
are always seen in life, and around them were
all those rosy and pearly tints, as well as the
lashes, which cannot be represented without
the greatest subtlety. The eyebrows, through
his having shown the manner in which the
hairs spring from the flesh, here more close
and here more scanty, and curve according
to the pores of the skin, could not be more
natural. The nose, with its beautiful nostrils,
rosy and tender, appeared to be alive. The
mouth, with its opening, and with its ends

united by the red of the lips to the flesh-tints of the face, seemed, in truth, to be not colours but flesh. In the pit of the throat, if one gazed upon it intently, could be seen the beating of the pulse. And, indeed, it may be said that it was painted in such a manner as to make every valiant craftsman, be he who he may, tremble and lose heart. He made use, also, of this device: Mona Lisa being very beautiful, he always employed, while he was painting her portrait, persons to play or sing, and jesters, who might make her remain merry, in order to take away that melancholy which painters are often wont to give to the portraits that they paint. And in this work of Leonardo's there was a smile so pleasing, that it was a thing more divine than human to behold; and it was held to be something marvellous, since the reality was not more alive. . . .

There was very great disdain between Michelangelo Buonarrati and him, on account of which Michelangelo departed from Florence, with the excuse of Duke Giuliano, having been summoned by the Pope to the competition for the façade of S. Lorenzo. Leonardo, understanding this, departed and went into France, where the King, having had works by his hand, bore him great affection; and he desired that he should colour the cartoon of S. Anne, but Leonardo, according to his custom, put him off for a long time with words.

Finally, having grown old, he remained ill many months, and, feeling himself near to death, asked to have himself diligently informed of the teaching of the Catholic faith, and of the good way and holy Christian religion; and then, with many moans, he confessed and was penitent; and although he could not raise himself well on his feet, supporting himself on the arms of his friends and servants, he was pleased to take devoutly the most holy Sacrament, out of his bed. The King, who was wont often and lovingly to visit him, then came into the room; wherefore he, out of reverence, having raised himself to sit upon the bed, giving him an account of his sickness and the circumstances of it, showed withal how much he had offended God and mankind in not having worked at his art as he should have done. Thereupon he was seized by a paroxysm, the messenger of death; for which reason the King having risen and having taken his head, in order to assist him and show him favour, to the end that he might alleviate his pain, his spirit, which was divine, knowing that it could not have any greater honour, expired in the arms of the King, in the seventy-fifth year of his age.

QUESTIONS

1. If Leonardo is the classic example of the "Renaissance Man," how would you define the term?

2. What flaws does Vasari identify in Leonardo?

3. What might you deduce from Vasari's *Life* about the social position of the artist in Renaissance Italy?

4. Why was Leonardo such a successful painter?

5. How did the famous artists of Leonardo's time get along with one another?

54

■ *Niccolò Machiavelli* ■

THE PRINCE
(1513)

Niccolò Machiavelli (1469–1527) was born in Florence, the son of a struggling lawyer. Marked from his youth as a brilliant student, he received a sound humanist education, which he put to use in the service of the state. At the age of twenty-five, Machiavelli entered the service of the Republic of Florence as a diplomat and political advisor. His career brought him into contact with many of the most powerful figures of his age, but it was abruptly cut short in 1512 when the Republic was overthrown. Machiavelli was jailed and tortured before being sent into exile.

Forced into retirement, Machiavelli studied ancient history and began to write. In 1513, he finished *The Prince,* which remains one of the classics of Western political theory. A distillation of his experience in government and colored by his own cynical view of human nature, *The Prince* is a treatise on the art of governing successfully; Machiavelli wrote it in hope of being allowed to return to government service, and it reflects his passionate desire for the restoration of political stability in Florence.

Niccolò Machiavelli to the Magnificent Lorenzo de' Medici

It is a frequent custom for those who seek the favor of a prince to make him presents of those things they value most highly or which they know are most pleasing to him. Hence one often sees gifts consisting of horses, weapons, cloth of gold, precious stones, and similar ornaments suitable for men of noble rank. I too would like to commend myself to Your Magnificence with some token of my readiness to serve you; and I have not found among my belongings anything I prize so much or value so highly as my knowledge of the actions of men, acquired through long experience of contemporary affairs and extended reading in those of antiquity. For a

long time I have thought carefully about these matters and examined them minutely; now I have condensed my thoughts into a little volume, and send it to Your Magnificence. My book is not stuffed with pompous phrases or elaborate, magnificent words, neither is it decorated with any form of extrinsic rhetorical embroidery, such as many authors use to present or adorn their materials. I wanted my book to be absolutely plain, or at least distinguished only by the variety of the examples and the importance of the subject.

I hope it will not be thought presumptuous if a man of low social rank undertakes to discuss the rule of princes and lay down principles for them. When painters want to represent land-scapes, they stand on low ground to get a true view of the mountains and hills; they climb to the tops of the mountains to get a panorama over the valleys. Similarly, to know the people well one must be a prince, and to know princes well one must be, oneself, of the people.

On Different Kinds of Troops, Especially Mercenaries

I said before that a prince must lay strong foundations, otherwise he is bound to come to grief. The chief foundations on which all states rest, whether they are new, old, or mixed, are good laws and good arms. And since there cannot be good laws where there are not good arms, and where there are good arms there are bound to be good laws, I shall set aside the topic of laws and talk about arms.

Let me say, then, that the armies with which a prince defends his state are either his own or are mercenaries, auxiliaries, or mixed. Mercenaries and auxiliaries are useless and dangerous. Any man who founds his state on mercenaries can never be safe or secure. The reason is that they have no other passions or incentives to hold the field, except their desire for a bit of money, and that is not enough to make them die for you.

Military Duties of the Prince

A prince, therefore, should have no other object, no other thought, no other subject of study, than war, its rules and disciplines; this is the only art for a man who commands, and it is of such value [*virtù*] that it not only keeps born princes in place, but often raises men from private citizens to princely fortune. On the other hand, it is clear that when princes have thought more about the refinements of life than about war, they have lost their positions. The quickest way to lose a state is to neglect this art; the quickest way to get one is to study it. Because he was a soldier, Francesco Sforza raised himself from private citizen to duke of Milan; his successors, who tried to avoid the hardships of warfare, became private citizens after being dukes. Apart from the other evils it brings

with it, being defenseless makes you contemptible. This is one of the disgraces from which a prince must guard himself, as we shall see later. Between a man with arms and a man without them there is no proportion at all. It is not reasonable to expect an armed man to obey one who is unarmed, nor an unarmed man to be safe among armed servants; because, what with the contempt of the former and the mistrust of the latter, there's no living together. Thus a prince who knows nothing of warfare, apart from his other troubles already described, can't hope for respect from his soldiers or put any trust in them.

On the Reasons Why Men Are Praised or Blamed—Especially Princes

It remains now to be seen what style and principles a prince ought to adopt in dealing with his subjects and friends. I know the subject has been treated frequently before, and I'm afraid people will think me rash for trying to do so again, especially since I intend to differ in this discussion from what others have said. But since I intend to write something useful to an understanding reader, it seemed better to go after the real truth of the matter than to repeat what people have imagined. A great many men have imagined states and princedoms such as nobody ever saw or knew in the real world, for there's such a difference between the way we really live and the way we ought to live that the man who neglects the real to study the ideal will learn how to accomplish his ruin, not his salvation. Any man who tries to be good all the time is bound to come to ruin among the great number who are not good. Hence a prince who wants to keep his post must learn how not to be good, and use that knowledge, or refrain from using it, as necessity requires.

Putting aside, then, all the imaginary things that are said about princes, and getting down to the truth, let me say that whenever men are discussed (and especially princes because they are prominent), there are certain qualities that bring them either praise or blame. Thus some are considered generous, others stingy; some are givers, others grabbers; some cruel, others merciful; one man is treacherous, another faithful; one is feeble and effeminate, another fierce and spirited; one humane, another proud; one lustful, another chaste; one straightforward, another sly; one harsh, another gentle; one serious, another playful; one religious, another skeptical, and so on. I know everyone will agree that among these many qualities a prince certainly ought to have all those that are considered good. But since it is impossible to have and exercise them all, because the conditions of human life simply do not allow it, a prince must be shrewd enough to avoid the public disgrace of those vices that would lose him his state. If he possibly can, he should also guard against vices that will not lose him his state; but if he cannot prevent them, he should not be too worried about indulging them. And furthermore, he should not be too worried about incurring blame for any vice without which he would find it hard to save his state. For if you look at matters carefully, you will see that something resembling virtue, if you follow it, may be your ruin, while something else resembling vice will lead, if you follow it, to your security and wellbeing.

On Cruelty and Clemency: Whether It Is Better to Be Loved or Feared

The question arises: is it better to be loved than feared, or vice versa? I don't doubt that every prince would like to be both; but since it is hard to accommodate these qualities, if you have to make a choice, to be feared is much safer than to be loved. For it is a good general rule about men, that they are ungrateful, fickle, liars and deceivers, fearful of danger and greedy for gain. While you serve their welfare, they are all yours, but when the danger is close at hand, they turn against you. People are less concerned with offending a man who makes himself loved than one who makes himself feared: the reason is that love is a link of obligation which men, because they are rotten, will break any time they think doing so serves

their advantage; but fear involves dread of punishment, from which they can never escape.

Still, a prince should make himself feared in such a way that, even if he gets no love, he gets no hate either; because it is perfectly possible to be feared and not hated, and this will be the result if only the prince will keep his hands off the property of his subjects or citizens, and off their women. When he does have to shed blood, he should be sure to have a strong justification and manifest cause; but above all, he should not confiscate people's property, because men are quicker to forget the death of a father than the loss of a patrimony.

Returning to the question of being feared or loved, I conclude that since men love at their own inclination but can be made to fear at the inclination of the prince, a shrewd prince will lay his foundations on what is under his own control, not on what is controlled by others. He should simply take pains not to be hated, as I said.

The Way Princes Should Keep Their Word

How praiseworthy it is for a prince to keep his word and live with integrity rather than by craftiness, everyone understands; yet we see from recent experience that those princes have accomplished most who paid little heed to keeping their promises, but who knew how craftily to manipulate the minds of men. In the end, they won out over those who tried to act honestly.

You should consider then, that there are two ways of fighting, one with laws and the other with force. The first is properly a human method, the second belongs to beasts. But as the first method does not always suffice, you sometimes have to turn to the second. Thus a prince must know how to make good use of both the beast and the man. Ancient writers made subtle note of this fact when they wrote that Achilles and many other princes of antiquity were sent to be reared by Chiron the centaur, who trained them in his discipline. Having a teacher who is half man and half beast can only mean that a prince must know how to use both these two natures, and that one without the other has no lasting effect.

Since a prince must know how to use the character of beasts, he should pick for imitation the fox and the lion. As the lion cannot protect himself from traps, and the fox cannot defend himself from wolves, you have to be a fox in order to be wary of traps, and a lion to overawe the wolves. Those who try to live by the lion alone are badly mistaken. Thus a prudent prince cannot and should not keep his word when to do so would go against his interest, or when the reasons that made him pledge it no longer apply. Doubtless if all men were good, this rule would be bad; but since they are a sad lot, and keep no faith with you, you in your turn are under no obligation to keep it with them.

How a Prince Should Act to Acquire Reputation

Nothing gives a prince more prestige than undertaking great enterprises and setting a splendid example for his people.

A prince ought to show himself an admirer of talent, giving recognition to men of ability and honoring those who excel in a particular art. Moreover, he should encourage his citizens to ply their callings in peace, whether in commerce, agriculture, or in any other business. The man who improves his holdings should not be made to fear that they will be taken away from him; the man who opens up a branch of trade should not have to fear that he will be taxed out of existence. Instead, the prince should bestow prizes on the men who do these things, and on anyone else who takes the pains to enrich the city or state in some special way. He should also, at fitting times of the year, entertain his people with festivals and spectacles.

The Influence of Luck on Human Affairs and the Ways to Counter It

I realize that many people have thought, and still do think, that events are so governed in this world that the wisdom of men cannot possibly avail against them, indeed is altogether useless. On this basis, you might say that there is no point in sweating over anything, we should simply leave all matters to fate. This opinion has been the more popular in our own times because of the tremendous change in things during our lifetime, that actually is still going on today, beyond what anyone could have imagined. Indeed, sometimes when I think of it, I incline toward this opinion myself. Still, rather than give up on our free will altogether, I think it may be true that Fortune governs half of our actions, but that even so she leaves the other half more or less, in our power to control.

I conclude, then, that so long as Fortune varies and men stand still, they will prosper while they suit the times, and fail when they do not. But I do feel this: that it is better to be rash than timid, for Fortune is a woman, and the man who wants to hold her down must beat and bully her. We see that she yields more often to men of this stripe than to those who come coldly toward her. Like a woman, too, she is always a friend of the young, because they are less timid, more brutal, and take charge of her more recklessly.

QUESTIONS

1. Why does Machiavelli think that he is fit to offer advice to princes?

2. How important is force in the rule of states?

3. What seems to be Machiavelli's view of human nature?

4. Machiavelli addressed his book to a prince. How do you think this fact shaped the book?

5. Many people believed *The Prince* was immoral, and yet it was very widely read. How do you think it might have been useful?

6. Contemporaries saw Machiavelli as a dangerous man. Does *The Prince* offer any ground for this opinion?

55

■ *Desiderius Erasmus* ■

IN PRAISE OF FOLLY
(1509)

Desiderius Erasmus (ca. 1466–1536) was the leading intellectual light of the early sixteenth century. An orphan, Erasmus was educated in a monastery and became a monk. His intellectual gifts were so great that he was allowed to travel throughout the continent searching for ancient manuscripts and perfecting his skills as a linguist, philologist, and writer. His principal scholarly achievements, an edition of the Greek New Testament and of the Writings of Saint Jerome, were both published in 1516. But Erasmus was better known for his popular writings, especially his *Adages* and the satirical *In Praise of Folly*.

In Praise of Folly was written for Sir Thomas More, with whom Erasmus had made friends on his first trip to England. It is a spoof in which Folly demands praise for all of the ways of the world. It is under Folly's influence that people behave as they do and that institutions are organized with an upside-down logic. Erasmus was particularly scathing in his description of the state of religion and of the Catholic Church. Historians are fond of saying that Erasmus laid the egg that Luther hatched.

The next to be placed among the regiment of fools are such as make a trade of telling or inquiring after incredible stories of miracles and prodigies: never doubting that a lie will choke them, they will muster up a thousand several strange relations of spirits, ghosts, apparitions, raising of the devil, and such like bugbears of superstition, which the farther they are from being probably true, the more greedily they are swallowed, and the more devoutly believed. And these absurdities do not only bring an empty pleasure, and cheap divertisement, but they are a good trade, and procure a comfortable income to such priests and friars as by this craft get their gain. To these again are nearly related such others as attribute strange virtues to the shrines and images of saints and martyrs, and so would make their credulous proselytes believe, that if they pay their devotion to St. Christopher in the morning, they shall be guarded and secured the day following from all dangers and misfortunes: if soldiers, when they first take arms, shall come and mumble over such a set prayer before the picture of St. Barbara, they shall return safe from all engagements: or if any pray to Erasmus on such particular holidays, with the ceremony of wax candles, and other fopperies, he shall in a short time be rewarded with a plentiful increase of wealth and riches.

The next to these are another sort of brain-sick fools, who style themselves monks and of religious orders, though they assume both titles very unjustly: for as to the last, they have very little religion in them; and as to the former, the etymology of the word monk implies a solitariness, or being alone; whereas they are so thick abroad that we cannot pass any street or alley without meeting them. Now I cannot imagine what one degree of men would be more hopelessly wretched, if I did not stand their friend, and buoy them up in that lake of misery, which by the engagements of a holy vow they have voluntarily immerged themselves in. But when this sort of men are so unwelcome to others, as that the very sight of them is thought ominous, I yet make them highly in love with themselves, and fond admirers of their own happiness. The first step whereunto they esteem a profound ignorance, thinking carnal knowledge a great enemy to their spiritual welfare, and seem confident of becoming greater proficients in divine mysteries the less they are poisoned with any human learning. They imagine that they bear a sweet consort with the heavenly choir, when they tone out their daily tally of psalms, which they rehearse only by rote, without permitting their understanding or affections to go along with their voice.

Among these some make a good profitable trade of beggary, going about from house to house, not like the apostles, to break, but to beg, their bread; nay, thrust into all public-houses, come aboard the passage-boats, get into the travelling waggons, and omit no opportunity of time or place for the craving people's charity; doing a great deal of injury to common highway beggars by interloping in their traffic of alms. And when they are thus voluntarily poor, destitute, not provided with two coats, nor with any money in their purse, they have the impudence to pretend that they imitate the first disciples, whom their master expressly sent out in such an equipage.

It is pretty to observe how they regulate all their actions as it were by weight and measure to so exact a proportion, as if the whole loss of their religion depended upon the omission of the least punctilio. Thus they must be very critical in the precise number of knots to the tying on of their sandals; what distinct colours their respective habits, and what stuff made of; how broad and long their girdles; how big, and in what fashion, their hoods; whether their bald crowns be to a hair's-breadth of the right cut; how many hours they must sleep, at what minute rise to prayers, and so on. And these several customs are altered according to the humours of different persons and places. While they are sworn to the superstitious observance of these trifles, they do not only despise all others, but are very inclinable to fall out among themselves; for though they make profession of an apostolic charity, yet they will pick a quarrel, and be implacably passionate for such poor provocations, as the girting on a coat the wrong way, for the wearing of clothes a little too darkish coloured or any such nicety not worth the speaking of.

Some are so obstinately superstitious that they will wear their upper garment of some coarse dog's hair stuff, and that next their skin as soft as silk: but others on the contrary will have linen frocks outermost, and their shirts of wool, or hair. Some again will not touch a piece of money, though they make no scruple of the sin of drunkenness, and the lust of the flesh. All their several orders are mindful of nothing more than of their being distinguished from each other by their different customs and habits. They seem indeed not so careful of becoming like Christ, and of being known to be his disciples, as the being unlike to one another, and distinguishable for followers of their several founders.

Most of them place their greatest stress for salvation on a strict conformity to their foppish ceremonies, and a belief of their legendary traditions; wherein they fancy to have acquitted themselves with so much of supererogation, that one heaven can never be a condign reward for their meritorious life; little thinking that the Judge of all the earth at the last day shall put them off, with a who hath required these things at your hands; and call them to account only for the stewardship of his legacy, which was the precept of love and charity. It will be pretty to hear their pleas before the great tribunal: one will brag how he mortified his carnal appetite by feeding only upon fish: another will urge that he spent most of his time on earth in the divine exercise of singing psalms: a third will tell how many days he fasted, and what severe penance he imposed on himself for the bringing his body into subjection: another shall produce in his own behalf as many ceremonies as would load a fleet of merchantmen: a fifth shall plead that in threescore years he never so much as touched a piece of money, except he fingered it through a thick pair of gloves: a sixth, to testify his former humility, shall bring along with him his sacred hood, so old and nasty, that any seaman had rather stand bare headed on the deck, than put it on to defend his ears in the sharpest storms: the next that comes to answer for himself shall plead, that for fifty years together, he had lived like a sponge upon the same place, and was content never to change his homely habitation: another shall whisper softly, and tell the judge he has lost his voice by a continual singing of holy hymns and anthems: the next shall confess how he fell into a lethargy by a strict, reserved, and sedentary life: and the last shall intimate that he

has forgot to speak, by having always kept silence, in obedience to the injunction of taking heed lest he should have offended with his tongue.

Now as to the popes of Rome, who pretend themselves Christ's vicars, if they would but imitate his exemplary life, in the being employed in an unintermitted course of preaching; in the being attended with poverty, nakedness, hunger, and a contempt of this world; if they did but consider the import of the word pope, which signifies a father; or if they did but practice their surname of most holy, what order or degrees of men would be in a worse condition? There would be then no such vigorous making of parties, and buying of votes, in the conclave upon a vacancy of that see: and those who by bribery, or other indirect courses, should get themselves elected, would never secure their sitting firm in the chair by pistol, poison, force, and violence.

How much of their pleasure would be abated if they were but endowed with one dram of wisdom? Wisdom, did I say? Nay, with one grain of that salt which our Saviour bid them not lose the savour of. All their riches, all their honour, their jurisdictions, their Peter's patrimony, their offices, their dispensations, their licences, their indulgences, their long train and attendants (see in how short a compass I have abbreviated all their marketing of religion); in a word, all their perquisites would be forfeited and lost; and in their room would succeed watchings, fastings, tears, prayers, sermons, hard studies, repenting sighs, and a thousand such like severe penalties: nay, what's yet more deplorable, it would then follow, that all their clerks, amanuenses, notaries, advocates, proctors, secretaries, the offices of grooms, ostlers, serving-men, pimps (and somewhat else, which for modesty's sake I shall not mention); in short, all these troops of attendants, which depend on his holiness, would all lose their several employments. This indeed would be hard, but what yet remains would be more dreadful: the very Head of the Church, the spiritual prince, would then be brought from all his splendour to the poor equipage of a scrip and staff.

But all this is upon the supposition only that they understood what circumstances they are placed in; whereas now, by a wholesome neglect of thinking, they live as well as heart can wish: whatever of toil and drudgery belongs to their office that they assign over to St. Peter, or St. Paul, who have time enough to mind it; but if there be any thing of pleasure and grandeur, that they assume to themselves, as being hereunto called: so that by my influence no sort of people live more to their own ease and content. They think to satisfy that Master they pretend to serve, our Lord and Saviour, with their great state and magnificence, with the ceremonies of instalments, with the titles of reverence and holiness, and with exercising their episcopal function only in blessing and cursing. The working of miracles is old and out-dated; to teach the people is too laborious; to interpret scripture is to invade the prerogative of the schoolmen; to pray is too idle; to shed tears is cowardly and unmanly; to fast is too mean and sordid; to be easy and familiar is beneath the grandeur of him, who, without being sued to and intreated, will scarce give princes the honour of kissing his toe; finally, to die for religion is too self-denying; and to be crucified as their Lord of Life, is base and ignominious.

Their only weapons ought to be those of the Spirit; and of these indeed they are mighty liberal, as of their interdicts, their suspensions, their denunciations, their aggravations, their greater and lesser excommunications, and their roaring bulls, that fright whomever they are thundered against; and these most holy fathers never issue them out more frequently than against those, who, at the instigation of the devil, and not having the fear of God before their eyes, do feloniously and maliciously attempt to lessen and impair St. Peter's patrimony: and though that apostle tells our Saviour in the gospel, in the name of all the other disciples, we have left all, and followed you, yet they challenge as his inheritance, fields, towns, treasures, and large dominions; for the defending whereof, inflamed with a holy zeal, they fight with fire and sword, to the great loss and effusion of Christian blood, thinking they are apostolical maintainers of Christ's spouse, the church, when they have murdered all such as they call her enemies; though indeed the church has no enemies more bloody and tyrannical than such impious popes, who give dispensations for the not preaching of Christ; evacuate the main effect and design of our redemption by their pecuniary bribes and sales; adulterate the gospel by their forced interpretations, and undermining traditions; and lastly, by their lusts and wickedness grieve the Holy Spirit, and make their Saviour's wounds to bleed anew.

QUESTIONS

1. How has superstition affected the message of the Church, according to Erasmus?

2. What is wrong with most members of religious orders?

3. The papacy, Erasmus says, is also corrupt. How? How might it be reformed?

4. Erasmus identifies many serious failings in the Church. Why do you think people allowed them to continue? What purpose was the Church serving?

5. The Church comes in for a great deal of criticism from Erasmus. Do you think he contributed to the origins of the Reformation? How might the scope of his criticism have been limited by his choice of forum?

56

■ *Sir Thomas More* ■

UTOPIA
(1516)

Sir Thomas More (1477–1535) began his public career in London. A brilliant lawyer, he came to the attention of King Henry VIII, who was impressed by his intellect and sense of humor. The two became friends, and More rose in public service to become Lord Chancellor, the highest legal officer in the land. More was a member of the humanist community in England and a close friend of Erasmus. A believer in education for both men and women, More raised his daughters according to humanist principles; they became internationally renowned for their learning.

When Henry VIII broke with the Catholic Church over the issue of his divorce, More refused to follow the king along the paths of Protestantism. He would not lend his support to the divorce or to the declaration of the king's supremacy in religious matters. Accused of treason and beheaded in 1535, More was subsequently canonized by the Catholic Church.

Utopia is an expression of More's humanist ideals. The first part, known as the Book of Counsel, contains a long debate over whether a humanist should become advisor to a king, a question which in More's case was to prove prophetic. The second part, from which the following excerpts are taken, describes the imaginary society of Utopia, which has lent its name to all subsequent proposals for ideal communities.

Occupations

Agriculture is the one pursuit which is common to all, both men and women, without exception. They are all instructed in it from childhood, partly by principles taught in school, partly by field trips to the farms closer to the city as if for recreation. Here they do not merely look on, but, as opportunity arises for bodily exercise, they do the actual work.

Besides agriculture (which is, as I said, common to all), each is taught one particular craft

as his own. This is generally either wool-working or linen-making or masonry or metal-working or carpentry. There is no other pursuit which occupies any number worth mentioning. As for clothes, these are of one and the same pattern throughout the island and down the centuries, though there is a distinction between the sexes and between the single and married. The garments are comely to the eye, convenient for bodily movement, and fit for wear in heat and cold. Each family, I say, does its own tailoring.

Of the other crafts, one is learned by each person, and not the men only, but the women too. The latter as the weaker sex have the lighter occupations and generally work wool and flax. To the men are committed the remaining more laborious crafts. For the most part, each is brought up in his father's craft, for which most have a natural inclination. But if anyone is attracted to another occupation, he is transferred by adoption to a family pursuing that craft for which he has a liking.

Social Relations

But now, it seems, I must explain the behavior of the citizens toward one another, the nature of their social relations, and the method of distribution of goods. Since the city consists of households, households as a rule are made up of those related by blood. Girls, upon reaching womanhood and upon being settled in marriage, go to their husbands' domiciles. On the other hand, male children and then grandchildren remain in the family and are subject to the oldest parent, unless he has become a dotard with old age. In the latter case the next oldest is put in his place.

Every city is divided into four equal districts. In the middle of each quarter is a market of all kinds of commodities. To designated market buildings the products of each family are conveyed. Each kind of goods is arranged separately in storehouses. From the latter any head of a household seeks what he and his require and, without money or any kind of compensation, carries off what he seeks. Why should anything be refused? First, there is a plentiful supply of all things, and secondly, there is no underlying fear that anyone will demand more than he needs. Why should there be any suspicion that someone may demand an excessive amount when he is certain of never being in want? No doubt about it, avarice and greed are aroused in every kind of living creature by the fear of want, but only in man are they motivated by pride alone—pride which counts it a personal glory to excel others by superfluous display of possessions. The latter vice can have no place at all in the Utopian scheme of things.

Meanwhile, gold and silver, of which money is made, are so treated by them that no one values them more highly than their true nature deserves. Who does not see that they are far inferior to iron in usefulness since without iron mortals cannot live any more than without fire and water? To gold and silver, however, nature has given no use that we cannot dispense with, if the folly of men had not made them valuable because they are rare. On the other hand, like a most kind and indulgent mother, she has exposed to view all that is best, like air and water and earth itself, but has removed as far as possible from us all vain and unprofitable things.

"The Island of Utopia." This illustration was the frontispiece in Sir Thomas More's Utopia, *published in 1516.*

If in Utopia these metals were kept locked up in a tower, it might be suspected that the governor and the senate—for such is the foolish imagination of the common folk—were deceiving the people by the scheme and they themselves were deriving some benefit therefrom. Moreover, if they made them into drinking vessels and other such skillful handiwork, then if occasion arose for them all to be melted down again and applied to the pay of soldiers, they realize that people would be unwilling to be deprived of what they had once begun to treasure.

In that part of philosophy which deals with morals, they carry on the same debates as we do. They inquire into the good: of the soul and of the body and of external gifts. They ask also whether the name of good may be applied to all three or simply belongs to the endowments of the soul. They discuss virtue and pleasure, but their principal and chief debate is in what thing or things, one or more, they are to hold that happiness consists. In this matter they seem to lean more than they should to the school that espouses pleasure as the object by which to define either the whole or the chief part of human happiness.

What is more astonishing is that they seek a defense for this soft doctrine from their religion, which is serious and strict, almost solemn and hard. They never have a discussion of happiness without uniting certain principles taken from religion as well as from philosophy, which uses rational arguments. Without these principles they think reason insufficient and weak by itself for the investigation of true happiness. The following are examples of these principles. The soul is immortal and by the goodness of God born for happiness. After this life rewards are appointed for our virtues and good deeds, punishment for our crimes. Though these principles belong to religion, yet they hold that reason leads men to believe and to admit them.

As it is, they hold happiness rests not in every kind of pleasure but only in good and decent pleasure. To such, as to the supreme good, our nature is drawn by virtue itself, to which the opposite school alone attributes happiness. The Utopians define virtue as living according to nature since to this end we were created by God. That individual, they say, is following the guidance of nature who, in desiring one thing and avoiding another, obeys the dictates of reason.

Women do not marry till eighteen, men not till they are four years older. If before marriage a man or woman is convicted of secret intercourse, he or she is severely punished, and they are forbidden to marry altogether unless the governor's pardon remits their guilt. In addition, both father and mother of the family in whose house the offense was committed incur great disgrace as having been neglectful in doing their duties. The reason why they punish this offense so severely is their foreknowledge that, unless persons are carefully restrained from promiscuous intercourse, few will unite in married love, in which state a whole life must be spent with one companion and all the troubles incidental to it must be patiently borne.

In choosing mates, they seriously and strictly espouse a custom which seemed to us very foolish and extremely ridiculous. The woman, whether maiden or widow, is shown naked to the suitor by a worthy and respectable matron, and similarly the suitor is presented naked before the maiden by a discreet man. We laughed at this custom and condemned it as foolish. They, on the other hand, marvelled at the remarkable folly of all other nations. In buying a colt, where there is question of only a little money, persons are so cautious that though it is almost bare they will not buy until they have taken off the saddle and removed all the trappings for fear some sore lies concealed under these coverings. Yet in the choice of a wife, an action which will cause either pleasure or disgust to follow them the rest of their lives, they are so careless that, while the rest of her body is covered with clothes, they estimate the value of the whole woman from hardly a single handbreadth of her, only the face being visible, and clasp her to themselves not without great danger of their agreeing ill together if something afterwards gives them offense.

They have very few laws because very few are needed for persons so educated. The chief fault they find with other peoples is that almost innumerable books of laws and commentaries are not sufficient. They themselves think it most unfair that any group of men should be bound by laws which are either too numerous to be read through or too obscure to be understood by anyone.

Moreover, they absolutely banish from their country all lawyers, who cleverly manipulate cases and cunningly argue legal points. They consider it a good thing that every man should plead his own cause and say the same to the judge as he would tell his counsel. Thus there is less ambiguity and the truth is more easily elicited when a man, uncoached in deception by a lawyer, conducts his own case and the judge skillfully weighs each statement and helps untutored minds to defeat the false accusations of the crafty. To secure these advantages in other countries is difficult, owing to the immense mass of extremely complicated laws. First, they have, as I said, very few laws and, secondly, they regard the most obvious interpretation of the law as the most fair interpretation.

This policy follows from their reasoning that, since all laws are promulgated to remind every man of his duty, the more recondite interpretation reminds only very few (for there are few who can arrive at it) whereas the more simple and obvious sense of the laws is open to all. Otherwise, what difference would it make for the common people, who are the most numerous and also most in need of instruction, whether you framed no law at all or whether the interpretation of the law you framed was such that no one could elicit it except by great ingenuity and long argument? Now, the untrained judgment of the common people cannot attain to the meaning of such an interpretation nor can their lives be long enough, seeing that they are wholly taken up with getting a living.

QUESTIONS

1. What do you think More's purpose was in writing *Utopia*? Do you think he expected such a society could ever be formed?

2. Musings on a perfect society can tell us much about the existing society from which they emanate. What were More's main concerns about the real world?

3. How does the Utopian economy function?

4. Utopians are not Christians, but More's account of their religion is a sympathetic one. What principle is at the heart of their religious beliefs?

5. How do Utopians choose their mates? What contemporary problem do you suppose More was reacting to when he invented this novel way of selecting a spouse?

6. How are humanist ideals reflected in *Utopia*?

THE NEW WORLDS AND THE AGE OF EXPLORATION

57

■ *Ibn Battuta* ■

TRAVELS IN AFRICA

(1354)

Abu Abdullah Muhammad Ibn Abdullah Al Lawati Al Tanji Ibn Battuta (1304–1368), known simply as Ibn Battuta, recorded his great adventures traveling around the world, including trips to Europe, India, China, and sub-Saharan Africa. No other traveler of his time ever visited every Muslim state and it is estimated that he traversed over 75,000 miles during his lifetime, a distance probably not accomplished by any other traveler until the introduction of steamships. Born and raised into a Muslim Berber family of legal scholars in Morocco, he began traveling after embarking on Hajj (Muslim Pilgrimage) to Mecca at the age of twenty-one. After performing his religious duty, he continued traveling for twenty-four years. He witnessed not only the very height of Muslim power and influence but also the destructive civil wars that began to erode Muslim power. Though most of his travels were accomplished in large caravans on the known routes such as the Silk Road, he also chanced long sea voyages around the Horn of Africa.

Soon after his return home, he wrote an account of his travels at the request of the Sultan of Morocco. This passage comes from this work, called the *Rihla* ("The Journey"), and deals with his trip to sub-Saharan African, which seemed a world away from his home in North Africa. The work gives us a unique perspective on the society and culture of fourteenth-century Black Africa. However, we must remember that his observations were shaped by his own background, religion, and sense of cultural superiority.

Thereupon I set out on the Ist Muharram of the year [seven hundred and] fifty-three [18th February 1352] with a caravan including, amongst others, a number of the merchants of Sijilmása. After twenty-five days we reached Tagházá, an unattractive village, with the curious feature that its houses and mosques are built of blocks of salt, roofed with camel skins. There are no trees there, nothing but sand. In the sand is a salt mine; they dig for the salt, and find it in thick slabs, lying one on top of the other, as though they had been tool-squared and laid under the surface of the earth.

A camel will carry two of these slabs. No one lives at Tagházá except the slaves of the Massúfa tribe, who dig for the salt; they subsist on dates imported from Dar'a and Sijilmása, camels' flesh, and millet imported from the Negrolands. The negroes come up from their country and take away the salt from there. At Iwálátan a load of salt brings eight to ten *mithqáls*; in the town of Mállí it sells for twenty to thirty, and sometimes as much as forty. The negroes use salt as a medium of exchange, just as gold and silver is used [elsewhere]; they cut it up into pieces and buy and sell with it. The business done at Tagházá, for all its meanness, amounts to an enormous figure in terms of hundredweights of gold-dust.

We passed ten days of discomfort there, because the water is brackish and the place is plagued with flies. Water supplies are laid in at Tagházá for the crossing of the desert which lies beyond it, which is a ten-nights' journey with no water on the way except on rare occasions. We indeed had the good fortune to find water in plenty, in pools left by the rain. One day we found a pool of sweet water between two rocky prominences. We quenched our thirst at it and then washed our clothes. Truffles are plentiful in this desert and it swarms with lice, so that people wear string necklaces containing mercury, which kills them. At that time we used to go ahead of the caravan, and when we found a place suitable for pasturage we would graze our beasts. We went on doing this until one of our party was lost in the desert; after that I neither went ahead nor lagged behind. We passed a caravan on the way and they told us that some of their party had become separated from them. We found one of them dead under a shrub, of the sort that grows in the sand, with his clothes on and a whip in his hand. The water was only about a mile away from him.

We came next to Tásarahlá, a place of subterranean water-beds, where the caravans halt. They stay there three days to rest, mend their waterskins, fill them with water, and sew on them covers of sack-cloth as a precaution against the wind. From this point the *takshíf* is despatched.

The *takshíf* is a name given to any man of the Massúfa tribe who is hired by the persons in the caravan to go ahead to Iwálátan, carrying letters from them to their friends there, so that they may take lodgings for them. These persons then come out a distance of four nights' journey to meet the caravan, and bring water with them. Anyone who has no friend in Iwálátan writes to some merchant well known for his worthy character, who then undertakes the same services for him. It often happens that the *takshíf* perishes in this desert, with the result that the people of Iwálátan know nothing about the caravan, and all or most of those who are with it perish. That desert is haunted by demons; if the *takshíf* be alone, they make sport of him and disorder his mind, so that he loses his way and perishes. For there is no visible road or track in these parts—nothing but sand blown hither and thither by the wind. You see hills of sand in one place, and afterwards you will see them moved to quite another place. The guide there is one who has made the journey frequently in both directions, and who is gifted with a quick intelligence. I remarked, as a strange thing, that the guide whom we had was blind in one eye, and diseased in the other, yet he had the best knowledge of the road of any man. We hired the *takshíf* on this journey for a hundred gold *mithqáls*; he was a man of the Massúfa. On the night of the seventh day [from Tásarahlá] we saw with joy the fires of the party who had come out to meet us.

Thus we reached the town of Iwálátan [Walata] after a journey from Sijilmása of two months to a day. Iwálátan is the northernmost province of the negroes, and the sultan's representative there was one Farbá Husayn, *farbá* meaning deputy [in their language]. When we arrived there, the merchants deposited their goods in an open square, where the blacks undertook to guard them, and went to the *farbá*. He was sitting on a carpet under an archway, with his guards before him carrying lances and bows in their hands, and the headmen of the Massúfa behind him. The merchants remained standing in front of him while he spoke to them through an interpreter, although they were close to him, to show his contempt for them. It was then that I repented of having come to their country, because of their lack of manners and their contempt for the whites.

I went to visit Ibn Baddá, a worthy man of Salá [Sallee, Rabát], to whom I had written requesting him to hire a house for me, and who had done so. Later on the *mushrif* [inspector] of Íwálátan, whose name was Manshá Jú, invited all those who had come with the caravan to partake of his hospitality. At first I refused to attend, but my companions urged me very strongly, so I went with the rest. The repast was served—some pounded millet mixed with a little honey and milk, put in a half calabash shaped like a large bowl. The guests drank and retired. I said to them "Was it for this that the black invited us?" They answered "Yes; and it is in their opinion the highest form of hospitality." This convinced me that there was no good to be hoped for from these people, and I made up my mind to travel [back to Morocco at once] with the pilgrim caravan from Íwálátan. Afterwards, however, I thought it best to go to see the capital of their king [at Málli].

My stay at Íwálátan lasted about fifty days; and I was shown honour and entertained by its inhabitants. It is an excessively hot place, and boasts a few small date-palms, in the shade of which they sow watermelons. Its water comes from underground water-beds at that point, and there is plenty of mutton to be had. The garments of its inhabitants, most of whom belong to the Massúfa tribe, are of fine Egyptian fabrics. Their women are of surpassing beauty, and are shown more respect than the men. The state of affairs amongst these people is indeed extraordinary. Their men show no signs of jealousy whatever; no one claims descent from his father, but on the contrary from his mother's brother. A person's heirs are his sister's sons, not his own sons. This is a thing which I have seen nowhere in the world except among the Indians of Malabar. But those are heathens; *these* people are Muslims, punctilious in observing the hours of prayer, studying books of

law, and memorizing the Koran. Yet their women show no bashfulness before men and do not veil themselves, though they are assiduous in attending the prayers. Any man who wishes to marry one of them may do so, but they do not travel with their husbands, and even if one desired to do so her family would not allow her to go.

The women there have "friends" and "companions" amongst the men outside their own families, and the men in the same way have "companions" amongst the women of other families. A man may go into his house and find his wife entertaining her "companion" but he takes no objection to it. One day at Íwálátan I went into the qádi's house, after asking his permission to enter, and found with him a young woman of remarkable beauty. When I saw her I was shocked and turned to go out, but she laughed at me, instead of being overcome by shame, and the qádi said to me "Why are you going out? She is my companion." I was amazed at their conduct, for he was a theologian and a pilgrim to boot. I was told that he had asked the sultan's permission to make the pilgrimage that year with his "companion" (whether this one or not I cannot say) but the sultan would not grant it.

• • •

A traveller in this country carries no provisions, whether plain food or seasonings, and neither gold nor silver. He takes nothing but pieces of salt and glass ornaments, which the people call beads, and some aromatic goods. When he comes to a village the womenfolk of the blacks bring out millet, milk, chickens, pulped lotus fruit, rice, *fúní* (a grain resembling mustard seed, from which *kuskusú*[8] and gruel are made), and pounded haricot beans. The traveller buys what of these he wants, but their rice causes sickness to whites when it is eaten, and the *fúní* is preferable to it.

• • •

I saw a crocodile in this part of the Nile, close to the bank; it looked just like a small boat.

One day I went down to the river to satisfy a need, and lo, one of the blacks came and stood between me and the river. I was amazed at such lack of manners and decency on his part, and spoke of it to someone or other. He answered "His purpose in doing that was solely to protect you from the crocodile, by placing himself between you and it."

We set out thereafter from Karsakhú and came to the river of Sansara, which is about ten miles from Mállí. It is their custom that no persons except those who have obtained permission are allowed to enter the city. I had already written to the white community [there] requesting them to hire a house for me, so when I arrived at this river, I crossed by the ferry without interference. Thus I reached the city of Mállí, the capital of the king of the blacks.[19]

• • •

The negroes possess some admirable qualities. They are seldom unjust, and have a greater abhorrence of injustice than any other people. Their sultan shows no mercy to anyone who is guilty of the least act of it. There is complete security in their country. Neither traveller nor inhabitant in it has anything to fear from robbers or men of violence. They do not confiscate the property of any white man who dies in their country, even if it be uncounted wealth. On the contrary, they give it into the charge of some trustworthy person among the whites, until the rightful heir takes possession of it. They are careful to observe the hours of prayer, and assiduous in attending them in congregations, and in bringing up their children to them. On Fridays, if a man does not go early to the mosque, he cannot find a corner to pray in, on account of the crowd. It is a custom of theirs to send each man his boy [to the mosque] with his prayer-mat; the boy spreads it out for his master in a place befitting him [and remains on it] until he comes to the mosque. Their prayer-mats are made of the leaves of a tree resembling a date-palm, but without fruit.

Another of their good qualities is their habit of wearing clean white garments on Fridays. Even if a man has nothing but an old worn shirt, he washes it and cleans it, and wears it to the Friday service. Yet another is their zeal for learning the Koran by heart. They put their children in chains if they show any backwardness in memorizing it, and they are not set free until they have it by heart. I visited the qádí in his house on the day of the festival. His children were chained up, so I said to him "Will you not let them loose?" He replied "I shall not do so until they learn the Koran by heart." Among their bad qualities are the following. The women servants, slave-girls, and young girls go about in front of everyone naked, without a stitch of clothing on them. Women go into the sultan's presence naked and without coverings, and his daughters also go about naked. Then there is their custom of putting dust and ashes on their heads, as a mark of respect, and the grotesque ceremonies we have described when the poets recite their verses. Another reprehensible practice among many of them is the eating of carrion, dogs, and asses.

QUESTIONS

1. What were the conditions like for a traveler to Africa in the fourteenth century?

2. Why does Ibn Battuta at first refuse to go the party hosted by Mansha Ju? What dissatisfies him about the hospitality he finds there?

3. How does Ibn Battuta categorize the people he meets? What characteristics does he use to define them?

4. What did Ibn Battuta find unusual about the customs of the people with whom he came in contact? What do these observations tell us about Ibn Battuta's own culture in Morocco?

5. What role did religion play in Ibn Battuta's life? How about in the life of the people of Malli? How did their practices of Islam differ?

58

■ *Christopher Columbus* ■

LETTER FROM THE FIRST VOYAGE
(1493)

The Italian Christopher Columbus (1451–1506) dreamed of making his fortune in the spice trade. As a young mariner, he had worked with a mapmaker and became obsessed with the idea of reaching the Spice Islands via a western route. This was as much a practical as a theoretical idea—Muslim conquests had disrupted the traditional Mediterranean trade, and the Portuguese had to make the long journey around Africa in stages. Columbus lobbied for his plan in both Portugal and Spain before convincing Queen Isabella of Castile to provide limited financial backing in return for a hefty share of any profits from the voyage. In 1492, Columbus sailed west from the Canary Islands in command of three ships and landed in the Caribbean, which he believed was a string of islands off the China mainland.

This letter is one of Columbus's early communications, though it was written nearly six months after his discovery. It was obviously composed for public consumption and was one of the most widely printed documents from the voyages of discovery.

A Letter addressed to the noble Lord Raphael Sanchez, Treasurer to their most invincible Majesties, Ferdinand and Isabella, King and Queen of Spain, by Christopher Columbus, to whom our age is greatly indebted, treating of the islands of India recently discovered beyond the Ganges, to explore which he had been sent eight months before under the auspices and at the expense of their said Majesties.

Knowing that it will afford you pleasure to learn that I have brought my undertaking to a successful termination, I have decided upon writing you this letter to acquaint you with all the events which have occurred in my voyage, and the discoveries which have resulted from it. Thirty-three days after my departure from Cadiz I reached the Indian sea, where I discovered many

islands, thickly peopled, of which I took possession without resistance in the name of our most
illustrious Monarch, by public proclamation and
with unfurled banners. To the first of these
islands, which is called by the Indians Guanahani,
I gave the name of the blessed Saviour (San
Salvador), relying upon whose protection I had
reached this as well as the other islands; to each of
these I also gave a name. In the mean time I had
learned from some Indians whom I had seized,
that that country was certainly an island: and
therefore I sailed towards the east, coasting to the
distance of three hundred and twenty-two miles,
which brought us to the extremity of it; from this
point I saw lying eastwards another island, fifty-
four miles distant from Juana, to which I gave the
name of Española: I went thither, and steered my
course eastward as I had done at Juana, even to
the distance of five hundred and sixty-four miles
along the north coast. This said island of Juana is
exceedingly fertile, as indeed are all the others; it
is surrounded with many bays, spacious, very
secure, and surpassing any that I have ever seen;
numerous large and healthful rivers intersect it,
and it also contains many very lofty mountains.
All these islands are very beautiful, and distinguished by a diversity of scenery; they are filled
with a great variety of trees of immense height,
and which I believe to retain their foliage in all
seasons; for when I saw them they were as verdant
and luxuriant as they usually are in Spain in the
month of May—some of them were blossoming,
some bearing fruit, and all flourishing in the
greatest perfection, according to their respective
stages of growth, and the nature and quality of
each: yet the islands are not so thickly wooded as
to be impassable. The nightingale and various
birds were singing in countless numbers, and that
in November, the month in which I arrived there.
There are besides in the same island of Juana
seven or eight kinds of palm trees, which, like all
the other trees, herbs, and fruits, considerably
surpass ours in height and beauty. The pines also
are very handsome, and there are very extensive
fields and meadows, a variety of birds, different

kinds of honey, and many sorts of metals, but no
iron. In that island also which I have before said
we named Española, there are mountains of very
great size and beauty, vast plains, groves, and very
fruitful fields, admirably adapted for tillage,
pasture, and habitation. The inhabitants of both
sexes in this island, and in all the others which
I have seen, or of which I have received information, go always naked as they were born, with the
exception of some of the women, who use the
covering of a leaf, or small bough, or an apron of
cotton which they prepare for that purpose. None
of them are possessed of any iron, neither have
they weapons, being unacquainted with, and
indeed incompetent to use them, not from any
deformity of body (for they are well-formed), but
because they are timid and full of fear.

They carry however in lieu of arms, canes
dried in the sun, on the ends of which they fix
heads of dried wood sharpened to a point, and
even these they dare not use habitually; for it has
often occurred when I have sent two or three of
my men to any of the villages to speak with the
natives, that they have come out in a disorderly
troop, and have fled in such haste at the
approach of our men, that the fathers forsook
their children and the children their fathers.
This timidity did not arise from any loss or injury
that they had received from us; for, on the contrary, I gave to all I approached whatever articles
I had about me, such as cloth and many other
things, taking nothing of theirs in return: but
they are naturally timid and fearful. As soon however as they see that they are safe, and have laid
aside all fear, they are very simple and honest,
and exceedingly liberal with all they have; none
of them refusing any thing he may possess when
he is asked for it, but on the contrary inviting us
to ask them. They exhibit great love towards all
others in preference to themselves: they also give
objects of great value for trifles, and content
themselves with very little or nothing in return.

I however forbade that these trifles and
articles of no value (such as pieces of dishes,
plates, and glass, keys, and leather straps) should

be given to them, although if they could obtain them, they imagined themselves to be possessed of the most beautiful trinkets in the world. It even happened that a sailor received for a leather strap as much gold as was worth three golden nobles, and for things of more trifling value offered by our men, especially newly coined blancas, or any gold coins, the Indians would give whatever the seller required; as, for instance, an ounce and a half or two ounces of gold, or thirty or forty pounds of cotton, with which commodity they were already acquainted. Thus they bartered, like idiots, cotton and gold for fragments of bows, glasses, bottles, and jars; which I forbade as being unjust, and myself gave them many beautiful and acceptable articles which I had brought with me, taking nothing from them in return; I did this in order that I might the more easily conciliate them, that they might be led to become Christians, and be inclined to entertain a regard for the King and Queen, our Princes and all Spaniards, and that I might induce them to take an interest in seeking out, and collecting, and delivering to us such things as they possessed in abundance, but which we greatly needed.

They practise no kind of idolatry, but have a firm belief that all strength and power, and indeed all good things, are in heaven, and that I had descended from thence with these ships and sailors, and under this impression was I received after they had thrown aside their fears. Nor are they slow or stupid, but of very clear understanding; and those men who have crossed to the neighbouring islands give an admirable description of everything they observed; but they never saw any people clothed, nor any ships like ours.

In all these islands there is no difference of physiognomy, of manners, or of language, but they all clearly understand each other, a circumstance very propitious for the realization of what I conceive to be the principal wish of our most serene King, namely, the conversion of these people to the holy faith of Christ, to which indeed, as far as I can judge, they are very favourable and well-disposed. There was one large town in Española of which especially I took possession, situated in a remarkably favourable spot, and in every way convenient for the purposes of gain and commerce. To this town I gave the name of Navidad del Señor, and ordered a fortress to be built there, which must by this time be completed, in which I left as many men as I thought necessary, with all sorts of arms, and enough provisions for more than a year. I also left them one caravel, and skilful workmen both in ship-building and other arts, and engaged the favor and friendship of the King of the island in their behalf, to a degree that would not be believed, for these people are so amiable and friendly that even the King took a pride in calling me his brother. But supposing their feelings should become changed, and they should wish to injure those who have remained in the fortress, they could not do so, for they have no arms, they go naked, and are moreover too cowardly; so that those who hold the said fortress, can easily keep the whole island in check, without any pressing danger to themselves, provided they do not transgress the directions and regulations which I have given them.

As far as I have learned, every man throughout these islands is united to but one wife, with the exception of the kings and princes, who are allowed to have twenty: the women seem to work more than the men. I could not clearly understand whether the people possess any private property, for I observed that one man had the charge of distributing various things to the rest, but especially meat and provisions and the like. I did not find, as some of us had expected, any cannibals amongst them, but on the contrary men of great deference and kindness. Neither are they black, like the Ethiopians: their hair is smooth and straight: for they do not dwell where the rays of the sun strike most vividly, and the sun has intense power there, the distance from the equinoctial line being, it appears, but six-and-twenty degrees. On the tops of the mountains the cold is very great, but the effect of this upon the Indians is lessened by their being accustomed to the climate, and by their frequently indulging in the use of very hot meats and drinks.

Finally, to compress into few words the entire summary of my voyage and speedy return, and of the advantages derivable therefrom, I promise, that with a little assistance afforded me by our most invincible sovereigns, I will procure them as much gold as they need, as great a quantity of spices, of cotton, and of mastic (which is only found in Chios), and as many men for the service of the navy as their Majesties may require. I promise also rhubarb and other sorts of drugs, which I am persuaded the men whom I have left in the aforesaid fortress have found already and will continue to find; for I myself have tarried no where longer than I was compelled to do by the winds, except in the city of Navidad, while I provided for the building of the fortress, and took the necessary precautions for the perfect security of the men I left there. Although all I have related may appear to be wonderful and unheard of, yet the results of my voyage would have been more astonishing if I had had at my disposal such ships as I required.

But these great and marvellous results are not to be attributed to any merit of mine, but to the holy Christian faith, and to the piety and religion of our Sovereigns; for that which the unaided intellect of man could not compass, the spirit of God has granted to human exertions, for God is wont to hear the prayers of his servants who love his precepts even to the performance of apparent impossibilities. Thus it has happened to me in the present instance, who have accomplished a task to which the powers of mortal men had never hitherto attained; for if there have been those who have anywhere written or spoken of these islands, they have done so with doubts and conjectures, and no one has ever asserted that he has seen them, on which account their writings have been looked upon as little else than fables. Therefore let the king and queen, our princes and their most happy kingdoms, and all the other provinces of Christendom, render thanks to our Lord and Savior Jesus Christ, who has granted us so great a victory and such prosperity. Let processions be made, and sacred feasts be held, and the temples be adorned with festive boughs. Let Christ rejoice on earth, as he rejoices in heaven in the prospect of the salvation of the souls of so many nations hitherto lost. Let us also rejoice, as well on account of the exaltation of our faith, as on account of the increase of our temporal prosperity, of which not only Spain, but all Christendom will be partakers.

Such are the events which I have briefly described. Farewell.

Lisbon, the 14th of March.

CHRISTOPHER COLUMBUS
Admiral of the Fleet of the Ocean

QUESTIONS

1. What was Columbus's purpose when he wrote this letter?

2. Columbus found the islands he explored to be "thickly peopled." What seems to be his attitude toward the inhabitants of the islands?

3. The Europeans engaged in trade with the Indians and prided themselves upon getting a good deal. How did the trade work? Do you think the Indians felt the same way?

4. What appear to be the overall goals of the Spanish explorers?

5. Can you make some generalizations about fifteenth-century European views of alien cultures?

59

■ *Gomes de Zurara* ■

CHRONICLE OF GUINEA
(1453)

Gomes de Zurara (1410?–1474) was a historian and biographer who is one of the principal sources for the life of Prince Henry the Navigator. Little is known for certain about Zurara's early life. Probably the son of a priest, he learned to read and write, though it was said that he had not had the benefit of much formal education. His early life might have been spent in the military. He became a member of the Order of Christ, one of the more important of the lay religious societies in Portugal and one that would have enabled him to make the acquaintance of many powerful patrons. He obtained preferment of a position in the Royal Library and by 1452 appears to have become the Royal Chronicler, an official position at court. He was commissioned by King Alfonso V to collect all of the extant information concerning the life of Prince Henry, and much of it is contained in the Chronicle of Guinea that was presented to the King in 1453.

The Chronicle of Guinea celebrates Portuguese exploration of the coast of Africa under the direction of Prince Henry. It is now recognized that Zurara freely embellished his account both of Henry's role in these events and of his character and conduct. Nevertheless, Zurara provides much rich detail of the exploration of Africa from the point of view of those Europeans who first arrived there. In this section of the work, Zurara recounts the capture of Africans he calls "Moors" and their enslavement. This is the first reliable account of how the Portuguese captured African villagers, assigned them as chattel to the various royal and naval authorities (Prince Henry is here identified as the Infant), and then sold them. Throughout the account, Zurara is sympathetic to the plight of the natives but from a distinctly Christian point of view.

Chapter XXIV

How the caravels arrived at Lagos, and of the account that Lançarote gave to the Infant.

The caravels arrived at Lagos, whence they had set out, having excellent weather for their voyage, for fortune was not less gracious to them in the serenity of the weather than it had been to them before in the capture of their booty.

And from Lagos the news reached the Infant, who happened to have arrived there a few hours before, from other parts where he had been for some days. And as you see that people are desirous of knowledge, some endeavoured to get near the shore; and others put themselves into the boats they found moored along the beach, and went to welcome their relations and friends; so that in a short time the news of their good fortune was well known, and all were much rejoiced at it. And for that day it sufficed for those who had led the enterprize to kiss the hand of the Infant their Lord, and to give him a short account of their exploits: after which they took their rest, as men who had come to their fatherland and their own homes; and you may guess what would be their joy among their wives and children.

And next day Lançarote, as he who had taken the main charge of the expedition, said to the Infant: "My Lord, your grace well knoweth that you have to receive the fifth of these Moors, and of all that we have gained in that land, whither you sent us for the service of God and of yourself.

"And now these Moors, because of the long time we have been at sea; as well as for the great sorrow that you must consider they have at heart, at seeing themselves away from the land of their birth, and placed in captivity, without having any understanding of what their end is to be;—and moreover because they have not been accustomed to a life on shipboard—for all these reasons are poorly and out of condition; wherefore it seemeth to me that it would be well to order them to be taken out of the caravels at dawn, and to be placed in that field which lies outside the city gate, and there to be divided into five parts, according to custom; and that your Grace should come there and choose one of these parts, whichever you prefer."

The Infant said that he was well pleased, and on the next day very early, Lançarote bade the masters of the caravels that they should put out the captives, and take them to that field, where they were to make the divisions, as he had said already. But before they did anything else in that matter, they took as an offering the best of those Moors to the Church of that place; and another little Moor, who afterwards became a friar of St. Francis, they sent to St. Vincent do Cabo,

where he lived ever after as a Catholic Christian, without having understanding or perception of any other law than that true and holy law in which all we Christians hope for our salvation. And the Moors of that capture were in number 235.

Chapter XXV

Wherein the Author reasoneth somewhat concerning the pity inspired by the captives, and of how the division was made.

O, Thou heavenly Father—who with Thy powerful hand, without alteration of Thy divine essence, governest all the infinite company of Thy Holy City, and controllest all the revolutions of higher worlds, divided into nine spheres, making the duration of ages long or short according as it pleaseth Thee—I pray Thee that my tears may not wrong my conscience; for it is not their religion but their humanity that maketh mine to weep in pity for their sufferings. And if the brute animals, with their bestial feelings, by a natural instinct understand the sufferings of their own kind, what wouldst Thou have my human nature to do on seeing before my eyes that miserable company, and remembering that they too are of the generation of the sons of Adam?

On the next day, which was the 8th of the month of August, very early in the morning, by reason of the heat, the seamen began to make ready their boats, and to take out those captives, and carry them on shore, as they were commanded. And these, placed all together in that field, were a marvellous sight; for amongst them were some white enough, fair to look upon, and well proportioned; others were less white like mulattoes; others again were as black as Ethiops, and so ugly, both in features and in body, as almost to appear (to those who saw them) the images of a lower hemisphere. But what heart could be so hard as not to be pierced with piteous feeling to see that company? For some kept their heads low and their faces bathed in tears, looking one upon another; others stood groaning very dolorously, looking up to the height of heaven, fixing their eyes upon it, crying out loudly, as if asking help of the Father of Nature; others struck their faces with the palms of their hands, throwing themselves at full length upon the ground; others made their lamentations in the manner of a dirge, after the custom of their country. And though we could not understand the words of their language, the sound of it right well accorded with the measure of their sadness. But to increase their sufferings still more, there now arrived those who had charge of the division of the captives, and who began to separate one from another, in order to make an equal partition of the fifths; and then was it needful to part fathers from sons, husbands from wives, brothers from brothers. No respect was shewn either to friends or relations, but each fell where his lot took him.

O powerful fortune, that with thy wheels doest and undoest, compassing the matters of this world as pleaseth thee, do thou at least put before the eyes of that miserable race some understanding of matters to come; that they may receive some consolation in the midst of their great sorrow. And you who are so busy in making that division of the captives, look with pity upon so much misery; and see how they cling one to the other, so that you can hardly separate them.

And who could finish that partition without very great toil? for as often as they had placed them in one part the sons, seeing their fathers in another, rose with great energy and rushed over to them; the mothers clasped their other children in their arms, and threw themselves flat on the ground with them, receiving blows with little pity for their own flesh, if only they might not be torn from them.

And so troublously they finished the partition; for besides the toil they had with the captives, the field was quite full of people, both from the town and from the surrounding villages and districts, who for that day gave rest to their hands (in which lay their power to get their living) for the sole purpose of beholding this novelty. And with what they saw, while some were weeping and others separating the captives, they caused such a tumult as greatly to confuse those who directed the partition.

The Infant was there, mounted upon a powerful steed, and accompanied by his retinue, making distribution of his favours, as a man who sought to gain but small treasure from his share; for of the forty-six souls that fell to him as his fifth, he made a very speedy partition of these; for his chief riches lay in his purpose; for he reflected with great pleasure upon the salvation of those souls that before were lost.

And certainly his expectation was not in vain; for, as we said before, as soon as they understood our language they turned Christians with very little ado; and I who put together this history into this volume, saw in the town of Lagos boys and girls (the children and grandchildren of those first captives, born in this land) as good and true Christians as if they had directly descended, from the beginning of the dispensation of Christ, from those who were first baptised.

Chapter XXVI

How the Infant Don Henry made Lançarote a Knight.

Although the sorrow of those captives was for the present very great, especially after the partition was finished and each one took his own share aside (while some sold their captives, the which they took to other districts); and although it chanced that among the prisoners the father often remained in Lagos, while the mother was taken to Lisbon, and the children to another part (in which partition their sorrow doubled the first grief)—yet this sorrow was less felt among those who happened to remain in company. For as saith the text, the wretched find a consolation in having comrades in misfortune. But from this time forth they began to acquire some knowledge of our country; in which they found great abundance, and our men began to treat them with great favour. For as our people did not find them hardened in the belief of the other Moors; and saw how they came in unto the law of Christ with a good will; they make no difference between them and their free servants, born in our own country; but those whom they took while still young, they caused to be instructed in mechanical arts, and those whom they saw fitted for managing property; they set free and married to women who were natives of the land; making with them a division of their property, as if they had been bestowed on those who married them by the will of their own fathers, and for the merits of their service they were bound to act in a like manner. Yea, and some widows of good family who bought some of these female slaves, either adopted them or left them a portion of their estate by will; so that in the future they married right well; treating them as entirely free. Suffice it that I never saw one of these slaves put in irons like other captives, and scarcely any one who did not turn Christian and was not very gently treated.

And I have been asked by their lords to the baptisms and marriages of such, at which they, whose slaves they were before, made no less solemnity than if they had been their children or relations.

And so their lot was now quite the contrary of what it had been; since before they had lived in perdition of soul and body; of their souls, in that they were yet pagans, without the clearness and the light of the holy faith; and of their bodies, in that they lived like beasts, without any custom of reasonable beings—for they had no knowledge of bread or wine, and they were without the covering of clothes, or the lodgment of houses; and worse than all, through the great ignorance that was in them, in that they had no

understanding of good, but only knew how to live in a bestial sloth.

But as soon as they began to come to this land, and men gave them prepared food and coverings for their bodies, their bellies began to swell, and for a time they were ill; until they were accustomed to the nature of the country; but some of them were so made that they were not able to endure it and died, but as Christians.

Now there were four things in these captives that were very different from the condition of the other Moors who were taken prisoners from this part. First, that after they had come to this land of Portugal, they never more tried to fly, but rather in time forgot all about their own country, as soon as they began to taste the good things of this one; secondly, that they were very loyal and obedient servants, without malice; thirdly, that they were not so inclined to lechery as the others; fourthly, that after they began to use clothing they were for the most part very fond of display, so that they took great delight in robes of showy colours, and such was their love of finery, that they picked up the rags that fell from the coats of the other people of the country and sewed them on to their garments, taking great pleasure in these, as though it were matter of some greater perfection. And what was still better, as I have already said, they turned themselves with a good will into the path of the true belief, and in this same they died. And now reflect what a guerdon should be that of the Infant in the presence of the Lord God; for thus bringing to true salvation, not only those, but many others, whom you will find in this history later on.

QUESTIONS

1. How were the captive Moors divided? What was the share of Prince Henry (the Infant)?

2. What about the Moors moved Zurara?

3. What is Zurara's attitude to race?

4. What was the experience of the Moors in Portugal?

60

■ *Bartolomé de Las Casas* ■

APOLOGETIC HISTORY OF THE INDIES
(1566)

Bartolomé de Las Casas (1474–1566) was a Dominican friar, a bishop in the New World, and the Spanish government's unofficial "Protector of the Indians." Born in the bustling port of Seville, Las Casas witnessed Columbus's triumphant return from his first voyage. The exotic goods and the exotic tales with which the mariners returned fired the young friar's imagination. In 1498, Las Casas was presented with an Indian for use as a personal servant, and he was entranced by the simplicity and gentle nature of the Native Americans; he thereupon decided to devote his life to their salvation.

Arriving in the New World in 1502, Las Casas set about his mission, preaching among the Indians and baptizing those that he converted. He was appalled by the harsh treatment some Spaniards meted out to these innocent people. He returned to Spain in 1515 and launched a vigorous campaign to ensure the Indians' protection. The *Apologetic History* was a reflection of Las Casas's belief in the inherent goodness of the Native Americans, and of his conviction that all of humanity were God's children.

Apologetic and Summary History Treating the Qualities, Disposition, Description, Skies and Soil of These Lands; and the Natural Conditions, Governance, Nations, Ways of Life and Customs of the Peoples of These Western and Southern Indies, Whose Sovereign Realm Belongs to the Monarchs of Castile.

Argument of the Work

The ultimate cause for writing this work was to gain knowledge of all the many nations of this vast new world. They had been defamed by persons who feared neither God nor the charge, so grievous before divine judgment, of defaming even a single man and causing him to lose his esteem and honor. From such slander can come great harm and terrible calamity, particularly when large numbers of men are concerned and, even more so, a whole new world. It has been written that these peoples of the Indies, lacking human governance and ordered nations, did not have the power of reason to govern themselves—which was inferred only from their having been found to be gentle, patient and humble. It has been implied that God became careless in creating so immense a number of rational souls and let human nature, which He so largely determined and provided for, go astray in the almost infinitesimal part of the human lineage which they comprise. From this it follows that they have all proven themselves unsocial and therefore monstrous, contrary to the natural bent of all peoples of the world; and that He did not allow any other species of corruptible creature to err in this way, excepting a strange and occasional case. In order to demonstrate the truth, which is the opposite, this book brings together and compiles certain natural, special and accidental causes which are specified below. . . . Not only have [the Indians] shown themselves to be very wise peoples and possessed of lively and marked understanding, prudently governing and providing for their nations (as much as they can be nations, without faith in or knowledge of the true God) and making them prosper in justice; but they have equalled many diverse nations of the world, past and present, that have been praised for their governance, politics and customs, and exceed by no small measure the wisest of all these, such as the Greeks and Romans, in adherence to the rules of natural reason. This advantage and superiority, along with everything said above, will appear quite clearly when, if it please God, the peoples are compared one with another. This history has been written with the aforesaid aim in mind by Fray Bartolomé de Las Casas, or Casaus, a monk of the Dominican Order and sometime bishop of Chiapa, who promises before the divine word that everything said and referred to is the truth, and that nothing of an untruthful nature appears to the best of his knowledge.

Chapter CXXVII. The Indians Possessed More Enlightenment and Natural Knowledge of God Than the Greeks and Romans

. . . These Indian peoples surpassed the Greeks and Romans in selecting for their gods, not sinful and criminal men noted for their great baseness, but virtuous ones—to the extent that virtue exists among people who lack the knowledge of the true God that is gained by faith. . . .

The following argument can be formed for the proof of the above: The Indian nations seem to show themselves to be or to have been of better rational judgment and more prudent and upright in what they considered God to be. For nations which have reached the knowledge that there is a God hold in common the natural concept that God is the best of all things that can be imagined. Therefore the nation which has elected virtuous men as God or gods, though it might have erred in not selecting the true God, has a better concept and estimation of God and more natural purity than one which has selected and accepted for God or gods men known to be sinful and criminal. The latter was the case of the Greek and Roman states, which the former is that of all these Indian nations. . . . It seems probable that none of these Indian peoples will be more difficult of conversion than the ancient idolaters. First, because, as we have proved and are still proving, all these peoples are of good reason. Second, because they show less duplicity and more simplicity of heart than others. Third, because they are in their natural persons better adjusted, as has been proved above—a quality characteristic of men who may more easily be persuaded of the truth. Fourth, because an infinite number in their midst have already been converted (although some with certain difficulty, namely, those who worshiped many gods; for it is not possible except by a great miracle for a religion so aged, mellowed and time-honored to be abandoned suddenly, in a short time or with ease—as proven by all of the world's past and ancient idolaters). . . .

Chapter CCLXII. From All That Has Been Said It Is Inferred That the Indian Nations Equalled and Even Surpassed All the Ancient Ones in Good Laws and Customs

. . . Let us compare [the ancients] with the people of the realms of Peru as concerns women, marriage and chastity. The [Peruvian] kings honored and favored marriages with their presence and performed them themselves or through their proconsuls and delegates. They themselves exhorted the newlyweds to live happily, and in this these people were superior to all nations. They were certainly superior to the Assyrians and Babylonians, . . . even to our own Spaniards of Cantabria, . . . more especially to the renowned isle of England . . . and to many others. . . . To whom were they not superior in the election and succession of kings and those who were to govern the country? They always chose the wisest, most virtuous and most worthy of ruling, those who had subordinated all natural and sensual affection and were free and clean of repugnant ambition and all private interest.

They were likewise more than moderate in exacting tribute of vassals and, so that the people should not be molested, in levying the costs of war. Their industries existed so that nations might communicate among each other and all live in peace. They had a frequent and meticulous census of all deaths and births and of the exact number of people in all estates of the realms. All persons had professions, and each one busied himself and worked to gain his necessary livelihood. They possessed abundant deposits of provisions which met all the necessities of their warriors, reduced the burden and trouble for the subjects and were distributed in the lean years. . . . Who of the peoples and kings of the world ever kept the men of their armies under such discipline that they would not dare to touch even a single fruit hanging over the road from a tree behind a wall? Not the Greeks, nor Alexander, nor the Romans, nor even our own Christian monarchs. Has anyone read of soldiers who, no matter where they were marching when not in battle, were as well commanded, trained, sober and orderly as good friars in a procession? They established order and laws for the obedience which vassals must show toward their immediate lords and for reverence between each other, the humble

to the humble and the mighty to the mighty. The rearing of children, in which parents inculcate the obedience and faithfulness owed to superiors—where is it surpassed? . . . Has anyone read of any prince in the world among the ancient unbelievers of the past or subsequently among Christians, excepting St. Louis of France, who so attentively assisted and provided for the poor among his vassals— those not only of his own village or city but of all his large and extensive realms? They issued public edicts and personal commands to all nobles and provincial governors, of whom there were many, that all poor, widows and orphans in each province should be provided for from their own royal rents and riches, and that alms should be given according to the need, poverty and desert of each person. Where and among what people or nation was there a prince endowed with such piety and beneficence that he never dined unless three or four poor people ate from his plate and at his table? . . . Then, there is that miracle—such it may be called for being the most remarkable, singular and skilful construction of its kind, I believe, in the world—of the two highways . . . across the mountains and along the coast. The finer and more admirable of these extends for a least six and perhaps eight hundred leagues and is said to reach the provinces of Chile. . . . In Spain and Italy I have seen portions of the highway said to have been built by the Romans from Spain to Italy, but it is quite crude in comparison with the one built by these peoples. . . .

Chapter CCLXIII. The Indians Are as Capable as Any Other Nations to Receive the Gospel

Thus it remains stated, demonstrated and openly concluded . . . throughout this book that all these peoples of the Indies possessed— as far as is possible through natural and human means and without the light of faith—nations, towns, villages and cities, most fully and abundantly provided for. With a few exceptions in varying degrees they lacked nothing, and some were endowed in full perfection for political and social life and for attaining and enjoying that civic happiness which in this world any good, rational, well provided and happy republic wishes to have and enjoy; for all are by nature of very subtle, lively, clear and most capable understanding. This they received (after the will of God, Who wished to create them in this way) from the favorable influence of the heavens, the gentle attributes of the regions which God gave them to inhabit, the clement and soft weather; from the composition of their limbs and internal and external sensory organs; from the quality and sobriety of their diet; from the fine disposition and healthfulness of the lands, towns and local winds; from their temperance and moderation in food and drink; from the tranquility, calmness and quiescence of their sensual desires; from their lack of concern and worry over the worldly matters that stir the passions of the soul, these being joy, love, wrath, grief and the rest; and also, *a posteriori,* from the works they accomplished and the effects of these. From all these causes, universal and superior, particular and inferior, natural and accidental, it followed, first by nature and then by their industry and experience, that they were endowed with the three types of prudence: the monastic, by which man

knows how to rule himself; the economic, which teaches him to rule his house; and the political, which sets forth and ordains the rule of his cities. As for the divisions of this last type (which presupposes the first two types of prudence to be perfect) into workers, artisans, warriors, rich men, religion (temples, priests and sacrifices), judges and magistrates, governors, customs and into everything which concerns acts of understanding and will, . . . they were equal to many nations of the world outstanding and famous for being politic and reasonable. . . . We have, then, but slight occasion to be surprised at defects and uncouth and immoderate customs which we might find among our Indian peoples and to disparage them for these; for many and perhaps all other peoples of the world have been much more perverse, irrational and corrupted by depravity, and in their governments and in many virtues and moral qualities much less temperate and orderly. Our own forbears were much worse, as revealed in irrationality and confused government and in vices and brutish customs throughout the length and breadth of this our Spain, which has been shown in many places above. Let us, then, finish this book and give immense thanks to God for having given us enough life, strength and help to see it finished.

QUESTIONS

1. Does Las Casas's view of the Indians differ from Columbus's? How? In what ways do they operate from the same assumptions?

2. How did some Europeans justify the mistreatment of Native Americans? How does Las Casas refute those arguments?

3. In his letter Columbus depicted a simple, almost primitive society. Does Las Casas find this to be the case?

4. Why, according to Las Casas, were the Indians a more admirable people than the ancient Greeks and Romans?

61

■ *Bernal Díaz* ■

THE TRUE HISTORY OF THE CONQUEST OF NEW SPAIN
(1552–1568)

Bernal Díaz del Castillo (ca. 1492–1581) was one of the soldiers who accompanied Hernán Cortés on the conquest of the Aztecs. Díaz left Spain for the New World at the age of eighteen and had explored both Cuba and the Yucatan Peninsula before he joined Cortés's expedition. After the conquest of Mexico, Díaz accompanied Cortés on his unsuccessful expedition into Honduras. He remained in Central America for most of his life, settling in what is now Guatemala, where his papers, including the manuscript copy of his *True History*, remain.

Díaz wrote *The True History of the Conquest of New Spain* to refute what he regarded as inaccurate accounts of the conquest. Although he was an eyewitness and participant, his history was not written until many years later and was undoubtedly colored by his polemical purpose. Nevertheless, his description of Tenochtitlán, capital of Montezuma's empire, remains compelling.

As we had already been in Mexico for four days and none of us had left our quarters except to go to the houses and gardens, Cortés told us it would be a good idea to go to the main plaza and see the great temple of their Uichilobos.... Many of Montezuma's chiefs were sent to accompany us, and when we arrived at the great square we were struck by the throngs of people and the amount of merchandise they displayed, at the efficiency and administration of everything.

The chiefs who accompanied us showed us how each kind of merchandise was kept separate and had its place marked out. Let us start with the dealers in gold, silver, and precious stones, feathers, cloth, and embroidered goods, and other merchandise in the form of men and women to be sold as slaves. There were as many here as the Negroes brought from Guinea by the Portuguese. Some were tied to long poles with collars around their necks so they couldn't escape, and others were left free. Then there were merchants who sold homespun clothing, cotton, and thread, and others who sold cacao, so that one could see every sort of goods that is to be found in all of New Spain, set out the way it's done where I come from, Medina del Campo, during fair time....

I wonder why I waste all these words in telling what they sold in that great square, for I shall never finish describing everything in detail. But I must mention the paper, which is called *amal*, the little pipes scented with liquidambar and filled with tobacco, and the yellow ointments and other things of the same sort, all sold separately. Cochineal was sold under the arcades, and herbs and many other kinds of goods. There were buildings where three judges sat, and magistrates who inspected the merchandise.... I wish I could get through with telling all the things they sold there, but only to finish looking and inquiring about everything in that great square filled with people would have taken two days, and then you wouldn't have seen everything. . . .

. . . When we climbed to the top of the great *cu* [stairway] there was a kind of platform, with huge stones where they put the poor Indians to be sacrificed, and an image like a dragon and other evil figures, with a great deal of blood that had been shed that day.

Montezuma, accompanied by two priests, came out from an oratory dedicated to the worship of his cursed idols at the top of the *cu,* and said with great deference toward all of us, "You must be tired, Señor Malinche, after climbing up this great temple of ours."

Through our interpreters, who went with us, Cortés replied that neither he nor the rest of us ever got tired from anything. Then Montezuma took him by the hand and bade him look at his great city and at all the other cities rising from the water, and the many towns around the lake; and if he had not seen the market place well, he said, he could see it from here much better.

There we stood looking, for that large and evil temple was so high that it towered over everything. From there we could see all three of the causeways that led into Mexico: the road from Iztapalapa, by which we had entered four days earlier; the Tacuba road, by which we fled the night of our great rout; and the road from Tepeaquilla.

We saw the fresh water that came from Chapultepec, which supplied the city, and the bridges on the three causeways, built at certain intervals so the water could go from one part of the lake to another, and a multitude of canoes, some arriving with provisions and others leaving with merchandise. We saw that every house in this great city and in the others built on the water could be reached only by wooden draw-bridges or by canoe. We saw temples built like towers and fortresses in these cities, all white-washed; it was a sight to see. We could look down on the flat-roofed houses and other little towers and temples like fortresses along the causeways.

After taking a good look and considering all that we had seen, we looked again at the great square and the throngs of people, some buying and others selling. The buzzing of their voices could be heard more than a league away. There were soldiers among us who had been in many parts of the world, in Constantinople and Rome and all over Italy, who said that they had never before seen a market place so large and so well laid out, and so filled with people. . . .

Then Cortés said to Montezuma, through Doña Marina, "Your Highness is indeed a great prince, and it has delighted us to see your cities. Now that we are here in your temple, will you show us your gods?"

Montezuma replied that he would first have to consult with his priests. After he had spoken with them, he bade us enter a small tower room, a kind of hall where there were two altars with very richly painted planks on the ceiling. On each altar there were two giant figures, their bodies very tall and stout. The first one, to the right, they said was Uichilobos, their god of war. It had a very broad face with monstrous, horrible eyes, and the whole body was covered with precious stones, gold, and pearls that were stuck on with a paste they make in this country out of roots. The body was circled with great snakes made of gold and precious stones, and in one hand he held a bow and in the other some arrows. A small idol standing by him they said was his page; he held a short lance and a shield rich with gold and precious stones. Around the neck of Uichilobos were silver Indian faces and things that we took to be the hearts of these Indians, made of gold and decorated with many precious blue stones. There were braziers with copal incense, and they were burning in them the hearts of three Indians they had sacrificed that day. All the walls and floor were black with crusted blood, and the whole place stank.

To the left stood another great figure, the height of Uichilobos, with the face of a bear and

The Founding of Tenochtitlán. *The first two Aztec conquests, Culhuacán and Tenayucán, are depicted at the bottom of the drawing. From the* Codex Mendoza.

glittering eyes made of their mirrors, which they call *tezcal*. It was decorated with precious stones the same as Uichilobos, for they said that the two were brothers. This Tezcatepuca was the god of hell and had charge of the souls of the Mexicans. His body was girded with figures like little devils, with snakelike tails. The walls were so crusted with blood and the floor was so bathed in it that in the slaughterhouses of Castile there was no such stink. They had offered to this idol five hearts from the day's sacrifices.

In the highest part of the *cu* there was another recess, the wood of which was very

richly carved, where there was another figure, half man and half lizard, covered with precious stones and with a mantle over half of it. They said that its body was filled with all the seeds there are in all the world. It was the god of sowing and ripening, but I do not remember its name. Everything was covered with blood, the walls as well as the altar, and it stank so much that we couldn't get out fast enough. . . .

Our captain said to Montezuma, half laughingly, "Lord Montezuma, I do not understand how such a great prince and wise man as yourself can have failed to come to the conclusion that these idols of yours are not gods, but evil things—devils is the term for them. So that you and your priests may see it clearly, do me a favor: Let us put a cross on top of this tower, and in one part of these oratories, where your Uichilobos and Tezcatepuca are, we will set up an image of Our Lady [an image that Montezuma had already seen], and you will see how afraid of it these idols that have deceived you are."

The two priests with Montezuma looked hostile, and Montezuma replied with annoyance, "Señor Malinche, if I had thought that you would so insult my gods, I would not have shown them to you. We think they are very good, for they give us health, water, good seedtimes and weather, and all the victories we desire. We must worship and make sacrifices to them. Please do not say another word to their dishonor."

When our captain heard this and saw how changed Montezuma was, he didn't argue with him any more, but smiled and said, "It is time for Your Highness and ourselves to go."

Montezuma agreed, but he said that before he left he had to pray and make certain offerings to atone for the great sin he had committed in permitting us to climb the great *cu* and see his gods, and for being the cause of the dishonor that we had done them by speaking ill of them.

QUESTIONS

1. What impressed Díaz most about the city? Is his list of the merchandise he saw for sale random or ordered?

2. Why does Díaz describe the Aztec gods as devils?

3. How does the fact that the Aztecs sacrificed humans color Díaz's account of their religion?

4. Who do you have more sympathy for, Cortés or Montezuma? How does Díaz manipulate your sympathies?

62

■ *Juan Gonzalez de Mendoza* ■

THE HISTORY OF THE GREAT AND MIGHTIE KINGDOM OF CHINA

(1585)

Juan Gonzalez de Mendoza was a Spanish missionary who spent most of his early life abroad. He went first to Mexico City where he was involved with the earliest missions from Spanish America to the Philippines. His interest in missionary work in Asia led to his return to Spain and to an audience with King Philip II. Although Mendoza hoped to be appointed to a second mission to the Philippines, instead he remained in Madrid to process the reports sent back from the Asian missions. In 1580, he was appointed one of the heads of a new mission to China, but by the time he reached Spanish America the mission had been postponed. Mendoza returned to Europe, was called to Rome and commissioned by the Pope to collect all of the information that was known about China. The result was *The History of the Great and Mightie Kingdom of China* (1585), one of the most popular books of the sixteenth century, going through forty-six editions in fifteen years.

Mendoza compiled his history from the few eyewitness accounts of early Portuguese ambassadors and from the dispatches of Christian missionaries. He read everything that had previously been written about China and synthesized it in a lively and direct style. His work is notable for its description of the political structure of Ming rule as well as for its description of social customs. The following selection includes his famous description of the custom of foot-binding.

Both men and women of this countrie are of a good disposition of their bodies, well proportioned and gallant men, somewhat tall: they are all for the most part brode faced, little eyes and flat noses, and without bearde save only upon the ball of the chinne: but yet there be some that have great eyes and goodly beardes, and their faces well proportioned, yet of these sorts (in respect of the others) are verie few: and it is to bee beleeved that these kinde of people doo proceede of some strange nation, who in times past when it was lawful to deale out of that countrie did joyne one with another.

Those of the province of Canton (which is a hot country) be browne of colour like to the Moores: but those that be farther within the countrie be like unto Almaines, Italians and Spanyardes, white and redde, and somewhat swart. All of them do suffer their nailes of their left hande to grow very long, but the right hand they do cut: they have long haire, and esteeme it very much and maintaine it with curiositie: of both they make a superstition, for that they say thereby they shall be carried into heaven. They do binde their haire up to the crowne of their heade, in calles of golde verie curious, and with pinnes of the same.

The garments which the nobles and principals do use, bee of silke of different colours, of the which they have excellent good and verie perfite: the common and poore people doo apparell themselves with another kinde of silke more courser, and with linnen, serge, and cotton: of all the which there is great abundance. And for that the countrie for the most part is temperate, they may suffer this kinde of apparell, which is the heaviest that they doo use: for in all the whole kingdome they have no cloth, neither doo they suffer it to be made, although they have great aboundance of woolle, and very good cheape: they do use their coates according unto our old use of antiquitie, with long skirts and full of plaites, and a flappe over the brest to be made fast under the left side, the sleeves verie bigge and wide: upon their coates they doo use cassockes or long garments according unto the possibilitie of either of them, made according as wee doo use, but only their sleeves are more wider. They of royall bloode and such as are constituted unto dignitie, do differ in their apparell from the other ordinarie gentlemen: for that the first have their garments laide on with gold and silver downe to the waste, and the others alonely garnished on the edges, or hem: they do use hose verie well made and stitched, shoes and buskins of velvet, verie curious. In the winter (although it be not very colde,) they have their garments furred with beasts skins, but in especiall with Martas Cevellinas, of the which they have great aboundance (as aforesaid) and generally they do use them at all times about their necks. They that be not married doo differ from them that be married, in that they do kirrle their haire on their foreheade, and wear higher hattes. Their women do apparell themselves verie curiouslie, much after the fashion of Spaine: they use many jewels of gold and precious stones: their gownes have wide sleeves; that wherewith they do apparel themselves is of cloath of gold and silver and divers sortes of silkes, whereof they have great plentie, as aforesaid, and excellent good, and good cheape: and the poore folks doo apparell themselves with velvet, unshorne velvet and serge. They have verie faire haire, and doo combe it with great care and diligence, as do the women of Genouay, and do binde it about their heade with a broad silke lace, set full of pearles and precious stones, and they say it doth become them verie well: they doo use to paint themselves, and in some place in excesse.

Amongst them they account it for gentilitie and a gallant thing to have little feete, and therefore from their youth they so swadell and binde them verie straight, and do suffer it with patience: for that she who hath the least feete is accounted the gallantest dame. They say that the men hath induced them unto this custome, for to binde their feete so harde, that almost they doo loose the forme of them, and remaine halfe lame, so that their going is verie ill, and with great travell: which is the occasion that they goe but little abroad, and fewe times doo rise up from their worke that they do; and was invented onely for the same intent. This custome hath indured manie yeares, and will indure many more, for that it is stablished for a law: and that woman which doth breake it, and not use it with her children, shalbe counted as evill, yea shalbe punished for the same. They are very secreat and honest, in such sort that you shall not see at any time a woman at her window nor at her doores: and if her husband doo invite any person to dinner, she is never seene nor eateth not at the table, except the gest be a kinsman or a very friende: when they go abroade to visite their father, mother, or any other kinsfolkes, they are carried in a little chaire by foure men, the which is made close, and with lattices rounde about made of golde wyre and with silver, and curteines of silke; that although they doo see them that be in the streete, yet they cannot be seene. They have many servants waiting on them. So that it is a great marvell when that you shall meete a principall woman in the streete, yea you will thinke that there are none in the citie, their keeping in is such: the lameness of their feet is a great helpe thereunto. The women as well as the men be ingenious; they doo use drawne workes and carved works, excellent painters of flowers, birds and beasts, as it is to be seene upon beddes and bords that is brought from thence. I did see my selfe, one that was brought unto Lysborne in the yeare 1582, by Captaine Ribera, chiefe sergant of Manilla, that it was to be wondred at the excellencie thereof: it caused the kings majestie to have admyration, and he is a person that little wondreth at things. All the people did wonder at it: yea the famous imbroiderers did marvaile at the curiousnesse thereof. They are great inventers of things, that although they have amongst them many coches and wagons that goe with sailes, and made with such industrie and policie that they do governe them with great ease: this is crediblie informed

by many that have seen it: besides that, there be many in the Indies, and in Portugall, that have seene them painted upon clothes, and on their earthen vessell that is brought from thence to be solde: so that it is a signe that their painting hath some foundation. In their buying and selling they are verie subtill, in such sort that they will depart a haire. Such merchants as do keepe shoppes (of whom in every citie there is a great number) they have a table or signe hanging at their doore, whereon is written all such merchandise as is within to be sold.

That which is commonly sold in their shops is cloth of golde and silver, cloth of tissue, silkes of divers sorts and excellent colours: others there be of poorer sort that selleth serges, peeces of cotton, linnen and fustian of all colours; yet both the one and the other is verie goode cheape, for that there is great aboundance, and many workemen that do make it. The apothecarie that selleth simples, hath the like table: there be also shops full of earthen vessels of divers making, redde, greene, yellow, and gilt; it is so good cheape that for foure rials of plate they give fiftie peeces: very strong earth, the which they doo breake all to peeces and grinde it, and put it into sesternes with water, made of lime and stone; and after that they have well tumbled and tossed it in the water, of the creame that is upon it they make the finest sort of them, and the lower they go, spending that substance that is the courser: they make them after the forme and fashion as they do here, and afterward they do gild them, and make them of what colour they please, the which will never be lost: then they put them into their killes and burne them. This hath beene seene and is of a truth, as appeareth in a booke set foorth in the Italian toonge, by Duardo Banbosa, that they do make them of periwinkle shelles of the sea: the which they do grinde and put them under the ground to refine them, whereas they lie 100 years: and many other things he doth treat of to this effect. But if that were true, they should not make so great a number of them as is made in that kingdome, and is brought into Portugall, and carried into the Peru, and Nova Espania, and into other parts of the world: which is a sufficient proofe for that which is said. And the Chinos do agree for this to be true. The finest sort of this is never carried out of the countrie, for that it is spent in the service of the king, and his governours, and is so fine and deere, that it seemeth to be of fine and perfite cristal: that which is made in the province of Saxii is the best and finest. Artificers and mechanicall officers doo dwell in streets appointed, whereas none do dwell amongst them, but such as be of the same occupation or arte: in such sort that if you doo come at the beginning of the street, looke what craft or art they are there, it is to be understood that all that streete are of that occupation. It is ordayned by a law and statute, that the sonne shall inherite his fathers occupation, and shall not use any other without licence of the justice: if one of them bee verie rich and will not worke, yet he cannot let but

have in his shop men that must worke of his occupation. Therefore they that do use it, by reason that they are brought up in it from their youth, they are famous and verie curious in that which they do worke, as it is plainelie seene in that which is brought fro thence to Manilla, and into the Indies, and unto Portugall. Their currant monie of that kingdome is made of golde and silver, without any signe or print, but goeth by waight: so that all men carrieth a balances with them, and little peeces of silver and golde, for to buy such things as they have neede of. And for things of a greater quantitie they have bigger ballances in their houses, and waights, that are sealed, for to give to every man that which is theirs: for therein the justices have great care. In the government of the Chincheo they have copper monie coyned, but it is nothing woorth out of that province.

QUESTIONS

1. To whom does Mendoza compare the Chinese people? Why?

2. What does the passage tell us about the position of women in Chinese society?

3. What does he think about the custom of foot-binding?

4. Why do you think Mendoza's *History* was so popular in the sixteenth century?

RELIGIOUS REFORM

63

■ *Bernard Gui* ■

A MANUAL FOR INQUISITORS

(1331)

Bernard Gui (1261–1331) was one of the most famous medieval inquisitors, leading the Roman Catholic Church's attack, or "Inquisition," against heresies. Gui was also an historian, bishop, and theologian. When he was not yet twenty years old, he joined the Order of the Preachers (often called the Dominicans after their founder, St. Dominic). This was a mendicant sect of monks that sought to address the spiritual problems brought on by the explosive growth of cities in the thirteenth century. French by birth, Gui spent his early years as a Dominican in southern France dedicated to a life of the mind—studying logic, grammar, and philosophy. At this time, France was racked by political and religious unrest. A number of heretical sects not only deviated from Catholic orthodox doctrine and practice but also threatened to undermine the entire Catholic political order. To defend the faith, the Pope authorized the two largest mendicant orders, the Dominicans and the Franciscans, to suppress these heretics. Gui, already known as an excellent administrator, was given charge of organizing these efforts. As an inquisitor he had nearly unchecked power. Secular powers were ordered to provide him with assistance and he could arrest and even execute on his own authority. The Inquisition became an effective weapon for the Pope and a feared institution for the people.

Though specifically charged with uprooting local heresies, Gui was determined to undermine a whole array of perceived heretical groups and individuals, including Jews, sorcerers, and the female heretics called the Beguines. Seeking to aid other inquisitors, Gui recorded his experiences and advice in his most famous work: *The Manual for Inquisitors.* As its name suggests, it is a handbook in which he sets out the history of various heresies and proposes models for the apprehension, conviction, and punishment of heretics. The selected passage focuses on one such heretical group, known as the Waldensians, discussing their origins, their erroneous beliefs, and the ways to uncover their heterodox views.

11   THE SECT OF THE WALDENSIANS

The sect of the Waldensians, beginning with their origin and date

The sect and heresy of the Waldensians or the Poor of Lyon first started in the year of Our Lord 1170. It was begun by a citizen of Lyon called Waldes or Waldo, whose followers took their name from his. He was a rich man who made a stand, abandoned all his property and decided to observe poverty and the perfection of the gospels as the apostles had done. And when he had had the gospels and some other books of the Bible written for him in the Gallic verna-cular,[1] together with important passages from the saints Augustine, Jerome, Ambrose and Gregory set out in sections which he and his followers called Sentences, often reading them on their own and without any understanding, then these uneducated persons, puffed up with their own opinions, usurped the role of the apostles and presumed to preach the gospel in the streets and public squares. And this Waldo caused very many men and women to join him in this presumptuous behaviour and sent them out like disciples to preach.

These foolish and ignorant people, men and women as well, ran about in towns and got into houses, they preached in public squares and even in churches, the men especially, and spread many errors abroad.

Summoned by Lord John Fair Hands,[2] Archbishop of Lyon, and commanded by him to stop this presumptuous behaviour, they refused to obey, cloaking their folly by saying that it was better to obey God than man, that God had ordered his apostles to preach the gospel to all creatures, and arrogating to themselves what had been said to the apostles, whose imitators and successors they dared to call themselves,

under a pretence of poverty and a false image of holiness. They poured scorn on prelates and clergy because these enjoyed great wealth and lived lives of pleasure.

Usurping the role of preachers with such presumption, they made themselves masters of error. They were told to stop preaching but refused to do so and were declared contumacious; then they were excommunicated and expelled from that city and country. At last, as they remained obdurate they were judged to be in schism and therefore condemned as heretics at a certain council held in Rome at the Lateran.[3] With their numbers thus increased, they spread across that province and neighbouring areas as far as the borders of Lombardy, and as they were cut off from the Church and mixed with other heretics, acquiring new errors from them, they added ancient errors and heresies to their own imaginings.

•••

Of the errors of today's Waldensians, for previously they had many more

The first heresy of these Waldensians, in which they persist, is contempt of the Church's authority. For this reason they were excommunicated and handed over to Satan, who drove them into countless errors so that they added the errors of ancient heretics to those they had invented themselves.

Thus the erring followers and profane teachers of this sect hold and teach that they are not subject to the lord pope or the Roman pontiff or other prelates of the Roman Church, asserting that this Church unjustly and undeservedly persecutes and condemns them. They also assert that they cannot be excommunicated by this Roman pontiff and these prelates and that they do not owe them any obedience when they order the followers and teachers of this sect to abandon and abjure it, even though this sect has been condemned as heretical by the Church of Rome.

---

[1] Gui says in *vulgari gallico*; this would be 'in French', not Occitan. Linda M. Paterson's *World of the Troubadors* places the northern boundary of Occitan well to the south of Lyon.
[2] Johanne de Bellis Manibus, but Mollat p. 36 says to read 'Blanches-Mains', White Hands.

---

[3] The fourth Lateran Council, 1215.

Furthermore they hold and teach that God has forbidden all oaths, in law courts or elsewhere, as wicked and sinful, without exception or explanation, applying the words of the gospel and of St James against taking oaths in a sense as crazy as it is extreme, in spite of the sane teaching of the saints and doctors of the Church, in spite of the tradition of this holy Catholic Church and even of the recent decree against this error, 'if any of them through damnable superstition reject the sanctity of an oath and refuse to swear, let them therefore be considered heretics'.

Yet it must be noted that the Waldensians grant dispensations to themselves. They may take an oath to save their own or another's life or even to avoid naming their accomplices or revealing the secrets of their sect. For they say that it is an unforgivable crime and a sin against the Holy Spirit to hand over one of their sect's 'perfects'.

And from the same source comes this error: that all judging is forbidden by God and is therefore a sin, that a judge who condemns anyone for any reason to a physical punishment involving bloodshed or death is disobeying God. It is written in the holy gospel, 'Judge not, that you may not be judged',[4] and 'Thou shalt not kill'[5] and other similar passages, and they use these texts without due exposition, not understanding or accepting the interpretation that the holy Roman Church wisely offers to the faithful according to the teaching of the fathers and teachers and the canonical decrees.

Also this sect, wandering from the way and the right path, does not accept or respect the canonical decrees or the decisions of the sovereign pontiffs nor the feast days and fasts to be observed nor the decrees of the fathers, but despises, condemns and rejects them.

• • •

---

[4]Matthew, 7, i.
[5]Matthew, 5, xxi.

The method or rite by which they celebrate mass

This is the way they usually celebrate mass: It is only done once a year, on the day of the Lord's Supper.[6] At nightfall the one who presides, although not a priest ordained by a Catholic bishop, calls together his whole household, both men and women. He has a suitable bench or chest prepared in front of them, has it spread with a clean cloth, and on this they place a full cup of good pure wine and a flat cake or loaf of unleavened bread. Then the person presiding says to those with him, 'Let us ask our God in his mercy to forgive us our sins and offences and to fulfil for his mercy's sake the petitions we rightly make, and let us repeat the Lord's Prayer seven times in honour of God and the holy Trinity, so that he may do this.' And then they all kneel, recite the Lord's Prayer seven times, and then stand up.

After this he makes the sign of the cross on the bread and the cup of wine, and breaking the bread he gives a piece to all those present, then gives them to drink from the cup; and all this time they remain standing. And so they finish their sacrifice. And they believe firmly and confess that this is the body and blood of Our Lord Jesus Christ. If there is anything left over from the sacrifice, they keep it until Easter[7] and it is then consumed. Throughout the rest of the year they give only wine and blessed bread to their sick people.

All these Poor of Lyon or Waldensians used to use the same rite of consecration before the division that took place among them when they separated into the Lombard Poor and the Poor on this side of the mountains.[8]

These Waldensians also state that there is no purgatory for souls after this life, and therefore prayers, almsgiving, masses and other works of piety for the dead can do them no good.

---

[6]Maundy Thursday, the day before Good Friday.
[7]The following Sunday.
[8]This split began in 1205 and was confirmed at a meeting at Bergamo in 1218.

Also they belittle the condition of the prelates, clerics and religious of the Roman Church, criticise and condemn it, and say that they are blind men leading the blind, who neither preserve the truth of the gospel nor follow apostolic poverty. And they lie most bitterly in calling the Church of Rome itself the house of falsehood. These fools glory in being, as they say, like the apostles who led a life of perfection, they claim to be their heirs, equal to them in merit, and they boast that it is they who uphold the apostolic perfection of the gospel.

Furthermore they declare that they have three orders in their Church, those of deacons, priests and bishops, claiming that the authority of each and all of these derives solely from themselves and not from the Roman Church; all the more so because they do not believe that the holy orders of the Roman Church come from God but from human tradition. In this way they can the more easily deceive, by asserting that they believe in the sacred orders of the episcopate, priesthood and diaconate of the holy Church, by which they mean their own.

Also they say that none of the miracles worked in the Church through the merits and prayers of the saints are genuine, because none of them ever performed any miracles. Privately they claim that the saints in heaven do not hear the prayers of the faithful or take any notice of the honour we show them on earth, that the saints do not pray for us and therefore we do not need to ask for their intercessions. Therefore they despise the solemnities we celebrate in honour of the saints and all the other ways in which we venerate them, and if they can do so safely, they work on holy days.

These three points, however, they do not reveal indiscriminately to their believers but keep them private among themselves, the 'perfects' of the sect; that is, that the miracles of the saints are not genuine, that their intercessions should not be asked for and that no days are to be kept holy except the Lord's day and the day of the blessed Virgin Mary, and, say some of them, those of the apostles and evangelists.

They teach these beliefs, and the many false and wild ideas to which they lead, secretly to their believers in their conventicles. They also preach to them about the gospels, epistles and other sacred scriptures, distorting them like the masters of error that they are, who have never learned how to study truth, although preaching is utterly forbidden to lay persons.

After they have been received into this society or brotherhood as they call it, and promised to obey their superior and to live in gospel poverty, they must from then on remain chaste and own no possessions. They must sell everything they have, put the profits into a common fund and live on alms given by those who believe in and support their sect. The oldest among them distributes these funds according to each one's need.

The Waldensians speak in praise of chastity to their believers, but they allow them to satisfy a burning passion, in however foul a manner. Their apostles explain the text, 'It is better to marry than to be burnt',[9] by saying that it is better to satisfy passion, however shamefully, than to be tempted in the heart. But they keep this very dark, so as not to lose credit with their believers.

They make collections among their believers and friends and bring what they have gathered to their superior.

They hold one or two chapters general every year in some appointed town, as secretly as they can, meeting in a house which one or more believers have previously hired, as if they were traders. And in these chapters the most senior person present arranges and decides about priests and deacons and those who are to be sent to different districts and regions to visit believers and friends, to hear confessions and collect alms, and he hears and receives details of income and expenses.

After becoming 'perfects', these no longer work with their hands or do any kind of work to earn money, except perhaps as a means of disguise, to avoid being identified or arrested.

---

[9] I Corinthians, 7, ix.

They address each other as brothers and call themselves the Poor of Christ or the Poor of Lyon.

Sometimes, for protection, they will mix with religious and clerics in false friendship, and will give them gifts in token of humility and service, so that they and their followers may the more easily remain hidden, may live and injure souls.

They attend churches and hear sermons and in all ways behave in an apparently devout and proper manner and are careful to talk in honeyed and discreet terms.

QUESTIONS

1. What about the Waldensians makes them heretical in the eyes of Gui?

2. Gui claims that the Waldensians' first crime is "contempt of Church authority." What beliefs and actions of the Waldensians undermine the authority of the Pope and his Church? How?

3. According to this text, Waldensians forbid all oaths. The Church insists on oaths. Why might this be important for an inquisitor to know? How might this make it more difficult to detect Waldensians?

4. Gui describes in a number of places the difference in the ways that the Church and the Waldensians read the Bible. What are these differences? What can they tell us about the underlying religious debates at this time?

5. Why do you think it is important for Gui to offer the history of the Waldensians' origins and founding?

64

■ *Martin Luther* ■

THE FREEDOM OF A CHRISTIAN
(1520)

OF MARRIAGE AND CELIBACY
(1566)

Martin Luther (1483–1546) was undoubtedly the central figure of the sixteenth century. Trained for the law, he underwent a spiritual crisis that led him to enter an Augustinian monastery. There his extraordinary gifts were recognized, and he quickly distinguished himself as a scholar, teacher, and pastor. In 1517, he protested against the sale of indulgences and found himself at the center of a political and religious controversy. Luther refused to recant his views and was condemned by both the Pope and the Holy Roman Emperor. He broke from the Roman Catholic Church and founded his own religious movement, first called Protestantism and later Lutheranism.

Throughout his political struggles, Luther wrote incessantly. The spread of his message and his movement was aided by the invention of printing and by the increase of literacy. He translated parts of the Bible into German, prepared a new church service, and even wrote hymns. But his most important works were the explanations of his faith. *The Freedom of a Christian* is one of the central statements of Luther's theology.

Among the many church reforms that Luther undertook was permitting clergy to marry. In his later years, he took a wife, a former nun from a dissolved monastery. Luther's views on marriage, however, were not part of his systematic theology. They were collected in *The Table Talk,* a work compiled by his followers after his death.

THE FREEDOM OF A CHRISTIAN

Many people have considered Christian faith an easy thing, and not a few have given it a place among the virtues. They do this because they have not experienced it and have never tasted the great strength there is in faith. It is impossible to write well about it or to understand what has been written about it unless one has at one time or another experienced the courage which faith gives a man when trials oppress him. But he who has had even a faint taste of it can never write, speak, meditate, or hear enough concerning it. It is a living "spring of water welling up to eternal life," as Christ calls it in John 4[:14].

As for me, although I have no wealth of faith to boast of and know how scant my supply is, I nevertheless hope that I have attained to a little faith, even though I have been assailed by great and various temptations; and I hope that I can discuss it, if not more elegantly, certainly more to the point, than those literalists and subtle disputants have previously done, who have not even understood what they have written.

To make the way smoother for the unlearned—for only them do I serve—I shall set down the following two propositions concerning the freedom and the bondage of the spirit:

A Christian is a perfectly free lord of all, subject to none.

A Christian is a perfectly dutiful servant of all, subject to all.

These two theses seem to contradict each other. If, however, they should be found to fit together they would serve our purpose beautifully. Both are Paul's own statements, who says in I Cor. 9[:19], "For though I am free from all men, I have made myself a slave to all," and in Rom. 13[:8], "Owe no one anything, except to love one another." Love by its very nature is ready to serve and be subject to him who is loved. So Christ, although he was Lord of all, was "born of woman, born under the law" [Gal. 4:4], and therefore was at the same time a free man and a servant, "in the form of God" and "of a servant" [Phil. 2:6–7].

Let us start, however, with something more remote from our subject, but more obvious. Man has a twofold nature, a spiritual and a bodily one. According to the spiritual nature, which men refer to as the soul, he is called a spiritual, inner, or new man. According to the bodily nature, which men refer to as flesh, he is called a carnal, outward, or old man. Because of this diversity of nature the Scriptures assert contradictory things concerning the same man, since these two men in the same man contradict each other, "for the desires of the flesh are against the Spirit, and the desires of the Spirit are against the flesh," according to Gal. 5[:17].

First, let us consider the inner man to see how a righteous, free, and pious Christian, that is, a spiritual, new, and inner man becomes what he is. It is evident that no external thing has any influence in producing Christian righteousness or freedom, or in producing unrighteousness or servitude. A simple argument will furnish the proof of this statement. What can it profit the soul if the body is well, free, and active, and eats, drinks, and does as it pleases? For in these respects even the most godless slaves of vice may prosper. On the other hand, how will poor health or imprisonment or hunger or thirst or any other external misfortune harm the soul?

One thing, and only one thing, is necessary for Christian life, righteousness, and freedom. That one thing is the most holy Word of God, the gospel of Christ, as Christ says, John 11[:25], "I am the resurrection and the life; he who believes in me, though he die, yet shall he live"; and John 8[:36], "So if the Son makes you free, you will be free indeed"; and Matt. 4[:4], "Man shall not live by bread alone, but by every word that proceeds from the mouth of God." Let us then consider it certain and firmly established that the soul can do without anything except the Word of God and that where the Word of God is missing there is no help at all for the soul. If it has the Word of God it is rich and lacks nothing since it is the Word of life, truth, light, peace, righteousness, salvation, joy, liberty, wisdom, power, grace, glory and of every incalculable blessing.

You may ask, "What then is the Word of God, and how shall it be used, since there are so many words of God?" I answer: The Apostle explains this in Romans 1. The Word is the gospel of God concerning his Son, who was made flesh, suffered, rose from the dead, and was glorified through the Spirit who sanctifies. Faith alone is the saving and efficacious use of the Word of God, according to Rom. 10[:9]: "If you confess with your lips that Jesus is Lord and believe in your heart that God raised him from the dead, you will be saved." Furthermore, "Christ is the end of the law, that every one who has faith may be justified" [Rom. 10:4]. Again, in Rom. 1[:17], "He who through faith is righteous shall live." The Word of God cannot be received and cherished by any works whatever but only by faith. Therefore it is clear that, as the soul needs only the Word of God for its life and righteousness, so it is justified by faith alone and not any works; for if it could be justified by anything else, it would not need the Word, and consequently it would not need faith.

Should you ask how it happens that faith alone justifies and offers us such a treasure of great benefits without works in view of the fact that so many works, ceremonies, and laws are prescribed in the Scriptures, I answer: First of all, remember what has been said, namely, that faith alone, without works, justifies, frees, and saves; we shall make this clearer later on. Here we must point out that the entire Scripture of God is divided into two parts: commandments and promises. Although the commandments teach things that are good, the things taught are not done as soon as they are taught, for the commandments show us what we ought to do but do not give us the power to do it. They are intended to teach man to know himself, that through them he may recognize his inability to do good and may despair of his own ability. That is why they are called the Old Testament and constitute the Old Testament. For example, the commandment, "You shall not covet" [Exod. 20:17], is a command which proves us all to be sinners, for no one can avoid coveting no matter how much he may struggle against it. Therefore, in order not to covet and to fulfil the commandment, man is compelled to despair of himself, to seek the help which he does not find in himself elsewhere and from someone else, as stated in Hosea [13:9]: "Destruction is your own, O Israel: your help is only in me." As we fare with respect to one commandment, so we fare with all, for it is equally impossible for us to keep any one of them.

Now when a man has learned through the commandments to recognize his helplessness and is distressed about how he might satisfy the law—since the law must be fulfilled so that not a jot or tittle shall be lost, otherwise man will be condemned without hope—then, being truly humbled and reduced to nothing in his own eyes, he finds in himself nothing whereby he may be justified and saved. Here the second part of Scripture comes to our aid, namely, the promises of God which declare the glory of God, saying, "If you wish to fulfil the law and not covet, as the law demands, come, believe in Christ in whom grace, righteousness, peace, liberty, and all things are promised you. If you believe, you shall have all things; if you do not believe, you shall lack all things."

The following statements are therefore true: "Good works do not make a good man, but a good man does good works; evil works do not make a wicked man, but a wicked man does evil works." Consequently it is always necessary that the substance or person himself be good before there can be any good works, and that good works follow and proceed from the good person, as Christ also says, "A good tree cannot bear evil fruit, nor can a bad tree bear good fruit" [Matt. 7:18]. It is clear that the fruits do not bear the tree and that the tree does not grow the fruits, also that, on the contrary, the trees bear the fruits and the fruits grow on the trees. As it is necessary, therefore, that the trees exist before their fruits and the fruits do not make trees either good or bad, but rather as the trees are, so are the fruits they bear; so a man must first be good or wicked before he does a good or wicked work, and his works do not make him good or wicked, but he himself makes his works either good or wicked.

Illustrations of the same truth can be seen in all trades. A good or bad house does not make a good or a bad builder; but a good or a bad builder makes a good or a bad house. And in general, the work never makes the workman like itself, but the workman makes the work like himself. So it is with the works of man. As the man is, whether believer or unbeliever, so also is his work—good if it was done in faith, wicked if it was done in unbelief. But the converse is not true, that the work makes the man either a believer or an unbeliever. As works do not make a man a believer, so also they do not make him righteous. But as faith makes a man a believer and righteous, so faith does good works. Since, then, works justify no one, and a man must be righteous before he does a good work, it is very evident that it is faith alone which, because of the pure mercy of God through Christ and in his Word, worthily and sufficiently justifies and saves the person. A Christian has no need of any work or law in order to be saved since through faith he is free from every law and does everything out of pure liberty and freely. He seeks neither benefit nor salvation since he already abounds in all things and is saved through the grace of God because in his faith he now seeks only to please God.

So a Christian, like Christ his head, is filled and made rich by faith and should be content with this form of God which he has obtained by faith; only, as I have said, he should increase this faith until it is made perfect. For this faith is his life, his righteousness, and his salvation: it saves him and makes him acceptable, and bestows upon him all things that are Christ's, as has been said above, and as Paul asserts in Gal.2[:20] when he says, "And the life I now live in the flesh I live by faith in the Son of God." Although the Christian is thus free from all works, he ought in this liberty to empty himself, take upon himself the form of a servant, be made in the likeness of men, be found in human form, and to serve, help, and in every way deal with his neighbor as he sees that God through Christ has dealt and still deals with him. This he should do freely, having regard for nothing but divine approval.

He ought to think: "Although I am an unworthy and condemned man, my God has given me in Christ all the riches of righteousness and salvation without any merit on my part, out of pure, free mercy, so that from now on I need nothing except faith which believes that this is true. Why should I not therefore freely, joyfully, with all my heart, and with an eager will do all things which I know are pleasing and acceptable to such a Father who has overwhelmed me with his inestimable riches? I will therefore give myself as a Christ to my neighbor, just as Christ offered himself to me; I will do nothing in this life except what I see is necessary, profitable, and salutary to my neighbor, since through faith I have an abundance of all good things in Christ."

Behold, from faith thus flow forth love and joy in the Lord, and from love a joyful, willing, and free mind that serves one's neighbor willingly and takes no account of gratitude or ingratitude, of praise or blame, of gain or loss. For a man does not serve that he may put men under obligations. He does not distinguish between friends and enemies or anticipate their thankfulness or unthankfulness, but he most freely and most willingly spends himself and all that he has, whether he wastes all on the thankless or whether he gains a reward. As his Father does, distributing all things to all men richly and freely, making "his sun rise on the evil and on the good" [Matt. 5:45], so also the son does all things and suffers all things with that freely bestowing joy which is his delight when through Christ he sees it in God, the dispenser of such great benefits.

Therefore, if we recognize the great and precious things which are given us, as Paul says [Rom. 5:5], our hearts will be filled by the Holy Spirit with the love which makes us free, joyful, almighty workers and conquerors over all tribulations, servants of our neighbors, and yet lords of all. For those who do not recognize the gifts bestowed upon them through Christ, however, Christ has been born in vain; they go their way with their works and shall never come to taste or feel those things. Just as our neighbor is in need and lacks that in which we abound, so we were in need before God and lacked his mercy. Hence, as our

heavenly Father has in Christ freely come to our aid, we also ought freely to help our neighbor through our body and its works, each one should become as it were a Christ to the other that we may be Christs to one another and Christ may be same in all, that is, that we may be truly Christians.

OF MARRIAGE AND CELIBACY

DCCXV

A preacher of the gospel, being regularly called, ought, above all things, first, to purify himself before he teaches others. Is he able, with a good conscience, to remain unmarried? let him so remain; but if he cannot abstain living chastely, then let him take a wife; God has made that plaster for that sore.

DCCXVI

It is written in the first book of Moses, concerning matrimony: God created a man and a woman and blessed them. Now, although this sentence was chiefly spoken of human creatures, yet we may apply it to all the creatures of the world—to the fowls of the air, the fish in the waters, and the beasts of the field, wherein we find a male and a female consorting together, engendering and increasing. In all these, God has placed before our eyes the state of matrimony. We have its image, also, even in the trees and earth.

DCCXVII

Between husband and wife there should be no question as to *meum* and *tuum*. All things should be in common between them, without any distinction or means of distinguishing.

DCCXVIII

St. Augustine said, finely: A marriage without children is the world without the sun.

DCCXIX

Maternity is a glorious thing, since all mankind have been conceived, born, and nourished of women. All human laws should encourage the multiplication of families.

DCCXX

The world regards not, nor comprehends the works of God. Who can sufficiently admire the state of conjugal union, which God has instituted and founded, and whence all human creatures, yea, all states proceed. Where were we, if it existed not? But neither God's ordinance, nor the gracious presence of children, the fruit of matrimony, moves the ungodly world, which beholds only the temporal difficulties and troubles of matrimony, but sees not the great treasure that is hid therein. We were all born of women—emperors, kings, princes, yea, Christ himself, the Son of God, did not disdain to be born of a virgin. Let the contemners and rejecters of matrimony go hang, the Anabaptists and Adamites, who recognise not marriage, but live all together like animals, and the papists, who reject married life, and yet have strumpets; if they must needs contemn matrimony, let them be consistent and keep no concubines.

DCCXXI

The state of matrimony is the chief in the world after religion; but people shun it because of its inconveniences, like one who, running out of the rain, falls into the river. We ought herein to have more regard to God's command and ordinance, for the sake of the generation, and the bringing up of children, than to our untoward humours and cogitations; and further, we should consider that it is a physic against sin and unchastity. None, indeed, should be compelled to marry; the matter should be left to each man's conscience, for bride-love may not be forced.

God has said, "It is not good that the man should be alone;" and St. Paul compares the church to a spouse, or bride and a bridegroom. But let us ever take heed that, in marrying, we esteem neither money nor wealth, great descent, nobility, nor lasciviousness.

DCCXXII

The Lord has never changed the rules he imposed on marriage, but in the case of the conception of his Son Jesus Christ. The Turks, however, are of opinion that 'tis no uncommon thing for a virgin to bear a child. I would by no means introduce this belief into my family.

DCCXXV

Men have broad and large chests, and small narrow hips, and more understanding than the women, who have but small and narrow breasts, and broad hips, to the end they should remain at home, sit still, keep house, and bear and bring up children.

DCCXXVI

Marrying cannot be without women, nor can the world subsist without them. To marry is physic against incontinence. A woman is, or at least should be, a friendly, courteous, and merry companion in life, whence they are named, by the Holy Ghost, house-honours, the honour and ornament of the house, and inclined to tenderness, for thereunto are they chiefly created, to bear children, and be the pleasure, joy, and solace of their husbands.

DCCXVII

Dr. Luther said one day to his wife: You make me do what you will; you have full sovereignty here, and I award you, with all my heart, the command in all household matters, reserving my rights in other points. Never any good came out of female domination. God created Adam master and lord of living creatures, but Eve spoilt all, when she persuaded him to set himself above God's will. 'Tis you women, with your tricks and artifices, that lead men into error.

QUESTIONS

1. What role does faith play in Luther's thought?

2. How important is the Word of God? What is it, according to Luther?

3. Luther believes that faith offers more hope for salvation than good works. Why is this?

4. *Of Marriage and Celibacy* is composed of words spoken by Luther taken down by his followers. How does this make it different from *The Freedom of a Christian?*

5. Why does Luther think clergy should be allowed to marry?

6. Why is matrimony important?

7. What is Luther's view of women? What does he see as their role in marriage, and how does he think they should be treated?

8. Luther spent most of his early adulthood as a celibate monk. How do you think this might have affected his views of marriage?

65

■ *John Calvin* ■

INSTITUTES OF THE CHRISTIAN RELIGION CATECHISM
(1534) (CA. 1540)

John Calvin (1509–1564) was the seminal thinker among the post-Luther generation of religious reformers. French by birth and a lawyer by training, Calvin found himself the leader of the Reformation in the Swiss city of Geneva. There he helped establish a new form of church government that depended not upon a hierarchy of priests and bishops as in the Catholic

Church but instead gave power to individual congregations of believers. Calvin's principal theological contribution was to emphasize the doctrine of predestination as the foundation of individual salvation.

Institutes of the Christian Religion was first written for the purpose of gaining acceptance for Protestantism in France. Through successive editions, Calvin expanded and refined his theology.

Calvin's *Catechism,* first published in about 1540, was designed as a simple statement of the Church's doctrine. Before formal admission to the congregation, children memorized the answers to the minister's questions and proved that they understood the essentials of Calvinist theology. The question and answer format, a Protestant version of the Socratic method, was thought to be the most effective way to teach children complex ideas. The selections reproduced here focus on the nature of the Church and on salvation.

INSTITUTES OF THE CHRISTIAN RELIGION

Knowledge of God Involves Trust and Reverence

What is God? Men who pose this question are merely toying with idle speculation. It is far better for us to inquire, "What is his nature?" and to know what is consistent with his nature. What good is it to profess with Epicurus some sort of God who has cast aside the care of the world only to amuse himself in idleness? What help is it, in short, to know a God with whom we have nothing to do? Rather, our knowledge should serve first to teach us fear and reverence; secondly, with it as our guide and teacher, we should learn to seek every good from him, and having received it, to credit it to his account. For how can the thought of God penetrate your mind without your realizing immediately that, since you are his handiwork, you have been made over and bound to his command by right of creation, that you owe your life to him?—that whatever you undertake, whatever you do, ought to be ascribed to him? If this be so, it now assuredly follows that your life is wickedly corrupt unless it be disposed to his service, seeing that his will ought for us to be the law by which we live. Again, you cannot behold him clearly

unless you acknowledge him to be the fountainhead and source of every good. From this too would arise the desire to cleave to him and trust in him, but for the fact that man's depravity seduces his mind from rightly seeking him.

Because it acknowledges him as Lord and Father, the pious mind also deems it meet and right to observe his authority in all things, reverence his majesty, take care to advance his glory, and obey his commandments. Because it sees him to be a righteous judge, armed with severity to punish wickedness, it ever holds his judgment seat before its gaze, and through fear of him restrains itself from provoking his anger. And yet it is not so terrified by the awareness of his judgment as to wish to withdraw, even if some way of escape were open. But it embraces him no less as punisher of the wicked than as benefactor of the pious. For the pious mind realizes that the punishment of the impious and wicked and the reward of life eternal for the righteous equally pertain to God's glory. Besides, this mind restrains itself from sinning, not out of dread of punishment alone; but, because it loves and reveres God as Father, it worships and adores him as Lord. Even if there were no hell, it would still shudder at offending him alone.

Here indeed is pure and real religion; faith so joined with an earnest fear of God that this fear also embraces willing reverence, and carries with it such legitimate worship as is prescribed in the law. And we ought to note this fact even more diligently: all men have a vague general veneration for God, but very few really reverence him; and wherever there is great ostentation in ceremonies, sincerity of heart is rare indeed. ·

Superstition

Experience teaches that the seed of religion has been divinely planted in all men. But barely one man in a hundred can be found who nourishes in his own heart what he has conceived; and not even one in whom it matures, much less bears fruit in its season (cf. Ps. 1:3). Now some lose themselves in their own superstition, while others of their own evil intention revolt from God, yet all fall away from true knowledge of him. As a result, no real piety remains in the world. But as to my statement that some erroneously slip into superstition, I do not mean by this that their ingenuousness should free them from blame. For the blindness under which they labor is almost always mixed with proud vanity and obstinacy. Indeed, vanity joined with pride can be detected in the fact that, in seeking God, miserable men do not rise above themselves as they should, but measure him by the yardstick of their own carnal stupidity, and neglect sound investigation; thus out of curiosity they fly off into empty speculations. They do not therefore apprehend God as he offers himself, but imagine him as they have fashioned him in their own presumption. When this gulf opens, in whatever direction they move their feet, they cannot but plunge headlong into ruin. Indeed, whatever they afterward attempt by way of worship or service of God, they cannot bring as tribute to him, for they are worshiping not God but a figment and a dream of their own heart. Paul eloquently notes this wickedness: "Striving to be wise, they make fools of themselves" (Rom. 1:22f.). He had said before that "they became futile in their thinking" (Rom. 1:21). In order, however, that no one might excuse their guilt, he adds that they

are justly blinded. For not content with sobriety but claiming for themselves more than is right, they wantonly bring darkness upon themselves— in fact, they become fools in their empty and perverse haughtiness. From this it follows that their stupidity is not excusable, since it is caused not only by vain curiosity but by an inordinate desire to know more than is fitting, joined with a false confidence.

The Divine Wisdom Displayed for All to See

There are innumerable evidences both in heaven and on earth that declare his wonderful wisdom; not only those more recondite matters for the closer observation of which astronomy, medicine, and all natural science are intended, but also those which thrust themselves upon the sight of even the most untutored and ignorant persons, so that they cannot open their eyes without being compelled to witness them. Indeed, men who have either quaffed or even tasted the liberal arts penetrate with their aid far more deeply into the secrets of the divine wisdom. Yet ignorance of them prevents no one from seeing more than enough of God's workmanship in his creation to lead him to break forth in admiration of the Artificer. To be sure, there is need of art and of more exacting toil in order to investigate the motion of the stars, to determine their assigned stations, to measure their intervals, to note their properties. As God's providence shows itself more explicitly when one observes these, so the mind must rise to a somewhat higher level to look upon his glory. Even the common folk and the most untutored, who have been taught only by the aid of the eyes, cannot be unaware of the excellence of divine art, for it reveals itself in this innumerable and yet distinct and well-ordered variety of the heavenly host. It is, accordingly, clear that there is no one to whom the Lord does not abundantly show his wisdom. Likewise, in regard to the structure of the human body one must have the greatest keenness in order to weigh, with Galen's skill, its articulation, symmetry, beauty, and use. But yet, as all acknowledge, the human body shows itself to be a composition so ingenious that its Artificer is rightly judged a wonder-worker.

Man as the Loftiest Proof of Divine Wisdom

Certain philosophers, accordingly, long ago not ineptly called a man a microcosm because he is a rare example of God's power, goodness, and wisdom, and contains within himself enough miracles to occupy our minds, if only we are not irked at paying attention to them. Paul, having stated that the blind can find God by feeling after him, immediately adds that he ought not to be sought afar off (Acts 17:27). For each one undoubtedly feels within the heavenly grace that quickens him. Indeed, if there is no need to go outside ourselves to comprehend God, what pardon will the indolence of that man deserve who is loath to descend within himself to find God? For the same reason, David, when he has briefly praised the admirable name and glory of God, which shine everywhere, immediately exclaims: "What is man that thou art mindful of him?" (Ps. 8:4). Likewise, "Out of the mouths of babes and sucklings thou hast established strength" (Ps. 8:2). Indeed, he not only declares that a clear mirror of God's works is in humankind, but that infants, while they nurse at their mother's breasts, have tongues so eloquent to preach his glory that there is no need at all of other orators. Consequently, also, he does not hesitate to bring their infant speech into the debate, as if they were thoroughly instructed, to refute the madness of those who might desire to extinguish God's name in favor of their own devilish pride. Consequently, too, there comes in that which Paul quotes from Aratus, that we are God's offspring (Acts 17:28), because by adorning us with such great excellence he testifies that he is our Father. In the same way the secular poets, out of a common feeling and, as it were, at the dictation of experience, called him "the Father of men." Indeed, no one gives himself freely and willingly to God's service unless, having tasted his fatherly love, he is drawn to love and worship him in return.

God Bestows the Actual Knowledge of Himself upon Us Only in the Scriptures

That brightness which is borne in upon the eyes of all men both in heaven and on earth is more than enough to withdraw all support from men's ingratitude—just as God, to involve the human race in the same guilt, sets forth to all without exception his presence portrayed in his creatures. Despite this, it is needful that another and better help be added to direct us aright to the very Creator of the universe. It was not in vain, then, that he added the light of his Word by which to become known unto salvation; and he regarded as worthy of this privilege those whom he pleased to gather more closely and intimately to himself. For because he saw the minds of all men tossed and agitated, after he chose the Jews as his very own flock, he fenced them about that they might not sink into oblivion as others had. With good reason he holds us by the same means in the pure knowledge of himself, since otherwise even those who seem to stand firm before all others would soon melt away. Just as old or bleary-eyed men and those with weak vision, if you thrust before them a most beautiful volume, even if they recognize it to be some sort of writing, yet can scarcely construe two words, but with the aid of spectacles will begin to read distinctly; so Scripture, gathering up the otherwise confused knowledge of God in our minds, having dispersed our dullness, clearly shows us the true God.

The Word of God as Holy Scripture

But whether God became known to the patriarchs through oracles and visions or by the work and ministry of men, he put into their minds what they should then hand down to their posterity. At any rate, there is no doubt that firm certainty of doctrine was engraved in their hearts, so that they were convinced and understood that what they had learned proceeded from God. For by his Word, God rendered faith unambiguous forever, a faith that should be superior to all opinion. Finally, in order that truth might abide forever in the world with a continuing succession of teaching and survive through all ages, the same oracles he had given to the patriarchs it was his pleasure to have recorded, as it were, on public tablets. With this intent the law was published, and the prophets afterward added as its interpreters. For even though the use of the law was manifold, as will be seen more clearly in its place, it was especially committed to Moses and all the prophets to teach the way of reconciliation between God and men, whence also Paul calls "Christ the end of the law" (Rom. 10:4). Yet I repeat once more: besides the specific doctrine of faith and repentance that sets forth Christ as Mediator, Scripture adorns with unmistakable marks and tokens the one true God, in that he has created and governs the universe, in order that he may not be mixed up with the throng of false gods. Therefore, however fitting it may be for man seriously to turn his eyes to contemplate God's works, since he has been placed in this most glorious theater to be a spectator of them, it is fitting that he prick up his ears to the Word, the better to profit. And it is therefore no wonder that those who were born in darkness become more and more hardened in their insensibility; for there are very few who, to contain themselves within bounds, apply themselves teachably to God's Word, but they rather exult in their own vanity. Now, in order that true religion may shine upon us, we ought to hold that it must take its beginning from heavenly doctrine and that no one can get even the slightest taste of right and sound doctrine unless he be a pupil of Scripture. Hence, there also emerges the beginning of true understanding when we reverently embrace what it pleases God there to witness of himself. But not only faith, perfect and in every way complete, but all right knowledge of God is born of obedience. And surely in this respect God has, by his singular providence, taken thought for mortals through all ages.

Faith Rests upon God's Word

This, then, is the true knowledge of Christ, if we receive him as he is offered by the Father: namely, clothed with his gospel. For just as he has been appointed as the goal of our faith, so we cannot take the right road to him unless the gospel goes before us. And there, surely, the treasures of grace are opened to us; for if they had been closed, Christ would have benefited us little. Thus Paul yokes faith to teaching, as an inseparable companion, with these words: "You did not so learn Christ if indeed you were taught what is the truth in Christ" (Eph. 4:20–21 p.).

Yet I do not so restrict faith to the gospel without confessing that what sufficed for building it up had been handed down by Moses and the prophets. But because a fuller manifestation of Christ has been revealed in the gospel, Paul justly calls it the "doctrine of faith" (cf. I Tim. 4:6). For this reason, he says in another passage that by the coming of faith the law was abolished (Rom. 10:4; cf. Gal. 3:25). He understands by this term the new and extraordinary kind of teaching by which Christ, after he became our teacher, has more clearly set forth the mercy of the Father, and has more surely testified to our salvation.

Yet it will be an easier and more suitable method if we descend by degrees from general to particular. First, we must be reminded that there is a permanent relationship between faith and the Word. He could not separate one from the other any more than we could separate the rays from the sun from which they come. For this reason, God exclaims in The Book of Isaiah: "Hear me and your soul shall live" (ch 55:3). And John shows this same wellspring of faith in these words: "These things have been written that you may believe" (John 20:31). The prophet, also, desiring to exhort the people to faith, says: "Today if you will hear his voice" (Ps. 95:7; 94:8, Vg.). "To hear" is generally understood as meaning to believe. In short, it is not without reason that in The Book of Isaiah, God distinguishes the children of the church from outsiders by this mark: he will teach all his children (Isa. 54:13; John 6:45) that they may learn of him (cf. John 6:45). For if benefits were indiscriminately given, why would he have directed his Word to a few? To this corresponds the fact that the Evangelists commonly use the words "believers" and "disciples" as synonyms. This is especially Luke's usage in The Acts of the Apostles: indeed he extends this title even to a woman in Acts 9:36.

Therefore if faith turns away even in the slightest degree from this goal toward which it should aim, it does not keep its own nature, but becomes uncertain credulity and vague error of mind. The same Word is the basis whereby faith is supported and sustained; if it turns away from the Word, it falls. Therefore, take away the Word and no faith will then remain.

We are not here discussing whether a human ministry is necessary for the sowing of God's Word, from which faith may be conceived. This we shall discuss in another place. But we say that the Word itself, however it be imparted to us, is like a mirror in which faith may contemplate God. Whether, therefore, God makes use of man's help in this or works by his own power alone, he always represents himself through his Word to those whom he wills to draw to himself. And for this reason, Paul defines faith as that obedience which is given to the gospel (Rom. 1:5), and elsewhere praises allegiance to faith in Philippians (Phil. 1:3–5; cf. I Thess. 2:13). In understanding faith it is not merely a question of knowing that God exists, but also—and this especially—of knowing what is his will toward us. For it is not so much our concern to know who he is in himself, as what he wills to be toward us.

Now, therefore, we hold faith to be a knowledge of God's will toward us, perceived from his Word. But the foundation of this is a preconceived conviction of God's truth. As for its certainty, so long as your mind is at war with itself, the Word will be of doubtful and weak authority, or rather of none. And it is not even enough to believe that God is trustworthy (cf. Rom. 3:3), who can neither deceive nor lie (cf. Titus 1:2), unless you hold to be beyond doubt that whatever proceeds from him is sacred and inviolable truth.

CATECHISM

M[INISTER].   What is the Church?

C[HILD].   The body and society of believers, whom God has predestinated unto eternal life.

M.   Is this article necessary to be believed?

C.   Yes, truly, unless we would render the death of Christ without effect, and account all that we have said, for nothing. For this is the sole purpose of all, that there should be a Church. . . .

M.   But why do you call the Church Holy?

C.   Because those whom God elects, he justifies, and purifies in holiness and innocence of life, to make his glory shine forth in them. And this is what Paul means, when he says, that Christ sanctified the Church, which he redeemed, that it might be glorious and pure from every spot.

M.   What do you mean by the epithet Catholick or universal?

C.   By that we are taught, that as there is one head of all believers, so it becomes all to be united in one body, that there may be one Church and no more, spread throughout all the world.

M.   What is the meaning of what is next added, *the communion of saints*?

C.   This is laid down, to express more clearly the unity which is among the members of the Church. At the same time, it intimates, that whatever benefits God bestows on the Church, respect the common good of all, as all have a communion among themselves.

M.   But is this holiness, which you attribute to the Church, already perfect?

C. Not yet, not so long, indeed, as it is militant in this world. For it will always labour under infirmities; nor will it ever be entirely purified from the remains of corruption, until it shall be completely united to Christ its head, by whom it is sanctified.

M. Can this Church be otherwise known, than as it is discerned by Faith?

C. There is indeed a visible Church of God, which he has designated to us by certain signs and tokens; but we now treat expressly of the congregation of those, whom he has elected to salvation. But this is neither known by signs, nor at any time discerned by the eyes.

M. What article follows next?

C. *I believe the forgiveness of sins.*

M. What does the word forgiveness signify?

C. That God, by his gratuitous goodness, will pardon and remit the sins of believers, so that they shall neither come into judgment, nor have punishment exacted of them.

M. Hence it follows, that we can by no means merit, by personal satisfactions, that pardon of sins, which we obtain from the Lord.

C. It is true. For Christ alone, by suffering the penalty, has finished the satisfaction. As to ourselves, we have nothing at all, which we can offer to God as a compensation; but we receive the benefit of pardon from his pure goodness and liberality.

M. Why do you connect forgiveness of sins with the Church?

C. Because no one obtains it, only as he is first united to the people of God, and perseveringly cherishes this union with the body of Christ even to the end; and in that manner gives evidence, that he is a true member of the Church.

M. By this rule you determine, that there is no condemnation or destruction, except to those who are without the Church?

C. It is so. For from those who make a separation from the body of Christ, and by factions destroy its unity, all hope of salvation is cut off, in so far as they continue in this separation.

M. Recite the last article.

C. *I believe the resurrection of the body, and the life everlasting.*

M. For what purpose is this article of Faith put in the Confession?

C. To admonish us that our happiness is not to be placed in this world. The knowledge of this has a twofold advantage and use. By it we are taught, first, that this world is to be passed through by us, merely as strangers—that we may think continually of our departure, and not suffer our hearts to be entangled with earthly anxieties. And secondly, that we should not, in the mean time, despair in our minds, but patiently wait for those things which are as yet hidden and concealed from our eyes, being the fruits of grace, laid up for us in Christ, until the day of revelation.

M. What will be the order of this resurrection?

C. Those who were before dead will receive the same bodies in which they dwelt on earth; but endowed with a new quality, that is, to be no more obnoxious to death and corruption. But those who shall be living at that day, God will marvellously raise up with a sudden change.

M. But will it be common at once to the just and the unjust?

C. There will be one resurrection of all; but the condition will be different: Some will be raised to salvation and glory; others to condemnation, and final misery . . . . .

M. Since we hold the foundation on which Faith depends, it will be easy to infer from thence the definition of true Faith.

C. It is so, and thus we may define it— Faith is the certain and stable knowledge of the paternal benevolence of God towards us, according to his testimony in the Gospel; that he will be to us, for the sake of Christ, a Father and a Saviour.

M. Do we obtain that of ourselves, or do we receive it from God?

C. The scriptures teach us, that it is the special gift of God, and experience confirms the testimony.

M.   Inform me what experience.

C.   Truly, our understandings are too weak to comprehend that spiritual knowledge of God, which is revealed to us by Faith; and our hearts have too strong a propensity to distrust God, and to put a perverse confidence in ourselves or the creatures, for us to submit to him of our own mere motion. But the Holy Spirit makes us capable, by his own illumination, of understanding those things, which would otherwise very far exceed our capacity, and forms in us a sure persuasion, by sealing in our hearts the promises of salvation.

M.   What benefit arises to us from this Faith, when we have once obtained it?

C.   It justifies us before God, and by this justification makes us heirs of eternal life.

M.   What? Are not men justified by good works, when by living an innocent and holy life, they study to approve themselves to God?

C.   If anyone could be found thus perfect, he might well be called just; but since we are all sinners, in many ways guilty before God, that worthiness which may reconcile us to him must be sought by us in some other way.

M.   But are all the works of men so polluted, and of no value, that they deserve no favour with God?

C.   In the first place, all those things which proceed from us, as they are properly called ours, are polluted, and therefore avail nothing, but to displease God, and be rejected by him.

M.   You say then, that before we are born again, and created anew by the Spirit of God, we can do nothing but sin; as a corrupt tree brings forth only corrupt fruit.

C.   It is wholly so; for whatever appearance our works may have in the eyes of men, they are altogether evil, as long as the heart is corrupt; at which God especially looks.

M.   Hence you infer, that we cannot, by any merits of our own, come before God and challenge his favour: but rather, in all our undertakings and pursuits, we expose ourselves to his wrath and condemnation.

C.   So I think. Therefore it is of his mere mercy, and not from any respect to our works, that he freely embraces us in Christ, and holds us accepted, by accounting that righteousness of his, which is accepted by us, as our own; and not imputing our sins unto us.

M.   In what manner then do you say that we are justified by Faith?

C.   When by a sure confidence of heart, we embrace the promises of the gospel, then we obtain possession of this righteousness. . . .

M.   Must we then conclude, that the good works of believers are useless?

C.   No, for God has promised a reward to them, both in this world and in the life to come. But this reward proceeds from the gratuitous love of God as from a fountain; as he first embraces us as sons; and then by blotting out the remembrance of our sins, he follows with his favour those things which we do.

M.   But can that righteousness be separated from good works; so that he who has that may be destitute of these?

C.   This cannot be done. For to believe in Christ is to receive him as he offers himself to us. Now he not only promises to us deliverance from death, and reconciliation with God, but at the same time also, the grace of the Holy Spirit, by which we are regenerated in newness of life. It is necessary that these things be united together, unless we would divide Christ from himself.

M.   It follows from this, that Faith is the root, from which all good works originate; and cannot, by any means, make us slothful about them.

C.   It is true: And therefore the whole doctrine of the gospel is contained in these two points, *Faith and Repentance*.

M.   What is Repentance?

C.   It is a hatred of sin and a love of righteousness, proceeding from the fear of God; leading us to a denial and mortification of the flesh, so that we may give up ourselves to be governed by the Holy Spirit, and perform all the actions of our lives in obedience to the will of God. . . .

QUESTIONS

1. As shown in the first reading, what seems to be Calvin's view of human nature? How does he believe God reveals himself?

2. Historians have often noted the importance of Scripture in Protestant thought. What is Calvin's view? What do you think the practical effect of this might have been for society?

3. How does Calvin's background as a lawyer and literate member of the professional class affect his work?

4. According to the *Catechism,* what is the Church? How does one become a member of it?

5. Why, according to the *Catechism,* are good works insufficient to assure salvation? What does salvation depend upon in this view?

6. Why do you think Calvin believed the *Catechism* was necessary? What purposes might such a book serve?

7. How effective a method of teaching religious doctrine do you think the *Catechism* was? What does the use of this particular form tell us about how people learned and taught in early modern Europe?

8. Both Calvin and Luther are Protestants, but they have very different theological views. Can you detect some of these differences in their writings?

66

■ *Ignatius Loyola* ■

SPIRITUAL EXERCISES
(1548)

Ignatius of Loyola (1491–1556), the founder of the best-known Catholic religious order of the Counter-reformation, the Society of Jesus (or the Jesuits), was born in the Basque region of northern Spain. We know little of his youth, though he served in several courts as a page, and at twenty-five, was a soldier in the service of the small kingdom of Navarre. While fighting the French at the siege of Pamplona in 1521, Loyola was badly wounded, forcing an end to his military career. He went home to recuperate, and it was during this period that he received what he believed was divine inspiration. From 1522, he devoted himself to the Church, first by performing an ambitious pilgrimage to the Holy Land, and later by offering his services to the papacy.

Loyola believed strongly in the benefits of education, and he made higher education an essential prerequisite for membership in the Society of Jesus, the order he founded with the permission of Pope Paul III in 1540. Jesuits, directed by Loyola, fanned out across the globe, advancing the cause of Catholicism. By the time he died in 1556, the Society had 1,000 members and was known as the most formidable of all the missionary orders. Ignatius Loyola was canonized by the Roman Catholic Church in 1662.

Loyola's *Spiritual Exercises,* a selection of which is reproduced here, is still used as a religious guide today. The *Exercises* were meant to encourage Christians to lead an active life in the pursuit of salvation, to avoid sin and encourage godliness.

RULES FOR PERCEIVING AND KNOWING IN SOME MANNER

The Different Movements Which Are Caused in the Soul

THE GOOD, TO RECEIVE THEM, AND THE BAD TO REJECT THEM

First Rule. The first Rule: In the persons who go from mortal sin to mortal sin, the enemy is commonly used to propose to them apparent pleasures, making them imagine sensual delights and pleasures in order to hold them more and make them grow in their vices and sins. In these persons the good spirit uses the opposite method, pricking them and biting their consciences through the process of reason.

Second Rule. The second: In the persons who are going on intensely cleansing their sins and rising from good to better in the service of God our Lord, it is the method contrary to that in the first Rule, for then it is the way of the evil spirit to bite, sadden and put obstacles, disquieting with false reasons, that one may not go on; and it is proper to the good to give courage and strength, consolations, tears, inspirations and quiet, easing, and putting away all obstacles, that one may go on in well doing.

Third Rule. The third: OF SPIRITUAL CONSOLATION. I call it consolation when some interior movement in the soul is caused, through which the soul comes to be inflamed with love of its Creator and Lord; and when it can in consequence love no created thing on the face for the earth in itself, but in the Creator of them all.

Likewise, when it shed tears that move to love of its Lord, whether out of sorrow of one's sins, or for the Passion of Christ our Lord, or because of other things directly connected with His service and praise.

Finally, I call consolation every increase of hope, faith and charity, and all interior joy which calls and attract to heavenly things and to the salvation of one's soul, quieting it and giving it peace in its Creator and Lord.

Fourth Rule. The fourth: OF SPIRITUAL DESOLATION. I call desolation all the contrary of the third rule, such as darkness of soul, disturbance in it, movement to things low and earthly, the unquiet of different agitations and temptations, moving to want of confidence, without hope, without love, when one finds oneself all lazy, tepid, sad, and as if separated from his Creator and Lord. Because, as consolation is contrary to desolation, in the same way the thoughts which come from consolation are contrary to the thoughts which come from desolation.

Ninth Rule. The ninth: There are three principal reasons why we find ourselves desolate.

The first is, because of our being tepid, lazy, or negligent in our spiritual exercises; and so through our faults, spiritual consolation withdraws from us.

The second, to try us and see how much we are and how much we let ourselves out in His service and praise without such great pay of consolation and great graces.

The third, to give us true acquaintance and knowledge, that we may interiorly feel that it is not ours to get or keep great devotion, intense love, tears, or any other spiritual consolation, but that all is the gift and grace of God our Lord, and that we may not build a nest in a thing not ours, raising our intellect into some pride or vainglory, attributing to us devotion or the other things of the spiritual consolation.

Twelfth Rule. The twelfth: The enemy acts like a woman, in being weak against vigor and strong of will. Because, as it is the way of the woman when she is quarrelling with some man to lose heart, taking flight when the man shows her much courage: and on the contrary, if the man, losing heart, begins to fly, the wrath, revenge, and ferocity of the woman is very great, and so without bounds; in the same manner, it is the way of the enemy to weaken and lose heart, his temptations taking flight, when the person who is exercising himself in spiritual things opposes a bold front against the temptations of the enemy, doing diametrically the opposite. And on the contrary, if the person who is exercising himself commences to have fear and lose heart in suffering the temptations, there is no beast so wild on the face of the earth as the enemy of human nature in following out his damnable intentions with so great malice.

Thirteenth Rule. The thirteenth: Likewise, he acts as a licentious lover in wanting to be secret and not revealed. For, as the licentious man who, speaking for an evil purpose, solicits a daughter of a good father or a wife of a good husband, wants his words and persuasions to be a secret, and the contrary displeases him much, when the daughter reveals to her father or the wife to her husband his licentious words and depraved intention, because he easily gathers that he will not be able to succeed with the undertaking begun: in the same way, when the enemy of human nature brings his wiles and persuasion to the just soul, he wants and desires that they be received and kept in secret; but when one reveals them to his good Confessor or to another spiritual person that knows his deceits and evil ends, it is very grievous to him, because he gathers, from his manifest deceits being discovered that he will not be able to succeed with his wickedness begun.

Fourteenth Rule. The fourteenth: Likewise, he behaves as a chief bent on conquering and robbing what he desires: for, as a captain and chief of the army, pitching his camp, and looking at the forces or defenses of a stronghold, attacks it on the weakest side, in like manner the enemy of human nature, roaming about, looks in turn at all our virtues, theological, cardinal, and moral; and where he finds us weakest and most in need for our eternal salvation, there he attacks us and aims at taking us.

To Have The True Sentiment

WHICH WE OUGHT TO HAVE IN THE CHURCH MILITANT

Let the following Rules be observed.

First Rule. The first: All judgment laid aside, we ought to have our mind ready and prompt to obey, in all, the true Spouse of Christ our Lord, which is our holy Mother the Church Hierarchical.

Second Rule. The second: to praise confession to a Priest, and the reception of the most Holy Sacrament of the Altar once in the year, and much more each month, and much better from week to week, with the conditions required and due.

Third Rule. The third: To praise the hearing of Mass often, likewise hymns, psalms, and long prayers, in the church and out of it; likewise the hours set at the time fixed for each Divine Office and for all prayer and all Canonical Hours.

Fourth Rule. The Fourth: To praise much Religious Orders, virginity and continence, and not so much marriage as any of these.

Fifth Rule. The fifth: To praise vows of Religion, of obedience, of poverty, of chastity and of other perfections of supererogation. And it is to be noted that as the vow is about the things which approach to Evangelical perfection, a vow ought not to be made in the things which withdraw from it, such as to be a merchant, or to be married, etc.

Sixth Rule. To praise relics of the Saints, giving veneration to them and praying to the Saints; and to praise Stations, pilgrimages, Indulgences, pardons, Cruzadas, and candles lighted in the churches.

Seventh Rule. To praise Constitutions about fasts and abstinence, as of Lent, Ember Days, Vigils, Friday and Saturday; likewise penances, not only interior, but also exterior.

Eighth Rule. To praise the ornaments and the buildings of churches; likewise images, and to venerate them according to what they represent.

Ninth Rule. Finally, to praise all precepts of the Church, keeping the mind prompt to find reasons in their defense and in no manner against them.

Tenth Rule. We ought to be more prompt to find good and praise as well the Constitutions and recommendations as the ways of our Superiors. Because, although some are not or have not been such, to speak against them, whether preaching in public or discoursing before the common people, would rather give rise to fault-finding and scandal than profit; and so the people would be incensed against their Superiors, whether temporal or spiritual. So that,

as it does harm to speak evil to the common people of Superiors in their absence, so it can make profit to speak of the evil ways to the persons themselves who can remedy them.

Eleventh Rule. To praise positive and scholastic learning. Because, as it is more proper to the Positive Doctors, as St. Jerome, St. Augustine and St. Gregory, etc., to move the heart to love and serve God our Lord in everything; so it is more proper to the Scholastics, as St. Thomas, St. Bonaventure, and to the Master of the Sentences, etc., to define or explain for our times the things necessary for eternal salvation; and to combat and explain better all errors and all fallacies. For the Scholastic Doctors, as they are more modern, not only help themselves with the true understanding of the Sacred Scripture and of the Positive and holy Doctors, but also, they being enlightened and clarified by the Divine virtue, help themselves by the Councils, Canons and Constitutions of our holy Mother the Church.

Twelfth Rule. We ought to be on our guard in making comparison of those of us who are alive to the blessed passed away, because error is committed not a little in this; that is to say, in saying, this one knows more than St. Augustine; he is another, or greater than, St. Francis; he is another St. Paul in goodness, holiness, etc.

Thirteenth Rule. To be right in everything, we ought always to hold that the white which I see, is black, if the Hierarchical Church so decides it, believing that between Christ our Lord, the Bridegroom, and the Church, His Bride, there is the same Spirit which governs and directs us for the salvation of our souls. Because by the same Spirit and our Lord Who gave the ten Commandments, our holy Mother the Church is directed and governed.

Fourteenth Rule. Although there is much truth in the assertion that no one can save himself without being predestined and without having faith and grace; we must be very cautious in the manner of speaking and communicating with others about all these things

Fifteenth Rule. We ought not, by way of custom, to speak much of predestination; but if in some way and at some times one speaks, let him so speak that the common people may not come into any error, as sometimes happens, saying: Whether I have to be saved or condemned is already determined, and no other thing can now be, through my doing well or ill; and with this, growing lazy, they become negligent in the works which lead to the salvation and the spiritual profit of their souls.

Sixteenth Rule. In the same way, we must be on our guard that by talking much and with much insistence of faith, without any distinction and explanation, occasion be not given to the people to be lazy and slothful in works, whether before faith is formed in charity or after.

Seventeenth Rule. Likewise, we ought not to speak so much with insistence on grace that the poison of discarding liberty be engendered.

So that of faith and grace one can speak as much as is possible with the Divine help for the greater praise of His Divine Majesty, but not in such way, nor in such manners, especially in our so dangerous times, that works and free will receive any harm, or be held for nothing.

Eighteenth Rule. Although serving God our Lord much out of pure love is to be esteemed above all; we ought to praise much the fear of His Divine Majesty, because not only filial fear is a thing pious and most holy, but even servile fear—when the man reaches nothing else better or more useful—helps much to get out of mortal sin. And when he is out, he easily come to filial fear, which is all acceptable and grateful to God our Lord, as being at one with the Divine Love.

QUESTIONS

1. What is the difference between what Loyola describes as "spiritual consolation" and "spiritual desolation"?

2. The *Exercises* contain certain assumptions about the differences between the genders. What are they?

3. What is Loyola's attitude toward authority and hierarchy in the Church and society?

4. Loyola, who insisted upon a life of action on behalf of the "Church militant," is often contrasted to mystics such as St. Teresa of Avila. Do the *Exercises* support this generalization?

5. Loyola, and the order which he founded, was known for his firm belief in the importance of education. How is that reflected in the *Exercises?* How do you think that this emphasis might have been useful in the context of the Counter-reformation?

67

■ *Teresa of Ávila* ■

THE LIFE OF ST. TERESA
(1611)

One of the most remarkable women of her age, Teresa de Cepeda (1515–1582) was born at Ávila into a prosperous Spanish family. From childhood she was extremely pious and believed that she had been singled out for some special service to the Lord. Over the objections of her father, she entered a Carmelite convent at the age of twenty-one. There she undertook a rigorous spiritual regimen that ultimately broke her health. During this period she had visions that convinced her that her mission was to travel throughout Spain founding new monasteries and convents. Against the objections of leaders of her order, Teresa followed this spiritual guidance. A prolific author of devotional works, Teresa was widely revered during her lifetime and canonized as St. Teresa of Ávila in 1622.

In her autobiography, which was published after her death, St. Teresa describes her intensely personal and mystical relationship with God. Her writings had a profound impact on ordinary men and women who identified with the new spiritual rebirth of Spanish Catholicism.

I was one day in prayer, when I found myself in a moment, without knowing how, plunged apparently into hell. I understood that it was our Lord's will I should see the place which the devils kept in readiness for me, and which I had deserved by my sins. It was but a moment, but it seems to me impossible I should ever forget it even if I were to live many years.

The entrance seemed to be by a long and narrow pass, like a furnace, very low, dark, and close. The ground seemed to be saturated with water, mere mud, exceedingly foul, sending forth pestilential odours, and covered with loathsome vermin. At the end was a hollow place in the wall, like a closet, and in that I saw myself confined. All this was even pleasant to behold in comparison with what I felt there. There is no exaggeration in what I am saying.

But as to what I then felt, I do not know where to begin, if I were to describe it; it is utterly inexplicable. I felt a fire in my soul. I cannot see how it is possible to describe it. My bodily sufferings were unendurable. I have undergone most painful sufferings in this life, and, as the physicians say, the greatest that can be borne, such as the contraction of my sinews when I was paralysed, without speaking of others of different kinds, yea, even those of which I have also spoken, inflicted on me by Satan; yet all these were as nothing in comparison with what I felt then, especially when I saw that there would be no intermission, nor any end to them.

These sufferings were nothing in comparison with the anguish of my soul, a sense of oppression, of stifling, and of pain so keen, accompanied by so hopeless and cruel an infliction, that I know not how to speak of it. If I said that the soul is continually being torn from the body, it would be nothing, for that implies the destruction of life by the hands of another; but here it is the soul itself that is tearing itself in pieces. I cannot describe that inward fire or that despair, surpassing all torments and all pain. I did not see who it was that tormented me, but I felt myself on fire, and torn to pieces, as it seemed to me; and, I repeat it, this inward fire and despair are the greatest torments of all.

Left in that pestilential place, and utterly without the power to hope for comfort, I could neither sit nor lie down; there was no room. I was placed as it were in a hole in the wall; and those walls, terrible to look on of themselves, hemmed me in on every side. I could not breathe. There was no light, but all was thick darkness. I do not understand how it is; though there was no light, yet everything that can give pain by being seen was visible.

I know not how it was, but I understood distinctly that it was a great mercy that our Lord would have me see with mine own eyes the very place from which His compassion saved me. I have listened to people speaking of these things, and I have at other times dwelt on the various torments of hell, though not often, because my soul made no progress by the way of fear; and I have read of the divers tortures, and how the devils tear the flesh with red-hot pincers. But all is as nothing before this; it is a wholly different matter. In short, the one is a reality, the other a picture; and all burning here in this life is as nothing in comparison with the fire that is there.

Ever since that time, as I was saying, everything seems endurable in comparison with one instant of sufferings such as those I had then to bear in hell. I am filled with fear when I see that, after frequently reading books which describe in some manner the pains of hell, I was not afraid of them, nor made any account of them. Where was I? How could I possibly take any pleasure in those things which led me directly to so dreadful a place? Blessed for ever be Thou, O my God! and oh, how manifest is it that Thou didst love me much more than I did love Thee! How, often, O Lord, didst Thou save me from that fearful prison! and how I used to get back to it contrary to Thy will!

It was that vision that filled me with the very great distress which I feel at the sight of so many lost souls, especially of the Lutherans—for they were once members of the Church by baptism—and also gave me the most vehement desires for the salvation of souls; for certainly I believe that, to save even one from those overwhelming torments, I would most willingly endure many deaths. If here on earth we see one whom we specially love in great trouble or pain, our very nature seems to bid us compassionate him; and if those pains be great, we are troubled ourselves. What, then, must it be to see a soul in danger of pain, the most grievous of all pains, for ever? Who can endure it? It is a thought no heart can bear without great anguish. Here we know that pain ends with life at last, and that there are limits to it; yet the sight of it moves our compassion so greatly. That other pain has no ending; and I know not how we can be calm, when we see Satan carry so many souls daily away.

The Effects of the Divine Graces in the Soul—the Inestimable Greatness of One Degree of Glory

It is painful to me to recount more of the graces which our Lord gave me than these already spoken of; and they are so many, that nobody can believe they were ever given to one so wicked: but in obedience to our Lord, who has commanded me to do it, and you, my fathers, I will speak of some of them to His glory. May it please His Majesty it may be to the profit of some soul! For if our Lord has been thus gracious to so miserable a thing as myself, what will He be to those who shall serve Him truly? Let all people resolve to please His Majesty, seeing that He gives such pledges as these even in this life.

My love of, and trust in, our Lord, after I had seen Him in a vision, began to grow, for my converse with Him was so continual. I saw that, though He was God, He was man also; that He is not surprised at the frailties of men; that He understands our miserable nature, liable to fall continually, because of the first sin, for the reparation of which He had come. I could speak to Him as a friend, though He is my Lord, because I do not consider Him as one of our earthly lords, who affect a power they do not possess, who give audience at fixed hours, and to whom only certain persons may speak. If a poor man have any business with these, it will cost him many goings and comings, and currying favour with others, together with much pain and labour before he can speak to them. Ah, if such a one has business with a king! Poor people, not of gentle blood, cannot approach him, for they must apply to those who are his friends; and certainly these are not persons who tread the world under their feet; for they who do this speak the truth, fear nothing, and ought to fear nothing; they are not courtiers, because it is not the custom of a court, where they must be silent about those things they dislike, must not even dare to think about them, lest they should fall into disgrace.

O my Lord! O my King! who can describe Thy Majesty? It is impossible not to see that Thou art Thyself the great Ruler of all, that the beholding of Thy Majesty fills men with awe. But I am filled with greater awe, O my Lord, when I consider Thy humility, and the love Thou hast for such as I am. We can converse and speak with Thee about everything whenever we will; and when we lose our first fear and awe at the vision of Thy Majesty, we have a greater dread of offending Thee—not arising out of the fear of punishment, O my Lord, for that is as nothing in comparison with the loss of Thee!

I am not yet fifty, and yet I have seen so many changes during my life, that I do not know how

Gianlorenzo Bernini, The Ecstasy of St. *Teresa, ca. 1645.*

to live. What will they do who are only just born, and who may live many years? Certainly I am sorry for those spiritual people who, for certain holy purposes, are obliged to live in the world; the cross they have to carry is a dreadful one.

Certain Heavenly Secrets, Visions, and Revelations

One night I was so unwell that I thought I might be excused making my prayer; so I took my rosary, that I might employ myself in vocal prayer, trying not to be recollected in my understanding, though outwardly I was recollected, being in my oratory. These little precautions are of no use when our Lord will have it otherwise.

I remained there but a few moments thus, when I was rapt in spirit with such violence that I could make no resistance whatever. It seemed to me that I was taken up to heaven; and the first persons I saw there were my father and my mother. I saw other things also; but the time was no longer than that in which the *Ave Maria* might be said, and I was amazed at it, looking on it all as too great a grace for me. But as to the shortness of the time, it might have been longer, only it was all done in a very short space.

It happened, also, as time went on, and it happens now from time to time, that our Lord showed me still greater secrets. The soul, even if it would, has neither the means nor the power to see more than what He shows it; and so, each time, I saw nothing more than what our Lord was pleased to let me see. But such was the vision, that the least part of it was enough to make my soul amazed, and to raise it so high that it esteems and counts as nothing all the things of this life. I wish I could describe in some measure, the smallest portion of what I saw; but when I think of doing it, I find it impossible; for the mere difference alone between the light we have here below, and that which is seen in a vision—both being light—is so great, that there

is no comparison between them; the brightness of the sun itself seems to be something exceedingly loathsome. In a word, the imagination, however strong it may be, can neither conceive nor picture to itself this light, nor any one of the things which our Lord showed me in a joy so supreme that it cannot be described; for then all the senses exult so deeply and so sweetly, that no description is possible.

I was in this state once for more than an hour, our Lord showing me wonderful things. He seemed as if He would not leave me. He said to me: "See, My daughter, what they lose who are against Me; do not fail to tell them of it." Ah, my Lord, how little good my words will do them, who are made blind by their own conduct, if Thy Majesty will not give them light! Some, to whom Thou hast given it, there are, who have profited by the knowledge of Thy greatness; but as they see it revealed to one so wicked and base as I am, I look upon it as a great thing if there should be any found to believe me. Blessed be Thy name, and blessed be Thy compassion; for I can trace, at least in my own soul, a visible improvement. Afterwards I wished I had continued in that trance for ever, and that I had not returned to consciousness.

QUESTIONS

1. How does Teresa's gender affect her account of her life? Can you note any differences from male religious writers of the period?

2. What, according to Teresa's vision, was hell like?

3. What sort of relationship did Teresa have with God?

4. Judging from Teresa's work, what sort of generalizations might you make about contemporary views of heaven and hell?

5. Why do you think Teresa wrote about her experiences? How do you think society responded to her?

THE EARLY MODERN WORLD

68

■ *Anonymous* ■

LAZARILLO DE TORMES
(1554)

Lazarillo de Tormes is among the first modern novels, one of a variety of sixteenth-century Spanish stories that are called *picaresque,* named after the wandering beggars who are their heroes. In contrast to traditional adventure stories, which took chivalrous knights as their subjects and were a combination of fantasy and romance, *Lazarillo de Tormes* is steeped in realism. It takes a boy of the lowest social origins as its hero and follows his pathetic life.

The story begins after Lazarillo's father has died and his mother can no longer afford to keep him. He is first employed as a servant to a blind beggar and then to a series of evil masters. Lazarillo finally becomes town crier of Toledo, the officer who accompanies the condemned to their executions.

Although the picaresque novel was a fictional account, much of the descriptive detail accurately portrays the social condition of the vast majority of the Spanish population in the so-called Golden Age.

We went out of Salamanca, and as you approach the bridge there is a stone animal at the entrance, almost in the shape of a bull, and the blind man bade me go close to the animal, and when I was there, said to me: "Lazaro, put thine ear close to this bull and shalt hear a great noise inside." Naïvely I went, believing this to be so; and when he perceived that I had my head close to the stone, he swung out his hand hard and gave my head a great blow against the devil of a bull, so that for three days the pain of the butting remained, and said to me: "Silly fool, learn that the blind man's boy has to know one point more than the devil," and laughed a great deal at the joke. It seemed to me that in that instant I awoke from the childish simplicity in which I had always been asleep. I said to myself: "This man says the truth, for it behooves me to open mine eyes and look about, since I am alone, and to consider how to take care of myself."

We began our journey, and in a very few days he taught me thieves' jargon, and when he saw me to be of a good wit, was well pleased, and used to say: "Gold or silver I cannot give thee, but I will show thee many pointers about life." And it was so; for after God this man gave me my life, and although blind lighted and guided me in the career of living.

He used to carry bread and everything else in a linen sack which closed at the mouth with an iron ring and a padlock and key, and when he put things in and took them out, it was with so much attention, so well counted, that the whole world wouldn't have been equal to making it a crumb less. But I would take what stingy bit he gave me, and finish it in less than two mouthfuls. After he had fastened the lock and stopped worrying about it, thinking me to be engaged in other things, by a little seam, which I unsewed and sewed up again many times in the side of the sack, I used to bleed the miserly sack, taking out bread—not measured quantities but good pieces—and slices of bacon and sausage; and thus would seek a convenient time to make good the devilish state of want which the wicked blind man left me in.

When we ate he used to put a little jug of wine near him. I would quickly seize it and give it a couple of silent kisses and return it to its place; but this plan didn't work long, for he noticed the deficiency in his draughts, and in order to keep his wine safe, he never after let go the jug, but kept hold of the handle. But there is no lodestone that draws things to it so strongly as I with a long rye straw, which I had prepared for that purpose, and placing which in the mouth of the jug, I would suck up the wine to a fare-ye-well. But the villain was so clever that I think he heard me; and from then on he changed procedure and set his jug between his legs and covered it with his hand, and thus drank secure. Now that I had grown accustomed to wine, I was dying for it; and seeing that the straw-cure was no longer helping me, I decided to make a tiny hole in the bottom of the jug for a little drain, and to bung it neatly with a very thin cake of wax, and at dinner-time, pretending to be cold, I got between the wretched blind man's legs to warm me at the miserable fire we had, in whose heat the wax being soon melted, for there was very little, the streamlet began to drain into my mouth, which I held in such a way that never a drop was lost.

We were at Escalona, town of the Duke of that ilk, in an inn, and he gave me a piece of sausage to roast. When he had basted the sausage and eaten the basting, he took a maravedi from his purse and bade me fetch wine from the tavern. The devil put the occasion before my eyes, which, as the saying is, makes the thief; and it was this: there lay by the fire a small turnip, rather long and bad, and which must have been thrown there because it was not fit for the stew. And as nobody was there at the time but him and me alone, as I had an appetite whetted by having got the toothsome odour of the sausage inside me (the only part, as I knew, that I had to enjoy myself with), not considering what might follow, all fear set aside in order to comply with desire—while the blind man was taking the money out of his purse, I took the sausage, and quickly put the above-mentioned turnip on the spit, which my master grasped, when he had given me the money for the wine, and began to turn before the fire, trying to roast what through its demerit had escaped being boiled. I went for the wine, and on the way did not delay in despatching the sausage, and when I came back I found the sinner of a blind man holding the turnip ready between two slices of bread, for he had not yet recognized it, because he had not tried it with his hand. When he took the slices of bread and bit into them, thinking to get part of the sausage too, he found himself chilled by the chilly turnip; he grew angry and said: "What is this, Lazarillo?" "Poor Lazaro," said I, "if you want to blame me for anything. Haven't I just come back with the wine? Somebody was here, and must have done this for a joke." "No, no," said he, "for I've not let the spit out of my hand. It's not possible." I again swore and forswore that I was innocent of the exchange, but little did it avail me, for nothing was hid from the sharpness of the confounded blind man. He got up and seized me by the head and came close up to smell me; and since he must have caught the scent like a good hound, the better to satisfy himself of the truth in the great agony he was suffering, he seized me with his hands, opened my mouth wider than it ought to go, and unconsideringly thrust in his nose, which was long and sharp, and at that crisis a palm longer from rage, with the point of which he reached my gorge; what with this and with the great fright I was in, and the short time the black sausage had had to get settled in my stomach, and most of all, with the tickling of his huge nose nearly half-choking me, all these things conjointly were the cause that my misconduct and gluttony were made evident, and his own returned to my master; for before the wicked blind man withdrew his bugle from my mouth, my stomach was so upset that it abandoned its stolen goods, and thus his nose and the wretched, half-masticated sausage went out of my mouth at the same time.

O great God, that I had been buried at that hour! for dead I already was. Such was the depraved blind man's fury, that if they had not come to my assistance at the noise, I think he had not left me alive. They dragged me from out his hands, leaving them full of what few hairs I had, my face scratched and my neck and throat clawed; and well my throat deserved this, for such abuse befell me through its viciousness. The wicked blind man related my disgraceful actions to all that approached, and gave them the history once and again, both of the wine-jug and of the bunch of grapes, and now of the actual trouble. Everybody laughed so much that all the passers-by came in to see the fun; for the blind man related my doings with so much wit and sprightliness that although I was thus abused and weeping, it seemed to me that I was doing him injustice not to laugh.

In view of this and the evil tricks the blind man played me, I decided to leave him once and for all, and as I had everything thought out and in my mind, on his playing me this last game I determined on it more fully. And so it was that the next day we went out about town to beg alms, and it had rained a great deal the night before; and as it was still raining that day he walked in prayer under some arcades which there were in that town, where we didn't get wet; but as night was coming on and the rain didn't stop, the blind man said to me: "Lazaro, this

water is very persistent, and the more night shuts down, the heavier it is: let us get back to the inn in time." To go there we had to cross a gutter which was running full because of all the water; I said to him: "Uncle, the gutter runs very wide; but if you wish, I see where we can get over more quickly without wetting us, for there it becomes much narrower, and by jumping we can cross with dry feet." This seemed good advice to him, and he said: "Thou art clever, I like thee for that. Bring me to the place where the gutter contracts, for it is winter now and water is disagreeable, and going with wet feet still more so." Seeing the scheme unfolding as I desired, I led him out from the arcades and brought him in front of a pillar or stone post which was in the square, and upon which and others like it projections of the houses rested, and said to him, "Uncle, this is the narrowest crossing there is in the gutter." As it was raining hard, and the poor creature was getting wet, and what with the haste we made to get out of the water that was falling on us, and most of all because God blinded his intelligence in that hour—it was to give me revenge on him—he trusted me and said: "Place me quite straight, and do thou jump the gutter." I placed him quite straight in front of the pillar, and gave a jump, and put myself behind the post like one who awaits the charge of a bull, and said to him: "Hey, jump all you can, so as to get to this side of the water." Scarcely had I finished saying it, when the poor blind man charged like a goat and with all his might came on, taking a step back before he ran, for to make a bigger jump, and struck the post with his head, which sounded as loud as if he had struck it with a big gourd, and fell straight down backwards half dead and with his head split open. "What, thou smeltest the sausage and not the post? Smell, smell!" said I, and left him in charge of many folk who had come to help him, and took the towngate on foot in a trot, and before night had struck into Torrijos. I knew no more of what God did with him, nor cared to know.

QUESTIONS

1. A very prominent theme in *Lazarillo* is food—getting it, keeping it, and losing it. What does this tell us about the life of the poor in sixteenth-century Spain?

2. How are wanderers like Lazarillo and his blind master treated by Spanish society?

3. What is the relationship between Lazarillo and the blind man like? Who benefits most from their partnership?

4. What sort of a person is Lazarillo? Does his character say anything about people's expectations of wandering beggars?

5. *Lazarillo de Tormes* is a very early form of a novel. In what ways is it similar to and different from modern novels?

69

■ *Martin Luther* ■

THE TWELVE ARTICLES OF THE PEASANTS OF SWABIA

(1524)

ADMONITION TO PEACE

(1525)

Changing social and economic conditions in the early sixteenth century had a disruptive effect on the lives of common people. Ancient feudal relations stretched the bonds between landlord and peasant at the same time that the military demands of the princes were increasing local taxation. In 1524, a series of local protests over economic conditions coalesced into one of the largest concerted peasant risings in German history. The Peasants' Revolt was not a spontaneous rising of the hungry and dispossessed, but rather a carefully coordinated movement that attempted to win widespread social reforms.

The Twelve Articles show both the nature of the peasants' grievances and the peasants' ability to articulate them. The leaders of the movement believed that their program would appeal to the religious reforms of Martin Luther. In a stinging rebuke, *Admonition to Peace,* Luther set forth the doctrine of passive obedience and instructed the peasants to lay down their arms.

THE TWELVE ARTICLES

Peace to the Christian reader and the grace of God through Christ:

There are many evil writings put forth of late which take occasion, on account of the assembling of the peasants, to cast scorn upon the gospel, saying, "Is this the fruit of the new teaching, that no one should obey but that all should everywhere rise in revolt, and rush together to reform, or perhaps destroy altogether, the authorities, both ecclesiastic and lay?" The articles below shall answer these godless and criminal fault-finders, and serve, in the first place, to remove the reproach from the word of God, and, in the second place, to give a Christian excuse for the disobedience or even the revolt of the entire peasantry.

In the first place, the gospel is not the cause of revolt and disorder, since it is the message of Christ, the promised Messiah; the word of life, teaching only love, peace, patience, and concord. Thus all who believe in Christ should learn to be loving, peaceful, long-suffering, and harmonious. This is the foundation of all the articles of the peasants (as will be seen), who accept the gospel and live according to it. How then can the evil reports declare the gospel to be a cause of revolt and disobedience? That the authors of the evil reports and the enemies of the gospel oppose themselves to these demands is due, not to the gospel, but to the devil, the worst enemy of the gospel, who causes this opposition by raising doubts in the minds of his followers, and thus the word of God, which teaches love, peace, and concord, is overcome.

In the second place, it is clear that the peasants demand that this gospel be taught them as a guide in life, and they ought not to be called disobedient or disorderly. Whether God grant the peasants (earnestly wishing to live according to his word) their requests or no, who

shall find fault with the will of the Most High? Who shall meddle in his judgments or oppose his majesty? Did he not hear the children of Israel when they called upon him and saved them out of the hands of Pharaoh? Can he not save his own today? Yea, he will save them and that speedily. Therefore Christian reader, read the following articles with care and then judge. Here follow the articles:

The First Article. First, it is our humble petition and desire, as also our will and resolution, that in the future we should have power and authority so that each community should choose and appoint a pastor, and that we should have the right to depose him should he conduct himself improperly. The pastor thus chosen should teach us the gospel pure and simple, without any addition, doctrine, or ordinance of man.

The Second Article. According as the just tithe is established by the Old Testament and fulfilled in the New, we are ready and willing to pay the fair tithe of grain. The word of God plainly provides that in giving rightly to God and distributing to his people the services of a pastor are required. We will that for the future our church provost, whomsoever the community may appoint, shall gather and receive this tithe. From this he shall give to the pastor, elected by the whole community, a decent and sufficient maintenance for him and his, as shall seem right to the whole community. What remains over shall be given to the poor of the place, as the circumstances and the general opinion demand. Should anything farther remain, let it be kept, lest any one should have to leave the country from poverty. The small tithes, whether ecclesiastical or lay, we will not pay at all, for the Lord God created cattle for the free use of man. We will not, therefore, pay farther an unseemly tithe which is of man's invention.

The Third Article. It has been the custom hitherto for men to hold us as their own property, which is pitiable enough, considering that Christ has delivered and redeemed us all, without exception, by the shedding of his precious blood, the lowly as well as the great. Accordingly it is consistent with Scripture that we should be free and should wish to be so. Not that we would wish to be absolutely free and under no authority. God does not teach us that we should lead a disorderly life in the lusts of the flesh, but that we should love the Lord our God and our neighbor. We would gladly observe all this as God has commanded us in the celebration of the communion. He has not commanded us not to obey the authorities, but rather that we should be humble, not only towards those in authority, but towards every one. We are thus ready to yield obedience according to God's law to our elected and regular authorities in all proper things becoming to a Christian. We therefore take it for granted that you will release us from serfdom as true Christians, unless it should be shown us from the gospel that we are serfs.

The Fourth Article. In the fourth place, it has been the custom heretofore that no poor man should be allowed to touch venison or wild fowl, or fish in flowing water, which seems to us quite unseemly and unbrotherly as well as selfish and not agreeable to the word of God. In some places the authorities preserve the game to our great annoyance and loss, recklessly permitting the unreasoning animals to destroy to no purpose our crops, which God suffers to grow for the use of man; and yet we must submit quietly. This is neither godly nor neighborly; for when God created man he gave him dominion over all the animals, over the birds of the air and over the fish in the water. Accordingly it is our desire, if a man holds possession of waters, that he should prove from satisfactory documents that his right has been unwittingly acquired by purchase. We do not wish to take it from him by force, but his rights should be exercised in a Christian and brotherly fashion. But whosoever cannot produce such evidence should surrender his claim with good grace.

The Fifth Article. In the fifth place, we are aggrieved in the matter of woodcutting, for the noble folk have appropriated all the woods to themselves alone. If a poor man requires wood, he must pay two pieces of money for it. It is our opinion in regard to a wood which has fallen into the hands of a lord, whether spiritual or temporal, that unless it was duly purchased it should revert again to the community. It should, moreover, be free to every member of the community to help himself to such firewood as he needs in his home.

The Sixth Article. Our sixth complaint is in regard to the excessive services which are demanded of us and which are increased from day to day. We ask that this matter be properly looked into, so that we shall not continue to be oppressed in this way, but that some gracious consideration be given to us, since our forefathers were required only to serve according to the word of God.

The Seventh Article. Seventh, we will not hereafter allow ourselves to be farther oppressed by our lords, but will let them demand only what is just and proper according to the word of the agreement between the lord and the peasant. The lord should no longer try to force more services or other dues from the peasant without payment, but permit the peasant to enjoy his holding in peace and quiet. The peasant should, however, help the lord when it is necessary, and at proper times, when it will not be disadvantageous to the peasant, and for a suitable payment.

The Eighth Article. In the eighth place, we are greatly burdened by holdings which cannot support the rent exacted from them. The peasants suffer loss in this way and are ruined; and we ask that the lords may appoint persons of honor to inspect these holdings, and fix a rent in accordance with justice, so that the peasant shall not work for nothing, since the laborer is worthy of his hire.

The Ninth Article. In the ninth place, we are burdened with a great evil in the constant making of new laws. We are not judged according to the offense, but sometimes with great ill-will, and sometimes much too leniently. In our opinion, we should be judged according to the old written law, so that the case shall be decided according to its merits, and not with partiality.

The Tenth Article. In the tenth place, we are aggrieved by the appropriation by individuals of meadows and fields which at one time belonged to a community. These we will take again into our own hands. It may, however, happen that the land was rightfully purchased. When, however, the land has unfortunately been purchased in this way, some brotherly arrangement should be made according to circumstances.

The Eleventh Article. In the eleventh place, we will entirely abolish the due called "heriot," and will no longer endure it, nor allow widows and orphans to be thus shamefully robbed against God's will.

Conclusion. In the twelfth place, it is our conclusion and final resolution that if any one or more of the articles here set forth should not be in agreement with the word of God, as we think they are, such article we will willingly retract if it is proved really to be against the word of God by a clear explanation of the Scripture. Or if articles should now be conceded to us that are hereafter discovered to be unjust, from that hour they shall be dead and null and without force. Likewise, if more complaints should be discovered which are based upon truth and the Scriptures and relate to offenses against God and our neighbor, we have determined to reserve the right to present these also, and to exercise ourselves in all Christian teaching. For this we shall pray to God, since he can grant our demands, and he alone. The peace of Christ abide with us all.

LUTHER'S ADMONITION TO PEACE

To the peasants. So far, dear friends, for the princes; now let me, in all kindness and charity, address myself to you. I have acknowledged that the princes and lords who prohibit the preaching of the gospel, and who load the people with intolerable burdens, have well merited that the Almighty should cast them from their seats, seeing that they have sinned against God and against man, and are without excuse.

Nevertheless, though your complaints are just, and your demands reasonable, it behoves you to prosecute those demands with moderation, conscience, and justice. If you act with conscience, moderation, and justice, God will aid you; and even though subdued for the moment, you will triumph in the end; and those of you who may perish in the struggle, will be saved. But if you have justice and conscience against you, you will fail; and even though you were not to fail, even though you were to kill all the princes, you, body and soul, would be none the less eternally damned.

Believe me, this is no trifling or jesting matter; it is a matter in which your body and soul are intimately concerned. What you have to consider, is not your own strength or the wrongs you have sustained from your adversaries, but whether the course you pursue is consistent with justice and conscience.

Put no trust, I pray you, in the prophets of murder whom Satan has raised up amongst you, and who proceed directly from him, though they sacrilegiously invoke the name of the holy gospel. They will hate me, I know, for the counsel I give you, they will call me hypocrite, but this I heed not a whit. What I desire is, to save from the anger of God the good and honest among you; I care not for the rest, I heed them not, I fear them not; let them despise me, if they will, I know One who is stronger than all of them put together, and he tells me in the 3rd Psalm to do that which I am now doing. The

ACKER CONCZ.

KLOS WVCZER.

IM BAVEREN KRIEG

1525

1544
ISB

Drummer and standard bearer at the time of the
Peasants' Revolt (1524–1526) in Germany.

tens of thousands, and the hundreds of thousands, intimidate not me. . . .

But say you, authority is wicked, cruel, intolerable; it will not allow us the gospel, it overwhelms us with burdens beyond all reason or endurance; it ruins us, soul and body. To this I reply, that the wickedness and injustice of authority are no warrant for revolt, seeing that it befits not all men indiscriminately to take upon themselves the punishment of wickedness. Besides which, the natural law says that no man shall be the judge in his own cause, nor revenge his own quarrel. The divine law

teaches us the same lesson: *Vengeance is mine, saith the Lord, I will repay.* Your enterprise, therefore, is not only wrong according to Bible and gospel law, but it is opposed also to natural law and to equity; and you cannot properly persevere in it, unless you prove that you are called to it by a new commandment of God, especially directed to you, and confirmed by miracles.

You see the mote in the eye of authority, but you see not the beam in your own. Authority is unjust, in that it interdicts the Gospel, and oppresses you with burdens; but you are still more in the wrong even than authority, you who, not content with interdicting the Word of God, trample it under foot, and arrogate to yourselves the power reserved to God alone. Which (I refer the decision of the question to yourselves) is the greatest robber: he who takes a part, or he who takes the whole? Now authority, it is not to be denied, unjustly deprives you of your property, but you seek to deprive authority, not only of property, but also of body and of life. You say, indeed, that you will leave it something; but who will believe you? You aim to take from it power; he who takes all, does not hesitate, at will, to take also the part; when the wolf eats the sheep, he eats the ears also.

Do you not perceive, my friends, that if your doctrine were tenable, there would remain upon the earth neither authority, nor order, nor any species of justice. Every man would act entirely as his own judge, his own vindicator, and nought would be seen but murder, rapine, and desolation.

I say all this unto you, my dear friends, that you may see to what an extent you are profaning the name of Christ and of his holy law; however just your demands may be, it befits not a Christian to draw the sword, or to employ violence; you should rather suffer yourselves to be defrauded, according to the law which has been given unto you (1 Corinthians, vi.). At all events, if you persist in carrying out the dictates of a perverse will, desecrate not the name of Christ, nor impiously make use of it as a pretext and cloak for your unrighteous conduct. I will not permit you to do so; I will not excuse it; I will wrest that name from you by any effort of which I am capable, sacrificing, if necessary, the last drop of blood in my veins. . . .

It is absolutely essential, then, that you should either abandon your enterprise, and consent to endure the wrongs that men may do unto you, if you desire still to bear the name of Christians; or else, if you persist in your resolutions, that you should throw aside that name, and assume some other. Choose one or the other of these alternatives: there is no medium.

Answer to Article 1.—If authority will not support a pastor who is agreeable to the feelings of a particular parish, the parish should support him at its own expense. If authority will not permit this pastor to preach, the faithful should follow him elsewhere.

Answer to Article 2.—You seek to dispose of a tithe which does not belong to you; this would be a spoliation and robbery. If you wish to do good, let it be with your own money, and not with that of other people. God himself has told us that he despises an offering which is the product of theft.

Answer to Article 3.—You wish to apply to the flesh the Christian liberty taught by the gospel, but I would ask you did not Abraham and the other patriarchs, as well as the prophets, keep bondmen? St. Paul himself tells us that the empire of this world cannot subsist without an inequality of persons.

Answer to the eight last Articles.—As to your propositions respecting game, wood, feudal services, assessment of payments, &c., I refer these matters to the lawyers; I am not called upon to decide respecting them; but I repeat to you that the Christian is a martyr, and that he has no care for all these things; cease, then, to speak of the Christian law, and say rather that it is the human law, the natural law that you assert, for the Christian law commands you to suffer as to all these things, and to make your complaint to God alone.

QUESTIONS

1. What does the promulgation of the Twelve Articles suggest about the nature and organization of the Peasants' Revolt? How sophisticated were the rebels?

2. What were the primary grievances of the peasantry?

3. How does Protestant thought affect the demands of the peasants?

4. What should peasants do when oppressed by their rulers, according to Luther?

5. Why should peasants never take action against their superiors? What does Luther fear will result from rebellion?

70

■ *Francis Xavier* ■

LETTER FROM INDIA

(1543)

Francis Xavier (1506–1552) was born in the mountain kingdom of Navarre that straddled the warring states of France and Spain. During his childhood this Basque country was ruled by the kings of Spain to whom his father served as president of the council. Francis grew up in privileged circumstances, his ancestral home was a hilltop castle, and it was expected that he would receive the best education possible. In 1525, he was sent to the University of Paris, then the leading center of intellectual life in France. While at university, he fell in with another Basque countryman also studying in Paris, Ignatius Loyola. Loyola had recently experienced a profound religious conversion and had pledged to live his life in imitation of Jesus. After much persuasion he convinced Francis Xavier to do the same, and they became founding members of the Society of Jesus. Xavier left his studies to enter the service of the pope; his first assignment was under the direction of the king of Portugal, whose eastern empire included many non-Christians. Francis Xavier arrived in India in 1542 to establish a mission there. He lived amongst the poorest populations and by translating a catechism into native dialect was able to bring the message of Christianity to the villagers. He baptized and converted thousands. He traveled widely throughout Asia, making a mission to the savage Spice Islands and visiting Japan, whose people he much admired. His final objective was to reach China and establish a mission there, but he died in 1552 before he could fulfill this dream.

Throughout his time in Asia, Francis Xavier reported his experiences to his Jesuit colleagues who remained at home. Many of his letters were private documents, but some were thought so important to the cause of the counter-reformation that they were published and widely distributed. Only two of his letters from the interior of India have survived. In the letter reprinted here, he tells of his experiences among the native peoples whom he calls the Paravas.

We have in these parts a class of men among the pagans who are called Brahmins. They keep up the worship of the gods, the superstitious rites of religion, frequenting the temples and taking care of the idols. They are as perverse and wicked a set as can anywhere be found, and I always apply to them the words of holy David, *"from an unholy race and a wicked and crafty man deliver me, O Lord."* They are liars and cheats to the very backbone. Their whole study is, how to deceive most cunningly the simplicity and ignorance of the people. They give out publicly that the gods command certain offerings to be made to their temples, which offerings are simply the things that the Brahmins themselves wish for, for their own maintenance and that of their wives, children, and servants. Thus they make the poor folk believe that the images of their gods eat and drink, dine and sup like men, and some devout persons are found who really offer to the idol twice a day, before dinner and supper, a certain sum of money. The Brahmins eat sumptuous meals to the sound of drums, and make the ignorant believe that the gods are banqueting. When they are in need of any supplies, and even before, they give out to the people that the gods are angry because the things they have asked for have not been sent, and that if the people do not take care, the gods will punish them by slaughter, disease, and the assaults of the devils. And the poor ignorant creatures, with the fear of the gods before them, obey them implicitly. These Brahmins have barely a tincture of literature, but they make up for their poverty in learning by cunning and malice. Those who belong to these parts are very indignant with me for exposing their tricks. Whenever they talk to me with no one by to hear them they acknowledge that they have no other patrimony but the idols, by their lies about which they procure their support from the people. They say that I, poor creature as I am, know more than all of them put together. They often send me a civil message and presents, and make a great complaint when I send them all back again. Their object is to bribe me to connive at their evil deeds. So they declare that they are convinced that there is only one God, and that they will pray to Him for me. And I, to return the favour, answer whatever occurs to me, and then lay bare, as far as I can, to the ignorant people whose blind superstitions have made them their slaves, their imposture and tricks, and this has induced many to leave the worship of the false gods, and eagerly become Christians. If it were not for the opposition of the Brahmins,

we should have them all embracing the religion of Jesus Christ.

The heathen inhabitants of the country are commonly ignorant of letters, but by no means ignorant of wickedness. All the time I have been here in this country I have only converted one Brahmin, a virtuous young man, who has now undertaken to teach the Catechism to children. As I go through the Christian villages, I often pass by the temples of the Brahmins, which they call pagodas. One day lately, I happened to enter a pagoda where there were about two hundred of them, and most of them came to meet me. We had a long conversation, after which I asked them what their gods enjoined them in order to obtain the life of the blessed. There was a long discussion amongst them as to who should answer me. At last, by common consent, the commission was given to one of them, of greater age and experience than the rest, an old man, of more than eighty years. He asked me in return, what commands the God of the Christians laid on them. I saw the old man's perversity, and I refused to speak a word till he had first answered my question. So he was obliged to expose his ignorance, and replied that their gods required two duties of those who desired to go to them hereafter, one of which was to abstain from killing cows, because under that form the gods were adored; the other was to show kindness to the Brahmins, who were the worshippers of the gods. This answer moved my indignation, for I could not but grieve intensely at the thought of the devils being worshipped instead of God by these blind heathen, and I asked them to listen to me in turn. Then I, in a loud voice, repeated the Apostles' Creed and the Ten Commandments. After this I gave in their own language a short explanation, and told them what Paradise is, and what Hell is, and also who they are who go to Heaven to join the company of the blessed, and who are to be sent to the eternal punishments of hell. Upon hearing these things they all rose up and vied with one another in embracing me, and in confessing that the God of the

Christians is the true God, as His laws are so agreeable to reason. Then they asked me if the souls of men like those of other animals perished together with the body. God put into my mouth arguments of such a sort, and so suited to their ways of thinking, that to their great joy I was able to prove to them the immortality of the soul. I find, by the way, that the arguments, which are to convince these ignorant people must by no means be subtle, such as those which are found in the books of learned schoolmen, but must be such as their minds can understand. They asked me again how the soul of a dying person goes out of the body, how it was, whether it was as happens to us in dreams, when we seem to be conversing with our friends and acquaintance? (Ah, how often this happens to me, dearest brothers, when I am dreaming of you!) Was this because the soul then leaves the body? And again, whether God was black or white? For as there is so great a variety of colour among men, and the Indians being black themselves, consider their own colour the best, they believe that their gods are black. On this account the great majority of their idols are as black as black can be, and moreover are generally so rubbed over with oil as to smell detestably, and seem to be as dirty as they are ugly and horrible to look at. To all these questions I was able to reply so as to satisfy them entirely. But when I came to the point at last, and urged them to embrace the religion which they felt to be true, they made that same objection which we hear from many Christians when urged to change their life,—that they would set men talking about them if they altered their ways and their religion, and besides, they said that they should be afraid that, if they did so, they would have nothing to live on and support themselves by.

I have found just one Brahmin and no more in all this coast who is a man of learning: he is said to have studied in a very famous Academy. Knowing this, I took measures to converse with him alone. He then told me at last, as a great secret, that the students of this Academy are at the outset made by their masters to take an oath not to reveal their mysteries, but that, out of friendship for me, he would disclose them to me. One of these mysteries was that there only exists one God, the Creator and Lord of heaven and earth, whom men are bound to worship, for the idols are simply images of devils. The Brahmins have certain books of sacred literature which contain, as they say, the laws of God. The masters teach in a learned tongue, as we do in Latin. He also explained to me these divine precepts one by one; but it would be a long business to write out his commentary, and indeed not worth the trouble. Their sages keep as a feast our Sunday. On this day they repeat at different hours this one prayer: "I adore Thee, O God; and I implore Thy help for ever." They are bound by oath to repeat this prayer frequently, and in a low voice. My friend added, that the law of nature permitted them to have more wives than one, and their sacred books predicted that the time would come when all men should embrace the same religion. After all this he asked me in my turn to explain the principal mysteries of the Christian religion, promising to keep them secret. I replied, that I would not tell him a word about them unless he promised beforehand to publish abroad what I should tell him of the religion of Jesus Christ. He made the promise, and then I carefully explained to him those words of Jesus Christ in which our religion is summed up: "He who believes and is baptized shall be saved." This text, with my commentary on it, which embraced the whole of the Apostles' Creed, he wrote down carefully, as well as the Commandments, on account of their close connection with the Creed. He told me also that one night he had dreamt that he had been made a Christian to his immense delight, and that he had become my brother and companion. He ended by begging me to make him a Christian secretly. But as he made certain conditions opposed to right and justice, I put off his baptism. I don't doubt but that by God's mercy he will one day be a Christian. I charged him to teach the ignorant and unlearned that there is only one God, Creator of heaven and earth; but he pleaded the obligation of his oath, and said he could not do so, especially as he was much afraid that if he did it he should become possessed by an evil spirit.

And now I have nothing more to tell you except that so great is the intensity and abundance of the joy which God is accustomed to bestow upon those workmen of His vineyard who labour diligently in cultivating this barbarous part of the same, that for my part I do really believe that if there is in this life any true and solid happiness, it is here. It often happens to me to hear one whose lot it is to labour in this field cry out, *"O Lord, I beseech Thee overwhelm me not now in this life with so much delight, or at least, since in Thy boundless goodness and mercy Thou dost so overwhelm me, take me away to the abode of the blessed. For any one who has once known what it is to taste in his soul Thy ineffable sweetness must of necessity think it very bitter to live any longer without seeing Thee face to face."*

It is one of my greatest consolations, dearest brethren, to think often of you, and to call to mind that sweet and tender intercourse with you which God of His immense goodness vouchsafed to me of old. At the same time it makes me think over and feel very keenly, how much precious time I then spent uselessly, and gathered to little fruit from your holy example and conversation, and from knowledge of the things of God. However, I owe it to your prayers for me that God has given me the blessing, absent as I am from you in the body, of having, by means of

your care and intercession for me, the infinite number of my sins shown to me from God, and of having courage and strength given me to cultivate with all diligence the soil of heathendom. Endless thanks to God's goodness, and to your charity!

Among the many great blessings of my life past and present, and for which I have to thank the mercy of God, I count it as the greatest that I have heard the tidings of the approbation and confirmation of our Institute by the Holy Father. I give God endless thanks that He has now at last ordained to be publicly ratified by His Vicar, so as to be remembered by posterity for ever, that same rule of life which He Himself laid down in secret to His servant our Father Ignatius.

Here, then, I will leave off writing, begging of God that since in His goodness He has united us in a common way to life, and then has separated us so widely for the good of the Christian religion, so also He will be pleased to bring us together again in the abode and home of the Blessed. That He may grant us this grace, let us, if you will, plead the prayers, among others, of the infants and children whom I have baptized with my own hand, here, and whom God has called away to His mansions in heaven before they had lost their robe of innocence. They are, I think, more than a thousand in number, and I pray to them over and over again, begging that they will obtain for us from God that for what remains of this life, or rather of this time of exile, He will teach us to do His will, and to do it so completely as to accomplish all that He requires of us exactly as He Himself desires it to be done.

QUESTIONS

1. What is Xavier's opinion of the Brahmins?

2. Why can't Xavier convert the Brahmin?

3. What was Francis Xavier's reaction to questions about the race of God?

4. Do you believe Xavier's account of how he converted the Paravas?

71

■ *Marguerite de Navarre* ■

HEPTAMERON

(1558)

Marguerite de Navarre (1492–1549), elder sister of Francis I, king of France, was educated in the humanist tradition. She developed a lifelong attachment to learning, patronized humanist thinkers, and protected Protestants in the kingdom of Navarre, of which she became queen by marriage. She wrote a number of devotional tracts including *Mirror for a Sinful Soul* (1531), which was widely reprinted.

The *Heptameron* is a collection of seventy stories published in 1558, nearly ten years after Marguerite's death. There is considerable dispute over its actual authorship, but it is clear that the queen had a hand in its production. The tales are told by ten different characters, and there is reason to believe that all the stories were based on actual occurrences.

Story Five

At the port of Coulon near Niort, there was once a woman whose job it was to ferry people night and day across the river. One day she found herself alone in her boat with two Franciscan friars from Niort. Now this is one of the longest crossings on any river in France, and the two friars took it into their heads that she would find it less boring if they made amorous proposals to her. But, as was only right and proper, she refused to listen. However, the two were not to be deterred. They had not exactly had their strength sapped by rowing, nor their ardours chilled by the chilly water nor, indeed, their consciences pricked by the woman's refusals. So they decided to rape her, both of them, and if she resisted, to throw her into the river. But she was as sensible and shrewd as they were vicious and stupid.

'I'm not as ungracious as you might think,' she said to them, 'and if you'll just grant me two little things, you'll see I'm just as keen to do what you want as you are.'

The Cordeliers swore by the good Saint Francis that they'd let her have anything she asked for, if she'd just let them have what they wanted.

'First of all, you must promise on your oath the neither of you will tell a soul about it,' she said.

To this they readily agreed.

'Secondly, you must do what you want with me one at a time—I'd be too embarrassed to have both of you looking at me. So decide between you who's to have me first.'

They thought this too was a very reasonable request, and the younger of the two offered to let the older man go first. As they sailed past a small island in the river, the ferrywoman said to the younger one: 'Now my good father, jump ashore and say your prayers while I take your friend here to another island. If he's satisfied with me when he gets back, we'll drop him off here, and then you can come with me.'

So he jumped out of the boat to wait on the island till his companion came back. The ferry-woman then took the other one to another island in the river, and while she pretended to be making the boat fast to a tree, told him to go and find a convenient spot.

He jumped out, and went off to look for a good place. No sooner was he on dry land than the ferrywoman shoved off with a kick against the tree, and sailed off down the river, leaving the two good friars stranded.

'You can wait till God sends an angel to console you, Messieurs!' she bawled at them. 'You're not going to get anything out of me today!'

The poor friars saw they had been hood-winked. They ran to the water's edge and pleaded on bended knees that she would take them to the port. They promised not to ask her for any more favours. But she went on rowing, and called back: 'I'd be even more stupid to let myself get caught again, now I've escaped!'

As soon as she landed on the other side, she went into the village, fetched her husband and called out the officers of the law to go and round up these two ravenous wolves, from whose jaws she had just by the grace of God been delivered. They had plenty of willing helpers. There was no one in the village, great or small, who was not anxious to join in the hunt and have his share of the fun. When the two good brothers, each on his own island, saw this huge band coming after them, they did their best to hide—even as Adam hid from the presence of the Lord God, when he saw that he was naked. They were half dead for shame at this exposure of their sins, and trembled in terror at the thought of the punishment that surely awaited them. But there was nothing they could do. They were seized and bound, and led through the village to the shouts and jeers of every man and woman in the place. Some people said: 'There they go, those good fathers who preach chastity to us yet want to take it from our wives!' Others said: 'They are whited sepulchres, outwardly beautiful, but within full of dead men's bones and all uncleanness!' And someone else called out, 'Every tree is known by his own fruit!' In fact, they hurled at the two captives every text in the Gospels that condemns hypocrites. In the end their Father Superior came to the rescue. He lost no time in requesting their custody, reassuring the officers of the law that he would punish them more severely than secular law could. By way of reparation, they would, he promised, be made to say as many prayers and masses as might be required! [The Father Superior was a worthy man, so the judge granted his request and sent the two prisoners back to their convent, where they were brought before the full Chapter and severely reprimanded.] Never again did they take a ferry across a river, without making the sign of the cross and commending their souls to God!

'Now consider this story carefully, Ladies. We have here a humble ferrywoman who had the sense to frustrate the evil intentions of two vicious men. What then ought we to expect from women who all their lives have seen nothing but good examples, read of nothing but good examples and, in short, had examples of feminine virtue constantly paraded before them? If well-fed women are virtuous, is it not just as much a matter of custom as of virtue? But it's quite another matter if you're talking about women who have no education, who probably don't hear two decent sermons in a year, who have time for nothing but thinking how to make a meagre living, and who, in spite of all this, diligently resist all pressures in order to preserve their chastity. It is in the heart of such women as these that one finds pure virtue, for in the hearts of those we regard as inferior in body and mind the spirit of God performs his greatest works. Woe to those women who do not guard their treasure with the utmost care, for it is a treasure that brings them great honour if it is well guarded and great dishonour if it is squandered!'

'If you ask me, Geburon,' observed Longarine, 'there's nothing very virtuous in rejecting the advances of a friar. I don't know how anyone could possibly feel any affection at all for them.'

'Longarine,' he replied, 'women who are not so used as you are to having refined gentlemen to serve them find friars far from unpleasant. They're often just as good-looking as we are, just as well-built and less worn out, because they've not been knocked about in battle. What is more, they talk like angels and are as persistent as devils. That's why I think that any woman who's seen nothing better than the coarse cloth of monks' habits should be considered extremely virtuous if she manages to escape their clutches.'

'Good Heavens!' exclaimed Nomerfide loudly. 'You may say what you like, but I'd rather be thrown in the river any day, than go to bed with a friar!'

'So you're a strong swimmer, are you then!' said Oisille, laughing.

Nomerfide took this in bad part, thinking that Oisille did not give her as much credit as she would have liked, and said heatedly: 'There *are* plenty of people who've refused better men than friars, without blowing their trumpets about it!'

'Yes, and they've been even more careful not to beat their drums about ones they've accepted and given in to!' retorted Oisille, amused to see that she was annoyed.

'I can see that Nomerfide would like to speak,' Geburon intervened, 'so I invite her to take over from me, in order that she may unburden herself by telling us a good story.'

Story Fifty-five

In the town of Saragossa there was a rich merchant. Seeing that his death was near, and that he could not take his wealth with him—wealth which perhaps he had not acquired altogether honestly—he thought that he might make some amends for his sins by making some little donation or other to God. As if God grants his grace in return for money! Anyway, he made arrangements regarding his house, and gave instructions that a fine Spanish horse of his should be sold, and the proceeds distributed to the poor [mendicants]. It was his wife whom he

requested to carry out these instructions as soon as possible after his death. No sooner was the burial over and the first few tears shed, then the wife, who to say the least was no more stupid than Spanish women in general, approached her servant, who had also heard her husband's wishes.

'I think I've lost enough,' said she, 'in losing my husband whom I loved so dearly, without losing his property as well. Not that I want to disobey his instructions. In fact, I want to carry out his wishes even better than he intended. You see, the poor man was so taken in by those greedy priests. He thought he would make a sacrifice to God after his death by giving away a sum of money, not a single écu of which he would have given away during his lifetime, however great the need, as you know. So I've made up my mind that we shall do what he instructed us to do after his death—indeed we shall do better, and do what he *would* have done himself, had he lived a fortnight longer. Only not a soul must hear of it!'

The servant gave his word, and she went on: 'You will go and sell his horse, and when they ask you how much you want, you will say one ducat. But I also have an excellent cat that I want to sell, and you will sell it at the same time, for ninety-nine ducats. Together the horse and the cat will fetch a hundred ducats, which is what my husband wanted for the horse alone.'

So the servant promptly went off to do as his mistress requested. As he was leading the horse across the square, carrying the cat in his arms, he was approached by a certain nobleman who had seen the horse before and was interested in acquiring it. Having asked the price, the nobleman received the answer: 'One ducat!'

'I should be obliged if you would be serious,' said the man.

'I assure you, Monsieur, that the price is one ducat. You have to buy the cat with it, of course. I can't let the cat go for less than ninety-nine ducats!'

The nobleman thought this was a fair enough bargain. On the spot he paid one ducat for the horse, and ninety-nine for the cat, as requested, and led his purchases away. The servant took the money back to his mistress, who was extremely pleased, and lost no time in giving away the proceeds from the sale of the horse to the poor mendicants. As for the rest, that went to provide for the wants of herself and her children.

'Well, what do you think of her? Wasn't she wiser than her husband, and wasn't she just as much concerned about his conscience as she was about doing well for her family?'

'I think she loved her husband,' said Parlamente, 'but realized that most men's minds wander when they're on their deathbeds, and knowing what his real intention was, she wanted to interpret his wishes for the benefit of their children, and I think it was very wise of her to do so.'

'What!' exclaimed Geburon. 'Do you not think it a grave error to fail to execute the last will and testament of deceased friends?'

'Indeed I do!' replied Parlamente. 'Provided the testator is sound of mind and not deranged.'

'Do you call it deranged,' replied Geburon, 'to give away one's goods to the Church and to the poor mendicants?'

'I do not call it deranged,' she replied, 'if a man distributes to the poor that which God has placed within his power. But to give away as alms what belongs to other people—I do not think that shows great wisdom. It's all too common to see the world's greatest usurers putting up ornate and impressive chapels, in the hope of appeasing God for hundreds of thousands of ducats' worth of sheer robbery by spending ten thousand ducats on a building! As if God didn't know how to count!'

'Indeed, I am frequently astonished,' said Oisille, 'that they presume to be able to appease God by means of the very things, which, when He came to earth, He condemned—things such as fine buildings, gilded ornaments, decorations and paintings. But, if they had rightly understood what God has said of human offerings in a certain passage—that "the sacrifice of God is a troubled spirit: a broken and contrite heart, O God, shalt thou not despise"—and again, in another passage, what Saint Paul has said—that "ye are the temple of the living God, in which He will dwell"—if they had rightly heard these words, I say, they would have taken pains to adorn their conscience while they were yet alive. They would not have waited till a time when man can do neither good nor evil. Nor would they have done what is even worse and placed upon those who remain the burden of dispensing their alms to those upon whom, during their lifetime, they did not even deign to look. But He who reads men's hearts will not be deceived, and He will judge them not only according to their works, but according to the faith and charity that they have shown towards Him.'

'Why is it, then,' said Geburon, 'that the Franciscans and Mendicants talk of nothing else when a man's dying but of how we ought to make bequests to their monasteries, with the assurance that they will send us to Paradise whether we want or not?'

'What, Geburon!' broke in Hirca. 'Have you forgotten your story about the Franciscans, that you're asking how men like that can possibly lie? I'll tell you, as far as I'm concerned, there's no one on this earth tells lies like they do. It may be that those who speak for the good of their community as a whole aren't to be criticized; but there are some who forget their vow of poverty in order to satisfy their own greed.'

QUESTIONS

1. What sort of picture does the fifth story paint of clergymen? How are the friars treated by the villagers?

2. Marguerite notes that both rich and poor women have similar interests. What are these?

3. *Story Fifty-five* reveals something of the contemporary view of merchants and commerce. How did society view such pursuits?

4. Marguerite was sympathetic to Protestantism. Is this revealed in her stories? How?

72

■ *Philippe Duplessis-Mornay* ■

A DEFENSE OF LIBERTY AGAINST TYRANTS
(1579)

Philippe Duplessis-Mornay (1549–1623), a French nobleman of Huguenot extraction, entered the service of Henry of Navarre, the leading Huguenot prince, and became his chief advisor by 1573. Duplessis-Mornay took up arms during the Wars of Religion and was captured by Catholic forces. He avoided paying a ruinous fine by escaping in disguise and making his way back to the Huguenot lines. He continued in his role as advisor to the new king, Henry IV, but broke with him when Henry publicly converted to Catholicism. Duplessis-Mornay died in obscurity in 1623.

A Defense of Liberty was the most influential of Duplessis-Mornay's many writings. Although there remains some controversy over whether it was written alone or in collaboration, the *Defense* was the first Huguenot tract that attempted to justify resistance to lawful authority. It is a seminal work in the history of resistance theory.

First Question: Must Subjects Obey Princes Who Issue Orders Counter to the Law of God?

At first sight this question might appear to waste our time to no purpose because it seems to call the most evident axiom of Christianity into doubt as if it were still controversial, although it has been corroborated by so many testimonies of sacred Scripture, so many examples accumulated over the centuries, and the pyres of so many pious martyrs. What other reason, it might

be asked, could explain the willingness of the pious to undergo such extraordinary suffering if not their conviction that God is to be obeyed simply and absolutely, kings, however, only so long as they do not issue orders counter to the law of God? How else are we to understand the apostolic precept to obey God rather than men? And since God's will alone is always just, whereas the will of anybody else can be unjust at any time, who could doubt that only the former is to be obeyed without exception, but the latter always with reservations?

There are, however, many princes nowadays who boast the name of Christ, yet dare to arrogate an immense power that most assuredly does not depend from God. There are also many adulators who worship them as gods on earth, and many others seized by fear, or else coerced by force, who either really believe that obedience is never to be denied to princes or at least wish to seem to believe it. The vice of our times indeed appears to be that nothing is so firm as that it could not be uprooted, nothing so certain that it could not be disputed, and nothing so sacred that it could not be violated. Therefore I am afraid that anyone carefully weighing the matter will consider this question to be not only far from useless, but even absolutely necessary, especially in our century. . . .

The question then is whether subjects are obliged to obey kings whose orders are in conflict with the law of God. Who of the two, in other words, is rather to be obeyed, God or the king? If an answer can be given for the king, whose power is deemed the greatest of all, the same answer will apply to other magistrates.

In short, we see that kings are invested with their kingdoms by God in almost the same manner in which vassals are invested with their fiefs by their superior lords, and that they are deprived of their benefices for the same reasons. Therefore we must on all counts conclude that the former are in an almost identical place as the latter and that all kings are vassals of God. Having said this, our question is easily finished. For if God occupies the place of a superior lord, and the king that of a vassal, who will not declare that one should rather obey the lord than the vassal? If God commands this, and the king the other, who will consider someone refusing to obey the king as a rebel? Who will not on the contrary condemn it as rebellion if he fails to obey God promptly or if he obeys the king instead? And finally, if the king calls us to this choice and God to that, who will not declare that

we must desert the king in order to fight for God? Thus we are not only not obliged to obey a king who orders something against the law of God, but we even commit rebellion if we do obey him, in no other way than a landholder does who fights for a senior vassal against the king, or who prefers to obey the edict of the inferior rather than the superior, of the vicar rather than the prince, and of the minister rather than the king. . . .

Second Question: May Private Individuals Resist with Arms?

It only remains to deal with private persons. First of all, individuals as such are not bound by the covenant that is established between God and the people as a whole, that they should be God's people. For just as what is owed to a community is not owed to individuals, so individuals do not owe what the community owes. Furthermore they have none of the duties of office. The obligation to serve God depends upon the position to which one has been called. Private individuals, however, have no power, perform no magistracy, have no dominion and no power of punishment. God did not give the sword to private persons and therefore does not require them to use it. To private persons it is said: "Put thy sword into its scabbard"; to magistrates, however: "You do not bear the sword in vain." The former are guilty if they draw the sword, the latter are guilty of grave negligence unless they draw it when necessary.

But, you may ask, is there no covenant between God and the individuals at all, as there is between God and the community? No covenant with private persons as with magistrates? What could then be the purpose of circumcision and baptism? Why else is this sacred covenant mentioned over and over again in Scripture? Of course there is a covenant, but of a wholly different sort. For just as all the subjects of a just prince in general, of whatever rank they may be, are obliged to obey him, but only some of them have a special obligation, for example in the form of a magistracy, to take care that the others will be obedient, too, so all human beings in general are indeed obliged to serve God, but only some of them have taken on a greater burden along with their higher position so that, if they neglect their duty, they are responsible up to a point for the guilt of the rest. Kings, the community, and magistrates who have received the sword from the community must take care that the body of the church is governed according to the rite. Individuals, however, have no other function than to be members of that church. The former must pay heed that the temple of the lord is not polluted and does not collapse, but is safe from all internal corruption and external injury; the latter only that their body, which is the temple of God, is not impure, so that God's spirit can live in it. "Whosoever shall destroy God's temple, which you are," says Paul, "him shall God destroy." This is the reason why the former have been given a sword that can be fastened to their belts, whereas only the sword of the spirit has been entrusted to the latter, that is, the word of the lord with which Paul girds all Christians against the devil's attack.

When then shall private individuals do when the king urges impious rites upon them? If the nobles with authority from the entire people, or at least their own magistrates, oppose themselves to the king, they shall obey, follow, and assist the pious striving of the pious with all of their might as soldiers of God. If the nobles and magistrates applaud a raging king, however, or if at least they fail to resist him, the advice of Christ should be taken to heart: they should withdraw to another city. But if there is nowhere to escape to, they should rather forsake their lives than God, rather let themselves be crucified than, as the apostle says, crucify Christ once again. Do not, says our lord, fear those who can only kill the body, a lesson that has been taught to us by his own example as well as that of the apostles and innumerable pious martyrs.

Is no private person at all then permitted to resist with arms? But what about Moses, who led Israel out of Egypt against the will of Pharaoh? What about Ehud, who killed king Eglon of Moab and liberated Israel from the yoke of the Moabites after their rule had already lasted for eighteen years, when they might have seemed to acquire a right to the kingdom? And what about Jehu, who killed king Jehoram, for whom he himself had used to fight, who destroyed the line of Ahab and killed all the worshipers of Baal? Were they not private persons? As such you may of course consider them as private persons because they were not equipped with power in the normal way. But since we know them to have been called by extraordinary means, God himself, so to speak, evidently girding them with their swords, we may regard them not only as more than mere private persons, but also as placed above anyone equipped with power by ordinary means. The vocation of Moses is confirmed by an express word of God and by the most obvious signs. Ehud is explicitly said to have been incited by God to kill the tyrant and save Israel. And Jehu, anointed at the command of the prophet Elijah, was ordered to destroy the line of Ahab, although the leading people had greeted him as the king earlier on. The same can be shown for all others like them who can be adduced from Scripture.

But when God has spoken neither himself nor through prophets out of the ordinary, we must be especially sober and circumspect. If someone arrogates authority by reason of divine inspiration, he must find out whether he is not rather swelled up with arrogance, does not confuse God with himself, and creates his great spirits out of himself, lest he should conceive vanity and beget a lie. And the people, although they may be desiring to fight under the sign of Christ, must find out whether they are not perhaps fighting to their own great damage. I do not say that the same God who is sending us Pharaohs and Ahabs in this century does not occasionally also inspire liberators in an extraordinary way. His justice and his mercy have certainly never waned. But when external signs are lacking, we must at least recognize the inner ones by their effects, a mind devoid of all ambition, true and fervid zeal, good conscience, and knowledge, too, lest someone misled by error should serve false gods or being driven mad by ambition should serve himself rather than the true God.

Third Question: Is it Permitted to Resist a Prince Who Oppresses or Destroys the Commonwealth? To What Extent, by Whom, in What Fashion, and by What Right?

Kings Are Created by the People

We have previously shown that it is God who sets up kings, gives them their kingdoms, and chooses them. Now we add that it is the people who constitute kings, deliver them their kingdoms, and approve their election by vote. God wanted it to be like that so that, next to himself, the kings would receive all of their authority and power from the people. That is why they should devote all of their care, thought, and energy to the good of the people, but should not deem themselves to have been raised above the rest by some natural preeminence, as men are raised above sheep and cattle. They should rather remember that they have been born to exactly the same lot as all other human beings and that they have been raised from the earth to their rank by the votes of the people, as if by shoulders on which the burdens of the commonwealth may later for the greater part fall back again. . . .

In general, since no one is born as a king, can turn himself into a king, or is able to rule without a people, whereas the people can very well exist on their own before there are kings, all kings were obviously first created by the people. Although the sons and nephews of kings may seem to have turned their kingdoms into hereditary possessions by imitating their fathers' virtues, and although the power of free election

seems to have vanished in certain regions, it thus remains the custom in all well-established kingdoms that children do not succeed to their fathers until they are constituted by the people, as if they had had no claims upon the throne at all. They are not born to their fathers as heirs of a family property, but are only considered kings as soon as those who represent the people's majesty have invested them with the kingdom through scepter and crown. Even in Christian kingdoms that are nowadays said to descend by hereditary succession there are obvious traces of this fact. In France, Spain, England, and other countries it thus is the custom that kings are inaugurated and put in possession of the kingdom, so to speak, by the estates of the realm, the peers, the patricians, and the magnates who represent the community of the people.

The Nature of Tyranny

So far we have described a king. Now we shall describe tyrants a little more accurately. We have said that a king is someone legitimately ruling over a kingdom conveyed to him by inheritance or election and properly committed to his care. It follows that a tyrant, is the direct opposite of a king, is someone who has either usurped power by force or fraud or who governs a kingdom that has been freely conveyed to him against human and divine law and persists in administering it in violation of the laws and pacts to which he has bound himself by oath. A single individual may of course fall into both kinds of tyranny at the same time. The former is commonly called a tyrant without title, the latter a tyrant by conduct. It can, however, also happen that someone governs justly over a kingdom that he has occupied by force, or governs unjustly over a kingdom legally conveyed to him. In that case, since kingship is a matter of right rather than of heredity, a function rather than a possession, someone administering his office badly is worthier of being called a tyrant than someone who has not entered his office in the proper way. . . .

Natural law, first of all, teaches us to preserve and protect our lives and liberty, without which life can hardly be lived, against all violence and injury. This is what nature has instilled in dogs against wolves, bulls against lions, doves against hawks, and chickens against kites. So much the more in man against man, if man becomes a wolf to man. Hence no doubt is permitted whether one should fight back, for nature herself is fighting here.

In addition there is the law of peoples, which distinguishes between countries, fixes limits and sets up borders that everybody is obliged to defend against foreign enemies. Hence it is just as permissible to resist Alexander if he mounts an enormous fleet in order to invade a people over which he has no rights and from which he has suffered no harm as it is to resist the pirate Diomedes if he raids the sea with but a single ship. Under such circumstances Alexander outdoes Diomedes, not by his greater right, but merely by his greater impunity. One may also resist Alexander's devastation of a region as though he were a vagabond stealing a cloak, and resist an enemy putting a city under siege as though he were a burglar breaking into a house.

Above all there is civil law, by which all human societies are constituted according to particular laws, so that each of them is governed by its own laws. Some societies are ruled by one man, others by several, and still others by all; some reject government by women, others accept it; some elect kings from a specific line, others do not; and so on. If anyone should try to break this law by force or fraud, all are obliged to resist him, because he violates society, to which everything is owed, and undermines the foundations of the fatherland, to which we are bound by nature, laws, and sacred oaths. If we neglect to resist him, we are truly traitors of our fatherland, deserters of human society, and contemners of law. Since the laws of nature, of peoples, and civil law all command us to take up arms against tyrants of that kind, no reason at all can be offered to dissuade us from our obligation. No oath, no pact, no obligation of any kind,

whether private or public, can intervene. Even a private individual is therefore permitted to resist usurpations by a tyrant of this sort . . . .

These considerations apply while the tyranny is still in the happening, as they say, that is, while the tyrant is still getting in motion, plotting, and tunneling. As soon, however, as he has gotten so much control over things that the people are conquered and swear an oath to him, that the commonwealth has been suppressed and transferred its power to him, and that the kingdom has regularly consented to a change in its laws, he has acquired the title that he was formerly lacking. He is then not only in factual but also in legal possession. Even though the people has only superficially agreed to accept his yoke, but has acted against the will of its heart, it is nevertheless right for it to obey and calmly to acquiesce in the will of God, who transfers kingdoms from one hand to another as he pleases. Otherwise there would be no kingdom at all whose jurisdiction could not be called into doubt. But this shall only apply if he who used to be a tyrant without title governs legitimately after he has acquired his title and does not continue to act as a tyrant by conduct. . . .

What the Law Permits to Be Done Against Tyrants by Conduct

We must be rather careful in examining the case of those who are tyrants by conduct, regardless of whether they acquired power by law or by force. First of all we must take into consideration that all princes are mere human beings. Their reason cannot be protected from passion any more than their souls can be separated from their bodies. It is therefore not the case that we should wish for none but perfect princes. We should rather regard ourselves lucky if we have been furnished middling ones. If a prince occasionally exceeds the proper measure, if he does not always follow reason, if he is a little lazy about the public good, a little negligent about providing justice, or not so keen on military defense, he is not really a tyrant at all times. Since a man does not govern other men as a god, as men do with oxen, but rather as a human being born to the same lot as they, it is not only presumptuous of a prince to mistreat human beings as though they were brutes, but also iniquitous of the people to look for a god in their prince, and a divinity in his fallible nature. If the prince, however, overturns the commonwealth on purpose, if he unabashedly demolishes the laws, if he cares not a bit about promises, conventions, justice, and piety, if he becomes an enemy to his people, and finally if he exercises all or the most important tyrannical skills that we have mentioned, then he can really be judged a tyrant, that is (although there was a time when that word had more pleasant connotations) an enemy of God and man.

QUESTIONS

1. Duplessis-Mornay was a Protestant living under the rule of a Roman Catholic. How might his status affect his political theory?

2. How might a monarch, like King James, argue against Duplessis-Mornay's theories?

3. How are the powers of a king limited?

4. Under what circumstances is resistance to a lawful ruler allowable? Who may offer resistance?

5. Absolute monarchs maintain that they received their authority from God. How does Duplessis-Mornay think monarchs get their power?

73

■ *Magdalena and Balthasar Paumgartner* ■

LETTERS
(1592–1596)

Balthasar Paumgartner (1551–1600) and his wife, Magdalena Behaim (1555–1642), lived in Nuremberg, in south-central Germany. Children of prominent families, they were never famous themselves, and belonged to that solid class of merchants who provided much of the dynamism of early modern business. Balthasar spent long periods on the road traveling on business to the great markets of southern Germany and Northern Italy. His travels were long and dangerous, but they did provide his family with a measure of prosperity. Magdalena, who rarely traveled herself, remained behind in Nuremberg, but, as her letters show, her role in her husband's business was an important one. Most European trade of the time was carried on by people like the Paumgartners, working on a small scale within a network of family and kinship in which both men and women played important roles. These family firms dealt in goods from as close as the next town to as far as Asia, but in every case business involved a high degree of risk and was ultimately dependent upon personal relations among merchants and their families.

Magdalena's letters reveal much about life in Europe during a period of dramatic religious, political, and social change, though these matters are as often as not subordinated to news of family and business.

Magdalena to Balthasar

19 April 1596, in Nuremberg

Honest, kind, dear Paumgartner:

Your pleasing letter reached me last Saturday through brother-in-law Jörg. I understand from it what I must get from Andreas Imhoff and Torisani. It will be done most diligently. I must also reserve with Torisani a barrel of wine [from a shipment] coming to him for the holidays; Hans Christoph Scheurl has also been promised one. However, he recently told brother-in-law Paul that if no one has need of it, he would allot it to him so we have the one we need for [Adam] Krämer, to whom I have already sent 2½ kegs. Wilhelm Kress has taken 1½ kegs. I think the wine will have proved too expensive for Hans Christoph; it will come to 9 gulden before excise taxes. They say that one now may buy good wine at the marketplace for 5 gulden because, praise God, we have had the necessary good weather. Among the peasants at market Paul could get only 10½ to 11 gulden before excise taxes for last year's new wine. I took it and distributed the wine.

[Adam] Krämer this week sent us as a gift 2½ kegs of strong Egerich beer. He writes about how ill his wife is. . . . I thanked him for the beer; I must send him a Dutch cheese right away.

I am happy to hear that you are beginning your journey home so soon, on Tuesday, after the servant departs. May Almighty God give you luck and safety on your journey and help bring us together again in joy and health! Amen.

Hans Albrecht wrote to you this week, but as there was nothing pressing in the letter, I decided not to send it on to you. He writes mainly to say that we should undertake our planned trip as soon as possible. So I beg you most earnestly, dear Paumgartner, to let me know where around Fürth you have in mind for us to meet you, and, depending on when you depart [Frankfurt] and when the springs [of Langenschwalbach] have refreshed you, about what time you should be arriving there. We very much want to come out and meet you with our two wagons full [of family and friends]. Just let me know from Frankfurt, or from whatever you can, so that we do not make the trip in vain.

If you see something that is rare and special when you are in Mainz or at the springs, please get it for me. Should you forget, I already have enough in you for which to give God thanks.

Brother-in-law Paul has wondered why you have not written a reply to his letter concerning the land purchase.

Otherwise, I have nothing especially new to report, except that Hans Flenz is being buried today in the new *Bau*. I was asked whether you might also join the funeral train. Yesterday Rosenthaler on Dieling Street died.

Herewith is the newspaper from Herr König, who sends greetings. I went myself from vespers to fetch it from him. He says he is sorry he has not seen you for so long.

I know nothing else to say to you, dear Paumgartner, except to ask that you take care of yourself. I do not know how you will be provided for in the kitchen. May it always be well with you! I have long wanted to hitch the three horses and, with brother-in-law Paul, come to you. But then I have thought better of it, [remembering that] you have not given me permission to do so, and it would also be expensive. And you have also said that you do not need me at this time. So I have restrained myself. Otherwise, I have devoted my week to cleaning and scrubbing.

Take my greetings into your heart of hearts, you chosen treasure, until God helps us come together again in joy. Brother-in-law Paul, Stephen Bair, his wife, and Christoph Behaim send sincere greetings. And Madela says that I should greet Uncle warmly. She must be watching what I am doing, because there is nothing in your letter for her.

Be commended to Almighty God in grace,
Magdalena Balthasar Paumgartner

Magdalena to Balthasar

18 April 1594, in Nuremberg

Honest, kind, dear Paumgartner:
Your letter from Augsburg has come. I will hope in Almighty God that when this letter reaches [Lucca], you will also, with God's help, already have arrived there. May he again grant you his divine grace!

I am happy to learn that the horses [you are planning to buy] have been well cared for up to now.

I paid the tailor already after your departure, but he tells me there is no woolen material left over.

When [our servant] Hans arrives, I will send him also to the count, as you instruct.

I have given your brother Jörg the money that belongs to Bartel Albrecht to deliver to him. Brother-in-law Jörg tells me that someone has already written to you about your estimated expenses for shipments to Frankfurt.

I will not neglect to admonish the peasants [in Wöhrd], and I will see that brother-in-law Paul does so in Engelthal.

The wine, or rather new wine, came the Sunday after your departure. Brother-in-law Jörg has calculated the cost at 23 gulden per large measure, no less. I have sent one to [your] father, to Wilhelm Imhoff, and to Wilhelm Kress. Since [Paul] Behaim did not want one, Kress asked me to let him have it. So I have laid aside only one for ourselves. One for [Wolf] Rehlein; the Pfauds one. When I get the bill for the excise tax, which Jörg calculated for me on each measure, I will send each one a bill for his share.

Otherwise the matter is settled. I did, however, have a fight with the wine controller. When I sent him the money, 34 gulden, he sent it back to me, tore up the original bill, and said he had to make a new one because an additional barrel bought at the market must be added. I twice sent word to him that I knew of no such purchase and that you bought no wine whatsoever at the market, otherwise one would know about it. Finally, brother-in-law Jörg went there, returned, and asked if perhaps Hans had taken a barrel on your behalf, and it then dawned on me for the first time that the barrel we had drunk so quickly you had gotten with Hans. So I had to send him $40^3/_4$ gulden. He informed me that it had been a good nine weeks since he had given you the bill for that barrel. I am puzzled why you have been so slow to pay it.

Kind, dear treasure, I have nothing more to write at this time, except that the delivery of invitations [to brother Paul's wedding] has gone well, four happy tables [of guests have promised to come]. May God grant that the wedding also goes well.

Magdalena to Bathasar

1592

Your letter arrived today, Wednesday, only a short time ago. In the great affliction so recently brought upon me by God, I had waited longingly for it on Monday. After I had written to you last Thursday, he [little Balthasar] had a very bad night, so bad that I did not leave his bed then or on the following night because his breathing had become so difficult and continued that way until Saturday noon. All the while he was constantly talking, although not in such a way that any could understand him. Finally he wanted to get out of bed. Seeing that he was too weak to do so, we started to lift him up, whereupon he began to convulse. Within a quarter hour he was dead. . . . May God now keep him safe until we come to him!

I must now accept these facts: that we had him for so short a time, that he has not really been ours [but rather God's], and that we have unfortunately known in him a short-lived joy. I must accept God's will and let him go in peace to God, for there is nothing left in this for me now except suffering, heartache, and tears. I must learn to block it from my mind as best I can and you must do the same, my heart's treasure. You must strike it from your mind and be patient. Perhaps God will again be merciful to us and help us to forget this now that he has afflicted us so much. I know that if you were here all my suffering would be so much easier! For me every day now becomes as three. I trust you will make your way home in advance of the [merchants'] convoy, if you possibly can. I worry, however, that when you receive this tragic news from cousin Paul Scheurl's letter and from mine you will not want to hurry home ahead of the convoy. I will, however, hope better of you. May God help us to be together again in joy and without any more misfortune. I know from your letter that the Lord God has helped you make your way safely there; may he now grant you a good fair. I have faithfully buried our son as one who now lives in another body that knows no human suffering. Too early the clergy and the choir carried him away, too soon the bells were tolled for him.

QUESTIONS

1. What are Magdalena's duties as a merchant's wife?

2. Some historians have argued that early modern people avoided too close an attachment to their children because of high death rates. Does this argument hold true in the Paumgartners' case? How can you tell?

3. What is Magdalena and Balthasar's relationship like? How different does their marriage seem from its modern equivalent?

4. Compare Magdalena's letters with those written by Margaret Paston. How do their concerns differ? How are they alike?

5. Letter-writing has been described as a "lost art" in the modern world, but it was obviously alive and well in the sixteenth century. What purpose did letters serve?

PART
IV

■ ■ ■

THE ANCIEN RÉGIME

THE WARS OF RELIGION
74. Henry IV, *The Edict of Nantes* (1598)
75. Cardinal Richelieu, *The Political Testament* (1638)
76. Hans von Grimmelshausen, *Simplicissimus* (1669)

SUBJECTS AND SOVEREIGNS
77. James I, *True Law of a Free Monarchy* (1598)
78. Thomas Hobbes, *Leviathan* (1651)
79. John Locke, *Second Treatise of Government* (1689)
80. *The English Bill of Rights* (1689)
81. Duc de Saint-Simon, *Memoirs* (1694–1723)
82. Napoleon Bonaparte, *The Napoleonic Code (The French Civil Code)* (1804)

THE WARS OF RELIGION

74

■ *Henry IV* ■

THE EDICT OF NANTES

(1598)

Henry IV (1589–1610) was the Protestant king of Navarre who led the Huguenot cause during the French wars of religion. His grandmother was Marguerite de Navarre and his mother Jeanne d'Albret, both educated and remarkably talented women. Henry achieved the French throne through a series of accidents, the last of which was the assassination of Henry III in 1589. It was clear that no Protestant could ever command the allegiance of the mass of French people or peacefully rule in the Catholic capital of Paris. Henry converted to Catholicism, defeated his enemies, and ended the long years of religious warfare.

The Edict of Nantes was the compromise settlement that granted limited toleration for the Huguenots. It was a landmark in the history of religious toleration, though its main features were watered down under Louis XIII. The Edict was finally rescinded under Louis XIV in 1685.

Henry, by the grace of God king of France and of Navarre, to all to whom these presents come, greeting:

Among the infinite benefits which it has pleased God to heap upon us, the most signal and precious is his granting us the strength and ability to withstand the fearful disorders and troubles which prevailed on our advent in this kingdom. The realm was so torn by innumerable factions and sects that the most legitimate of all the parties was fewest in numbers. God has given us strength to stand out against this storm; we have finally surmounted the waves and made our port of safety—peace for our state. For which his be the glory all in all, and ours a free recognition of his grace in making use of our instrumentality

in the good work. . . . We implore and await from the Divine Goodness the same protection and favor which he has ever granted to this kingdom from the beginning. . . .

We have, by this perpetual and irrevocable edict, established and proclaimed and do establish and proclaim:

First, that the recollection of everything done by one party or the other between March, 1585, and our accession to the crown, and during all the preceding period of troubles, remain obliterated and forgotten, as if no such things had ever happened.

We ordain that the Catholic Apostolic and Roman religion shall be restored and reestablished in all places and localities of this our kingdom and countries subject to our sway, where the exercise of the same has been interrupted, in order that it may be peaceably and freely exercised, without any trouble or hindrance; forbidding very expressly all persons, of whatsoever estate, quality, or condition, from troubling, molesting, or disturbing ecclesiastics in the celebration of divine service, in the enjoyment or collection of tithes, fruits, or revenues of their benefices, and all other rights and dues belonging to them; and that all those who during the troubles have taken possession of churches, houses, goods or revenues, belonging to the said ecclesiastics, shall surrender to them entire possession and peaceable enjoyment of such rights, liberties, and sureties as they had before they were deprived of them.

And in order to leave no occasion for troubles or differences between our subjects, we have permitted, and herewith permit, those of the said religion called Reformed to live and abide in all the cities and places of this our kingdom and countries of our sway, without being annoyed, molested, or compelled to do anything in the matter of religion contrary to their consciences . . . upon condition that they comport themselves in other respects according to that which is contained in this our present edict.

It is permitted to all lords, gentlemen, and other persons making profession of the said religion called Reformed, holding the right of high justice [or a certain feudal tenure], to exercise the said religion in their houses.

We also permit those of the said religion to make and continue the exercise of the same in all villages and places of our dominion where it was established by them and publicly enjoyed several and divers times in the year 1597, up to the end of the month of August, notwithstanding all decrees and judgements to the contrary.

We very expressly forbid to all those of the said religion its exercise, either in respect to ministry, regulation, discipline, or the public instruction of children, or otherwise, in this our kingdom and lands of our dominion, otherwise than in the places permitted and granted by the present edict.

It is forbidden as well to perform any function of the said religion in our court or retinue, or in our lands and territories beyond the mountains, or in our city of Paris, or within five leagues of the said city.

We also forbid all our subjects, of whatever quality and condition, from carrying off by force or persuasion, against the will of their parents, the children of the said religion, in order to cause them to be baptized or confirmed in the Catholic Apostolic and Roman Church; and the same is forbidden to those of the said religion called Reformed, upon penalty of being punished with especial severity.

Books concerning the said religion called Reformed may not be printed and publicly sold, except in cities and places where the public exercise of the said religion is permitted.

We ordain that there shall be no difference or distinction made in respect to the said religion, in receiving pupils to be instructed in universities, colleges, and schools; nor in receiving the sick and poor into hospitals, retreats and public charities.

Those of the said religion called Reformed shall be obliged to respect the laws of the Catholic Apostolic and Roman Church, recognized in this our kingdom, for the consummation of marriages contracted, or to be contracted, as regards the degrees of consanguinity and kinship.

QUESTIONS

1. Does Henry IV grant complete liberty of conscience in his edict? If not, how is freedom of religion restricted?

2. What is the position of the Catholic Church under the edict?

3. *The Edict of Nantes* is often seen as a step toward religious toleration. How tolerant is it?

4. Although the edict helped restore order to France, many people argued that it created more problems than it solved. Can you think what some of these might have been?

5. The edict was a declaration made by the king alone, without the advice or assistance of any other governmental institution. What does it reveal about the power of the monarch? About the king's role in religious affairs?

75

■ *Cardinal Richelieu* ■

THE POLITICAL TESTAMENT

(1638)

Armand Jean du Plessis, Cardinal and Duke Richelieu (1585–1642), was the son of a minor official of the French court. He was trained for church service and made his mark as a delegate to the Estates-General of 1614. He was brought into the service of Louis XIII by the Queen Regent, Marie de Médicis, and eventually became the king's favorite and chief advisor. An able diplomat and a master politician, Richelieu played an important role in the consolidation of the royal state. His principal goal was to centralize administration and to harness the power of the nobility and localities. He was chiefly responsible for French foreign policy, including France's participation in the Thirty Years' War.

Written for the instruction of Louis XIII, Richelieu's *Political Testament* contains the cardinal's assessment of his own achievements. It was composed over the course of several years, with the last events mentioned dating from 1638. It was not published for another half century, and then only in a pirated Dutch edition.

When Your Majesty resolved to admit me both to your council and to an important place in your confidence for the direction of your affairs, I may say that the Huguenots shared the state with you; that the nobles conducted themselves as if they were not your subjects, and the most powerful governors of the provinces as if they were sovereign in their offices.

I may say that the bad example of all of these was so prejudicial to the welfare of this realm that even the best courts were affected by it, and endeavored, in certain cases, to diminish your legitimate authority as far as it was possible in order to carry their own powers beyond the limits of reason.

I may say that everyone measured his own merit by his audacity; that in place of esteeming the benefits which they received from Your Majesty at their proper worth, they all valued them only as they satisfied the demands of their imaginations; that the most scheming were held to be the wisest, and often found themselves the most prosperous.

In broadest outline, Sire, these have been the matters with which Your Majesty's reign has thus far been concerned. I would consider them most happily concluded if they were followed by an era of repose during which you could introduce into your realm a wealth of benefits of all types. In order to present the problem to you, it is necessary to look into the nature of the various classes in your realm and the state which it comprises, together with your own role, both as a private and a public person. In sum, what will be indicated is the need for a competent and faithful council, whose advice should be listened to and followed in governing the state. It is to the detailed explanation and urging of this that the remainder of my testament will be devoted.

While the nobility merits to be generously treated if it does well, it is necessary at the same time to be severe with it if it ever fails in what its status demands of it. I do not hesitate to say that those nobles who, degenerating from the virtuous conduct of their forebears, fail to serve the crown constantly and courageously with both their swords and their lives, as the laws of the state require, deserve the loss of the privileges of their birth and should be reduced to sharing the burdens of the common people. Since honor should be more dear to them than life itself, it would be much more of a punishment to them to be deprived of the former than the latter.

All students of politics agree that when the common people are too well off it is impossible to keep them peaceable. The explanation for this is that they are less well informed than the members of the other orders in the state, who are much more cultivated and enlightened, and so if not preoccupied with the search for the necessities of existence, find it difficult to remain within the limits imposed by both common sense and the law.

It would not be sound to relieve them of all taxation and similar charges, since in such a case they would lose the mark of their subjection and consequently the awareness of their station. Thus being free from paying tribute, they would consider themselves exempted from obedience. One should compare them with mules, which being accustomed to work, suffer more when long idle than when kept busy. But just as this work should be reasonable, with the burdens placed upon these animals proportionate to their strength, so it is likewise with the burdens placed upon the people. If they are not moderate, even when put to good public use, they are certainly unjust. I realize that when a king undertakes a program of public works it is correct to say that what the people gain from it is returned by paying the taille. In the same fashion it can be maintained that what a king takes from the people returns to them, and that they advance it to him only to draw upon it for the enjoyment of their leisure and their investments, which would be impossible if they did not contribute to the support of the state.

I also know that many princes have lost their countries and ruined their subjects by failing to maintain sufficient military forces for their protection, fearing to tax them too heavily. Some people have even fallen into slavery under their enemies because they have wanted too much liberty under their natural sovereign. There is, however, a certain level which one cannot exceed without injustice, common sense indicating in each instance the proportion which should prevail between the burden and the ability of those who sustain it. This consideration ought always to be religiously observed, although a prince cannot be esteemed good just because he taxes his subjects no more than necessary, nor considered evil because occasionally he takes more.

Also, just as when a man is wounded, his heart, weakened by the loss of blood, draws upon the reserves of the lower parts of the body only after the upper parts are exhausted, so in moments of great public need the king should, in so far as he is able, make use of the abundance of the rich before bleeding the poor heavily. This is the best advice Your Majesty can follow, and it is easy to put into practice since in the future you will draw the principal income for your state from the general tax farms, which are much closer to the interests of the rich than of the poor, since the latter, spending less, contribute less to the total.

The public interest ought to be the sole objective of the prince and his councillors, or, at the least, both are obliged to have it foremost in mind, and preferred to all private gain. It is impossible to overestimate the good which a prince and those serving him in government can do if they religiously follow this principle, and one can hardly imagine the evils which befall a state if private interest is preferred to the public good and actually gains the ascendency. True philosophy, as well as the precepts of both Christianity and sound politics, teach this truth so clearly that a prince's councillors can hardly too often remind him of so necessary a principle, nor the prince punish too severely those members of his council despicable enough not to practice it.

Princes ordinarily easily consent to the overall plans proposed for their states because in so doing they have nothing in mind save reason and justice, which they easily accept when they meet no obstacle which turns them off the path. When the occasion arises, however, of putting into practical action the wise programs they have adopted, they do not always show the same firmness. Distracting interests, pity and compassion, favoritism and importunities of all sorts obstruct their best intentions to a degree they often cannot overcome sufficiently to ignore private consideration, which ought never influence public affairs. It is in such matters that they should summon up all their strength against inclinations toward weakness, keeping before their eyes the fact that those whom God has destined to protect others should have no characteristics but those advantageous to the public interest, and to which they should adhere inflexibly.

Power being one of the things most necessary to the grandeur of kings and the success of their governments, those who have the principal management of states are particularly obliged to omit nothing which could contribute to making their masters fully and universally respected. As goodness is the object of love, so power is the cause of fear. It is certain that of all the forces capable of producing results in public affairs, fear, if based on both esteem and reverence, is the most effective, since it can drive everyone to do his duty. If sthis principle is of great efficacy with regard to internal affairs, it is of no less value externally, since both foreigners and subjects take the same view of redoubtable power and both refrain from offending a prince whom they recognize as being able to hurt them if he so wishes. I have said already that this power of which I speak should be based on esteem and respect. I hasten to add that this is so necessary that if it is based on anything else there is the grave danger that instead of producing a reasonable fear the result will be a hatred of princes, for whom the worst possible fate is to incur public disapprobation.

There are several kinds of power which can make princes respected and feared—it is a tree with various branches, all nourished by the same root. The prince ought to be powerful because of his good reputation, because of a reasonable number of soldiers kept continuously under arms, because of a sufficient revenue to meet his ordinary expenses, plus a special sum of money in his treasury to cover frequent but unexpected contingencies, and, finally, because of the possession of the hearts of his subjects, as we will clearly demonstrate.

A good reputation is especially necessary to a prince, for if we hold him in high regard he can accomplish more with his name alone than a less well esteemed ruler can with great armies at his command. It is imperative that he guard it above life itself, and it is better to risk fortune and grandeur than to allow the slightest blemish to fall upon it, since it is certain that the first lessening of his reputation, no matter how slight, is a step in the most dangerous of directions and can lead to his ruin.

Those who guide themselves by the rules and precepts contained in this testament will without doubt acquire names of no little weight

in the minds of both their subjects and their foreign neighbors. This is particularly so if, being devoted to God, they are also devoted to themselves; that is, if they keep their word and are faithful to their promises. These are indispensable conditions to the maintenance of the reputation of a prince, for just as he who is destitute of them is esteemed by no one, so he who possess them is revered and trusted by all.

QUESTIONS

1. What problems did Richelieu face when he took power?

2. Richelieu is in a delicate position, because he is totally dependent upon the king's goodwill for his success. How is his weakness reflected in his testament?

3. Richelieu compares the common people with mules. Why? What does this analogy reflect about his view of society and social relations?

4. What, according to Richelieu, is the most important prop of a king's power?

5. Does the cardinal's advice resemble Machiavelli's program in any way? How do they differ?

76

■ *Hans von Grimmelshausen* ■

SIMPLICISSIMUS

(1669)

Hans von Grimmelshausen (ca. 1622–1676) was the son of a German innkeeper. Orphaned as a youth, he was carried away by soldiers during the Thirty Years' War. He was soon pressed into service as a musketeer in the imperial army. His literary skills, however, gained him a job as a secretary to a general and then as a clerk to a noble family. A charge of embezzlement brought his career full circle, for he ended his life as an innkeeper.

Grimmelshausen began his writings while still a soldier. He specialized in satires and in picaresque stories, of which *Simplicissimus* was the most famous. The title is translated as "The Simplest of the Simple." Much of the early part of the work (which includes the section excerpted here) is thought to be autobiographical. No other work of the period so vividly depicts the horror of the Thirty Years' War.

Although it was not my intention to lead these riders to my dad's farm, truth demands that I leave to posterity the cruelties committed in this our German war, to prove these evils were done to our advantage. Who else would have told me there was a God in Heaven if the warriors had not destroyed my father's house and forced me, through my captivity, to meet other people, for till this moment I had imagined my dad, mum and the rest of our household to be the sole inhabitants of this earth as no other man nor human dwelling were known to me but the one where I daily went in and out. Soon I had to learn man's origin in this world. I was merely a human in shape and a Christian only in name, otherwise just an animal. Our gracious God looked upon my innocence with pity and wished to bring me both to his and my awareness, and although there were a thousand ways of doing this, he used the one by which my dad and mum were punished as an example to others for their careless education of me.

The first thing that the riders did was to stable their horses. After that each one started his own business which indicated nothing but ruin and destruction. While some started to slaughter, cook and fry, so that it looked as though they wished to prepare a gay feast, others stormed through the house from top to bottom as if the golden fleece of Colchis were hidden there. Others again took linen, clothing and other goods, making them into bundles as if they intended going to market; what they did not want was broken up and destroyed. Some stabbed their swords through hay and straw as if they had not enough pigs to stab. Some shook the feathers out of the beds and filled the ticks

with ham and dried meat as if they could sleep more comfortably on these. Others smashed the ovens and windows as if to announce an eternal summer. They beat copper and pewter vessels into lumps and packed the mangled pieces away. Bedsteads, tables, chairs and benches were burned although many stacks of dried wood stood in the yard. Earthenware pots and pans were all broken, perhaps because our guests preferred roasted meats, or perhaps they intended to eat only one meal with us. Our maid had been treated in the stable in such a way that she could not leave it any more—a shameful thing to tell! They bound the farm-hand and laid him on the earth, put a clamp of wood in his mouth, and emptied a milking churn full of horrid dung water into his belly. This they called the Swedish drink, and they forced him to lead a party of soldiers to another place, where they looted men and cattle and brought them back to our yard. Among them were my dad, my mum and Ursula.

The soldiers now started to take the flints out of their pistols and in their stead screwed the thumbs of the peasants, and they tortured the poor wretches as if they were burning witches. They put one of the captive peasants into the baking-oven and put fire on him, although he had confessed nothing. Then they tied a rope round the head of another one, and twisted it with the help of a stick so tightly that blood gushed out through his mouth, nose and ears. In short everybody had his own invention to torture the peasants and each peasant suffered his own martyrdom. My dad alone appeared to me the most fortunate for he confessed with laughter what others were forced to say under pains and miserable lament, and such honour was done to him without doubt because he was the master of the house. They put him next to a fire, tied him so that he could move neither hands nor feet, and rubbed the soles of his feet with wet salt, which our old goat had to lick off. This tickled him so much that he almost wanted to burst with laughter, and it seemed to me so gentle and pleasant—for I had never seen nor heard my dad making such long-lasting laughter—that I half in companionship and half in ignorance joined heartily with him. In such merriment he confessed his guilt and revealed the hidden treasure, which was richer in gold, pearls and jewels than might have been expected of a peasant. What happened to the captive women, maids and daughters I do not know as the soldiers would not let me watch how they dealt with them. I only very well remember that I heard them miserably crying in corners here and there, and I believe my mum and Ursula had no better fate than the others.

In the midst of this misery I turned the spit and did not worry as I hardly understood what all this meant. In the afternoon I helped to water the horses and so found our maid in the stable looking amazingly dishevelled. I did not recognise her but she spoke to me with pitiful voice:

'Oh, run away, boy, or the soldiers will take you with them. Look out, escape! Can't you see how evil. . . .'

More she could not say.

So I made my way to a village but when I arrived found it in full flame; a troop of horsemen had just looted it and put it on fire. They had killed some of the peasants, driven away many and captured a few amongst whom was the vicar. Oh, God, how human life is full of pain and misery! Scarcely one misfortune has ended when we are overcome by another. The riders were ready to go and were leading the vicar on a rope. Some shouted: 'Shoot the rascal down!', and others demanded money from him. He raised his hands and asked for the sake of the Last Judgment for pardon and Christian charity. But in vain. One of them rode toward him giving

him a blow over the head so that he fell to the ground and recommended his soul to God. Nor had the other captive peasants any better fate.

The day following the burning of the village, as I was sitting in my hut saying my prayers and cooking carrots for sustenance, about forty to fifty musketeers surrounded me. These, although astonished at my unusual appearance, stormed through my hut seeking that which was not to be found; for I had nothing but books which they threw about as they were of no value to them. Finally, looking at me more carefully and seeing what a poor bird they had trapped, they realised that there was no good booty to be gained from me. My hard life amazed them and they had great pity for my tender youth, especially the officer who was in command. Indeed he honoured me and politely requested me to show him and his men the way out of the wood in which they had been lost for a long time. I did not refuse but led them by the nearest path toward the village where the vicar had been so badly treated, as I knew no other way. Before we left the wood we saw about ten peasants partly armed with blunderbusses and others occupied in burying something. The musketeers went up to them shouting: 'Halt! Halt!' The peasants answered with their guns but when they saw they were overpowered by the soldiers, they dispersed so that the tired musketeers could not follow them.

When I arrived back I discovered that my flintbox and all my belongings, including my whole store of miserable victuals, which I had grown all through the summer in my garden and saved up for the winter, had disappeared. Whither now, I thought. Need taught me to pray the more. I exercised all my poor wit to find out what to do and what not to do—but with my small experience I could not come to any real decision. The best was to recommend myself to God and put all my trust in him, otherwise I would have despaired and perished. My mind was still full of that which I had seen and heard that very day. I did not think so much about food and my own preservation as about the hatred between soldiers and peasants, and in my foolishness there seemed no other explanation than that there must undoubtedly be two kinds of men in the world, not one single stock derived from Adam, but as different as wild and tame animals, for they persecute each other so cruelly.

Once at the end of May when I again in my usual although forbidden way crept into a farmyard to fetch my food, I found myself in the kitchen, but soon realised that the folk were still awake (where dogs hung about I wisely never went). I kept the kitchen door leading into the courtyard wide open so that if danger came I should be able to run away, and there I remained quiet as a mouse, waiting until the people would go to bed. In the meantime I noticed a slit in the kitchen-hatch leading to the living room. There I stealthily crept to see whether the peasants would not soon go to sleep. But my hopes came to nothing, as they had just dressed themselves, and instead of a candle a sulphurous blue flame stood on a bench, near which they smeared grease on sticks, brooms, forks, stools and benches, and rode out on these through the windows. At this I was terribly amazed and felt great horror, but as I had been accustomed to still more horrible things and had all my life neither read nor heard of witches, I did not take it too seriously, mostly because everything happened so quietly.

After all had flown away, I went into the room and here I considered what I could take with me and where to look for it. With such thoughts I sat down astride on a bench but as soon as I did so, I flew with the bench out through the window, leaving behind knapsack and blunderbuss, which I had put down almost as a reward for witches' ointment. My sitting down, flying off and descent happened in one moment, for I arrived as it seemed to me instantly amongst a great mass of people; possibly because of fear I did not realise the length of my journey. These people were dancing a remarkable dance such as I had never seen in my life. They held hands and turned their backs inwards as one has seen the Three Graces painted, so that their faces turned outwards, forming many rings one within the other. The innermost ring consisted of seven or eight persons; the next one of double this number; the third more than both, and so on, so that in the outer circle were more than two hundred. And as always once circle danced to the left and the other to the right, I could not see how many rings they had formed nor what stood in the middle around which they danced. It looked strange and horrid as all bobbed their heads ludicrously, and just as strange was the music. Everyone, it appeared to me, sang as he danced which gave an amazing harmony. My bench which carried me there came to rest near the musicians who stood about outside the rings of the dancers. Some of the musicians had instead of flutes, bagpipes and shawms, nothing but adders, vipers and blind-worms, on which they whistled merrily. Some had cats into whose behinds they blew and fingered on the tail, which sounded similar to bagpipes. Others bowed on the skulls of horses as on the best fiddles, and others played the harp upon cow skeletons like those which lie in the flayer's pit. One held a bitch under his arm whose tail he turned and fingered her teats. In between devils trumpeted through their noses that the whole forest echoed, and when the dance came to an end, the whole hellish crowd started to rage, shriek, rustle, roar, howl and storm as if they were all mad and senseless. And so one can imagine how I was struck by horror and fear.

In this turmoil a fellow approached me with a gigantic toad under his arm, easily as big as a kettledrum. Its guts had been pulled out through the arse and pushed into its mouth, which looked so revolting that I had to vomit.

'Look here, Simplicius,' he said, 'I know that you are a good lute player. Let's hear a fine tune!'

I was so terrified that I almost fell down on hearing the fellow call me by name; out of fear I became completely speechless and imagined I lay in a deep dream and prayed fervently in my heart that I might wake up. The fellow with the toad however, at whom I stared, pushed his nose forwards and backwards like a Calcutta cock, and at last he knocked me with it on the breast so that I nearly choked. At this I started to cry loudly to God and thereupon the whole host disappeared, and in a flash it was pitch dark and my heart felt so fearful that I fell to the ground, making the sign of the cross well nigh a hundred times.

QUESTIONS

1. What is the nature of war in the seventeenth century? Who appears to suffer most?

2. Why were soldiers so brutal toward the common people who crossed their paths?

3. *Simplicissimus* speculates that peasants and soldiers must have been different species; yet in fact most soldiers were of peasant stock themselves. What might this fact indicate about the peasantry and about the military?

4. How might Grimmelshausen's status as a village innkeeper have biased his views of peasants?

5. Grimmelshausen's description of a witches' coven is typical of many such accounts. What is it like? How does it demonstrate the taboos and dark fears of the age?

SUBJECTS AND SOVEREIGNS

77

■ *James I* ■

TRUE LAW OF A FREE MONARCHY
(1598)

James VI of Scotland (1567–1625), who also reigned as James I of England from 1603 to 1625, was the product of the ill-fated love affair between Mary, Queen of Scots, and Henry, Lord Darnley. He was raised as a Presbyterian by the Protestant lords who declared that Mary had vacated the throne of Scotland. James fancied himself a theologian and scholar and wrote a number of works on both scholarly and popular issues, including an attack on the use of tobacco. He became king of England at the death of Elizabeth I in 1603 and ruled there for over twenty years. He was considered generous to a fault, but his rough Scottish speech and manner came in for more than their fair share of criticism.

While still king of Scotland, James composed the *True Law of a Free Monarchy* for the instruction of his subjects. It is one of the clearest statements of both the powers and restrictions placed upon a divine right monarch.

THE TREW LAW OF FREE MONARCHIES: OR THE RECIPROCK AND MUTUALL DUTIE BETWIXT A FREE KING AND HIS NATURALL SUBJECTS

As there is not a thing so necessarie to be knowne by the people of any land, next the knowledge of their God, as the right knowledge of their alleageance, according to the forme of governement established among them, especially in a *Monarchie* (which forme of government, as resembling the Divinitie, approacheth nearest to perfection, as all the learned and wise men from the beginning have agreed upon; Unitie being the perfection of all things). So hath the ignorance, and (which is worse) the seduced opinion of the multitude blinded by them, who

thinke themselves able to teach and instruct the ignorants, procured the wracke and overthrow of sundry flourishing Common-wealths; and heaped heavy calamities, threatening utter destruction upon others. And the smiling successe, that unlawfull rebellions have oftentimes had against Princes in ages past (such hath bene the misery, and iniquitie of the time) hath by way of practise strengthened many in their errour: albeit there cannot be a more deceivable argument; then to judge by the justnesse of the cause by the event thereof; as hereafter shall be proved more at length. And among others, no Common-wealth, that ever hath bene since the beginning, hath had greater need of the trew knowledge of this ground, then this our so long disordered, and distracted Common-wealth hath: the misknowledge hereof being the onely spring, from whence have flowed so many endlesse calamities, miseries, and confusions, as is better felt by many, then the cause thereof well knowne, and deepely considered. The naturall zeale therefore, that I beare to this my native countrie, with the great pittie I have to see the so-long disturbance thereof for lack of the trew knowledge of this ground (as I have said before) hath compelled me at last to breake silence, to discharge my conscience to you my deare country men herein, that knowing the ground from whence these your many endlesse troubles have proceeded, as well as ye have already too-long tasted the bitter fruites thereof, ye may by knowledge, and eschewing of the cause escape, and divert the lamentable effects that ever necessarily follow thereupon. I have chosen then onely to set downe in this short Treatise, the trew grounds of the mutuall duty, and alleageance betwixt a free and absolute *Monarche,* and his people.

First then, I will set downe the trew grounds, whereupon I am to build, out of the Scriptures, since *Monarchie* is the trew paterne of Divinitie, as I have already said: next, from the fundamental Lawes of our owne Kingdome, which nearest must concerne us: thirdly, from the law of Nature, by divers similitudes drawne out of the same.

By the Law of Nature the King becomes a naturall Father to all his Lieges at his Coronation: And as the Father of his fatherly duty is bound to care for the nourishing, education, and vertuous government of his children; even so is the king bound to care for all his subjects. As all the toile and paine that the father can take for his children, will be thought light and well bestowed by him, so that the effect thereof redound to their profite and weale; so ought the Prince to doe towards his people. As the kindly father ought to foresee all inconvenients and dangers that may arise towards his children, and though with the hazard of his owne person presse to prevent the same; so ought the King towards his people. As the fathers wrath and correction upon any of his children that offendeth, ought to be by a fatherly chastisement seasoned with pitie, as long as there is any hope of amendment in them;

so ought the King towards any of his Lieges that offend in that measure. And shortly, as the Fathers chiefe joy ought to be in procuring his childrens welfare, rejoycing at their weale, sorrowing and pitying at their evil, to hazard for their safetie, travell for their rest, wake for their sleepe; and in a word, to thinke that his earthly felicitie and life standeth and liveth more in them, nor in himselfe; so ought a good Prince thinke of his people.

As to the other branch of this mutuall and reciprock band, is the duty and alleageance that the Lieges owe to their King: the ground whereof, I take out of the words of *Samuel,* dited by Gods Spirit, when God had given him commandement to heare the peoples voice in choosing and annointing them a King. And because that place of Scripture being well understood, is so pertinent for our purpose, I have insert herein the very words of the Text.

10. So *Samuel* tolde all the wordes of the Lord unto the people that asked a King of him.

11. And he said, this shall be the maner of the King that shall raigne over you: he will take your sonnes, and appoint them to his Charets, and to be his horsemen, and some shall runne before his Charet.

12. Also, hee will make them his captaines over thousands, and captaines over fifties, and to eare his ground, and to reape his harvest, and to make instruments of warre and the things that serve for his charets:

13. Hee will also take your daughters, and make them Apothicaries, and Cookes, and Bakers.

14. And hee will take your fields, and your vineyards, and your best Olive trees, and give them to his servants.

15. And he will take the tenth of your seed, and of your Vineyards, and give it to his Eunuches, and to his servants.

16. And he will take your men servants, and your maid-servants, and the chiefe of your young men, and your asses, and put them to his worke.

17. He will take the tenth of your sheepe: and ye shall be his servants.

18. And ye shall cry out at that day, because of your King, whom ye have chosen you: and the Lord God will not heare you at that day.

19. But the people would not heare the voice of *Samuel,* but did say: Nay, but there shalbe a King over us.

20. And we also will be all like other Nations, and our King shall judge us, and goe out before us, and fight our battels.

As likewise, although I have said, a good king will frame all his actions to be according to the Law; yet is hee not bound thereto but of his good will, and for good example-giving to his subjects: For as in the law of abstaining from eating of flesh in *Lenton,* the king will, for examples sake, make his owne house to observe the Law; yet no man will thinke he needs to take a licence to eate flesh. And although by our Lawes, the bearing and wearing of hag-buts, and pistolets be forbidden, yet no man can find any fault in the King, for causing his traine use them in any raide upon the Borderers, or other male-factours or rebellious subjects. So as I have alreadie said, a good King, although hee be above the Law, will subject and frame his actions thereto, for examples sake to his subjects, and of his owne free-will, but not as subject or bound thereto.

And the agreement of the Law of nature in this our ground with the Lawes and constitutions of God, and man, already alledged, will by two similitudes easily appeare. The King towards his people is rightly compared to a father of children, and to a head of a body composed of divers members: For as fathers, the good Princes, and Magistrates of the people of God acknowledged themselves to their subjects. And for all other well ruled Common-wealths, the stile of *Pater patriae* was ever, and is commonly used to Kings. And the proper office of a King towards his Subjects, agrees very wel with the office of the head towards the body, and all members thereof: For from the head, being the seate of Judgement, proceedeth the care and foresight of guiding, and preventing all evill that may come to the body or any part thereof. The head cares for the body, so doeth the King for his people. As the discourse and direction flowes from the head, and the execution according thereunto belongs to the rest of the members, every one according to their office: so it is betwixt a wise Prince, and his people. As the judgement comming from the head may not onely imploy the members, every one in their owne office, as long as they are able for it; but likewise in case any of them be affected with any infirmitie must care and provide for their remedy, in-case it be curable, and if otherwise, gar cut them off for feare of infecting

Portrait of James I (1567–1625) by Van Somer.

of the rest: even so is it betwixt the Prince, and his people. And as there is ever hope of curing any diseased member by the direction of the head, as long as it is whole; but by the contrary, if it be troubled, all the members are partakers of that paine, so is it betwixt the Prince and his people.

And now first for the fathers part (whose naturally love to his children I described in the first part of this my discourse, speaking of the duty that Kings owe to their Subjects) consider, I pray you what duty his children owe to him, & whether upon any pretext whatsoever, it will not be thought monstrous and unnaturall to his sons, to rise up against him, to control him at their appetite, and when they thinke good to sley him, or to cut him off, and adopt to themselves any other they please in his roome: Or can any pretence of wickednes or rigor on his part be a just excuse for his children to put hand into him? And although wee see by the course of nature, that love useth to descend more than to ascend, in case it were trew, that the father hated and wronged the children never so much, will any man, endued with the least sponke of reason, thinke it lawful for them to meet him with the line? Yea, suppose the father were furiously following his sonnes with a drawn sword, is it lawful for them to turne and strike againe, or make any resistance but by flight? I thinke surely, if there were no more but the example of bruit beasts & unreasonable creatures, it may serve well enough to qualifie and prove this my argument. We reade often the pietie that the Storkes have to their olde and decayed parents: And generally wee know, that there are many sorts of beasts and fowles, that with violence and many bloody strokes will beat and banish their yong ones from them, how soone they perceive them to be able to fend themselves; but wee never read or heard of any resistance on their part, except among the vipers; which prooves such persons, as ought to be reasonable creatures, and yet unnaturally follow this example, to be endued with their viperous nature.

And it is here likewi... ... ..., that the duty and alleageance, which ... ...ple sweareth to their prince, is not only bound to themselves, but likewise to their lawfull heires and posterity, the lineall succession of crowns being begun among the people of God, and happily continued in divers christian common-wealths: So as no objection either of heresie, or whatsoever private statute or law may free the people from their oathgiving to their king, and his succession, established by the old fundamentall lawes of the kingdom: For, as hee is their heritable over-lord, and so by birth, not by any right in the coronation, commeth to his crowne; it is a like unlawful (the crowne ever standing full) to displace him that succeedeth thereto, as to eject the former: For at the very moment of the expiring of the king reigning, the nearest and lawful heire e ntrude another, is not to holde out uncomming in, but to expell and put out their righteous King. And I trust at this time whole *France* acknowledgeth the superstitious rebellion of the liguers, who upon pretence of heresie, by force of armes held so long out, to the great desolation of their whole country, their native and righteous king from possessing of his owne crowne and naturall kingdome.

Not that by all this former discourse of mine, and Apologie for kings, I meane that whatsoever errors and intollerable abominations a sovereigne prince commit, hee ought to escape all punishment, as if thereby the world were only ordained for kings, & they without controlment to turne it upside down at their pleasure: but by the contrary, by remitting them to God (who is their onely ordinary Judge) I remit them to the sorest and sharpest schoolmaster that can be devised for them: for the further a king is preferred by God above all other ranks & degrees of men, and the higher that his seat is above theirs, the greater is his obligation to his maker. And therfore in case he forget himselfe (his unthankfulness being in the same measure of height) the sadder and sharper will his correction be; and according to the greatnes of the height he is in, the weight of his fall wil recompense the same: for the further that any person is obliged to God, his offence becomes and growes so much the greater, then it would be in any other. *Joves* thunderclaps light oftner and sorer upon the high & stately oakes, then on the low and supple willow trees: and the highest bench is sliddriest to sit upon. Neither is it ever heard that any king forgets himselfe towards God, or in his vocation; but God with the greatnesse of the plague revengeth the greatnes of his ingratitude: Neither thinke I by the force and argument of this my discourse so to perswade the people, that none will hereafter be raised up, and rebell against wicked Princes. But remitting to the justice and providence of God to stirre up such scourges as pleaseth him, for punishment of wicked kings (who made the very vermine and filthy dust of the earth to bridle the insolencie of proud *Pharaoh*) my onely purpose and intention in this treatise is to perswade, as farre as lieth in me, by these sure and infallible grounds, all such good Christian readers, as beare not onely the naked name of a Christian, but kith the fruites thereof in their daily forme of life, to keep their hearts and hands free from such monstrous and unnaturall rebellions, whensoever the wickednesse of a Prince shall procure the same at Gods hands: that, when it shall please God to cast such scourges of princes, and

instruments of his fury in the fire, ye may stand up with cleane handes, and unspotted consciences, having prooved your selves in all your actions trew Christians toward God, and dutifull subjects towards your King, having remitted the judgement and punishment of all his wrongs to him, whom to onely of right it appertaineth.

But craving at God, and hoping that God shall continue his blessing with us, in not sending such fearefull desolation, I heartily wish our kings behaviour so to be, and continue among us, as our God in earth, and loving Father, endued with such properties as I described a King in the first part of this Treatise. And that ye (my deare countreymen, and charitable readers) may presse by all means to procure the prosperitie and welfare of your King; that as hee must on the one part thinke all his earthly felicitie and happinesse grounded upon your weale, caring more for himselfe for your sake then for his owne, thinking himselfe onely ordained for your weale; such holy and happy emulation may arise betwixt him and you, as his care for your quietnes, and your care for his honour and preservation, may in all your actions daily strive together, that the Land may thinke themselves blessed with such a King, and the king may thinke himselfe most happy in ruling over so loving and obedient subjects.

QUESTIONS

1. How is a king's power limited, according to James?

2. James's mother and predecessor on the Scottish throne, Queen Mary, was overthrown and driven into exile. How is this fact reflected in the king's political views?

3. Why is a strong monarchy the best form of government?

4. What are the two main metaphors James employs in describing a king's power? How do they differ from modern political images such as the "ship of state"?

5. Although James, of course, has an interest in arguing for a powerful monarchy, how would such a government be advantageous to a king's subjects?

78

■ *Thomas Hobbes* ■

LEVIATHAN
(1651)

Thomas Hobbes (1588–1679), the son of a quarrelsome minister of the Church of England, was the greatest English philosopher of the seventeenth century. Raised by an uncle following his father's early death, Hobbes went to Oxford University in 1603. Unsatisfied with the medieval curriculum at Oxford, Hobbes was a lackluster student who preferred to design his own education by reading books independently. After his graduation, he began a career as a tutor in the household of the Earl of Devonshire. Hobbes spent most of the rest of his life closely associated with the heirs of the Devonshire title, who paid him an annual pension until his death. A major part of his duties as tutor was to guide his charges during their European tours. This allowed Hobbes entry into the increasingly international world of scholarship. He befriended Galileo and earned the enmity of the famous French philosopher Descartes when on a trip to Paris. The Civil Wars in England broke out and his patron chose the losing Royalist side. This resulted in a long Parisian exile, during which Hobbes began to formulate the ideas which later became a part of *Leviathan*. Following the Restoration of Charles II, Hobbes returned to England, where he spent much of his time refining his ideas and defending himself from the attacks of his enemies, who claimed that his work was anti-Christian and subversive.

Leviathan, published in 1651 while Hobbes was in exile, was the fruit of his experience as the subject of a kingdom torn apart by civil war. In later years, his work was condemned as an apology for the military dictatorship of Oliver Cromwell, although in fact most of it was written well before Cromwell came to power. The selection reproduced here reflects Hobbes's vision of human nature.

Of the Naturall Condition *of Mankind, as* Concerning Their Felicity, and Misery

Nature hath made men so equall, in the faculties of body, and mind; as that though there bee found one man sometimes manifestly stronger in body, or of quicker mind than another; yet when all is reckoned together, the difference between man, and man, is not so considerable, as that one man can thereupon claim to himselfe any benefit, to which another may not pretend, as well as he. For as to the strength of body, the weakest has strength enough to kill the strongest, either by secret machination, or by confederacy with others, that are in the same danger with himselfe.

And as to the faculties of the mind, . . . I find yet a greater equality amongst men, than that of strength. For Prudence, is but Experience; which equall time, equally bestowes on all men, in those things they equally apply themselves unto. That which may perhaps make such equality incredible, is but a vain conceipt of ones owne wisdome, which almost all men think they have in a greater degree, than the Vulgar; that is, than all men but themselves, and a few others, whom by Fame, or for concurring with themselves, they approve. For such is the nature of men, that howsoever they may acknowledge many others to be more witty, or more eloquent, or more learned; Yet they will hardly believe there be many so wise as themselves: For they see their own wit at hand, and other mens at a distance. But this proveth rather that men are in that point equall, than unequall. For there is not ordinarily a greater signe of the equall distribution of any thing, than that every man is contented with his share.

From this equality of ability, ariseth equality of hope in the attaining of our Ends. And therefore if any two men desire the same thing, which neverthelesse they cannot both enjoy, they become enemies; and in the way to their End, (which is principally their owne conservation, and sometimes their delectation only,) endeavour to destroy, or subdue one an other. And from hence it comes to passe, that where an Invader hath no more to feare, than an other mans single power; if one plant, sow, build, or possesse a convenient Seat, others may probably be expected to come prepared with forces united, to dispossesse, and deprive him, not only of the fruit of his labour, but also of his life, or liberty. And the Invader again is in the like danger of another.

And from this diffidence of one another, there is no way for any man to secure himselfe, so reasonable, as Anticipation; that is, by force, or wiles, to master the persons of all men he can, so long, till he see no other power great enough to endanger him: And this is no more than his own conservation requireth, and is generally allowed. Also because there be some, that taking pleasure in contemplating their own power in the acts of conquest, which they pursue farther than their security requires; if others, that otherwise would be glad to be at ease within modest bounds, should not by invasion increase their power, they would not be able, long time, by standing only on their defence, to subsist. And by consequence, such augmentation of dominion over men, being necessary to a mans conservation, it ought to be allowed him.

Againe, men have no pleasure, (but on the contrary a great deale of griefe) in keeping company, where there is no power able to over-awe them all. For every man looketh that his companion should value him, at the same rate he sets upon himselfe: And upon all signes of contempt, or undervaluing, naturally endeavours, as far as he dares (which amongst them that have no common power to keep them in quiet, is far enough to make them destroy each other,) to extort a greater value from his contemners, by dommage; and from others, by the example.

So that in the nature of man, we find three principall causes of quarrell. First, Competition; Secondly, Diffidence; Thirdly, Glory.

The first, maketh men invade for Gain; the second, for Safety; and the third, for Reputation. The first use Violence, to make themselves Masters of other mens persons, wives, children, and cattell; the second, to defend them; the third, for trifles, as a word, a smile, a different opinion, and any other signe of undervalue, either direct in their Persons, or by reflexion in their Kindred, their Friends, their Nation, their Profession, or their Name.

Hereby it is manifest, that during the time men live without a common Power to keep them all in awe, they are in that condition which is called *Warre;* and such a warre, as is of every man, against every man. For *Warre,* consisteth not in Battell onely, or the act of fighting; but in a tract of time, wherein the Will to contend by Battell is sufficiently known: and therefore the notion of *Time,* is to be considered in the nature of Warre;

as it is in the nature of Weather. For as the nature of Foule weather, lyeth not in a showre or two of rain; but in an inclination thereto of many dayes together: So the nature of War, consisteth not in actual fighting; but in the known disposition thereto, during all the time there is no assurance to the contrary. All other time is PEACE.

Whatsoever therefore is consequent to a time of Warre, where every man is Enemy to every man; the same is consequent to the time, wherein men live without other security, than what their own strength, and their own invention shall furnish them withall. In such condition, there is no place for Industry; because the fruit thereof is uncertain: and consequently no Culture of the Earth; no Navigation, nor use of the commodities that may be imported by Sea; no commodious Building; no Instruments of moving, and removing such things as require much force; no Knowledge of the face of the Earth; no account of Time; no Arts; no Letters; no Society; and which is worst of all, continuall feare, and danger of violent death; and the life of man, solitary, poore, nasty, brutish, and short.

It may seem strange to some man, that has not well weighed these things; that Nature should thus dissociate, and render men apt to invade, and destroy one another: and he may therefore, not trusting to this Inference, made from the Passions, desire perhaps to have the same confirmed by Experience. Let him therefore consider with himself, when taking a journey, he armes himselfe, and seeks to go well accompanied; when going to sleep, he locks his dores; when even in his house he locks his chests; and this when he knowes there bee Lawes, and publike Officers, armed, to revenge all injuries shall bee done him; what opinion he has of his fellow subjects, when he rides armed; of his fellow Citizens, when he locks his dores; and of his children, and servants, when he locks his chests. Does he not there as much accuse mankind by his actions, as I do by my words? But neither of us accuse mans nature in it. The Desires, and other Passions of man, are in themselves no Sin. No more are the Actions, that

proceed from those Passions, till they know a Law that forbids them: which till Lawes be made they cannot know: nor can any Law be made, till they have agreed upon the Person that shall make it.

It may peradventure be thought, there was never such a time, nor condition of warre as this; and I believe it was never generally so, over all the world: but there are many places, where they live so now. For the savage people in many places of *America,* except the government of small Families, the concord whereof dependeth on naturall lust, have no government at all; and live at this day in that brutish manner, as I said before. Howsoever, it may be perceived what manner of life there would be, where there were no common Power to feare; by the manner of life, which men that have formerly lived under a peaceful government, use to degenerate into, in a civil Warre.

But though there had never been any time, wherein particular men were in a condition of warre one against another; yet in all times, Kings, and Persons of Soveraigne authority, because of their Independency, are in continual jealousies, and in the state and posture of Gladiators; having their weapons pointing, and their eyes fixed on one another; that is, their Forts, Garrisons, and Guns upon the Frontiers of their Kingdomes; and continuall Spyes upon their neighbours; which is a posture of War. But because they uphold thereby, the Industry of their Subjects; there does not follow from it, that misery, which accompanies the Liberty of particular men.

To this warre of every man against every man, this also is consequent; that nothing can be Unjust. The notions of Right and Wrong, Justice and Injustice have there no place. Where there is no common Power, there is no Law: where no Law, no Injustice. Force, and Fraud, are in warre, the two Cardinall vertues. Justice, and Injustice are none of the Faculties neither of the Body, nor Mind. If they were, they might be in a man that were alone in the world, as well as his Senses, and Passions. They are Qualities, that relate to men in Society, not in Solitude. It is consequent also to the same condition, that there be no Propriety, no Dominion, no *Mine* and *Thine* distinct; but onely that to be every mans, that he can get; and for so long, as he can keep it. And thus much for the ill condition, which man by meer Nature is actually placed in; though with a possibility to come out of it, consisting partly in the Passions, partly in his Reason.

The Passions that encline men to Peace, are Feare of Death; Desire of such things as are necessary to commodious living; and a Hope by their Industry to obtain them. And Reason suggesteth convenient Articles of Peace, upon which men may be drawn to agreement. These Articles, are they, which otherwise are called the Lawes of Nature.

QUESTIONS

1. Hobbes argues that "Nature hath made men . . . equall." What sort of equality is he talking about? How are people equal?

2. What is Hobbes's view of human nature? Is it a pessimistic or an optimistic view? Why?

3. Why do people quarrel, according to Hobbes? What sort of society is the product of the "state of nature"?

4. How do you think Hobbes's experience of the English Civil Wars might have affected his point of view?

5. How do you think Hobbes's war of "every man against every man" could be stopped? What sort of government could break the natural human tendency toward war?

79

■ *John Locke* ■

SECOND TREATISE OF GOVERNMENT

(1689)

John Locke (1632–1704) is one of the most influential political theorists in Western history. His *Two Treatises of Government* not only inspired the English tradition of parliamentary democracy, but also influenced the French Enlightenment through the writing of Montesquieu and most famously became the foundation for the American Declaration of Independence and Constitution. Locke was educated at Oxford after which he became a physician.

His early intellectual endeavors were devoted to science and he was elected to the Royal Society in 1668. In the employ of the earl of Shaftesbury, Locke wrote an *Essay Concerning Toleration* (1667), which argued for the peaceful coexistence of diverse religious groups in England. He wrote his most important philosophical work, *Essay Concerning Human Understanding* (1689), while recovering his health in France. Locke was actively engaged in domestic politics during the reign of Charles II, and he wrote his *Two Treatises on Government* during the Exclusion Crisis (1679–1681) to defend the principles that government originated in the consent of the governed and for their benefit alone. His account of an idyllic state of nature from which man emerged voluntarily to form companionable society was in sharp contrast to the brutal state of nature theorized by Hobbes. Locke was associated with the Whig party in England and he followed Lord Shaftesbury into self-imposed exile in Holland after the accession of James II, returning only after the Revolution of 1688. He served briefly in the government of William III, mostly as a financial advisor, but ill health limited his public career. Locke died in 1704.

The *Second Treatise of Government* (1689) is one of the enduring works of political theory in the western tradition. Although it was written in 1681 as a polemical tract, Locke attempted to prove his ideas about the nature of government by returning first principles and stating them in simple, didactic terms. In this section on the Beginning of Political Society, Locke demonstrates how a political nation came into existence and how it was ruled by the will of the majority.

§ 87. Man being born, as has been proved, with a title to perfect freedom, and uncontrolled enjoyment of all the rights and privileges of the law of nature, equally with any other man, or number of men in the world, hath by nature a power, not only to preserve his property, that is, his life, liberty, and estate, against the injuries and attempts of other men; but to judge of and punish the breaches of that law in others, as he is persuaded the offence deserves, even with death itself, in crimes where the heinousness of the fact, in his opinion, requires it. But because no political society can be, nor subsist, without having in itself the power to preserve the property, and, in order thereunto, punish the offences of all those of that society; there and there only is political society, where every one of the members hath quitted his natural power, resigned it up into the hands of the community in all cases that excludes him not from appealing for protection to the law established by it. And thus all private judgment of every particular member being excluded, the community comes to be umpire by settled standing rules, indifferent, and the same to all parties; and by men having authority from the community, for the execution of those rules, decides all the differences that may happen between any members of that society concerning any matter of right; and punishes those offences which any member hath committed against the society, with such penalties as the law has established, whereby it is easy to discern, who are, and who are not, in political society together. Those who are united into one body, and have a common established law and judicature to appeal to, with authority to decide controversies between them, and punish offenders, are in civil society one with another; but those who have no such common appeal, I mean on earth, are still in the state of nature, each being, where these is no other, judge for himself, and executioner; which is, as I have before showed, the perfect state of nature.

§ 88. And thus the commonwealth comes by a power to set down what punishment shall belong to the several transgressions which they think worthy of it, committed amongst the members of that society, (which is the power of making laws) as well as it has the power to punish any injury done unto any of its members, by any one that is not of it, (which is the power of war and peace,) and all this for the preservation of the property of all the members of that society, as far as is possible. But though every man who has entered into civil society, and is become a member of any commonwealth, has thereby quitted his power to punish offences against the law of nature, in prosecution of his own private judgment; yet with the judgment of offences, which he has given up to the legislative in all cases, where he can appeal to the magistrate, he has given a right to the commonwealth to employ his force, for the execution of the judgments of the commonwealth, whenever he shall be called to it; which indeed are his own judgments, they being made by himself, or his representative. And herein we have the original of the legislative and executive power of civil society, which is to judge by standing laws, how far offences are to be punished, when committed within the commonwealth; and also to determine, by occasional judgments founded on the present circumstances of the fact, how far injuries from without are to be vindicated; and in both these to employ all the force of all the members, when there shall be need.

§ 89. Whenever therefore any number of men are so united into one society, as to quit every one his executive power of the law of nature, and to resign it to the public, there and there only is a political, or civil society. And this is done, wherever any number of men, in the state of nature, enter into society to make one people, one body politic, under one supreme government; or else when any one joins himself to, and incorporates with any government already made: for hereby he authorizes the society, or, which is all one, the legislative thereof, to make laws for him, as the public good of the society shall require; to the executive whereof, his own assistance (as to his own degrees) is due. And this puts men out of a state of nature into that of a commonwealth, by setting up a judge on earth, with authority to determine all the controversies, and redress the injuries that may happen to any member of the commonwealth: which judge is the legislative, or magistrate appointed by it. And wherever there are any number of men, however associated, that have no such decisive power to appeal to, there they are still in the state of nature.

§ 90. Hence it is evident, that absolute monarchy, which by some men is counted the only government in the world, is indeed inconsistent with civil society, and so can be no form of civil government at all; for the end of civil society being to avoid and remedy these inconveniencies of the state of nature, which necessarily follow from every man being judge in his own case, by setting up a known authority, to which every one of that society may appeal upon any injury received, or controversy that may arise, and which every one of the society ought to obey; wherever any persons are, who have not such an authority to appeal to for the decision of any difference between, there those persons are still in the state of nature; and so is every absolute prince, in respect of those who are under his dominion.

§ 91. For he being supposed to have all, both legislative and executive power in himself alone, there is no judge to be found, no appeal lies open to any one, who may fairly, and indifferently, and with authority decide, and from whose decision relief and redress may be expected of any injury or inconveniency that may be suffered from the prince, or by his order: so that such a man, however intitled, czar, or grand seignior, or how you please, is as much in the state of nature, with all under his dominion, as he is with the rest of mankind: for wherever any two men are, who have no standing rule, and common judge to appeal to on earth, for the determination of controversies of right betwixt them, there they are still in the state of nature, and under all the inconveniencies of it, with only this woful difference to the subject, or rather slave of an absolute prince; that whereas in the ordinary state of nature he has a liberty to judge of his right, and, according to the best of his power, to maintain it; now, whenever his property is invaded by the will and order of his monarch, he has not only no appeal, as those in society ought to have, but, as if he were degraded from the common state of rational creatures, is denied a liberty to judge of, or to defend his right; and so is exposed to all the misery and inconveniencies, that a man can fear from one, who being in the unrestrained state of nature, is yet corrupted with flattery, and armed with power.

§ 92. For he that thinks absolute power purifies men's blood, and corrects the baseness of human nature, need read but the history of this or any other age, to be convinced of the contrary. He that would have been so insolent and injurious in the woods of America, would not probably be much better in a throne; where perhaps learning and religion shall be found out to justify all that he shall do to his subjects, and the sword presently silence all those that dare question it: for what the protection of absolute monarchy is, what kind of fathers of their countries it makes princes to be, and to what a degree of happiness and security it carries civil society, where this sort of government is grown to perfection; he that will look into the late relation of Ceylon, may easily see.

§ 93. In absolute monarchies, indeed, as well as other governments of the world, the subjects have an appeal to the law, and judges to decide any controversies, and restrain any violence that may happen betwixt the subjects themselves, one amongst another. This every one thinks necessary, and believes he deserves to be thought a declared enemy to society and mankind, who should go about to take it away. But whether this be from a true love of mankind and society, and

such a charity as we all owe one to another, there is reason to doubt: for this is no more than what every man, who loves his own power, profit, or greatness, may and naturally must do, keep those animals from hurting, or destroying one another, who labour and drudge only for his pleasure and advantage; and so are taken care of, not out of any love the master has for them, but love of himself, and the profit they bring him: for if it be asked, what security, what fence is there, in such a state, against the violence and oppression of this absolute ruler? the very question can scarce be borne. They are ready to tell you, that it deserves death only to ask after safety. Betwixt subject and subject, they will grant, there must be measures, laws, and judges, for their mutual peace and security: but as for the ruler he ought to be absolute, and is above all such circumstances; because he has power to do more hurt and wrong, it is right when he does it. To ask how you may be guarded from harm, injury, on that side where the strongest hand is to do it, is presently the voice of faction and rebellion: as if when men quitting the state of nature entered into society, they agreed that all of them but one should be under the restraint of laws, but that he should still retain all the liberty of the state of nature, increased with power, and made licentious by impunity. This is to think, that men are so foolish, that they take care to avoid what mischiefs may be done them by polecats, or foxes; but are content, nay think it safety, to be devoured by lions.

§ 94. But whatever flatterers may talk to amuse people's understandings, it hinders not men from feeling; and when they perceive, that any man, in what station soever, is out of the bounds of the civil society which they are of, and that they have no appeal on earth against any harm they may receive from him, they are apt to think themselves in the state of nature, in respect of him whom they find to be so: and to take care, as soon as they can, to have that safety and security in civil society, for which it was instituted, and for which only they entered into it. And therefore, though perhaps at first, (as shall be showed more at large hereafter in the following part of this discourse) some one good and excellent man having got a pre-eminency amongst the rest, had this deference paid to his goodness and virtue, as to a kind of natural authority, that the chief rule, with arbitration of their differences, by a tacit consent devolved into his hands, without any other caution, but the assurance they had of his uprightness and wisdom; yet when time, giving authority, and (as some men would persuade us) sacredness to customs, which the negligent and unforeseen innocence of the first ages began, had brought in successors of another stamp; the people finding their own properties not secure under the government, as then it was, (whereas government has no other end but the preservation of property) could never be safe nor at rest, nor think themselves in civil society, till the legislature was placed in collective

bodies of men, call them senate, parliament, or what you please. By which means every single person became subject, equally with other the meanest men, to those laws, which he himself, as part of the legislative, had established; nor could any one, by his own authority, avoid the force of the law, when once made; nor by any pretence of superiority plead exemption, thereby to license his won, or the miscarriages of any of his dependents. "No man in civil society can be exempted from the laws of it:" for if any man may do what he thinks fit, and there be no appeal on earth, for redress or security against any harm he shall do; I ask, whether he be not perfectly still in the state of nature, and so can be no part or member of that civil society: unless any one will say, the state of nature and civil society are one and the same thing, which I have never yet found any one so great a patron of anarchy as to affirm.

QUESTIONS

1. What is the relationship between civil society and property?

2. Where does the power of law making come from?

3. What is Locke's definition of a civil society?

4. Why does Locke believe that absolute monarchy is an illegitimate form of government?

80

THE ENGLISH BILL OF RIGHTS
(1689)

For more than two hundred years before 1689, when the Bill of Rights was enacted, English subjects and their kings disagreed over the prerogatives of the king and the responsibilities of the subject. Law, taxes, and the succession were particularly contentious matters. These disagreements caused conflicts, rebellions, and even civil wars. The last of these disagreements happened in 1688. The Catholic King James II violated the laws of the realm, and certain of his subjects believed this meant that he had forfeited the right to be king. They invited the king's son-in-law, the Dutch Protestant Prince William of Orange, to invade. James, frightened that his subjects had turned against him and fearing he would lose the war against William, fled England. Englishmen who had supported James' right to the throne became convinced that leaving England meant that James had abandoned the right to be king as well.

After much debate, James' former supporters and his former opponents agreed on the Bill of Rights to settle their disagreements about how the English state worked. In hopes of averting future conflict, they informed William and his wife, Mary, of the contents of the Bill of Rights before they were crowned as the new king and queen.

An Act Declaring the Rights and Liberties of the Subject and Settling the Succession of the Crown.

Whereas the Lords Spiritual and Temporal and Commons assembled at Westminster, lawfully, fully and freely representing all the estates of the people of this realm, did upon the thirteenth day of February in the year of our Lord one thousand six hundred eighty-eight [old style date] present unto their Majesties, then called and known by the names and style of William and Mary, prince and princess of Orange, being present in their proper persons, a certain declaration in writing made by the said Lords and Commons in the words following, viz.:

Whereas the late King James the Second, by the assistance of divers evil counsellors, judges and ministers employed by him, did endeavour to subvert and extirpate the Protestant religion and the laws and liberties of this kingdom;

By assuming and exercising a power of dispensing with and suspending of laws and the execution of laws without consent of Parliament;

By committing and prosecuting divers worthy prelates for humbly petitioning to be excused from concurring to the said assumed power;

By issuing and causing to be executed a commission under the great seal for erecting a court called the Court of Commissioners for Ecclesiastical Causes;

By levying money for and to the use of the Crown by pretence of prerogative for other time and in other manner than the same was granted by Parliament;

By raising and keeping a standing army within this kingdom in time of peace without consent of Parliament, and quartering soldiers contrary to law;

By causing several good subjects being Protestants to be disarmed at the same time when papists were both armed and employed contrary to law;

By violating the freedom of election of members to serve in Parliament;

By prosecutions in the Court of King's Bench for matters and causes cognizable only in Parliament, and by divers other arbitrary and illegal courses;

And whereas of late years partial corrupt and unqualified persons have been returned and served on juries in trials, and particularly divers jurors in trials for high treason which were not freeholders;

And excessive bail hath been required of persons committed in criminal cases to elude the benefit of the laws made for the liberty of the subjects;

And excessive fines have been imposed;

And illegal and cruel punishments inflicted;

And several grants and promises made of fines and forfeitures before any conviction or judgment against the persons upon whom the same were to be levied;

All which are utterly and directly contrary to the known laws and statutes and freedom of this realm;

And whereas the said late King James the Second having abdicated the government and the throne being thereby vacant, his Highness the prince of Orange (whom it hath pleased Almighty God to make the glorious instrument of delivering this kingdom from popery and arbitrary power) did (by the advice of the Lords Spiritual and Temporal and divers principal persons of the Commons) cause letters to be written to the Lords Spiritual and Temporal being Protestants, and other letters to the several counties, cities, universities, boroughs and cinque ports, for the choosing of such persons to represent them as were of right to be sent to Parliament, to meet and sit at Westminster upon the two and twentieth day of January in this year one thousand six hundred eighty and eight, in order to such an establishment as that their religion, laws and liberties might not again be in danger of being subverted, upon which letters elections having been accordingly made;

And thereupon the said Lords Spiritual and Temporal and Commons, pursuant to their respective letters and elections, being now assembled in a full and free representative of this nation, taking into their most serious consideration the best means for attaining the ends aforesaid, do in the first place (as their ancestors in like case have usually done) for the vindicating and asserting their ancient rights and liberties declare

That the pretended power of suspending the laws or the execution of laws by regal authority without consent of Parliament is illegal;

That the pretended power of dispensing with laws or the execution of laws by regal authority, as it hath been assumed and exercised of late, is illegal;

That the commission for erecting the late Court of Commissioners for Ecclesiastical Causes, and all other commissions and courts of like nature, are illegal and pernicious;

That levying money for or to the use of the Crown by pretence of prerogative, without grant of Parliament, for longer time, or in other manner than the same is or shall be granted, is illegal;

That it is the right of the subjects to petition the king, and all commitments and prosecutions for such petitioning are illegal;

That the raising or keeping a standing army within the kingdom in time of peace, unless it be with consent of Parliament, is against law;

That the subjects which are Protestants may have arms for their defence suitable to their conditions and as allowed by law;

That election of members of Parliament ought to be free;

That the freedom of speech and debates or proceedings in Parliament ought not to be impeached or questioned in any court or place out of Parliament;

That excessive bail ought not to be required, nor excessive fines imposed, nor cruel and unusual punishments inflicted;

That jurors ought to be duly impanelled and returned, and jurors which pass upon men in trials for high treason ought to be freeholders;

That all grants and promises of fines and forfeitures of particular persons before conviction are illegal and void;

And that for redress of all grievances, and for the amending, strengthening and preserving of the laws, Parliaments ought to be held frequently.

And they do claim, demand and insist upon all and singular the premises as their undoubted rights and liberties, and that no declarations, judgments, doings or proceedings to the prejudice of the people in any of the said premises ought in any wise to be drawn hereafter into consequence or example; to which demand of their rights they are particularly encouraged by the declaration of his

Highness the prince of Orange as being the only means for obtaining a full redress and remedy therein. Having therefore an entire confidence that his said Highness the prince of Orange will perfect the deliverance so far advanced by him, and will still preserve them from the violation of their rights which they have here asserted, and from all other attempts upon their religion, rights and liberties, the said Lords Spiritual and Temporal and Commons assembled at Westminster do resolve that William and Mary, prince and princess of Orange, be and be declared king and queen of England, France and Ireland and the dominions thereunto belonging, to hold the crown and royal dignity of the said kingdoms and dominions to them, the said prince and princess, during their lives and the life of the survivor to them, and that the sole and full exercise of the regal power be only in and executed by the said prince of Orange in the names of the said prince and princess during their joint lives, and after their deceases the said crown and royal dignity of the same kingdoms and dominions to be to the heirs of the body of the said princess, and for default of such issue to the Princess Anne of Denmark and the heirs of her body, and for default of such issue to the heirs of the body of the said prince of Orange. And the Lords Spiritual and Temporal and Commons do pray the said prince and princess to accept the same accordingly.

And that the oaths hereafter mentioned be taken by all persons of whom the oaths have allegiance and supremacy might be required by law, instead of them; and that the said oaths of allegiance and supremacy be abrogated.

I, A.B., do sincerely promise and swear that I will be faithful and bear true allegiance to their Majesties King William and Queen Mary. So help me God.

I, A.B., do swear that I do from my heart abhor, detest and abjure as impious and heretical this damnable doctrine and position, that princes excommunicated or deprived by the Pope or any authority of the see of Rome may be deposed or murdered by their subjects or any other whatsoever. And I do declare that no foreign prince, person, prelate, state or potentate hath or ought to have any jurisdiction, power, superiority, pre-eminence or authority, ecclesiastical or spiritual, within this realm. So help me God.

Upon which their said Majesties did accept the crown and royal dignity of the kingdoms of England, France and Ireland, and the dominions thereunto belonging, according to the resolution and desire of the said Lords and Commons contained in the said declaration. And thereupon their Majesties were pleased that the said Lords Spiritual and Temporal and Commons, being the two Houses of Parliament, should continue to sit, and with their Majesties' royal concurrence make effectual provision for the settlement of the religion, laws and liberties of this kingdom, so that the same for the future might not be in danger again of being subverted, to which the said Lords Spiritual and Temporal and Commons did agree, and proceed to act accordingly. Now in pursuance of the premises the said Lords Spiritual and Temporal and Commons in Parliament assembled, for the ratifying, confirming and establishing the said declaration and the articles, clauses, matters and things therein contained by the force of law made in due form by authority of Parliament, do pray that it may be declared and enacted that all and singular the rights and liberties asserted and claimed in the said declaration are the true, ancient and indubitable rights and liberties of the people of this kingdom, and so shall be esteemed, allowed, adjudged, deemed and taken to be; and that all and every the particulars aforesaid shall be firmly and strictly holden and observed as they are expressed in the said declaration, and all officers and ministers whatsoever shall serve their Majesties and their successors according to the same in all time to come. And the said Lords Spiritual and Temporal and

Commons, seriously considering how it hath pleased Almighty God in his marvellous providence and merciful goodness to this nation to provide and preserve their said Majesties' royal persons most happily to reign over us upon the throne of their ancestors, for which they render unto him from the bottom of their hearts their humblest thanks and praises, do truly, firmly, assuredly and in the sincerity of their hearts think, and do hereby recognize, acknowledge and declare, that King James the Second having abdicated the government, and their Majesties having accepted the crown and royal dignity as aforesaid, their said Majesties did become, were, are and of right ought to be by the laws of this realm our sovereign liege lord and lady, king and queen of England, France and Ireland and the dominions thereunto belonging, in and to whose princely persons the royal state, crown and dignity of the said realms with all honours, styles, titles, regalities, prerogatives, powers, jurisdictions and authorities to the same belonging and appertaining are most fully, rightfully and entirely invested and incorporated, united and annexed. And for preventing all questions and divisions in this realm by reason of any pretended titles to the crown, and for preserving a certainty in the succession thereof, in and upon which the unity, peace, tranquility and safety of this nation doth under God wholly consist and depend, the said Lords Spiritual and Temporal and Commons do beseech their Majesties that it may be enacted, established and declared, that the crown and regal government of the said kingdoms and dominions, with all and singular the premises thereunto belonging and appertaining, shall be and continue to their said Majesties and the survivor of them during their lives and the life of the survivor of them, and that the entire, perfect and full exercise of the regal power and government be only in and executed by his Majesty in the names of both their Majesties during their joint lives; and after their deceases the said crown and premises

shall be and remain to the heirs of the body of her Majesty, and for default of such issue to her Royal Highness the Princess Anne of Denmark and the heirs of the body of his said Majesty; and thereunto the said Lords Spiritual and Temporal and Commons do in the name of all the people aforesaid most humbly and faithfully submit themselves, their heirs and posterities for ever, and do faithfully promise that they will stand to, maintain and defend their said Majesties, and also the limitation and succession of the crown herein specified and contained, to the utmost of their powers with their lives and estates against all persons whatsoever that shall attempt anything to the contrary. And whereas it hath been found by experience that it is inconsistent with the safety and welfare of this Protestant kingdom to be governed by a popish prince, or by any king or queen marrying a papist, the said Lords Spiritual and Temporal and Commons do further pray that it may be enacted, that all and every person and persons that is, are or shall be reconciled to or shall hold communion with the see or Church of Rome, or shall profess the popish religion, or shall marry a papist, shall be excluded and be for ever incapable to inherit, possess or enjoy the crown and government of this realm and Ireland and the dominions thereunto belonging or any part of the same, or to have, use or exercise any regal power, authority or jurisdiction within the same; and in all and every such case or cases the people of these realms shall be and are hereby absolved of their allegiance; and the said crown and government shall from time to time descend to and be enjoyed by such person or persons being Protestants as should have inherited and enjoyed the same in case the said person or persons so reconciled, holding communion or professing or marrying as aforesaid were naturally dead; and that every king and queen of this realm who at any time hereafter shall come to and succeed in the imperial crown of this kingdom shall on the first day of the meeting of the first Parliament next after his or her coming to the crown, sitting in his or her throne in the House of Peers in the presence of the Lords and Commons therein assembled, or at his or her coronation before such person or persons who shall administer the coronation oath to him or her at the time of his or her taking the said oath (which shall first happen), make, subscribe and audibly repeat the declaration mentioned in the statute made in the thirtieth year of the reign of King Charles the Second entitled, *An Act for the more effectual preserving the king's person and government by disabling papists from sitting in either House of Parliament.* But if it shall happen that such king or queen upon his or her succession to the crown of this realm shall be under the age of twelve years, then every such king or queen shall make, subscribe and audibly repeat the same declaration at his or her coronation or the first day of the meeting of the first Parliament as aforesaid which shall first happen after such king or queen shall have attained the said age of twelve years. All which their Majesties are contented and pleased shall be declared, enacted and established by authority of this present Parliament, and shall stand, remain and be the law of this realm for ever; and the same are by their said Majesties, by and with the advice and consent of the Lords Spiritual and Temporal and Commons in Parliament assembled and by the authority of the same, declared, enacted and established accordingly.

II. And be it further declared and enacted by the authority aforesaid, that from and after this present session of Parliament no dispensation by *non obstante* of or to any statute or any part thereof shall be allowed, but that the same shall be held void and of no effect, except a dispensation be allowed of in such statute, and except in such cases as shall be specially provided for by one or more bill or bills to be passed during this present session of Parliament.

III. Provided that no charter or grant or pardon granted before the three and twentieth day of October in the year of our Lord one thousand six hundred eighty-nine shall be any ways impeached or invalidated by this Act, but that the same shall be and remain of the same force and effect in law and no other than as if this Act had never been made.

QUESTIONS

1. Does the Bill of Rights require monarchs of England to subscribe to a certain religion?

2. Does the Bill of Rights provide for freedom of speech? If so, in what arena may people speak freely?

3. What is the king's role in making law as described in the Bill of Rights?

4. What were the authors of the Bill of Rights referring to when they said that James had abdicated and left the throne vacant? Did different Englishmen think it meant different things?

81

■ *Duc de Saint-Simon* ■

MEMOIRS

(1694–1723)

Louis de Rouvroy, Duke of Saint-Simon (1675–1755), led a privileged life at the very heart of the French absolute state. A godson of Louis XIV, Saint-Simon was brought up in Versailles in the shadow of the Sun King. Although he served briefly as an ambassador and as an officer in the French army, Saint-Simon never carved out a place for himself in either government service or court life. He tended to blame Louis XIV for his failures, but his record of achievement in the next reign was equally unimpressive. He died bitter and resentful in 1755.

Saint-Simon is remembered only for his voluminous *Memoirs*, from which much of our knowledge of the day-to-day life at the court of Versailles derives. He began keeping them when he was nineteen and continued on into middle age; the *Memoirs* show his talent for observation, particularly of social detail, and his ear for the latest court gossip. His character sketches, such as the one of Louis XIV presented here, always unearth the darker side of the subject under study. There is always as much of Saint-Simon in his portrayals as there is of the people he is describing.

I shall pass over the stormy period of Louis XIV's minority. At twenty-three years of age he entered the great world as King, under the most favourable auspices. His ministers were the most skilful in all Europe; his generals the best; his Court was filled with illustrious and clever men, formed during the troubles which had followed the death of Louis XIII.

Louis XIV was made for a brilliant Court. In the midst of other men, his figure, his courage, his grace, his beauty, his grand mien, even the tone of his voice and the majestic and natural charm of all his person, distinguished him till his death as the King Bee, and showed that if he had only been born a simple private gentleman, he would equally have excelled in fêtes, pleasures, and gallantry, and would have had the greatest success in love. The intrigues and adventures which early in life he had been engaged in—when the Comtesse de Soissons lodged at the Tuileries, as superintendent of the Queen's household, and was the centre figure of the Court roup—had exercised an unfortunate influence upon him: he received those impressions with which he could never after successfully struggle. From this time, intellect, education, nobility of sentiment, and high principle, in others, became objects of suspicion to him, and soon of hatred. The more he advanced in years the more this sentiment was confirmed in him. He wished to reign by himself. His jealousy on this point unceasingly became weakness. He reigned, indeed, in little things; the great he could never reach: even in the former, too, he was often governed. The superior ability of his early ministers and his early generals soon wearied him. He liked nobody to be in any way superior to him. Thus he chose his ministers, not for their knowledge, but for their ignorance; not for their capacity, but for their want of it. He liked to form them, as he said; liked to teach them even the most trifling things. It was the same with his generals. He took credit to himself for instructing them; wished it to be thought that from his cabinet he commanded and directed all his armies. Naturally fond of trifles, he unceasingly occupied himself with the most petty details of his troops, his household, his mansions; would even instruct his cooks, who received, like novices, lessons they had known by heart for years. This vanity, this unmeasured and unreasonable love of admiration, was his ruin. His ministers, his generals, his mistresses, his courtiers, soon perceived his weakness. They praised him with emulation and spoiled him. Praises, or to say truth, flattery, pleased him to such an extent, that the coarsest was well received, the vilest even better relished. It was the sole means by which you could approach him. Those whom he liked owed his affection for them, to their untiring flatteries. This is what gave his ministers so much authority, and the opportunities they had for adulating him, of attributing everything to him, and of pretending to learn everything from him. Suppleness, meanness, an admiring, dependent, cringing manner—above all, an air of nothingness—were the sole means of pleasing him.

This poison spread. It spread, too, to an incredible extent, in a prince who, although of intellect beneath mediocrity, was not utterly without sense, and who had had some experience. Without voice or musical knowledge, he use to sing, in private, the passages of the opera prologues that were fullest of his praises! He was drowned in vanity; and so deeply, that at his public suppers—all the Court present, musicians also— he would hum these self-same praises between his teeth, when the music they were set to was played!

And yet, it must be admitted, he might have done better. Though his intellect, as I have said, was beneath mediocrity, it was capable of being formed. He loved glory, was fond of order and regularity; was by disposition prudent, moderate,

discreet, master of his movements and his tongue. Will it be believed? He was also by disposition good and just! God had sufficiently gifted him to enable him to be a good King; perhaps even *a tolerably great King!* All the evil came to him from elsewhere. His early education was so neglected that nobody dared approach his apartment. He has often been heard to speak of those times with bitterness, and even to relate that, one evening he was found in the basin of the Palais Royale garden fountain, into which he had fallen! He was scarcely taught how to read or write, and remained so ignorant, that the most familiar historical and other facts were utterly unknown to him! He fell, accordingly, and sometimes even in public, into the grossest absurdities.

It was his vanity, his desire for glory, that led him, soon after the death of the King of Spain, to make that event the pretext for war; in spite of renunciations so recently made, so carefully stipulated, in the marriage contract. He marched into Flanders; his conquests there were rapid; the passage of the Rhine was admirable; the triple alliance of England, Sweden, and Holland only animated him. In the midst of winter he took Franche-Comté, by restoring which at the peace of Aix-la-Chapelle, he preserved his conquests in Flanders. All was flourishing then in the state. Riches everywhere. Colbert had placed the finances, the navy, commerce, manufactures, letters even, upon the highest point; and this age, like that of Augustus, produced in abundance illustrious men of all kinds—even those illustrious only in pleasures.

Thus, we see this monarch grand, rich, conquering, the arbiter of Europe; feared and admired as long as the ministers and captains existed who really deserved the name. When they were no more, the machine kept moving some time by impulsion, and from their influence. But soon afterwards we saw beneath the surface; faults and errors were multiplied, and decay came on with giant strides; without, however, opening the eyes of that despotic master, so anxious to do everything and direct everything himself, and who seemed to indemnify himself for disdain abroad by increasing fear and trembling at home.

So much for the reign of this vain-glorious monarch.

Let me touch now upon some other incidents in his career, and upon some points in his character.

He early showed a disinclination for Paris. The troubles that had taken place there during the minority made him regard the place as dangerous; he wished, too, to render himself venerable by hiding himself from the eyes of the multitude; all these considerations fixed him at St. Germains soon after the death of the Queen, his mother. It was to that place he began to attract the world by fêtes and gallantries, and by making it felt that he wished to be often seen.

His love for Madame de la Vallière, which was at first kept secret, occasioned frequent excursions to Versailles, then a little card castle, which had been built by Louis XIII—annoyed, and his suite still more so, at being frequently obliged to sleep in a wretched inn there, after he had been out hunting in the forest of Saint Leger. That monarch rarely slept at Versailles more than one night, and then from necessity; the King, his son, slept there, so that he might be more in private with his mistress, pleasures unknown to the hero and just man, worthy son of Saint Louis, who built the little château.

These excursions of Louis XIV by degrees gave birth to those immense buildings he erected at Versailles; and their convenience for a numerous court, so different from the apartments at St. Germains, led him to take up his abode there entirely shortly after the death of the Queen. He built an infinite number of apartments, which were asked for by those who wished to pay their court to him; whereas at St. Germains nearly everybody was obliged to lodge in the town, and the few who found accommodation at the château were strangely inconvenienced.

The frequent fêtes, the private promenades at Versailles, the journeys, were means on which the King seized in order to distinguish or mortify the courtiers, and thus render them more assiduous in pleasing him. He felt that of real favours he had not enough to bestow; in order to keep up the spirit of devotion, he therefore unceasingly invented all sorts of ideal ones, little preferences and petty distinctions, which answered his purpose as well.

He was exceedingly jealous of the attention paid him. Not only did he notice the presence of the most distinguished courtiers, but those of inferior degree also. He looked to the right and to the left, not only upon rising but upon going to bed, at his meals, in passing through his apartments, or his gardens of Versailles, where alone the courtiers were allowed to follow him; he saw and noticed everybody; not one escaped him, not even those who hoped to remain unnoticed. He marked well all absentees from the court, found out the reason of their absence, and never lost an opportunity of acting towards them as the occasion might seem to justify. With some of the courtiers (the most distinguished), it was a demerit not to make the court their ordinary abode; with others it was a fault to come but rarely; for those who never or scarcely ever came it was certain disgrace. When their names were in any way mentioned, "I do not know them," the King would reply haughtily. Those who presented themselves but seldom were thus characterised: "They are people I never see"; these decrees were irrevocable. He could not bear people who liked Paris.

Louis XIV took great pains to be well informed of all that passed everywhere; in the public places, in the private houses, in society and familiar intercourse. His spies and tell-tales were infinite. He had them of all species; many who were ignorant that their information reached him; others who knew it; others who wrote to him direct, sending their letters through channels he indicated; and all these letters were seen by him alone, and always before everything else; others who sometimes spoke to him secretly in his cabinet, entering by the back stairs. These unknown means ruined an infinite number of people of all classes, who never could discover the cause; often ruined them very unjustly; for the King, once prejudiced, never altered his opinion, or so rarely, that nothing was more rare. He had, too, another fault, very dangerous for others and often for himself, since it deprived him of good subjects. He had an excellent memory; in this way, that if he saw a man who, twenty years before, perhaps, had in some manner offended him, he did not forget the man, though he might forget the offence. This was enough, however, to exclude the person from all favour. The representations of a minister, of a general, of his confessor even, could not move the King. He would not yield.

The most cruel means by which the King was informed of what was passing—for many years before anybody knew it—was that of opening letters. The promptitude and dexterity with which they were opened passes understanding.

He saw extracts from all the letters in which there were passages that the chiefs of the post-office, and then the minister who governed it, thought ought to go before him; entire letters, too, were sent to him, when their contents seemed to justify the sending. Thus the chiefs of the post, nay, the principal clerks were in a position to suppose what they pleased and against whom they pleased. A word of contempt against the King or the government, a joke, a detached phrase, was enough. It is incredible how many people, justly or unjustly, were more or less ruined, always without resource, without trial, and without knowing why. The secret was impenetrable; for nothing ever cost the King less than profound silence and dissimulation.

QUESTIONS

1. What qualities did Saint-Simon admire in Louis XIV?

2. To what does Saint-Simon attribute Louis's early successes?

3. Judging from Saint-Simon's description of courtly life, what did a courtier need to get along?

4. On balance, Saint-Simon believed Louis to have been a failure. Why?

5. What sort of a picture does Saint-Simon present of the workings of the absolutist state?

82

■ *Napoleon Bonaparte* ■

THE NAPOLEONIC CODE (THE FRENCH CIVIL CODE)
(1804)

The Emperor Napoleon Bonaparte (1769–1821) is remembered as France's greatest military and political leader, as well as one of the most significant figures in modern world history. His name has been associated with a pastry, a psychological complex and is a synonym for a dictator. The son of Italian nobles from the French-controlled island of Corsica, Napoleon studied in France and joined the French military before the French Revolution broke out in 1789. During the war, he supported the radical Jacobins, a group that acted as enforcers of the Reign of Terror. At the end of the revolution, Napoleon earned a name (and wealth) by crushing a pro-royalist insurrection through innovative use of artillery. Working his way up the military ranks, he also became a respected voice in French politics, particularly by publishing a newspaper from the front lines. After a series of military campaigns, including a failed attempt to capture Egypt from the British, Bonaparte took part in a coup to overthrow the French Republic's government. In 1799, Bonaparte had himself elected First Consul, a throwback to Roman governmental titles. He crowned himself Emperor Napoleon I on December 2, 1804.

Both as First Consul and as Emperor, Napoleon enacted extensive reforms in a France that had been virtually bankrupted by decades of civil and external warfare. These highly successful initiatives included a centralization of government administration, a central bank, building new infrastructure around the country, establishment of a system of higher education, and a new tax code. But perhaps his most lasting and influential reform was the French Civil Code, more commonly known as the Napoleonic Code. Ratified in 1804, this law code enacted many of the values that had spurred the French Revolution. In particular, it enshrined a meritocracy, undermining the political and social privileges that had previously gone to the nobility. The Code also established legal specifications for marital and familial relationships. The Code overrode local laws that had proliferated around France and united the country under one legal system. The Napoleonic Code set a standard by which many other Western countries created their own civil law codes. It remains the foundation of the legal system in the state of Louisiana.

Napoleonic Code

. . .

Preliminary Title: Of the Publication, Effect, and Application of the Laws in General

1. The laws are executory throughout the whole French territory, by virtue of the promulgation thereof made by the First Consul.
2. They shall be executed in every part of the Republic, from the moment at which their promulgation can have been known.
3. The promulgation made by the First Consul shall be taken to be known in the department which shall be the seat of government, one day after the promulgation; and in each of the other departments, after the expiration of the same interval augmented by one day for every ten myriameters (about twenty ancient leagues) between the town in which the promulgation shall have been made, and the chief place of each department.
4. The law ordains for the future only; it has no retrospective operation.

5. The laws of police and public security bind all the inhabitants of the territory. Immovable property, although in the possession of foreigners, is governed by the French law. The laws relating to the condition and privileges of persons govern Frenchmen, although residing in a foreign country. . . .

6. Private agreements must not contravene the laws which concern public order and good morals.

Book I: Of Persons

Title I: Of the Enjoyment and Privation of Civil Rights

7. The exercise of civil rights is independent of the quality of citizen, which is only acquired and preserved conformably to the constitutional law.

8. Every Frenchman shall enjoy civil rights.

Chapter VI: Of the Respective Rights and Duties of Married Persons

212. Married persons owe to each other fidelity, succor, assistance.

213. The husband owes protection to his wife, the wife obedience to her husband.

214. The wife is obliged to live with her husband, and to follow him to every place where he may judge it convenient to reside: the husband is obliged to receive her, and to furnish her with every necessity for the wants of life, according to his means and station.

215. The wife cannot plead in her own name, without the authority of her husband, even though she should be a public trader, or noncommunicant, or separate in property.

216. The authority of the husband is not necessary when the wife is prosecuted in a criminal manner, or relating to police.

217. A wife, although noncommunicant or separate in property, cannot give, pledge, or acquire by free or chargeable title, without the concurrence of her husband in the act, or his consent in writing.

218. If the husband refuses to authorize his wife to plead in her own name, the judge may give her authority.

219. If the husband refuses to authorize his wife to pass an act, the wife may cause her husband to be cited directly before the court of the first instance, of the circle of their common domicil[e], which may give or refuse its authority, after the husband shall have been heard, or duly summoned before the chamber of council.

220. The wife, if she is a public trader, may, without the authority of her husband, bind herself for that which concerns her trade; and in the said case she binds also her husband, if there be a community between them.

She is not reputed a public trader if she merely retails goods in her husband's trade, but only when she carries on a separate business.

221. When the husband is subjected to a condemnation, carrying with it an afflictive or infamous punishment, although it may have been pronounced merely for contumacy, the wife, though of age, cannot, during the continuance of such punishment, plead in her own name or contract, until after authority given by the judge, who may in such case give his authority without hearing or summoning the husband.

222. If the husband is interdicted or absent, the judge, on cognizance of the cause, may authorize . . . [the] wife either to plead in her own name or to contract.

223. Every general authority, though stipulated by the contract of marriage, is invalid, except as respects the administration of the property of the wife.

224. If the husband is a minor, the authority of the judge is necessary for his wife, either to appear in court, or to contract.

225. A nullity, founded on defect of authority, can be opposed by the wife, by the husband, or by their heirs.

226. The wife may make a will without the authority of her husband.

Title VI: Of Divorce

Section II: Of the Provisional Measures to Which the Petition for Cause Determinate May Give Rise

267. The provisional management of the children shall rest with the husband, petitioner, or defendant, in the suit for divorce, unless it be otherwise ordered for the greater advantage of the children, on petition of either the mother, or the family, or the government commissioner.

268. The wife, petitioner or defendant in divorce, shall be at liberty to quit the residence of her husband during the prosecution, and demand an alimentary pension proportioned to the means of the husband. The court shall point out the house in which the wife shall be bound to reside, and shall fix, if there be ground, the alimentary provision which the husband shall be obliged to pay her.

269. The wife shall be bound to prove her residence in the house appointed. As often as she shall be thereto required; in default of such proof, the husband may refuse the alimentary pension and if the wife is the petitioner for divorce, may cause her to be declared incapable of continuing her prosecution.

270. The wife having community of goods, plaintiff or defendant in divorce, shall be at liberty, in every stage of the cause, commencing with the date of the order mentioned in article 238, to require, for the preservation of her rights, that seals should be affixed to the movable goods in community. These seals shall not be taken off until an inventory and appraisal is made, and on the undertaking of the husband to produce the article contained in the inventory, or to answer for their value, as their legal keeper.

271. Every obligation contracted by the husband at the expense of the community, every alienation made by him of immovable property dependent upon it, subsequent to the date of the order mentioned in article 238, shall be declared void, if proof be given, moreover, that it has been made or contracted in fraud of the rights of the wife.

Section III: Of Exceptions of Law Against the Suit of Divorce for Cause Determinate

272. The suit for divorce shall be extinguished by the reconciliation of the parties, whether occurring subsequently to the facts which might have authorized such suit, or subsequently to the petition for divorce.

273. In either case the petitioner shall be declared incapable of pursuing the action; a new one may, nevertheless, be instituted for cause accruing subsequently to the reconciliation, and the ancient causes may then be employed in support of such new petition.

297. In case of divorce by mutual consent, neither of the parties shall be allowed to contract a new marriage until the expiration of three years from the pronunciation of the divorce.

298. In case of divorce admitted by law for cause of adultery, the guilty party shall never be permitted to marry with his accomplice. The wife adulteress shall be condemned in the same judgment; and, on the request of the public minister, to confinement in a house of correction, for a determined period, which shall not be less than three months nor exceed two years.

299. For whatever cause a divorce shall take place, except in the case of mutual consent, the married party against whom the divorce shall have been established shall lose all the advantage conferred by the other party, whether by their contract or marriage, or since the marriage contracted.

300. The married party who shall have obtained the divorce shall preserve the advantages conferred by the other spouse, although they may have made stipulations and such reciprocity has not taken place.

QUESTIONS

1. What is the procedure for getting divorced in nineteenth-century France? Who can decide to get divorced? What features are similar or different to divorce in our own times?

2. Why do you think it is important for the writers of the Code to stress that it only operates from the time of its ratification, and not for the past?

3. How much power does a father have over his children according to this Code? How about a mother?

4. Do you think this law code makes women free and equal? In what ways? In what ways does it subordinate women?

5. From what you have read about the ideals of the French Revolution, discuss the ways in which these sections of the Napoleonic law code uphold those values, and in what ways they undermine those values.

ACKNOWLEDGMENTS

1. From "The Flood" in *The Epic of Gilgamesh,* translated by N.K. Sandars, pp. 108–112 (Penguin Classics 1960, Third Edition 1972). Copyright © N.K. Sandars, 1960, 1964, 1972. Reproduced by permission of Penguin Books Ltd.
2. *The Creation Epic. The Creation Epic,* in Morris Jastrow, *The Civilizations of Babylonia and Assyria* (Philadelphia: J. B. Lippincott Company, 1915), pp. 428–441 passim.
3. *The Book of Genesis.* Genesis from the Holy Bible, King James Version.
4. From Hesiod, *Theogony and Works and Days* (1988), edited and translated by M.L. West. By permission of Oxford University Press.
5. From "The Code of Hammurabi" from *Ancient Near Eastern Texts Relating to the Old Testament—Third Edition with Supplement,* ed. by James Pritchard. © 1950, 1955, 1969, renewed 1978 by Princeton University Press. Reprinted by permission of Princeton University Press.
6. From "The Book of the Dead" from *Ancient Near Eastern Texts Relating to the Old Testament—Third Edition with Supplement,* ed. by James Pritchard. © 1950, 1955, 1969, renewed 1978 by Princeton University Press. Reprinted by permission of Princeton University Press.
7. *The Book of Exodus.* From the Revised Standard Version of the Bible, copyright 1946, 1952, 1971 by the Division of Christian Education of the National Council of the Churches of Christ in the USA. Used by permission.
8. *The Book of Isaiah.* From the Revised Standard Version of the Bible, copyright 1946, 1952, 1971 by the Division of Christian Education of the National Council of the Churches of Christ in the USA. Used by permission.
9. From Pritchard, James B. (ed.) *The Ancient Near East.* © 1958 Princeton University Press. 1986 renewed PUP Reprinted by permission of Princeton University Press.
10. From "The Death of Hector" by Homer, from *The Iliad* by Homer, translated by Robert Fagles. Copyright © 1990 by Robert Fagles. Used by permission of Viking Penguin, a division of Penguin Group (USA) Inc.
11. Sappho of Lesbos, *Poems.* From *Sappho of Lesbos: The Poems,* translated by Terence DuQuesne. Copyright © 1989 by Terence DuQuesne. Reprinted by permission.
12. Thucydides, *History of the Peloponnesian War.* Excerpt from *Thucydides* by B. Jowett, M. A.
13. Reprinted by permission of the publishers and the Trustees of the Loeb Classical Library from *Xenophon: Volume VII,* Loeb Classical Library Volume 183, translated by E.C. Marchant, pp. 137–153. Cambridge, Mass.: Harvard University Press, 1925. The Loeb Classical Library ® is a registered trademark of the president and fellows of Harvard College.
14. Plato, *Apology.* From *The Best Known Works of Plato,* translated into English by B. Jowett, M.A. (Garden City, NY: Blue Ribbon Books, 1942).
15. Plato, *The Republic.* Plato, *The Republic of Plato,* translated by B. Jowett (Oxford: Clarendon Press, 1888), pp. 214–221.
16. Aristotle, *Politics.* Aristotle, *The Politics,* in *The Politics of Economics of Aristotle,* translated by Edward Walford (London: Bell & Daldy, 1866), pp. 239–243, 245–250.
17. From "Alexander" in *The Age of Alexander: Nine Greek Lives* by Plutarch, translated and annotated by Ian Scott-Kilvert, Introduction by G.T. Griffith, pp. 255–260; 263–267; 269–271; 274–277. (Penguin Classics, 1973). Translation and notes copyright © Ian Scott-Kilvert, 1973. Introduction copyright G.T. Griffith, 1973. Reproduced by permission of Penguin Books Ltd.
18. Reprinted by permission of the publishers and the Trustees of the Loeb Classical Library from *Polybius; Volume III,* Loeb Classical Library Volume 138, translated by W.R. Paton, pp. 293, 295, 297, 299, 301, 303, 305, 307, 309, 311. Cambridge, Mass.: Harvard University Press, 1923. The Loeb Classical Library ® is a registered trademark of the president and fellows of Harvard College.
19. From *Murder Trials* by Cicero, translated with an introduction by Michael Grant, pp. 127–129; 131; 234; 237; 245; 248. (Penguin Classics, 1975). Copyright © Michael Grant Publications Ltd, 1973. Reproduced by permission of Penguin Books Ltd.
20. Virgil, *Aeneid.* Virgil, *The Aeneid,* translated by Theodore C. Williams (Boston: Houghton Mifflin, 1910), pp. 1–2, 8–14.
21. Juvenal, *Satires.* From *Juvenal, The Satires,* translated and with an introduction and notes by Charles Plumb. Reprinted by permission of the translator.
22. Plutarch, *The Life of Cato the Elder.* Plutarch, *Life of Cato.* In *Plutarch's Lives,* Vol. 2, revised translation by Arthur Hugh Clough (Philadelphia: The John C. Winston Co., 1908), pp. 658–663, 682, 689–690.

363

23. Suetonius, *The Life of Augustus*. Suetonius, *Life of Augustus*, in *The Lives of the Twelve Caesars*, translated by Alexander Thomson, revised by T. Forester (London: George Bell & Sons, 1909), pp. 87–92, 96–97, 115–116, 129–130, 145–146.

24. *The Sermon on the Mount*. From the Revised Standard Version of the Bible, copyright 1946, 1952, 1971 by the Division of Christian Education of the National Council of the Churches of Christ in the USA. Used by permission.

25. St. Paul, *Epistle to the Romans*. From the Revised Standard Version of the Bible, copyright 1946, 1952, 1971 by the Division of Christian Education of the National Council of the Churches of Christ in the USA. Used by permission.

26. Tacitus, *Germania*. Tacitus, *The Germania*, the Oxford Translation, Revised (New York: Arthur Hinds & Co., n.d.), pp. 3, 11–13, 15–16, 19–26.

27. Excerpted from *In Praise of Constantine: A Historical Study and New Translation of Eusebius' Tricennial Orations* by H.A. Drake. (Berkeley: University of California Press, 1976), pp. 85–90, 102. Reprinted by permission of H.A. Drake.

28. Augustine of Hippo, *The City of God*. From *The City of God* by St. Augustine, 1945 edition. Reprinted by permission of Everyman's Library (J. M. Dent & Sons Ltd.).

29. Benedict of Nursia, *Rule of Saint Benedict*. Saint Benedict of Nursia, *The Rule*. Translated by Dom Justin McCann (Latrobe, PA: The Archabbey Press, 1950), pp. 63ff.

30. From *The Burgundian Code*, translated by Katherine Fischer Drew, pp. 17–18, 23, 29, 30, 31, 32, 35, 40, 45, 46, 50. Copyright 1949, 1972 University of Pennsylvania Press, reprinted by permission of the University of Pennsylvania Press.

31. Gregory of Tours, *History of the Franks*. From *Records of Civilization: Sources and Studies*, edited by James T. Shotwell (New York: Columbia University Press, 1916).

32. Bede, *The Ecclesiastical History of England*. Excerpt from *The Venerable Bede's Ecclesiastical History of England*, edited by J. A. Giles.

33. Einhard, *The Life of Charlemagne*. From *Early Lives of Charlemagne* by Einhard and the Monk of St. Gall, translated and edited by Professor A. J. Grant (Cooper Square Publishers, Inc., New York, 1966).

34. Justinian, *Code*. From *The Digest of Justinian*. Latin text edited by Theodor Mommsen with the aid of Paul Krueger. English translation edited by Alan Watson. Vol. II. Copyright © 1985 by the University of Pennsylvania Press. Reprinted by permission.

35. Procopius, *Secret History*. From *Secret History* by Procopius, translated by Richard Atwater (Ann Arbor: The University of Michigan Press, 1961). Reprinted by permission of The University of Michigan Press.

36. *The Koran*. Reprinted by permission from *The Short Koran*, edited by George M. Lamsa. Copyright © 1949 by Ziff-Davis Publishing Company.

37. Michael Psellus, *Chronographia*. From *Fourteen Byzantine Rulers* by Marcus Psellus, translated by E. R. A. Sewter (Penguin Classics 1966), copyright © E. R. A. Sewter, 1966. Used by permission of The Penguin Group (UK).

38. Ibn Al-Qalanisi, *The Damascus Chronicle*. From *The Damascus Chronicle of the Crusaders*, extracted and translated from the *Chronicle of Ibn Al-Qalanisi*, by H. A. R. Gibb. Reprinted by permission of Luzac Oriental Ltd.

39. Ibn Ishaq, *The Life of Muhammad*, ed. by Ibn Hisham, taken from a translation by Edward Rehatsek, c. 1891.

40. *Feudal Documents*. From *Translations and Reprints from the Original Sources of European History*, Volume IV. Reprinted by permission of the University of Pennsylvania Press.

41. From *Readings in Medieval History, Third Edition, Volume Two: The Later Middle Ages*, edited by Patrick J. Geary, pp. 1–8. Peterborough, Ont.: Broadview Press, 2003. Copyright © 2003. Reprinted by permission of Broadview Press.

42. From *Fulcher of Chartres: Chronicle of the First Crusade*, translated by Martha Evelyn McGinty, pp. 9–17, 66–72. Copyright © 1941 University of Pennsylvania Press. Reprinted by permission of the University of Pennsylvania Press.

43. From *Song of Roland*, translated by Robert Harrison. Copyright © 1970 by Robert Harrison. Used by permission of Dutton Signet, a division of Penguin Group (USA) Inc.

44. *Magna Carta*. Boyd C. Barrington, ed., *Magna Carta* (Philadelphia: William J. Campbell, 1900), pp. 228–234, 237–240, 244, 246–250.

45. Francis of Assisi, *Admonitions*. From *The Admonitions of St. Francis of Assisi* by Lothar Hardick, O.F.M., translated by David Smith. Reprinted by permission of Franciscan Herald Press.

46. Thomas Aquinas, *Summa Theologica*. From *Summa Theologica* by St. Thomas Aquinas. Translated by Fathers of the English Dominican Province. Copyright 1948 by Beniziger Brothers, Inc. Reprinted by permission of Glencoe Publishing Co., Inc.

47. Dante, *The Divine Comedy*. Dante, *The Divine Comedy* (London: J. M. Dent & Sons, 1931), pp. 13–15, 17–18, 417–421.

48. Catherine of Siena, *Letters*. From *The Letters of St. Catherine of Siena*, Vol. I, translated by Suzanne Noffke. Copyright © 1988 by the Center for Medieval and Renaissance Studies. Reprinted by permission.

49. Christine de Pisan, *The Book of the City of Ladies*. Excerpts from *Book of the City of Ladies* by Christine de Pisan, translated by Daniel Gordon from Ph.D. dissertation "The Livre de la cite des dames" by Maureen Cheney Curnow. Reprinted by permission.

50. Margaret Paston, *Letters*. Extract from Folio edition of *The Pastons: A Family in the War of the Roses* edited by Richard Barber. Reprinted by permission of Boydell and Brewer Ltd.

51. Francesco Petrarca, *Letters*. Petrarch, *Letters*. Translated by James Harvey Robinson and Henry Winchester Rolfe (New York: G. P. Putnam's Sons, 1909), pp. 59–65, 207–209, 213, 239–251.

52. Leon Battista Alberti, *On the Family*. From *The Family in Renaissance Florence*, a translation by Renee Neu Watkins of *I Libri della Famiglia* by Leon Battista Alberti. Copyright © 1969 by Renee Watkins. Reprinted by permission.

53. Giorgio Vasari, *The Life of Leonardo da Vinci*. Giorgio Vasari, *Lives of the Most Eminent Painters, Sculptors, and Architects*, translated by Gaston DuC. DeVere (London: Philip Lee Warner, Publishers, 1912–1914), pp. 89–92, 95–101, 104–105.

54. From *The Prince: A Norton Critical Edition*, Second Edition, by Niccolo Machiavelli, translated by Robert M. Adams. Copyright © 1992, 1977 by W.W. Norton & Company, Inc. Used by permission of W.W. Norton & Company, Inc.

55. Desiderius Erasmus, *In Praise of Folly*. Erasmus, *In Praise of Folly* (London: Reeves & Turner, 1876), pp. 81–82, 134–138, 139, 156–160.

56. Excerpts from Thomas More, "Occupations," pp. 68–69 and "Social Relations," pp. 75–77 in *Utopia: Selected Works of St. Thomas More*, edited. by Edward Surtz, S.J. Copyright © 1964 by Yale University. Reprinted by permission of Yale University Press.

57. From Ibn Battuta, *Travels in Asia and Africa*, translated and selected by H.A.R. Gibb. Pages 317–323, 329–331. Copyright © 1957 Reprinted by permission of Taylor & Francis Group.

58. Christopher Columbus, *Letter from the First Voyage*. Christopher Columbus, *Letters*, translated and edited by R. H. Major (London: Hakluyt Society, 1847), pp. 1–17.

59. Gomes Eannes de Zurara, *Chronicle of Guinea*. From *The Chronicle of the Discovery and Conquest of Guinea*, Volume I, translated by Charles Raymond Beazley and Edgar Prestage (London: The Hakluyt Society, 1896), Chapters XXIV–XXVI.

60. Bartolomé de Las Casas, *Apologetic History of the Indies*. From *Introduction to Contemporary Civilization in the West*, a sourcebook prepared by the Contemporary Civilization Staff of Columbia College, Volume I, 3rd edition. Copyright © 1946, 1954, 1960, Columbia University Press. Reprinted by permission.

61. From *The Bernal Diaz Chronicles*, translated by Albert Idell, copyright © 1956 by Albert Idell. Used by permission of Doubleday, a division of Random House, Inc.

62. Juan Gonzalez de Mendoza, *The History of the Great and Mighty Kingdom of China*.

63. From *The Inquisitor's Guide*, edited and translated by Janet Shirley. Copyright © 2006 Reprinted by permission of Janet Shirley.

64. Martin Luther, *The Freedom of a Christian*. Adapted and reprinted from *Luther's Works*, Vol. 31, copyright © 1957 by Fortress Press. Used by permission of Augsburg Fortress. Martin Luther, *Of Marriage and Celibacy*. Martin Luther, *Table Talk*, translated and edited by William Hazlitt (London: George Bell and Sons, 1895), pp. 297–300.

65. John Calvin, *Institutes of the Christian Religion*. From *John Calvin, Selections from His Writings*, edited and with an introduction by John Dillenberger. Copyright © 1975 by American Academy of Religion. Reprinted by permission of Scholars Press. John Calvin, *Catechism*. From John Calvin, *The Catechism of the Church of Geneva*, translated by Elijah Waterman (Hartford: Sheldon & Goodwin, 1815), pp. 31–40.

66. Ignatius Loyola, *Spiritual Exercises*. Excerpt from *The Spiritual Exercises of St. Ignatius of Loyola*, translated by Father Elder Mullan, S. J.

67. Teresa of Ávila, *The Life of St. Teresa*. From *The Life of St. Teresa of Ávila*, written by herself. Translated from the Spanish by David Lewis. Reprinted by permission of Burnes and Oates Ltd.

68. Anonymous, *Lazarillo de Tormes*. From Louis How, translator and editor, *The Life of Lazarillo de Tormes*, with an introduction by Charles Philip Wagner (New York: Michael Kennerly, 1917), pp. 9–11, 13–16, 24–32.

69. *The Twelve Articles of the Peasants of Swabia*. "The Peasants' Revolt" in *Readings in European History*, Volume II: *From the Opening of the Protestant Revolt to the Present Day*, edited by James Harvey Robinson (Boston: Ginn & Company, 1906), pp. 94–99. Martin Luther, *Admonition to Peace*. From Martin Luther, *The Life of Luther*, translated by William Hazlitt (London: Bell & Daldy, 1872), pp. 170–172, 174, 176–177.

70. Francis Xavier, "Letter from India" in *The Life and Letters of St. Francis Xavier*, translated by Henry James Coleridge. (London: Burns and Oates, 1874), pp. 157–163.

71. Marguerite de Navarre, *Heptameron*. Stories Five and Fifty-five from *The Heptameron* by Marguerite de Navarre, translated by P. A. Chilton. Copyright © 1984 by P. A. Chilton. Reproduced by permission of Penguin Books Ltd.

72. From *University of Chicago Readings in Western Civilization*, Volume 6, edited by Cochrane, Gray, and Kishlansky; General eds. Boyer and Kirshner, pp. 81–89. Copyright © 1987 University of Chicago. Reprinted by Permission of University of Chicago Press.

73. Reprinted with permission of Simon & Schuster Adult Publishing Group from *Magdalena and Balthasar* by Steven Ozment. Copyright © 1986 by The Steven Ozment Family Trust.

74. Henry IV, *The Edict of Nantes*. From *Readings in European History*, Vol. II: *From the Opening of the Protestant Revolt to the Present Day*, edited by James Harvey Robinson (Boston: Ginn & Company, 1906), pp. 183–185.

75. Cardinal Richelieu, *The Political Testament*. From *The Political Testament of Cardinal Richelieu*, translated by Henry Bertram Hill. Copyright © 1961 by the Regents of the University of Wisconsin. Reprinted by permission of the University of Wisconsin Press.

76. Hans von Grimmelshausen, *Simplicissimus*. From *Simplicius Simplicissimus* by Jans Jacob Christoffel von Grimmelshausen, translated from the original German edition of 1669 by Helmuth Weissenborn and Lesley Macdonald. Copyright © 1984 by the translators. Reprinted by permission of John Calder Publishers Ltd.

77. From *The Political Works of James I, Reprinted from the Edition of 1616*, with an introduction by Charles Howard McIlwain. (Cambridge: Harvard University Press, 1918).

78. Thomas Hobbes, *Leviathan*. From Thomas Hobbes, *Leviathan*, edited by A. R. Waller (Cambridge: University Press, 1904).

79. John Locke, *Second Treatise of Government*.

80. *English Bill of Rights*, 1689.

81. Duc de Saint-Simon, *Memoirs*. Duc de Saint-Simon, *Memoirs*, translated by Bayle St. John (London: Swan Sonnonschein & Co., 1900), pp. 357–365.

82. From R.A. Arnold (ed. and trans.) *A Documentary Survey of Napoleonic France*, as it appears in *The French Revolution: A Document Collection*, by Laura Mason and Tracey Rizzo (eds.) Copyright © 1993. Reprinted by permission of Rowman & Littlefield.

PHOTO CREDITS